Cases on Enhancing Business Sustainability Through Knowledge Management Systems

Meir Russ
University of Wisconsin-Green Bay, USA & Stellenbosch University, South Africa

IGI Global
PUBLISHER of TIMELY KNOWLEDGE

A volume in the Advances in Business Information Systems and Analytics (ABISA) Book Series

Published in the United States of America by
IGI Global
Business Science Reference (an imprint of IGI Global)
701 E. Chocolate Avenue
Hershey PA, USA 17033
Tel: 717-533-8845
Fax: 717-533-8661
E-mail: cust@igi-global.com
Web site: http://www.igi-global.com

Library of Congress Cataloging-in-Publication Data

Names: Russ, Meir, 1968- editor.
Title: Cases on enhancing business sustainability through knowledge management systems / edited by: Meir Russ.
Description: Hershey PA : Business Science Reference, [2023] | Includes bibliographical references. | Summary: "This book will present teaching case studies exploring the formulating and implementing of knowledge management systems (KMS) in organizations, framed by the changes and the model mentioned above; and by deficiencies of teaching cases that I (and others) observed while teaching KM classes at the advanced undergraduate and graduate levels"-- Provided by publisher.
Identifiers: LCCN 2022054941 (print) | LCCN 2022054942 (ebook) | ISBN 9781668458594 (hardcover) | ISBN 9781668458600 (paperback) | ISBN 9781668458617 (ebook)
Subjects: LCSH: Knowledge management--Case studies. | Information technology--Management--Case studies. | Automation--Case studies. | Artificial intelligence--Industrial applications--Case studies. | Sustainable development--Case studies.
Classification: LCC HD30.2 .C37875 2023 (print) | LCC HD30.2 (ebook) | DDC 658.4/038--dc23/eng/20230227
LC record available at https://lccn.loc.gov/2022054941
LC ebook record available at https://lccn.loc.gov/2022054942

This book is published in the IGI Global book series Advances in Business Information Systems and Analytics (ABISA) (ISSN: 2327-3275; eISSN: 2327-3283)

British Cataloguing in Publication Data
A Cataloguing in Publication record for this book is available from the British Library.
All work contributed to this book is new, previously-unpublished material. The views expressed in this book are those of the authors, but not necessarily of the publisher.
For electronic access to this publication, please contact: eresources@igi-global.com.

Advances in Business Information Systems and Analytics (ABISA) Book Series

Madjid Tavana
La Salle University, USA

ISSN:2327-3275
EISSN:2327-3283

Mission

The successful development and management of information systems and business analytics is crucial to the success of an organization. New technological developments and methods for data analysis have allowed organizations to not only improve their processes and allow for greater productivity, but have also provided businesses with a venue through which to cut costs, plan for the future, and maintain competitive advantage in the information age.

The **Advances in Business Information Systems and Analytics (ABISA) Book Series** aims to present diverse and timely research in the development, deployment, and management of business information systems and business analytics for continued organizational development and improved business value.

Coverage

- Strategic Information Systems
- Data Governance
- Statistics
- Business Information Security
- Data Strategy
- Decision Support Systems
- Forecasting
- Management Information Systems
- Geo-BIS
- Performance Metrics

IGI Global is currently accepting manuscripts for publication within this series. To submit a proposal for a volume in this series, please contact our Acquisition Editors at Acquisitions@igi-global.com or visit: http://www.igi-global.com/publish/.

The Advances in Business Information Systems and Analytics (ABISA) Book Series (ISSN 2327-3275) is published by IGI Global, 701 E. Chocolate Avenue, Hershey, PA 17033-1240, USA, www.igi-global.com. This series is composed of titles available for purchase individually; each title is edited to be contextually exclusive from any other title within the series. For pricing and ordering information please visit http://www.igi-global.com/book-series/advances-business-information-systems-analytics/37155. Postmaster: Send all address changes to above address.

Titles in this Series

For a list of additional titles in this series, please visit: http://www.igi-global.com/book-series/advances-business-information-systems-analytics/37155

Data-Driven Approaches for Effective Managerial Decision Making
Anubha (Jaipuria Institute of Management, Ghaziabad, India) and Himanshu Sharma (IILM Institute for Higher Education, New Delhi, India)
Business Science Reference • © 2023 • 336pp • H/C (ISBN: 9781668475683) • US $255.00

Handbook of Research on AI and Machine Learning Applications in Customer Support and Analytics
Md Shamim Hossain (Hajee Mohammad Danesh Science and Technology University, Bangladesh) Ree Chan Ho (Taylor's University, Malaysia) and Goran Trajkovski (Western Governors University, USA)
Business Science Reference • © 2023 • 423pp • H/C (ISBN: 9781668471050) • US $325.00

Building Secure Business Models Through Blockchain Technology Tactics, Methods, Limitations, and Performance
Shweta Dewangan (ICFAI University, Raipur, India) Sapna Singh Kshatri (Shri Shankaracharya Institute of Professional Management and Technology, India) Astha Bhanot (Princess Nourah Bint Abdulrahman University, Saudi Arabia) and Mushtaq Ahmed Shah (Lovely Professional University, India)
Business Science Reference • © 2023 • 283pp • H/C (ISBN: 9781668478080) • US $250.00

Enhancing Business Communications and Collaboration Through Data Science Applications
Nuno Geada (ISCTE - University Institute of Lisbon, Portugal) and George Leal Jamil (Informações em Rede Consultoria e Treinamento, Brazil)
Business Science Reference • © 2023 • 262pp • H/C (ISBN: 9781668467862) • US $270.00

Revolutionizing Business Practices Through Artificial Intelligence and Data-Rich Environments
Manisha Gupta (Sharda University, India) Deergha Sharma (The NorthCap University, India) and Himani Gupta (Jagannath International Management School, India)
Business Science Reference • © 2022 • 300pp • H/C (ISBN: 9781668449509) • US $250.00

AI-Driven Intelligent Models for Business Excellence
Samala Nagaraj (Woxsen University, India) and Korupalli V. Rajesh Kumar (Woxsen University, India)
Business Science Reference • © 2023 • 267pp • H/C (ISBN: 9781668442463) • US $250.00

Handbook of Research on Foundations and Applications of Intelligent Business Analytics
Zhaohao Sun (Papua New Guinea University of Technology, Papua New Guinea) and Zhiyou Wu (Chongqing Normal University, China)
Business Science Reference • © 2022 • 425pp • H/C (ISBN: 9781799890164) • US $325.00

IGI Global
PUBLISHER of TIMELY KNOWLEDGE

701 East Chocolate Avenue, Hershey, PA 17033, USA
Tel: 717-533-8845 x100 • Fax: 717-533-8661
E-Mail: cust@igi-global.com • www.igi-global.com

To Fay, my one and only, for everything.

Editorial Advisory Board

Table of Contents

Section 3
Business Case Studies

Section 4
Technology Reviews and Case Studies

Detailed Table of Contents

This chapter aims to explore the knowledge sharing model in virtual communities within the metaverse domain and proposes a way to enhance knowledge sharing and innovation in these communities. The study takes into account the practical implications of digital ethics and digital citizenship and the impact they have on the shaping of digital ethics. Based on the analysis of relevant practices and prior research, a knowledge sharing model for virtual communities in the metaverse is constructed. The results show that the basic process of knowledge sharing involves the selection and acquisition of community knowledge in three dimensions, internalization and absorption of situational knowledge to form a "knowledge black box," and finally, sharing through private domain knowledge broadcasting and diffusion. The current practices in virtual communities within the metaverse domain are limited and lack empirical evidence.

The Fourth Industrial Revolution has profoundly affected all sectors, quickly leading to significant technological changes. This new revolution has also affected aviation systems that have a direct connection with technology. This revolution has brought about rapid changes especially in airport systems and led to the emergence of the concept of "smart airport." In this study, the case of Istanbul Airport has been analyzed in terms of digital transformation in order to exemplify the digital applications in an airport. In this scope, the aim of the study is to present a new projection, integrated with a digital business strategy, to businesses operating in the airline industry, where they can successfully realize the digital transformation process and manage this process strategically.

Projects have been increasingly used in the implementation of organizations' business operations. Knowledge sharing has been considered essential in the project environment; therefore, the integration of knowledge management within project management becomes crucial for project success. The objective of this research is to study how knowledge sharing is integrated within the context of a project, and what is the perception of project team members about it. A case study was carried out in a company within the financial sector, focused on a project team of the entity. The results revealed that project managers, other professionals in project management, and the organization itself are very much aware of the importance of knowledge sharing. The results also emphasized that, regardless of the lack of incentives by top management, project team members consider that knowledge sharing highly contributes to a successful execution of projects.

Preface

This book was envisioned as a manuscript that presents case studies exploring the formulation and implementation of knowledge management systems in organizations at times when Artificial Intelligence (AI) is becoming a reality for pioneering organizations while they are facing complex multifaceted aspects of business sustainability and the post-COVID-19 reality, with ambiguous and changing ethical norms and vague or not existing legislation regarding the adaptation of the new AI algorithms.

INTRODUCTION

The first quarter of the 21st century was identified as the beginning of the continuous, ongoing, and accelerating wave of simultaneous 'general purpose technologies' revolutions causing accelerated shrinkage of the half-life of knowledge. At such a pace of change, one would experience multiple paradigm shifts during their lifetime leaving no time in between to allow the individual, organizations, and/or society to adjust; forcing society at large and organizations to develop and adopt a different set of new tools, systems, and procedures (Russ, 2021a).

One such tool is a new framework model of knowledge management for sustainable development (see Figure 1), which incorporates the most recent developments of big data and machine learning in the context of cybersecurity and humanistic paradigms, steering toward a circular and 'smart' sustainable economy. This model proposed a three-layer model of knowledge management (KM) that incorporates a human layer, a machine layer, and a unifying new knowledge development and knowledge sharing layer, incorporating the knowledge management cycle. Each one of the two layers (the human layer and the machine layer) is comprised of human actors that learn and decide as well as systems that learn and decide. Of course, there are interactions between human actors and the systems. The systems could include numerous different technologies (e.g., AI, Robotics, Cyber security algorithms) that of course could interact as well among themselves as well as with human actors. Finally, the model suggests combining decision-making and learning into a unified, synergistic managerial activity as critical aspects for human and machine actors (Russ, 2021a, 2021b).

This book presents teaching case studies exploring the formulation and implementation of knowledge management systems (KMS) in organizations, as well as relevant technologies and systems, as framed by the model (in context) mentioned above; and by deficiencies of teaching cases that the editor (and others) observed while teaching KM classes at the advanced undergraduate and graduate levels. KM is taught as a standalone class and/or as a module in classes, in business, decision-making, information systems, and computer sciences (among others), sometimes under a different title. Such teaching includes models, tools, and some theoretical aspects (depending on the discipline), but usually lacks updated, relevant, and detailed teaching cases, which could enable a fruitful class discussion, covering technological, organizational, and human aspects, including managerial, design, moral and ethical dilemmas. This manuscript intended to close such a gap.

Figure 1. The mesosystem model of knowledge management
Source: Russ (2021a, Figure 3)

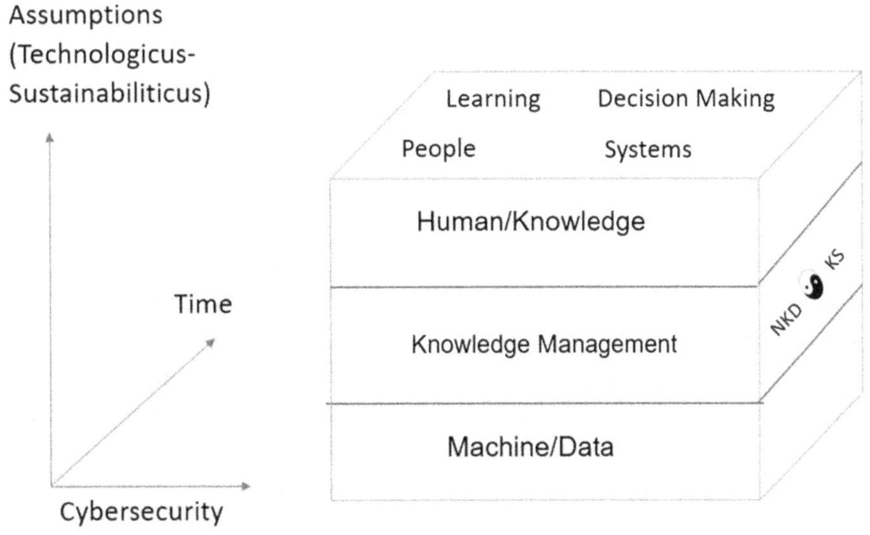

Specifically, the call for chapters was soliciting chapter proposals of teaching case studies of organizations formulating and implementing KMS where the AI algorithms and/or big data systems are infused with human-centered knowledge while supporting economic, social, and/or environmental sustainability issues. The call hoped to attract contributions from different countries, covering different industries, discussing different aspects of KMS during their complete life cycle, and covering a diverse set of technologies and processes. The focus of the cases was expected to be on the decision-making and learning opportunities at the individual, team, organizational, and inter-organizational levels while uncovering business, sustainability, and ethical dilemmas facing the learning and decision-making actors.

For the call for chapters, the broad and holistic definition of KMS as defined by ISO 30401:2018 was used. KMS is defined as the set of interrelated or interacting elements of organizations that establish, embed, and enable knowledge management policies and objectives, as well as the processes to achieve those objectives (ISO, 2018). Those objectives must (or at least have the potential to) create value (Russ et al., 2010) for a set (or subset) of stakeholders.

The call for chapters attracted a broad variety of cases. In this volume, the reader will find traditional teaching business cases, as well as academic case studies that can serve as teaching case studies. The volume also includes cases of new technologies that businesses can use (as illustrated by the cases) and recent implementations of diverse Artificial Intelligence tools.

The chapters in this collection of cases discuss different units' levels of organizations starting with project units within companies, small and large organizations, supply chains, and virtual communities, both from the for-profit and not-for-profit/government segments of the economy. The cases also cover a wide variety of industries and are originated by authors from all over the world, from underdeveloped, developing, and developed countries.

The cases are organized into three sections: 1) "Business Teaching Cases," 2) "Business Case Studies," and 3) "Technology Reviews and Case Studies."

Finally, each case includes in the end several questions, as suggested by the authors of the cases that could facilitate class discussion.

And now, to the chapters.

The first chapter, written by Jaime J. González-Masip and titled "Mapping Knowledge Management for Sustainability and Information Technology," is providing the instructor and discussion facilitator with a conceptual map of the academic areas of interest covered by the cases in this book. The chapter identified ten major clusters of study in the KM for sustainability research context that can be combined into three major areas of study: Big-data, innovation, and governance. The chapter also identified two leading themes of research: utilizing corporate social responsibility for competitive advantage and the use of green innovation to promote sustainability profitably. The mapping provided by this chapter can provide the instructor with an opportunity to broaden the scope of their class discussions and extend them in different directions. For example, how can AI and green innovation facilitate sustainable development in salmon-based aquaculture (see Chapter 6)? On the other hand, a researcher can investigate the use of AI while using the autopoietic parading in the educational context (see Chapter 3) and by using the case in Chapter 3, see how they can extend the research of Artificial Intelligent systems and Projects Management by studying the adoption of Large Language Model (LLM) algorithms into educational systems.

The second chapter, written by Liz Kheng and titled "Walmart: A Case Study in Knowledge Management," is a teaching business case study (developed by using publicly available secondary data and an interview with a Walmart Executive) that explores Walmart's development of omnichannel capabilities, supply chain automation, smart store rollouts, and human resource management development through virtual reality training. The author describes the use of knowledge management across multiple spectrums that work together to anticipate customer needs and enhance their shopping experience. The chapter also discusses Walmart's use of artificial intelligence and data analytics to improve in-store and warehouse processes, as well as how Walmart uses data for decision-making and improving the consumer shopping experience.

The third chapter, written by Beth A Kiernan Ferrigno and titled "Transforming Education Through Autopoiesis, AI, and Collaboration: Harborwoods Central School District's Journey to Social-Emotional Wellness," is a teaching business case study (using a fictitious organization and names, developed by using publicly available secondary data and the many years of the author's experience in this sector in several positions) that showcases the successful development of a Knowledge Management System (KMS) in support of a school district's five-year strategic plan to enhance Social Emotional Wellness. This case study explores the district's adoption of an autonomous approach, utilization of AI and technology tools, implementation of structured project management strategies, and commitment to continuous collaboration and innovation. The author suggests that the main reasons behind the district's success resulted from analyzing key success drivers. The case study also highlights the transformative impact of these initiatives on educators, students, and the overall educational ecosystem. This transformative journey emphasizes the power of knowledge management in revolutionizing education.

The fourth chapter, written by Liz Kheng and titled "Knowledge Management Data Collection for Public Safety Priority Communications: Ohio FirstNet Public Safety Broadband Network," describes the early stages of the implementation of the network. Following the signage into law of the designation of the 700-megahertz band block D spectrum allocated to public safety by President Obama (as part of the Middle-Class Tax Relief and Job Creation Act of 2012) the state of Ohio issued a Request for Quotation (RFQ) seeking a vendor for OhioFirst.Net National Public Safety Broadband Network (NPSBN) State and Local Implementation Grant Program (SLIGP) Support (State of Ohio Office of Information Technology. The winning vendors, Advocate Technical Services and Televate were tasked with building a project plan for Ohio First and gathering data to help the state of Ohio develop a business plan for National FirstNet. This business case study follows the early stages of the implementation of the Ohio FirstNet Project from the knowledge management perspective.

The fifth chapter, written by Brenda Gross and titled "Challenges Faced by a Global Organization and Their KMS Implementation," portrays the implementation challenges of a Knowledge Management System (KMS) in an unnamed global communication company. The case study describes the process the company followed in selecting and implementing Helpjuice (their choice of the KMS). The author depicts several challenges faced by the company, affecting revenues, shareholder dividends, employee retention, and an inexperienced and less knowledgeable workforce unable to complete assigned tasks. Also, lengthy connectivity outages have impacted emergency services, leading to record-high fines imposed by the FCC. To overcome these challenges, the company established a team to analyze the affordability and return on investment (ROI) of implementing a KMS. As a result of the analysis, the team recommended that the company implement Helpjuice as its KMS. This case study describes the affordability and ROI analysis, challenges and SWOT analysis, organizational culture, KMS implementation, and audit process, as affected by multicultural perspectives of the global company.

The sixth chapter, written by Knut Ingar Westeren and titled "Innovative Technologies and Knowledge Developments for Sustainability in Salmon-Based Aquaculture," portrays the use of knowledge management to enhance sustainability while scaling up production in aquaculture. The author suggests that counterintuitively, more sustainable rigorous regulations can help companies to develop new technologies that while complying with tougher regulations, can increase productivity and profitability. To do so, the author suggests that the company should have a flat organizational structure and effective human capital (focus on training) and Knowledge Management (upgrading of knowledge levels and dissemination) strategies.

The seventh chapter, written by Ismail Olatunji Adeyemi and titled "Knowledge Sharing Practices Among Social Media Marketers and Significance for Business Sustainability in Nigeria," provides evidence of knowledge sharing for market advantage, promotion of adaptability/positive changes, and increased innovation and creativity for social media marketers in Nigeria. The case discusses and analyzes specific knowledge-sharing practices, including their drivers and specific implementation means used by social media marketers in Nigeria.

The eighth chapter, written by Mohammad Daradkeh and titled "Exploring the Knowledge Sharing Dynamics in Virtual Communities Within the Metaverse Domain," explores a model of knowledge sharing and proposes a way to enhance such knowledge sharing and boost innovation in virtual communities within the Metaverse domain. The model of knowledge sharing discussed by the author considers the practical implications of digital citizenship and the impact they have on influencing digital ethics. The author's research suggests that the basic process of knowledge sharing in such communities involves the selection and acquisition of community knowledge in three dimensions, namely: internalization, and absorption of situational knowledge to form a "knowledge black box", and finally, sharing through private domain knowledge broadcasting and diffusion. The case concludes with the tender that the proposed knowledge sharing model can improve knowledge sharing and innovation in virtual communities in the Metaverse while promoting digital ethics and digital citizenship.

The ninth chapter, written by Filiz Mizrak and Gonca Reyhan Akkartal and titled "Strategic Management of Digital Transformation Process in the Aviation Industry: The Case of the Istanbul Airport as a Smart Airport," describes the makeover process of an organization within the aviation industry into a digital (smart) entity. The case defines the concept of a 'smart airport' and the digital applications are epitomized. The authors then analyze the transition of Istanbul Airport into a 'smart airport' including the discussion of the strategic management aspects of the digital transformation process. In conclusion, the authors briefly suggest the next steps for the organization.

The tenth chapter, written by Zinga Novais, Jorge Vareda Gomes, and Mario Romão and titled "Sharing Knowledge for Projects," integrates the literature of knowledge management and project management, as the author considers the growing importance of projects as they are recently implemented more frequently by organizations. The authors then pursue a more in-depth analysis of how knowledge sharing is integrated within the context of a project, and what is the perception of project team members about it. Specifically, their research focused on an organization within the financial sector. Their findings revealed that project managers as well as other professionals in project management are very much aware of the importance of knowledge sharing in the project context. Their results also emphasized that, regardless of the lack of incentives by top management, project team members consider knowledge sharing as highly valuable for the successful implementation and completion of projects.

The eleventh chapter, written by Özden Özkanlısoy and Füsun Bulutlar and titled "Impact of Sustainability on Supply Chain: Contributions and New Performance Measurements in the Disruptive Technology Era," identifies a gap in the academic literature regarding the comprehensiveness of the sustainability measurement in the context of supply chain management. The authors reconstitute sustainability performance measurements, considering the contributions of disruptive technologies to determine them. As a background for such analysis, the authors briefly explain disruptive technologies, determine the contributions of these technologies to sustainability and investigate the technology-based contributions of them to supply chain sustainability performance separately. Finally, the authors provide a guide for companies and their supply chains that could enhance their supply chain sustainability performance by utilizing disruptive technologies.

The twelfth chapter by Sahana P. Shankar and her colleagues is titled "Enhancing DevOps Using Intelligent Techniques: Application of Artificial Intelligence and Machine Learning Techniques to DevOps." It depicts the application of the Development and Operations (DevOps for short) model for application development. DevOps is the practice of having a single team that manages all aspects of the application development life cycle and combines various practices and effective tools to improve the speed with which applications and services are delivered. DevOps is used especially when it is necessary to incorporate security into the software development life cycle at a rapid scale while minimizing risks, ensuring compliance, and reducing friction and costs, since it is based on the active participation of both operational and development teams at all stages of product development. Incorporating DevOps into the development process is also recommended when creating an agile and scalable system that has to be ready for rapid change and growth if required. The authors also developed a specific method to improve the implementation of the DevOps model, which is described in the chapter.

Finally, Chapter 13, written by José G Vargas-Hernandez, Muhammad Mahboob Ali, and Omar C. Vargas-González, titled "Socio-Ecological and Green Innovation Management System Performance: An Approach Towards Green Enterprises," discusses how utilizing green innovation may work as a catalyst to safeguard the environment through improved managerial functions for which multiple green enterprises should be instigated. Green enterprises are expected to improve business and social performance by solving sustainability issues while creating opportunities and generating ideas for human skill development. According to the authors, the integration of several domains, dimensions, and sectors of socio-ecological-economic systems with political economy, and the elements of the humanitarian domain may lead to a system that can combine the green industrial revolution and Industry 5.0 simultaneously and successfully.

Lastly, since this manuscript was framed by the KM Model discussed above, the editor took the liberty of reviewing the thirteen cases summarized above, to identify which areas/components of the model were covered/discussed by the cases and if any new aspects emerge from the cases described here.

The results of such an endeavor can be seen in Table 1.

Table 1. Components of the mesosystem model of knowledge management as illustrated by the cases

	L_1P	L_1L	L_1DM	L_1S	KS_2	NKD_2	L_3P	L_3L	L_3DM	L_3S
Chapter 2	X	X	X	X	X	X	X	X	X	X
Chapter 3	X	X	X	X	X	X				X
Chapter 4	X	X	X	X	X					
Chapter 5	X	X	X	X	X	X				
Chapter 6	X	X	X	X	X	X	X		X	X
Chapter 7	X	X		X	X					
Chapter 8	X	X		X	X	X	X			X
Chapter 9	X	X	X	X	X	X	X			X
Chapter 10	X	X	X	X	X	X				
Chapter 11	X		X	X		X	X	X	X	X
Chapter 12	X	X	X	X	X		X	X	X	X
Chapter 13	X	X	X	X		X				X

Note: The human layer-$L_{(1)}$, The unified new knowledge development and knowledge sharing layer$_{(2)}$; and the machine layer-$L_{(3)}$. P-People; L-Learning; DM-Decision Making; S-Systems; KS-Knowledge Sharing; NKD-New Knowledge Development.

The following are some observations that follow:

Only about a third of the cases discuss either knowledge sharing or new knowledge development, but not both. The other two-thirds cover both.

Only three cases have no evidence of the data/machine layer.

In several cases, the data/AI presence is discussed but their decision-making and/or learning are omitted, or not observed.

The vast majority of the cases discuss both learning and decision-making within the human/knowledge layer. Only three cases discuss one of the two (learning or decision-making) but not both. It seems though that the timing (as well as the actors and the 'place') of learning and decision-making are exclusive.

The complex interactions between different actors within components (for example different systems interacting within the 'system" component in the human (1) layer; or between components within and between the layers are not represented in detail by the mesosystem model, which does not capture well such richness.

The major research recommendation the editor would have for future case studies will be for the researchers to try and capture the richness of the interactions between the different actors, systems, processes, and activities on the time dimension since the timing for many aspects of knowledge and data management very shortly (if not present already) will be dictated by the AI algorithms.

Meir Russ
University of Wisconsin-Green Bay, USA

REFERENCES

ISO. (2018). *ISO 30401:2018. Knowledge management systems-Requirements*. https://www.iso.org/obp/ui/#iso:std:iso:30401:ed-1:v1:en

Russ, M. (2021a). Knowledge management for sustainable development in the era of continuously accelerating technological revolutions: A framework and models. *Sustainability (Basel), 13*(6), 3353. doi:10.3390u13063353

Russ, M. (2021b). The individual and the organizational model of quantum decision-making and learning: An introduction and the application of the quadruple loop learning. *Merits, 1*(1), 34-46. https://www.mdpi.com/2673-8104/1/1/5

Russ, M., Fineman, R., & Jones, J. K. (2010). Conceptual Theory: What Do You Know? In M. Russ (Ed.), *Knowledge Management Strategies for Business Development: 1-22*. Business Science Reference. doi:10.4018/978-1-60566-348-7.ch001

Acknowledgment

This book will not be in your hands without the help and support that I have received in the last two-plus years from various collaborators. First, the editorial advisory board and the IGI editorial staff, especially Elizabeth Barrantes provided continuous moral and practical support when the response to the call for chapters was minimal at best. The authors of the chapters themselves as writers and as reviewers deserve a big thank you for responding to my continuous nagging and requests. Special thanks go to Liz Kheng and Beth A. Kiernan Ferrigno who during their doctoral studies devoted their time again and again to reviewing the papers I asked them to review. I also want to thank my good friends Knut Ingar Westeren and Mohammad Daradkeh who went beyond their expected responsibilities and helped me when help was needed. Finally, without the help of my family, especially my one and only, allowing me to take the time needed for thinking, editing, and writing, this book would not have come to fruition.

Section 1
Introduction

Chapter 1
Mapping Knowledge Management for Sustainability and Information Technology: Trends and Opportunities

Jaime J. González-Masip
https://orcid.org/0000-0001-9352-7896
Universidad Politécnica de Madrid, Spain

EXECUTIVE SUMMARY

Knowledge management became a relevant topic for academics and practitioners. Information and communication technologies are important tools for supporting knowledge management practices. In this sense, artificial intelligence has recently acquired great prominence. On the other hand, there is great interest in fitting organizational strategies in the so-called sustainability paradigm due to the urgency perceived by the different stakeholders. This chapter presents the results of a mapping bibliometric analysis of the academic literature that jointly addresses these three concepts using SciMAT software. These results include bibliometric performance metrics of publications and graphical representations of the cognitive structures (conceptual themes) hidden in the selected bibliographic sample. The work shows the most and least studied topics in the field. Also, a series of recommendations on possible lines of research work in the field are included.

INTRODUCTION

Knowledge economies are advancing and consolidating, making knowledge and its management a key piece in the value creation and productivity of organizations (Sheehan & Houghton, 2000). They can be defined as "production and services based on knowledge-intensive activities that contribute to an accelerated pace of technical and scientific advance, as well as rapid obsolescence" (Powell & Snellman, 2004, p.199). Knowledge management is a set of systematic and disciplined actions that an organization can take to obtain the greatest value from the available knowledge (Marwick, 2001). Well-done knowledge

DOI: 10.4018/978-1-6684-5859-4.ch001

management is based on the adequate use of technologies that allow processing and systematizing information in an optimal way to be used in decision-making (Liao, 2003). Artificial intelligence is one of the technologies at the foundation of knowledge management (Baskerville & Dulipovici, 2006). Artificial intelligence, together with massive data analysis, is gaining relevance due to the technical advances that these technologies are experiencing. Currently, a distinction can be made between human knowledge, processed or shared knowledge, and machine knowledge or artificial intelligence (Russ, 2021).

On the other hand, there is a notable concern and urgency to understanding everything related to the environmental and social impact that the economic activity of organizations is generating (Gond & Crane, 2010). Organizations and regulators must adopt sustainability strategies, that enable them to fit their proposals and activities within the sustainable development framework to positively manage their impact (Curran, 2009). Thus, academics and practitioners already know that, in addition to growth and profitability, organizations must pursue objectives related to sustainable development such as environmental protection, social justice, and equity (Wilson, 2003).

Taking these three aspects into account, this study aims to identify the topics that have been studied most in the academic literature that deals jointly with knowledge management, sustainability, and the use of technologies (which we will call 'KST studies'). This allows us to assess the scientific relevance of some issues in the field and possible research opportunities or knowledge gaps that may represent important contributions. To carry out the study, a science mapping analysis will be made, which helps to identify the most commonly studied topics or themes and their relations (Mura, Longo, Micheli, & Bolzani, 2018), as well as under-explored or emerging conceptual areas of research (Shiffrin & Borner, 2004; Van Raan & Noyons, 2002). Web of Science is used as a data source and the SciMAT software is used as an analytical tool (Cobo, López-Herrera, Herrera-Viedma, & Herrera, 2012).

This work provides two main novelties. First, the results of the mapping analysis show descriptively the state of the art in the field, organized by topics of interest. It is accompanied by data on the bibliometric performance of the publications and the conceptual structures or themes identified in the analysis. Secondly, a series of questions are answered on the presence in the literature of the KST dimensions studied from different perspectives. At the end of these questions, present and future possible lines of research are raised based on the topics found.

The chapter is structured in several parts. First, a brief theoretical analysis is made to justify the convenience of the study. Second, the bibliometric method used is explained step by step. Third, the results of the bibliometric analysis and the science mapping analysis are shown. Next, the results are analyzed by answering a series of questions aimed at identifying the presence of the three KST elements under study. Finally, a series of conclusions are drawn, including recommendations for further research based on this field.

BACKGROUND

This section presents the theoretical foundations underpinning this study, which aims to provide evidence of the existing cognitive structures in the academic literature on knowledge management (KM), sustainability, and the use of technology, all together. The following lines show the conceptual connection between these three topics, which gives meaning to the results of the subsequent bibliometric analysis.

Knowledge management "is the collection, integration, and classification of disordered information, technology, and expertise in an enterprise and provides systematic and organized information for internal employees or management-level staff to consult when undertaking new tasks and decision-making" (Huang & Shih, 2009, p.36). A proper KM leads to obtaining innovations in the organizations, by search, absorption, and sharing of knowledge, so it is a consolidated activity for the achievement of competitive advantages in organizations and therefore, a key strategic resource (Martins, Rampasso, Anholon, Quelhas, & Leal Filho, 2019).

Due to the increasing volume of information handled by organizations and the need to automate its processing, information and communication technologies (ICTs or ITs) act as a support tool for fostering the creation of new knowledge by people at different levels and in different contexts. Thus, ICTs are key resources in the KM of organizations, existing tools, software, or systems for specific functions, scenarios, or sectors of activity, generically called 'knowledge management systems' (Edwards, Shaw, & Collier, 2005; Saito, Umemoto, & Ikeda, 2007). As a general concept, it is said that a "knowledge management systems (KMS) refer to a class of information systems applied to managing organizational knowledge", and they define them as "IT-based systems developed to support and enhance the organizational processes of knowledge creation, storage/retrieval, transfer, and application" (Alavi & Leidner, 2001, p.114). Artificial intelligence (IA) is a prominent technology that can be used as a tool for knowledge creation and management and decision-making (Liebowitz, 2001; Nemati, Steiger, Iyer, & Herschel, 2002). On its own, or combined with other technologies, such as big data, it can be applied to different contexts and operational issues (e.g., Abubakar, Behravesh, Rezapouraghdam, & Yildiz, 2019). AI shows capabilities for autonomous information processing and the generation of large amounts of knowledge. For this reason, some authors differentiate between three main sources: human knowledge, processed knowledge, and machine knowledge (Russ, 2021).

Organizations need to face the challenge of adapting themselves to the paradigm of sustainable development and the United Nations' Agenda 2030 project (Leal Filho, Manolas, & Pace, 2015). Corporate sustainability (CS) and corporate social responsibility (CSR) are two strategic initiative models that organizations can adopt for this purpose. Both have been used as equivalent terms a in multitude of academic contexts to work on the link between the company and its social and environmental surroundings (Strand, Freeman, & Hockerts, 2015). Nevertheless, there are arguments to consider both as different concepts (González-Masip, 2020). A consensual perspective is to fit *sustainability* within the conceptual framework of *sustainable development*, understood as "to ensure that it meets the needs of the present without compromising the ability of future generations to meet their own needs" (World Commission on Environment and Development, 1987, p. 15). Therefore, the approach to sustainability has a systemic vision, since it analyzes the impact on economic, social and environmental capital (Kleine & von Hauff, 2009). On the other hand, CSR is more concerned with how organizations decide to manage and incorporate stakeholder demands into their strategies, and the ethical analysis of what organizations should do (Gond & Crane, 2010). Stakeholders are defined as "people who affect or are affected by corporate policies and practices" (Garriga & Melé, 2004, p. 59). Effective organizational practices come in part from knowledge transferred from stakeholders and are consolidated when they are re-evaluated by them (Riege & Lindsay, 2006). Involving stakeholders in the organization's strategy means exchanging information with them.

Both sustainability and KM are complex strategies that organizations must plan for the long term and dedicate specific resources to. However, the coexistence of both is possible: the presence of KM in organizations can improve sustainability through their core processes and activities (Sanguankaew & Vathanophas Ractham, 2019). For example, KM allows to increase the knowledge of the company and to foster better practices for sustainability through dialogue with its stakeholders (Tsalis, Malamateniou,

Koulouriotis, & Nikolaou, 2020), so it is an effective means of making decisions for sustainability. Thus, KM plays an important mediating role between stakeholder demands and sustainability practices, also reinforcing the image of commitment and responsibility (Shahzad, Qu, Zafar, Ding, & Rehman, 2020). The latest technological advances have given much social prominence to KM technologies like artificial intelligence, due to the changes that it can potentially produce in numerous sectors of economic activity. It is interesting to explore how this technology, among others, can contribute to the achievement of better sustainability impacts by organizations and the Sustainable Development Goals (Nishant, Kennedy, & Corbett, 2020; Vinuesa et al., 2020).

For all these reasons expressed above, we propose to select publications that address the topics of knowledge management, sustainability (from the perspective of sustainable development) and technology (called KST scope), and to find the intellectual structure of that literature. The objective is to identify in this body of literature the topics mainly addressed by previous research in the field, as well as the opportunities that researchers may have to contribute with new knowledge.

METHODOLOGY

Bibliometric studies allow an algorithmic analysis of metadata fields and textual content of sets of publications in a systematic and semi-automatic way (using specific software). In this study, the analysis process has two phases (see Figure 1), both of which are considered bibliometric analysis methods (Noyons, Moed, & Luwel, 1999). In the first phase, bibliometric performance analysis begins with the collection of documents from a bibliographic database and provides in the end data on the bibliographic impact of the publications analyzed. In the second phase, science mapping analysis allows us to identify the conceptual or intellectual structure of the analyzed bibliographic body.

Figure 1. Bibliometric analysis process overview
Source: Author elaboration

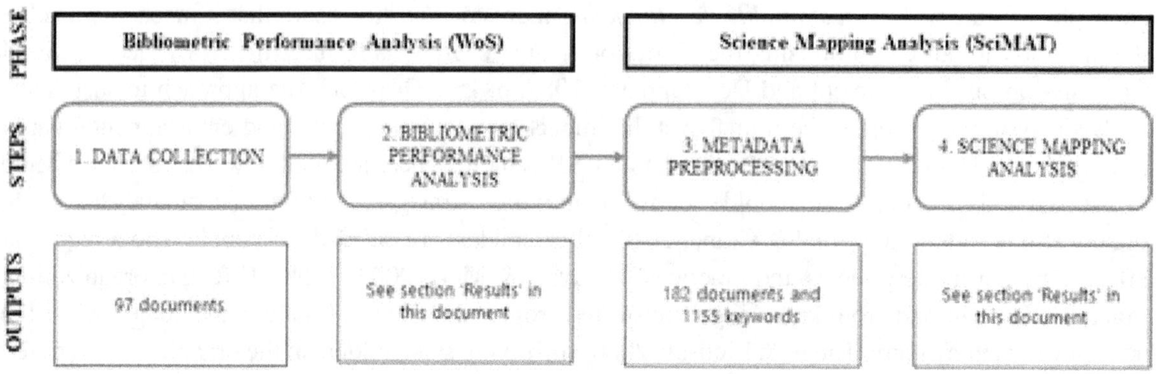

The science mapping analysis methodology is systematic but not deterministic. Its results highly depend on the analysis parameters provided to the algorithm. For this reason, as will be seen below, three different parameter settings were used to test the stability of the results obtained. Anyway, it is important to consider the results as a descriptive approximation of the intellectual content undercover in the sample of documents analyzed.

Data Collection

Document sample was selected from the Social Science Citation Index (SSCI) of the Web of Science™ Core Collection (Martín-de Castro, Amores-Salvadó, & Díez-Vial, 2022; Ye, Kueh, Hou, Liu, & Yu, 2020), Table 1 lists all search and selection parameters applied for document extraction.

Table 1. Data collection parameters

Selection Filter	Value or Criteria
Data Base	Web of Science Core Collection.
Index	Social Science Citation Index (SSCI).
Language	English.
Type of document	Any (articles, early access, review article, proceeding paper).
Search Query	TS= ("knowledge management") AND TS= (sustainable* and development) AND TS= (technology or ICT or AI or "artificial intelligence" or machine* or information* or comput*) NOT TS= ("sustainable competitive" or "competitive advantage")"
Date	7 April 2023

Source: Author elaboration

The search query is composed of three groups of concepts that are applied together to select the intersection of documents that meet the three criteria. First, knowledge management is the main topic. Secondly, those derived from the 'sustainability' and 'development' words, referring to sustainable development (Tsalis et al., 2020). We try to avoid cases where "sustainable" is meaning "long-lasting" or "stable over time". Third, we include the topics to select the publications that deal with or mention technological issues. The last condition in the search is to discard documents that include the concepts "sustainable competitive" or "competitive advantage" as they are not the desired approach to sustainability. The wildcard character * at the end of the search terms allows you to select documents using derived terms. All these terms are matched with the TOPIC metadata field of the documents in Web of Science (WoS), which encompasses the TITLE, ABSTRACT and KEYWORDS in each document. The search query was launched on April 7th, 2023, resulting in the collection of 182 documents.

Bibliometric Performance Analysis

Bibliometric performance analysis is a descriptive analysis of the distribution of a set of publications according to different criteria, and their relevance or impact on the academic community (Noyons, Moed, & Van Raan, 1999). Aggregated data from the sample are shown in Table 3. We also show the distribution of the number of publications per year and citations received by the total set of documents in each year (López-Robles et al., 2021), the distribution of publications by the different WoS Categories (González-Alcaide, 2021), and the number of publications by authors' country of affiliation.

Science Mapping Analysis

As mentioned before, science mapping analysis allows to identify and represent graphically hidden conceptual structures into a set of documents (Börner, Chen, & Boyack, 2003; Van den Besselaar & Heimeriks, 2006). There are different types of analysis. When performing a co-word analysis (keyword pairing), we assume that pair of words in the same document jointly contribute value to the construction of conceptual elements (Callon, Courtial, Turner, & Bauin, 1983). Before running this analysis, we must review the keyword pool to be analyzed. It means merging similar concepts in one word, and dropping generic words that do not provide relevant interpretation and words related to analysis methods used in research articles. Also, we drop words used in the search query if they appear over-represented in the sample, as they can produce a bias in the results.

Table 2 compiles the parameters used for running the analysis. To verify the validity of the results obtained, different parametric configurations were iteratively compared until a stable solution was reached.

Table 2. Science mapping analysis parameters

Analysis Parameter	Value or Criteria	Function	Description	References
Software tool	SciMAT	Bibliometric mapping analysis software.	Developed by the Universidad de Granada (Spain).	Cobo, López-Herrera, Herrera-Viedma, & Herrera (2012)
Unit of Analysis	Keywords (author's and source's).	Network extraction.	It identifies pairs of keywords used simultaneously in the same documents.	Olawumi & Chan (2018)
Kind of Matrix	Co-occurrence.			
Frequency reduction	2	It allows filtering out words that are under-represented in the sample.	It selects words that appear at least two times in the sample.	
Edge value reduction	2	It allows for filtering out word pairs that are under-represented in the sample.	It selects word pairs that appear at least two times in the sample.	
Normalization Measure	Equivalence Index.	It normalizes the intensity or strength of keyword pairs.	It compares the times two words appear together in the same document concerning to times they appear in the sample.	Santana & Lopez-Cabrales (2019)
Clustering Algorithm	Simple Center Algorithm.	It creates clusters iteratively by grouping nodes that represent keywords.	It adds new nodes to a cluster by calculating its *density* and *centrality* indexes.	Coulter, Monarch, & Konda (1998)
Cluster size	a) Min 3 / max 6. b) Min 3 / max 9. c) Min 3 / max 12.	Maximum and minimum allowed cluster size.	We compare three different configurations.	
Aggregation function	Union document mapper.	It allows the management of the documents, backing the clusters' keywords resulting from the analysis.	Algebraic union of the set of documents linked to a cluster	Cobo et al. (2012)
Performance metrics	H-index, document sum, citations sum.			

Source: Author elaboration.

The *simple center algorithm* constructs clusters by adding new nodes until the defined maximum cluster size is reached prioritizing the strongest links. The clusters obtained are visually represented in a strategic diagram according to their *density* and *centrality* index values (Callon, Courtial, & Laville, 1991). A high value on the *density index* indicates strong internal conceptual coherence and ease of interpretation of the cluster, and a high value on the *centrality index* indicates a strong conceptual influence on other clusters (Figure 2). Themes that are highly developed internally and strongly linked to other conceptual aspects are called *motor themes*. The so-called *isolated themes* have strong internal links and are highly developed in the field but show weak connections to other concepts. *Basic and transversal themes* group topics that are widely used in the field of study and linked extensively. *Emerging or declining themes* are internally loosely cohesive themes with little external linkage. In general, themes with low density index are difficult to interpret conceptually due to their weak cohesion and the diversity of internal topics.

Figure 2. Cluster mapping strategic diagram
Source: Cobo et al. (2011)

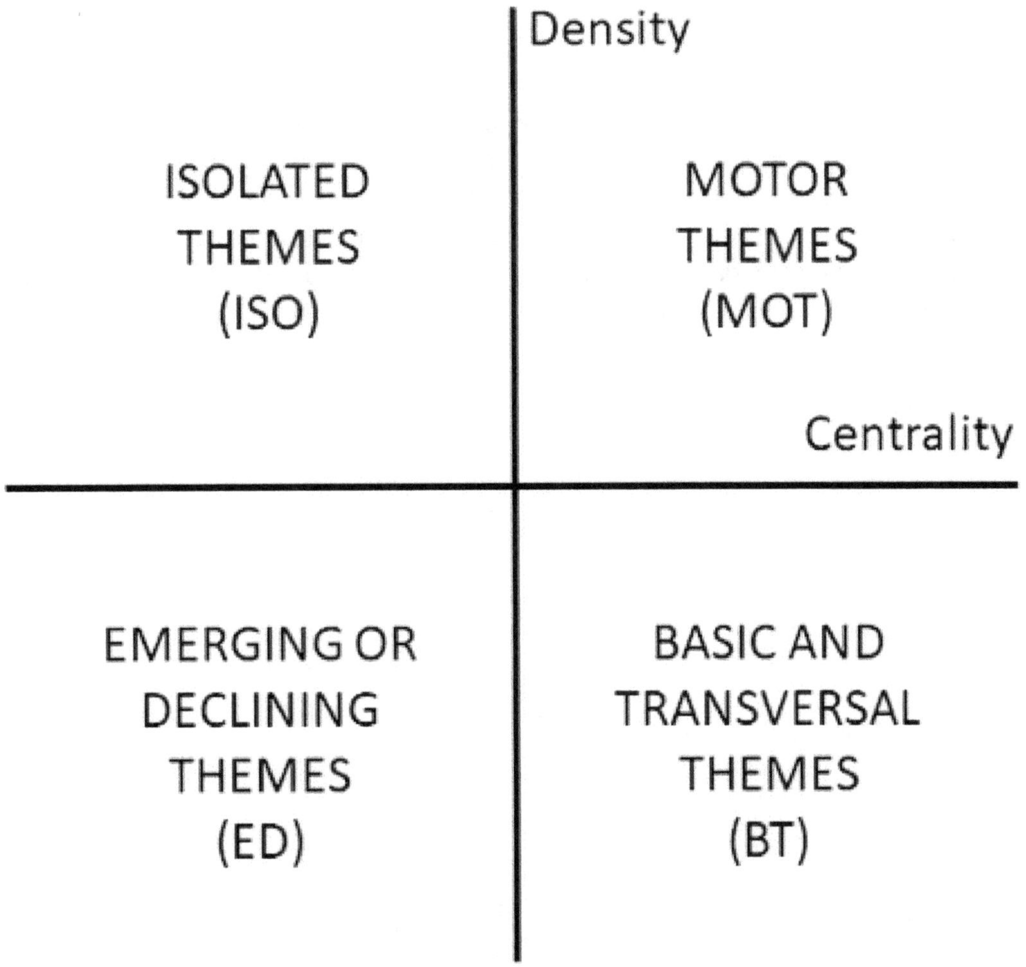

RESULTS

This section includes the results obtained in the complete analysis process. Table 3 shows a summary of the main bibliometric measures of the sample obtained. The number of documents in the dataset is 182, with a total word count of 1195. Among them, 233 are within the defined limits to participate in the study because they appear at least twice in the sample.

Table 3. Summary bibliometric report

Descriptive Parameter	Sample's Value
Documents count	182
The sum of the times cited	4,504
Average citations per item	24.75
h-index	31
Words count	1155
Words with frequency >= 2	233 (20,1%)

Source: Author elaboration

Figure 3 shows the number of publications per year, and the growth of citations received by the set of documents analyzed. The publications cover the period from 2000 to the present year 2023. Growth in the number of publications is observed from 2015 onwards, with a relatively small number of publications until that year. Precisely, this reduced number of publications in the first half of the temporal range prevents the creation of more than one temporal subperiod for the analysis. Therefore, the study is carried out considering a single overall period.

Figure 3. Documents and citations per year
Source: Author elaboration

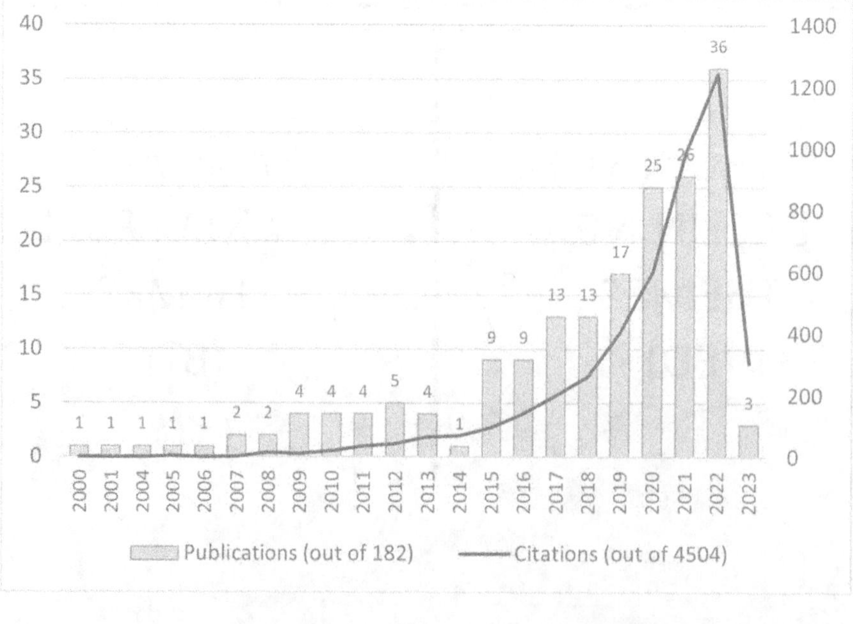

Figure 4 shows the distribution of publications among the different WoS Social Science Citation Index (SSCI) categories. The main ones are Green Sustainable Science Technology, Environmental Sciences, Environmental Studies, Management, and to a lesser extent the categories of Business and Information Science Library Science. The remaining categories do not show an outstanding bibliometric performance, although the large number of these (47 categories in total) is surprising. Publications are concentrated in fields related to business and management, environment, and information management. In WoS SSCI publications can be linked to more than one category.

Figure 5 shows the distribution of the documents according to the countries of the academic entities to which the authors are affiliated. As can be seen, there is a wide diversity of countries and continents within the set of countries with the highest bibliometric performance.

Figure 4. Documents per WoS Categories (best 25 out of 47)
Source: Author elaboration

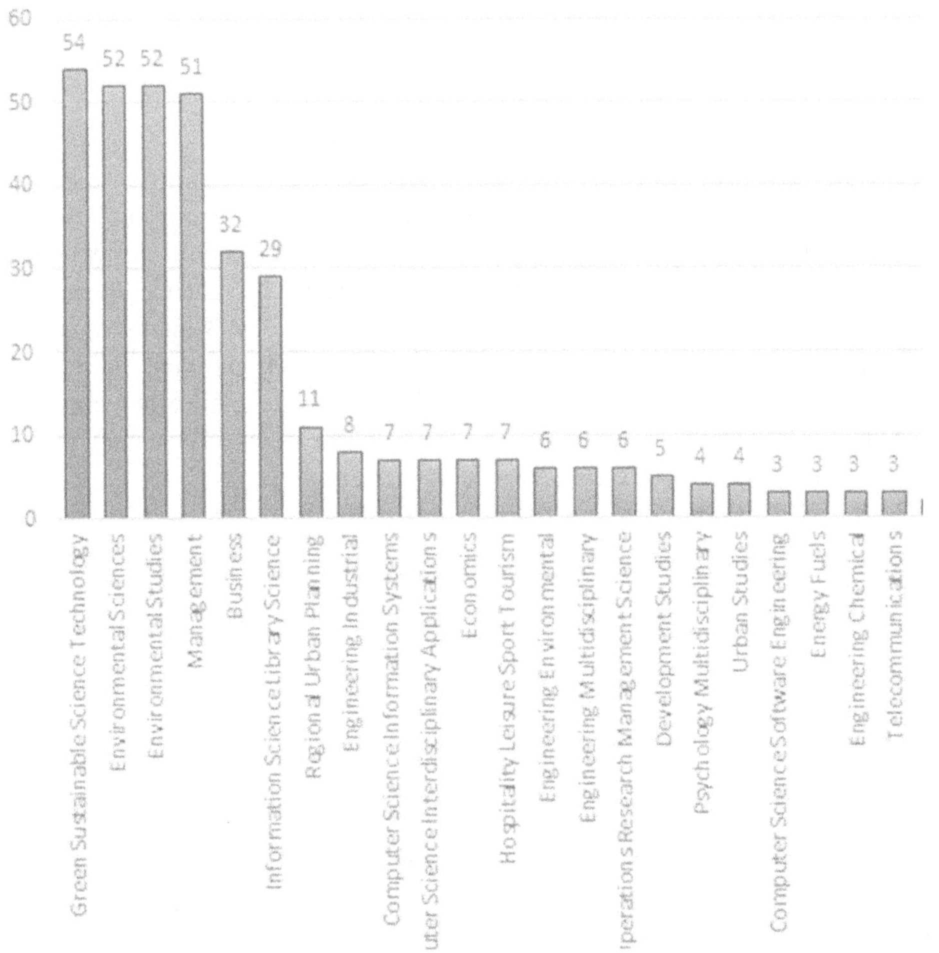

Figure 5. Documents per author's affiliation country (best 25)
Source: Author elaboration

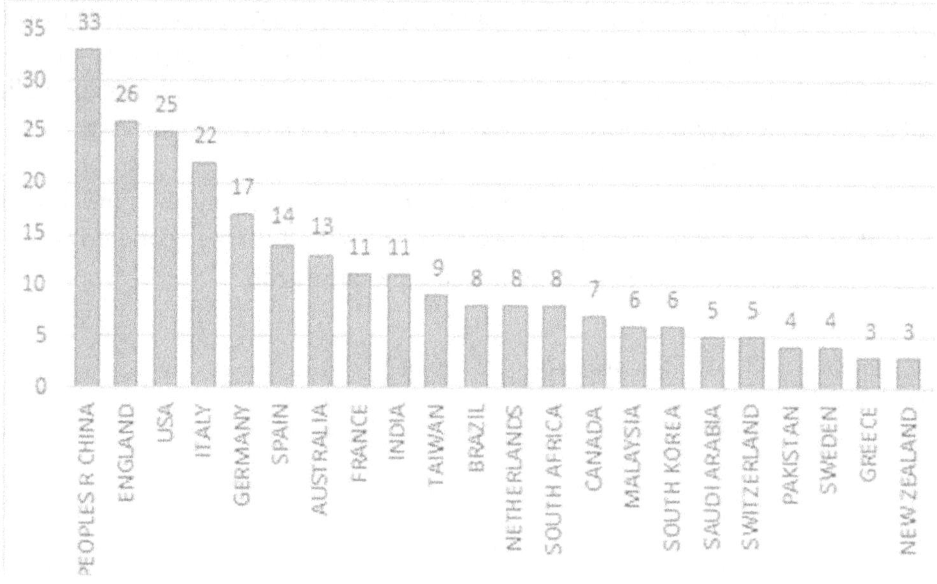

Figure 6 includes the strategic cluster diagrams obtained in the mapping analysis process. The results are shown for three different configurations of minimum and maximum cluster size (3-6, 3-9, and 3-12 respectively), to assess the stability of the results obtained. The strategic diagram located in the center (Figure 7B), obtained with the parameters minimum cluster size 3 and maximum cluster size 9, is considered the selected result (which we will call the *reference configuration*). Each cluster represents a conceptual theme related to the scope of analysis. The label is the name of the cluster keyword best connected to the other keywords within the cluster. The diameter represents the number of unique documents (*union document*) that support the keywords of each cluster.

Figure 6. Clusters' strategic diagram (documents count)
Source: Author elaboration

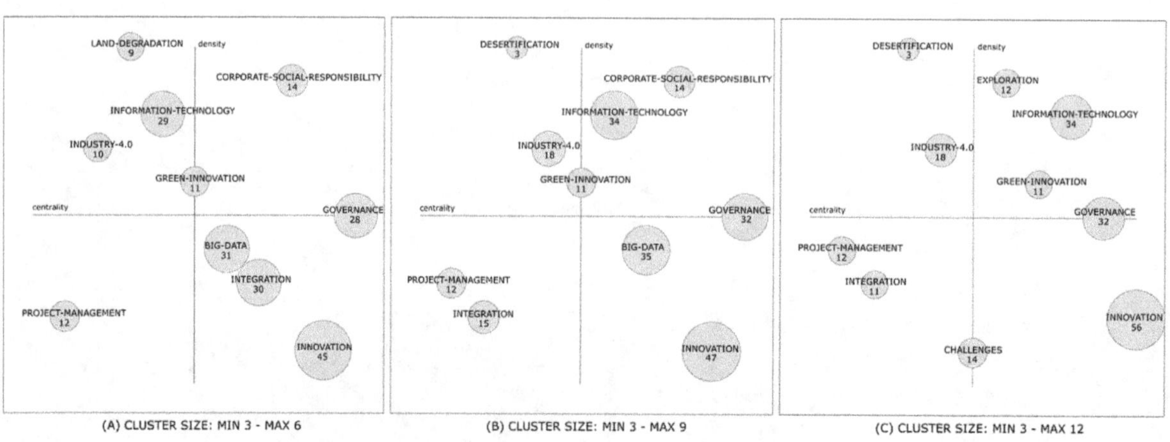

Table 4 shows the performance values of the 10 clusters resulting from by using the reference configuration (cluster size between 3 and 9 nodes or keywords). The list of clusters is sorted according to the document count column, according to *union document mapping* criteria. Also, for each cluster, are shown the h-index values, the sum of citations, the max citations number of any document linked to the cluster, and the centrality and density values in the range 0 to 1, which locate the clusters in the strategic diagram (see Figure 7B). The columns *average citations* and *normalized-h* allow displaying normalized values of bibliometric performance considering the size of each cluster in document number. Average citations are calculated by dividing the total sum of citations by the document count. On the other hand, we introduce the 'normalized-h index' calculated by dividing, for each cluster, the square of its h-index value by its document count. This index bonuses those clusters that have an h-index close to their documents count (i.e., their maximum possible h-index value) and penalizes otherwise. Starting from two clusters with equal h-index, the normalized-h index will have a higher value in the cluster with a lower document count, since their document average performance is higher.

Table 4. Clusters' bibliometric performance (clusters size 3-9 nodes)

Cluster	Docs. Count	h-Index	Sum. Citations	Max. Citations	Avg. Citations	Norm-h	Centrality Range	Density Range
INNOVATION	47	20	1655	351	35,21	8,51	0,90	0,10
BIG-DATA	35	17	1278	351	36,51	8,26	0,70	0,40
INFORMATION-TECHNOLOGY	34	15	1116	327	32,82	6,62	0,60	0,80
GOVERNANCE	32	16	797	128	24,91	8,00	1,00	0,50
INDUSTRY-4.0	18	12	817	327	45,39	8,00	0,40	0,70
INTEGRATION	15	8	144	42	9,60	4,27	0,20	0,20
CORPORATE-SOCIAL-RESPONSIBILITY	14	8	330	114	23,57	4,57	0,80	0,90
PROJECT-MANAGEMENT	12	7	279	108	23,25	4,08	0,10	0,30
GREEN-INNOVATION	11	8	582	196	52,91	5,82	0,50	0,60
DESERTIFICATION	3	2	149	97	49,67	1,33	0,30	1,00

Source: Author elaboration.

Finally, Table 5 shows the list of keywords (or *topics*) included within each cluster and the number of documents supporting each of them, for each of the three cluster size configurations. This allows us to evaluate the intellectual content of each cluster and its internal coherence. The two columns in the center show the data resulting from the reference configuration, which will be analyzed in the next section. The names of the clusters (or *conceptual themes*) are accompanied by the number of unique documents that support them and the strategic diagram quadrant in which they are located.

Table 5. Clusters' content depends on the selected cluster size.

Clusters Size: 3-6 Nodes		Clusters Size: 3-9 Nodes (Reference Configuration)		Clusters Size: 3-12 Nodes	
CLUSTER (Docs. Count, Quadrant)	**NODES (Documents Count)**	**CLUSTER (Docs. Count, Quadrant)**	**NODES (Documents Count)**	**CLUSTER (Docs. Count, Quadrant)**	**NODES (Documents Count)**
INNOVATION (45, BT)	AGRICULTURAL TECHNOLOGIES (2) BUSINESS (6) CAPABILITY (11) DATA ANALYTICS (2) INNOVATION (36) SERVICES (5) STAKEHOLDER-ENGAGEMENT (2)	**INNOVATION (47, BT)**	AGRICULTURAL TECHNOLOGIES (2) BUSINESS (6) CAPABILITY (11) DATA ANALYTICS (2) DECISION-SUPPORT (4) ENTREPRENEURSHIP (5) INNOVATION (36) SERVICES (5) STAKEHOLDER-ENGAGEMENT (2)	**INNOVATION (56, BT)**	AGRICULTURAL TECHNOLOGIES (2) BIG DATA (9)* BUSINESS (6) CAPABILITY (11) DATA ANALYTICS (2) DECISION-SUPPORT (4) ENTREPRENEURSHIP (5) FIRM-PERFORMANCE (6)* INNOVATION (36) RESOURCE-BASED-VIEW (5)* SERVICES (5) STAKEHOLDER-ENGAGEMENT (2)
BIG-DATA (31, BT)	ARTIFICIAL INTELLIGENCE (5) BIG DATA (9) CHALLENGES (10) DECISION-SUPPORT (4) DIGITALIZATION (4)* KNOWLEDGE-MANAGEMENT-SYSTEMS (5) SMART-CITIES (9)	**BIG-DATA (35, BT)**	ARTIFICIAL INTELLIGENCE (5) BIG DATA (9) CHALLENGES (10) DECISION-MAKING (11) KNOWLEDGE-MANAGEMENT-SYSTEMS (5) SMART-CITIES (9)	**CHALLENGES (14, ED/BT)**	ARTIFICIAL INTELLIGENCE (5) CHALLENGES (10) OPPORTUNITIES (3)*
INFORMATION-TECHNOLOGY (29, ISO)	ABSORPTIVE CAPACITY (8) INFORMATION TECHNOLOGY (10) INTERNET (4) IOT (4) KNOWLEDGE-SHARING (11) PERCEIVED USEFULNESS (2) USER ACCEPTANCE (3)	**INFORMATION-TECHNOLOGY (34, MOT)**	ABSORPTIVE CAPACITY (8) INFORMATION TECHNOLOGY (10) INTERNET (4) IOT (4) KNOWLEDGE-SHARING (11) PERCEIVED USEFULNESS (2) SUPPLY-CHAIN-MANAGEMENT (7) USER ACCEPTANCE (3)	**INFORMATION-TECHNOLOGY (34, MOT)**	ABSORPTIVE CAPACITY (8) INFORMATION TECHNOLOGY (10) INTERNET (4) IOT (4) KNOWLEDGE-SHARING (11) PERCEIVED USEFULNESS (2) SUPPLY-CHAIN-MANAGEMENT (7) USER ACCEPTANCE (3)
GOVERNANCE (28, MOT/BT)	COMMUNITIES (11) ENTREPRENEURSHIP (5)* GOVERNANCE (9) PARTICIPATION (4) PRODUCT DEVELOPMENT (5) SCIENCE (7) VALUE-CREATION (5)	**GOVERNANCE (32, MOT/BT)**	COMMUNITIES (11) GOVERNANCE (9) ORGANIZATIONS (9) PARTICIPATION (4) PRODUCT DEVELOPMENT (5) SCIENCE (7) VALUE-CREATION (5)	**GOVERNANCE (32, MOT/BT)**	COMMUNITIES (11) GOVERNANCE (9) ORGANIZATIONS (9) PARTICIPATION (4) PRODUCT DEVELOPMENT (5) SCIENCE (7) VALUE-CREATION (5)
INDUSTRY-4.0 (10, ISO)	BUSINESS MODELS (3) CIRCULAR ECONOMY (4) CYBER-PHYSICAL-SYSTEMS (2) ENVIRONMENTAL-SUSTAINABILITY (2) INDUSTRY-4.0 (7) PERFORMANCE MEASUREMENT (3) SOCIAL-SUSTAINABILITY (2)	**INDUSTRY-4.0 (18, ISO)**	BUSINESS MODELS (3) CIRCULAR ECONOMY (4) CYBER-PHYSICAL-SYSTEMS (2) DIGITALIZATION (4) ENVIRONMENTAL-SUSTAINABILITY (2) INDUSTRY-4.0 (7) PERFORMANCE MEASUREMENT (3) SOCIAL-SUSTAINABILITY (2) SUSTAINABLE-DEVELOPMENT-GOALS (8)	**INDUSTRY-4.0 (18, ISO)**	BUSINESS MODELS (3) CIRCULAR ECONOMY (4) CYBER-PHYSICAL-SYSTEMS (2) DIGITALIZATION (4) ENVIRONMENTAL-SUSTAINABILITY (2) INDUSTRY-4.0 (7) PERFORMANCE MEASUREMENT (3) SOCIAL-SUSTAINABILITY (2) SUSTAINABLE-DEVELOPMENT-GOALS (8)

Continued on following page

Table 5. Continued

Clusters Size: 3-6 Nodes		Clusters Size: 3-9 Nodes (Reference Configuration)		Clusters Size: 3-12 Nodes	
CLUSTER (Docs. Count, Quadrant)	**NODES (Documents Count)**	**CLUSTER (Docs. Count, Quadrant)**	**NODES (Documents Count)**	**CLUSTER (Docs. Count, Quadrant)**	**NODES (Documents Count)**
INTEGRATION (30, BT)	DYNAMIC CAPABILITIES (3) ENVIRONMENT (4) FIRM-PERFORMANCE (6) FUTURE (6)* INTEGRATION (8) ORGANIZATIONS (9)* SUPPLY-CHAIN-MANAGEMENT (7)*	**INTEGRATION (15, ED)**	DYNAMIC CAPABILITIES (3) ENVIRONMENT (4) FIRM-PERFORMANCE (6) INTEGRATION (8)	**INTEGRATION (15, ED)**	DYNAMIC CAPABILITIES (3) ENVIRONMENT (4) INTEGRATION (8)
CORPORATE-SOCIAL-RESPONSIBILITY (14, MOT)	CORPORATE-SOCIAL-RESPONSIBILITY (7) EXPLOITATION (3) EXPLORATION (3) FINANCIAL PERFORMANCE (5) RENEWABLE-ENERGY-SECTOR (2) RESOURCE-BASED-VIEW (5) RESOURCES (3)	**CORPORATE-SOCIAL-RESPONSIBILITY (14, MOT)**	CORPORATE-SOCIAL-RESPONSIBILITY (7) EXPLOITATION (3) EXPLORATION (3) FINANCIAL PERFORMANCE (5) RENEWABLE-ENERGY-SECTOR (2) RESOURCE-BASED-VIEW (5) RESOURCES (3)	**EXPLORATION (12, MOT)**	AMBIDEXTERITY (3)* CORPORATE-SOCIAL-RESPONSIBILITY (7) EXPLOITATION (3) EXPLORATION (3) FINANCIAL PERFORMANCE (5) RENEWABLE-ENERGY-SECTOR (2)
PROJECT-MANAGEMENT (12, ED)	CONSTRUCTION (4) INFORMATION SYSTEMS (7) PROJECT MANAGEMENT (5)	**PROJECT-MANAGEMENT (12, ED)**	CONSTRUCTION (4) INFORMATION SYSTEMS (7) PROJECT MANAGEMENT (5)	**PROJECT-MANAGEMENT (12, ED)**	CONSTRUCTION (4) INFORMATION SYSTEMS (7) PROJECT MANAGEMENT (5)
GREEN-INNOVATION (11, ISO/MOT)	ECO-INNOVATION (4) GREEN INNOVATION (6) RESEARCH-AND-DEVELOPMENT (7)	**GREEN-INNOVATION (11, ISO/MOT)**	ECO-INNOVATION (4) GREEN INNOVATION (6) RESEARCH-AND-DEVELOPMENT (7)	**GREEN-INNOVATION (11, MOT)**	ECO-INNOVATION (4) GREEN INNOVATION (6) RESEARCH-AND-DEVELOPMENT (7)
LAND-DEGRADATION (9, ISO)	DESERTIFICATION (2) LAND-DEGRADATION (3) SUSTAINABLE-DEVELOPMENT-GOALS (8)* SUSTAINABLE LAND MANAGEMENT (2) UNCCD (2)	**DESERTIFICATION (3, ISO)**	DESERTIFICATION (2) LAND-DEGRADATION (3) SUSTAINABLE LAND MANAGEMENT (2) UNCCD (2)	**DESERTIFICATION (3, ISO)**	DESERTIFICATION (2) LAND-DEGRADATION (3) SUSTAINABLE LAND MANAGEMENT (2) UNCCD (2)
* The topic does not exist in the equivalent theme in the "Cluster Size: 3-9 nodes" configuration (reference configuration). MOT: Motor theme; ISO: Isolated theme; BT: Basic and transversal theme; ED: Emerging or declining theme. ISO/MOT, MOT/BT or ED/BT: The theme lies in the division between these two quadrants.					

Source: Author elaboration

DISCUSSION

In this section, we try to answer several questions related to the most relevant cognitive areas identified in the obtained results and the topics included in them. First, we analyze the temporal evolution of the number of publications over the years. Second, we identify and comment on the themes that have the greatest internal cohesion and are most developed, as well as the topics that are most widespread and used in the set of documents analyzed. Then, we analyze how technology concepts connect with other topics within the different themes. Finally, we analyze the presence of the sustainability dimensions within the themes, and topics that conceptually can be related to different types of stakeholders. It is important to consider that the results obtained are always limited to the scope of intellectual content defined in the database query, i.e., to literature that mentions knowledge management, sustainability, and technology in the way they have been expressed in the search. The results must therefore be interpreted with an understanding of how they fit within that chosen scope. To make the text more understandable, the names of the clusters or themes are written in capital letters, and the names of the topics are written in italics with words joined by hyphens.

Is the Research Topic of Interest to Academics?

As we saw in Figure 3, the publications obtained in the sample range from 2000 to 2023. We can identify two periods with two trends in the publications count. There is a first period, between 2000 and 2014, with a reduced and stable annual number of publications over the years. Then there is another period from 2015 onwards, with a steadily increasing number of annual publications. The acceleration of publications after 2016 coincides with the launching of the United Nations' Sustainable Development Goals program (United Nations, 2020) and the implementation of the 2030 Agenda.

The total number of documents is not high. However, their evolution is clearly upward or incremental. Therefore, given the growth rate of annual publications, it can be said that the topic analyzed is of growing interest to researchers. This affirmation could be verified in the next few years by re-launching the query to confirm the upward trend.

What Are the Most Cohesive and Well-Defined Conceptual Themes?

The most strongly cohesive and well-defined conceptual themes can be easily identified in the strategic diagram (Figure 7B): those with over-average *Callon's density* values (Callon et al., 1991). Strongly cohesive and well-defined conceptual themes are those positioned in the top two quadrants. Those are *isolated* themes and *motor* themes (see Figure 4). In our study, these clusters are not the best bibliometric performers (Table 4), but they should be the ones that best represent publication trends.

The corporate social responsibility theme shows the best balance between both dimensions in the strategic diagram. The topics included in this cluster refer to *resource-based-view* approaches and strategic management of knowledge (*exploitation* and *exploration*), with an explicit link to *financial performance*. This instrumental perspective on the use of CSR by companies has been widely addressed in the literature (Aguilera, Rupp, Williams, & Ganapathi, 2007).

The *motor* theme information technology not only gathers topics related to ICTs, such as the *internet* or *IoT* but also others about knowledge management technologies use context. *Knowledge-sharing, absorptive capacity,* and *supply chain management* refer to the exchange, assimilation, and use of knowledge coming from other 'agents' or stakeholders (Tsalis et al., 2020). We can find in this cluster also the topics *perceived-usefulness* and *user-acceptance*, both related to "the degree to which a person believes that using a particular system would enhance his/her job performance" (Davis, 1985, p.26). Therefore, this theme deals with the capacity to exchange and absorb knowledge, as well as the predisposition of users to adopt new technologies.

The green innovation theme, located between the *isolated* and *motor* themes quadrant, appears self-differentiated and separated from the generic innovation concept (another cluster). This theme has only three topics, which remain stable in the three configurations of analysis carried out, so it has a strong cohesion. Along with *green innovation*, the other two topics included in the cluster are *eco-innovation* and *research and development*. A clear trend can be identified in the joint use of the concepts in this case. Eco-innovation and green innovation are similar concepts in the academic literature (Bossle, de Barcellos, Vieira, & Sauvée, 2016; Cheng & Shiu, 2012). Eco-innovation is a tool that organizations can develop to protect the environment with a positive impact on the economy and society by reducing impacts on the environment, increasing resilience against external pressures, and using resources more efficiently (European Commission, 2022).

The conceptual theme Industry 4.0 refers to the so-called fourth industrial revolution, characterized mainly by the presence of digital transformation and networking, cyber-physical systems, and the integration of a socially responsible and sustainable approach to production (Ghobakhloo, 2020; Lasi, Fettke, Kemper, Feld, & Hoffmann, 2014). Although no specific technologies are mentioned, we can identify in the cluster, on one hand, the topics of *digitalization* and *cyber-physical systems*, and on the other hand, in relation to sustainability, the topics of *circular economy*, *environmental sustainability,* and *social sustainability*. Also, and showing a practical vision of integration with technology, we can find the topics of *performance measurement* and *sustainable development goals*, both related to the definition and use of indicators (easier thanks to technology). All this is encompassed in *business models* (another topic in the cluster). This conceptual theme is stable across the different configurations tested in the analysis, which reinforces the proposition that it has its own cognitive identity and internal strength.

The desertification theme is the last of the set of clusters with high internal cohesion. Conceptually related to the phenomenon of global warming (Herrmann & Hutchinson, 2005; Park et al., 2018), this cluster relates specifically to the topics of *land degradation*, *sustainable land management,* and *UNCCD*, which stands for United Nations Convention to Combat Desertification (UNCCD, 2023). Desertification and land degradation look well-fitting specific topics for the KST field. It is therefore a clearly differentiated specific research niche aligned, in this case, with the interests of public entities and administrations. In cluster configuration 3-6 we observe in this theme the presence of the *sustainable-development-goals* topic, which in the reference configuration 3-9 jumps to the Industry 4.0 cluster. This phenomenon indicates a conceptual proximity between *desertification* and *sustainable development goals*, which is compatible with other arguments mentioned about this cluster.

What Are the Most Used Topics in the Literature?

To answer this question, we can look at the themes that appear in the quadrant of *basic and transversal* themes in the strategic diagram (Figure 4 and Figure 7b). These themes have a high bibliometric performance (number of documents, number of citations, h-index...), but have little internal cohesion, so and more difficult to interpret. Their topics are strongly related to topics existing in other clusters. Therefore, they are usually related to diverse and varied research aspects within the scope of the study.

The big data theme gathers topics that can be grouped into three groups. First are technology topics, such as *big data* and *artificial intelligence*. The latter was included in the literature search query, so it could have a positive bias in the results obtained, but the former was not. However, it is noted that both *big data* and *artificial intelligence* are frequently linked in the knowledge management literature (Haenlein & Kaplan, 2019; Smuts & Van der Merwe, 2022). The second group is related to decision-making and includes the topics of *challenges*, *decision-making,* and *knowledge management systems* (Russ, 2021). Finally, can we find the *smart-cities* topic, which corresponds to publications that consider big data as a key resource for the governance and management of smart cities and the assurance of positive sustainable performance (Israilidis, Odusanya, & Mazhar, 2021) Indeed, these places require the compilation and exploitation of large amounts of data for their operations and services.

The innovation theme shows a high internal conceptual diversity, but it is still possible to find an argumentative thread that brings its topics altogether. The presence of the topics *data analytics* and *decision support*, on the one hand, and *entrepreneurship* and *business* on the other, is noteworthy, as they have a strong two-to-two relationship, but also as a whole. The first pair of topics are related since decision support usually refers to systems or tools, and data analytics is precisely a powerful method of decision support (Power, 2014). *Entrepreneurship* is strongly linked to *innovation* and the creation of new value proposals (Wong, Ho, & Autio, 2005). These proposals are usually constituted with business purposes, and structured in business models (Morris, Schindehutte, & Allen, 2005). If we consider the definition of the business model as the basis for strategic decision-making in companies, we can close the circle that links all these concepts (Hacklin & Wallnöfer, 2012). Another important topic we can find in this theme is *stakeholder-engagement*. The reason behind this is that some literature publications affirm that knowledge sourced from engagement with internal and external stakeholders fosters a firm's innovation for sustainability (Ayuso, Rodríguez, García-Castro, & Ariño, 2011). Indeed, stakeholders can be a very valuable source of knowledge for companies if they can establish collaborative links with them. In addition, proper stakeholder management ensures a positive sustainable strategic approach.

Regarding the theme of governance, it compiles, on one hand, topics related to groups or collectives, such as *communities* and *organizations*, which together with topics like *participation* and *science*, refer to the management of knowledge generation and knowledge exchange in the context of sustainable development (Mohamed, Stankosky, & Mohamed, 2009; Nguyen, Young, & Cooke, 2017). On the other hand, concepts such as *product development* and *value creation* refer to the need for management and support in the development of ongoing value-creation processes that require monitoring and validation (Lubberink, Blok, Van Ophem, & Omta, 2017). *Product development* refers in a multitude of cases to *innovation*, eco-innovation, or open-innovation processes (Orlando, Ballestra, Scuotto, Pironti, & Del Giudice, 2022; Rodríguez-Rebés, Navío-Marco, & Ibar-Alonso, 2021), which can have conceptual connections with the themes innovation and green innovation. Taking the conceptual meaning of these topics together, we could say that it refers to the management, supported by technology, of the creation of value and development of products with a positive sustainability impact, through the exchange of knowledge and the collaboration of organizations, communities, and researchers.

Among these three themes analyzed, big data and innovation are the two with the lowest Callon's density. This is reflected in the variability shown in the results of the analysis, comparing the three cluster configurations used in the study (columns in Table 5). Both themes exchange the *big-data* topic when changing the analysis parameters from cluster size 3-9 to cluster size 3-12. It happens, as well, that the topics *decision-support* (in innovation) and *decision-making* (in big data) have semantic closeness, even though they are in different themes. The governance theme includes topics that refer to innovation processes and entrepreneurship (*product development* and *value-creation*), which are also represented in other themes. All these phenomena give clues about the themes, in the quadrant of *basic* and *transversal* themes, acting as repositories of generic topics. Due to the ease with which they interchange topics with each other in some cases, or the conceptual closeness between them, that quadrant could be considered as a pool of interchangeable topics, which can be studied as a block.

Table 6. Topics in the strategic diagram' basic and transversal themes quadrant

Topics in Basic and Transversal Themes	Docs. Count
INNOVATION	36
CAPABILITY	11
DECISION-MAKING	11
COMMUNITIES	11
CHALLENGES	10
BIG-DATA	9
SMART-CITIES	9
GOVERNANCE	9
ORGANIZATIONS	9
SCIENCE	7
BUSINESS	6
ENTREPRENEURSHIP	5
SERVICES	5
ARTIFICIAL-INTELLIGENCE	5
KNOWLEDGE-MANAGEMENT-SYSTEMS	5
PRODUCT-DEVELOPMENT	5
VALUE-CREATION	5
DECISION-SUPPORT	4
PARTICIPATION	4
AGRICULTURAL-TECHNOLOGIES	2
DATA-ANALYTICS	2
STAKEHOLDER-ENGAGEMENT	2

Source: Author elaboration

Table 6 shows the list of *basic and transversal* topics, ordered by the number of documents that support each keyword. The average value of the number of occurrences for each keyword is 7.8, higher than, for example, the occurrences of any keyword in the corporate social responsibility cluster, which is of the *motor* theme type. It can be said that this list includes the most common topics covered in this field's literature. Therefore, the combination of words in this set could represent the intellectual scope of the publications in the field and their objectives (see, Di Vaio, Palladino, Hassan, & Escobar, 2020).

To Which Conceptual Themes Are the Technology Concepts Most Linked?

We can identify in the results a list of technological topics. They are compiled in Table 7, together with the number of documents in which they appear, the cluster in which they are located, and the type of cluster to which they belong.

Table 7. Technology topics found in results (shorted by document count)

Topic	Docs. Count	Cluster	Quadrant
INFORMATION-TECHNOLOGY	10	INFORMATION-TECHNOLOGY	MOT
BIG-DATA	9	BIG-DATA	BT
INFORMATION-SYSTEMS	7	PROJECT-MANAGEMENT	ED
ARTIFICIAL-INTELLIGENCE	5	BIG-DATA	BT
KNOWLEDGE-MANAGEMENT-SYSTEMS	5	BIG-DATA	BT
INTERNET	4	INFORMATION-TECHNOLOGY	MOT
IOT	4	INFORMATION-TECHNOLOGY	MOT
DIGITALIZATION	4	INDUSTRY-4.0	ISO
DATA-ANALYTICS	2	INNOVATION	BT

Source: Author elaboration

Considering the document selection criteria when performing the search (see Table 1), we can differentiate between the terms that appear in the query itself and those that do not. Thus, *information technology*, *information systems,* and *artificial intelligence* would have been selected by the search engine and could therefore be overrepresented in the sample.

Information systems, with a backing of seven documents (above the mean of the table) is in the *emerging or disappearing* project management cluster. The internal weakness of this cluster suggests that its topics connect to a broad set of other topics, not only within the cluster itself. However, the cluster remains stable in the three configurations of analysis applied (Table 5), so it seems that the internal links have conceptual logic (see, Hanafizadeh & Mehrabioun, 2018; Umar, 2022). The publications that incorporate these keywords are in a recent range, so it could be said that, in the KST context, the study of the application of technology in project management is an emerging phenomenon in the literature.

All other keywords in Table 7 appear in the results without being part of the search query. We could differentiate between the more generic topics, which belong to *basic and transversal* clusters, and those that appear in clusters with high conceptual cohesion. In the first set are *big data, knowledge management systems,* and *data analytics*, which show the importance of data in knowledge management for sustainability (Castro, Fernandez, & Colsa, 2021; Smuts & Van der Merwe, 2022). This is the first group of technology concepts highlighted that we could name 'data technologies for sustainability knowledge management'. In the second set, we find the topics *internet, IoT,* and *digitalization*, which represent, for sustainability contexts, the presence of digital communications and the transformation of business processes towards digital models, with greater technological presence (see, Carmela Annosi, Brunetta, Capo, & Heideveld, 2020; Manavalan & Jayakrishna, 2019). The themes with these technological keywords would belong to a stream of publications that we could name 'digital processes for sustainability knowledge management'.

There are other technology keywords that, due to their low frequency or representation in the sample, have not had any relevance in the results of applying the algorithm. It should be remembered that the search criteria on sustainability have restricted the resulting sample. For example, we found among the keywords in our sample terms referring to technology-based business processes, such as *ERP*, *CRM,* or *GIS* tools. We also found terms referring to digital computing processes such as *cloud computing, computational tools*, *healthcare computing, digital systems,* or *computing systems and software*. We can also find references to digital economies such as *economics-of-information systems* or the *digital revolution*. It would be necessary to wait some time to incorporate in the sample possible new publications dealing with these topics, to see them reflected in the results of the bibliometric analysis.

Which Topics Related to CSR or Sustainability Appear in the Results?

In this section, we will analyze another important component in the search query, which is related to sustainability. Topics related to sustainability are classified into three groups: sustainability dimensions, stakeholders, and sustainable industry and business processes. The complete list of topics can be found in Table 8.

Table 8. Sustainability topics found in results (shorted by cluster)

Topic	Docs. Count	Cluster	Quadrant
CORPORATE-SOCIAL-RESPONSIBILITY	7.0	CORPORATE-SOCIAL-RESPONSIBILITY	MOT
SUSTAINABLE-LAND-MANAGEMENT	2.0	DESERTIFICATION	ISO
UNCCD	2.0	DESERTIFICATION	ISO
COMMUNITIES	11.0	GOVERNANCE	MOT/BT
ORGANIZATIONS	9.0	GOVERNANCE	MOT/BT
ECO-INNOVATION	4.0	GREEN-INNOVATION	ISO/MOT
GREEN-INNOVATION	6.0	GREEN-INNOVATION	ISO/MOT
CIRCULAR-ECONOMY	4.0	INDUSTRY-4.0	ISO
ENVIRONMENTAL-SUSTAINABILITY	2.0	INDUSTRY-4.0	ISO
INDUSTRY-4.0	7.0	INDUSTRY-4.0	ISO
SOCIAL-SUSTAINABILITY	2.0	INDUSTRY-4.0	ISO
SUSTAINABLE-DEVELOPMENT-GOALS	8.0	INDUSTRY-4.0	ISO
USER-ACCEPTANCE	3.0	INFORMATION-TECHNOLOGY	MOT
STAKEHOLDER-ENGAGEMENT	2.0	INNOVATION	BT

Source: Author elaboration

The topics related to sustainability dimensions are grouped in the Industry 4.0 theme, and these topics are *environmental sustainability*, *social sustainability*, and *sustainable development goals*. The so-called 'fourth industrial revolution' is a technological development framework that supports the incorporation of the sustainable paradigm in the industry (Bai, Dallasega, Orzes, & Sarkis, 2020). A similar statement can be found in the literature on knowledge management. (e.g., Patyal, Sarma, Modgil, Nag, & Dennehy, 2022; Pinzone et al., 2020). It may be surprising not to see the *environment* topic (in the integration theme) listed in Table 8. After reviewing the documents that support this keyword in the sample, it has been verified that it refers to the organization's operating environment, and not to the natural environment. This is a common phenomenon when conducting bibliometric studies on sustainability, which requires special attention when analyzing the results.

The topics related to stakeholders, a fundamental concept when analyzing sustainable organizations, are *stakeholder-engagement*, *user-acceptance*, *communities*, *organizations*, and *corporate-social-responsibility*. One of the most commonly accepted definitions of stakeholder is "group or individual who can affect or is affected by the achievement of the organization's objectives" (Freeman, 1984, p.46). 'Stakeholder engagement' and CSR are general concepts liked with stakeholder management. The former refers to the strategy adopted by companies to establish relations with stakeholders, and can be defined as "the aims, activities, and impacts of stakeholder relations in a moral, strategic, and/ or pragmatic manner" (Kujala, Sachs, Leinonen, Heikkinen, & Laude, 2022, p. 1139). For example, in the literature on knowledge management we can read that knowledge sourced from engagement with stakeholders foster a firm's innovation for sustainability (Ayuso et al., 2011). On the other hand, CSR is related to stakeholders in its very foundation, since CSR is "a concept whereby companies integrate social and environmental concerns in their business operations and their interaction with their stakeholders voluntarily." (European Commission, 2001, p.6). *Communities* are stakeholders (Clarkson, 1995) that may vary depending on the context of each organization, so it remains an abstract and generalist concept. Something similar happens when considering *organizations* as stakeholders, which could refer to a multitude of entities, such as suppliers, competitors, trade unions, consumer associations, media, etc. (Henriques & Sadorsky, 1999).

The last topic to be reviewed is *user acceptance* since users of products and services, processes, or technology platforms can be considered stakeholders (Maguire & Bevan, 2002). They are similar in nature to customers, although without the need for purchase transactions. Three arguments to support this assertion are as follows. First, the user can be a defined role of stakeholders using specific tools within the context of contributing to sustainability (O'Dwyer, Unerman, & Hession, 2005). Second, we can talk about 'ease of use' by stakeholders (Djimesah et al., 2022). Last, and referring exclusively to the stakeholders' use of technology, we can talk about *user adoption* and *user acceptance* (Sneesl, Jusoh, Jabar, & Abdullah, 2022).

The third group of topics includes processes or models for sustainability. In the set are included the words *circular economy*, *eco-innovation*, *green-innovation*, *sustainable-land-management*, and *UNCCD*. The first of these is included in the Industry 4.0 theme, which reinforces the approach of the fourth industrial revolution paradigm as a framework that merges technology, knowledge, and sustainable development principles (Rajput & Singh, 2019; Rosa, Sassanelli, Urbinati, Chiaroni, & Terzi, 2020). As it was mentioned before, e*co-innovation* and *green innovation* can be considered equivalent concepts in the literature (Sezen & Cankaya, 2013). They have their conceptual theme, together with the topic of *research and development*. It confirms the idea that green innovation is a specific theme isolated from the rest (Orlando et al., 2022). Finally, *sustainable land management* and *UNCCD*, which appear together in the desertification theme, represent another *specific and isolated* research theme referring to academic initiatives that develop their own indicators and knowledge management and show a high presence of measurement technology (Reed et al., 2011).

CONCLUSION

This study provides a graphical representation of the conceptual structures existing in the research literature on the combined concepts of knowledge management, sustainability, and information and communication technology (KST). As main contributions, the discussion section in this chapter answers the following questions: How have publications evolved in number over time? Which topics in the literature are more cohesive and differentiated from the rest? Which topics are the most generally used in this field? Which technology concepts are most relevant and to which other concepts do they relate? And finally, what are the sustainability concepts mentioned in the literature and how are they distributed within the conceptual map? The total number of papers published on the subject is relatively low, starting in 2000. However, the rate of publications has progressively increased over the years until today, showing its academic interest. The number of publications has grown especially since 2016, a date that coincides with the launch of the United Nations' Sustainable Development Goals project.

This chapter makes two outstanding methodological contributions. First, the incorporation of two weighted bibliometric performance measures called 'average citations' and 'normalized h-index' (*norm-h*), which facilitate the assessment of the bibliometric impact of the identified themes or conceptual clusters. In particular, 'norm-h' allows highlighting those clusters that have an h-index close to the maximum value they can reach according to the number of documents they possess, which implies a high quality of all their publications, as opposed to others with a high h-index but far from the potential limit they could achieve, which implies that a majority of their documents is of low quality. The other methodological contribution is the comparison of the mapping analysis results obtained in the application of different parameters of maximum and minimum cluster size, as a method of assessing the strength of the links between topics, and the stability and conceptual coherence of each theme.

Concerning the mapping analysis, the reader is provided with the list of topics in each cluster. Results obtained can still respond to diverse meta-analysis questions depending on what has been found and what has not. This naturally leads to a series of research recommendations for academics interested in the subject. One important conclusion is that the strongly cohesive and well-defined conceptual topics identified are not, in this study, the ones with the best bibliometric results (see Table 4), but they are the ones that best represent the publication trends in the field. Researchers can see in them opportunities for publication.

Strategic Aspects

Analyzing from a strategic perspective, two research topics have stood out notably in the results. The first of these is corporate social responsibility, which appears on the strategic diagram as a *motor* theme. CSR has been extensively studied as a resource for achieving sustainable competitive advantages and improving financial performance in organizations (Cochran & Wood, 1984). The presence in the cluster of the *resource-base-view* and *financial-performance* topics suggests that interpretation. Two other aspects of knowledge management strategy are included in this theme: *exploitation* and *exploration*. Both fit, as well, in the *resource-base-view* perspective, specifically with the attainment of valuable resources and their exploitation.

The second topic is innovation, and more specifically green innovation (or *eco-innovation*). Innovation processes include research and development activities that affect strategic plans, both in their definition, allocation of resources, and results management. Green innovation leads to the creation of eco-efficiencies that consist of optimizing production while reducing resource consumption. In other words, it is about the delivery of competitive goods and services that satisfy human needs and bring quality of life, while progressively reducing ecological impacts (Schmidheiny, WBCSD, & Unotec Holding Ag, 1992).

In all cases, there is a strategic use of CSR or sustainability with a utilitarian or instrumental approach, aimed at increasing financial results or cost savings. In general, there is no evidence of publication trends that raise ethical or moral dilemmas in the results that have been analyzed. This could be a disruptive line of publication, especially given the consolidation shortly of specific technologies of dubious impact on society, such as artificial intelligence.

Human Aspects

Following the interpretation of the results made above, we assume that the human aspects of knowledge management for sustainability reside in the organizations' stakeholders. In addition to conditioning the companies' strategy, the stakeholders of an organization can be a source of knowledge when properly managed (Ayuso et al., 2011).

The set of documents collected for the study is biased by the presence of technical terms in their title, abstract, or keywords. This may limit the presence of keywords that conceptually symbolize stakeholders. However, we note the existence of stakeholders-related generic concepts such as CSR or 'stakeholder management', and some collective stakeholder terms such as 'communities' and 'organizations'. The absence of any mention of workers in the literature, especially those linked to the exploitation of technologies, or knowledge workers, is striking.

In this text, we defend the proposal to consider 'technology users' as stakeholders of technology-intensive organizations. These users would not always be customers, but also employees or collaborators. According to the definition of stakeholders, technology users would be those with an interest in the company adopting or developing technologies that meet certain characteristics or functionalities.

Environmental Aspects

Regarding topics on the natural environment, the two differentiated themes green innovation and desertification stand out among the results. Both themes show a strong internal cohesion and isolation and, therefore, conceptual identity. They have been previously commented and both are an interesting research opportunity. desertification and *sustainable land management* offer the possibility of fitting the research into a larger framework proposal, with specific institutional projects, such as the UNCCD.

Also, we can find, within the Industry 4.0 theme, two other important topics, which are *circular economy* and *environmental sustainability*. Regarding the circular economy, it should be noted that it meets a multitude of KST scope requirements. Therefore, it seems a very promising topic for research in this field.

Technology and Machine Aspects

Technology concepts are spread throughout the results obtained. Table 6 shows that a large number of technology topics have a wide presence in the conceptual map. Among the themes detected, information technology and big data stand out. The first one is a *motor-type* theme, so it is cohesive and well-defined. Among its nodes, technological concepts coexist with others that guide about the usual uses given to technology for knowledge management. We can perceive inside the cluster, research trends like human-machine interaction, learning capacity (present in the term *absorptive capacity*), and knowledge sharing. The case of the big data theme is different, as it is a *basic and transversal* theme, although its global interpretation has remarkable logic. Within it, we find connections between *decision-making*, *smart cities,* and *artificial intelligence* (all three clear scenarios for the application of big data solutions).

It is reasonable to think that there will be an evolution in research where both artificial intelligence (Metaxiotis, Ergazakis, Samouilidis, & Psarras, 2003) and smart cities (Hashem et al., 2016; Israilidis et al., 2021) become independent and relevance themes in the future.

The discussion section of this document shows a proposed grouping of the technologies identified in the study. These are, on the one hand, the so-called 'data technologies for sustainability knowledge management' which groups together concepts such as *big data*, *knowledge management systems,* and *data analytics*, and the so-called 'digital processes for sustainability knowledge management', which groups together the concepts of *internet*, *IoT,* and *digitalization*. It is proposed to future researchers in the field, as well as practitioners, to deepen in both sets, taking advantage of this conceptual division detected between digital data management and digital processes management for knowledge management for sustainability.

Decision-Making (DM) Aspects

Among the results obtained, the topics *decision-making* (in the big data theme), and decision-support (in the innovation theme) fit in this subsection. Both belong to a *basic and transversal* cluster type, so probably are two keywords widely linked to other concepts in the field. Moreover, as can be seen in Table 6, *decision-making* ranks third in the number of occurrences, which indicates that it is a highly relevant topic. Notice that *decision-making* and *big data* appear together.

Decision-making is an important aspect of project management processes (Liberatore & Pollack-Johnson, 2013). Project management could be defined as an orderly and planned succession of decision-making that pursues an end goal by a given date, using limited resources, and going through stages and intermediate deliverables. In our case, project management is a conceptual theme in the quadrant of *emerging or disappearing* themes and contains the particularly relevant topic *information systems*.

Finally, since governance can be understood, in a broad sense, as the decision-making rules (Mansourian, 2017), we can mention in this section the governance theme. It is a cluster halfway between *motor* and *basic and transversal* quadrants, so its keywords are important in the field, and it has a certain degree of conceptual autonomy. Within this cluster, we find the *product development* and *value-creation* topics, which represent complex processes or projects that need to be managed.

The results obtained indicate that decision-making is an important aspect in the literature on knowledge management when considering technology and data as a medium, and sustainability as a conditioning factor. It is not clear whether project management, specifically in this field, is an emerging topic, although we can assume that it is. On the other hand, governance is a research topic in the process of consolidation.

Industry-Specific Aspects

There are some mentions of specific activity sectors or industries in the conceptual map obtained, all with a low bibliometric impact. The most represented one is the construction industry with four publications supporting the word *construction* in the project management theme. In addition, we can see the words *renewable-energy-sector* in the corporate social responsibility theme, and *agricultural-technologies* in the innovation theme, both with two publications each.

If we consider the fourth industrial revolution as a generic framework that groups activity sectors that share similar production models, we could include the Industry 4.0 theme in this subsection. As can be read above, this is an isolated theme with high internal cohesion and a combination of factors that makes it a perfect fit for KST's scope. This topic is a candidate for in-depth analysis and research.

What Has Not Yet Been Written on the Subject

Due to the double limitation imposed in the bibliographic search (technology and sustainability), research contexts that usually could have relevance in knowledge management, do not have a relevant representation in our obtained results. In the previous sections, it has been mentioned that some keywords do not have enough weight in the sample to be selected by the algorithm that maps and visualizes the documents' contents. For these reasons, the non-appearance in the results does not imply the non-existence of isolated publications on certain topics.

Researchers and practitioners are encouraged to identify, in addition to those consolidated thematic lines, possible gaps in the literature that could represent relevant contributions according to new trends and existing needs. In this way, they would join the identified interest in the field, which materialized in the increases in publication ratios. In addition, in terms of sustainability, all contributions will be useful, given the urgency for the implementation and improvement of such measures. The human context of the future is conditioned by the appropriate use of knowledge and the planet's limited resources. Technology can optimize processes, but a rational design of uses and objectives will be necessary.

REFERENCES

Abubakar, A. M., Behravesh, E., Rezapouraghdam, H., & Yildiz, S. B. (2019). Applying artificial intelligence techniques to predict knowledge-hiding behavior. *International Journal of Information Management*, *49*, 45–57. doi:10.1016/j.ijinfomgt.2019.02.006

Aguilera, R. V., Rupp, D. E., Williams, C. A., & Ganapathi, J. (2007). Putting the S back in corporate social responsibility: A multilevel theory of social change in organizations. *Academy of Management Review*, *32*(3), 836–863. doi:10.5465/amr.2007.25275678

Alavi, M., & Leidner, D. E. (2001). Knowledge management and knowledge management systems: Conceptual foundations and research issues. *Management Information Systems Quarterly*, *25*(1), 107–136. doi:10.2307/3250961

Ayuso, S., Rodríguez, M. Á., García-Castro, R., & Ariño, M. Á. (2011). Does stakeholder engagement promote sustainable innovation orientation? *Industrial Management & Data Systems*, *111*(9), 1399–1417. doi:10.1108/02635571111182764

Bai, C., Dallasega, P., Orzes, G., & Sarkis, J. (2020). Industry 4.0 technologies assessment: A sustainability perspective. *International Journal of Production Economics*, *229*, 107776. doi:10.1016/j.ijpe.2020.107776

Baskerville, R., & Dulipovici, A. (2006). The theoretical foundations of knowledge management. *Knowledge Management Research and Practice*, *4*(2), 83–105. doi:10.1057/palgrave.kmrp.8500090

Börner, K., Chen, C., & Boyack, K. W. (2003). Visualizing knowledge domains. *Annual Review of Information Science & Technology*, *37*(1), 179–255. doi:10.1002/aris.1440370106

Bossle, M. B., de Barcellos, M. D., Vieira, L. M., & Sauvée, L. (2016). The drivers for adoption of eco-innovation. *Journal of Cleaner Production, 113*, 861–872. doi:10.1016/j.jclepro.2015.11.033

Callon, M., Courtial, J., & Laville, F. (1991). Co-word analysis as a tool for describing the network of interactions between basic and technological research: The case of polymer chemistry. *Scientometrics, 22*(1), 155–205. doi:10.1007/BF02019280

Callon, M., Courtial, J., Turner, W. A., & Bauin, S. (1983). From translations to problematic networks: An introduction to co-word analysis. *Social Sciences Information. Information Sur les Sciences Sociales, 22*(2), 191–235. doi:10.1177/053901883022002003

Carmela Annosi, M., Brunetta, F., Capo, F., & Heideveld, L. (2020). Digitalization in the agri-food industry: The relationship between technology and sustainable development. *Management Decision, 58*(8), 1737–1757. doi:10.1108/MD-09-2019-1328

Castro, G. D. R., Fernandez, M. C. G., & Colsa, A. U. (2021). Unleashing the convergence amid digitalization and sustainability towards pursuing the sustainable development goals (SDGs): A holistic review. *Journal of Cleaner Production, 280*, 122204. doi:10.1016/j.jclepro.2020.122204

Cheng, C. C., & Shiu, E. C. (2012). Validation of a proposed instrument for measuring eco-innovation: An implementation perspective. *Technovation, 32*(6), 329–344. doi:10.1016/j.technovation.2012.02.001

Clarkson, M. B. E. (1995). A stakeholder framework for analyzing and evaluating corporate social performance. *Academy of Management Review, 20*(1), 92. doi:10.2307/258888

Cobo, M. J., López-Herrera, A. G., Herrera-Viedma, E., & Herrera, F. (2011). An approach for detecting, quantifying, and visualizing the evolution of a research field: A practical application to the fuzzy sets theory field. *Journal of Informetrics, 5*(1), 146–166. doi:10.1016/j.joi.2010.10.002

Cobo, M. J., López-Herrera, A. G., Herrera-Viedma, E., & Herrera, F. (2012). SciMAT: A new science mapping analysis software tool. *Journal of the American Society for Information Science and Technology, 63*(8), 1609–1630. doi:10.1002/asi.22688

Cochran, P. L., & Wood, R. A. (1984). Corporate social responsibility and financial performance. *Academy of Management Journal, 27*(1), 42.

Coulter, N., Monarch, I., & Konda, S. (1998). Software engineering as seen through its research literature: A study in co-word analysis. *Journal of the American Society for Information Science, 49*(13), 1206–1223. doi:10.1002/(SICI)1097-4571(1998)49:13<1206::AID-ASI7>3.0.CO;2-F

Curran, M. A. (2009). Wrapping our brains around sustainability. *Sustainability (Basel), 1*(1), 5–13. doi:10.3390u1010005

Davis, F. D. (1985). *A technology acceptance model for empirically testing new end-user information systems: Theory and results* [Doctoral dissertation, Massachusetts Institute of Technology]. https://dspace.mit.edu/bitstream/handle/1721.1/15192/14927137-MIT.pdf

Di Vaio, A., Palladino, R., Hassan, R., & Escobar, O. (2020). Artificial intelligence and business models in the sustainable development goals perspective: A systematic literature review. *Journal of Business Research, 121*, 283–314. doi:10.1016/j.jbusres.2020.08.019

Djimesah, I. E., Zhao, H., Okine, A. N. D., Li, Y., Duah, E., & Mireku, K. K. (2022). Analyzing the technology of acceptance model of Ghanaian crowdfunding stakeholders. *Technological Forecasting and Social Change*, *175*, 121323. doi:10.1016/j.techfore.2021.121323

Edwards, J. S., Shaw, D., & Collier, P. M. (2005). Knowledge management systems: Finding a way with technology. *Journal of Knowledge Management*, *9*(1), 113–125. doi:10.1108/13673270510583009

European Commission. (2001). *Green paper. promoting a European framework for corporate social responsibility*. European Commission.

European Commission. (2022). *Eco-innovation at the heart of European policies*. Retrieved from https://green-business.ec.europa.eu/eco-innovation_en

Freeman, R. E. (1984). *Strategic management: A stakeholder approach*. Pittman.

Garriga, E., & Melé, D. (2004). Corporate social responsibility theories: Mapping the territory. *Journal of Business Ethics*, *53*(1-2), 51–71. doi:10.1023/B:BUSI.0000039399.90587.34

Ghobakhloo, M. (2020). Industry 4.0, digitization, and opportunities for sustainability. *Journal of Cleaner Production*, *252*, 119869. doi:10.1016/j.jclepro.2019.119869

Gond, J., & Crane, A. (2010). Corporate social performance disoriented: Saving the lost paradigm? *Business & Society*, *49*(4), 677–703. doi:10.1177/0007650308315510

González-Alcaide, G. (2021). Bibliometric studies outside the information science and library science field: Uncontainable or uncontrollable? *Scientometrics*, *126*(8), 6837–6870. doi:10.100711192-021-04061-3

González-Masip, J. (2020). Corporate sustainability, business sustainability, or corporate social responsibility: Some relevant criteria for choosing the right one. In G. Martín-de Castro, & J. González-Masip (Eds.), Knowledge management for corporate social responsibility (pp. 45-62). Business Science Reference (IGI Global). doi:10.4018/978-1-7998-4833-2.ch003

Hacklin, F., & Wallnöfer, M. (2012). The business model in the practice of strategic decision making: Insights from a case study. *Management Decision*, *50*(2), 166–188. doi:10.1108/00251741211203515

Haenlein, M., & Kaplan, A. (2019). A brief history of artificial intelligence: On the past, present, and future of artificial intelligence. *California Management Review*, *61*(4), 5–14. doi:10.1177/0008125619864925

Hanafizadeh, P., & Mehrabioun, M. (2018). Application of SSM in tackling problematical situations from academicians' viewpoints. *Systemic Practice and Action Research*, *31*(2), 179–220. doi:10.100711213-017-9422-y

Hashem, I. A. T., Chang, V., Anuar, N. B., Adewole, K., Yaqoob, I., Gani, A., Ahmed, E., & Chiroma, H. (2016). The role of big data in a smart city. *International Journal of Information Management*, *36*(5), 748–758. doi:10.1016/j.ijinfomgt.2016.05.002

Henriques, I., & Sadorsky, P. (1999). The relationship between environmental commitment and managerial perceptions of stakeholder importance. *Academy of Management Journal*, *42*(1), 87–99. doi:10.2307/256876

Herrmann, S. M., & Hutchinson, C. F. (2005). The changing contexts of the desertification debate. *Journal of Arid Environments*, *63*(3), 538–555. doi:10.1016/j.jaridenv.2005.03.003

Huang, P., & Shih, L. (2009). Effective environmental management through environmental knowledge management. *International Journal of Environmental Science and Technology*, *6*(1), 35–50. doi:10.1007/BF03326058

Israilidis, J., Odusanya, K., & Mazhar, M. U. (2021). Exploring knowledge management perspectives in smart city research: A review and future research agenda. *International Journal of Information Management*, *56*, 101989. doi:10.1016/j.ijinfomgt.2019.07.015

Kleine, A., & von Hauff, M. (2009). Sustainability-driven implementation of corporate social responsibility: Application of the integrative sustainability triangle. *Journal of Business Ethics*, *85*(S3), 517–533. doi:10.100710551-009-0212-z

Kujala, J., Sachs, S., Leinonen, H., Heikkinen, A., & Laude, D. (2022). Stakeholder engagement: Past, present, and future. *Business & Society*, *61*(5), 1136–1196. doi:10.1177/00076503211066595

Lasi, H., Fettke, P., Kemper, H., Feld, T., & Hoffmann, M. (2014). Industry 4.0. *Business & Information Systems Engineering*, *6*(4), 239–242. doi:10.100712599-014-0334-4

Leal Filho, W., Manolas, E., & Pace, P. (2015). The future we want: Key issues on sustainable development in higher education after Rio and the UN decade of education for sustainable development. *International Journal of Sustainability in Higher Education*, *16*(1), 112–129. doi:10.1108/IJSHE-03-2014-0036

Liao, S. (2003). Knowledge management technologies and applications: A literature review from 1995 to 2002. *Expert Systems with Applications*, *25*(2), 155–164. doi:10.1016/S0957-4174(03)00043-5

Liberatore, M. J., & Pollack-Johnson, B. (2013). Improving project management decision-making by modeling quality, time, and cost continuously. *IEEE Transactions on Engineering Management*, *60*(3), 518–528. doi:10.1109/TEM.2012.2219586

Liebowitz, J. (2001). Knowledge management and its link to artificial intelligence. *Expert Systems with Applications*, *20*(1), 1–6. doi:10.1016/S0957-4174(00)00044-0

López-Robles, J. R., Cobo, M. J., Gutiérrez-Salcedo, M., Martínez-Sánchez, M., Gamboa-Rosales, N. K., & Herrera-Viedma, E. (2021). 30th anniversary of applied intelligence: A combination of bibliometrics and thematic analysis using SciMAT. *Applied Intelligence*, *51*(9), 6547–6568. doi:10.100710489-021-02584-z

Lubberink, R., Blok, V., Van Ophem, J., & Omta, O. (2017). Lessons for responsible innovation in the business context: A systematic literature review of responsible, social and sustainable innovation practices. *Sustainability (Basel)*, *9*(5), 721. doi:10.3390u9050721

Maguire, M., & Bevan, N. (2002). User requirements analysis: A review of supporting methods. In J. Hammond, T. Gross, & J. Wesson (Eds.), Usability. Gaining a Competitive Edge (pp. 133-148). Springer Science+Business Media. doi:10.1007/978-0-387-35610-5

Manavalan, E., & Jayakrishna, K. (2019). A review of Internet of Things (IoT) embedded sustainable supply chain for industry 4.0 requirements. *Computers & Industrial Engineering*, *127*, 925–953. doi:10.1016/j.cie.2018.11.030

Mansourian, S. (2017). Governance and forest landscape restoration: A framework to support decision-making. *Journal for Nature Conservation*, *37*, 21–30. doi:10.1016/j.jnc.2017.02.010

Martín-de Castro, G., Amores-Salvadó, J., & Díez-Vial, I. (2022). Framing the evolution of the "environmental strategy" concept: Exploring a key construct for the environmental policy agenda. *Business Strategy and the Environment*.

Martins, V. W. B., Rampasso, I. S., Anholon, R., Quelhas, O. L. G., & Leal Filho, W. (2019). Knowledge management in the context of sustainability: Literature review and opportunities for future research. *Journal of Cleaner Production*, *229*, 489–500. doi:10.1016/j.jclepro.2019.04.354

Marwick, A. D. (2001). Knowledge management technology. *IBM Systems Journal*, *40*(4), 814–830. doi:10.1147j.404.0814

Metaxiotis, K., Ergazakis, K., Samouilidis, E., & Psarras, J. (2003). Decision support through knowledge management: The role of the artificial intelligence. *Information Management & Computer Security*, *11*(5), 216–221. doi:10.1108/09685220310500126

Mohamed, M., Stankosky, M., & Mohamed, M. (2009). An empirical assessment of knowledge management criticality for sustainable development. *Journal of Knowledge Management*, *13*(5), 271–286. doi:10.1108/13673270910988105

Morris, M., Schindehutte, M., & Allen, J. (2005). The entrepreneur's business model: Toward a unified perspective. *Journal of Business Research*, *58*(6), 726–735. doi:10.1016/j.jbusres.2003.11.001

Mura, M., Longo, M., Micheli, P., & Bolzani, D. (2018). The evolution of sustainability measurement research. *International Journal of Management Reviews*, *20*(3), 661–695. doi:10.1111/ijmr.12179

Nemati, H. R., Steiger, D. M., Iyer, L. S., & Herschel, R. T. (2002). Knowledge warehouse: An architectural integration of knowledge management, decision support, artificial intelligence and data warehousing. *Decision Support Systems*, *33*(2), 143–161. doi:10.1016/S0167-9236(01)00141-5

Nguyen, V. M., Young, N., & Cooke, S. J. (2017). A roadmap for knowledge exchange and mobilization research in conservation and natural resource management. *Conservation Biology*, *31*(4), 789–798. doi:10.1111/cobi.12857 PMID:27767241

Nishant, R., Kennedy, M., & Corbett, J. (2020). Artificial intelligence for sustainability: Challenges, opportunities, and a research agenda. *International Journal of Information Management*, *53*, 102104. doi:10.1016/j.ijinfomgt.2020.102104

Noyons, E. C. M., Moed, H., & Van Raan, A. (1999). Integrating research performance analysis and science mapping. *Scientometrics*, *46*(3), 591–604. doi:10.1007/BF02459614

Noyons, E. C. M., Moed, H. F., & Luwel, M. (1999). Combining mapping and citation analysis for evaluative bibliometric purposes: A bibliometric study. *Journal of the American Society for Information Science*, *50*(2), 115–131. doi:10.1002/(SICI)1097-4571(1999)50:2<115::AID-ASI3>3.0.CO;2-J

O'Dwyer, B., Unerman, J., & Hession, E. (2005). User needs in sustainability reporting: Perspectives of stakeholders in Ireland. *European Accounting Review*, *14*(4), 759–787. doi:10.1080/09638180500104766

Olawumi, T. O., & Chan, D. W. (2018). A scientometric review of global research on sustainability and sustainable development. *Journal of Cleaner Production*, *183*, 231–250. doi:10.1016/j.jclepro.2018.02.162

Orlando, B., Ballestra, L. V., Scuotto, V., Pironti, M., & Del Giudice, M. (2022). The impact of R&D investments on eco-innovation: A cross-cultural perspective of green technology management. *IEEE Transactions on Engineering Management*, *69*(5), 2275–2284. doi:10.1109/TEM.2020.3005525

Park, C., Jeong, S., Joshi, M., Osborn, T. J., Ho, C., Piao, S., ... Park, H. (2018). Keeping global warming within 1.5 C constrains the emergence of aridification. *Nature Climate Change*, *8*(1), 70–74. doi:10.103841558-017-0034-4

Patyal, V. S., Sarma, P., Modgil, S., Nag, T., & Dennehy, D. (2022). Mapping the links between industry 4.0, circular economy and sustainability: A systematic literature review. *Journal of Enterprise Information Management*, *35*(1), 1–35. doi:10.1108/JEIM-05-2021-0197

Pinzone, M., Albè, F., Orlandelli, D., Barletta, I., Berlin, C., Johansson, B., & Taisch, M. (2020). A framework for operative and social sustainability functionalities in human-centric cyber-physical production systems. *Computers & Industrial Engineering*, *139*, 105132. doi:10.1016/j.cie.2018.03.028

Powell, W. W., & Snellman, K. (2004). The knowledge economy. *Annual Review of Sociology*, *30*(1), 199–220. doi:10.1146/annurev.soc.29.010202.100037

Power, D. J. (2014). Using 'Big data for analytics and decision support. *Journal of Decision Systems*, *23*(2), 222–228. doi:10.1080/12460125.2014.888848

Rajput, S., & Singh, S. P. (2019). Connecting circular economy and industry 4.0. *International Journal of Information Management*, *49*, 98–113. doi:10.1016/j.ijinfomgt.2019.03.002

Reed, M. S., Buenemann, M., Atlhopheng, J., Akhtar-Schuster, M., Bachmann, F., Bastin, G., ... Essahli, W. (2011). Cross-scale monitoring and assessment of land degradation and sustainable land management: A methodological framework for knowledge management. *Land Degradation & Development*, *22*(2), 261–271. doi:10.1002/ldr.1087

Riege, A., & Lindsay, N. (2006). Knowledge management in the public sector: Stakeholder partnerships in the public policy development. *Journal of Knowledge Management*, *10*(3), 24–39. doi:10.1108/13673270610670830

Rodríguez-Rebés, L., Navío-Marco, J., & Ibar-Alonso, R. (2021). Influence of organisational innovation and innovation in general on eco-innovation in European companies. *Journal of Intellectual Capital*, *22*(5), 840–867. doi:10.1108/JIC-06-2020-0203

Rosa, P., Sassanelli, C., Urbinati, A., Chiaroni, D., & Terzi, S. (2020). Assessing relations between circular economy and industry 4.0: A systematic literature review. *International Journal of Production Research*, *58*(6), 1662–1687. doi:10.1080/00207543.2019.1680896

Russ, M. (2021). Knowledge management for sustainable development in the era of continuously accelerating technological revolutions: A framework and models. *Sustainability (Basel), 13*(6), 3353. doi:10.3390u13063353

Saito, A., Umemoto, K., & Ikeda, M. (2007). A strategy-based ontology of knowledge management technologies. *Journal of Knowledge Management, 11*(1), 97–114. doi:10.1108/13673270710728268

Sanguankaew, P., & Vathanophas Ractham, V. (2019). Bibliometric review of research on knowledge management and sustainability, 1994–2018. *Sustainability (Basel), 11*(16), 4388. doi:10.3390u11164388

Santana, M., & Lopez-Cabrales, A. (2019). Sustainable development and human resource management: A science mapping approach. *Corporate Social Responsibility and Environmental Management, 26*(6), 1171–1183. doi:10.1002/csr.1765

Schmidheiny, S., WBCSD, & Unotec Holding Ag. (1992). Changing course. A global business perspective on development and the environment. The MIT Press.

Sezen, B., & Cankaya, S. Y. (2013). Effects of green manufacturing and eco-innovation on sustainability performance. *Procedia: Social and Behavioral Sciences, 99*, 154–163. doi:10.1016/j.sbspro.2013.10.481

Shahzad, M., Qu, Y., Zafar, A. U., Ding, X., & Rehman, S. U. (2020). Translating stakeholders' pressure into environmental practices–The mediating role of knowledge management. *Journal of Cleaner Production, 275*, 124163. doi:10.1016/j.jclepro.2020.124163

Sheehan, P., & Houghton, J. W. (2000). *A primer on the knowledge economy*. Centre for Strategic Economic Studies.

Shiffrin, R. M., & Borner, K. (2004). Mapping knowledge domains. *Proceedings of the National Academy of Sciences of the United States of America, 101*(Suppl 1), 5183-5185. 10.1073/pnas.0307852100

Smuts, H., & Van der Merwe, A. (2022). Knowledge management in society 5.0: A sustainability perspective. *Sustainability (Basel), 14*(11), 6878. doi:10.3390u14116878

Sneesl, R., Jusoh, Y. Y., Jabar, M. A., & Abdullah, S. (2022). Revising technology adoption factors for IoT-based smart campuses: A systematic review. *Sustainability (Basel), 14*(8), 4840. doi:10.3390u14084840

Strand, R., Freeman, R. E., & Hockerts, K. (2015). Corporate social responsibility and sustainability in Scandinavia: An overview. *Journal of Business Ethics, 127*(1), 1–15. doi:10.100710551-014-2224-6

Tsalis, T. A., Malamateniou, K. E., Koulouriotis, D., & Nikolaou, I. E. (2020). New challenges for corporate sustainability reporting: United Nations' 2030 agenda for sustainable development and the sustainable development goals. *Corporate Social Responsibility and Environmental Management, 27*(4), 1617–1629. doi:10.1002/csr.1910

Umar, T. (2022). Challenges of BIM implementation in GCC construction industry. *Engineering, Construction, and Architectural Management, 29*(3), 1139–1168.

UNCCD. (2023). *United Nations convention to combat desertification*. Retrieved from https://www.unccd.int/

United Nations. (2020). *Sustainable development goals*. Retrieved from https://www.un.org/sustainabledevelopment/sustainable-development-goals/

Van den Besselaar, P., & Heimeriks, G. (2006). Mapping research topics using word-reference co-occurrences: A method and an exploratory case study. *Scientometrics*, *68*(3), 377–393. doi:10.100711192-006-0118-9

Van Raan, A. F. J., & Noyons, E. C. M. (2002). Discovery of patterns of scientific and technological development and knowledge transfer. *Proceedings of the 6th International Conference on Current Research Information Systems,* 105-112.

Vinuesa, R., Azizpour, H., Leite, I., Balaam, M., Dignum, V., Domisch, S., Felländer, A., Langhans, S. D., Tegmark, M., & Fuso Nerini, F. (2020). The role of artificial intelligence in achieving the sustainable development goals. *Nature Communications*, *11*(1), 233. doi:10.103841467-019-14108-y PMID:31932590

Wilson, M. (2003). Corporate sustainability: What is it and where does it come from? *Ivey Business Journal*, *67*(6), 1–5.

Wong, P. K., Ho, Y. P., & Autio, E. (2005). Entrepreneurship, innovation and economic growth: Evidence from GEM data. *Small Business Economics*, *24*(3), 335–350. doi:10.100711187-005-2000-1

World Commission on Environment and Development. (1987). *Our common future*. United Nations.

Ye, N., Kueh, T., Hou, L., Liu, Y., & Yu, H. (2020). A bibliometric analysis of corporate social responsibility in sustainable development. *Journal of Cleaner Production*, *272*, 122679. doi:10.1016/j.jclepro.2020.122679

Section 2
Business Teaching Cases

Chapter 2
Walmart:
A Business Case Study in Knowledge Management, Walmart's Secret Sauce – The Use of Machine Learning, Automation, and Virtual Reality

Liz Kheng
Franklin University, USA

EXECUTIVE SUMMARY

The world's largest retailer is more than just a superstore. Their knowledge management runs across multiple spectrums that work together to anticipate customer needs and enhance the shopping experience. Walmart eCommerce offers a seamless shopping experience integrated across digital and physical storefronts, and Walmart International serves millions of customers across 23 countries. Each of these segments works towards one goal, using technology to connect all sales channels to increase productivity and efficiency. This illustrative business case study explores Walmart's development of omnichannel capabilities, supply chain automation, smart store rollouts, and human resource management development through virtual reality training. It provides a seamless shopping experience between web, mobile, and brick-and-mortar stores. This case study also discusses Walmart's use of artificial intelligence and data analytics to improve in-store and warehouse processes. Lastly, this case study examines how Walmart uses data for decision-making and improving the consumer shopping experience.

INTRODUCTION

The average consumer sees Walmart as a convenient superstore with low prices. This illustrative business case study takes a knowledge management approach and allows a peek behind the proverbial curtain that the average consumer does not see. This case study aims to provide firsthand insight into Walmart's knowledge management and technology decisions. It will also offer a blueprint for other aspiring businesses to follow in its footsteps. The case study will discuss the history of Walmart,

DOI: 10.4018/978-1-6684-5859-4.ch002

its international footprint, supply chain management, cutting-edge technological advancements, and lessons learned. This study employed several methods of data collection to build the narrative. The author collected historical data from digital archives, news articles, and credible websites. Data from some sections of this paper were gathered from Walmart's press releases, Walmart's corporate website, an interview with a Walmart executive, and peer-reviewed journals. At the same time, others were collected from management review journals, tech review websites, and business management websites.

BACKGROUND

Humble Beginnings and Rapid Growth

On July 2, 1962, Sam Walton opened the first Walmart store in Rogers, Arkansas. Within five years, it expanded to 24 stores. By 1969, the company was officially incorporated as Wal-Mart Stores, Inc., and soon became publicly traded. Its first stock sold at $16.50 per share, equal to $126.20 in today's economy. In 1971, Walmart opened the doors to its new home office and first distribution center in Bentonville, Arkansas. Nearly 60 years after opening its first retail store, Walmart is now a multi-national corporation offering several lines of business, including big-box retail stores, healthcare, video streaming services, eCommerce, philanthropic programs, and a comprehensive international supply chain.

Walmart has been known for its scale and rapid growth since its inception. The company attributes its growth and sustainability to its everyday low-price (EDLP) business model. Many experts have explored the company's history and strategic business decisions to discover the company's secret sauce for success. Behind the EDLP business model are the inner workings of Walmart's knowledge management and technology business decisions that keep them on the cutting edge, which goes unseen by the everyday consumer. This case study takes a knowledge management approach to understand Walmart's success, which currently operates over 10,000 stores and Sam's Clubs under 46 brands in 24 countries and employs 2.3 million associates, with more than half working in the US.

The company has five divisions: Walmart US, eCommerce, Supply Chain Division, Walmart International, and Sam's Club. The first Sam's Club store opened its doors in 1983 to support small businesses by offering bulk items at discounted prices. The average Sam's Club store spans about 134,000 square feet and provides products and services to fulfill small business and family needs, such as food and beverages and specialty services, including travel, auto buying, pharmacy, optical, hearing aid centers, and tire and battery centers. Walmart operates 600 clubs across the US and more than 200 internationally and employs approximately 100,000 club associates.

Walmart's US retail division operates several stores across the United States, including supercenters, discount stores, and neighborhood markets, making up the world's largest brick-and-mortar retail store. Walmart eCommerce offers a seamless shopping experience integrated across digital and physical storefronts. Walmart International (WI) serves millions of customers across 23 countries, operates 5,100 retail units, and employs more than 550,000 associates. Its footprint is across countries like China, India, Mexico, Chile, and several African countries. Walmart also holds equity interests in Brazil, Japan, and the United Kingdom. Walmart's international supply chain includes 210 distribution centers (DCs) and is one of the world's largest. Each distribution center spans over one million square feet and employs more than 600 personnel. The distribution centers utilize a fleet of 9,000 tractors, 80,000 trailers, and more than 11,000 drivers.

Omnichannel Capabilities and Robotics to Enhance Job Function

A recent interview with Mr. Henry Akwa-Mensah revealed some insight into Walmart's supply chain strategy. Mr. Akwa-Mensah, who was Walmart's international supply chain director of innovations and insight at the time of the interview, is integral to the organization's technological growth and sustainability. He is now the director of product and user experience (UX). His background in operations management and supply chain innovations has allowed him to anticipate market needs and conceptualize technologies to fulfill these needs. In an interview, he shared his experiences at Walmart and how his lessons learned have helped with corporate sustainability.

After studying resource economics in Germany, the Ghana native moved to Las Vegas for an internship at the University of Nevada Reno, ultimately leading him to Walmart. So what is a Director of Innovations and Insight for Walmart's international supply chain? With a team of highly skilled engineers and a state-of-the-art test lab, Henry led the charge by developing a roadmap for the global market by providing a framework to test emerging technology for market challenges. Technologies such as augmented reality, virtual reality, robotics, and automation, and develop analytics to validate market problems and cost-benefit analyses for solutions. His team helped to support the international markets by developing innovative strategies for omnichannel acceleration. Omnichannel convergence is one of their biggest initiatives.

Omnichannel, or Omni, is a physical and digital commerce convergence. The serviceability of omnichannel capabilities gives the modern consumer access to all products and services under one metaphorical roof. It provides a seamless shopping experience between web, mobile, and brick-and-mortar stores. Firms like Accenture, Salesforce, and ConnexOne lead the charge for the omnichannel approach. Market research found that 45% of today's consumers prefer receiving real-time promotions delivered to their mobile devices while in a brick-and-mortar store. However, only 28% of retailers currently offer this functionality (Accenture, 2015).

Additionally, 42% of shoppers surveyed indicated that they found it easy to complete a purchase using their mobile device. However, when asked what aspect of the shopping experience needed an upgrade, 39% stated the physical store. Survey responses also indicated the following areas of the in-store experience needed improvement, merchandise availability (19%), free Wi-Fi (15%), and the ability to buy out-of-stock products on a mobile device while in-store (36%). Dave Richards, the global managing director of Accenture retail practice, said in a press release,

Physical and digital commerce are converging at an incredible pace. The fact that many consumers use their mobile devices to check inventory availability while on their way to a store and are looking for real-time promotions to be sent to their phones means retailers have an opportunity to capitalize on the power of these devices. By investing in mobile applications and frictionless digital payment tools that incorporate loyalty, coupons, and rewards in-store, retailers can provide a seamless bridge between customers' online and offline experiences. All sales channels must be equally desirable to the consumer so that the path to purchase is not chosen based on satisfaction in one channel over another, but simply on what is most convenient at that time. (Accenture, 2015, para. 7)

Walmart understands that today's consumers look for choice, consistency, and convenience across all shopping channels. Their omnichannel journey began by integrating Walmart's US retail and eCommerce divisions to provide a more streamlined customer experience. During the height of COVID-19, when the state of the world's economy was unknown, Walmart prepared for an uptick in online sales and delivery services. As customers sheltered themselves from the unforeseen future, services like grocery pickup and home delivery became a fundamental requisite to daily life. In December 2020, former Vice President of Walmart International Distribution and Supply Chain Jeff Loafman issued a press release stating the importance of meeting customer expectations through an omnichannel approach.

Whether by building innovative distribution center formats to deliver products faster or by launching our shopping apps in new languages to enable more people to access them, Walmart is continuing to invest to serve our customers in international markets. . . . For example, many of Walmart's markets—the United States, Canada, Mexico, and China–have advanced eCommerce capabilities, such as faster express home delivery services and various pickup options such as lockers and towers. (Loafman, 2020, para. 2)

Walmart's omnichannel methodology is a three-pronged approach to minimize operational steps: innovating in today's market, improving infrastructure, and investing in the future. In markets like India, which operates Flipkart Wholesale, the digital marketplace connects retail operations with local manufacturers, offering sustainability and growth opportunities for local small and medium-sized retail stores during the pandemic. In China, partners like JD Daojia help expand delivery services so that more than 400 stores can offer one-hour delivery. In markets like Chile, specialized distribution centers, and depots, provide direct delivery to consumers. For example, Walmart de México y Centroamérica, in Merida, Mexico, is building a $42 million distribution center to allow customers to shop for groceries and pick them up at a local bodega. In the next several years, customers in Canada will see an overhaul in operations from the $3.5 billion investment designated to omnichannel capabilities.

Loafman concluded his press release with:

Walmart is leading the future of retail around the world, and eCommerce and omnichannel are becoming more important. Our investments reflect our confidence in this approach. Most importantly, we want customers in our international markets to know they can count on a seamless, safe, and convenient shopping experience at Walmart (Loafman, 2020, para. 15).

MAN VS. MACHINE OR MAN AND MACHINE?

Using Robotics to Enhance Job Function

Technology and automation are on the fast track to disrupting the human workforce. According to a 2017 report by the Kinsey Global Institute, by the year 2030, as many as 375 million people may need to switch occupational categories due to workplace automation (Manika et al., 2017). A large number of organizations use automation to increase production, streamline processes and improve their bottom line. Automation has also helped front-line jobs become less repetitive and may replace some dangerous front-line tasks required in extreme work. A recent report from the World Economic Forum (WEF) stated: "A new generation of smart machines, fueled by rapid advances in artificial intelligence (AI) and robotics, could potentially replace a large proportion of existing human jobs" (Kelly, 2020, para 2). The same report stated that by 2025 more than 85 million jobs would be replaced by robotics, automation, and artificial intelligence. Automation has undoubtedly affected the workforce. However, is the workforce being replaced or supplemented by automation with job category shifts and streamlined processes?

The WEF says not to fear artificial intelligence, which will lead to long-term job growth. The COVID-19 pandemic has accelerated automation technology from contactless point-of-sale terminals to delivery robots. While the first industrial revolution used steam engines to maximize production, the current revolution comprises artificial intelligence, robotics, and the Internet of Things (IoT). Corporations like Walmart have focused on research and development efforts to enhance the customer's shopping experience.

Walmart has distributed automated technology in over 1,500 stores (Harwell, 2019). These stores have thousands of automated shelf scanners, box unloaders, AI cameras, and cleaning robots. With the new automated technologies, stores have become hyper-efficient, making it hard for some employees to keep up with the machines, making a co-existence with them hard to manage. Although the technologies have increased efficiency, employees are still tasked with some of the physical work. As a result, the new technologies have added a layer of discomfort and complexity to the company culture.

Walmart's president and CEO, Doug McMillion, believes that machine technology is a part of the company's effort to trim waste and operate with discipline. "The robots don't complain, ask for raises, or require vacations and bathroom breaks" (Harwell, 2019, para 17). Machines increase the bottom line and cost less than the human workforce. Economists Pascual Restrepo and Daron Acemoglu have argued that today's automation is not designed to increase productivity but to replace the more costly option, humans (Harwell, 2019). As Walmart announces the deployment of thousands of robots to do physical tasks, the fear of being replaced, which has loomed over workers for years, may become a reality. These workers are not alone. Among US workers between the ages of 18 and 34, 37% are concerned that automation will replace them in the workplace (Douglas, 2019).

The fear of job loss can lead to adverse negative outcomes for the company. The effects can decrease employee morale, create an unhappy work environment, and decrease human productivity. It can also lead to negative public perception, bad press, and loss of customer loyalty. Is it worth the increased bottom line? Walmart executives face a human versus machine dilemma. How can this dilemma be mitigated? A paradigm shift is needed.

Expanded Employee Training for New Roles: A Shift in Paradigm

Regional knowledge management (RKM) is a management theory that focuses on the knowledge acquisition and transfer of a specified region (Zhao & de Pablos, 2010). The concept of regional knowledge management goes back to the late 1990s when Storper (1997) suggested the importance of regional knowledge, which focuses on a community's economic, social, cultural, and political activities that help improve citizen welfare (Zhao & de Pablos, 2010). Applying the principle of RKM to the man versus machine dilemma by expanding training and knowledge programs to include regional knowledge concepts. According to Zhao and de Pablos (2010), regional learning concepts include:

- Marketing strategies
- Local supply chain management processes
- Agricultural or industrial localization
- Regional development and innovation

New knowledge can create new roles. Understanding regional nuances increases efficiency and helps with decision-making. RKM also helps with recruiting and retention by creating new positions and increasing employee engagement.

Man–Machine Collaboration

In the dilemma of man versus machine, someone will lose. Do the two genuinely have to compete? Collaborative knowledge management (CKM) pulls concepts from the collaborative cognition model (CCM) by Salisbury (2001), which explores the knowledge lifecycle in an organization. CCM can be used to design and evaluate the whole knowledge management process, including primary and subsidiary operations providing knowledge and human-computer interfaces (Abdullah et al., 2018). Using the principles of collaborative knowledge management and the collaborative cognition model, an organization can develop human–automation sub-groups within each retail division for the workers to oversee quality control and manage, maintain, and mitigate computer malfunctions.

Several years after announcing self-scanning robots, Walmart canceled its five-year contract with its robotics partner Bossa Nova Robotics. Although the shelf-scanning robots are no longer part of the customer experience, Walmart has yet to be deterred from all robotics and artificial intelligence. Distribution centers are seeing increased use of robotics. In 2021 Walmart partnered with Massachusetts-based company Symbotic to introduce robots to 25 US distribution centers. In May of 2022, the partnership announced an expansion of its efforts to deploy robots to all US distribution centers (DC) over the next eight years (Heater, 2022).

The DC robots are a part of the company's strategy to support its retail stores by modernizing the supply chain. The robots and associates work together to pick, pack and sort inventory into pallets assigned to retail departments, allowing products to get from the distribution center to retail shelves faster and more precisely. With the help of Knapp, a tech company for intelligent fulfillment solutions, Walmart reduced its 12-step fulfillment process into five steps. The following is the patent-pending five-step process:

- **Unloading** merchandise from suppliers and manufacturers
- **Receiving** and breaking down pallets and placing inventory into totes
- **Picking** (retrieving) the items from the designated distribution location
- **Packing** the items in boxes
- **Shipping** items to their final destination

Associates help oversee each of the automated steps, which helps ensure quality control. First, the specialized totes are transported into a primarily automated storage system and shuttled to their designated location. Once the customer places an online order, the automated storage system can retrieve the items, put them into a tote, and shuttle them to a picking station. Associates then pack the items into a customized cardboard box folded to match the needed dimensions. The packages are finally taped and shipped to their final destinations. From building new, high-tech fulfillment centers to retrofitting our regional distribution centers, we continue to modernize and transform our supply chain by adding game-changing automation technology to our facilities. Our ability to test, embed, and scale automation rapidly is powered by Walmart Control Services, a technology platform developed by Walmart Global Technology that gives us the flexibility to plug automated solutions from partners like Knapp, Symbotic, and Witron into our vast supply chain network. (David Guggina—Walmart's senior vice president of innovation and automation, 2022).

Building Human Capital: Increasing Knowledge With the Walmart System

Walmart's scale and reach have expanded exponentially over the years. In the last five years alone, they have acquired 12 companies, including Flipkart in India, Bare Necessities, and Groupo de Narváez in Argentina. Front-line and administrative workers, the human factor, are the organization's backbone. The human element is essential to growth and is a substantial factor in Walmart's strategy. So much so Walmart has developed an associate training and development program called Walmart Academy (WA) to improve retention and increase skills and capabilities to promote employee growth.

"It's more than just training. It helps our associates see a clear path to advancement" (Walmart, 2017, para. 2). In 2016, Walmart opened the first WA and graduated more than 52,000 employees. Each location is built in or near a Walmart Superstore designed for front-line hourly supervisors, department managers, and assistant managers to receive up to six weeks of training. WA has about 200 locations. Each location serves up to 26 community stores and has a dedicated teaching staff. The training curriculum promotes higher-skilled jobs, encourages cross-training, develops digital acumen, and enhances knowledge acquisition.

In the wake of social distancing, COVID-19 precautions, and the temporary cessation of in-store shopping Walmart implemented a strategic plan for its employees, promising to improve job security. According to Walmart (2022), 62% of service workers have limited literacy skills, and 72% have limited numeracy skills. The impact of COVID-19 includes more than 50% of displaced low-wage workers and 25% of workers needing to switch occupations. Additionally, due to automation, 25% of retail salespeople and 24% of cashiers could potentially lose their jobs. The intersection of these three components creates an urgency to upskill, which provides the opportunity for a more advanced skill set through additional training and education. WA offers such opportunities.

Walmart designed a job development model called a *lattice of opportunity*. The model is akin to the omnichannel services model. The lattice offers several entry points and allows for vertical, horizontal, and even diagonal job shifts. These entry points include retail, logistics, healthcare, and technology. Walmart understands that training is a critical component of associate growth and success. Therefore, WA offers immersive teaching that combines technology, classroom training, and ongoing coaching on the sales floor (Walmart, 2022). The immersive learning experience provided to Walmart associates has become a trailblazing approach to corporate learning and development (L&D).

In 2022 Walmart announced the launch of one global WA to serve each of its associates worldwide (Stomski, 2022). As one of the world's largest learning ecosystems, it offers a hybrid learning experience, providing job-specific training to over 2.3 million associates. The academy focuses on three areas, developing on-the-job skills, growing future skills for associates, and building leadership skills for future managers. WA has also announced the College2Career Program, allowing associates to gain corporate office experience through an internship program while in college (Stomski, 2022).

Human Resource Development and Virtual Reality Training

From an academic perspective, VR and immersion theory have been studied extensively. According to Gutierrez et al. (2008), the physical configuration of VR can be classified as fully immersive systems, semi-immersive systems, or non-immersive systems. Fully immersive systems require head-mounted devices which isolate the user from the outside environment (Khandelwal & Upadhyay, 2021). Not unlike Walmart's training devices. Brock McKeel, Walmart's senior director of digital operations, brought VR training to Walmart's training curriculum by partnering with Strivr, a virtual reality training solutions company. Strivr's immersive technology uses behavioral science data to design VR learning programs that reduce training time and increases employee retention. "Overall associate engagement is significantly higher when we use this type of training, and the knowledge retention is significantly higher" (Strivr, 2022, para 1).

The initial pilot increased employee satisfaction by 30%, assessment scores by 70%, and knowledge rates by 15%. Walmart soon rolled out VR training to all of its academic training facilities.

WHAT DATA MEANS TO WALMART

Data and Decision-Making

Data is an integral part of Walmart's decision-making process. As with many companies, data provides insight into customer behaviors to facilitate daily and long-term decision-making. Walmart has five approaches to data use: pharmacy efficiency, improving the in-store checkout process, supply chain management, optimizing product assortment, and improving the customer shopping experience. Data determines pharmacy staffing needs to reduce costs and quickly fill prescription orders. Decision-makers use data and predictive analytics to assess cashier staffing needs at checkout lanes. This data determines the number of cashiers and the kind of checkout lanes required, such as express checkout lanes, standard checkout lanes, or self-checkout lanes that need facilitating.

Supply chain management is critical to operations. The company uses simulations from the collected data to improve efficiency and determine the physical steps to move products from the receiving dock to the store. With the help of companies like Kapp and Symbotic, Walmart has reduced the number of manual tasks required for order fulfillment. They developed ways to optimize routes, reduce the handling time of products, and improve trucking fleet and logistics costs. Walmart has also utilized data to improve the customer shopping experience by personalizing rollback deals and optimizing in-store and online product assortment. By analyzing customer preferences, shopping patterns, and behaviors, Walmart can determine which retail outlets should stock and display specific merchandise.

Data and Product Sustainability

Walmart's leadership has a split focus between profits and corporate responsibility. These commitments do not have to be mutually exclusive. In 2005, H. Lee Scott, Walmart's CEO from 2000 to 2009, announced a new initiative, an undertaking that he envisioned would make the world a better place. In the initiative, Lee outlines three goals for Walmart's upcoming strategies: produce zero waste, be fueled by 100% renewable energy, and sell products that sustain people and the environment (Spicer & Hyatt, 2017). How did Walmart plan to turn Lee's vision into concrete results? Spicer and Hyatt (2017) presented the findings from the multi-year project on how Walmart implemented the strategy.

The first challenge was *process tracing*, Walmart's emergent strategy, used to implement its environmental and social initiatives. An emergent strategy employs initiatives that anticipate unplanned actions, which contrasts with deliberate actions (Stobierski, 2020). In 2011–2012, the researchers interviewed 28 former Walmart employees and seven stakeholders for a process tracing narrative. The findings were publicly announced in 2015 (Spicer & Hyatt, 2017):

1. Move away from product-specific sustainability claims toward projects to develop a more generalizable and holistic sustainability index.
2. In institution-oriented strategies, the language justifying an initiative switched from what was just good for Walmart to what would be good for the entire set of private and public actors interested in providing customers with more credible and meaningful information.
3. The implementation of scorecard-based product initiatives emphasized communications with suppliers, better to identify low-cost innovations that improved economic or social performance without raising prices.

Corporations love to boast of their successes by telling stories; Walmart is no exception. Stories create excitement and build anticipation for the future. However, that is all they are: stories. Consumers and stakeholders were demanding quantifiable answers. Challenge two was recognizing a demand to define, measure and compare product sustainability. Part of the strategy to fulfill the demand began with a broader packaging initiative. Reducing the packaging size of products contributes to multiple environmental and sustainability goals, lowered packing and transportation costs, and fuel efficiency. Although these attributes could be measured, they came with their own challenges. First, by investigating the data, analysts found that some of Walmart's manufacturers were falsifying sustainability data and contracting with sweatshops. Analysts also found it nearly impossible to standardize the measurement and labeling of the sustainability of many of Walmart's products. The problem was that each supplier had its own set of standards to define sustainability.

Spicer and Hyatt (2017) described how Walmart develops its comprehensive solution to "holistically" measure and label sustainability across various products. Walmart developed an index modeled after one created by a company called GoodGuide. GoodGuide, the creator of The Index Project, developed a mobile app that rates green, healthy, and socially responsible products on a scale of 1 to 10 (Hodgkins, 2014). Walmart's Sustainability Index rates products on a scale of 1–5. It provided an overall product rating for consumers to compare. H. Lee Scott envisioned a better world, and data paved the path of that journey. Spicer and Hyatt used process tracing by interviewing former Walmart employees and stakeholders. They evaluated the methods by developing a narrative for Walmart's leadership. Spicer and Hyatt (2017) used quantitative data to assess corporate-wide waste reduction and cost savings for products and fuel. Data also improved consumer transparency by providing a sustainability index on products.

Deep Learning Artificial Intelligence and Big Data

Initially piloted in 2013, Walmart's curbside pickup service enables customers to order grocery items online and deliver them curbside. Once the customer orders, a personal shopper gathers the items and loads the completed order into the customer's car. Curbside service became integral to Walmart's brick-and-mortar operation during the COVID-19 pandemic. Customers were still able to get their much-needed groceries while practicing social distancing. However, the uptick in curbside orders created a challenge for personal shoppers when item stock became low or out of stock. Walmart explored deep learning and artificial intelligence to assist personal shoppers with this challenge.

Deep learning is a machine learning approach based on artificial neural networks. It uses algorithms for learning and decision-making. "The decision on how to substitute is complex and highly personal to each customer. If the wrong choice is made, it can negatively impact customer satisfaction and increase costs" (Venkatesan, 2021, para. 3). Walmart's artificial intelligence (AI) uses a deep learning approach to consider hundreds of variables, such as brand, price, type, preference, and available inventory. When a requested item is out of stock, the technology preemptively notifies the customer of available substitutes. Each time feedback is received, data sets are collected, and learning algorithms begin to improve the accuracy of future options. The data collected becomes large data sets used for decision-making.

According to Oracle, one of the leading providers of cloud and on-premises data infrastructure platforms, large data sets that are too complex to be analyzed using traditional data-processing applications are called *big data* (Oracle, 2023). These data sets also require more processing power than traditional data sets. Traditional data is structured and requires data taxonomy, a hierarchical structure that separates data into specific classes of data based on common characteristics. Big data can be structured or unstructured; volumes range from petabytes to zettabytes or exabytes. It is fitting that the world's largest retailer plans to build the largest cloud, capable of processing 2.5 petabytes of data every hour (Marr, 2021). Walmart's analytics hub, aptly named the Data Café, has already processed 40 petabytes of transactional, meteorological, economic, social media, and Nielsen data. One such data source is Walmart's Neighborhood Market in Levittown, New York.

In 2019 Walmart transformed its Levittown Neighborhood Market into a live retail laboratory. The Intelligent Retail Lab (IRL) is an entirely new concept of artificial intelligence retail space in a brick-and-mortar store. It is housed in a tech incubator called Store No. 8, containing over 30,000 items for purchase. The 50,000-square-foot space is equipped with thousands of cameras, sensors, and processors which collect enough data in seconds to stream three years of music. The cameras and sensors allow real-time data collection, analysis, and action. For example, suppose a customer takes the last two-pound tray of ground beef (the system can detect the difference between a one-pound tray and a two-pound tray). The sensor can detect an empty shelf and notify the store associate of a restocking need.

The new IRL experience has not only affected the customer experience but also increased associate knowledge and capabilities. AI was not intended to replace associates but to enhance their jobs and expand their skill sets (Smith, 2019). IRL store associates participate in experiments and simulations to help improve in-store processes and increase efficiencies. This associate–AI collaboration is evidence that Walmart's human capital is not being replaced by technology but enhanced. Over the last several years, Walmart has hired over 200,000 employees for technology-empowered roles (Walmart, 2022).

Lessons Learned and Future Directions in Knowledge Management

The twenty-first century is data-centric, emphasizing insights and knowledge. Modern companies have focused on digital transformation, data analysis, and predictive analytics to gain insight into practical decision-making. Knowledge is the basis of this insight. Why is knowledge management critical? The modern-day company exists in a *knowledge economy*, focusing on data, information, and knowledge as the most critical organizational resources (Jelenic, 2001). The steps made by Walmart demonstrate a precise alignment with the concepts of a knowledge economy. The world's largest retailer shares lessons learned.

Over the last decade, Walmart has been growing organically and through acquisitions. The company's strategic growth is divided into three categories: learning and innovating, growing current segments, and expanding into new segments to adopt new customer needs. Unbeknownst to the general public, many of Walmart's acquisitions were not all retail companies. In 2001, Walmart acquired a social media startup called Kosmix to help drive innovation (Weinand, 2019). In 2016, Walmart acquired Jet.com, which drove online sales up more than 40%. In 2019, Walmart acquired Aspectiva to advance Walmart's AI and machine-learning capabilities. Still, only some companies can afford to spend $3 billion on an eCommerce startup.

So what suggestions does Walmart have for the little guy? Walmart suggests focusing on innovating segments of an organization rather than the entire company. They have embraced the digital culture, investing billions in gathering and analyzing data. They have enhanced their knowledge management strategy by implementing new technologies and increasing employee knowledge and skills.

CONCLUSION

Sam Walton was a visionary, but did he foresee what Walmart has become? It is now a multibillion-dollar conglomerate, with an international footprint, in various sectors. Walmart serves millions of customers worldwide in over twenty countries. Its global supply chain is one of the largest, which includes 210 distribution centers, with plans to build four more next-generation fulfillment centers (Unglesbee, 2022). This illustrative business case study provided a narrative into knowledge management and technology decisions that helped Walmart succeed. An interview with Henry Akwa-Mensah revealed Walmart's strategy for physical and digital commerce convergence and how Walmart uses data to improve the consumer shopping experience.

The narrative explored the man-versus-machine paradigm. The case study discussed how Walmart shifted the paradigm to man and machine by enhancing job function rather than replacing jobs. Walmart uses machines to increase precision and speed fulfillment times for distribution centers. Virtual reality devices improve human resource development and build human capital.

Lastly, data is a crucial part of knowledge management. This business case study described some of the creative ways Walmart used data. The various aspects of improving the consumer shopping experience include pharmacy efficiency, in-store checkout process, supply chain management, optimizing product assortment, and appropriately staffing cashiers at peak times. Walmart also used data as a measure of corporate social responsibility. For example, they developed the sustainability index to increase product transparency and help consumers make informed buying decisions.

As for the secret to success, concluding words from Mr. Akwa-Mensah: "Success is not about what you know, but how you use it." (Akwa-Mensah, interview, June 8, 2022).

Questions for Discussion

1. Discuss the type of knowledge Walmart currently uses. Are there other forms of knowledge that they should consider?
2. Discuss the implications of knowledge management if Walmart were to merge Walmart US and Walmart International.
3. What innovations would you explore if Walmart hired you as the new director of innovations and insight? How would you use data?
4. You are the owner of a small business. What have you learned from this case study? How could you apply it to your company's plan for growth and sustainability?
5. How can Walmart determine the most effective combination of man and machine efforts in the man-versus-machine dilemma?
6. What factors should Walmart consider when deciding on test markets for new smart stores?
7. How does Walmart use data for business operations or decision-making in each example?

REFERENCES

Accenture. (2015, March 25). *U.S. retailers struggling to meet consumer expectations around mobile and in-store experience, Accenture study finds* [Press Release]. https://newsroom.accenture.com/news/us-retailers-struggling-to-meet-consumer-expectations-around-mobile-and-in-store-experience-accenture-study-finds.htm

Douglas, J. (2019). *These American workers are the most afraid of A.I. taking their jobs.* CNBC. https://www.cnbc.com/2019/11/07/these-american-workers-are-the-most-afraid-of-ai-taking-their-jobs.html

Guggina, D. (2022). *A new era of fulfillment: Introducing Walmart's next generation fulfillment centers.* Walmart. https://corporate.walmart.com/newsroom/2022/06/03/a-new-era-of-fulfillment-introducing-walmarts-next-generation-fulfillment-centers

Harwell, D. (2019). As Walmart turns to robots, it's the human workers who feel like machines. *The Washington Post.* https://www.washingtonpost.com/technology/2019/06/06/walmart-turns-robots-its-human-workers-who-feel-like-machines/

Heater, B. (2022, May 23). Walmart adding Symbotic robots to warehouses throughout US. *TechCrunch.* https://social.techcrunch.com/2022/05/23/walmart-is-adding-symbotic-robots-to-warehouses-across-the-country/

Hodgkins, K. (2014). Daily app: GoodGuide helps you find green, healthy and socially responsible products. *Engadget.* https://www.engadget.com/2014-04-22-daily-app-goodguide-helps-you-find-green-healthy- and-socially.html

Jelenic, D. The importance of knowledge management in Organizations–with emphasis on the balanced scorecard learning and growth Perspective. *Knowledge and Learning, International Conference,* 453-483.

Kande, M., & Sonmez, M. (2020). *Don't fear AI: The tech will lead to long-term job growth.* World Economic Forum. https://www.weforum.org/agenda/2020/10/dont-fear-ai-it-will-lead-to-long-term-job-growth/

Khandelwal, K., & Upadhyay, A. K. (2021). Virtual reality interventions in developing and managing human resources. *Human Resource Development International, 24*(2), 219–233. doi:10.1080/13678868.2019.1569920

Loafman, J. (2020). *Choice and convenience: Omnichannel around the world, today and into the future.* Walmart. https://corporate.walmart.com/newsroom/2020/12/09/choice-and-convenience-omnichannel-around-the-world-today-and-into-the-future

Manika, J., Lund, S., Chui, M., Bughin, J., Woetzel, J., Brata, P., Ko, R., & Sanghvi, S. (2017). *Jobs lost, jobs gained: Workforce transitions in a time of automation.* McKinsey Global Institute.

Marr, B. (2021). *Walmart: Big data analytics at the world's biggest retailer.* https://bernardmarr.com/walmart-big-data-analytics-at-the-worlds-biggest-retailer/

Oracle. (2023). *What is big data?* https://www.oracle.com/big-data/what-is-big-data/

Salisbury, M., & Plass, J. (2001). A conceptual framework for a knowledge management system. *Human Resource Development International, 4*(4), 451–464. doi:10.1080/13678860010016913

Smith, M. (2019). *Walmart's new Intelligent Retail Lab shows a glimpse into the future of retail, IRL.* Walmart. https://corporate.walmart.com/newsroom/2019/04/25/walmarts-new-intelligent-retail-lab-shows-a-glimpse-into-the-future-of-retail-irl

Spicer, A., & Hyatt, D. (2017). Walmart's emergent low-cost sustainable product strategy. *California Management Review, 59*(2), 116–141. doi:10.1177/0008125617695287

Stobierski, T. (2020). *Emergent vs. deliberate strategy: How & when to use each.* https://online.hbs.edu/blog/post/emergent-vs-deliberate-strategy#:~:text=What%20Is%20an%20Emergent%20Strategy,initiatives%20from%20within%20an%20organization

Stomski, L. (2022). *Walmart launches one global Walmart Academy to help 2.3 million associates build and grow their careers.* Walmart. https://corporate.walmart.com/newsroom/2022/06/02/walmart-launches-one-global-walmart-academy-to-help-2-3-million-associates-build-and-grow-their-careers

Storper, M. (1997). *The regional world: territorial development in a global economy*. Routledge.

Strivr. (2022). *Elevate performance through immersive experience*. https://www.strivr.com/lp/elevate-performance/

Unglesbee, B. (2022). Walmart plots 4 new "next generation" fulfillment centers. *Retail Dive*. https://www.retaildive.com/news/walmart-plots-fulfillment-centers-jobs/624868

Venkatesan, S. (2021). *How Walmart is using A.I. to make smarter substitutions in online grocery orders*. Walmart. https://corporate.walmart.com/newsroom/2021/06/24/headline-how-walmart-is-using-a-i-to-make-smarter-substitutions-in-online-grocery-orders

Walmart. (2017). *What is a Walmart Academy? How they're building confidence and careers*. https://corporate.walmart.com/newsroom/opportunity/20170417/what-is-a-walmart-academy-how-theyre-building-confidence-and-careers

Walmart. (2022). *Human capital: Good jobs and advancement for associates*. https://corporate.walmart.com/esgreport/esg-issues/human-capital

Weinand, D. (2019). *Lessons from Walmart: Smart strategies for retailers of all sizes*. Incisiv. https://www.incisiv.com/blog/lessons-from-walmart-smart-strategies-for-retailers-of-all-sizes

Zhao, J., & de Pablos, P. O. (2010). Regional knowledge management: The perspective of management theory. *Behaviour & Information Technology*, *7*(3), 39–49.

Chapter 3
An Innovative Approach to Knowledge Management:
How Scaling Social Emotional Learning Through Technology Led to Systemic Change

Beth A. Kiernan Ferrigno
https://orcid.org/0009-0006-3113-4492
Franklin University, USA

EXECUTIVE SUMMARY

This chapter summarizes a case study of the Harborwoods Central School District's successful implementation of a knowledge management system to improve social emotional learning for students and teachers. The case study highlights the challenges faced by K12 education in the realm of EdTech, including high costs, wasted instructional time, and tools that do not align with district goals. The COVID-19 pandemic has led to an increase in the adoption of EdTech solutions without proper professional development. The case study explores how Harborwoods transformed resistant teachers into tech-savvy experts and how they supported their school community through social emotional learning, AI, and collaboration. The analysis identifies an autonomous approach, adopting AI and technology tools, structured project management, and continuous collaboration and innovation as the main drivers behind Harborwoods' success. The findings can help school leaders to develop effective strategies for improving EdTech usage, saving time and money for school systems, and enhancing learning outcomes.

INTRODUCTION

Harborwoods Central School District (HCSD) is a school district educating approximately 4,000 students from grades K through 12 (K12). The goal of the Harborwoods Central School District is to educate students and develop life-long learners who can navigate a "diverse global society." To meet this goal, superintendent Dr. Williams and a team of district leaders created a 5-year strategic technology plan ad-

DOI: 10.4018/978-1-6684-5859-4.ch003

dressing the issues they deemed critical to achieving their goals. Sheila Ferguson, Assistant Superintendent for Business, led a team that included Denise Cowley, Assistant Superintendent for Human Resources and Administration, and Dr. Danielle Lombardi, Assistant Superintendent for Curriculum and Instruction. Along with crucial educators and building leaders, this team identified three overarching goals for the school year 2022-2023: Innovation, Curriculum, and Finance. Dr. Lombardi led the development of a knowledge management system (KMS), to address one of the curricular goals, improving Social Emotional Learning (SEL). The HCSD team wanted to try a novel approach to address their SEL goals by integrating a technology solution along with new professional development strategies. The strategic plan and district goals align with their vision and mission, which are as follows:

The mission of Harborwoods CSD is to provide an innovative and collaborative learning environment where all students are empowered to realize their unique potential while striving for academic excellence...Harborwoods is committed to developing life-long learners with the intellectual, social, and emotional skills necessary to achieve success as active citizens within their local community and in an ever-changing diverse global society.

To achieve its goals, HCSD needed to implement a district-wide KMS that was clear, aligned to outcomes, and measurable. Dr. Williams knew that developing a strategic KM (knowledge management) plan and ensuring its effectiveness required a multifaceted set of metrics embedded throughout the plan's implementation. Embracing new technologies and a shift in professional development were key strategies to achieve their goals, especially after past failed attempts at scaled change. The Harborwoods KMS aimed to avoid the problems encountered with previous initiatives by aligning tech initiatives, professional development, and a scalable approach to learning.

LITERATURE REVIEW

The implementation of EdTech in K12 organizations has been fraught with challenges for district leaders in the United States. The current state of education, specifically regarding EdTech, has led to various issues such as educator dissatisfaction, increased costs, and wasted instructional time, among others (BCG, 2021; Graham, 2021; Jotkoff, 2022). The market is flooded with over 9,000 EdTech tools, including 1,500 academic tools (Cauthen, 2021). K12 school systems are spending nearly $31 billion per year on tech solutions for their students and staff, and this amount is projected to increase to $45 billion by 2025 (Holon IQ, 2021). Unfortunately, students use an average of 74 different EdTech tools, while educators use 86, and half of them are underused, ineffective, or not used at all (Kuykendall April 2022, June 2022). The selection and implementation of EdTech in educational institutions are multifaceted processes that involve various factors such as funding, administrative support, optimism, and uncertainty (Lestari & Subriadi, 2021). One significant driver for the rapid increase in EdTech use was the shift to remote and hybrid learning during the COVID-19 pandemic, which changed how educators previously used tech solutions. Before, these solutions were used to provide ancillary support and instruction to students, but now they are used as a primary delivery tool for academic content, to manage student information, deliver instruction, and assess learning (Železný-Green, 2022). Districts sought to include multiple stakeholders in the decision-making process, knowing that a committee process for selecting

EdTech can provide diverse perspectives. But it can also be slow and lack the resources to evaluate all available tools effectively (Morrison et al., 2019).

Once the tech is selected, it must be implemented effectively in the classroom for the best return on investment. Explicit instruction in the form of professional development (PD) is crucial in increasing EdTech adoption rates, but it needs to be ongoing, flexible, and tailored to the specific needs of users. When teachers are required to implement new tech solutions without sufficient PD (BCG, 2021), the result is that educators leave school systems due to decreasing motivation and increasing expectations (Graham, 2021, BCG, 2021). Part of the dissatisfaction could be related to how EdTech was selected and implemented. Data indicates that almost three-quarters of tech purchasers are unhappy with their products or paying for tools they don't use (Fernandez et al., 2022).

Thus, education institutions must take a strategic approach to EdTech procurement, implementation, and knowledge sharing that considers the unique needs of their students, teachers, and staff. Studies by Bai and Lehman (2003) and Nazaretsky et al. (2022) have found that PD aimed at increasing faculty members' use of technology and improving teachers' trust in AI-powered educational technology can positively impact their perceptions and use of technology. Providing teachers and students with adequate training and support is essential to ensure they can effectively use the technology and see its benefits to their work. Without proper PD, users may not fully understand how to use the technology, leading to frustration and a lack of adoption (Archambault et al., 2010).

Scaling PD involves the use of Knowledge Management (KM) strategies, ensuring that all stakeholders have access to the information they need to be successful. An effective KM strategy includes the acquisition, use, and preservation of knowledge (Raudeliūnienė et al., 2018) over time to further support educators and school leaders in achieving their strategic goals. Ongoing, flexible, and tailored PD that leverages technology and digital tools can help teachers stay current and improve their teaching practices, according to Archambault et al. (2010). The sustainability of outcomes from explicit instruction depends on various factors, such as the nature of PD, the type of faculty, and the institutional context, according to Derting et al. (2016).

Harborwoods leaders needed to consider several areas for their SEL project: what technology would support their goals, how to ensure all participants understood their role in achieving a successful outcome, and to deliver professional development that aligned with best practices.

Preparing for Success

For the KMS to succeed, Williams and his team knew they had to rely on the strengths of the HCSD community. These strengths included a strong leadership structure supported by workers (teachers, administrators, and staff) and community members. Their original proposal was generic without well-defined metrics; measuring success would again challenge Harborwoods leaders unless they tried a new approach for their SEL strategy.

While alignment can help initiatives succeed, too much alignment across stakeholder groups can pose unique challenges if there are few opportunities for innovative ideas to be introduced and accepted. For HCSD, groupthink led to a narrow vision without measurable KPIs. With past initiatives, district committee leaders would propose new curricula or software, but there was minimal impact across all stakeholder groups. One recent example was the district's purchase of a new career readiness software program in 2018. Although district teachers were trained on the platform, there was minimal implementation support and even less leadership enforcement. The software program was discarded in favor of old practices and resulted in wasted district time and money for an underused tool and a poor return on investment.

Williams believed that HCSD leaders could improve upon prior experience by quantifying their goals for improved staff and student SEL. Lombardi was tasked with using the 5-year plan as an opportunity for the organization to refine and define metrics, and to help students achieve the "skills necessary to achieve success," as stated in their mission.

A Problem...

To achieve this organizational transformation, Williams and Lombardi had to rectify the problems within their current system. They knew that the gap between the district's strategic plan and specific, measurable, actionable KPIs would result in yet another poorly executed initiative. If they chose not to move forward with a vision that was accessible to all stakeholders, they would struggle to effect change as in the past—and their goal for social emotional learning was important enough to try something different. Social emotional learning was an existing part of the district's instructional practices, with some classroom teachers incorporating SEL as standalone lessons and others infusing SEL across their curriculum. How could they scale this initiative to align with their 5-year strategic plan? HCSD leadership team knew that improving organizational processes would result in more classroom time to accomplish district goals, so Williams and Lombardi proposed a KMS to resolve this issue. They decided to connect their 5-year plan with a strategy for implementing an SEL program with the potential to expand the process across other district goals and initiatives.

...A Plan

Williams and Lombardi knew they needed to start with a training initiative to support the change necessary for success. Current practices include top-down initiatives that lacked consistency within and across grade levels. District-wide training sessions would support the end-users and enable further efficiency when the SEL program was launched. If the SEL plan was going to work at scale, students, teachers, and community members needed to be aligned in their goals and able to act independently to achieve them.

In the case of the career readiness tool, standards and expectations were delivered by administrators or committees and expected to be followed within a semester or school year. Decisions and behaviors were driven by top-down compliance-based processes where administrators reviewed lesson planners to see if the career-focused lessons were planned or completed. This was already happening across the district with their existing SEL instruction--SEL lessons were treated as checklist items to be completed. Some limitations to scaling SEL and other new initiatives were due to a disconnect between the availability of data to measure success and the lack of time allotted for joint discussion and planning within and across grades and subject areas. District professionals used Microsoft Office tools to manage their communication, but there was little sharing within grades and across the district. Hundreds of custom lesson plans, folders, and inconsistent naming conventions led to a very crowded file structure. It was nearly impossible for teachers to find previously created materials, leading them to just develop them from scratch. There was also no method to share success. The SEL lessons were taught without evaluation or assessment, preventing iterative improvements.

Amidst the confusion, there were bright spots across the district.

- HS principal Dr. Michelle Newman shared that in some classrooms, students considered the SEL lessons and how they impacted their learning experience. Follow-up activities were aligned with cross-curricular lessons such as literature and history, and teachers and students reflect on how SEL benefits them personally.
- MS principal Elizabeth Corrigan shared that some of her more innovative educators have created new processes for teaching. Teachers partner up with colleagues from other curriculum areas to build cross-curricular units of study.
- And Sandra Whitson, elementary school principal, shared that teachers in her building have built their elementary curriculum to meet state academic standards while achieving the SEL goals as stated in the five-year plan. These teachers planned together, captured data to track student progress quickly, communicated among themselves, and allowed students more latitude in meeting academic goals.

While these educators embraced strategies to embed the SEL goals into various aspects of the student learning experience, individual classroom strategies hadn't changed the overall organizational practices. Lombardi was convinced that implementing an effective KMS would result in the district increasing its ability to scale its SEL goals across all stakeholders. But first, she needed to ensure that the HCSD community understood their roles in improving SEL across the district. To improve their ability to succeed, professional development for all stakeholders would require time and effort to achieve the district SEL goal. Lombardi felt that autopoietic epistemology would work as a foundation for the proposed KMS.

The proposed KMS focused on the processes of knowledge development as a foundational step in achieving their goals, starting with a tech-enabled strategy of collecting and sharing information across stakeholder groups. Subsequent steps included acquiring, using, and preserving knowledge (Raudeliūnienė et al., 2018) to support further educators and school leaders in achieving their strategic goals.

A New Approach

For HCSD to find success, leaders needed to address their previous challenges and build their systemic understanding of SEL and how to implement new strategies via knowledge sharing across stakeholder groups. Autopoietic epistemology would address the issue of siloed implementations and improve the potential for success by increasing the understanding of autonomously operating learning organizations (Russ et al., 2009). The KMS for HCSD was based on explicit instruction on the autopoietic epistemology for all stakeholders, school leaders, educators, and students (Parker, 2022).

To set the stage, Williams and Lombardi partnered with Denise Cowley, Asst. Supt. for HR and Administration to build a training initiative and secured funding to build an internal reward system with Asst. Supt. for Business, Sheila Ferguson.

Cowley led a team of coaches and trainers to develop an initiative geared toward role-specific outcomes. Since the implementation of the SEL strategy would be occurring within individual classrooms, training on autonomy was a key initiative. Lombardi and Cowley also worked together to ensure that instructional strategies relied upon more than recall but embedded complex learning in their teaching practices.

The training included:

- District-wide training initiative for building and district leaders on autopoietic epistemology, the benefits of an autonomously operating learning organization, and the practical measures needed to support educators.
- District-wide training initiative for educators on autopoietic epistemology, the benefits of an autonomously operating classroom, and the practical measures needed to support students.
- Explicit, ongoing instruction for educators and school leaders on autopoietic organizations and strategies to improve how they can achieve organizational goals related to SEL (Parker, 2022).
- House KM resources in MS Teams for educators and leaders and Google Classroom for students.

Figure 1 illustrates the pre-implementation activities by phase and task over time.

Figure 1. Gantt chart: Pre-implementation activities

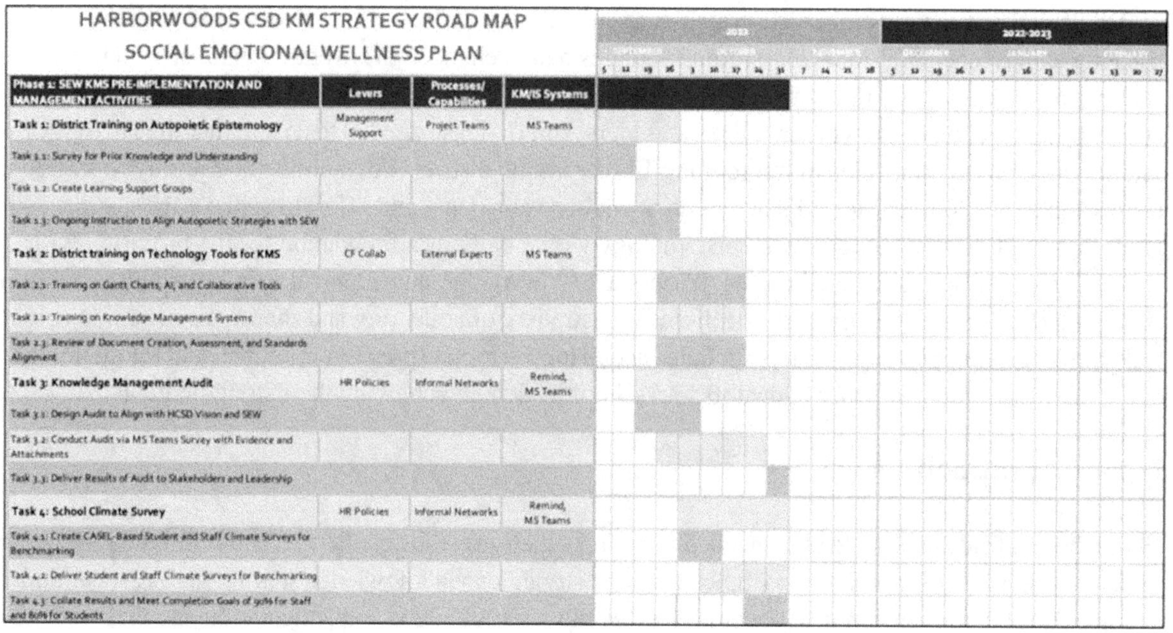

To save time in creating training materials, Cowley used artificial intelligence to write first drafts. ChatGPT, an OpenAI tool, followed her prompts on how school systems can use autopoietic epistemology to improve knowledge management:

Autopoietic epistemology can help school systems improve knowledge management by recognizing that knowledge is a dynamic process generated through interactions between people and their environment. To support self-organization and self-generation of knowledge, schools can create an environment that encourages active engagement and problem-based and project-based learning, as well as collaborative learning. By providing opportunities for students to reflect on their learning and understanding, schools can foster autonomy and creativity, which can improve problem-solving and critical-thinking skills. (OpenAI, 2020)

Using ChatGPT during this session helped participants understand the tool and embrace AI when building the KMS. After completing the district-wide autopoietic epistemology training sessions, Cowley and her team created an SEL committee with educators and leaders across the district to oversee the details of the knowledge management plan (OpenAI, 2020).

The KMS Process

Williams, Cowley, and Lombardi were pleased with the ease of integrating AI technology into their training plan and sought to do the same for the KM plan. An effective KM strategy has four pillars: goals, levers, processes, and systems (Massingham, 2019). HCSD's 5-year plan had general district goals but no clear levers, processes, or systems in place to support the attainment of their goals. Their stated goals for the HCSD strategic roadmap were vague and difficult to measure. Their goal for "Social and Emotional Learning" lacked levers and was as follows:

Together with the Harborwoods Community, students and staff will create a culture where the acquisition of self-awareness, positive relationships, social consciousness, and reflective decision-making skills enables students to thrive in their personal pursuits and chosen endeavors.

The district's stated processes to achieve that goal were documented in its plan. The four goals were generic and difficult to measure:

1. Ensure that the culture of the Harborwoods School Community is conducive to prioritizing social-emotional Learning (SEL) for ALL of its members.
2. Through the lens of Social Emotional Learning, develop core values representing our community.
3. Through the lens of Social Emotional Learning, examine the existing curriculum and consider alignment, enhancement, and implementation of standards where appropriate.
4. Enhance community and citizenship connections and opportunities for all students to support the growth of all students to thrive in their pursuits.

With no identified systems to support stakeholders or participants as they attempted to achieve the district's goals, challenges and frustrations prevented success for educators and district administrators. They needed a new approach with strong leadership. Dr. Andrew Schein, HS assistant principal, was tasked with leading the KMS development team as they worked to meet the district's SEL goals. For HCSD, Schein and other district leaders needed to ensure the tools and resources were available to key stakeholders, so the KMS achieved its intended outcomes.

Schein started with a Gantt chart which became the strategic roadmap to assist the team in achieving its KM goals by managing goal levers, metrics, and KPIs and tracking progress by critical stakeholders. Schein used AI to ensure they captured project milestones that may not have been considered by the HCSD team. The Gantt chart's goals were clearly defined within each overall strategy, and the enablers are detailed for each:

- KM levers are detailed for the underlying tasks within the three strategies.
- Processes and capabilities are defined to assist in achieving the goals.
- SM and IT systems are detailed as tools to support KM.

Project milestones were also identified on the Gantt chart, which was further defined as the KM strategy was developed with SMEs (subject matter experts) and project stakeholders. Schein and the project management team used the chart to:

- Define the SEL project scope and objectives
- Track staff training progress on the use of the new system and program
- Evaluate the effectiveness of the system and program
- Continuously monitor, maintain, and improve the KMS and program

The Gantt chart was used to ensure all employees understood their role in achieving HCSD's stated goals and became the one source of truth for the entire project.

KM Audit

Before implementing the KMS, Schein and his team had to understand the existing knowledge assets housed in the Microsoft Office files. The district's existing knowledge assets were audited to clarify the organization's current knowledge and what new or updated knowledge assets are needed. They followed the three components of designing a KM audit as defined by Handa et al. (2019).

The first component was designing the audit. To accomplish this, the KMS team started by asking questions addressing existing practices and processes within HCSD as related to SEL. The purpose was defined in the vision statement, "Each Child, Each Day, One Harborwoods Family." The KM team then defined the evidence needed. Evidence included mission statements, lesson plans, textbooks, library books, and state standards that align with SEL.

The second component was conducting the asset audit. The staff audit was in the form of an MS Teams survey with the ability to upload evidence to demonstrate alignment with SEL goals. The audit was conducted through system-wide tools for staff and students that acted as repositories for the social emotional learning knowledge assets. Microsoft Teams and MS Suite housed documentation and survey data for staff, and participating students used Google Classroom to complete pre- and post-surveys and SEL activities. The audit team collected the responses and again, used AI to analyze large amounts of data, identify patterns and insights, and make decisions based on that information. This helped the teams to identify historical practices that should be continued, and others that should not.

As part of the KM audit, all attachments required source identification (Handa et al., 2019). If this was not possible, the team evaluated the evidence to determine ownership. Assets that did not have an identifiable source were not used in the KMS. If there were duplicate assets, the SMEs determined which was of the highest quality, or whether to merge similar resources resulting in an improved tool. AI helped them to predict what would work in the SEL project and to decide what knowledge resources should be prioritized in their new KMS. The evidence was categorized and aligned to specific goals defined in the strategy roadmap.

The third and final component of the KM audit was delivering the results of the audit. For this KMS, the team provided the results of the audit in multiple formats based on role. Formats included a complete report for district leaders and project participants, a business brief for district staff, and a presentation of results to the BOE, district staff, and community members. Once the existing knowledge assets were identified and the results were presented, the committee started the work of building out the system.

Tools and Technologies

To support asynchronous collaboration, Schein sought additional technology solutions. He knew that he needed to move beyond the existing technology tools in the district if he was going to transform how they implemented new initiatives. Developing and sharing knowledge through technology-enabled communication tools and a clearly defined project management tool helped project stakeholders collect, share, and preserve knowledge.

Schein leveraged AI to support collaboration and knowledge sharing by providing his team with the ability to communicate and share information across different departments. Managing the project also required a new approach, Schein used an Excel Gantt chart to assign responsibility and track progress. These tools, along with the existing district systems, helped committee members work asynchronously to identify potential improvements and create new processes for future projects. Miro also helped with asynchronous brainstorming activities.

Schein and the rest of the district leadership team closely monitored the progress of the SEL plan. Their goal was for future projects to focus on acquiring and using knowledge across all groups, including educators, students, and community members, so following a detailed strategy was essential. The Gantt chart became a strategy roadmap to detail how each group would capture information and measure progress toward implementing their SEL goals. Specifically, participants accomplished the following through this KMS:

1. Developed knowledge by brainstorming SEL strategies within groups, documenting results using Miro, and then tracking the completion of tasks on the Gantt chart.
2. Shared knowledge by connecting or building off each other's strategies using Miro's multi-group connection capabilities and tracking the completion of tasks on the shared Gantt chart.
3. Built on shared knowledge to define and refine the district's SEL strategy. The Miro and Gantt charts help collect, share, and preserve information across all stakeholders.

A Road Map for Success

Williams and Lombardi decided to build upon existing innovative practices to test how HCSD could achieve its SEL goals, improve its KM issues, and scale the SEL instructional strategy to include all classrooms. The HCSD top-down and bottom-up approach was foundational and occurred before the start of the scaled SEL plan.

The first step in HCSD's KM road map was building the interactive Gantt chart, seen in Figures 1, 2, and 3, ensuring each stakeholder group can manage its aspect of the strategy autonomously. The committee managed task completion throughout the project (figure 2 details the SEL implementation activities). A CASEL (CASEL, 2023) SEL school climate survey was the baseline measure to determine the impact of embedding the new SEL lessons throughout the district. A piloted use-case approach included use cases in first, fourth, seventh, and eleventh-grade levels for the broadest learning application. Finally, the committee distributed the CASEL (CASEL, 2023) post-survey to all students and then analyzed the results.

The KPIs used to determine effectiveness were a 30% decrease in student disciplinary actions and a 30% decrease in teacher sick days. If the district achieved those metrics, the program would be scaled to all K-12 classrooms starting with professional development at the end of the 22-23 school year and continuing through the 5-year strategic plan.

Figure 2. Gantt chart: Implementation activities

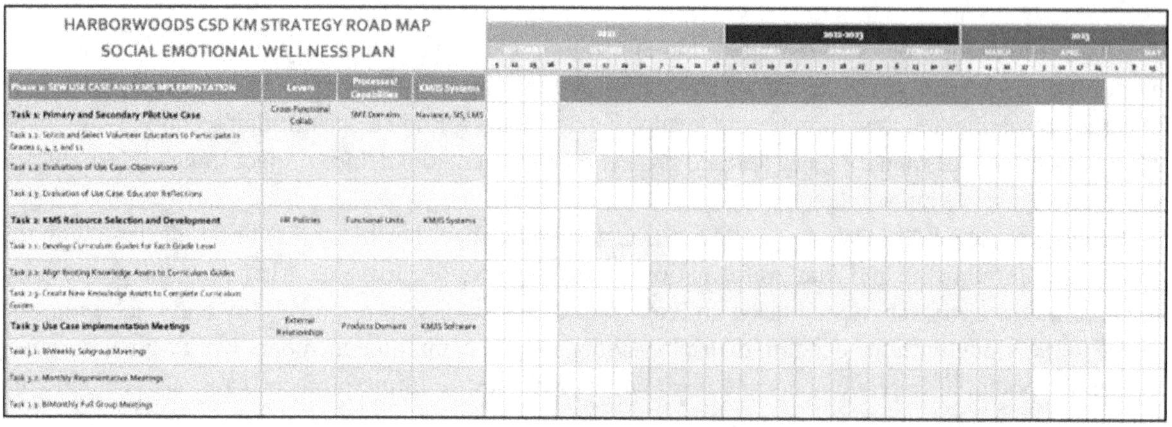

The district's strong culture helped leaders as they worked to align stakeholder groups throughout this project. Leadership support for other relevant management roles was another crucial success indicator (Pawlowsky et al., 2018, p.8). In a K12 organization, data privacy is essential, and staff must follow COPPA (FTC, 2022) and HIPAA (US Department of ED, 2021) rules. The KM leaders had to "balance between knowledge sharing and knowledge protection" (Pawlowski et al., 2018, p.8), especially when working on student social-emotional learning. The software solutions that were already in place (MS Office and Google) had security guardrails to ensure compliance with these regulations. Schein and his team went further by aligning their work with the district's Instructional Technology team's security standards and built data security compliance training into the KMS messaging.

The Timeline

Dr. Lombardi and Dr. Schein believed that if the SEL pilot was successful, it would result in an improved education system and more instructional time. The participating teachers were selected due to their expressed interest in the pilot and their grade level. A wide range of students and teachers from first, fourth, seventh, and eleventh-grade classes participated in this program. Lombardi and Schein felt that if they were going to scale this program, piloting with a cross-section of students and teachers would provide the most pertinent data.

The SEL committee developed a timeline to achieve this goal that was tracked on the Gantt project planning chart, illustrated in Figure 3. One of the key drivers to help teachers manage the extra work was the incentive program approved by Dr. Williams and Ms. Ferguson. Participating teachers had non-teaching duties relieved to allow time for planning and collaboration throughout the project. Teachers were also encouraged to attend SEL conferences to help gather and build additional knowledge resources for the KMS. This timeline gave participants enough flexibility to deliver the SEL lessons, and the district enough time to analyze results. The goal was to learn from the pilot, improve the KMS, and scale the program in the following school year.

Figure 3. Gantt chart: Assessment and evaluation activities

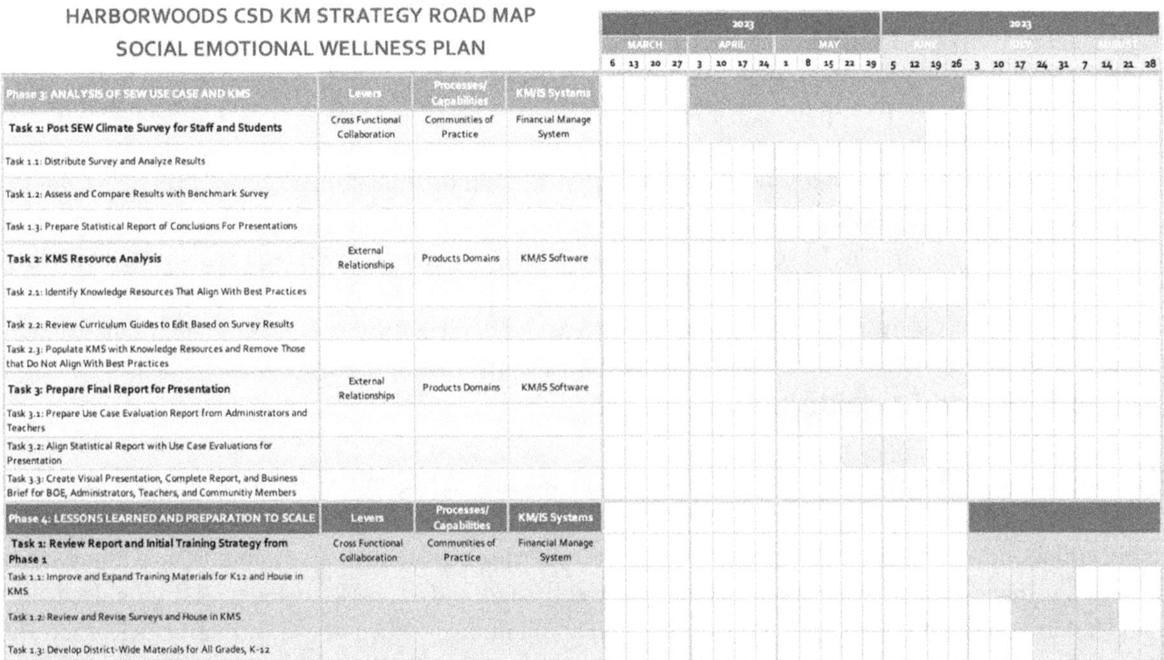

CONCLUSION

Under the leadership of Dr. Rory Williams, HCSD district leaders, educators, and students tried something new. The HCSD KMS used innovative solutions, from explicit instruction on autopoietic epistemology to embedded technology solutions, expanded stakeholder groups, and incentives for participants. The KM resource structures supported sharing information across participating groups without leadership input, leading to autonomy in classrooms and throughout the project.

Determining the success of their KMS required clear metrics to define expectations for all participants with achievable, repeatable KPIs across the organization. HCSD leaders, educators, students, and community members achieved their goals by starting with a knowledge management strategy that accurately captured and created new knowledge to share and disseminate across groups. The HCSD strategy of building a KM system to support the implementation of their social-emotional learning program is built on a foundation of shared understanding and goals.

This KMS proposal acted as a use case for implementing other district goals as leaders work through their 5-year strategic plan. The tools described in this project plan helped school leaders, teachers, and students to stay on a timeline to support their initiative and increase the district's chance of success. Innovative strategies helped committee members identify potential improvements and create new processes for future projects.

In conclusion, the current state of K12 education regarding EdTech has led to challenges such as increased costs, wasted instructional time, and tools that don't align with district goals. The COVID-19 pandemic has only exacerbated these challenges as teachers are required to implement new EdTech solutions without sufficient PD. Consequently, educators leave the school systems due to decreasing motivation and increasing expectations.

This study investigates how K12 districts select their EdTech tools and what PD strategies can be implemented to increase EdTech adoption rates. The results of this research can help school leaders to improve processes, leading to more efficient and effective EdTech usage and saving time and money for the school systems.

The significance of this study lies in the fact that how an organization selects EdTech and the PD provided to users can significantly impact EdTech adoption rates. This study has the potential to provide valuable insights into how K12 school systems can effectively integrate EdTech tools into their classrooms. By identifying best practices for EdTech procurement and implementation, school leaders can ensure that EdTech solutions align with academic goals and contribute positively to student achievement.

Reflections and Considerations

The choice of HCSD leaders to implement a KMS for their SEL initiative highlighted the power of technology, community, and autonomy. A system that provides visibility to all stakeholders can lead to a more collaborative and open organizational culture, fostering a more inclusive and practical approach to knowledge management, where staff and students freely share and access knowledge. Individual teachers and leaders working for the HCSD will know to act autonomously when new information is learned and focus on organizational goals without specific and direct input from leaders (Russ, 2021). Upon reflection, what the leaders built for their organization was an autopoietic system where the individual educator is empowered to act as "an autonomous, simultaneously open and ...self-referencing" individual (Russ et al., 2009). This type of school culture can embrace some of what has made autopoietic organizational structures so effective in Japanese businesses through explicit instruction across all stakeholders—administrators, educators, and students (Parker, 2022). Autopoietic epistemology is so different from what American workers are used to; substantive change will likely only come with explicit instruction that relates the autopoiesis with organizational goals.

Reflecting on the work of HCSD leaders, building processes to enable knowledge sharing is crucial in driving organizational change and helping educational institutions break through their siloed structures. An organizational culture prioritizing knowledge will have innovative business models, fluid boundaries, and a flexible knowledge base (Massingham, 2019). By eliminating the hierarchical structure that hampered previous initiatives, leaders expanded the SEL initiative and drove top-down and bottom-up success. To further advance the research, investigating the effects of implementing the KMS across an entire district and examining its efficacy with other initiatives would be valuable. It is essential to understand if HCSD's successful results of the SEL initiative can be replicated with other district goals and how the autopoietic organization adjusts and develops over time. Exploring these and other related inquiries is recommended.

Discussion Questions

1. What was the impetus for Harborwoods' Social Emotional Learning (SEL) program?
2. What were the key steps/building blocks of Harborwoods' district-wide SEL initiative? Why did they decide on using a knowledge management system (KMS) for this initiative?

3. How did Harborwoods use technology, knowledge, and knowledge management to empower educators and students? How does explicit instruction support the success of the KMS?
4. Why did Harborwoods start with SEL as a pilot case? What did the pilot implementation process look like for Harborwoods?
5. What methodology made the SEL plan possible? To what extent did this process serve as a role for future initiatives, and why? How was the SEL pilot leveraged to expand across the district?
6. To what extent did previous district-wide EdTech initiatives influence leadership in developing the SEL plan? How did economic factors impact the development of the SEL KMS? What will this mean for the other goals in the Harborwoods 5-Year Strategic Plan?
7. Following this analysis, what might be Harborwoods' strategies for future district-wide initiatives, in your opinion? What core competencies are captured by the procedures discussed in this case?
8. Describe the role of the Knowledge Base (KB) System depicted in this case study and identify the limitations of the tools described. Identify gaps in the existing infrastructure of HCSD.
9. Recommend an update to the systems (new infrastructure, tools, AI) and suggest concrete steps of implementation. Be sure to use the ISO 30401 Knowledge Management Systems Requirements to support your answer.

REFERENCES

Archambault, L., Wetzel, K., Foulger, T. S., & Kim Williams, M. (2010). Professional development 2.0: Transforming teacher education pedagogy with 21st-century tools. *J. Digital Learn. Teach. Educ.*, *27*(1), 4–11. doi:10.1080/21532974.2010.10784651

Bai, H., & Lehman, J. (2003). *Impact of a professional development project on university faculty members' perceptions and use of technology.* In D. Lassner & C. McNaught (Eds.), *Proceedings of ED-MEDIA–World Conference on Educational Multimedia, Hypermedia & Telecommunications, 2003* (pp. 1927–1934). Association for the Advancement of Computing in Education. Available online at https://www.learntechlib.org/p/14126/

Binkley, C. (2022, October 24). *Test scores show how COVID set kids back across the US PBS.* Retrieved January 6, 2023, from https://www.pbs.org/newshour/education/test-scores-show-how-covid-set-kids-back-across-the-u-s

Boston Consulting Group (BCG). (2021, December 5). *Teachers know best - Bill & Melinda Gates Foundation.* Retrieved June 23, 2022, from https://usprogram.gatesfoundation.org/-/media/dataimport/resources/pdf/2016/11/gates-pdmarketresearch-dec5.pdf

Cauthen, L. L. (2021). *The 2020 digital transition survey results are in: Just how large is the K12 ed-tech market?* The Learning Counsel. Retrieved August 12, 2022, from https://thelearningcounsel.com/article/2020-digital-transition-survey-results-are-just-how-large-k12-ed-tech-market

ChatGPT. (2022). *How can school systems use autopoietic epistemology to improve knowledge management strategies?* Retrieved from https://openai.com/chatgpt/

Dalkir, K. (2011). *Knowledge Management in Theory and Practice* (2nd ed.). MIT Press.

Derting, T. L., Ebert-May, D., Henkel, T. P., Maher, J. M., Arnold, B., & Passmore, H. A. (2016). Assessing faculty professional development in STEM higher education: Sustainability of outcomes. *Science Advances*, *2*(3), e1501422. doi:10.1126ciadv.1501422 PMID:27034985

Dubois, D., Niessing, J., & Kachan, K. (2020). A*nalytics-Driven Transformation at Majid Al Futtaim: Building a Data-Led, Test-&-Learn Culture to Generate Customer Value in the Middle East.* Insead, The Business School for the World. https://www.insead.edu/

Fernandez, R., Abdullahi, A., Shacklett, M., Greenberg, K., & Stone, B. (2022, July 28). *Most technology purchases come with high degree of Regret, Gartner says.* TechRepublic. Retrieved January 6, 2023, from https://www.techrepublic.com/article/most-technology-purchases-come-with-high-degree-of-regret-gartner-says/

FTC (2022, June 23). *Children's Online Privacy Protection Rule ("COPPA").* Federal Trade Commission.

Google. (n.d.). *Classroom Management Tools & Resources.* Google for Education. Retrieved November 20, 2022, from https://edu.google.com/workspace-for-education/classroom/

Graham, E. (2021, December 14). *Who is behind the attacks on educators and public schools?* NEA. Retrieved June 23, 2022, from https://www.nea.org/advocating-for-change/new-from-nea/who-behind-attacks-educators-and-public-schools

Handa, P., Pagani, J., & Bedford, D. (2019). *Knowledge assets and knowledge audits.* Emerald. doi:10.1108/9781789737714

Holon, I. Q. (2021, October 12). *K-12 digital instruction and assessment market to reach $42b by 2025.* HolonIQ. Global Impact Intelligence. Retrieved August 12, 2022, from https://www.holoniq.com/notes/k-12-digital-instruction-and-assessment-market-to-reach-42b-by-2025

Jotkoff, E. (2022, February 1). *NEA survey: Massive staff shortages in schools leading to educator burnout; alarming number of educators indicating they plan to leave the profession.* NEA. Retrieved June 23, 2022, from https://www.nea.org/about-nea/media-center/press-releases/nea-survey-massive-staff-shortages-schools-leading-educator

Kelly, P., Tejeda-Delgado, C., & Slate, J. R. (2008). Superintendents' Views on Financial and Non-Financial Incentives on Teacher Recruitment and Retention. *The International Journal of Educational Leadership Preparation*, *3*(1), n1.

Koenig, M. E. D. (2012, May 4). *What is KM? Knowledge management explained.* KMWorld.

Kuykendall, K. (2022, April 12). Report: Students used 74 different Ed Tech tools in fall 2021 semester, educators used 86. *THE Journal.* Retrieved June 23, 2022, from https://thejournal.com/articles/2022/04/12/students-used-74-different-ed-tech-tools-in-fall-2021-semester-while-educators-used-86.aspx

Lestari, N. D. I., & Subriadi, A. P. (2021, September). EdTech Investment: Optimism, Pessimism, and Uncertainty. In *2021 International Conference on Electrical and Information Technology (IEIT)* (pp. 239-245). IEEE. 10.1109/IEIT53149.2021.9587429

Massingham, P. (2019). *Knowledge Management.* SAGE Publications, Ltd.

Morrison, J. R., Ross, S. M., & Cheung, A. C. K. (2019). From the market to the classroom: How ed-tech products are procured by school districts interacting with vendors. *Educational Technology Research and Development*, *67*(2), 389–421. doi:10.100711423-019-09649-4

Nazaretsky, T., Ariely, M., Cukurova, M., & Alexandron, G. (2022). Teachers' trust in AI-powered educational technology and a professional development program to improve it. *British Journal of Educational Technology*, *53*(4), 914–931. doi:10.1111/bjet.13232

OpenAI. (2020). *ChatGPT: OpenAI's language model for conversation*. https://openai.com/research/chatgpt

Parker, K. (2022, November 9). Why explicit instruction matters, according to neuroscience. *Tes Magazine*.

Raudeliūnienė, J., Davidavičienė, V., & Jakubavičius, A. (2018). Knowledge management process model. *Entrepreneurship and Sustainability Issues*, *5*(3), 542–554. doi:10.9770/jesi.2018.5.3(10)

Ribeiro, J. (2016). Educational technology decision-making: Technology acquisition for 746,000 Ontario students. *Canadian Journal of Educational Administration and Policy*, 176.

Russ, M. (2010). *How Do We Get There? Strategy Action Framework–"Action Engine"*. IGI Global. doi:10.4018/978-1-60566-348-7.ch009

Russ, M. (2021). The individual and the organizational model of quantum decision-making and learning: An introduction and the application of the quadruple loop learning. *Merits*, *1*(1), 34–46. doi:10.3390/merits1010005

Russ, M., Fineman, R., & Jones, J.K. (2009). Conceptual theory: What do you know? *Knowledge Management Strategies for Business Development*, 1-22. . doi:10.4018/978-1-60566-348-7.ch001

Savage, J., & Savage, J. (2011). *Cross-curricular teaching and learning in the secondary school*. Routledge.

Sullivan, E. T. (2022, June 23). *Schools are looking for evidence from their Edtech. are companies ready to provide it?* EdSurge. Retrieved January 6, 2023, from https://www.edsurge.com/news/2022-06-23-schools-are-looking-for-evidence-from-their-edtech-are-companies-ready-to-provide-it)

The CASEL Guide to schoolwide social and emotional learning. (2023). CASEL. Retrieved December 3, 2022, from https://schoolguide.casel.org/

The visual collaboration platform for every team: Miro. (n.d.). Retrieved November 20, 2022, from https://miro.com/

What is Appreciative Inquiry? Examples & Resources for the Appreciative Inquiry Process. (2020, December 10). Benedictine University CVDL.

Železný-Green, D. R., Kagawa, F., & Giri, R. (2022, April 29). *Three reasons why the boost EdTech got from the COVID-19 pandemic may be short-lived.* Global Partnership for Education. Retrieved January 6, 2023, from https://www.globalpartnership.org/blog/three-reasons-why-boost-edtech-got-covid-19-pandemic-may-be-short-lived

KEY TERMS AND DEFINITIONS

Artificial Intelligence (AI): The development of computer systems capable of performing tasks that typically require human intelligence, such as understanding images, recognizing speech, making decisions, and translating languages (OpenAI, 2020).

Autopoietic Epistemology: A theory that highlights how individual and organizational learning lead to improved behaviors and outcomes. It emphasizes autonomous action and learning based on new information, without direct input from organizational leaders (Russ, 2009, 2021).

Knowledge Management: A framework for organizing, capturing, analyzing, and sharing knowledge within an organization. It involves creating a culture that supports knowledge sharing and collaboration and using technology to facilitate the management process (Koenig, 2012).

Social Emotional Learning: (SEL): The process by which individuals of all ages acquire and apply knowledge, skills, and attitudes to develop a healthy sense of self, manage emotions, achieve personal and collective goals, demonstrate empathy, build and maintain relationships, and make responsible decisions (CASEL, 2023).

Chapter 4
Knowledge Management Data Collection for Public Safety Priority Communications:
A Project Management Journey Through Ohio's FirstNet Public Safety Broadband Network

Liz Kheng
https://orcid.org/0009-0001-0731-9140
Franklin University, USA

EXECUTIVE SUMMARY

Many of the tragedies of 9/11 could have been prevented if not for the failure of commercial cellular networks that were flooded with public calls. These calls caused a bottleneck in the first responder communication systems. Because of these failures, President Obama signed the Middle-Class Tax Relief and Job Creation Act of 2012. Part of the law designates the 700 megahertz band block D spectrum allocated to public safety. In June 2014, the State of Ohio issued a Request for Quotation (RFQ) seeking a vendor for OhioFirst.Net National Public Safety Broadband Network (NPSBN) State and Local Implementation Grant Program (SLIGP) Support. The winning vendors, Advocate Technical Services and Televate, were tasked with building a project plan for Ohio First and gathering data to help the state of Ohio develop a business plan for National FirstNet. This business case study follows the Ohio FirstNet Project from a knowledge management perspective.

BACKGROUND

September 11, 2001, is forever etched in the minds of many Americans. Not only did the tragic events unfold at the World Trade Center and the Pentagon, but also the casualties that could have been prevented had emergency communications been prioritized for first responders. Cellular networks were flooded

DOI: 10.4018/978-1-6684-5859-4.ch004

with public calls on that tragic day, causing a failure in first responder communication systems (Orr, 2021). Like freeway congestion during an emergency evacuation caused by severe weather, the calling overload crippled the communication networks. Although many first responder agencies could still communicate using traditional mission-critical Land Mobile Radio (LMR) narrow-band voice systems (Police Executive Research Forum, 2017). Although reliable, this radio technology operated on a different designated spectrum and was not interoperable with other networks. The departments using them could not communicate outside of their agency. Senior Law Enforcement Officer at the First Responder Network Authority (FirstNet) Harry Markley wrote: *OUT OF TRAGEDY, A PUBLIC SAFETY NETWORK IS BORN*, and explained how,

The tragedies of 9/11 revealed fundamental problems with communication systems used by our nation's first responders. The radios relied on by police, fire, and paramedics did not efficiently operate across different agencies. Land and mobile phone lines were overwhelmed by a high volume of calls. First responders struggled to communicate with each other. (Markley, 2021, para. 8)

On February 22, 2012, President Obama signed the Middle-Class Tax Relief and Job Creation Act of 2012, Public Law 112-96 (Compton, 2012). Title VI of the law designates 700 megahertz band block D spectrum allocated to public safety. The term 700 MHz D block spectrum refers to the portion of the electromagnetic spectrum between the frequencies from 758 megahertz to 763 megahertz and between the frequencies from 788 megahertz to 793 megahertz. The designates 700 megahertz bands and allocates the necessary spectrum for a nationwide interoperable broadband network for first responders. In addition, it provides $7 billion for public safety broadband network build-out (Middle-Class Tax Relief and Job Creation Act of 2012, 2012).

The following is an excerpt from the legislative text of Section 6206 of the law [47 U.S.C. 1426] POWERS, DUTIES, AND RESPONSIBILITIES OF THE FIRST RESPONDER NETWORK AUTHORITY: STATE AND LOCAL PLANNING.—

(A) REQUIRED CONSULTATION.—In developing requests for proposals and otherwise carrying out its responsibilities under this Act, the First Responder Network Authority shall consult with regional, State, tribal, and local jurisdictions regarding the distribution and expenditure of any amounts required to carry out the policies established under paragraph (1), including concerning the—

- (i) construction of a core network and any radio access network build-out;
- (ii) placement of towers;
- (iii) coverage areas of the network, whether at the regional, State, tribal, or local level;
- (iv) adequacy of hardening, security, reliability, and resiliency requirements;
- (v) assignment of priority to local users;
- (vi) assignment of priority and selection of entities seeking access to or use of the nationwide public safety interoperable broadband network established under subsection (b); and
- (vii) training needs of local users. (Camp, 2012, p. 61)

THE STATE-ISSUED RFQ

Congress created the First Responder Network Authority (FirstNet) as part of the Middle-Class Tax Relief and Job Creation Act. Public law 112-96 required FirstNet to consult with federal, State, tribal, and local public safety entities to ensure that FirstNet meets the needs of public safety agencies across the country (First Responder Network Authority, 2022). These consultations guided states on the requirements to write and issue a Request for Quote (RFQ) to shape the plans for each State's customized build-out strategy. In June 2014, the State of Ohio Office of Information Technology (O.I.T.), through The Department of Administrative Services (D.A.S.), issued an RFQ seeking a vendor for OhioFirst. Net National Public Safety Broadband Network (NPSBN) State and Local Implementation Grant Program (SLIGP) Support (Anderson, 2014). The scope of work described in the RFQ listed nine detailed tasks in two separate phases.

Task one included a project mobilization strategy. In project management, mobilization refers to the initial stage of a project where preparations occur onsite before the commencement of any work, also referred to as the initiation phase in Project Management Body of Knowledge (PMBOK) terms. The mobilization phase requires diligent planning, identification of stakeholders, potential risks and bottlenecks, procurement of resources, and identify milestones and deliverables. It also includes documentation development, such as project and communication plans. The RFQ explicitly required the winning vendor to develop a Statewide Communications Interoperability Plan (SCIP) and the State and Local Implementation Grant Program (SLIGP) planning documents.

Task two was the development of the State's Public Safety Broadband Network Strategy and Implementation Methodology. The draft SLIGP, strategies, and methodologies plan presented to the State had to have the following items, structure, decision processes, high-level objectives, preparation and strategy, identification of goals for first responders and other needs, and build-out timeline priorities. In addition, the authors of the RFQ (the State of Ohio) anticipated that the SLIGP strategies and methodologies plan would be a living document maintained and updated throughout the project lifecycle.

Task three was to identify any potential broadband users and a stakeholder entity list. Potential broadband users include State, county, and local public safety officers. They may also include computer-aided dispatch centers (CAD), 911 dispatch centers, private and public patient transport companies, and hospital emergency rooms. Stakeholder entities may include highway departments, public health departments, other departments, critical infrastructure providers, public and private school districts (K-12), colleges and universities, and county and local management and administration.

Task four was to establish a complete familiarization with the organization, develop a government model for the public safety broadband needs assessment, and make recommendations. The winning bidder must develop a comprehensive understanding of organizational practices and protocols to assess and prepare suggestions regarding possible modification of processes or resources to optimize the organization, management, and execution of the SLIGP planning process. In addition, the contractor identified agencies as having potential network users (as specified in task three), determining agency personnel and their roles, and identifying agency decision-makers.

Task five was to evaluate and update any existing SLIGP planning documents developed as a requirement of task two. In addition, the task required the winning vendor to collaborate with the State to make any necessary improvements to the objectives or processes concerning its portion of the interoperable broadband network. Completing this task involved a critical review and updating the primary planning documents to ensure consistency with the State's strategy. Additionally, validate the durability of findings and conclusion on their utility in the execution of the State's strategy.

Task six was to conduct outreach and educational sessions for all stakeholders and participants within the state borders. Educational outreach sessions helped stakeholders effectively plan for the broadband implementation planning process. Educational material covered basic Long Term Evolution (LTE) capabilities, current and future applications, and transmission requirements. Supplemented educational sessions and offered detailed descriptions of the methods used to implement that plan. The plan included, among other methods, the use of some of the following: 1.) Classes of instruction, 2.) Online web-based training courses, 3.) Training materials, 4.) Educational documentation (printed or electronic), 5.) Web sites offering relevant educational materials, 6.) Presentations at meetings; and 7.) Facilitated Workshops.

Task seven required a secondary review of the Statewide Communications Interoperability Plan (SCIP) for updates. The contractor worked with the State to make any necessary updates to the existing SCIP. The implementation plan had to accord with the State's data and technology goals. In addition, any updates made had to align with the State's governance, standard operating procedures (S.O.P.), training and exercise, and usage. During the project's life cycle, the State expected two annual updates to the SCIP.

Task eight was to develop a plan for gathering stakeholder entity requirements. The plan had to include a description of the data type, its parameters, how to collect it, and the tools to use for collecting and compiling the data. The data must be tabular and graphical, accurately reflecting traffic flow in each state area, where coverage is required, and the quality of that coverage in the specified regions. Additionally, data had to include identifying relevant geographic priority areas, such as government buildings and schools. The completion of task eight concludes Phase I.

Task nine initiated Phase II of the project plan. It involved data discovery and collection as a part of the overall National FirstNet Agency and the National Telecommunications and Information Administration (NTIA) request. National data collection efforts would use all state and local data. The data collection process documented all existing infrastructure and other resources that would contribute to the design, implementation, maintenance, and operation of the National Public Safety Broadband Network (NPSBN). The data discovery and collection processes throughout all 88 Ohio counties included the availability and usefulness of potential assets such as communication sites, potential communication sites (government-owned lands and tall buildings), backhaul infrastructure, staff, human resources, coverage and non-coverage areas, and priority areas. After data discovery and collection, the contractor will develop an infrastructure report. The report was to be presented to the State for review and approval and must support the State's final business plan.

THE WINNING PARTNERSHIP

In July 2014, Advocate Technical Services (A.T.S.), a Columbus, Ohio-based IT consulting firm, partnered with Virginia-based Televate, experts in public safety communications, and submitted the winning proposal to the State of Ohio. Both companies had several decades of experience in the public sector, and each offered unique skill sets germane to the project's overall goal. The project team was collectively referred to as the Advocate-Televate Team. In the proposal cover letter submitted to the Ohio Department of Administrative Services, the following was how the Advocate-Televate team described their corporate experience:

The proposal response should address the Advocate-Televate Team's background, relationships, experience, and skills concerning public safety broadband wireless communications. As our proposal response will demonstrate, Advocate Technical Services has extensive experience delivering information technology services to various state and local governments, including the Department of Administrative Services (D.A.S.) Office of Information Technology (O.I.T.). Televate engaged in advancing public safety 700 MHz broadband initiatives over the past 14 years. Over this timeframe, Advocate-Televate has been a strong advocate for public safety broadband, has developed multiple broadband strategic plans, conducted national broadband financial analysis and business modeling, designed over a dozen public safety LTE networks across the country, assessed and implemented applications into live networks, and operated a 700 MHz broadband network in the District of Columbia. Televate provided SLIGP services to the states of Minnesota and North Dakota, and the District of Columbia, where they are currently engaged in Phase I activities. We are confident that our team's objectives will best position the State to define Ohio First.Net requirements and prepare for FirstNet consultation (Advocate Technical Services Televate, 2014, p. 5).

Advocate Technical Services (A.T.S.), later to be rebranded as T.S.G. Partners Ltd., is an Ohio-based IT consulting firm. Its expansive consultancy portfolio includes designing, implementing, and deploying unified communications networks, business growth, and solutions for state agencies, boards, commissions, and commercial customers; staffing solutions managed services; application development; and call center support. Its past clients include the Ohio Department of Job and Family Services, The Ohio Board of Nursing, Ohio Business Gateway, the Commonwealth of Massachusetts Department of Transitional Assistance, Cincinnati Bell Telephony Solutions (CBTS), and Franciscan Hospital Network.

Televate, headquartered in Vienna, Virginia, is an expert in business communications. Their business portfolio includes mission-critical communications for public safety personnel, public and private wireless networks, communications consulting, community broadband, and project and program management. Televate also offers fiber optic systems, LTE (Long Term Evolution) technologies, and Land Mobile Radio (LMR). Their client base includes the State of Vermont, the City of San Antonio, the Los Angeles Regional Interoperable Communications System (LA-RICS), and the State of North Dakota Information Technology Department.

PHASE I

Kickoff

In October 2014, the Advocate-Televate Team developed and presented a project plan to Mr. Daryl Anderson, the Statewide Interoperability Coordinator and Administrator of the Statewide Communication Interoperability. Following Mr. Anderson's approval, the official project kickoff meetings took place on November 12, 2014, and November 19, 2014. An Advocate-Televate team (ATST) representative Greg Berquist led the kickoff meetings. Mr. Berquist is a veteran in the public safety arena with a diverse background in law enforcement. As the project's public safety subject matter expert, Greg's knowledge network reach was invaluable to outreach efforts and identifying critical stakeholders.

User Population List and Point of Contact Database

The user population list had to encompass every user and subscriber from Ohio's 88 counties. These included police and sheriff offices and officers, Department of Corrections and officers, ambulance services and their drivers, computer-aided dispatch centers (911 centers), private security companies, the Ohio National Guard, the Ohio Department of Education, the American Red Cross (the Ohio Buckeye Region Disaster Reserve), the Ohio State University Police Department. In addition, these could include public and private K-12 schools, the Ohio Department of Parks and Recreation, the Ohio Department of Natural Resources, the Ohio Department of Public Safety, and the Ohio Department of Corrections. Another critical potential user population was any agency utilizing the Ohio MARCS Systems. MARCS is the Multi-Agency Radio Communication System for first responders and public safety (Ohio Department of Administrative Services, 2022).

Developing a point-of-contact database and stakeholder user population list was difficult. However, the point of contact database maintained ongoing communications with each organization. The email addresses of all points of contact were used to send out surveys, invitations, and mass communique. In addition, they used phone numbers when more personal correspondence was needed. Larger agencies often required phone conversations when losing communication between personnel.

User Population Survey

The User Population to provide the actual, quantifiable metrics for OFIP, including user population, specific barriers to adoption, adoption rates based on the availability of "value-added" features, and adoption rates over time. The survey is to be completed by the P.O.C. identified in the P.O.C. survey. The complete list of User Population Survey Questions is in Appendix A.

OFIP workgroups will vet the contents of the User Population Survey (see later section, "Statewide Requirements"). However, ATST anticipates, at a minimum, that the following information will be gathered through this survey:

- Potential number of NPSBN subscribers,
- Coverage requirements and use cases,
- Assess the preferred device types,
- Assess the current spending (commercial cellular, private mobile data, Land Mobile Radio),
- Assess the barriers to adoption (funding, computers, user terminals, mobile routers, I.T. resources, training, etc.).

Point of Contact (P.O.C.) Survey

The P.O.C. survey aims to develop a database of NPSBN contacts for all eligible user agencies throughout the State of Ohio. The P.O.C.'s responsibilities are to:

- Identify key contacts to facilitate requirements gathering and stakeholder participation,
- Provide the number of potential NPSBN subscribers for their agency,
- Provide input into the current spending on broadband communications within their agency,
- Assess user requirements for their agency,

- Provide information on available infrastructure,
- Assess terrestrial coverage (public safety agencies only) consultation (Advocate Technical Services Televate, 2014, pp. 57-58).

How was this information to be collected? ATST developed a targeted survey to establish an empirical basis and stakeholder statement for the State's requirement. The survey was emailed to each organization with an introduction and an explanation of the Ohio FirstNet Phase I goals. They provided links to Google surveys in the email for the point of contact (P.O.C.) to submit contact information for future correspondence and user population data. The surveys help collect P.O.C. information for 35 Red Cross Chapters, 884 Police Chiefs, 90 Sheriffs, 368 Public Safety Answering Point (PSAP) agencies, 94 transportation agencies, 219 hospitals, 382 schools, and 1,665 Fire Chiefs, totaling 3,739 points of contacts.

Once the P.O.C. and User Population lists were established, it was time to assess the current technology used by these organizations. ATST has gathered enough contact information to establish direct communication with the P.O.C.s. They sent another email survey requesting information about the organizations' current use of emergency communication technologies, level of technology expertise, and significant incident types. The surveys also gathered data on the type of devices utilized, application, required timetables for significant features, and other issues of interest to the State and the SIEC. The surveys also inquired about subscription services and cost expectations.

Education and Outreach

The education and outreach phase could begin now that ATST has a complete comprehensive contact list for each organization and a better understanding of agency communication needs. The education phase started by developing and publishing the OhioFirst.Net website and web-based training material. The training covered topics such as an introduction to OhioFirst.Net, public safety broadband, wireless data technologies for the non-technical person, LTE for radio experts, public safety broadband for the Public Safety Answering Point (PSAP), and data interoperability. Figure 1 shows screenshots from the web-based training found on YouTube.

Figure 1. Screenshots from the web-based training found on YouTube
Source: Abley (2016)

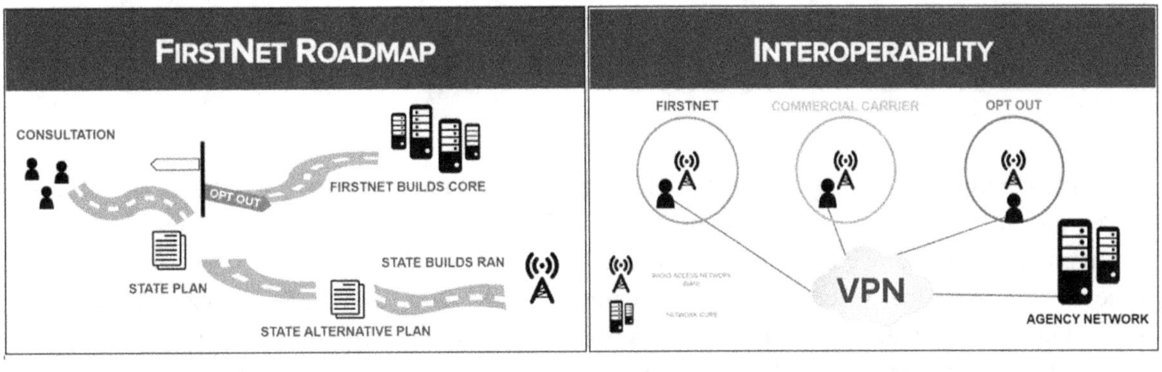

To enhance the learning experience, the ATST team developed a public safety video game simulating a fire and communications emergency where firefighters search for an unresponsive victim. According to Kelly Hill, a correspondent for R.C.R. Wireless News, the Ohio FirstNet video game showcases public safety LTE potential (Hill, 2016). The video game allows the player to sit in the driver's seat in a firefighter training scenario. The game also compares traditional communication technologies with an enhanced LTE mobile broadband network and applications such as integrated blueprints, real-time mapping and instructions, and thermal imaging to inform their actions (Hill, 2016).

On May 16, 2016, the Public Safety Broadband Summit in Washington, DC, showcased the PC-based video game. The OhioFirst.Net's Program Manager, Kelly Castle, told the federal FirstNet agency that the project was inspired by her son's love of video games. "After the first round of outreach, we decided that we needed a strategy that was going to fit hand and glove with the time frame that FirstNet put out so that we could keep our audiences interested," Castle said in a statement during the summit (Hill, 2016, para 2). Figure 2 shows screenshots from a demonstration of the video game.

Figure 2. Screenshots from a demonstration of the video game
Source: Abley (2017)

As a requirement to meet the outreach deliverables to the State of Ohio, ATST hosted five face-to-face kickoff meetings to present the findings of Phase I. These kickoff meetings offered real-time information and addressed any concerns from contract sponsors, agencies, and Ohio constituents. Invitees to the meeting were major stakeholders and members of the SIEC and NPSBN subcommittees. The focus included project status and next steps, a review of stakeholder requirements (coverage, capacity, devices, applications, and use cases), and other information of interest and value to the stakeholders. Each outreach session was scheduled based on the five Homeland Security Planning Regions; North-west, Northeast Lakeshore, West Central, Central, Northeast, Southwest, South Central, and Eastern. The map is shown in Figure 3.

Figure 3. Homeland security planning regions
Source: Abley (2014b)

PHASE II

Discovery and Data Collection for Infrastructure Database

The infrastructure database was the crux of this project. It provided evidence of the infrastructure and information on where it was unavailable (Abley, 2014a). Collecting infrastructure data for all 88 counties took over 16 months, requiring a dedicated team of five ATAS employees to accomplish the monumental task. Once again, the Phase II game plan began by contacting county P.O.C.s requesting contact information to develop a Computer Aided Dispatch Center (CAD) P.O.C. database. The ATST team compiled a database of over 130 CAD centers and then began requesting incident data. Below is the actual request:

This email was regarding a request for CAD data from your agency. The data will be used to help with the FirstNet consultation process. Table 1 is a sample of what we need. The most important data we are looking for is the location (address, latitude, and longitude), the priority of the incident, and the number of responding units. We are hoping you could provide data from the past three years (2012-2014) so we can proceed with scheduling your county coverage review (Personal Communications, Berquist, 2014, para. 1).

Table 1. Sample CAD requirements

Agency	Lat	Long	Address	Incident Priority	Responding Unit Count	Incident Duration (mins)
PD	90.6543	45.8468	3802 Smith Street, Columbus, Ohio	5	1	25
Fire	92.5465	43.1863	6479 Washington Blvd, Cincinnati, Ohio	4	1	30
Sheriff	91.6324	46.4863	6479 Washington Blvd, Cincinnati, Ohio	3	2	5
EMS	90.6543	45.8468	3802 Smith Street, Columbus, Ohio	4	2	6
Sheriff	90.6543	45.8468	3802 Smith Street, Columbus, Ohio	8	2	29

Source: Berquist (2014)

The extracted latitude and longitude data from the incident reports and imported them into Google Earth Pro to show a concentration of incidents in a particular area. Below is the actual screenshot of the data from the Columbus Police Department from 2012 to 2014. Each colored square represents an area of one-half mile, where the darker the color, the higher the concentration shown within the two years of data provided.

The combined data collection comprised thousands of incident records provided by the CAD data sets. Many data sets provided were only available to, address form and converted into geo-coded data in latitude and longitude format. Using a proprietary geographic information systems (G.I.S.) program, ATST analysts geo-coded (converted) incident addresses into latitude and longitude formats. For example, when geo-coded, the infamous address 1600 Pennsylvania Avenue NW, Washington, DC 20500, becomes 38.897957, -77.036560. Once the data sets were geo-coded, we imported them into Google Earth Pro Google Earth to create heatmaps files (.kml). Figure 4 shows the heat map of Columbus, Ohio's incident data from 2012 to 2014.

Figure 4. Heat map of Columbus, Ohio's incident data from 2012 to 2014
Source: Abley (2014b)

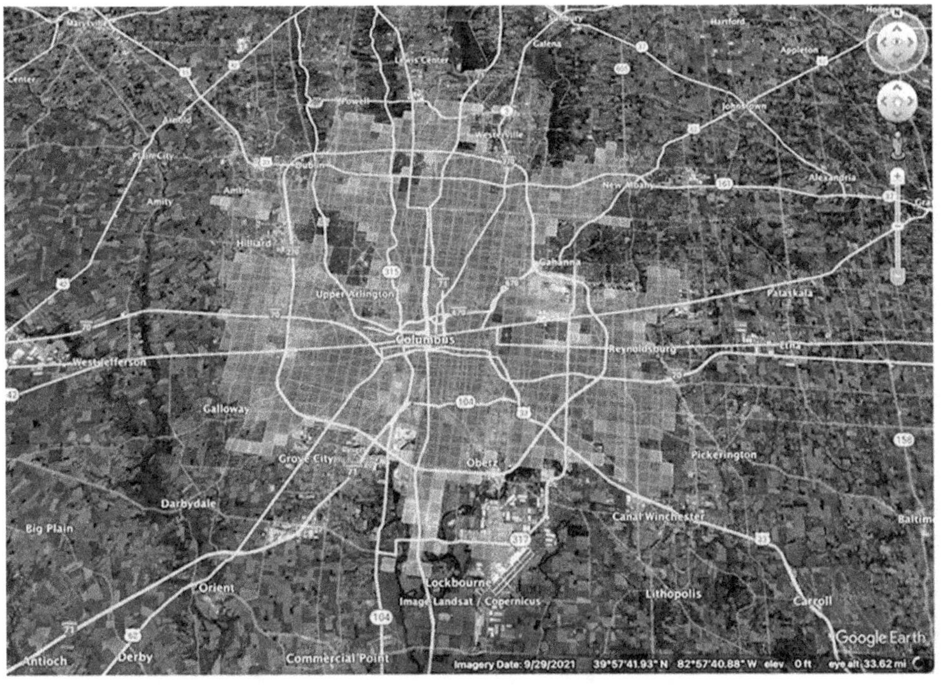

To further enhance geographic and infrastructure knowledge for Ohio's FirstNet Business Plan, ATST also scheduled coverage reviews with local public safety and administrative stakeholders. The coverage reviews were in-person and virtual consultations to identify geographic priority areas, coverage areas, emergency services areas, and priority assets (schools, towers, buildings, and critical private and government structures). We also collected coverage area data using Google Earth Pro. The projected a large screen during each coverage review session, displaying a topical view of the particular county. The aim was to consult with local stakeholders to identify their priority points of interest. Last, the coverage review consultations helped to identify emergency service areas (E.S.A.) and current service areas (C.S.A.) and graphically show where these areas did not converge. Figure 5 shows the screenshot of Mahoning County's C.S.A. (Red) and E.S.A. (Blue) areas and P.O.I.s.

Figure 5. Screenshot of Mahoning County's C.S.A. (red) and E.S.A. (blue) areas and P.O.I.s
Source: Abley (2014b)

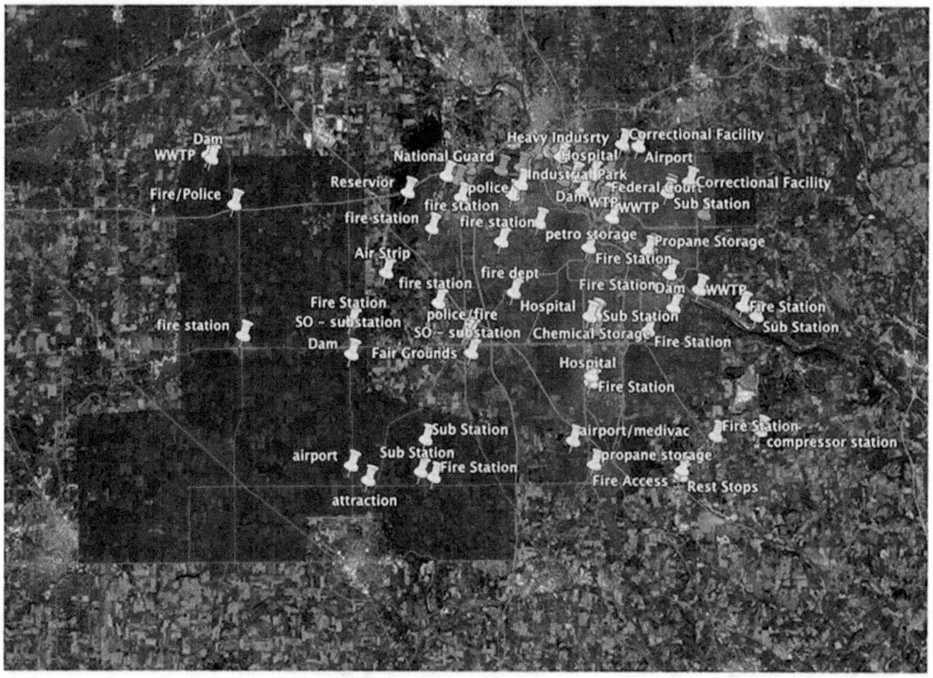

WHERE ARE WE NOW?

In November 2017, Ohio became the thirty-fifth State to opt officially into the FirstNet, the nation's first responder network (Aycock, 2017). By January 2018, every State joins the public safety network. In March of the same year, AT&T brought the network to life. Built from the group, AT&T "launched the dedicated, physically separate FirstNet network core, giving first responders access to a highly secure and truly specialized communications system that is distinct from commercial network offerings to keep their mission ready" (AT&T, 2016, para 3). By December 2019, over 10,000 agencies took part in National FirstNet, with over a million connections nationwide.

In November 2020, at the height of Covid-19, Ohio FirstNet, received a network expansion at more than a thousand cell sites (AT&T, 2020). The new infrastructure is part of Ohio FirstNet and its network expansion across the State to increase coverage capacity and capability for all public safety in Ohio. According to Commander Dennis Lowe, Major Crimes Unit at Fairfield and Athens Counties, a multijurisdictional task force, "connectivity has been a big plus with this platform" (The FirstNet Network Expands Across Ohio to Advance Public Safety Communications Capabilities. 2020, para 2). Deputy Fire Chief Nick Bergman of the Washington Township Fire Department in Montgomery County states, "FirstNet has provided us with several new resources that are not only helpful during the pandemic but year-round. This platform lets us quickly connect to other agencies and jurisdictions and track our assets and personnel." (The FirstNet Network Expands Across Ohio to Advance Public Safety Communications Capabilities. 2020).

The efforts by the State of Ohio and the consultants that collected data that helped build Ohio's business plan played no small part in this monumental undertaking. In addition, advocate Technical Services,

Televate, and the Ohio Department of Administrative Services should be applauded for their invaluable contribution to Ohio's public safety community and constituency in the form of this partnership. The next endeavor will be even more significant with the hard work already set forth. Isaac Newton once said, "If I have seen further, it is by standing on the shoulders of giants."

Discussion Questions

1. Why was it so important to build a P.O.C. list first?
2. What were the different types of data being collected throughout the project?
3. Suppose you were to have designed the User Population questions. What questions would you ask?
4. From a project management perspective, what improvements would you have made to this project?
5. What about from a knowledge management perspective?

REFERENCES

Abley, B. (2014a). *Advocate Technical Services Televate Proposal for Ohio SLIGP.* Academic Press.

Abley, B. (2014b). *OH Project Plan.* Academic Press.

Abley, B. (2016). *What is FirstNet?* YouTube. https://www.youtube.com/watch?v=w94UCxI-QuE

Abley, B. (2017). *OhioFirst.Net Next Generation FireFighter Demo.* YouTube. https://www.youtube.com/watch?v=4xmBUVoCKS8

Anderson, D. (2014). *OhioFirst.Net State and Local Implementation Grant Program Support Request for Quotation # OITRFQ093.* State of Ohio Procurement Services. https://procure.ohio.gov/bidders-and-suppliers/resources/03_OB_Solicitations_Contracts

Berquist, G. (2014). FirstNet Communication. Public Safety Agency.

Compton, M. (2012). *President Obama Signs the Payroll Tax Cut.* The Obama White House Archives. https://obamawhitehouse.archives.gov/blog/2012/02/22/president-obama-signs-payroll-tax-cut

Creating America's Public Safety Broadband Network Building a Network with First Responders (2016). Academic Press.

FirstNet: The History of our Nation's Public Safety Network. (2022). FirstNet Authority. https://www.firstnet.gov/about/history

Hill, K. (2015). *Ohio uses FirstNet video games to showcase public safety LTE potential.* RCR Wireless News. https://www.rcrwireless.com/20160517/featured/ohio-uses-firstnet-video-game-to-showcase-lte-potential-tag6

Markley, H. (2021). *Remembering 9/11 and how it changed public safety communications.* FirstNet. https://www.firstnet.gov/newsroom/blog/remembering-911-and-how-it-changed-public-safety-communications

Middle-Class Tax Relief and Job Creation Act of 2012. (2012). http://catalog.gpo.gov/fdlpdir/locate.jsp?ItemNumber=0575&SYS=000869737

Multi-Agency Radio Communication System. (2022). Ohio Department of Administrative Services. https://das.ohio.gov/technology-and-strategy/marcs

Orr, D. (2021). *How 9/11 Changed Me and First Responder Communications*. NIST. https://www.nist.gov/blogs/taking-measure/how-911-changed-me-and-first-responder-communications

The FirstNet Network Expands Across Ohio to Advance Public Safety Communications Capabilities. (2020). AT&T. https://about.att.com/story/2020/fn_ohio.html

The Revolution in Emergency Communications. (2017). https://www.policeforum.org/assets/EmergencyCommunications.pdf

APPENDIX A

User Population Survey Questions

User Demographics

- Number of Full-Time Employees
- Number of Part-Time Employees
- Number of Paid-on-Call or Duty Crew
- Number of Volunteers (Unpaid)
- How many emergency response vehicles are in your agency's fleet?
- How many non-response service vehicles are in your agency's fleet?
- Routine Emergency Incident (e.g., 911 call)
- Major Emergency Incident (e.g., natural disaster)
- Pre-planned incident (e.g., festival or sporting event)
- Pre-planned exercises (e.g., full-scale exercise or live training exercise)

Current Cellular Provider

- Choose which best applies:
- State Contract/Local Contract/Retail/G.S.A./Based on Price Quotes /Other/My agency does not utilize wireless service
- Does your agency have a direct sales/account relationship with the provider?
- Does your agency have a direct technical support relationship with the provider?
- Does the provider provide any additional or specialized services? (If yes, briefly explain)
- What is your average total monthly spending on voice/data devices, such as phones, NOT including additional costs and fees (taxes, apps, etc.)?
- What is your average total monthly spending on data-only devices, such as mobile routers and hotspots, NOT including additional costs and fees (taxes, apps, etc.)?
- On a scale of 1-5, how important is having a fixed rate plan?
- Who is responsible for the payment of the invoice? Choose one of the following that best describes your agency:
- Agency Pays/Individual User Pays/Hybrid/Administration
- What are the monthly data limits on the plan?
- What is the contract duration of your plan in years?
- What is your average monthly data usage per user in G.B.?
- Are employees allowed to use personally owned devices to perform work functions?
- If so, how many BYOD cellular devices does your agency support?
- Is the number above an estimate?
- Are personally owned devices allowed to connect to agency email?

- Are personal devices allowed to connect to official applications/services such as internal databases?
- What percentage of your devices are on the Verizon network?
- What percentage of your devices are on the Sprint network?
- What percentage of your devices are on the AT&T network?
- What percentage of your devices are on the T-Mobil network?
- What percentage of your devices are on the network besides those listed above?
- Does the BYOD device require a VPN connection?
- Does your agency have a policy on ownership of the information on a BYOD device?
- If you have a BYOD reimbursement policy, what is the monthly compensation?
- If you have a BYOD reimbursement policy, what is the compensation for purchasing a device?

Cost for Cellular Service

- The monthly cost is too high.
- Cost is not a barrier.
- The cost is fair, but my agency doesn't have enough funding.

Coverage

- My agency has excellent coverage.
- The coverage is poor, but we wouldn't purchase more services without better coverage.
- We would purchase more services if we had better coverage.

Network Performance

- My agency is very satisfied with network performance, reliability, and speed.
- The networks are too slow, and we would purchase more services if they were faster.
- The networks aren't reliable, and we would purchase more services if they were more reliable.

Security

- My agency is satisfied with security over commercial cellular networks.
- We would purchase more services if we had a more secure provider.
- We would NOT purchase more services if we had a more secure provider.

User Expertise

- My users have the sufficient technical understanding to utilize mobile data fully.

- We would purchase more mobile data if my users understood it better.
- My users don't understand mobile data, but we would NOT purchase more services if they did.

Perceived Usefulness

- This is not a barrier. On the contrary, my agency thinks mobile data is very useful to our organization.
- My users don't think mobile data is useful, and we would purchase more services if they did.

Device Inventory

How would you describe your paging system? Check all that apply.

- Application-Based (e.g., OnPage or Active911)
- My agency does not have a paging system.
- Commercial (subscription service)
- Private (owned by your agency)
- Local hospital operator calls my cell
- Application-Based (e.g., OnPage or Active911), s
- County-owned paging system
- V.H.F. radio paging
- Use County Radio System

How would you best describe your voice radio system?

- Fee-for-Service (e.g., MARCS)
- Cooperative (a system owned by your agency and multiple other agencies)
- Private (owned by your agency)
- Tax-based, county-wide infrastructure, agency-paid radios
- None

Enter the Number of Devices

- Number of Voice-only Phones
- Number of Smart Phones
- Number of Tables
- USB Modem or Wireless Card
- Laptop with Embedded Modem
- Mobile Hotspot
- Wearable Cameras

- Telemetry Devices (e.g., ShotSpotter)
- Biometry Devices (e.g., Blue Force)
- Wearable Heads-Up devices
- M2M Sensors
- Portable Radios
- Mobile Radios
- Base Station/Fixed Radios (e.g., Consolette)
- Pagers

Application Inventory

- On which devices do you use this application? Check all that apply.
- Mobile Laptop (e.g., in-car computer), Fixed Station (e.g., at dispatch),
- Mobile Device (e.g., phone or tablet)
- Fixed Station (e.g., at dispatch), Mobile Device (e.g., phone or tablet)
- Mobile Laptop (e.g., in-car computer)
- Mobile Laptop (e.g., in-car computer), Fixed Station (e.g., at dispatch

How Often on Average Does Your Typical End-User Utilize This Application?

- Daily
- Weekly
- Infrequently
- N/A (we do not use this application)

If you do not use this application today, when do you plan on using it? (Enter Date)
On which devices do you use this application? Check all that apply.

- Mobile Laptop (e.g., in-car computer),
- Fixed Station (e.g., at dispatch),
- Mobile Device (e.g., phone or tablet)
- None

Chapter 5
Challenges Faced by a Global Organization and Their KMS Implementation

Brenda Gross
Franklin University, USA

EXECUTIVE SUMMARY

Worldwide Connectivity Solutions (WCS) is a global enterprise. The purpose of this teaching case study is to describe the process WCS followed in selecting and implementing Helpjuice as its knowledge management system (KMS). Helpjuice is an easy-to-use WCS that faced numerous challenges that impacted revenues, shareholder dividends, employee retention, and a workforce needing more experience and knowledge to complete assigned tasks. Lengthy connectivity outages have impacted emergency services, leading to record-high fines imposed by the FCC. To overcome these challenges, WCS established a team to analyze the affordability of implementing a knowledge management system (KMS). As a result of the analysis, the team recommended that WCS implement Helpjuice as their KMS. This teaching case study describes the affordability analysis, challenges, strengths, organizational culture, KMS implementation, audit process, and multicultural perspectives. Lastly, a list of discussion topics and questions is included.

INTRODUCTION

This teaching case study is based on the experience of Worldwide Connectivity Solutions (WCS) in selecting and implementing a Knowledge Management System (KMS). It does not reflect how any company should conduct its business. However, challenges similar companies experienced were taken into consideration. Details have been enhanced to show how challenges, company culture, strengths, weaknesses, opportunities, and threats affect company operations and how implementing a KMS would overcome challenges and weaknesses and improve strengths and opportunities. For several years, companies in this communication sector (see below industry analysis) have been plagued with lawsuits and FCC fines resulting from poor customer service to interruptions to emergency connectivity services.

DOI: 10.4018/978-1-6684-5859-4.ch005

WCS is a global enterprise providing service across North America, Latin America, Europe, the Middle East and Africa (EMEA), and Asia Pacific that "provides high-performance, scalable, high-bandwidth connectivity worldwide" (Gross, 2022a, p. 2) services including cloud security, private cloud, multi-cloud management, network, cloud connect, voice, managed services, bid data as services, public cloud, SaaS apps, Internet, phone, and TV. The team of system administrators has faced challenges in meeting goals and productivity expectations because they lacked the experience and knowledge to complete assigned tasks. A contributing factor was high employee turnover owing to quarterly layoffs based on productivity expectations.

When quarterly reviews showed that revenue did not meet expectations, leadership leveraged productivity metrics to determine where improvements were needed. Often leadership was led to believe that laying off employees would increase revenues by reducing the expenses of employee salaries. The focus was on reducing expenses as opposed to increasing productivity. The quarterly review process resulted in employees fearing layoffs, which reduced employee loyalty and created an environment where employees lacked trust in management.

Unfortunately, after layoffs, leadership realized they needed more people to provide the services WCS was committed to delivering. Leadership would then request the Human Resources (HR) department to recruit new employees to fill positions. This was an endless cycle that had repeated itself for many years before leadership decided to explore options that had the potential to increase employee retention and develop their workforce.

The quarterly review output was an environmental, social, and governance (ESG) score and report. The 2023 ESG report stated that global workforce training offered relevant videos, books, and courses for various topics, including emotional and mental health, multicultural lessons in leadership, and today's racial landscape. WCS's mentoring programs offer a collection of mentoring relationships that build the competencies needed by future leaders. Leadership programs were designed to provide WCS employees with tools, training, and resources to engage, influence, coach, drive change, and increase a growth mindset across the WCS employee base. Tools include workspaces conducive to productivity, communication, and collaboration, software applications (software development applications, Microsoft Office products, communication applications such as Microsoft Teams, etc.), and equipment needed to complete assigned tasks, etc. (Stoddard, 2022). Unfortunately, the report was misleading in that the workforce had time constraints that prevented them from having time to participate in and complete the training offered.

To increase revenues by improving productivity and employee retention, WCS established a team to analyze the affordability of implementing a KMS. As a result, WCS determined that implementing a KMS would support its mission and vision by providing "access to a centralized location for storing information and knowledge captured for later review and sharing" (Gross, 2022a, p. 3). After WCS implemented Helpjuice, "employees began documenting processes, network diagrams, troubleshooting guides, and lessons learned" (Gross, 2022a, p. 3) for storage and future reference.

The purpose of this case study is to describe the challenges WCS faced and how it implemented Helpjuice to support its mission, vision, business strategies, and workforce development. Further, research was conducted to identify an affordable KMS to implement, support organizational growth, and align with WCS's strategies, mission, and vision.

LITERATURE REVIEW

Numerous factors may impact the level of success or failure of a KMS implementation. Studies reviewed and examined include the selection of KMS driven by organizational challenges, internal processes, implementation affected by industry and culture, and the impacts top management has on the success or failure of a KMS.

Greco et al. (2013, p. 1) define knowledge as the "sum of information – facts, procedures, concepts, interpretations, ideas, observations and/or judgments – that human beings can process and store in their minds," including tacit and organizational knowledge. Greco et al. (2013) also found that step one of a successful KMS implementation is selecting supportive criteria (Greco et al., 2013). Typologies to consider include document management system (DMS), learning platform (e-LP), virtual human resource management system (VHRMS), knowledge portal system (KPS), decision support system (DSS), customer relationship management system (CRMS), supply chain management system (SCMS), features and perspectives of KMSs, knowledge impact, knowledge creation, knowledge accumulation, knowledge transfer, knowledge diffusion, cost reduction, application, personalization, collaboration and communication, integration, tracking and monitoring, stakeholder satisfaction, customers, employees, shareholders, and suppliers (Greco et al., 2013). Analysis should be conducted to identify business activities (Greco et al., 2013) and requirements the KMS is expected to meet. Analysis results will include required features and application architecture (Greco et al., 2013). Additionally, the study found that "rigid organizational hierarchies, cultural acceptance, staff resistance, and the overlapping of initiatives can" (Greco et al., 2013, p. 8) impact KMS implementation.

Another area of consideration is organizational culture. A study by Ciganke et al. (2008) found that process-oriented and open communication affect KMS acceptance; results-oriented organizations have employees who tolerate risks more because they are not as concerned with the negative consequences of sharing knowledge. Ciganke et al. (2008, p. 441) stated that De Long & Fahey (2000), Grover & Davenport (2001), and Ruppel & Harrington (2001) "believed organizational culture is a major barrier to KMS acceptance." Further, Ruppel & Harrington (2001) stated that to prevent implementation failure, the organizational culture must be aligned with the cultural assumptions of the KMS (Ciganke et al., 2008). An organization must establish practices that "support knowledge creation, sharing and use" (De Long & Fahey, 2000, p. 16). Hofstede (1991) defined cultural practices as internal (invisible) and external (visible) (Ciganke et al., 2008). Opposed to job-oriented environments that focus on assignment and task completion to achieve organizational goals (Ciganke et al., 2008). The space shuttle Columbia disaster is an example of a KMS that failed. However, the organizational culture was just as much a factor as the piece of "insulation that fell off during launch" (Ciganke et al., 2008, p. 442). The NASA culture believed accidents were unavoidable; therefore, they did not take action to prevent known and preventable risks (Ciganke et al., 2008). Contributing factors were NASA employees who used the Lessons Learned Information System when needed, which reduced its usefulness (Ciganke et al., 2008), and an organizational culture that did not support open communication, sharing lessons learned, which resulted in additional resources that were not needed and a workforce resistance to guidance and recommendations (Ciganke et al., 2008). As a result, the author suggested that leadership should build and support a results-oriented work environment that encourages open communication (Ciganke et al., 2008).

The last study examined how technical and social aspects impact KMS's success (Cham et al., 2016) in the banking industry. Additionally, banking products and services depend on information and knowledge (Cham et al., 2016). This is significant because financial institutions offer the same products and services (Cham et al., 2016). As a result, financial institutions leverage knowledge to develop quality products and services (Cham et al., 2016). The study found that the success of a KMS was positively impacted by top management support and a supportive work environment (Cham et al., 2016). This is important in industries such as banking that require employees to use the KMS. Financial institutions do not give employees a choice whether to use the KMS implemented (Cham et al., 2016). In this case, top management must build employee trust and support knowledge sharing (Cham et al., 2016). When users trust the KMS, they are "more certain and comfortable to use the system in performing their jobs" (Cham et al., 2016, p. 7). Top management can build trust by communicating their confidence that the KMS will be reliable and meet organizational goals (Cham et al., 2016). The study found that user satisfaction in the banking industry depended on knowledge quality (Cham et al., 2016). To ensure reliability, usefulness, and knowledge quality, management teams must establish strategies and processes for evaluating, analyzing, and optimizing knowledge that will be stored in the KMS (Cham et al., 2016).

In summary, the studies found that organizational culture and management affect the level of success when implementing and using a KMS. KMS selection should begin by analyzing business activities and gathering requirements. Top management must support an organizational culture that builds user trust in the KMS, is results-oriented, and encourages open communication. Whether an organization requires employees to use the KMS or allows them to decide, the organizational culture must encourage and motivate employees to use the KMS. The space shuttle disaster was an example of a failed KMS because employees could choose how often they used their Lessons Learned Information System. In contrast, financial institutions do not give their employees the choice of using their KMS. In both cases, the organizational culture and top management must support and build an environment of trust, results-oriented, and open communication.

COMPANY OVERVIEW

WCS is a conglomerate of numerous companies and has conducted business under different names. Most recently, WCS had grown to over 29,000 employees globally, with more than $17 billion in revenues. WCS defined itself with the following mission and vision:

WCS Mission: To help customers achieve next-generation business goals by delivering exceptional networking, cloud, and security solutions.

WCS Vision: A continuing commitment to support environmental compliance and maintaining environmental, health, and safety efforts.

Over the years, WCS has experienced obstacles that resulted in negative impacts caused by connectivity outages that lasted longer than FCC regulations permitted. In three incidences, revenues have been impacted by significant FCC fines. The FCC fined a subsidiary a record $16 billion for failing to alert authorities of a preventable programming error that left close to 11 million people in seven states without access to emergency services for approximately six hours. FCC regulations require service providers to quickly alert Public Safety Answering Points (PSAP) when a 911 outage occurs (FCC, 2022). Years later, a "nationwide outage" caused 911 services to be disrupted across the country for about 12 hours and was the third shutdown of the year. The outage also widely affected ATMs and point-of-sale credit card machines. About two years later, the same business entity suffered another major technical outage owing to a misconfiguration in one of the company's data centers that impacted tech giants and resulted in fines imposed by the FCC.

Challenges

Over the years, WCS has faced numerous challenges, including low employee retention and revenues that did not meet expectations, negatively impacting shareholder dividends. Specifically, WCS laid off employees after quarterly reviews showed that stakeholder dividend expectations had not been met. As a result, fear of layoffs reduced employee loyalty (Gross, 2022b).

The workforce was faced with "time constraints created by multiple job functions which affected productivity, and conducting business reactively as opposed to proactive, and productivity-driven metrics" (Gross, 2022a, p. 3) that counted "the number of widgets clicked instead of focusing on quality services for their customers" (Gross, 2022a, p. 3) and on whether the actions effectively resolved the issue. Widgets are "lightweight applications designed for single specific tasks" (Xu, 2008, p. 3). In this case, widgets were developed to support communication architecture and framework (Xu, 2008). A significant factor was an organizational culture that discouraged communication and collaboration. Lastly, the HR department was burdened with continuously searching for and recruiting employees to fill open positions created by quarterly layoffs.

STRENGTHS, WEAKNESSES, OPPORTUNITIES, AND THREATS

SWOT, which stands for strengths, weaknesses, opportunities, and threats, is an analysis tool used to assess these aspects of an organization "related to business competition or project planning" (Wikipedia, 2023c, para. 1).

Strengths

The main selling point is that high-performance global bandwidth connectivity scalable to connect people, data, and applications digitally is offered. Conversations are initiated with customers to understand their needs so that design solutions meet customer needs (Gross, 2022c) and help them achieve their Fourth Industrial Revolution goals.

WCS has an advanced application delivery architecture explicitly designed to handle complex, data-intensive workloads of next-generation technology and business. This advanced technology empowers WCS's customers to utilize the full potential of their data, quickly adopt technologies that will revolutionize their business operations, and seamlessly deliver digital innovations that redefine everyday lives.

WCS has established business agreements, called competitive cooperation, "with other companies offering the same or similar products and services" (Gross, 2022b, p. 3). Competitive cooperation enables WCS to reduce the number and length of connectivity outages by other companies filling connectivity gaps when outages occur. This policy creates network redundancy, which is a method of "ensuring network availability" (Rouse, 2013, para. 1) by providing multiple "network devices, equipment, and communication mediums installed within network infrastructure" (Rouse, 2013, para. 1).

Weaknesses

By employing a workforce lacking experience and knowledge, WCS had inadvertently made itself vulnerable to security risks and threats. Employees were moved to teams without the experience and knowledge to complete tasks assigned to that team/division. Little knowledge sharing occurs when the company culture discourages communication and collaboration. As a result, trouble tickets responses times were high and often required rework. Trouble tickets are "automated requests for tracking and logging customer service requests" (Atchison, 2023, para. 2). A contributing factor to high response times was that trouble tickets were passed to different people until the trouble ticket was assigned to employees with the experience and knowledge to resolve the issue. Employees had to fulfill multiple job functions and face time constraints that prevented them from gaining new skills and knowledge. For instance, connectivity is a segmented network of circuits, "components, power sources, and signal sources, all connected so current can flow in a complete circle" (McAllister, 2023, para. 2), that employees do not completely understand; therefore, when outages occur, the employees were not equipped with the experience and knowledge to resolve the breakage and network collapse. Employees lacked knowledge of the processes before and after the segment they worked on, potentially impacting troubleshooting, service performance, and resolution time. These weaknesses negatively impacted productivity, created rework, and lessened the ability to maintain competitive advantage (Berry, 2023), all of which reduced revenue. Lastly, WCS risked becoming known for unstable networks and lengthy network outages.

Opportunities

The most significant opportunity was the availability of an advanced KMS that WCS could use. By implementing a KMS, WCS could build one team that communicates, collaborates, and shares information and knowledge. There were experienced and knowledgeable people available to hire. New HR policies will provide employees with training, mentorship, and coaching. WCS will expand its devices, equipment, and communication mediums (Rouse, 2013) to create network redundancy and reduce reliance on other companies to fill connectivity gaps.

Threats

Lengthy network outages impacting emergency services were caused by circuit and packet failures resulting in the FCC imposing fines. Circuits are "physical paths between the source and the destination" (GeeksforGeeks, 2023, para. 8). In contrast, with packets, "there is no physical path between the source and the destination" (GeeksforGeeks, 2023, para. 8). Additional contributing factors included inexperienced and less knowledgeable employees. This increases the chances that other companies will gain a competitive advantage over WCS and potentially lure customers away from WCS, which would negatively impact revenue.

INDUSTRY ANALYSIS

Three industry competitors were reviewed: Comcast, Equinix, and Lumen Technologies. Comcast Corporation is a global telecommunication (Wikipedia, 2023a) and media conglomerate providing broadband, mobile, and entertainment to customers (Comcast, n.d.); they "create, produce, and distribute leading entertainment, sports, and news" (Comcast, n.d., para. 3). Comcast has often been criticized for its "less-than-upstanding policies of employee relations" for years" (Wikipedia, 2023a, para. 7) and for having the "worst customer satisfaction rating of any company or government agency in the country" (Wikipedia, 2023a, para. 64). Corporate policies an obsession with sales opposed to customer service, reduced workforce, and employees who were poorly trained (Wikipedia, 2023a). In 2014 Comcast was awarded the "Worst Company in America" award" (Wikipedia, 2023a, para. 27). In 2016, Comcast was fined $2.3 million for "charging customers for unordered services and equipment" (Wikipedia, 2023a, para. 71). In subsequent years, a lawsuit was filed against Comcast for overcharging customers for products and services without their consent (Wikipedia, 2023a).

Lumen Technologies "offers communications, network services, security, cloud solutions, voice, and managed services" (Wikipedia, 2023b, para. 1). Since 2014, the FCC has imposed fines on a subsidiary of Lumen Technologies "for failing to alert authorities of a preventable programming error that left nearly 11 million people in seven states without access to emergency services" (Wikipedia, 2023b, para. 55). Another lengthy outage was caused by "misconfiguration in one of the company's data centers" (Wikipedia, 2023b, para. 56).

Equinix "interconnect industry-leading organizations such as finance, manufacturing, retail, transportation, government, healthcare, and education across a digital-first world" (Equinix, n.d., para. 1). In contrast to the workforce issues Comcast and Lumen Technologies experienced, Equinix "personalized development for employees through coaching" (The BetterUp Team, 2019, para. 1). Equinix chose to partner with BetterUp because of their "mobile platform that enabled" (The BetterUp Team, 2019, para. 7) Equinix "to provide customized and personalized development to employees at scale" (The BetterUp Team, 2019, para. 7). As a result, employees have shared "how much they love their coach, and that the work has impacted their performance and overall wellbeing. Many are requesting to extend their experience for another year" (The BetterUp Team, 2019, para. 11).

Comcast and Lumen Technologies have experienced many challenges and issues over the years that have resulted in FCC fines, poor customer service, and an undertrained workforce. In contrast, Equinix has proactively established a development program to enhance employee skills, morale, and satisfaction. It can be postulated that Equinix's coaching and development program has also increased employee retention. Could Comcast and Lumen Technologies benefit from similar workforce development programs?

ORGANIZATIONAL CULTURE

Organizational culture is critical to a company's success because it "is composed of beliefs and expectations shared by members of an organization" (Chalmers & Brannan, 2022, para. 1). It "consists of common norms, values, and beliefs of individuals within that group" (Chalmers & Brannan, 2022, para. 1). Additionally, "organizational culture determinants include an organization's structure, leadership, mission and strategy" (Chalmers & Brannon, 2022, para. 1). Consequently, organizational culture may have a positive or negative effect on whether the company is successful or not. For instance, organizational culture "can give employees a feeling of unity and purpose and can help a team cope with complex and dynamic changes" (Chalmers & Brannon, 2022, para. 1). Given the changes WCS faced, building a company culture that supported unity and change was pivotal in the success of their KMS implementation.

Company culture was driven by high productivity and revenue expectations. WCS leadership discouraged team communication and collaboration, which was counterproductive to productivity and revenue expectations and led to little knowledge sharing. Positions were isolated from others (siloed), which limited workforce skillsets (Gross, 2022a). Without an organizational culture change, employees would have been prevented from utilizing the implemented KMS. Over time, WCS began building a company culture that encouraged and motivated employees to share knowledge, learn, communicate, and collaborate as a team (Gross, 2022a).

IMPACT OF CHALLENGES ON THE OUTCOMES OF BUSINESS PROCESSES

An inexperienced and less knowledgeable workforce resulted in reworked issues because resolutions were ineffective and sometimes created additional issues. This cycle of issues negatively impacted revenues as more time was spent working on each resolution. Response time is essential to meeting customer expectations that issues are resolved in a reasonable amount of time and correctly. More importantly, response time is critical when resolving connectivity outages that impact emergency services. FCC imposed fines when outages were not resolved within the allowed time determined by the FCC.

To support the KMS implementation, WCS established processes that encouraged "communication and collaboration between employees" (Gross, 2022a, p. 10). Leadership was at the forefront of this new policy that required leadership to "be well-versed in managing change" (Gross, 2022a, p. 10). Because this was a significant shift from how WCS previously operated (Gross, 2022a), WCS contracted with an outside company specializing in change management. WCS recognized that "a big part of change management is communication in terms of sharing information with employees about what changes will occur, why and how the changes will impact them positively" (Gross, 2022a, p. 10). The change management team was tasked with "directing, motivating, inspiring, empowering and supporting" (ISO, 2018, p. 8) employees to contribute to the effectiveness of the KMS. As a result, WCS gained buy-in from employees, which was pivotal in their success.

WCS encouraged and led their workforce toward a culture that promoted knowledge sharing, learning, no negative implications when mistakes occurred (Gross, 2022a), and a mindset that "mistakes are an opportunity to learn what went wrong and why" (Gross, 2022a. p. 10). WCS leadership had to be committed to creating and supporting a knowledge culture for this to be possible. "Knowledge culture includes the different ways that people know things" (Roth, 2022, para. 3). It includes "the way they know things through experience, the way they know things through thinking, and the way they know things through reading" (Roth, 2022, para. 3). Oliver & Kandadi (2006) defined knowledge culture as "an organizational lifestyle which empowers individuals and motivates them to create, share and apply knowledge in order to reach consistent organizational success and benefits" (Dilmaghani et al., 2015, p. 4). Furthermore, Chang & Chang (2011) stated that "knowledge-based culture describes the extent to which the organizational culture supports knowledge as a valuable capital and source" (Dilmaghani et al., 2015, p. 4). Knowledge culture is leveraged to encourage and motivate employees "to identify and apply knowledge sharing as an appropriate behavior." (Romford, 2021, p. 1). As a result, WCS began noticing that employees were motivated to step out of their comfort zone to challenge themselves and learn new skills.

The HR department implemented numerous new processes to "improve employee retention and provide coaching and mentoring" (Gross, 2022a, p. 9) to employees. Policies were redefined in "areas of recruiting, selecting, hiring, training, developing, and rewarding new and current employees at all levels" (Russ et al., 2009, p. 13), as well as forming "company code of conduct expectations" (Gross, 2022a, p. 10).

MULTICULTURAL PERSPECTIVES

While implementing Helpjuice, WCS became aware that to build one team free of multicultural barriers, WCS must avoid stereotypes; calibrate communication style; learn, understand, respect, and leverage cultural differences; effectively communicate; build one team; make culturally correct decisions; foster cohesive relationships, build trust; and resolve conflicts quickly and peacefully Chgbesjp (2018).

WCS positioned itself to play for success (Chgbesjp, 2018), in which "team members work together as a team of ONE, understanding each other, supporting each other, and trusting each other, the whole team naturally becoming a winning team with the shared mindset and vision of success" (Chgbesjp, 2018).

Implementing Helpjuice was pivotal in WCS, creating one global team (Chgbesjp, 2018) by providing collaboration and communication functionality within groups, teams, and individuals. WCS's redesigned productivity guidelines to support collaboration and communication among teams and put less importance on the number of widget clicks.

In continued support of collaborative teams, WCS established communities of practice that are "people and teams in similar positions and similar disciplines" (Russ et al., 2019, p. 21) that began "to communicate for the common good" (Russ et al., 2019, p. 21). As a result, interpersonal relationships began "to emerge for the betterment of the organization as a whole and not for individual advancement" (Russ et al., 2019, p. 21). No longer were employees siloed in positions that limited their workforce skillsets (Gross, 2022a).

WCS established virtual workspaces that support communication, collaboration, and knowledge-sharing (Gross, 2022a). Cross-functional teams emerged that facilitated knowledge sharing by enabling WCS "to pool together a wide range of expertise from various units to accomplish complex tasks" (Davidow & Malone, 1992; Huang & Newell, 2003, p. 168; Baston & Haamann, 2018, p. 10).

KMS Affordability

WCS analyzed many KMSes, and selection was based on affordability, ROI, and whether the KMS fit the organizational vision, mission, and strategies. WCS also analyzed implementation expenses, managing costs, and "overhead, purchase, and utilization costs" (Gross, 2022a, p. 17). Five categories were considered "costs, including sunk costs, overhead costs, purchase costs, utilization costs, and life cycle costs" (Handa et al., 2019, p. 221). Overhead expenses included rent and the expense to purchase the facility for the company, utilities, office supplies, payroll, hardware, and so on. WCS's daily operations expenses already accounted for some of these expenses. However, additional costs, such as utilities, office supplies, office furniture, hardware, payroll for new employees, and administrative support, were included in calculating the ROI. Understanding how to calculate ROI differs depending on an employee's organizational role. For instance, employees may calculate ROI to support their project selection; managers may calculate ROI to give them greater insight into their team's performances; and executives may leverage ROI calculations to identify which projects should be approved (Stobierski, 2020). According to Stobierski (2020), the typical ROI formula is:

ROI = (Net profit/cost of investment) x 100

For project management, the ROI formula is written with different terms:

ROI = [(Financial value – project costs)/project cost] x 100

Stobierski (2020) offers the following example for calculating ROI for a project:

Total expenses and total expected revenues

Expected revenues = 1,000 x $3 = $3,000

Total expenses = (1,000 x $2) + $100 = $2,100

Net profit = $3,000 - $2,100 = $900

Expected ROI

ROI = ($900/$2,100) x 100 = 42.9%

Through analysis, WCS learned that implementing a KMS would improve decision-making and business processes, produce quicker problem-solving, increase innovation, improve knowledge sharing, support employee growth and development, and build better communication. (Invest Northern Ireland, n.d.). WCS calculated the ROI of each KMS to determine which KMS would provide the best ROI. As a result, WCS selected Helpjuice as its KMS. By conducting an affordability analysis, including ROI calculations, WCS was confident that it would "deliver value in a sustainable way" (Handa et al., 2019, p. 43).

Additionally, Helpjuice was a good choice because its easy-to-use design helps organizations scale customer support and team collaboration (Helpjuice, 2022). Helpjuice also provides functionality to manage access and create a daily backup schedule. Employees can "update articles and documents, collaborate on content and delete knowledge no longer useful or relevant" (Gross, 2022a, p. 9). The communication and collaboration feature of Helpjuice complements Microsoft Teams, which WCS continued to "utilize to encourage more informal communication, collaboration, and discussion" (Gross, 2022a, p. 8). WCS leveraged Microsoft Teams digital channels for users to post comments directly into articles and documents (Helpjuice, 2022a).

KMS IMPLEMENTATION

After selecting Helpjuice, WCS began recruiting software developers and system administrators to configure and customize functionality to meet WCS's requirements. Because Helpjuice is a commercial off-the-shelf (COTS) product, WCS was not burdened with building a custom KMS. The system administrators were required to have extensive experience and knowledge to support, troubleshoot, and maintain the servers and were tasked to design, install, and support the infrastructure for Helpjuice. Software developers were recruited based on their experience and knowledge of creating, designing, deploying, and supporting software and tasked to customize Helpjuice features and functionality to meet WCS's requirements.

KMS processes support seamless knowledge flow throughout organizations (Gross, 2022a, p. 4). To establish KMS processes, WCS identified bottlenecks, rerouted knowledge and information flows, and measured knowledge and information inputs and outputs (Harper, 2019). How knowledge flowed was standardized by using new processes, such as a seven-step cycle:

1. Create new knowledge—This happens every day, all the time, across all business areas.
2. Identify knowledge that is critical to strategy and operations.

3. Collect knowledge so that it can be shared with others.
4. Review knowledge to evaluate its relevancy, accuracy, and applicability.
5. Share knowledge through documentation, informal posts, and collaborative activities.
6. Access knowledge through pull (e.g., search) and push (e.g., alerts) mechanisms.
7. Use knowledge to solve problems faster and make more informed decisions (Harper, 2019, para. 6).

WCS used a KM strategy roadmap that included "workstreams, tasks, and milestones based on current state analysis and target state definition" (Little, 2019, p. 4). WCS found that KM workstreams added "value on their own, but ultimately created a more holistic solution when combined with other workstreams" (Little, 2019, p. 5). Tasks became the "discrete steps towards producing the deliverables in each workstream" (Little, 2019, p. 7), and milestones marked delivery dates of completed phases (Little, 2019).

WCS followed a seven-phase roadmap to customize and implement Helpjuice.

- **Phase 1:** Plan the KMS—Identify the project scope, establish an initial budget, estimate the level of effort, and identify resources needed.
- **Phase 2:** Analyze and define requirements, including evaluating infrastructure and system analysis (Suwandi, 2015)—Document KM system requirements.
- **Phase 3:** Verify that requirements are aligned with KM and WCS strategies (Suwandi, 2015)—Outline KMS strategies, outline WCS strategies, create a requirements matrix matching each requirement to strategies, and group related requirements into modules.
- **Phase 4:** Design the KM system, including the architecture and integration of existing infrastructure (Suwandi, 2015)—Design each module.
- **Phase 5:** KM system development, including testing (Suwandi, 2015)—Build and develop each module.
- **Phase 6:** Development and testing (Suwandi, 2015)—Deploy and test each module.
- **Phase 7:** Maintenance—Make a continual effort to maintain access availability, identify potential enhancements, identify and troubleshoot potential issues.

The first milestone included phases 1 through 4, which consisted of reviewing and acceptance approval from stakeholders before proceeding to the next phase (Gross, 2022a). Phases 5 and 6 consisted of "incremental deliveries, with each delivery marked as a milestone until all modules" (Gross, 2022a, p. 7) were "developed, deployed (Gross, 2022a, p. 7), tested, and validated and verified requirements were met (Gross, 2022a). Lastly, phase 7 continues as a maintenance effort to support accessibility and availability. The project schedule in Table 1 includes all the project phases and the timeline of the KMS implementation.

Table 1. Project schedule

		Duration (Days)	Start Date	End Date
	Project Duration	**217**	**3/1/2019**	**1/13/2020**
Phase 1	Planning	14	3/1/2019	3/21/2019
	Kickoff meeting	1	3/1/2019	3/1/2019
	Identify scope	5	3/4/2019	3/8/2019
	Estimate level of effort	3	3/11/2019	3/14/2019
	Identify resources needed	2	3/15/2019	3/18/2019
	Define budget	3	3/19/2019	3/21/2019
Phase 2	Analyze and define requirements	72	3/22/2019	7/5/2019
	Analysis process	62	3/22/2019	6/19/2019
	Define and document requirements	10	6/20/2019	7/5/2019
Phase 3	Requirements verification	15	7/8/2019	7/26/2019
	Outline KM strategies	3	7/8/2019	7/10/2019
	Outline WCS strategies	3	7/11/2019	7/15/2019
	Create requirements matrix	4	7/16/2019	7/19/2019
	Organize requirements into modules	5	7/22/2019	7/26/2019
Phase 4	Design each module (five modules)	75	7/29/2019	11/20/2019
	Module 1	15	7/29/2019	8/19/2019
	Module 2	15	8/20/2019	9/11/2019
	Module 3	15	9/12/2019	10/3/2019
	Module 4	15	10/4/2019	10/28/2019
	Module 5	15	10/29/2019	11/20/2019
Phase 5	Develop each module (five modules)	75	8/20/2019	12/9/2019
	Module 1	15	8/20/2019	9/11/2019
	Module 2	15	9/12/2019	10/3/2019
	Module 3	15	10/4/2019	10/28/2019
	Module 4	15	10/29/2019	11/20/2019
	Module 5	15	11/25/2019	12/17/2019
Phase 6	Test and deploy (five modules)	75	9/12/2019	1/13/2020
	Module 1	15	9/12/2019	10/3/2019
	Module 2	15	10/4/2019	10/28/2019
	Module 3	15	10/29/2019	11/20/2019
	Module 4	15	11/25/2019	12/17/2019
	Module 5	15	12/18/2019	1/13/2020
Phase 7	Maintenance			
	Identify potential enhancements	Continuous		
	Identify potential issues	Continuous		

During phases 2 through 5, the development team customized Helpjuice "to collect, review, share access, and use organizational information and knowledge and to improve communication and collaboration within groups and teams" (Gross, 2022, p. 8).

One goal was to create usable knowledge "to solve problems faster and make more informed decisions" (Harper, 2019, p. 8). To make this possible, the IT department developed and continues to manage an infrastructure that supports knowledge creation, identification, collection, reviewing, sharing, access, and use and "provides information storage and functionality to retrieve the proper knowledge at the right time — making the information and knowledge usable" (Gross, 2022a, p. 4).

After implementing Helpjuice, WCS reviewed its governance plan to ensure the KMS aligned with its goals as suggested by ISO (2018) and established a knowledge audit process to evaluate the strengths and weaknesses of the information and what it is used for.

Governance Plan

The governance plan consisted "of KMS strategies, policies, service level agreements, and codes of conduct" (Gross, 2022a, p. 10). The leadership of each department was "responsible for reviewing and establishing applicable policies" (Gross, 2022a, p. 10) that ensured KMS strategies aligned with their department goals.

A quarterly ESG report was written based on corporate governance scores courtesy of Institutional Shareholder Services (ISS) (2023). Scores indicate a decile rank relative to the index or region. A decile score of 1 indicates lower governance risk, whereas a 10 indicates higher governance risk. The following are the most recent results:

- Governance quality score 2023 = 4
- Audit = 4
- Board = 1
- Shareholder rights = 9
- Compensation = 3

A Corporate Governance Committee conducted quarterly ESG reviews and oversaw the ESG review process. This team routinely assesses disclosure and communication plans for their strengths, weaknesses, and effectiveness. An enterprise risk management committee assesses critical short- and long-term risks. It identifies mitigation efforts relating to financial reporting, strategic plans, operations, capital budgets, corporate functions, business units, and other operational risks. Lastly, the Sustainability Governance

Figure 1. Corporate governance committee organization chart

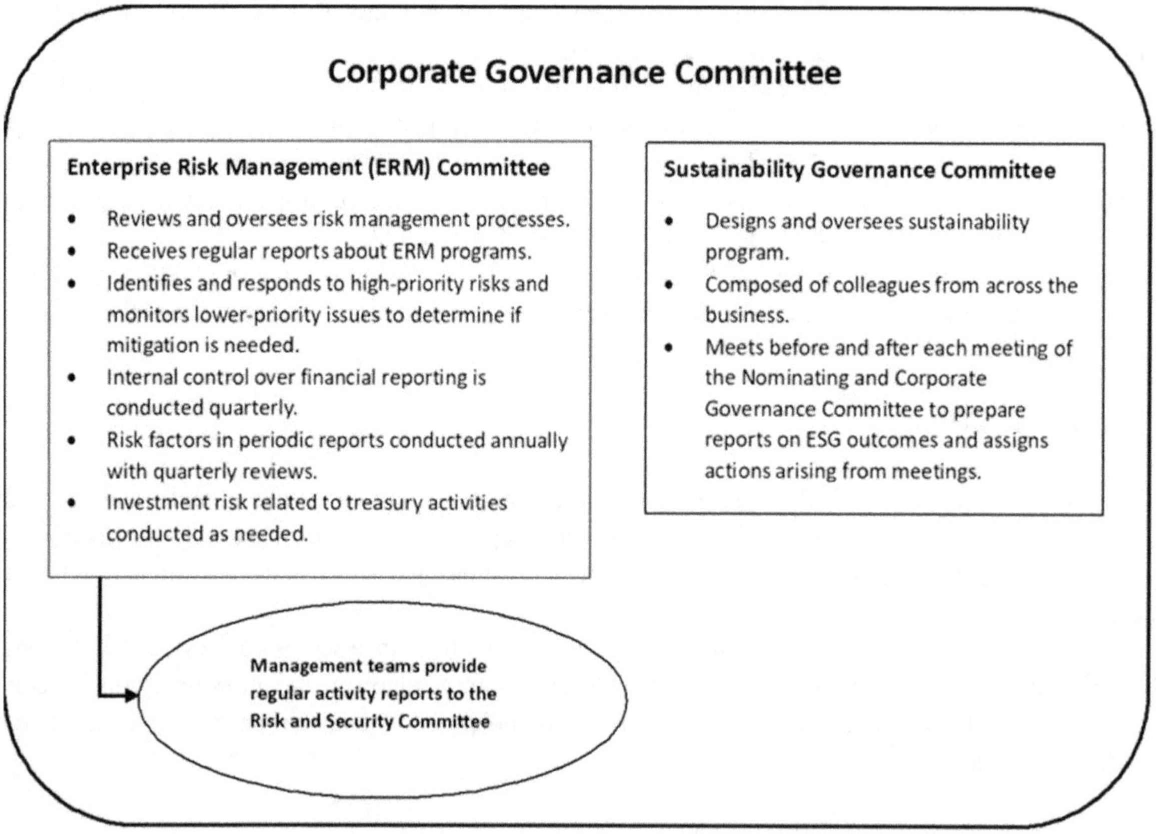

Committee designs and oversees the sustainability program. Figure 1 shows the primary responsibilities of each committee.

Voluntary employee engagement survey results were included in the ESG report. As of spring 2022, employee survey results were as follows:

- Overall company engagement increased from 67% to 69%.
- Overall well-being was 77%.
- Trusting relationships at work was 86%.
- Feeling positive about themselves at work was 80%.
- Highly favorable responses about being themselves and feeling comfortable voicing their opinions was 86%.

Knowledge Audit

WCS has a long history of focusing on "productivity-driven metrics that put a high degree of importance on the number of widgets clicked instead of focusing on quality service for their customers" (Gross, 2022a,

p. 3). As a result, to meet productivity expectations, inexperienced and less knowledgeable employees were more focused on clicking widgets than resolving issues effectively. To combat these issues, WCS relaxed productivity expectations to "allow time for employees to communicate and collaborate with other employees and teams" (Gross, 2022a, p. 4).

To answer the question of whether their knowledge assets added business value (Handa et al., 2019) and "where and how improvements" (Handa et al., 2019, p. 6) were achieved, WCS conducted audits of its structural capital, human capital, and relational capital. Structural capital, in this case, is defined as "the knowledge generated collectively by people across the organization — and formally expressed in documentation, procedures and operations and culture" (Handa et al., 2019, p. 48). In this case, human capital is defined as "tacit knowledge, skills and competencies, and attitudes and behaviors of individuals" (Handa et al., 2019, p. 48). Tacit knowledge, also referred to as implicit knowledge, "is knowledge that is difficult to express or extract, and thus more difficult to transfer to others by means of writing it down or verbalizing it" (Wikipedia, 2023d, para. 1). Lastly, relational capital is defined as "the knowledge inherent to the more extensive network of the organization — internal and external — and the reputations of all those individuals in the networks" (Handa et al., 2019, p. 48).

The first step was establishing an auditing team that began "collecting knowledge from employees" (Gross, 2022a, p. 11) and requesting "supporting evidence that their solutions are practical and resolve issues promptly" (Gross, 2022a, p. 11). This information was leveraged to assess the validity and reliability of knowledge assets. Knowledge value was measured by tracking when trouble tickets were submitted and completed and whether the solution resolved the issue (Gross, 2022a) or required rework. Additionally, the audit team assessed each source's competence, relevance, and reliability (Handa et al., 2019). With customers in mind, WCS collected "customer information to determine whether the solutions effectively resolved the issue" (Gross, 2022a, p. 11) and to measure customers' overall experience. The final step of the auditing process was to "diligently document all evidence and results" (Gross, 2022a, p. 11) and define "ownership and retention of audit documentation" (Handa et al., 2019, p. 57).

The productivity metrics were the "baseline for the audit results" (Gross, 2022a, p. 13). In addition to the number of widget clicks, metrics based on "how long it takes to resolve trouble tickets, whether the resolution was effective and if the resolution created issues" (Gross, 2022a, p. 13), leading to rework were collected as part of the baseline.

Effectiveness was "measured in terms of did the resolution solve the problem" (Gross, 2022a, p. 13). The expectation was that the KMS would increase productivity, reduce time to resolve trouble tickets, increase effectiveness, and lower adverse results (Gross, 2022a). As a result, WCS achieved less connectivity downtime but remained "challenged with providing network component redundancy" (Gross, 2022a, p. 13).

The preferable value strategy is "the internal rate of return used to estimate the profitability of potential investments" (Handa et al., 2019, p. 206). WCS estimated "the value of additional circuits" (Gross, 2022a, p. 12) it purchased, employees hired, and new processes defined and implemented (Gross, 2022a). Purchasing additional circuits was essential to WCS because more circuits added value by reducing the "number and length of time of connectivity interruptions and created redundancy" (Gross, 2022a, p. 12). Previously WCS recruited people to fill open positions "to ensure the work" (Handa et al., 2019, p. 206) was done with no regard to the "individual's tacit knowledge" (Handa et al., 2019, p. 206). After implementing a new productivity structure, WCS focused on recruiting people with tacit knowledge instead of filling vacancies (Gross, 2022a). Helpjuice defines tacit knowledge as "the knowledge, skills, and abilities an individual gains through experience that is often difficult to put into words or otherwise communicate" (Helpjuice, 2022, para. 2). This is important because capturing tacit knowledge is vital and "becomes even more valuable once" (Oragui, 2022, para. 11) documented. Four benefits of capturing tacit knowledge include being able to communicate organizational knowledge more effectively; differentiating the company from competitors; gaining knowledge capital and retaining organizational knowledge; and increasing productivity and organizational innovation (Oragui, 2022).

WCS leveraged net present value to estimate value by determining "if the projected future cash inflows" (Handa et al., 2019, p. 205) would "cover the future costs of starting and running the project" (Handa et al., 2019, p. 205). "Net present value is the difference between the present value of the cash inflows and the present value of cash outflows over a period of time" (Handa et al., 2019, p. 205).

"Time value as money is grounded on the assumption that the asset — in this case, money — has a time value" (Handa et al., 2019, p. 205). For instance, using knowledge as an example, knowledge does not depreciate over time as money does, nor does it lose value when not used (Handa et al., 2019). However, knowledge value increases when used and shared (Handa et al., 2019).

WCS estimated value based on what the employees brought, such as "their reputation and their personal network" (Handa et al., 2019, p. 207) and "skills and competencies to support" (Handa et al., 2019, p. 207) processes. For this reason, WCS leveraged net present value over human capital and structural and relational capital assets. WCS calculated knowledge value by calculating the "time utilized by the time spent learning" (Gross, 2022a, p. 13). Employees who used the new knowledge daily learned how to resolve issues (Gross, 2022a). As a result, knowledge learned improved resolution time and effectiveness and reduced the number of adverse effects resulting in rework (Gross, 2022a). WCS found that the "time-saved" (Cohen, 2006, para. 4) was not as important as "the quality of the output and its impact on the firm's reputation" (Cohen, 2006, para. 4).

Value calculations are essential so that organizations can measure success and have confidence that their actions positively impact revenue and services/products (Gross, 2022a).

Example 1: Value calculation

Value = time utilized/time spent learning
Employee hourly rate = $25.00
Employee weekly salary = $1,000.00
Time utilized: 3 hours a day * 5 days a week = 15 hours
Time spent learning: 8 hours a day * 5 days a week = 40 hours
(15 * 25)/(40 * 25) = (.375 * 1000) = $375.00

This calculation example was based on money saved on less rework to resolve issues. With the understanding that "knowledge loses value if it is stored or taken out of circulation" (Handa et al., 2019, p. 205), WCS leveraged Helpjuice to gain knowledge "interest through use and being in circulation" (Handa et al., 2019, p. 205). In other words, knowledge "creates new equity the minute it is used or put into circulation" (Handa et al., 2019, p. 205).

Example 2: Accuracy percentage and cost of rework

Cost of rework = Number of reworks performed/weekly productivity
Employee hourly rate = $25.00
Employee weekly salary = $1,000.00
Number of reworks = 20
Weekly productivity = 50
Accuracy rate = (20/50) = (.40 * 100) = (40 – (-100)) = 60%
Cost of rework = (1000 * .40) = $400.00

CONCLUSION

By implementing Helpjuice as its KMS, WCS overcame many challenges, notably an inexperienced and less knowledgeable workforce. WCS increased revenues, reduced the number of resolutions needing rework, built trust with employees, encouraged communication and collaboration, developed its workforce, and made one team globally. Employees were no longer constrained by time and productivity expectations driven by the number of widgets clicked.

WCS's growing workforce of knowledgeable employees positively impacts response times and reduces connectivity issues leading to outages. As a result, WCS has dramatically reduced FCC fines for outages that affected emergency services.

As WCS looks to the future, its leadership team is committed to an organizational culture that supports collaboration, communication, knowledge sharing, and workforce development.

Discussion Topics

A. Discuss the impact of implementing a KMS.
B. Discuss the impact of taking no action.
C. Discuss the benefits of implementing a KMS.
D. Discuss leadership styles and how each leadership style may impact the success of KMS implementation.
E. Discuss short- and long-term impacts of implementing a KMS.
F. Discuss KM tools and technologies.

Questions

1. How could the company increase employee retention?
2. What role does leadership play in the current situation?
3. How would the current leadership style impact the KMS implementation process?
4. What leadership styles would facilitate success and why?
5. How would WCS benefit from engaging a change management team before, during, and after implementing Helpjuice?
6. How does the KMS support and align with the company mission, values, and goals?

7. How could ROI be measured for implementing KMS?
8. What does the antagonist need to do to gain buy-in from stakeholders to implement a KMS?
9. What policy changes may be needed?
10. Who are the stakeholders?
11. What are the risks of not implementing a KMS?
12. How important are communication and transparency between leadership and employees?

REFERENCES

Atchison, E. (2023). *What's a Helpdesk Ticket? The Complete Guide*. Capacity. https://capacity.com/learn/helpdesk/helpdesk-ticket/#:~:text=A%20helpdesk%20ticket%20is%20an%20automated%20request%20for%20tracking%20and,to%20their%20product%20or%20service

Basten, D., & Haamann, T. (2018). Approaches for organizational learning: A literature review. *SAGE Open*, *8*(3). Advance online publication. doi:10.1177/2158244018794224

Berry, T. (2023). *How to do a SWOT analysis for better strategic planning*. Bplans.com. https://www.bplans.com/business-planning/how-to-write/marketing-sales/swot-analysis/

Chalmers, R., & Brannan, G. (2022). *Organizational Culture.* National Library of Medicine. StatPearls. https://www.ncbi.nlm.nih.gov/books/NBK560543/

Cham, T. H., Lim, Y. M., Cheng, B. L., & Lee, T. H. (2016). Determinants of knowledge management systems success in the banking industry. *VINE Journal of Information and Knowledge Management Systems*, *46*(1), 2–20. doi:10.1108/VJIKMS-03-2014-0021

Chang, T.-C., & Chuang, S.-H. (2009). Performance effects of knowledge management: Corporate management characteristics and competitive strategy enablers. *Asian Journal of Management and Humanity Sciences*, *4*(4), 181–199. doi:10.6413/AJMHS.200910.0181

Chgbesjp, P. V. (2018). *9 essential tips leading a multicultural team*. Personnel Communication. LinkedIn.

Ciganke, A. P., Mao, E., & Srite, M. (2008). Organizational culture for knowledge management systems: A study of corporate users. *International Journal of Knowledge Management*, *4*(1), 1–16. doi:10.4018/jkm.2008010101

Cohen, D. (2006). What is your return on knowledge? *Harvard Business Review*. https://hbr.org/2006/12/whats-your-return-on-knowledge

Comcast. (n.d.). *Our Company*. https://corporate.comcast.com/company

Davidow, W., & Malone, M. (1992). *The virtual corporation, structuring and revitalizing the corporation for the 21st century*. HarperBusiness.

De Long, D. W., & Fahey, L. (2000). Diagnosing cultural barriers to knowledge management. *The Academy of Management Perspectives, 14*(4), 113–127. doi:10.5465/ame.2000.3979820

Dilmaghani, M., Fahimnia, F., Ardakan, M. A., & Naghshineh, N. (2015). Function of knowledge culture in the effectiveness of knowledge management procedures: A case study of a knowledge-based organization. *Webology, 12*(1).

Equinix. (n.d.). *Who we are*. https://www.equinix.com/about

FCC. (2022). *911 Reliability, Network Outages, and Related Reporting Obligations*. Federal Communications Commission. https://www.fcc.gov/enforcement/areas/911-outages-reporting

GeeksforGeeks. (2023). *Difference between Circuit Switching and Packet Switching*. GeeksforGeeks. https://www.geeksforgeeks.org/difference-between-circuit-switching-and-packet-switching/

Greco, M., Grimaldi, M., & Hanandi, M. (2013). How to select knowledge management systems: A framework to support managers. *International Journal of Engineering Business Management, 5*, 6. doi:10.5772/56003

Gross, B. (2022a). *Worldwide connectivity solutions final project* [Unpublished paper]. Franklin University.

Gross, B. (2022b). *Worldwide connectivity solutions organizational analysis* [Unpublished paper]. Franklin University.

Gross, B. (2022c). *Worldwide connectivity solutions vision and roadmap* [Unpublished paper]. Franklin University.

Grover, V., & Davenport, T. (2001). General perspectives on knowledge management: Fostering a research agenda. *Journal of Management Information Systems, 18*(1), 5–21. doi:10.1080/07421222.2001.11045672

Handa, P., Pagani, J., & Bedford, D. (2019). *Knowledge assets and knowledge audits*. Emerald Publishing Ltd. doi:10.1108/9781789737714

Harper, M. (2019). *What are the best four components of knowledge management?* American Productivity & Quality Center (APQC). https://www.apqc.org/blog/what-are-best-four-components-knowledge-management#:~:text=The%20best%20four%20components%20of%20knowledge%20management%20are%20people%2C%20process,manage%20and%20measure%20knowledge%20flows

Helpjuice. (2022). *Helpjuice*. https://helpjuice.com/

Hofstede, G. (1991). *Cultures and organizations: Software of the mind*. McGraw-Hill.

Huang, J. C., & Newell, S. (2003). Knowledge integration processes and dynamics within the context of cross-functional projects. *International Journal of Project Management, 21*(3), 167–176. doi:10.1016/S0263-7863(02)00091-1

Institutional Shareholder Services, Inc. (2023). *ESG ratings & rankings*. https://www.issgovernance.com/esg/ratings/

Invest Northern Ireland. (n.d.). *Knowledge management and business growth: Advantages and disadvantages of knowledge management*. Nibusinessinfo.co.uk. https://www.nibusinessinfo.co.uk/content/advantages-and-disadvantages-knowledge-management

ISO. (2018). *Knowledge management systems*. https://www.iso.org

Little, M. (2019). *Building an agile KM roadmap*. KM Institute. https://www.kminstitute.org/blog/building-agile-km-roadmap

McAllister, W. (2023). *Circuit terminology*. Khan Academy. https://www.khanacademy.org/science/electrical-engineering/ee-circuit-analysis-topic/circuit-elements/a/ee-circuit-terminology

Oliver, S., & Kandadi, K. R. (2006). How to develop knowledge culture in organizations? A multiple case study of large distributed organizations. *Journal of Knowledge Management, 10*(4), 6–24. doi:10.1108/13673270610679336

Oragui, D. (2022). *Tacit knowledge: Definition, examples, and importance*. https://helpjuice.com/blog/tacit-knowledge

Romford, J. (2021). *Knowledge culture in knowledge management*. Agility Online Ltd. https://agilityportal.io/blog/knowledge-culture-in-knowledge-management#:~:text=in%20Knowledge%20Management-,Knowledge%20Culture%20in%20Knowledge%20Management,managing%20knowledge%20within%20an%20organizations

Roth, H. (2022). *Knowledge Culture — Its meaning in marketing & branding*. Neuroflash GmbH. https://neuroflash.com/blog/knowledge-culture-meaning-in-marketing-branding/

Rouse, M. (2013). *What does network redundancy mean?* Techopedia. https://www.techopedia.com/definition/29305/network-redundancy

Ruppel, C. P., & Harrington, S. J. (2001). Sharing knowledge through intranets: A study of organizational culture and intranet implementation. *IEEE Transactions on Professional Communication, 44*(1), 37-52.

Russ, M., Fineman, R., Paterni, R., & Jones, J. K. (2012). How do we get there? Strategy action framework-"Action engine.". In *Organizational learning and knowledge: Concepts, methodologies, tools and applications* (pp. 442–476). IGI Global. doi:10.4018/978-1-60960-783-8.ch204

Stobierski, T. (2020). *How to calculate ROI to justify a project*. Harvard Business School Online Business Insights Blog. https://online.hbs.edu/blog/post/how-to-calculate-roi-for-a-project

Stoddard, C. (2022). Give Your Employees the Tools They Need to be Productive. *Harvard Business Review*. https://hbr.org/sponsored/2022/11/give-your-employees-the-tools-they-need-to-be-productive

Suwandi, D. (2015). *Km roadmap & strategy*. SlideShare. https://www.slideshare.net/djatmikosuwandi/km-roadmap-strategy.to

The BetterUp Team. (2019). *Q&A with Equinix: Personalized development for employees through coaching*. BetterUp. https://www.betterup.com/blog/qanda-with-equinix-personalized-development-for-employees-through-coaching

Wikipedia. (2023a). Comcast. In *Wikipedia*. https://en.wikipedia.org/wiki/Comcast

Wikipedia. (2023b). Lumen Technologies. In *Wikipedia*. https://en.wikipedia.org/wiki/Lumen_Technologies

Wikipedia. (2023c). SWOT analysis. In *Wikipedia*. https://en.wikipedia.org/wiki/SWOT_analysis

Wikipedia. (2023d). Tacit knowledge. In *Wikipedia*. Wikipedia.

Xu, Y. (2008). *Widget Communication Architecture with Emphasis on Mobile Devices*. Academic Press.

Section 3
Business Case Studies

Chapter 6
Innovative and Knowledge Developments for Sustainability in Salmon-Based Aquaculture

Knut Ingar Westeren
Norwegian University of Science and Technology, Norway

EXECUTIVE SUMMARY

Coastal marine salmon-based aquaculture has grown considerably in produced volumes in recent years, and projections from FAO lay out possibilities for further increases. This can only be done by introducing stronger restrictions on sustainability, including fish health and environmental regulations. To solve environmental problems, the Norwegian aquaculture company Midt-Norsk Havbruk (now Salmonor AS) received development permits in 2017 for a project based on Aquatraz semi-closed steel cages. The study is based on documentation from the Aquatraz project and interviews with employees at Midt-Norsk Havbruk. The project has mainly been successful, as in the fourth generation of the Aquatraz cage put in operation in 2021/22 delousing was not required and escape did not take place. The projects also showed how knowledge management (KM) procedures were successfully changed during implementation of new innovative technologies, the main reason for this being a flat organizational structure and focus on training and upgrading of knowledge levels and dissemination.

AQUACULTURE AND SUSTAINABILITY IN A GLOBAL CONTEXT

Introduction

The situation for aquaculture has long been analyzed by the Food and Agriculture Organization (FAO) and the latest reports on global developments can be found in Bartley (2022), FAO (2018), and, with a special focus on sustainability, FAO (2020). In this report, the FAO discusses the relationship between the UN Sustainable Development Goals (SDGs) and developments in fishing and aquaculture. The FAO (2020, p. vi) states that "The fisheries and aquaculture sector has much to contribute to securing all the SDGs but is at the core of SDG 14 – Conserve and sustainably use the oceans, seas and marine resources

DOI: 10.4018/978-1-6684-5859-4.ch006

for sustainable development." Furthermore, we find in many FAO documents, such as FAO (2022), that sustainable aquaculture will contribute to most of the UN's SDGs. Implementation is now in the hands of the individual countries and the FAO's (2021) view on how this must be done is:

- *Better governance*
- *Increased investment*
- *Targeted support to environmentally-friendly production. (p. 36)*

Effective management systems that lead development in a sustainable direction are the key measures to achieving innovative investments that contribute to sustainable production, which gives rise to the following research questions:

- What are the sustainability problems for aquaculture in marine coastal areas when producing salmon and trout?
- How do we understand the concept of sustainability in an innovation and knowledge transfer context in aquaculture?
- How can innovative projects like Aquatraz contribute to solving sustainability problems with sea lice and escape and, at the same time, implement innovations and knowledge management (KM) procedures?

The Resource Situation

Commercial fishing in salt and fresh water has levelled off in produced volumes from around 1990, and aquaculture has taken over and is the form of production that is accounting for the increase in the production of food from marine sources to meet the needs of a growing population, see Figure 1.

Figure 1. Worldwide developments in commercial fishing and aquaculture 1980–2018, mill. tons
Source: Bartley (2022, p. 1)

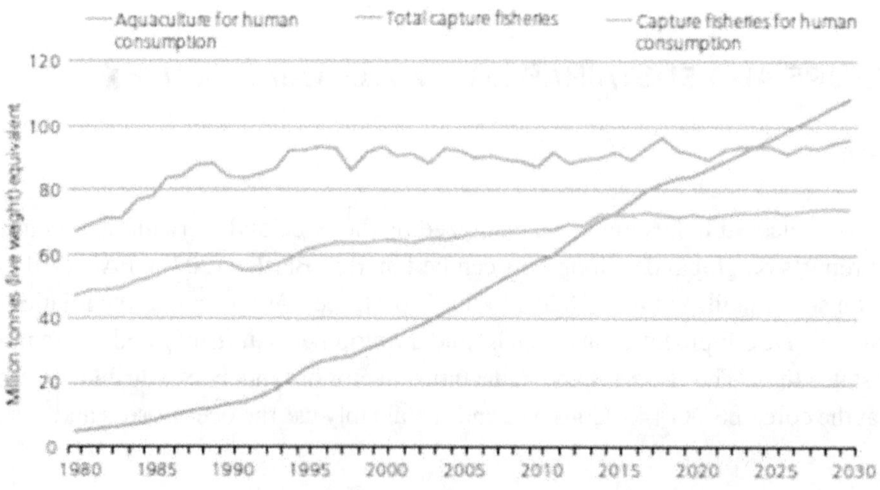

In Bartley (2022), we find projections for growth in aquaculture that the FAO believes is possible in relation to the production potential and that is needed to cover population growth (see Figure 1). The FAO projections assume that overall production from aquaculture will increase from 82 095 000 tons in 2018 to 108 517 000 tons in 2030 (i.e., a growth of 32%). These projections lies within the possibilities for sustainable development if countries meet the requirements set by the FAO. Freshwater aquaculture makes up the largest part of aquaculture today. The four largest countries/groups of countries producing salmon and trout in saltwater are listed in Table 1. For 2018, aquaculture-based production of salmon and trout in saltwater accounted for around 5.4% of the total production in aquaculture worldwide, and the projection for growth is 22% for the period 2018–2030.

Table 1. Aquaculture production for salmon and trout in salt water

Area	Production, 2018 (1000 Tons)	Estimated Production, 2030 (1000 Tons)	Growth in the Period in %
Norway	1355	1620	19.6
Chile	1266	1650	30.3
EUROPEAN UNION	1167	1320	13.1
USA + Canada	660	838	27.1
Sum	4448	5428	22.0

Note: Excerpts from FAO (2020, Table 17)

In summary, the global sustainability challenges for aquaculture to meet food needs, as stated in FAO reports (2018) and (2020), are significantly linked to China and countries such as India, Indonesia, and Vietnam, with an emphasis on freshwater aquaculture. The countries mentioned account for over 80% of aquaculture production globally. A major difference between marine aquaculture in Europe, Chile, and the USA/Canada compared to Asia is that the former mentioned countries have come much further in knowledge-based production, innovation, and management. Setting equal sustainability requirements for rich and developing countries is not realistic in either the short or medium term, and the FAO (2020) also recognizes this.

This chapter discusses salmon aquaculture which only constitutes about 5% of total aquaculture production. One subject of interest that could be looked at is how experiences from salmon aquaculture could be used to develop other saltwater aquaculture facing environmental challenges. There is limited research on this, but Handisyde et. al (2017) takes up this discussion and one conclusion is that it is not so easy to transfer knowledge because we have warmer water and different spices in saltwater outside countries like India, Malaysia and Philippines. On the other hand there is a huge potential for knowledge and technology developments in aquaculture the countries like the above mentioned.

This chapter tries to meet the focus of the on book enhancing business sustainability through knowledge management systems by using an actual project in aquaculture where sustainability was the common goal of both the authorities and the company. Salmon aquaculture in Norway has been through a fast technology development including innovative activities where the knowledge development in general and knowledge management in particular have seen more radical changes than other technology intensive productions. This has paved the way for knowledge management changes in aquaculture from mouth-to-mouth operational instructions to interpretations of computer based images from high end sonar equipment. The items this chapter takes up is more about the start of the development of business sustainability through knowledge management than the end of the story. We will look forward to dig more deep into how innovative behavior also plays a part together with the knowledge managerial changes.

PRODUCTION, SUSTAINABILITY, AND ENVIRONMENTAL MEASURES FOR SALMON AND TROUT IN NORWAY

The Government of Norway presented the Report to the Parliament, St. 16 (2014–2015) on "Predictable and environmentally sustainable growth in Norwegian salmon and trout farming" in March 2015 and this report states: "The Government believes that environmental sustainability must be used as the most important precondition for regulating further growth in the aquaculture industry" (Ministry of Trade, Industry, and Fisheries, 2015 p. 8). This principle has remained firm since the Report was presented, but the crucial factor is how it shall be implemented.

The biggest problems with both sustainability and fish health for salmon in cages in coastal areas are salmon lice and escaping from the cage. When lice accompany salmon out of the cage, this becomes an environmental problem and a threat to wild salmon. Farmed fish that escape from the cages have negative consequences for wild strains of salmonids, because they can wander up the waterways and spawn together with wild salmon, which in turn can affect the genetic diversity and productivity of wild salmon. Other substances from fish farming, like discharges of feed residue, fish excrement, copper from impregnated nets, pharmaceuticals, and other chemicals and foreign substances can also affect the marine environment. Norway has a severe control program to monitor all types of discharge from aquaculture, and the use of harmful chemicals from pharmaceuticals have been reduced considerably the later years.

There has been a rapid and significant development toward professionalization and knowledge-based operations in Norwegian aquaculture over the last two decades. The important reason for this is that measures to increase productivity and earnings have worked in the same direction as measures to protect the environment and increase sustainability. In recent years, we have also seen high salmon prices on the world market and large profit margins among companies, which has given the industry financial muscles to develop in these areas. It has also been in the industry's self-interest to develop sustainable solutions because costal sites are limited. Furthermore, it is envisaged that the requirements for "lice-free" and escape secure cage technologies are on the way in, which is a key point of this paper.

Norway has seen rapid growth in the volume of salmon and trout produced from aquaculture from 2007 (838 970 tons) to 2012, (1 1319 128 tons), that is a 57% increase over five years (see Fiskeridirektoratet, 2021). From 2012 to 2018, there have been smaller variations in produced volumes, with production averaging around 1.3 million tons, and from 2018 to 2020 we saw growth to 1.488 million tons in 2020. From 2012 to 2020, there have been major changes in regional distribution of production, with a significant shift in production from southern areas to North Norway. There have also been large variations in produced volumes in some areas. The value of slaughtered fish at current prices has more than doubled from 2012 to 2020, because the world market price for salmon has increased sharply.

In Nærings- og fiskeridepartementet (2015), the *Report to the Parliament on Aquaculture*, and in the subsequent risk assessment from the Norwegian Institute of Marine Research (Grefsrud et al., 2021), it is stated that sustainability is, and will be, the central theme for Norwegian aquaculture, because the country has about 500 million farmed fish at any time in cages along the coast, and there is a pressure to further increase production volume. A "traffic light system" has been established to evaluate changes in production volumes for fish farming based on a rule where environmental status is assessed on the basis of mortality of wild salmon due to the spread of lice from fish farms. Sea lice have thus become central both in relation to fish health for salmon in the cages and on the basis of environmental considerations in the coastal zone. Further information on the traffic light system can be found in Biering et al. (2021).

KM AND INNOVATION IN THEORY AND PRACTICE

KM Systems

New technologies and innovations require new knowledge, which means that the management of a company must develop new knowledge structures that penetrate the entire organization. Innovations are generally linked with uncertainty, so for a company to formulate specific knowledge development programs is not an easy task. Production in companies, like the aquaculture company we look at in this chapter, are routinized, and this is the backbone of secure production. Innovative initiatives involve saying that routines must be changed or scrapped, and this often brings uncertainty into production procedures. Innovations in action normally demand successful de-learning linked to Schumpeter's concept of creative destruction (see Westeren, 2016, 2018). Stead (2019) argues for a sharpened focus on open innovations in aquaculture for more efficiently to adapt to new technologies.

Figure 2. Simple flowchart: From knowledge management to innovation
Source: The author

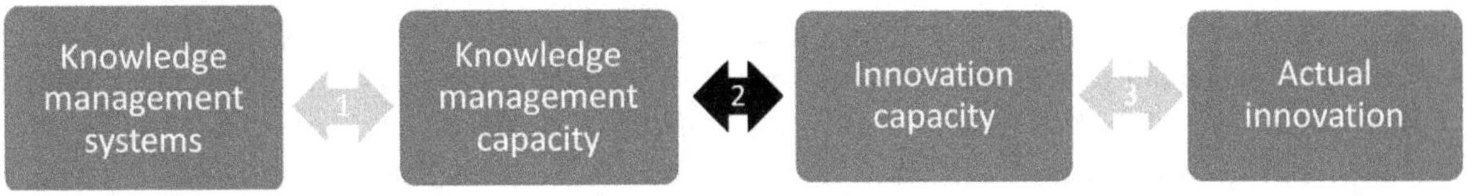

Thousands of articles have been written about the processes shown in and between the boxes in Figure 2. This approach started with Penrose (1958), who considered the company as a "collection of productive resources" (Penrose, 1959, p. 24) and stressed the unique character of each firm. In the 1990s, Barney (1991) developed the resource-based view of the firm, which was formed on the basis of a variety of developments focusing on:

- Intangible/invisible assets (Itami, 1987; Sveiby, 2001)
- Core competencies (Prahalad & Hamel, 1990)
- Dynamic capacity (Teece et al., 1997)
- Organizational structures (Williamson, 1996)
- Knowledge developments (Grant, 1996).

Out of this grew Knowledge Management (KM) as a tool for practitioners and as a subject for research, with early contributions such as Davenport and Prusak (2000), Alavi and Leidner (2001), and Hislop

(2013). In later years, research has pointed out differences and relationships between KM systems and KM capacity (Virji et al., 2012).

A KM System (KMS) is defined as the set of interrelated or interacting elements of an organization that establish, embed, and enable KM policies and objectives, as well as the processes to achieve those objectives (ISO, 2018). The KM capacity of an organization (like the company we analyze here) relates to how able and resourceful the organization is to put knowledge into action. Putting this into the three-layer system for KM, we first look at the machine/data and technology layer. Compared to Russ (2021), we use a broader understanding of this layer that also includes technology. The machine layer then consists of how knowledge linked to different data streams is transmitted from sources outside and inside the company. The example from the aquaculture company, Midt-Norsk Havbruk, implementing the Aquatraz project is describing how to manage feeding technologies, fish health surveillance, water quality, and oxygen content measurements; these are the most important examples. The fundamental thing here is that data for all these functions of the project are stored in IT databases that form the structure of the machine/data/technology layer of the KM system.

Two examples can illustrate how the different parts have very different IT and knowledge requirements. Modern feeding systems for salmon are based on a large number of indicators, including sea temperature, light penetration, oxygen saturation, and a number of other climate variables. In addition, salmon aquaculture production now uses sonar equipment to model how salmon behave. Sonars can deliver a scan of salmon behavior in the cage every 15 seconds, providing big data for analysis. Most important for fish health is monitoring sea lice, and all production sites in Norway must, by law, have a lice monitoring system. Several companies, such as Midt-Norsk Havbruk, have a more thorough test program than the law requires and use high tech biochemical equipment in the company and from collaborating laboratories. All these data are stored in IT systems, then retrieved and analyzed for use at the sites. When we add together all the equipment, technologies, and IT infrastructures, we have what we can call the machine/data and technology layer of the KM system. From the company side, we see very different KM requirements and sub-system developments depending on which function we look at.

The human layer of the KM system has (using Midt-Norsk Havbruk as the example) as its foundation, that all employees log all observations in a common database, and everyone is responsible for keeping themselves up-to-date and contacting their colleagues if necessary. Thus we can say that the human layer consists of an IT infrastructure filled in with human knowledge and experience.

The final layer in the three layer model of KM systems is a unified new knowledge development and sharing layer. This is interesting and relevant for the Aquatraz project and for innovation analysis in general. Most innovation, like Aquatraz, develops in stages. The first generation of Aquatraz had a KM structure set up adapted to the chosen technologies. Several technologies changed during the stages, and each new set-up required a new KM system, which is a new layer.

From KM Systems to KM Capacity

Figure 3 is a simplified illustration of the connections between KM systems and the other components; Lichtenthaler and Lichtenthaler (2009) look at KM capacity simply as the company's ability to manage knowledge in an innovation context. Both in theory (e.g., Chebbi et al., 2013), and in actual situations in companies, we divide between the internal and external ability to explore, utilize, and develop the knowledge that is in the system. From the Aquatraz project, we registered different abilities and success criteria for the employees when we compared feeding systems (mainly based on internal knowledge exchange and development) with fish health surveillance, which was based on a combination of internal and external relationships. The external KM capacity has similar aspects to the pathbreaking article by Cohen and Levinthal (1990) on absorptive capacity.

Another KM capacity has to do with connectiveness. Santoro et al. (2018, p. 349) looked at connective capacity as: "The ability to retain knowledge in inter-organizational relationships and the ability to create knowledge through co-R&D projects." Seen in the light of the Aquatraz project, the word "retain" in the quotation above becomes a little too narrow compared to what is happening in the real world. The Aquatraz connections were not limited to maintaining possession of (retaining) knowledge; it was even more important to let knowledge develop in circles—develop–change–retain— and one more circle was added on if the first did not fulfil its goals. This focuses further on the type of knowledge we are talking about. In the Aquatraz project, we saw some knowledge developments similar to the SEKI model (Nonaka & Takeuchi, 1995). In this model the movements between explicit and tacit knowledge follow a spiral development pattern; the SEKI model is explained in several standard textbooks on KM, such as Hislop (2013), and is mentioned by Russ (2021). The Aquatraz project revealed two of the most discussed items of the SEKI model: (a) how do we define tacit knowledge and (b) what is the importance of having a start-stop mechanism in the spiral movement. To understand tacit knowledge developments in the Aquatraz project, a process understanding of the concept directly building on Polanyi (1958) appears to be more fruitful than the SEKI model. The project also showed the necessity of introducing start-stop mechanisms for a better understanding of the knowledge processes that took place because of the differences in each stage of the project.

Considerations About Innovation and Innovative Capacity

Most Norwegian aquaculture companies have a significant innovation activity, with large variations both in terms of the type of measures and the size of the project. In this context, we explored an arrangement initiated by the Department of Fisheries called "Development permits," where the main criterion for being awarded such a permit is that the project entails significant innovation and significant investments and contributes to sustainable development. For public measures with requirements for innovativeness, it is not always clear what one means by the term, and we briefly discuss the concept of innovation here.

Innovation has become one of the most important, controversial, and widely used concepts in the scientific context, in practical politics, and in the public debate. If we take a quick look from about 1920 to around the year 2000, we start with Schumpeter (1934) and end up with the Oslo Manual (2020). The most interesting aspects, including the Oslo Manual, are based on Schumpeter (1934), where innovation is linked to new or significantly changed products, production methods (technologies), and markets. Furthermore, we must add to Schumpeter's criterion that an innovation must add value to society.

Since the 1990s, we have seen developments in innovation analysis focusing on different directions, including:

- The distinction between radical and incremental innovations (Henderson & Clark, 1990)
- "disruptive innovations" (Christensen, 2013)
- Innovation systems (Lundvall, 2010)
- The open innovation concept (Chesbrough et al., 2006)
- Eco-innovations (OECD, 2009)
- The connection between knowledge and innovation (Westeren et al., 2018).

Another important approach is looking at innovation as a process that can be divided into three phases, following Fagerberg et al. (2005):

1. The creative/idea-generating phase
2. The actual implementation of the innovation
3. Innovation management.

A main contribution to analyzing creativity and innovation comes from Amabile (1998), who used the following keywords as a basis for analyzing creativity: competence (knowledge); motivation (why do we engage in the project); and creative thinking (challenging the status quo). These three key phrases are featured in all standard textbooks on innovation, such as Dawson and Andriopoulos (2014), so we only comment briefly here. Competence relates to the need to have a knowledge platform to stand on to be creative. Over the past two decades, the aquaculture industry in Norway has pursued a profound increase in competence, especially with the development of new feeding technologies together with a focus on sustainability and fish health. We use Aquatraz as the central example here.

There are many models and suggestions for how to manage and lead innovations. A widely used starting point can be found in Tidd and Bessant (2020), who claim that an innovation must be analyzed as a central process in any organization. Adams et al. (2006) provide a summary of many studies of innovation management. The most commonly used indicators for discussing how an innovation should be implemented successfully can be summarized as follows:

1. Resource situation (such as labor, capital and financial resources)
2. Knowledge management (such as idea generation, level of knowledge and flow of knowledge)
3. Integration of the company's innovation strategy into the overall strategy
4. Organizational culture
5. Technology and technological cooperation
6. Use of IT-based solutions
7. Commercialization of the innovation
8. Risk

All these indicators are addressed when we discuss innovation in the Aquatraz project.

There have been many contributions to the analysis of innovations in aquaculture in recent years, much of this has been summed up by Joffre et al. (2019). One conclusion so far based on the literature review is that we have a "Lack of detailed analysis of the innovation process" (Joffre et al., 2019, p. 139).

Joffre et al. (2019) suggest an analysis of innovations in aquaculture based on the following categories:

- Technology driven
- Systemic
- Based on business needs

Our study of innovations shows that looking at how these three categories play together is of utmost importance. The Aquatraz project clearly has a technology-based starting point: the project is a matter of creating a technological solution that prevents lice from entering the cage, which must also be escape proof. The systemic perspective is related to sustainability and the environment, and there are several considerations that must be taken into account in dialogue with the authorities. The business need for innovations is indisputable because the new technologies required to meet environmental demands must also be profitable from the company's perspective — if not in the short term, then at least in the medium term (i.e., 6–8 years).

The technology-based innovative aspect of the Aquatraz project is made up of many solutions that vary across a wide range of technologies, from incremental to radical. On the radical side, we have the actual construction of the cage, which has dense side walls extending down about 20 meters, combined with a system for replacing water so that the oxygen content in the water inside the cage is high enough at all times. There are also several other incremental innovative technological solutions, including new surveillance equipment.

AQUATRAZ: CONTRIBUTING TO ENVIRONMENTAL SUSTAINABILITY AND INCREASED PRODUCTIVITY

Methodology: Analysis and Data Collection

Analyses can be either theory- or data-driven; usually there are elements of both, but the main emphasis must be on one of the options. In this case, study is theory driven in the sense that we ask questions that we try to answer based on the collected data. We can thus say that we are essentially engaging in deductive analysis. Data collection is primarily based on the gathering and review of documents and interviews. This study most closely approximates a hermeneutic approach.

The central elements of hermeneutics (Fuglesang & Olsen, 2007) are that we assume:

- That understanding is existential
- That understanding and interpretation precedes explanation
- That the social actors and phenomena studied are carriers of meaning
- That the concepts of time and language are central

Hermeneutics provides a suggestion for explaining how our understanding develops. This is believed to be a *circular movement*, which is called the *hermeneutic circle*. Put very simply, this means that we put layers of understanding and learning on top of each other so that our understanding continues to develop.

Data collection in this project started in 2018 with an interview with the project manager of the Aquatraz project. In 2019, we started gathering data by collecting reports from the project at Midt-Norsk Havbruk. New interviews were also conducted with the project manager and members of his team in the first months of 2022. There is extensive written documentation of all four phases of the project, see Midt-Norsk Havbruk (2020, 2021, 2022).

Development licenses: Combining Innovation and Sustainability

An important tool for managing the aquaculture sector in Norway is the "Laksetildelingsforskriften" (The Salmon Allocation Regulation; Lovdata, 2021); in section 22, there is a provision called "Special purposes" in which the Government can award development permits to facilitate the development of technology that can help solve one or more of the environmental and coastal use challenges facing the aquaculture industry. This can include the construction of prototypes and test facilities, new industrial design, and full-scale installation of new equipment. As of May 2, 2022, 24 projects have been granted permits, and 78 have been rejected.

This has been a popular initiative, which has stimulated numerous innovative projects. Another reason why these permits are so popular is that the Directorate of Fisheries can convert such permission to an ordinary production permit after the end of the project period if the criteria set for the project are met. Midt-Norsk Havbruk AS received four permits on April 28 for the Aquatraz project (i.e., the semi-closed cage). An important condition for the permit is that the project should contain a description of how it can affect the key sustainability indicators of reducing sea lice to a minimum and preventing escapes.

The Aquatraz Project

The main argument in Midt-Norsk Havbruk's application for development permits was to reduce the number of lice on the salmon to such a low level that one avoids delousing while maintaining fish health and welfare at a satisfactory level for the salmon and ensuring that there is no escape. Sea lice, *Lepeophtheirus salmonis*, live in the upper layers of the sea and flow with the current. The Aquatraz cage in generation 1 (AG1) had an 8-meter deep lice skirt (see Figure 3 for what a lice skirt can look like). AG1 started with 8-meter lice skirts to ensure that good water quality was maintained in the cages throughout the production cycle. It is particularly important to have adequate water replacement in the cage to maintain satisfactory oxygen levels. AG1 was in production at the site from October 2018 to August 2019 without delousing.

Aquatraz generation 2 (AG2) also had an 8-meter lice skirt and was put into operation at the site of Kyrøyan from October 2019 until September 2020. Kyrøyan, southwest of Rørvik in Norway, is a locality that is more exposed to lice. During the period of operation, the lice pressure around Kyrøyan was large and it turned out that 8-meter lice skirts were not sufficient to avoid the necessity for delousing. It was thus decided to increase the lice skirt to 18-meter for the third generation of Aquatraz (AG3) by installing cloths in the side windows in combination with steel structures (see Figure 3). Analyses were conducted with deeper lice skirts to check water circulation, water replacement, and oxygen levels. The results showed that with 18-meter deep lice skirts, four current setters were sufficient to maintain a good aquatic environment in the cage.

Figure 3. Aquatraz generation 3 is towed out to the site
Source: Midt-Norsk Havbruk (2022)

AG3 was used from June 2020 and throughout 2021 without delousing and no escapes. The majority of the water was collected from 20–25 meters deep, and the water replacement, water quality, and oxygen levels have been satisfactory. Aquatraz generation 4 (AQT4) was put into operation in Åretfjorden in January 2022 with 280,000 fish (see Figure 4). This version had a larger number of fish and improved water replacement equipment. Thus far, it has shown no need for delousing, there have been no escapes, and the fish health situation has been satisfactory.

The economics of the project are documented in Midt-Norsk Havbruk (2022), which compares the AQT4 cage to a conventional cage (KTR). The cost of the Aquatraz cage is around NOK 50 million, while a conventional cage costs NOK 1 million, which means that capital costs are significantly higher for the Aquatraz cage. On the other hand, the volume is larger, as is the density of salmon, so biological production becomes more than twice the size in AQT4 as in the conventional control cage. When all factors are brought into the calculation, the production cost per kilogram of salmon becomes quite similar, with Aquatraz yielding slightly better results: at NOK. 1.82 lower per kilogram in a cage that is both lice-proof and escape-proof, as documented in the reports from the project.

Figure 4. Aquatraz generation 4 in operation at the site
Source: Midt-Norsk Havbruk (2022)

DISCUSSION

The Aquatraz Project

Knowledge Management and Dissemination

In discussing the distinctions between KM and ordinary management, we build on Jensen (2008), who says that, in the case of KM, we must turn the authority pyramid upside down. This was also seen in this project, where it was obvious that more people in the Aquatraz project group have more detailed knowledge and professional insight into the project than the managerial team responsible in the company. On the other hand, the top management must be responsible for the decisions made. Everything indicates that the company managed this well—especially in relation to the views on organizational culture that have previously been mentioned.

In Midt-Norsk Havbruk (2022), it is pointed out that there were demands on knowledge level and flow at the beginning of the Aquatraz project. The general conclusion is that the project has generated a lot of new knowledge, especially in the areas of hydrodynamics, fish health, welfare indicators, and technical solutions. In the report, Midt-Norsk Havbruk (2022, p. 84; translated to English) notes: "it (is) important to emphasize that experiences and knowledge at all levels must be tied together if the results are to be good. The Aquatraz project has worked like this, where views and input from operating personnel, analysists, firm management, and cooperating partners have been taken seriously and formed the basis for development and change."

Sustainability was a central aspect of KM in the project. The requirements from the authorities were of a rather general nature—a reduction of lice to a very small number and an escape-free cage. Within this framework, the company was free to find solutions so long as they were within the requirements of the project and were innovative according to the development permits. The KM system was built up related to each sub-module. It was not possible to establish an overarching system covering all modules for several reasons. The knowledge needs were very different, with a high degree of specialization. Some of the sub-modules had co-operative agreements with external partners and were based on contracts with clauses on knowledge protection. There were also differences in risk assessments for the different sub-modules, which led to incredibly detailed knowledge requirements for some and low specifications for others. For the company, sustainability and KM considerations had to be linked together on a more general level. On a sub-module level (e.g., for the feeding systems) the sustainability and environmental standards were already built into the knowledge systems.

Innovation

Based on innovation theory, Aquatraz is clearly a process innovation—a significantly changed way of manufacturing a product. One would hardly say it is a product innovation because the salmon remain the same. On the other hand, we should not ignore the fact that the salmon market in the future may have a separate segment for sustainably produced fish or that it might become a requirement that all salmon be sustainably produced. From the criterion that innovation that creates new market opportunities, the Aquatraz project fits well, because a greater emphasis on environmental considerations will create a market for escape-proof cages where delousing is not necessary.

As explained, Aquatraz was a four-phase project with the construction of four generations of cages (AG1–AQT4). This emphasizes the need for successful innovation management, and based on the theoretical discussion, we address some of the key factors. The resource situation was crucial, and in this case, the company is a medium-sized aquaculture producer that, at the start of the project in 2019, had a turnover of about NOK 900 million and a pre-tax profit of about NOK 350 million. This means that the company had the financial muscle to initiate the project. The actual investment in the cages was high, at NOK 50 million per cage, but this was not a problem for the company.

The theoretical discussion highlights the importance of integrating innovation strategy into the company's overall strategy. The documentation from the project shows that this has gone well (see Midt-Norsk Havbruk, 2022). There are at least two reasons for this. When the project was initiated, Aquatraz was organized as a separate project with its own project organization, with the general manager of Midt-Norsk Havbruk as the person responsible. The Aquatraz cages were also all placed on sites together with other producing cages, so the Aquatraz cage had to be coordinated with all operations at the site. In general, Midt-Norsk Havbruk has a flat organizational structure, which also contributes to the efficient exchange of information. An adjacent point in innovation management is organizational culture, and this firm is characterized by short distances and a high degree of sharing of common values. In addition, the company has sustainability as one of its most prominent values—naturally, because the company is situated in a community where environmental considerations are important for local development.

The point on technology and technological cooperation has been solved by the fact that the entire project was linked between three main partners, Midt-Norsk Havbruk (now SalmoNor), Seafarming Systems, and Aqua Kompetanse. Midt-Norsk Havbruk was the project manager and responsible for the development permits and production of salmon in the Aquatraz cages. Seafarming Systems was the technology owner and responsible for technology, while Aqua Kompetanse was responsible for the project biology. The technology collaboration was grounded on the sharing of knowledge based on trust between Midt-Norsk Havbruk and Seafarming Systems. If we look at two important technological decisions—how deep the lice skirt should go and how the water replacement units should be implemented—the decisions were based on close cooperation between the two firms.

Commercialization of this innovation did not turn out to be a great leadership challenge. Aquaculture journals have regularly written about the project, and the company has published much material that is freely available on its website. It has been a requirement for development licenses from the Directorate of Fisheries that as much information as possible should be made public. The project has now been thoroughly assessed, and this is an important part of the commercialization process. The openness of the information flows from the project has given other companies and organizations the possibility to learn about how it is possible to enhance sustainability through knowledge management systems. This was one of the aims from the authorities for introducing development licenses and one of the reasons why the company was allowed to convert the development license to a regular license.

Another crucial point from the list of keywords about innovation management is risk. The company conducted a risk assessment study in connection with the application for the development license, but the experience from using lice skirts on conventional cages formed a modest basis for what a full-scale project in steel would entail. The project had risks in relation to (a) technical design, (b) in connection with feeding systems, (c) biological (fish health), and (d) economically. The company was aware of the risk and took it—one reason why this was possible was the company's solid financial basis. It was decided from the beginning of the project to run it in stages to reduce risk; however, the greater the emphasis placed on the innovative aspect of the project, the greater the risk (see Fagerberg et al., 2005).

Sustainability, KM, and Innovation

Eco-innovations (see OECD, 2009) have much in common with the thinking that underlies the criteria for development permits. Norway has also established innovation systems at the national and regional level. As was claimed in the section on aquaculture and sustainability, organizations such as the FAO emphasize the governance aspect for aquaculture to become sustainable. The argument of Lundvall (2010) about innovation systems is that the government must enforce regulations, so sustainability arguments enter into national and regional innovation measures. This is doable for aquaculture in Norway, which has a high degree of confidence in the public sector, generous public funding, and good routines for knowledge dissemination, but if we look at Chile (for example), the picture is somewhat different (see Westeren, 2020). Aquaculture in Chile has a more traditional industrial organization based on a pyramid like organizational structure where innovative ideas do not trickle down as easy as in Norway, Westeren (2020) and Barton et. al (2023).

Another issue addressed in this paper was the distinction between radical and incremental innovations (Henderson & Clark, 1990). New innovative solutions based on demands for sustainable development often require radical innovations. Aquatraz can be seen as a radical innovation because full-scale steel skirts had not previously been tested, and it was not known how deep down it was necessary to go or what water replacement systems were needed. An important aspect to remember is that that, within established innovation grant systems, application criteria must allow projects to fail.

CONCLUSION

In relation to the requirements the development licenses for projects to receive funding, the Aquatraz project was successful. For the AQT4, delousing was not required and escape did not take place. The salmon density was also high, water exchange/oxygen levels were satisfactory, and no problematic effects were found for fish health indicators. Contributions from recent innovation theory (e.g., Lundvall, 2010) argue that, especially for more societally oriented problems such as sustainability, system levels must be entered into the innovation management and coordination context.

Views on eco-innovations (OECD, 2009) are important, because they focus on sustainability and ecology as a field where new solutions must be found. The problem here is that one does not see where to look from the start. The eco-innovation concept must pave the way for greater acceptance that innovation initiatives can fail or be partly successful. For the company, sustainability and KM considerations had to be linked together on a more general level. On a sub-module level (e.g., feeding systems), the sustainability and environmental standards were already built into the knowledge systems. The link between projects based on sustainability and knowledge-driven innovations will become increasingly important in the years to come. If we look at aquaculture as an industry, this has rapidly developed towards advanced knowledge-driven production and the innovation needs we have seen, like Aquatraz, depend on evidence-based knowledge developments. The success of this project and the authorities use of development licenses is dependent of the fact that aquaculture is a profitable industry and one incentive for the company was increased profits. Projects like this in other countries and under other managerial circumstances may not be equally successful because companies financial muscles to carry out projects like this. Remember the cost increased from 1 million NOK for a traditional cage to 50 million NOK for the first commercial Aquatraz cage, and the company also had costs for knowledge upgrades. Norwegian authorities are in 2022/2023 introducing increased taxation of aquaculture production in Norway and the report KPMG (2022) argue that this will decrease the companies' possibilities to perform innovative sustainability projects.

On the managerial side, two factors in particular stand out. KM and the requirements for turning the pyramid of authority up/down were important for the Aquatraz project and for eco-innovations in general. Another experience from this project was that changing risk assessments had to be continuously built into the KM systems. The other field that needs both further focus and development is innovation management. This works well in a rich and highly skilled society like Norway, and the challenge is to be able to implement this in countries with lower levels of knowledge and more modest economic power.

The Aquatraz project has not found all solutions to all questions. It is now on target with phase 4, but this is based on very few cages and has not been tested in extreme weather conditions. There is therefore still much knowledge that needs to be gathered from both this and similar projects to solve sustainability problems in the longer term.

Questions for Discussion

1. Aquaculture has from about 2020 taken over as the main source for supply of fish for human consumption – what are the main challenges for further growth in aquaculture production?
2. Production of salmon and trout in saltwater accounts for around 5.4% of the total production in aquaculture worldwide – what are the main fish health challenges for this production?
3. Salmon and trout production has changed into knowledge based production – what are the main challenges for a country like Chile to encounter this?
4. Companies producing salmon and trout near the coastal line of the North Atlantic has earned large profits the last years and Norway plan to introduce a tax based on the exploitation of the environment – is this the right way to go?

5. We have seen a rapid development of innovations in aquaculture the last years – do you think the results companies have reached should be made public available?
6. Innovations must be managed successfully in aquaculture – discuss the most important steps to do this.
7. The Aquatraz project is an attempt to produce in a more environmentally friendly way and the company has received support from the public sector for this – discuss if there are seasons to regulate by law that all production shall change technology to this concept?
8. The Aquatraz technology is based on high tech and high knowledge developments – should a country like Chile have to change to this technology standard
9. How can it be possible to internationally introduce binding more environmentally friendly production standards in aquaculture
10. In high tech aquaculture production (like in other high tech productions as well) theory claim that there is a need for successful knowledge management to turn the pyramid of authority up/down – can you find any situations from the Aquatraz project where this seemed necessary.
11. Production procedures in aquaculture has changed considerably which has challenged knowledge management. Discuss the possibilities for on the job training compared to recruiting persons with more advanced education.

REFERENCES

Adams, R., Bessant, J., & Phelps, R. (2006). Innovation management measurement: A review. *International Journal of Management Reviews*, *8*(1), 21–47. doi:10.1111/j.1468-2370.2006.00119.x

Alavi, M., & Leidner, D. E. (2001). Knowledge management and knowledge management systems: Conceptual foundations and research issues. *Management Information Systems Quarterly*, *25*(1), 107–136. doi:10.2307/3250961

Amabile, T. M. (1998). How to kill creativity. *Harvard Business Review on Breakthrough Thinking*, *76*(5), 76–87. PMID:10185433

Bartley, D. (2022). *World Aquaculture 2020–A brief overview*. FAO.

Barton, J. R., Baeza-González, S., Hopp, J. Z., & Román, Á. (2023). Neostructural innovation and directionality in Chilean salmon aquaculture. *Marine Policy*, *150*, 105518. doi:10.1016/j.marpol.2023.105518

Biering, E., Boxaspen, K. K., & Næsje, T. F. (2021). *Styringsgruppens oppsummering og vurdering av lakseluspåvirkning på ville laksefisk 2021*. Havforskningsinstituttet.

Chebbi, H., Yahiaoui, D., Thrassou, A., & Vrontis, D. (2013). The exploration activity's added value into the innovation process. *Global Business and Economics Review*, *15*(2–3), 265–278. doi:10.1504/GBER.2013.053073

Chesbrough, H., Vanhaverbeke, W., & West, J. (2006). *Open innovation: Researching a new paradigm*. Oxford University Press.

Christensen, C. M. (2013). *The innovator's dilemma: When new technologies cause great firms to fail.* Harvard Business Review Press.

Dawson, P. M., & Andriopoulos, C. (2014). Managing change, creativity & innovation. *Sage (Atlanta, Ga.).*

Fagerberg, J., Mowery, D. C., & Nelson, R. R. (2005). *The Oxford handbook of innovation.* Oxford University Press.

FAO. (2018). *The future of food and agriculture—Alternative pathways to 2050.* FAO.

FAO. (2020). *The state of world fisheries and aquaculture 2020 (sustainability in action).* FAO.

FAO. (2021). *Strategic framework 2022-2031. Documents C 2021/7.* FAO.

Fiskeridirektoratet. (2017). *Utviklingstillatelser.* Bergen: Fiskeridirektoratet.

Fiskeridirektoratet. (2021). *Nøkkeltall fra norsk havbruksnæring 2020.* Bergen: Fiskeridirektoratet.

Fuglsang, L., & Olsen, P. (2007). *Videnskabsteori i samfunnsvidenskaberne.* Roskilde Universitetsforlag.

Grefsrud, E. S., Karlsen, Ø., Kvamme, B. O., Glover, K. A., Husa, V., Hansen, P. K., & Stien, L. H. (2021). *Risikorapport norsk fiskeoppdrett 2021-risikovurdering.* Havforskningsinstituttet.

Handisyde, N., Telfer, T. C., & Ross, L. G. (2017). Vulnerability of aquaculture-related livelihoods to changing climate at the global scale. *Fish and Fisheries, 18*(3), 466–488. doi:10.1111/faf.12186

Henderson, R. M., & Clark, K. B. (1990). Architectural innovation: The reconfiguration of existing product technologies and the failure of established firms. *Administrative Science Quarterly, 35*(1), 9–30. doi:10.2307/2393549

Hislop, D. (2013). *Knowledge management in organizations: A critical introduction.* Oxford University Press.

ISO. (2018). *ISO 30401:2018. Knowledge management systems—Requirements.*

Jensen, H. S. (2008). Knowledge Management in the Knowledge Economy. *The Journal of Regional Analysis & Policy, 38*(2), 130–137.

Joffre, O. M., Klerkx, L., Dickson, M., & Verdegem, M. (2017). How is innovation in aquaculture conceptualized and managed? A systematic literature review and reflection framework to inform analysis and action. *Aquaculture (Amsterdam, Netherlands), 470*, 129–148. doi:10.1016/j.aquaculture.2016.12.020

KPMG. (2022). *Taxation of Aquaculture 2022.* KPMG.

Lichtenthaler, U., & Lichtenthaler, E. (2009). A capability-based framework for open innovation: Complementing absorptive capacity. *Journal of Management Studies, 46*(8), 1315–1338. doi:10.1111/j.1467-6486.2009.00854.x

Lovdata. (2021). *Forskrift om endring av laksetildelingsforskriften - Fastsatt av Nærings- og fiskeridepartementet 1. juli 2021 med hjemmel i lov 17. juni 2005 nr. 79 om akvakultur (akvakulturloven) § 4, § 5, § 6 og § 7.* Oslo: Lovdata.

Lundvall, B.-Å. (2010). *National systems of innovation: Toward a theory of innovation and interactive learning.* Anthem press. doi:10.7135/UPO9781843318903

Midt-NorskHavbruk. (2020). *Installasjon og testing før utsett av fisk i Aquatraz G3–Driftserfaring fra Aquatraz G1, G2 og G3*. Rørvik.

Midt-NorskHavbruk. (2021). *Aquatraz: Sluttrapport for biologiprogram og tetthetsprogram – merdgenerasjon 3 på Årsetfjorden*. Rørvik.

Midt-NorskHavbruk. (2022). *Aquatrazprosjektet - Sluttrapport. Utvikling av semi-lukket stålmerd fra konsept til kommersielt produkt*. Rørvik.

Miljødirektoratet. (2022). *Miljøstatus.no, Påvirkning fra fiskeoppdrett*. Miljødirektoratet.

Nærings-ogfiskeridepartementet. (2015). *Meld. St. 16 (2014-2015) - Forutsigbar og miljømessig bærekraftig vekst i norsk lakse- og ørretoppdrett*. Oslo: Nærings-og fiskeridepartementet

OECD. (2009). *Eco-innovation, Framework, Practices and Measurement*. OECD.

OECD. (2020). *Guidelines for collecting and interpreting innovation data, 2005*. OECD.

Pine, B. J., Pine, J., & Gilmore, J. H. (1999). *The experience economy: Work is theatre & every business a stage*. Harvard Business Press.

Russ, M. (2021). Knowledge management for sustainable development in the era of continuously accelerating technological revolutions: A framework and models. *Sustainability (Basel), 13*(6), 3353. doi:10.3390u13063353

Santoro, G., Vrontis, D., Thrassou, A., & Dezi, L. (2018). The Internet of Things: Building a knowledge management system for open innovation and knowledge management capacity. *Technological Forecasting and Social Change, 136*, 347–354. doi:10.1016/j.techfore.2017.02.034

Schumpeter, J. A. (1934). *The theory of economic development: an inquiry into profits, capital, credit, interest, and the business cycle*. Harvard University Press.

Stead, S. M. (2019). Using systems thinking and open innovation to strengthen aquaculture policy for the United Nations Sustainable Development Goals. *Journal of Fish Biology, 94*(6), 837–844. doi:10.1111/jfb.13970 PMID:30887512

Tidd, J., & Bessant, J. R. (2020). *Managing innovation: Integrating technological, market and organizational change*. John Wiley & Sons.

Virji, H., Padgham, J., & Seipt, C. (2012). Capacity building to support knowledge systems for resilient development—Approaches, actions, and needs. *Current Opinion in Environmental Sustainability, 4*(1), 115–121. doi:10.1016/j.cosust.2012.01.005

Westeren, K. I. (2016). How transfer of knowledge can be linked to productivity and competitiveness of the firm-theoretical considerations and case study. *Informe Gepec, 20*(2), 156–171.

Westeren, K. I. (2020). Innovation processes in aquaculture: Comparing companies in Norway and Chile. In *Entrepreneurship-Contemporary Issues*. IntechOpen.

Westeren, K. I., Cader, H., de Fátima Sales, M., Similä, J. O., & Staduto, J. (2018). *Competitiveness and knowledge: An international comparison of traditional firms*. Routledge. doi:10.4324/9781315625331

Chapter 7
Knowledge Sharing Practices Among Social Media Marketers and the Significance for Business Sustainability

Ismail Olatunji Adeyemi
https://orcid.org/0000-0001-9822-5950
Kwara State University, Nigeria

EXECUTIVE SUMMARY

This chapter discusses knowledge sharing practices among social media marketers and their significance for business development. The study analysed the knowledge sharing practices among social media marketers, considering the rationale and means of sharing knowledge among these marketers. Using the views of the environment, economy, and society (three bottom line strategies), the chapter discusses the idea of business sustainability among social media marketers and other enterprises. Finally, the chapter provides an analysis of the importance of knowledge sharing practices for business sustainability providing evidence of its importance for market advantage, promotion of adaptability/positive changes, and increased innovation and creativity.

INTRODUCTION

Social media usage is becoming increasingly popular among the Nigerian populace. This has been supported by actual data from several empirical investigations (examples: Asibong et al., 2020; Sulaiman et al., 2020). This could shed light on the causes of the rise in social media campaigns, marketing, and advertising (ads) among Nigerians. These social media marketers are popularly referred to as "influencers" (Harrigan et al., 2021; Zhang et al., 2017). These "influencers" are employed on a contractual basis by various people, organizations, and groups to influence public opinion about a specific issue or phenomenon. Their actions are more noticeable in the Nigerian Twitter space, where they frequently operate in cliques. This factional idea of engagement is to propagate or make the tweets of those in a group more

DOI: 10.4018/978-1-6684-5859-4.ch007

visible via *like retweet*, and *comment*. That, however, does not mean there are no such practices on other social media spaces, most especially on Facebook, Instagram, and WhatsApp.

The recruitment of social media influencer in Nigeria's social media spaces is quite informal and subtle. Their sponsored posts are not tagged, and thus "consumers" are convinced by these posts unknowingly that they are sponsored. Aside from this model on Nigeria's social media space, the idea of social media marketing has been formalized. Different organizations have been established that carry out different social media campaigns for their clients. These organizations are more structured in engagements and practices. Some examples of these organizations are Wild Fusion, Mcjeh Digital, Realestateko Agency, Big Field Digital, Marketing Trybe, Rushing Tap, Simtech Creative, Brand Envoy Africa, Tech 0'clock, and so on. As much as these organizations operate separately, it has been observed that they share ideas. It has been observed that the emergence of these agencies is not unlikely, as the intrusion of digital marketing has had a devastating effect on the engagement of traditional marketing firms, which has indeed led some traditional agencies to adopt the blended approach, spelling a paradigm shift in the industry.

It has been observed that there is a practice of sharing ideas on how to enhance campaigns and ads. This chapter focuses on how these social media marketers share knowledge and its significance for business sustainability. The wide stakeholder portfolios of contemporary companies, which frequently have competing interests, place a high priority on concerns about business sustainability (Gupta et al., 2014). Social media marketers may be oblivious to the business sustainability concerns of an organization that gave them a marketing gig, which may lead to competing interests during the discharge of their duties and responsibilities. Consequently, social marketers' practices may cast an undue influence on the business sustainability strategies of the employing company.

Sharma et al. (2010) established that identification and marketing to the environmentally conscious consumer have received a lot of attention, despite the long-running arguments on ecological conservation and environmental practices in marketing. Less focus has been placed on marketing's function in an eco-friendly supply chain and how it interacts with eco-friendly products and operations. Here, eco-friendliness concerns practices that are not harmful to the larger environment. While Saura et al. (2020) have established that digital marketers consider and adopt sustainable strategies to carry out their online campaigns, little has been discussed on how these sustainable strategies or models have been shared among the different social media marketers. Thus, this chapter seeks to unpack these concerns from the perspectives of the knowledge-sharing practice of social media marketers.

BACKGROUND

Generally, knowledge is becoming increasingly important in this age. Thus, it has permeated every facet of life and provided an understanding of different phenomena. These necessitate and entrench the obligation of sharing knowledge to ensure that challenges are effectively addressed, and knotty issues are understood. Every individual needs the knowledge to progress in his/her endeavor. Having sound knowledge of one's culture, society, economy, and specifically business would entrench the development of an individual. In this wise, social media marketers are not left out of knowledge sharing for ensuring sustainable business practices. There is no generally accepted definition of who is a social media marketer. However, a social marketer is someone who engages in social media marketing. The advent of social media has eased marketing strategies for individuals and businesses. Thus, the growth in social media usage has led to an expansion in social media marketing.

Therefore, social media marketers can simply be described as individuals, groups of people, and/or organizations that adopt social media platforms to carry out advertisement and other promotional activities. Therefore, social media marketers adopt the practices of knowledge sharing in carrying out their promotions and ads to achieve a specific aim or target. Knowledge sharing is crucial to the development of a business organization. It was established that knowledge-sharing techniques are important to organizations to reduce the knowledge drain caused by high turnover rates (Ali, Paris & Gunasekaran, 2019), ensure competitive advantage (Abdul-Jaleel et al., 2013), and ultimately enhance organizational performance (Singh et al., 2021). This suggests the significance of knowledge-sharing practices in the running of a successful business and/or organization. Adeyemi et al. (2022) asserted that unused knowledge would be unproductive, hence the need to be strategic in knowledge sharing to ensure positive usage of the knowledge.

There is a need for a behavior change when there is a lack of cooperation or active knowledge sharing, especially when it concerns new creative technologies like social media (Razmerita et al., 2016). This underpins the importance of enhanced and active knowledge sharing on social media to facilitate engagement with potential clients or customers. Such practices would enable reaching out to a larger audience that can access the content shared through social media because of the organizational communication and collaboration that took place online (Oostervink et al., 2016). Expectedly, each social media marketer will have a different level at which context and audience are important hurdles to knowledge sharing. This is because they offer potential insights into how high-level affordances can permit and constrain knowledge-sharing practices, and thus social media marketers are encouraged to pay particular attention to the illustration of individual-organizational friction (Ellison et al., 2015).

There are varieties of ways to participate in knowledge sharing on social media, whether as an active or passive user. Majchrzak et al. (2013) assumed that social media provided four loci indicating different ways of engaging in knowledge-sharing conversations, which include metavoicing, triggered attending, network-informed associating, and generative role-taking. The authors described metavoicing as the reaction of people towards a post on social media, which may be in the form of a *retweet, like, online vote, upvote*, and so on. In this way, metavoicing can provide an indication of metaknowledge about a particular post on social media. Triggered attendance involves participating in online knowledge sharing by abstaining from content or discourse until one receives a timely automated alert informing of a change in the content. The authors discussed that network-informed association is the act of participating in the online knowledge discussion informed by relational and content linkages. Generative role-taking involves participating in the online knowledge discourse by acting in predictable ways and assuming roles that support the community to keep members engaged in a fruitful debate.

Meanwhile, Russ (2016) established that knowledge is an essential building block for a sustainable economy in the 21st Century. The author argued that society and economy unlike anything the human race has ever experienced are being created by the new knowledge-based economy and the unrelenting wave of technological innovations. Rahman et al. (2015) showed that social media, computerized records, and online marketing are all examples of modern technological innovation because they are based on technology and have an impact on how quickly new or improved processes and products are developed. It has been suggested that it is essential to design a framework that allows varied social media marketing and to capitalize on interpersonal networks to leverage the performance of the economy, which are likely to reinforce the importance of social media in the contemporary economic and business environment (Chen et al., 2018). Jacob and Teuteberg (2021) established that social media influences business sustainability and the individuals that are involved in business model development, value management, and stakeholders' integration. All of these underscore the importance of online knowledge sharing among social media marketers.

According to the findings of Chopra et al. (2021), knowledge management for sustainability has been supported by nine foundational clusters, including informed sustainability practice, firm performance, green innovation, sustainability assessment framework, global warming, knowledge management, innovative performance, social networks, and knowledge sharing culture. For this chapter, however, only two out of the nine clusters are adopted to enhance the discussion on business sustainability in the era of increasingly popular technological innovations. These clusters are the social networks and knowledge-sharing culture. This chapter seeks to analyze knowledge-sharing practices among social media marketers and their significance for business sustainability.

MAIN FOCUS OF THE CHAPTER

Knowledge Sharing Practices Among Social Media Marketers

Generally, knowledge-sharing practices can be described as synergistic and collaborative approaches to the exchange of knowledge. Knowledge sharing can be described as the exchange of ideas and thoughts about a particular phenomenon, which can be done via different platforms or avenues (Adeyemi et al., 2022). The exchange of knowledge can take place within an organization (Uyan et al., 2022; Vuori & Okkonen, 2012), or inter-organization (Adeyemi et al., 2022; Anatan, 2021; Qi et al., 2021). Among Nigerian social media marketers, the common knowledge-sharing practices are inter-individual, intra-organizational, and inter-organizational. Dwivedi et al. (2021) showed that there is a need for trust to entrench engagement and the sharing of knowledge among social media marketers. Hosen et al. (2021) established that knowledge sharing can be enhanced among social media marketers using social media functions such as document sharing, virtual communication, and knowledge formation.

While social media such as Twitter and Facebook have been the most widely used for knowledge sharing among social media marketers (Alves et al., 2016), other types of social media are also used for knowledge sharing depending on the discretion of the user (Sulaiman et al., 2020). However, it can be inferred that Twitter and Facebook are the most popular for knowledge-sharing practices. Effective knowledge-sharing practices on social media would enhance the knowledge management strategy of a business enterprise or an organization (Chatterjee et al., 2021), which is essentially providing information through available media. The enthusiasm to learn presupposes knowledge sharing on social media. Ansari and Khan (2020) found that there is a relationship between collaborative learning among peers on social media and knowledge-sharing practices. Also, Antunes and Pinheiro (2020) established the link between knowledge flows and organizational learning. The authors concluded that knowledge is an integral part of a company's strategic intangible resources, and social media, as a tool, encourages knowledge sharing.

Meanwhile, it is imperative to note that knowledge sharing among social media marketers can be entrenched by "viral marketing" strategies. Viral marketing is an effective way for both marketers and recipients to gain from the social network users' natural tendency to be helpful. Success depends on realizing how important it is for social media influencers to be seen as knowledgeable community members rather than as paid shills for marketers (Subramani & Rajagopalan, 2003). Campaigns that go viral on social media are said to offer several benefits over typical media campaigns, notably in terms of reach and affordability. As a result, viral marketing has caught the interest of researchers and marketers who are trying to determine the traits of knowledge shared online and what motivates sharing behavior via social media (Abass et al., 2021). More importantly, Hemsley and Mason (2012) concluded that extensive social media usage for marketing purposes develops a dynamic, recursive socio-technical information and knowledge-sharing system, or knowledge ecosystem (KE).

In this chapter, social media marketers in the Nigerian space are divided into informal and formal. On one hand, the informal sector is saturated by different individuals and requires no regulation whatsoever to partake in social media marketing. On the other hand, the formal sector comprises companies that are expected to be registered with the government through the Corporate Affairs Commission (CAC). Specifically, knowledge-sharing practices among those in the informal sector (individuals or groups of individuals) are usually loose and can lead to the spread of falsehood in the process (Sulaiman et al., 2020). This is often owing to the anonymity and absence of accountability in the Nigerian social media space. However, the formal sector has a defined approach to the sharing of knowledge through media such as meetings, conferences, collaboration, training, and workshops (Adeyemi et al., 2022).

Business Sustainability

Business sustainability is an element of the multidimensional concept of sustainability. Business sustainability has been defined as a company's ability to endure over time in terms of profitability, productivity, and financial performance as well as in terms of managing the natural and social resources that make up its capital (Giovannoni & Fabietti, 2013). ManhajanMahajan and Bose (2018) noted that business sustainability is the process of running a business while taking into account three major factors, namely environmental, social, and economic. Additionally, these three factors are not as part of the triple-bottom-line strategy for business development. Bansal and DesJardine (2014) described business sustainability as the ability of businesses to respond to their immediate financial requirements without jeopardizing their capacity to supply those needs. Ullah et al. (2021) established that green human capital has a positive significant effect on business sustainability. This will translate to a possible benefit for businesses operating in emerging economies and a beneficial impact on business sustainability.

It is argued in this chapter that strategy is important in ensuring business sustainability. There are different strategies for carrying out or entrenching business sustainability. Mahajan and Bose (2018) see business sustainability as philanthropy and corporate social responsibility (CSR). They also noted that there are three strategies to entrench business sustainability, which include resource optimization in business processes and supply chains using "recycle, re-use, and decrease" tactics; preserving the value of a brand through support from stakeholders and compliance with regulations; and selling to a niche market of environmentally conscious customers willing to pay more for goods and services. Bansal and DesJardine (2014) reported that the majority of strategy theorists argue that businesses can develop a competitive edge that lasts over time and enables them to produce above-average profits. For instance, social media marketers contend that businesses develop a long-term competitive advantage by investing in disruptive technologies that will enable them to successfully outdo their competitors.

Wang et al. (2022) demonstrated that green marketing is a crucial element in gaining a competitive edge and achieving long-term economic success. Also, the authors argued that sustainable success and competitive advantages are strongly impacted by green company culture. The competitive advantage was found to have a big impact on long-term corporate success. Varsei et al. (2014) recommended that a participatory governance approach and cooperative efforts can lead to sustainable development. In essence, sustainable development might be accomplished more effectively by building and propagating the ethos and codes of behavior in sustainable operations if the partners' values are in line with the main company's goals. Additionally, this ethos would promote the creation of business models that embrace such ideals. The business sustainability performance management systems must integrate easily with the current organizational infrastructure and develop over time to meet the corporation's changing internal and external circumstances (Searcy, 2012).

Baumgartner and Rauter (2017) discussed the importance of strategic management in corporate sustainability to clarify the various issues that concern corporate sustainability management. The three dimensions of strategic management in this wise include strategy content, context, and process. These dimensions can help establish how business sustainability can enhance social, economic, and environmental value. Johnson (2015) established that the most commonly used sustainability management tools are customized versions of traditional management tools like quality management systems and staff training and incentive schemes. It was further concluded that managers who are addressing sustainability issues for the first time should consider using tools from conventional business approaches and progressively incorporating social and environmental factors into these tools. From a strategic standpoint, these instruments can assist in the gradual development of a sustainability program that satisfies the business's financial objectives.

There are different approaches adopted by businesses in ensuring best practices in terms of business sustainability practices. Some of the reported best practices in business sustainability include promoting the organization's sustainability policies publicly; considering business sustainability while developing a plan of action; regularly meeting with all stakeholders (customers, employees, government agencies, and investors) and taking their feedbacks into account; excellent communication of the organization's performance and transparency; clearly defined strategic procedures that specify the owners' responsibilities and the effect of the process on output; ongoing financial support for social and environmental initiatives; a commitment to tracking trash production and polluting emissions, as well as taking specific steps to mitigate any unfavorable effects; driven to pursue certificates or accolades with the best possible performance (Alshehhi et al., 2018; Bansal & DesJardine, 2014; Meza-Ruiz et al., 2017).

Specifically, it can be observed that individual social media marketers have the ability to endure over time in terms of performance and productivity. This is because the majority of the influencers are often in cliques, and they ensure that members of their circles are sustained. For instance, if a member of a clique gets his/her account blocked, there is usually a concerted effort to ensure that the person's new account gets the visibility required to grow. Meanwhile, individual social media marketers participate in the act of "giveaway", which is philanthropic in nature. This is done to entrench engagement on their social media accounts. Several social media marketers do engage in social movement, which is regarded as "woke capital" (Fan, 2019).

Importance of Knowledge Sharing for Business Sustainability

Tajpour et al. (2022) revealed that the application of knowledge has an impact on the sustainability of technology-based enterprises by giving them a market advantage through data-driven decisions and enhancing business sustainability. Furthermore, it was stated that knowledge is used in technology-driven businesses to promote adaptability and positive changes inside the organization. Therefore, it is encouraged to foster innovation and creativity among technology-driven green marketers to enhance sustainability. By so doing, values are provided to their companies, and there would be an increased competitive edge. Chang and Hung (2021) showed that green group identification at the team level influences organizational members' knowledge-sharing and psychological ownership of green products. The study also showed that performance in green knowledge sharing, green creativity, and green product development is affected when members acquire psychological ownership of green products.

Mehdikhani and Valmohammadi (2019) found that strategic collaboration has a positive impact on internal and external knowledge sharing and sustainability management. Furthermore, it was demonstrated that knowledge exchange on the internal and external levels benefits sustainability management. The results also demonstrated that the relationship between strategic collaboration and sustainable management is fully mediated by both internal and external information exchange. Rastegar and Ruhanen (2021) concluded that it is important to establish forums or a secure environment where people can express their opinions in addition to simply knowing their thoughts and beliefs regarding justice and fairness. Similarly to this, giving stakeholders of an organization the chance to work together by exchanging knowledge might encourage knowledge-sharing behavior as a social obligation.

In a study of the knowledge-sharing behavior of green fashion communities online, Cervillon and Wernerfelt (2012) showed that there was a shift in knowledge content between the two periods (2007–2008 and 2010–2011), from an emphasis on sustainability to a focus on fashion. Additionally, the findings showed that the nature of knowledge content has changed over time, evolving from being originally subjective to becoming more objective and displaying competence during the most recent study period in the two periods for which data were collected for the study. Results showed that members of the communities were interested in exchanging detailed knowledge on a range of topics related to the sustainable supply chain, such as fabric, materials, manufacturing techniques, shipping, distribution, and recycling or reusing fashion goods, as the communities matured. This indicates that the kinds of knowledge shared among this homogenous group are those that concern their business activities. Batool et al. (2022) revealed that knowledge sharing affects organizational sustainability. Also, the results showed that creativity has a mediating role in the relationship between knowledge sharing and organizational sustainability.

Jilani et al. (2020) found that the relationship between knowledge sharing and long-term performance was mediated by employees' ambidexterity. Moreover, it was revealed that knowledge hiding does not affect the impact of knowledge sharing on employees' ambidexterity. This shows the significance of knowledge hiding and how knowledge sharing can inspire and drive workers to produce sustainable performance. Wong (2012) conducted a study on the electronic industry in China and showed that knowledge sharing mediates the association between green requirements and the commercial success of new green products as well as the relationship between green requirements and innovations in green products and processes. The direct positive effect of knowledge sharing is the most significant on the development of green processes. It was also determined that the areas where leverage may be used to best ensure the success of innovation are knowledge sharing and green process innovation.

Hung et al. (2013) showed that the performance of green management is significantly influenced by knowledge sharing. The results showed that supply chain social capital plays a significant role in motivating network members to get the resources needed on an individual basis. Nicolopoulou (2011) revealed that to effectively support the transfer of knowledge in terms of professionals in the field of sustainability, human resources management (HRM) issues such as new competencies and different approaches to career development options, talent retention and management, and a change in the terms of the employment contract must improve significantly. Muñoz-Pascual et al. (2019) found that a collaboration-oriented HRM system has a positive effect on knowledge sharing for sustainability-oriented performance. Moreover, it was shown that the age, size of the firm, and gender of the manager have positive influences on knowledge-sharing practices.

In Nigeria, different companies engage in social media marketing. In this chapter, those are the organizations/entities categorized as formal social media marketers in Nigeria. These organizations are founded to provide marketing and/or advertisement support for their clients and potential clients. The companies in Nigeria include Wild Fusion, Mcjeh Digital, Realestateko Agency, Big Field Digital, Rushing Tap, Simtech Creative, Brand Envoy Africa, Tech 0'clock, Four Eyes Media, Nelson Reids, Errand Media Limited, and so on. These companies have adopted social media in their marketing or advertisement campaigns to help achieve their client's aims and objectives. Social media marketing companies in Nigeria equip themselves with the necessary knowledge and support to discharge their duties.

CONCLUSION

This chapter focuses on knowledge-sharing practices among social media marketers and their importance for business sustainability. It is established that trust and collaborative learning are integral parts of knowledge sharing among social media marketers. Also, social media marketers use media such as document sharing, virtual communication, and knowledge formation for knowledge sharing. Essentially, it was concluded that business sustainability among different organizations concerns the environmental, social, and economic dimensions. These are the three pillars of business sustainability or green business. Meanwhile, philanthropy and corporate social responsibility are established as the common practices of entrenching green business (from the dimensions of environmental, social, and economic). Additionally, the chapter concludes that businesses should be conscious of using "recycle, reuse, and decrease" tactics to ensure environmental sustainability. Also, knowledge sharing among social media marketers enhances sustainability management. The importance of knowledge sharing for business sustainability among social media marketers includes enhanced market advantage; promotion of adaptability and positive changes; increased innovation and creativity through a technology-driven business model; and a sense of ownership of the products among social media marketers.

Questions for Discussion

1. What are the common series of knowledge shared among social media marketers?
2. Discuss the knowledge-sharing practices approaches by social media marketers?
3. What are the important factors that determine the credibility of the knowledge shared among social media marketers?
4. What are the major factors in business sustainability among social media marketers?

5. What are the sustainability management tools among social media marketers?
6. How can knowledge be applied to the sustainability of technology-based enterprises?
7. What is the impact of knowledge sharing on sustainability management?
8. What are the knowledge-sharing practices among social media marketers in Nigeria?
9. What are the perspectives of Nigerian social media marketers about sustainability?

This research received no specific grant from any funding agency in the public, commercial, or not-for-profit sectors.

REFERENCES

Abbas, A. A., Badawi, S., & Almahdi, M. H. (2021). Toward Successful Social Media Viral Marketing: A Knowledge Management Approach. In *International Conference on Business and Technology* (pp. 377-389). Springer. 10.1007/978-3-030-69221-6_28

Abdul-Jalal, H., Toulson, P., & Tweed, D. (2013). Knowledge sharing success for sustaining organizational competitive advantage. *Procedia Economics and Finance*, *7*, 150–157. doi:10.1016/S2212-5671(13)00229-3

Adeyemi, I. O., Uzamot, W. O., & Temim, F. M. (2022). Knowledge Transfer and Use as Predictors of Law Firm Performance: Nigerian Lawyer's Perspectives. *International Journal of Knowledge Management*, *18*(1), 1–17. doi:10.4018/IJKM.291097

Ali, A. A., Paris, L., & Gunasekaran, A. (2019). Key factors influencing knowledge-sharing practices and its relationship with organizational performance within the oil and gas industry. *Journal of Knowledge Management*, *23*(9), 1806–1837. doi:10.1108/JKM-06-2018-0394

Alshehhi, A., Nobanee, H., & Khare, N. (2018). The impact of sustainability practices on corporate financial performance: Literature trends and future research potential. *Sustainability (Basel)*, *10*(2), 494. doi:10.3390u10020494

Alves, H., Fernandes, C., & Raposo, M. (2016). Social media marketing: A literature review and implications. *Psychology and Marketing*, *33*(12), 1029–1038. doi:10.1002/mar.20936

Anatan, L. (2021). Interorganizational Knowledge Transfer Practices Toward MSMEs 4.0: A Proposed Conceptual Framework. *Review of Integrative Business and Economics Research*, *10*, 409–418. https://search.proquest.com/openview/2051203ec44ceeaedc2ebd8f7b81325a/1?pq-origsite=gscholar&cbl=2032316

Ansari, J. A. N., & Khan, N. A. (2020). Exploring the role of social media in collaborative learning the new domain of learning. *Smart Learning Environments*, *7*(1), 1-16. https://slejournal.springeropen.com/articles/10.1186/s40561-020-00118-7

Antunes, H. D. J. G., & Pinheiro, P. G. (2020). Linking knowledge management, organizational learning and memory. *Journal of Innovation & Knowledge*, *5*(2), 140–149. doi:10.1016/j.jik.2019.04.002

Asibong, U., Okafor, C. J., Asibong, I., Ayi, E., Omoronyia, O., & Owoidoho, U. (2020). Psychological distress and social media usage: A survey among undergraduates of a university in Calabar, Nigeria. *The Nigerian Postgraduate Medical Journal, 27*(2), 115–126. doi:10.4103/npmj.npmj_169_19 PMID:32295942

Bansal, P., & DesJardine, M. R. (2014). Business sustainability: It is about time. *Strategic Organization, 12*(1), 70–78. doi:10.1177/1476127013520265

Batool, F., Mohammad, J., Awang, S. R., & Ahmad, T. (2022). The effect of knowledge sharing and systems thinking on organizational sustainability: The mediating role of creativity. *Journal of Knowledge Management*. https://www.emerald.com/insight/content/doi/10.1108/JKM-10-2021-0785/full/html

Baumgartner, R. J., & Rauter, R. (2017). Strategic perspectives of corporate sustainability management to develop a sustainable organization. *Journal of Cleaner Production, 140*, 81–92. doi:10.1016/j.jclepro.2016.04.146

Cervellon, M. C., & Wernerfelt, A. S. (2012). Knowledge sharing among green fashion communities online: Lessons for the sustainable supply chain. *Journal of Fashion Marketing and Management, 16*(2), 176–192. doi:10.1108/13612021211222860

Chang, T. W., & Hung, C. Z. (2021). How to shape the employees' organization sustainable green knowledge sharing: Cross-level effect of green organizational identity effect on green management behavior and performance of members. *Sustainability (Basel), 13*(2), 626–645. doi:10.3390u13020626

Chatterjee, S., Chaudhuri, R., Vrontis, D., & Piccolo, R. (2021). Enterprise social network for knowledge sharing in MNCs: Examining the role of knowledge contributors and knowledge seekers for cross-country collaboration. *Journal of International Management, 27*(1), 100827. doi:10.1016/j.intman.2021.100827

Chen, F. W., Fu, L. W., Wang, K., Tsai, S. B., & Su, C. H. (2018). The influence of entrepreneurship and social networks on economic growth—From a sustainable innovation perspective. *Sustainability (Basel), 10*(7), 2510–2539. doi:10.3390u10072510

Chopra, M., Saini, N., Kumar, S., Varma, A., Mangla, S. K., & Lim, W. M. (2021). Past, present, and future of knowledge management for business sustainability. *Journal of Cleaner Production, 328*, 129592. doi:10.1016/j.jclepro.2021.129592

Dwivedi, Y. K., Ismagilova, E., Hughes, D. L., Carlson, J., Filieri, R., Jacobson, J., . . . Wang, Y. (2021). Setting the future of digital and social media marketing research: Perspectives and research propositions. *International Journal of Information Management, 59*, 102168. https://www.sciencedirect.com/science/article/pii/S0268401220308082

Ellison, N. B., Gibbs, J. L., & Weber, M. S. (2015). The use of enterprise social network sites for knowledge sharing in distributed organizations: The role of organizational affordances. *The American Behavioral Scientist, 59*(1), 103–123. doi:10.1177/0002764214540510

Fan, J. S. (2019). Woke Capital: The Role of Corporations in Social Movements. *Harvard Business Law Review, 9*(2), 441–494.

Giovannoni, E., & Fabietti, G. (2013). What is sustainability? A review of the concept and its applications. *Integrated Reporting*, 21-40. https://link.springer.com/chapter/10.1007/978-3-319-02168-3_2

Gupta, S., Rudd, J., & Lee, N. (2014). Business sustainability through successful integration of marketing and operations. *Industrial Marketing Management*, *43*(1), 3–5. doi:10.1016/j.indmarman.2013.10.004

Harrigan, P., Daly, T. M., Coussement, K., Lee, J. A., Soutar, G. N., & Evers, U. (2021). Identifying influencers on social media. *International Journal of Information Management*, *56*, 102246. doi:10.1016/j.ijinfomgt.2020.102246

Hemsley, J., & Mason, R. M. (2012). The nature of knowledge in the social media age: Implications for knowledge management models. In *2012 45th Hawaii International Conference on System Sciences* (pp. 3928-3937). IEEE.

Hosen, M., Ogbeibu, S., Giridharan, B., Cham, T. H., Lim, W. M., & Paul, J. (2021). Individual motivation and social media influence on student knowledge sharing and learning performance: Evidence from an emerging economy. *Computers & Education*, *172*, 104262. doi:10.1016/j.compedu.2021.104262

Hung, S. W., Chen, P. C., & Chung, C. F. (2014). Gaining or losing? The social capital perspective on supply chain members' knowledge sharing of green practices. *Technology Analysis and Strategic Management*, *26*(2), 189–206. doi:10.1080/09537325.2013.850475

Jacob, A., & Teuteberg, F. (2020). Towards a Taxonomy for Design options of social networking technologies in sustainable business models. *Sustainability (Basel)*, *13*(1), 81–100. doi:10.3390u13010081

Jilani, M. M. A. K., Fan, L., Islam, M. T., & Uddin, M. A. (2020). The influence of knowledge sharing on sustainable performance: A moderated mediation study. *Sustainability (Basel)*, *12*(3), 908–926. doi:10.3390u12030908

Johnson, M. P. (2015). Sustainability management and small and medium-sized enterprises: Managers' awareness and implementation of innovative tools. *Corporate Social Responsibility and Environmental Management*, *22*(5), 271–285. doi:10.1002/csr.1343

Mahajan, R., & Bose, M. (2018). Business sustainability: Exploring the meaning and significance. *ImiKonnect*, *7*(2), 8-13. https://www.researchgate.net/profile/Montu-Bose-2/publication/333078727_Business_Sustainability_Exploring_the_Meaning_and_Significance/links/5cda460f458515712ea950ba/Business-Sustainability-Exploring-the-Meaning-and-Significance.pdf

Majchrzak, A., Faraj, S., Kane, G. C., & Azad, B. (2013). The contradictory influence of social media affordances on online communal knowledge sharing. *Journal of Computer-Mediated Communication*, *19*(1), 38–55. doi:10.1111/jcc4.12030

Mehdikhani, R., & Valmohammadi, C. (2019). Strategic collaboration and sustainable supply chain management: The mediating role of internal and external knowledge sharing. *Journal of Enterprise Information Management*, *32*(5), 778–806. doi:10.1108/JEIM-07-2018-0166

Meza-Ruiz, I. D., Rocha-Lona, L., del Rocío Soto-Flores, M., Garza-Reyes, J. A., Kumar, V., & Lopez-Torres, G. C. (2017). Measuring business sustainability maturity-levels and best practices. *Procedia Manufacturing*, *11*, 751–759. doi:10.1016/j.promfg.2017.07.176

Muñoz-Pascual, L., Galende, J., & Curado, C. (2019). Human resource management contributions to knowledge sharing for a sustainability-oriented performance: A mixed methods approach. *Sustainability (Basel)*, *12*(1), 161–180. doi:10.3390u12010161

Nicolopoulou, K. (2011). Towards a theoretical framework for knowledge transfer in the field of CSR and sustainability. *Equality, Diversity and Inclusion*, *30*(6), 524–538. doi:10.1108/02610151111157738

Oostervink, N., Agterberg, M., & Huysman, M. (2016). Knowledge sharing on enterprise social media: Practices to cope with institutional complexity. *Journal of Computer-Mediated Communication*, *21*(2), 156–176. doi:10.1111/jcc4.12153

Qi, Y., Wang, X., Li, Y., Zhang, G., & Jin, H. (2021). The effects of inter-organizational compatibility on knowledge transfer in cross-border M&As. *Management Decision*, *59*(9), 2123–2142. doi:10.1108/MD-03-2020-0349

Rahman, N. A., Yaacob, Z., & Radzi, R. M. (2016). An overview of technological innovation on SME survival: A conceptual paper. *Procedia: Social and Behavioral Sciences*, *224*, 508–515. doi:10.1016/j.sbspro.2016.05.427

Rastegar, R., & Ruhanen, L. (2021). A safe space for local knowledge sharing in sustainable tourism: An organisational justice perspective. *Journal of Sustainable Tourism*, 1–17. https://www.tandfonline.com/doi/abs/10.1080/09669582.2021.1929261

Razmerita, L., Kirchner, K., & Nielsen, P. (2016). What factors influence knowledge sharing in organizations? A social dilemma perspective of social media communication. *Journal of Knowledge Management*, *20*(6), 1225–1246. doi:10.1108/JKM-03-2016-0112

Russ, M. (2016). The probable foundations of sustainabilism: Information, energy and entropy based definition of capital, Homo Sustainabiliticus and the need for a "new gold". *Ecological Economics*, *130*, 328–338. doi:10.1016/j.ecolecon.2016.07.013

Saura, J. R., Palos-Sanchez, P., & Rodríguez Herráez, B. (2020). Digital marketing for sustainable growth: Business models and online campaigns using sustainable strategies. *Sustainability (Basel)*, *12*(3), 1003–1023. doi:10.3390u12031003

Searcy, C. (2012). Corporate sustainability performance measurement systems: A review and research agenda. *Journal of Business Ethics*, *107*(3), 239–253. doi:10.100710551-011-1038-z

Sharma, A., Iyer, G. R., Mehrotra, A., & Krishnan, R. (2010). Sustainability and business-to-business marketing: A framework and implications. *Industrial Marketing Management*, *39*(2), 330–341. doi:10.1016/j.indmarman.2008.11.005

Singh, S. K., Gupta, S., Busso, D., & Kamboj, S. (2021). Top management knowledge value, knowledge sharing practices, open innovation and organizational performance. *Journal of Business Research*, *128*, 788–798. doi:10.1016/j.jbusres.2019.04.040

Subramani, M. R., & Rajagopalan, B. (2003). Knowledge-sharing and influence in online social networks via viral marketing. *Communications of the ACM, 46*(12), 300–307. doi:10.1145/953460.953514

Sulaiman, K. A., Adeyemi, I. O., & Ayegun, I. (2020). Information sharing and evaluation as determinants of spread of fake news on social media among Nigerian youths: Experience from COVID-19 pandemic. *International Journal of Knowledge Content Development & Technology, 10*(4), 65–82. https://www.koreascience.or.kr/article/JAKO202009252118722.page

Tajpour, M., Hosseini, E., Mohammadi, M., & Bahman-Zangi, B. (2022). The effect of knowledge management on the sustainability of technology-driven businesses in emerging markets: The mediating role of social media. *Sustainability (Basel), 14*(14), 8602. doi:10.3390u14148602

Ullah, H., Wang, Z., Bashir, S., Khan, A. R., Riaz, M., & Syed, N. (2021). Nexus between IT capability and green intellectual capital on sustainable businesses: Evidence from emerging economies. *Environmental Science and Pollution Research International, 28*(22), 27825–27843. doi:10.100711356-020-12245-2 PMID:33515153

Uyan, U., Şanal, M., & Ibin, A. (2022). A Theoretical Investigation on Intra-Firm Knowledge Sharing: The Roles of Contextual, Relational, and Socio-Cognitive Factors. In Understanding, Implementing, and Evaluating Knowledge Management in Business Settings (pp. 14-41). IGI Global.

Varsei, M., Soosay, C., Fahimnia, B., & Sarkis, J. (2014). Framing sustainability performance of supply chains with multidimensional indicators. *Supply Chain Management, 19*(3), 242–257. doi:10.1108/SCM-12-2013-0436

Vuori, V., & Okkonen, J. (2012). Knowledge sharing motivational factors of using an intra-organizational social media platform. *Journal of Knowledge Management, 16*(4), 592–603. doi:10.1108/13673271211246167

Wang, W., Zhang, D., Wang, H., Zhu, Q., & Morabbi Heravi, H. (2022). How do businesses achieve sustainable success and gain a competitive advantage in the green era? *Kybernetes*, 1–20. doi:10.1108/K-07-2021-0614

Wong, S. K. S. (2013). Environmental requirements, knowledge sharing and green innovation: Empirical evidence from the electronics industry in China. *Business Strategy and the Environment, 22*(5), 321–338. doi:10.1002/bse.1746

Zhang, Y., Moe, W. W., & Schweidel, D. A. (2017). Modeling the role of message content and influencers in social media rebroadcasting. *International Journal of Research in Marketing, 34*(1), 100–119. doi:10.1016/j.ijresmar.2016.07.003

KEY TERMS AND DEFINITIONS

Economic Sustainability: This can be described as an act of making financial decisions based on a commitment to engage in green practices.

Environmental Sustainability: This concerns obligations to maintain global ecosystems and conserve natural resources in order to support the health and welfare of today and in the future.

Knowledge Sharing: Knowledge sharing can be defined as the interchange of concepts and viewpoints regarding a specific phenomenon via a variety of media or channels.

Metaknowledge: This can simply be described as knowledge about knowledge.

Metavoicing: This is the response that users have to a social media post, such as a retweet, like, online vote, upvote, etc.

Social Media Marketers: These are those that help to provide advertising and marketing campaigns on social media.

Social Responsibility: This can be described as businesses abiding by ethics and ensuring transparency concerning taking up roles that enhance green practices.

Chapter 8
Exploring the Knowledge Sharing Dynamics in Virtual Communities Within the Metaverse Domain

Mohammad Daradkeh
University of Dubai, UAE & Yarmouk University, Jordan

EXECUTIVE SUMMARY

This chapter aims to explore the knowledge sharing model in virtual communities within the metaverse domain and proposes a way to enhance knowledge sharing and innovation in these communities. The study takes into account the practical implications of digital ethics and digital citizenship and the impact they have on the shaping of digital ethics. Based on the analysis of relevant practices and prior research, a knowledge sharing model for virtual communities in the metaverse is constructed. The results show that the basic process of knowledge sharing involves the selection and acquisition of community knowledge in three dimensions, internalization and absorption of situational knowledge to form a "knowledge black box," and finally, sharing through private domain knowledge broadcasting and diffusion. The current practices in virtual communities within the metaverse domain are limited and lack empirical evidence.

INTRODUCTION

The emergence of the metaverse has sparked an immense amount of creativity and scholarly debates regarding the evolution of human society. With the advent of technologies such as virtual reality, artificial intelligence, big data, 5G networks, and blockchain, the metaverse has gained the necessary technical support for its growth. As the metaverse continues to shape and influence the form of virtual communities, it has become imperative to study the knowledge sharing behaviors and models in these communities (Alpala, Quiroga-Parra, Torres, & Peluffo-Ordóñez, 2022; Buhalis, O'Connor, & Leung, 2023).

The popularity of virtual communities such as VRChat, Roblox, and Second Life highlights the potential for knowledge sharing in the metaverse. This chapter explores the existing research on the

DOI: 10.4018/978-1-6684-5859-4.ch008

metaverse, virtual communities, and knowledge sharing, and delves into the possible transformations of knowledge sharing models in virtual communities due to the impact of the metaverse. By taking into account the unique features of the metaverse, this chapter aims to construct a future knowledge sharing model for virtual communities and provide a roadmap for further research and development (Cappannari & Vitillo, 2022; Chen & Lee, 2021; Dahan et al., 2022).

The contribution of this chapter is significant as it sheds light on the importance of knowledge sharing in virtual communities in the metaverse domain, and highlights the need for a comprehensive understanding of the knowledge sharing models that are relevant to this space. The chapter also provides insights into the future of knowledge sharing in virtual communities, making it a valuable resource for researchers, practitioners, and anyone interested in the development of virtual communities (Dai, Wang, & Gao, 2022; De Ketelaere, Smeets, Verboven, Nicolaï, & Saeys, 2022; Hariharan, Risling, Felic, & Ostertag, 2023).

Moreover, this chapter sheds light on the challenges and opportunities that the metaverse presents for knowledge sharing in virtual communities. For example, the increased access to information and the diverse perspectives available in virtual communities may enhance the efficiency and effectiveness of knowledge sharing. However, these communities also face challenges such as information overload, information quality control, and the lack of trust among participants. To address these challenges, it is crucial to understand the existing knowledge sharing models and to identify the changes that the metaverse will bring to these models (Harisanty, Anna, Putri, Firdaus, & Noor Azizi, 2022; Huynh-The et al., 2023).

Additionally, this chapter highlights the importance of considering the cultural and social factors that influence knowledge sharing in virtual communities. In a metaverse, individuals from different cultural backgrounds may interact, leading to the emergence of new norms, values, and behaviors regarding knowledge sharing. Thus, it is crucial to take into account these cultural and social factors when constructing a future knowledge sharing model for virtual communities in the metaverse.

RESEARCH STATUS AND THEORETICAL BASIS

Connotation of Metaverse

The Metaverse refers to the overall meaning and perception associated with future versions of the Internet. It encompasses the continuous development of a virtual realm that is interconnected with our physical world. Extensive research and discussions have been devoted to exploring the concept and significance of the Metaverse in both academic and industry circles. The term was initially introduced in N. Stephenson's science fiction novel "Snow Crash" and it represents a shared virtual space with three-dimensional elements that are closely tied to a tangible virtual environment (De Ketelaere et al., 2022). The term gained attention following Facebook founder Mark Zuckerberg's declaration of his goal to turn Facebook into a metaverse company (Dubey, Gupta, Mikalef, & Akter, 2022). Since then, researchers and entrepreneurs have been exploring the meaning of the metaverse, with different perspectives on its definition and characteristics. Eom (2022) believes that the metaverse should have a high degree of realism and be capable of mapping people's real-life experiences to the virtual space. On the other hand, Faraboschi, Frachtenberg, Laplante, Milojicic, and Saracco (2022) see the metaverse as an independent and parallel virtual space that is becoming increasingly realistic. Duan et al. (2021), the founder of r. Beamable proposed a framework that classifies the metaverse into different levels.

The implementation of metaverse has been a topic of interest among companies and investors. Companies such as Roblox have already taken steps in building a metaverse ecosystem (Harisanty et al., 2022), and major manufacturers are investing in its development. Although there is no universally accepted definition of the metaverse, researchers and industry professionals agree that it holds the potential to bring about significant changes to our lives and society.

The goal of the metaverse is to create a virtual shared space that seamlessly integrates with the real world, requiring the integration of new technologies like big data, artificial intelligence, virtual reality, 5G, blockchain, and 3D engines (Hassani, Huang, & MacFeely, 2022; Huynh-The et al., 2023). The technical core of the metaverse depends on integration and application, and its underlying technologies are shown in Table 1. The success of the metaverse heavily depends on the effective integration and application of these technologies. This chapter focuses on the significance of knowledge sharing in virtual communities within the metaverse domain. It highlights the importance of understanding the knowledge sharing models that are relevant to this space and provides insights into the future of knowledge sharing in virtual communities. It is a valuable resource for researchers, practitioners, and anyone interested in the development of virtual communities. It is also crucial to take into account cultural and social factors when constructing a future knowledge sharing model for virtual communities in the metaverse. The interaction of individuals from different cultural backgrounds in a metaverse may lead to the emergence of new norms, values, and behaviors regarding knowledge sharing. Therefore, it is essential to consider these cultural and social factors in the development process.

Table 1. Major underlying technologies of the metaverse

Underlying Technologies	Implemented Functions
Artificial intelligence, digital twin	Meta-universe ecology
Blockchain	Access Verification
Artificial Intelligence, Cloud Computing	Underlying algorithms
The expanded reality, robotics, brain-computer interface	Virtual Reality Simulation
5G	Unhindered Networks

Current Status of Related Research

The idea of a metaverse has been discussed by scholars as early as 2003. At that time, the metaverse was considered an immersive network collection where users could freely create and trade (Hwang, 2023; Inder, 2023). The emergence of the 3D virtual game Second Life in the same period led to the best interpretation of the metaverse at that time and stimulated further thinking about the metaverse, such as the way of revenue creation in the metaverse (Jamil, Rahman, & Fawad, 2022), education model (Jeon, 2023), social patterns (Jin, Xu, & Leng, 2022), and possible inflation (Julian, Chung, & Wang, 2023) and moral issues (Keshmiri Neghab, Jamshidi, & Keshmiri Neghab, 2022).

A virtual community is a group of people who consciously and altruistically share information through the Internet, in which knowledge flows from individuals to groups (Kesselman & Esquivel, 2022). Research on knowledge sharing in virtual communities can be divided into two categories: micro and macro. One type of research analyzes the influencing factors that promote individual knowledge sharing behaviors in virtual communities from a micro perspective, such as classifying the main motivations that influence user-generated content in the Web 2. 0 environment from a theoretical perspective (Kraus et al., 2023), and attachment motivation, social support orientation, individual trust, altruism, and self-efficacy are important factors that influence knowledge sharing behaviors in communities (Kwanya, Stilwell, & Underwood, 2012; Maddahi & Chen, 2022; Mourtzis, Angelopoulos, & Panopoulos, 2023). These studies have been conducted from psychological, sociological, and social perspectives. These studies analyzed users' willingness to share in virtual communities from the perspectives of psychology and sociology and proposed corresponding measures to promote the development of knowledge sharing in virtual communities on this basis.

Another type of research studies the knowledge sharing behavior of virtual communities from a macro perspective, such as the SNS-based knowledge sharing model combined with Ikujiro Nonaka's knowledge spiral theory (Mystakidis, 2023), the coupling mechanism of knowledge sharing in virtual communities based on social system theory (Njoku, Nwakanma, Amaizu, & Kim, 2022), the multivariate derivation model of knowledge co-creation in virtual network communities (Park & Kim, 2022) and the knowledge exchange mechanism model of academic virtual communities (Pamucar, Deveci, Gokasar, Tavana, & Köppen, 2022). These studies focus on the whole picture of knowledge flow in virtual communities and the overall organic response of knowledge sharing in virtual communities with a system theory perspective. Unlike the transmission of information, knowledge sharing in virtual communities is a dynamic learning process, including not only the transmission of knowledge, but also the selection, absorption, and sublimation of knowledge (Popescu, Dragomir, Popescu, & Dragomir, 2022). The second type of research perspective is adopted to consider the whole process of virtual community knowledge sharing from the perspective of users, focusing on the complete process from knowledge selection, internalization, and innovation to the final sharing to other community users in the community.

In the existing metaverse research, the technical layout, social form, and situational knowledge reconstruction of virtual scenes provide references for the conception of the knowledge sharing model of virtual communities in the metaverse field. The knowledge sharing model of virtual communities in the metaverse field is constructed by using technologies such as big data, blockchain and virtual reality as the bones, contextualized knowledge modules as the flesh and blood, and social forms in the metaverse scene as the soul (Qamar, Anwar, & Afzal, 2023).

Theoretical Model Reference

Referring to the four forms of interconversion between tacit knowledge and explicit knowledge in the SECI model, this chapter analyzes the interaction process of knowledge transformation between users and communities based on the knowledge chain model and envisages the existence form of virtual community knowledge under the metaverse field based on immersion theory. The SECI model was proposed by Japanese scholars Nonaka and Takeuchi in 1995, which mainly describes four forms of interconversion of tacit knowledge and explicit knowledge: Socialization, Externalization, Combination, and Internalization (Rahaman, 2022). In 2000, the model was further refined to identify the sites where each transformation occurs, such as Originating Ba, Interacting/Dialoguing Ba, Systemizing Ba, and Exercising Ba. Meanwhile, Kwanya et al. (2012) proposed the knowledge chain model, which defines the link between organizational knowledge and core competence, dividing knowledge dissemination activities into five categories: knowledge acquisition, selection, generation, internalization, and externalization. This chapter delves into the interaction process of knowledge transformation between users and communities based on the SECI model's four forms of interconversion between tacit knowledge and explicit knowledge. Additionally, it examines the existence form of virtual community knowledge in the metaverse field through immersion theory.

KNOWLEDGE SHARING IN METAVERSE: AN EVOLUTION

The metaverse offers the possibility of transforming the existence of virtual communities from a two-dimensional Internet social platform to a three-dimensional virtual community with a three-dimensional field. In such a transformation, the "genes" of knowledge sharing, i.e., the core elements that constitute knowledge sharing, will also undergo a great transformation. This transformation is explained in the following four aspects: space, resources, behavior, and subjects.

Sharing Space in Three Dimensions

The existence of virtual communities in the future metaverse will change dramatically compared to the present. The existing virtual communities generally exist in the form of website forums, and users can only contact each other by posting in forums, which is not enough for spatial immersion and the form of interaction is too single. To a certain extent, this has led to a lack of motivation for users to participate in knowledge sharing in virtual communities and a low willingness to share (Sanji, Behzadi, & Gomroki, 2022).

Under the metaverse field, the virtual community will become a kind of "community" in the real sense, which consists of many private metaverses, and each user can have his own "private domain" in the community, where the community knowledge resources will be spread in three-dimensional modules. In front of users, users can select these knowledge modules to obtain corresponding knowledge. In addition to these private metaverses, the virtual community also has a corresponding public space, i.e., the "public domain", which provides the community users with a variety of knowledge interaction space, and this space can hold various activities such as academic conferences and virtual classes. Some examples of such forms of virtual communities have emerged in practice, such as VRchat, a massively multiplayer online virtual reality game in which players exist as avatars in a virtual space where they have their own "home" and can share the models they create in the commons (Şarlıoğlu, Boyacı, & Akca, 2023). A similar practice is Roblox, where players can not only experience virtual worlds, but also create games and build scenarios in a scene creation room, and then share their creations for other players to experience (Shen, Tan, Guo, Zhao, & Qin, 2021). These practices give the shape of a future virtual community space.

Situationalization of Shared Resources

In the future, knowledge sharing in three-dimensional virtual communities will also change the form of shared resources, and text and video with flat displays will be difficult to adapt to the development of virtual communities in the metaverse. The explicit knowledge displayed in three dimensions and the tacit knowledge contained in virtual scenarios will become the mainstream resources for knowledge sharing.

The three-dimensional presentation of explicit knowledge enables knowledge recipients to have a deeper immersion experience and a clearer understanding of the explicit knowledge they need in the process of knowledge sharing, which is essentially the transformation of explicit knowledge to explicit knowledge. In this process, the fragmented explicit knowledge content can be systematically integrated to form a more perfect three-dimensional module of explicit knowledge. In the traditional virtual community, tacit knowledge needs to be externalized into explicit knowledge in the form of text, etc., and then internalized and absorbed by users as their tacit knowledge. Unfortunately, this kind of knowledge transformation will inevitably cause certain loss and deviation, so the receiver cannot experience the full picture of the tacit knowledge completely and accurately when receiving the tacit knowledge (Siyaev & Jo, 2021). In the metaverse domain, knowledge resource reconstruction can reduce this loss to a certain extent. The situational reconstruction of tacit knowledge constructs a set of tacit knowledge occurrence scenarios in the form of virtual spatial processes. After receiving a set of knowledge modules, knowledge resource recipients enter the scenarios in the form of a three-dimensional unfolding and absorb the tacit knowledge that the publisher wants to convey precisely and immersively by experiencing the whole tacit knowledge generation process in its entirety. Situated reconstruction of tacit knowledge is a kind of knowledge externalization process, which is different from the traditional externalization method using words and language. With the virtual simulation of the tacit knowledge generation process, tacit knowledge is transformed into explicit knowledge in the meta-universe field.

Decentralization of Sharing Behavior

In the process of knowledge sharing in virtual communities in the past, knowledge sharing and publishing were generally carried out by the community platform, in which the virtual communities acted as a bridge to establish connections between users, and such a one-to-many relationship structure caused inconvenience in direct interaction between users to a certain extent and contradicted the concept of decentralized co-construction and sharing in the metaverse.

Under the metaverse, the behavior mode of knowledge sharing will be more decentralized. When users interact with knowledge, they can directly find the metaverse coordinates of knowledge exporters or knowledge receivers, and enter each other's "private domain" for knowledge interaction by inviting or applying for access, after getting authorization from users. Such direct face-to-face interaction can realize the socialization of tacit knowledge to tacit knowledge. The process of socialization of tacit knowledge in traditional virtual communities can only be carried out offline, but in the metaverse domain, users can realize remote interaction through avatars. Such peer-to-peer knowledge transfer can bypass the sharing center of the virtual community and realize peer-to-peer knowledge sharing and such knowledge sharing will form an intricate knowledge interaction network by intertwining in countless nodes of the metaverse community. The status of the traditional knowledge sharing center of the virtual community will gradually fade away in such a decentralized network. In this scenario, the role of the virtual community is more like a "sheriff" to manage the knowledge sharing of the community, to prevent the circulation of false information and illegal information in this network (Tait & Pierson, 2022; Teubner & Camacho, 2023). On the other hand, under the virtual experiment scenario of the metaverse, the near-accessible knowledge innovation output makes the number of users who share knowledge in traditional virtual communities, i.e., the core users, increase dramatically, and the group of users who share knowledge also becomes significantly decentralized.

Synergization of Sharing Subjects

The main body of virtual community knowledge sharing consists of virtual community and community users (Tlili et al., 2022). In the previous knowledge sharing in virtual communities, users usually show their knowledge alone through language and text or by making video images. The three-dimensional and contextualized construction of knowledge content in the metaverse field makes it difficult for knowledge exporters of different professional categories to build and share knowledge alone.

There are users with various knowledge backgrounds and abilities in the virtual community, and they may need to invoke multiple specialties when constructing a knowledge resource, and these users can interact with each other directly, with user privileges granted, through a metaverse "wormhole" - -a kind of channel connecting private metaverse, linking several user "private domains" to achieve the effect of collaborative knowledge construction. Admittedly, this collaborative approach is more dependent on users in the community who have the technology to build virtual resources. At this point, the role of the virtual community, another important subject of knowledge sharing, can be reflected. For example, Roblox provides development software for users to build scenarios, with corresponding development tutorials and classroom teaching (Tromp, 2022). In this way, user-user and user-virtual community collaborative knowledge building and sharing may become the mainstream of knowledge sharing in virtual communities in the future.

KNOWLEDGE SHARING IN METAVERSE VIRTUAL COMMUNITIES

The metaverse field is based on AI, XR, and blockchain technologies to reconstruct the virtual community field is reconstructed. The three-dimensionalization of shared space, the contextualization of shared resources, the decentralization of shared behavior, and the collaboration of shared subjects have become the main features of the metaverse. The new operating logic of virtual community knowledge sharing in the metaverse domain is based on AI, XR, and blockchain. The new operating logic of virtual community knowledge sharing under the metaverse field is the three-dimensionalization of sharing space, the contextualization of shared resources, the decentralization of sharing behavior, and the collaboration of sharing subjects (Weking, Desouza, Fielt, & Kowalkiewicz, 2023).

The knowledge sharing mode in the metaverse field can be reorganized by building a knowledge sharing mode of the virtual community based on the traditional knowledge sharing mode of the virtual community, combined with the new changes in the metaverse field. This knowledge sharing mode is designed from the perspective of users and includes four key components: content selection and acquisition, immersive experience learning, virtual experimental scene creation, and knowledge broadcasting module. The innovative knowledge in the "private domain" space is pushed to each node in the community through the knowledge broadcasting module, facilitating knowledge sharing and utilization. The emergence of metaverse technology is transforming virtual communities from two-dimensional platforms to three-dimensional virtual communities.

Case Example

To demonstrate the applicability and feasibility of a proposed knowledge sharing mode in the metaverse field, a case example of the scientific research community is presented. The scientific research community is one specific community that could greatly benefit from the transformation of virtual communities in the metaverse field. Scientists could use the immersive experiences provided by the metaverse to explore complex scientific concepts and collaborate with other scientists across different domains. This could lead to the emergence of new ideas and breakthroughs in scientific research. The immersive experiences provided by the metaverse could enhance knowledge sharing and collaboration among scientists across different domains, leading to new ideas and breakthroughs in scientific research. However, the transformation of virtual communities in the metaverse field also poses potential challenges and limitations to knowledge sharing. The specific knowledge sharing model is shown in Figure 1.

The purpose of this case study is to explore and analyze the potential challenges and limitations that may arise when sharing knowledge within virtual communities in the metaverse and to identify potential solutions to these issues.

The changes in the core elements of knowledge sharing in the metaverse field can be grouped into four aspects: space, resources, behavior, and subjects. The three-dimensionalization of shared space in the metaverse can provide immersive experiences, but a digital divide may impede knowledge sharing. Efforts should be made to ensure that necessary technology is accessible to all users. The quality and reliability of shared resources may vary greatly, and mechanisms should be put in place to ensure quality and reliability. The decentralization of shared behavior in the metaverse may lead to disorganized and chaotic knowledge sharing, and guidelines and standards should be established to structure and facilitate knowledge sharing. Collaboration across different domains and topics may lead to misunderstandings and communication breakdowns, and efforts should be made to ensure that users have a basic understanding of the domains and topics they are collaborating on, and that communication is clear and concise.

However, as with any new technology or platform, the transformation of virtual communities in the metaverse field poses potential challenges and limitations to knowledge sharing. These challenges can be grouped into four aspects: space, resources, behavior, and subjects.

- The first challenge is related to space. The three-dimensionalization of shared space in the metaverse can provide immersive experiences, but a digital divide may impede knowledge sharing. This is because not all users may have access to the necessary equipment or technology to access the metaverse. To address this challenge, efforts should be made to ensure that necessary technology is accessible to all users, regardless of their location or socio-economic status.
- The second challenge is related to resources. The contextualization of shared resources is another important aspect of the metaverse, but the quality and reliability of shared resources may vary greatly, depending on the source. This could potentially lead to misinformation being shared among users. To address this challenge, mechanisms could be put in place to ensure the quality and reliability of shared resources. For example, users could rate and review shared resources, or a system of peer review could be implemented.
- The third challenge is related to behavior. The decentralization of shared behavior in the metaverse may lead to disorganized and chaotic knowledge sharing. Guidelines and standards should be established to structure and facilitate knowledge sharing in a way that is productive and effective. This will ensure that knowledge sharing is structured and productive, rather than haphazard and disorganized.
- The fourth challenge is related to subjects. Collaboration across different domains and topics may lead to misunderstandings and communication breakdowns. This is because users may not have a basic understanding of the domains and topics they are collaborating on, leading to confusion

and potential misunderstandings. Efforts should be made to ensure that users have a basic understanding of the domains and topics they are collaborating on, and that communication is clear and concise.

To address these challenges, the proposed knowledge sharing mode in the metaverse field is based on a traditional knowledge sharing mode of a virtual community, combined with new changes in the metaverse field. The knowledge sharing mode is designed from the perspective of users, and it involves several components, including visual search, immersive experience learning, knowledge black box, and knowledge broadcasting.

- Visual search is the first component of the knowledge sharing mode. It involves the selection and acquisition of community knowledge content through visual search. This allows users to easily find relevant information and knowledge in the community.
- Immersive experience learning is the second component of the knowledge sharing mode. It involves the internalization and absorption of tacit knowledge through immersive experience learning of the knowledge scene modules required by oneself. This allows users to gain a deeper understanding of complex scientific concepts and ideas.
- The third component of the knowledge sharing mode is the creation and generation of a knowledge black box in the virtual experimental scene. This involves the consolidation and synthesis of knowledge and ideas, which can then be shared with others in the community.
- Finally, the knowledge broadcasting module is used to push innovative knowledge in the "private domain" space to each node in the community. This allows for the sharing of knowledge across the entire community and enables other users to absorb and utilize the innovative knowledge.

Overall, the proposed knowledge sharing mode in the metaverse field has the potential to greatly benefit the scientific research community and other communities that require complex knowledge sharing. However, efforts should be made to address the potential challenges and limitations to ensure that the knowledge sharing mode is accessible, reliable, structured, and productive.

Figure 1. Knowledge sharing model of virtual communities in the metaverse domain

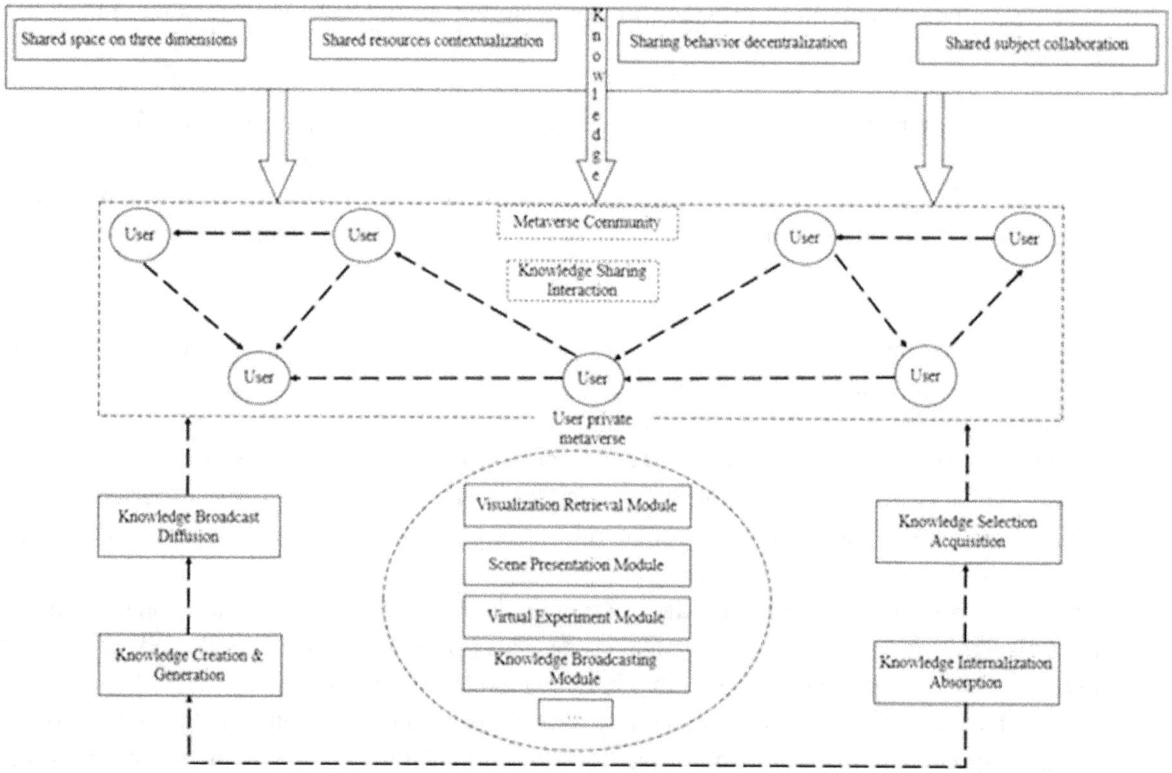

Stereoscopic Knowledge Selection and Acquisition

To enter the virtual community for knowledge sharing, users must first log in to the user's private metaverse, in which the community resources will surround the user avatar in a three-dimensional form, and each knowledge resource in the community will be a three-dimensional module for users to select and access. These modules contain explicit knowledge in 3D, such as 3D interactive books, a simulation that maps physical books into virtual three-dimensional space (Xiong & Wang, 2022), and tacit knowledge in the form of virtual scenarios.

The metaverse field provides a new form of shared resources for traditional virtual communities, and the three-dimensional explicit knowledge and situational tacit knowledge can be shared in this field, which gives a new connotation to the community knowledge selection and acquisition under the metaverse field. On the one hand, the traditional way of searching by keyword input in virtual communities seems to be unsuitable for the change of resource form, and AI technology in the base of metaverse technology will play an important role in the search for this new resource form. After users enter the private metaverse, they only need to issue language commands, and AI will retrieve the corresponding knowledge content blocks and visualize them according to the commands. On the other hand, the change of knowledge resource form will change the presentation of retrieval results, and users will not retrieve resources with a large number of figures, pictures, or videos, but a whole virtual scene. With XR technology, the user interaction interface will have better visibility and interactivity than the Web interface of traditional virtual communities, where users can enter the corresponding scenes by touching them to obtain the corresponding knowledge (Yang et al., 2022).

Contextualized Knowledge Internalization and Absorption

After users have visualized and selected the knowledge of virtual communities, they need to further internalize and absorb the acquired knowledge, to incorporate it into their knowledge system. In traditional virtual communities, there exists a large amount of explicit knowledge and tacit knowledge, which can be disseminated in the communities through posting and communication. In this process, the dissemination of tacit knowledge is usually difficult to be effectively realized in the knowledge sharing process.

Situated tacit knowledge in the metaverse refers to virtual scenarios that generate tacit knowledge in the metaverse, into which learners who need tacit knowledge can enter and acquire the corresponding skills and knowledge through repeated practice from the first-person perspective. The immersive learning of explicit knowledge of virtual scenes in the metaverse is the process of internalizing and absorbing the tacit knowledge contained in them, which is also the transformation of knowledge from explicit to tacit in the metaverse. Such practical scenarios already exist in practice. For example, the real-time simulation system of a pressurized water reactor nuclear power plant can simulate a typical nuclear power plant accident in real-time with the functions of pause, save, graphic output, etc. Through the pre-calculated display of accident occurrence, the implicit knowledge reserve of field staff facing emergencies is formed (Yu, 2022). Another example is the virtual simulation system for high-speed railroad operation and dispatching command, which trains the tacit knowledge of the staff on various situations faced in the operation and dispatching process through a virtual simulation of the complex process of high-speed railroad operation and dispatching [(Zhang et al., 2022). Under the metaverse domain, such a virtual simulation system can be constructed as virtual scenario modules, and users can obtain the corresponding tacit knowledge by selecting different virtual scenario modules.

Knowledge Black Box Creation and Generation

In the knowledge sharing of the metaverse virtual community, community users integrate and assimilate the acquired community knowledge, and when they find parts of the knowledge system that can be upgraded and improved, users can experiment and create in the virtual experimental scene in the private domain of the community, and the virtual experimental scene of the metaverse is a place where knowledge scene modules can be produced.

The term "black box" is a systems science term. It is a figurative description of a system whose internal mechanisms are largely unknown (Ahn, Kim, & Kim, 2022) and is used to describe how one does not consider its internal composition and dynamic mechanisms, but only sees it as a whole module and judges the function and structure of the system by its input-output relations. In the metaverse domain, the knowledge scenario module is actually a "black box" for the user." For example, the implicit knowledge scenario of "fire emergency avoidance" can be subdivided into different types of For example, the implicit knowledge scenario of "fire emergency avoidance" can be subdivided into different places of fire emergency avoidance. For example, the tacit knowledge scenario of "fire emergency avoidance" can be subdivided into fire emergency avoidance in different places. In the process of experiencing the knowledge black box, users do not need to consider its structure and elements but only need to substitute the first person into the generation process of tacit knowledge and obtain the corresponding tacit knowledge. The input of the "knowledge black box" is the user in the form of avatars, and the output is the physical user with the corresponding tacit knowledge. Meanwhile, users can also generate new explicit knowledge through experimental innovation in the virtual experiment scenario. Moreover, in the decentralized sharing process of the metaverse, the generated knowledge black boxes are recorded in the form of NFT (non-homogenized tokens) to ensure their authenticity and ownership.

Private Domain Knowledge Broadcast Diffusion

In the private domain of users, the knowledge black box generated by the virtual scenario construction of tacit knowledge needs to be authenticated and published by the group through the knowledge broadcasting module to achieve the effect of community knowledge sharing. In the metaverse domain, blockchain technology is a more suitable means to realize knowledge broadcasting of knowledge black boxes in the community.

Through the distributed storage and record of blockchain, when a private domain node in the community sends out knowledge sharing, all nodes in the whole community record and store the knowledge. Thanks to the NFT technology, the knowledge black box can be traced back to all backups when they are shared in the community, and the personal information of users who are authorized to modify the knowledge black box is included in the development history of the knowledge black box. When community users purchase the right to use the Knowledge Blackbox according to their needs, this transaction will also be recorded by all user nodes in the community. In this way, through the chain of knowledge black boxes and transaction records, knowledge sharing and transactions in the community are under the supervision and governance of the community. In addition, the publication of innovative knowledge needs to go through a certain authentication process to prove its quality. The "public domain" of virtual communities in the metaverse provides a suitable place for the authentication and sharing of knowledge communities, and through the black box display of knowledge in the public domain, we can obtain the community's evaluation of certain knowledge.

STRATEGIES FOR KNOWLEDGE SHARING IN VIRTUAL COMMUNITIES OF THE METAVERSE

The metaverse enables the knowledge sharing model of virtual communities to be reconstructed and to implement this model into virtual communities in the metaverse domain, improvements are needed in the following four areas.

Construction of a Community Resource Evaluation System for Knowledge Selection and Acquisition

When users enter the virtual community under the meta-field for knowledge visualization search, multiple results may appear, and how to let users choose relatively high-quality resources among many resources is the efficient basis for user knowledge selection and acquisition and community knowledge sharing. Therefore, establishing a community resource evaluation system is especially important for users' knowledge selection and acquisition (Alpala et al., 2022).

The most convenient sources for evaluating community resources are the experience of the resources and the users. In the future, when a knowledge module is authenticated and displayed in the public domain of a virtual community, the experience right can be opened to the users within the module, and then the experience score of the users within the knowledge module is recorded and visualized outside the module to form the initial score of the knowledge module. In the long run, in the subsequent transaction, use, and transformation of the knowledge module, all users can make scores, and the total score of the knowledge module is calculated by the scoring algorithm. Such dynamic scoring will accompany the whole life cycle of knowledge modules from creation to extinction. Under such a dynamic evaluation system, users can refer to the ratings when searching for the knowledge they need and select resources with the highest possible quality, thus facilitating the subsequent knowledge sharing process of the virtual community.

Reconstructing Virtual Community Resources for Knowledge Internalization and Absorption

The transformation of traditional virtual communities to the metaverse domain is, from a certain perspective, the "great migration" of information resources from the two-dimensional world to the three-dimensional world. Under such a change, the migration and reconstruction of knowledge resources of traditional virtual communities to the metaverse domain will be the key to realizing knowledge sharing in future virtual communities, and users of traditional virtual communities will also obtain virtual mapping in the metaverse domain, i.e., form a digital twin.

In terms of knowledge resources, virtual communities can simulate existing knowledge in 3D according to its classification, thus providing users with the realistic feeling of using knowledge in a virtual space. For tacit knowledge, the scenario process of knowledge content generation can be virtualized to provide users with a sense of immersion when acquiring knowledge. This realistic and immersive knowledge experience will promote efficient internalization and absorption of users. In terms of user resources, the user's digital twin is not just a virtual projection of the user's entity but will contain various information about the user's entity. With the user's setting, the virtual twin with the information set as the "in" and the virtual image as the "table" will reconstruct the user's form in the meta-universe domain. The information data as the "inside" will also become the basis for subsequent personalized knowledge push to the user to facilitate efficient knowledge absorption (Awasthi, Ahuja, & Sharma, 2022).

Construction of Community Research-Based Space for Knowledge Creation and Generation

Knowledge innovation can continuously inject new resources into the knowledge sharing process of virtual communities. In the traditional knowledge sharing process of virtual communities, knowledge innovation is rare and usually concentrated in research institutions and other places. In the Metaverse, the virtual experiment space provides a convenient place for users' knowledge innovation.

For this reason, private domains in virtual communities need to build corresponding research spaces. The research space applies to learners who have new discoveries and ideas about existing knowledge after absorbing and transforming the existing knowledge system in the community, and they can realize the creation and generation of knowledge by constructing corresponding virtual experiment spaces for research and creation. The research space can take real-world research institutions, laboratories, factories, etc. as the basic scenario template, or be constructed by the users themselves without pre-defined scenarios. In some cases, users can choose the corresponding research-based space when conducting different types of knowledge innovation. Taking automobile design as an example, users enter a virtual factory and continuously adjust and test cars in crash tests and wind tunnel tests through one-to-one physical simulations, to test the optimization of car structures under different conditions and output this optimal value. In addition, users can directly construct scenarios to generate a black box of tacit knowledge.

Personalized Pushing of Community Knowledge for Knowledge Diffusion

When knowledge under the metaverse is broadcasted in the community, it will be recorded in each private domain of the community based on blockchain technology, but this sharing behavior lacks certain purpose and relevance and cannot be personalized and recommended to the corresponding knowledge demanders, so certain personalized pushing needs to be implemented in the process of knowledge broadcast and proliferation (Huynh-The et al., 2023).

Big data technology in the foundation of metadata technology provides strong support for the personalized push. By collecting and acquiring users' avatar information in the community, such as occupation, gender, age, etc., we can build user profiles based on this information and analyze the knowledge they need or may be interested in. Based on this information, a user profile is built for each user and analyzes the knowledge they need or may be interested in, so that precise knowledge can be pushed to users (Buhalis et al., 2023; Dwivedi et al., 2022; Huynh-The et al., 2023; Hwang, 2023; Inder, 2023). On the other hand, big data mining techniques can also be used to classify users in a community into demand groups. On this basis, when a user searches for a piece of certain knowledge, a selection of corresponding knowledge searched by other users in the user group to which the user belongs can be pushed to the user in the form of highlighted results. Driven by the research-based space, the knowledge innovation within the reach of each individual will bring about an explosive chain reaction of community knowledge innovation. In the virtual community knowledge broadcasting and diffusion in the meta-space, if all the innovative knowledge is not highlighted but pushed indiscriminately to the private domain of other users in the community, it will lead to a certain degree of information confusion. This confusion can be largely avoided by using big data mining techniques to analyze users' knowledge needs and implement personalized pushing to them (Baghalzadeh Shishehgarkhaneh, Keivani, Moehler, Jelodari, & Roshdi Laleh, 2022; Batat & Hammedi, 2022; Bibri, 2022).

CONCLUSION

The analysis of knowledge flow in virtual communities in the metaverse domain shows that compared to traditional virtual communities, knowledge sharing in these communities will change in four aspects: sharing space, resources, behaviors, and subjects. The study defines a knowledge sharing model for metaverse virtual communities by combining the knowledge sharing model of traditional virtual communities with the user perspective. The model outlines a complete process, from three-dimensional selection and acquisition to scenario-based knowledge internalization and absorption to the creation of a knowledge black box, and finally, to broadcasting and diffusion across the entire community. This study provides a reference for future developments in knowledge sharing theory and practice in virtual communities.

This study has several limitations, including a lack of practical experience and insufficient empirical conditions in virtual communities in the metaverse domain. There are also many potential challenges to building virtual communities in the future, such as infrastructure security, resource monopoly, digital addiction, and platform security. These issues must be considered to avoid negative consequences and ensure the successful development of virtual communities in the metaverse.

In the future, further research is needed to explore the practical application of the knowledge sharing model in metaverse virtual communities, as well as to examine the cultural and social factors that influence knowledge sharing in these communities. Additionally, it is important to study the potential risks and challenges associated with the development of virtual communities in the metaverse and to find ways to mitigate these risks.

DISCUSSION QUESTIONS

The metaverse has the potential to revolutionize how knowledge is shared and distributed, fostering collaboration among individuals and communities globally. Nevertheless, as with any emerging technology, there are potential challenges to be addressed, such as a digital divide in access to technology and equipment, as well as the risk of misinformation and confusion among users. Therefore, it is crucial to address several significant issues related to equitable knowledge sharing, reliable and high-quality resources, effective communication, and ethical considerations. In this context, several critical discussion questions can guide our future research and exploration of knowledge sharing in the metaverse. The following questions will help us understand how to leverage the power of the metaverse while ensuring responsible and equitable knowledge sharing practices:

1. How can the potential digital divide in access to necessary technology and equipment to access the metaverse be addressed to ensure equitable knowledge sharing?
2. What mechanisms can be put in place to ensure the quality and reliability of shared resources in the metaverse to avoid misinformation and confusion among users?
3. How can guidelines and standards be established to structure and facilitate knowledge sharing in the metaverse to ensure that it is productive and effective?
4. What strategies can be employed to ensure that users have a basic understanding of the domains and topics they are collaborating on and that communication is clear and concise to avoid misunderstandings and communication breakdowns?
5. How can virtual experimental scene creation be used to enhance knowledge sharing and collaboration among scientists across different domains in the scientific research community?
6. What role can the knowledge broadcasting module play in facilitating the sharing and utilization of innovative knowledge in the "private domain" space of virtual communities in the metaverse?
7. How can immersive experience learning in the metaverse be leveraged to enhance knowledge sharing and collaboration among users across different domains and topics?
8. What ethical considerations need to be taken into account when sharing knowledge in virtual communities in the metaverse, and how can they be addressed to ensure responsible and ethical knowledge sharing practices?
9. How can we ensure that users have a positive and inclusive experience in virtual communities in the metaverse, and prevent discrimination or exclusion based on factors such as race, gender, or socio-economic status?

10. What are the potential ethical implications of knowledge sharing in the metaverse, and how can we ensure that users' privacy and data are protected?

REFERENCES

Ahn, S., Kim, J., & Kim, J. (2022). The Bifold Triadic Relationships Framework: A Theoretical Primer for Advertising Research in the Metaverse. *Journal of Advertising*, *51*(5), 592–607. doi:10.1080/00913367.2022.2111729

Alpala, L., Quiroga-Parra, D., Torres, J., & Peluffo-Ordóñez, D. (2022). Smart Factory Using Virtual Reality and Online Multi-User: Towards a Metaverse for Experimental Frameworks. *Applied Sciences (Basel, Switzerland)*, *12*(12), 6258. doi:10.3390/app12126258

Awasthi, S., Ahuja, R., & Sharma, S. (2022). Leadership and Emotional Intelligence: A Comparative Study. In D. Bathla & A. Singh (Eds.), *Applying Metalytics to Measure Customer Experience in the Metaverse* (pp. 99–110). IGI Global. doi:10.4018/978-1-6684-6133-4.ch009

Baghalzadeh Shishehgarkhaneh, M., Keivani, A., Moehler, R., Jelodari, N., & Roshdi Laleh, S. (2022). Internet of Things (IoT), Building Information Modeling (BIM), and Digital Twin (DT) in Construction Industry: A Review, Bibliometric, and Network Analysis. *Buildings*, *12*(10), 1503. doi:10.3390/buildings12101503

Batat, W., & Hammedi, W. (2022). The extended reality technology (ERT) framework for designing customer and service experiences in phygital settings: a service research agenda. *Journal of Service Management*. doi:10.1108/JOSM-08-2022-0289

Bibri, S. (2022). The Social Shaping of the Metaverse as an Alternative to the Imaginaries of Data-Driven Smart Cities: A Study in Science, Technology, and Society. *Smart Cities*, *5*(3), 832–874. doi:10.3390martcities5030043

Buhalis, D., O'Connor, P., & Leung, R. (2023). Smart hospitality: From smart cities and smart tourism towards agile business ecosystems in networked destinations. *International Journal of Contemporary Hospitality Management*, *35*(1), 369–393. doi:10.1108/IJCHM-04-2022-0497

Cappannari, L., & Vitillo, A. (2022). XR and Metaverse Software Platforms. In Roadmapping Extended Reality (pp. 135-156). doi:10.1002/9781119865810.ch6

Chen, Q., & Lee, S. (2021). Research Status and Trend of Digital Twin: Visual Knowledge Mapping Analysis. *International Journal of Advanced Smart Convergence*, *10*(4), 84–97. doi:10.7236/IJASC.2021.10.4.84

Dahan, N., Al-Razgan, M., Al-Laith, A., Alsoufi, M., Al-Asaly, M., & Alfakih, T. (2022). Metaverse Framework: A Case Study on E-Learning Environment (ELEM). *Electronics (Basel)*, *11*(10), 1616. doi:10.3390/electronics11101616

Dai, Y., Wang, J., & Gao, S. (2022). Advanced Electronics and Artificial Intelligence: Must-Have Technologies Toward Human Body Digital Twins. *Advanced Intelligent Systems*, *4*(7), 2100263. doi:10.1002/aisy.202100263

De Ketelaere, B., Smeets, B., Verboven, P., Nicolaï, B., & Saeys, W. (2022). Digital twins in quality engineering. *Quality Engineering*, *34*(3), 404–408. doi:10.1080/08982112.2022.2052731

Dubey, R., Gupta, M., Mikalef, P., & Akter, S. (2022). Incorporating blockchain technology in information systems research. *International Journal of Information Management*, *102573*. Advance online publication. doi:10.1016/j.ijinfomgt.2022.102573

Dwivedi, Y., Hughes, L., Baabdullah, A., Ribeiro-Navarrete, S., Giannakis, M., Al-Debei, M., Dennehy, D., Metri, B., Buhalis, D., Cheung, C. M. K., Conboy, K., Doyle, R., Dubey, R., Dutot, V., Felix, R., Goyal, D. P., Gustafsson, A., Hinsch, C., Jebabli, I., ... Wamba, S. (2022). Metaverse beyond the hype: Multidisciplinary perspectives on emerging challenges, opportunities, and agenda for research, practice and policy. *International Journal of Information Management*, *66*, 102542. doi:10.1016/j.ijinfomgt.2022.102542

Eom, S. (2022). The Emerging Digital Twin Bureaucracy in the 21st Century. *Perspectives on Public Management and Governance*, *5*(2), 174–186. doi:10.1093/ppmgov/gvac005

Faraboschi, P., Frachtenberg, E., Laplante, P., Milojicic, D., & Saracco, R. (2022). Virtual Worlds (Metaverse): From Skepticism, to Fear, to Immersive Opportunities. *Computer*, *55*(10), 100–106. doi:10.1109/MC.2022.3192702

Hariharan, A., Risling, M., Felic, A., & Ostertag, T. (2023). *Integration of Smart Glasses for Knowledge Transfer in Industrial Remote Maintenance: Learnings from Practice.* Paper presented at the Extended Reality and Metaverse, Cham, Switzerland.

Harisanty, D., Anna, N., Putri, T., Firdaus, A., & Noor Azizi, N. (2022). Leaders, practitioners and scientists' awareness of artificial intelligence in libraries: a pilot study. *Library Hi Tech*. doi:10.1108/LHT-10-2021-0356

Hassani, H., Huang, X., & MacFeely, S. (2022). Impactful Digital Twin in the Healthcare Revolution. *Big Data and Cognitive Computing*, *6*(3), 83. doi:10.3390/bdcc6030083

Huynh-The, T., Pham, Q., Pham, X., Nguyen, T., Han, Z., & Kim, D. (2023). Artificial intelligence for the metaverse: A survey. *Engineering Applications of Artificial Intelligence*, *117*, 105581. doi:10.1016/j.engappai.2022.105581

Hwang, Y. (2023). When makers meet the metaverse: Effects of creating NFT metaverse exhibition in maker education. *Computers & Education*, *194*, 104693. doi:10.1016/j.compedu.2022.104693

Inder, S. (2023). Entrepreneurial Opportunities in Metaverse. In M. Gupta, P. Jindal, & S. Bansal (Eds.), *Promoting Consumer Engagement Through Emotional Branding and Sensory Marketing* (pp. 52–62). IGI Global.

Jamil, S., Rahman, M., & Fawad, M. (2022). A Comprehensive Survey of Digital Twins and Federated Learning for Industrial Internet of Things (IIoT), Internet of Vehicles (IoV) and Internet of Drones (IoD). *Applied System Innovation*, *5*(3), 56. doi:10.3390/asi5030056

Jeon, J. (2023). The impact of XR applications' user experience-based design innovativeness on loyalty. *Cogent Business & Management*, *10*(1), 2161761. doi:10.1080/23311975.2022.2161761

Jin, J., Xu, H., & Leng, B. (2022). Adaptive Points Sampling for Implicit Field Reconstruction of Industrial Digital Twin. *Sensors (Basel), 22*(17), 6630. doi:10.339022176630 PMID:36081088

Julian, H., Chung, T., & Wang, Y. (2023). Adoption of Metaverse in South East Asia: Vietnam, Indonesia, Malaysia. In P. C. Lai (Ed.), *Strategies and Opportunities for Technology in the Metaverse World* (pp. 196–234). IGI Global. doi:10.4018/978-1-6684-5732-0.ch012

Keshmiri Neghab, H., Jamshidi, M., & Keshmiri Neghab, H. (2022). Digital Twin of a Magnetic Medical Microrobot with Stochastic Model Predictive Controller Boosted by Machine Learning in Cyber-Physical Healthcare Systems. *Information (Basel), 13*(7), 321. doi:10.3390/info13070321

Kesselman, M., & Esquivel, W. (2022). Technology on the move, Consumer Electronics Show 2022: The evolving metaverse and much more. *Library Hi Tech News, 39*(5), 1–4. doi:10.1108/LHTN-03-2022-0038

Kraus, S., Kumar, S., Lim, W., Kaur, J., Sharma, A., & Schiavone, F. (2023). From moon landing to metaverse: Tracing the evolution of Technological Forecasting and Social Change. *Technological Forecasting and Social Change, 189*, 122381. doi:10.1016/j.techfore.2023.122381

Kwanya, T., Stilwell, C., & Underwood, P. (2012). Intelligent libraries and apomediators: Distinguishing between Library 3.0 and Library 2.0. *Journal of Librarianship and Information Science, 45*(3), 187–197. doi:10.1177/0961000611435256

Maddahi, Y., & Chen, S. (2022). Applications of Digital Twins in the Healthcare Industry: Case Review of an IoT-Enabled Remote Technology in Dentistry. *Virtual Worlds, 1*(1), 20–41. doi:10.3390/virtualworlds1010003

Mourtzis, D., Angelopoulos, J., & Panopoulos, N. (2023). Blockchain Integration in the Era of Industrial Metaverse. *Applied Sciences (Basel, Switzerland), 13*(3), 1353. doi:10.3390/app13031353

Mystakidis, S. (2023). Sustainable Engagement in Open and Distance Learning With Play and Games in Virtual Reality: Playful and Gameful Distance Education in VR. In I. R. Management Association (Ed.), Research Anthology on Virtual Environments and Building the Metaverse (pp. 297-312). IGI Global.

Njoku, J., Nwakanma, C., Amaizu, G., & Kim, D. (2022). Prospects and challenges of Metaverse application in data-driven intelligent transportation systems. *IET Intelligent Transport Systems*. doi:10.1049/itr2.12252

Pamucar, D., Deveci, M., Gokasar, I., Tavana, M., & Köppen, M. (2022). A metaverse assessment model for sustainable transportation using ordinal priority approach and Aczel-Alsina norms. *Technological Forecasting and Social Change, 182*, 121778. doi:10.1016/j.techfore.2022.121778

Park, S., & Kim, Y. (2022). A Metaverse: Taxonomy, Components, Applications, and Open Challenges. *IEEE Access : Practical Innovations, Open Solutions, 10*, 4209–4251. doi:10.1109/ACCESS.2021.3140175

Popescu, D., Dragomir, M., Popescu, S., & Dragomir, D. (2022). Building Better Digital Twins for Production Systems by Incorporating Environmental Related Functions—Literature Analysis and Determining Alternatives. *Applied Sciences (Basel, Switzerland), 12*(17), 8657. doi:10.3390/app12178657

Qamar, S., Anwar, Z., & Afzal, M. (2023). A systematic threat analysis and defense strategies for the metaverse and extended reality systems. *Computers & Security, 128*, 103127. doi:10.1016/j.cose.2023.103127

Rahaman, T. (2022). Into the Metaverse – Perspectives on a New Reality. *Medical Reference Services Quarterly*, *41*(3), 330–337. doi:10.1080/02763869.2022.2096341 PMID:35980623

Sanji, M., Behzadi, H., & Gomroki, G. (2022). Chatbot: An intelligent tool for libraries. *Library Hi Tech News*, *39*(3), 17–20. doi:10.1108/LHTN-01-2021-0002

Şarlıoğlu, G., Boyacı, E., & Akca, M. (2023). Information and Communication Technologies in Logistics and Supply Chain Management in Turkey: Human Resource Practices and New Challenges. In N. Sharma & K. Shalender (Eds.), *Managing Technology Integration for Human Resources in Industry 5.0* (pp. 174–197). IGI Global. doi:10.4018/978-1-6684-6745-9.ch011

Shen, B., Tan, W., Guo, J., Zhao, L., & Qin, P. (2021). How to Promote User Purchase in Metaverse? A Systematic Literature Review on Consumer Behavior Research and Virtual Commerce Application Design. *Applied Sciences (Basel, Switzerland)*, *11*(23), 11087. doi:10.3390/app112311087

Siyaev, A., & Jo, G. (2021). Towards Aircraft Maintenance Metaverse Using Speech Interactions with Virtual Objects in Mixed Reality. *Sensors (Basel)*, *21*(6), 2066. doi:10.339021062066 PMID:33804253

Tait, E., & Pierson, C. (2022). Artificial Intelligence and Robots in Libraries: Opportunities in LIS Curriculum for Preparing the Librarians of Tomorrow. *Journal of the Australian Library and Information Association*, *71*(3), 256–274. doi:10.1080/24750158.2022.2081111

Teubner, T., & Camacho, S. (2023). Facing Reciprocity: How Photos and Avatars Promote Interaction in Micro-communities. *Group Decision and Negotiation*. Advance online publication. doi:10.100710726-023-09814-4

Tlili, A., Huang, R., Shehata, B., Liu, D., Zhao, J., Metwally, A., Wang, H., Denden, M., Bozkurt, A., Lee, L.-H., Beyoglu, D., Altinay, F., Sharma, R. C., Altinay, Z., Li, Z., Liu, J., Ahmad, F., Hu, Y., Salha, S., ... Burgos, D. (2022). Is Metaverse in education a blessing or a curse: A combined content and bibliometric analysis. *Smart Learning Environments*, *9*(1), 24. doi:10.118640561-022-00205-x

Tromp, J. (2022). Extended Reality & The Backbone: Towards a 3D Mirrorworld. In Roadmapping Extended Reality (pp. 193-227). Academic Press.

Weking, J., Desouza, K., Fielt, E., & Kowalkiewicz, M. (2023). Metaverse-enabled entrepreneurship. *Journal of Business Venturing Insights*, *19*, e00375. doi:10.1016/j.jbvi.2023.e00375

Xiong, M., & Wang, H. (2022). Digital twin applications in aviation industry: A review. *International Journal of Advanced Manufacturing Technology*, *121*(9), 5677–5692. doi:10.100700170-022-09717-9

Yang, C., Tu, X., Autiosalo, J., Ala-Laurinaho, R., Mattila, J., Salminen, P., & Tammi, K. (2022). Extended Reality Application Framework for a Digital-Twin-Based Smart Crane. *Applied Sciences (Basel, Switzerland)*, *12*(12), 6030. doi:10.3390/app12126030

Yu, J. (2022). Exploration of Educational Possibilities by Four Metaverse Types in Physical Education. *Technologies*, *10*(5), 104. doi:10.3390/technologies10050104

Zhang, Z., Wen, F., Sun, Z., Guo, X., He, T., & Lee, C. (2022). Artificial Intelligence-Enabled Sensing Technologies in the 5G/Internet of Things Era: From Virtual Reality/Augmented Reality to the Digital Twin. *Advanced Intelligent Systems*, *4*(7), 2100228. doi:10.1002/aisy.202100228

Chapter 9
Strategic Management of Digital Transformation Processes in the Aviation Industry: Case of Istanbul Airport

Filiz Mızrak
Istanbul Medipol University, Turkey

Gonca Reyhan Akkartal
Istanbul Medipol University, Turkey

EXECUTIVE SUMMARY

The Fourth Industrial Revolution has profoundly affected all sectors, quickly leading to significant technological changes. This new revolution has also affected aviation systems that have a direct connection with technology. This revolution has brought about rapid changes especially in airport systems and led to the emergence of the concept of "smart airport." In this study, the case of Istanbul Airport has been analyzed in terms of digital transformation in order to exemplify the digital applications in an airport. In this scope, the aim of the study is to present a new projection, integrated with a digital business strategy, to businesses operating in the airline industry, where they can successfully realize the digital transformation process and manage this process strategically.

INTRODUCTION

The rapid development of digital technologies changes paradigms in the business world as well as in daily life. Developments in digital technologies in recent years have led businesses to keep up with this process. Cloud technology, big data, artificial intelligence, virtual reality, and other innovative approaches and developments with digital technologies point to the necessity of realizing digital transformation in the entire world economy and businesses. The introduction of the internet, which rapidly has changed the world, and human and business habits, has also introduced the concept of

DOI: 10.4018/978-1-6684-5859-4.ch009

digitalization into our lives. This situation continues with the development of the internet and the digital technologies that developed afterward. These developments in technology and communication require businesses to keep up with the rapid flow. Businesses must realize digital transformation and adapt to their processes in today's digital age (Matt, Hess & Benlian, 2015). Digital transformation directly affects the decision-making mechanisms, production and design processes, services they provide to their customers, organizational structures, finance, and cost structures. In a market where competition is intense and globalization is increasing, it causes businesses to make radical decisions and transitions (Mitroulis & Kitsios, 2019).

Like in many sectors, an effective digital strategy is critical to long-term success in the aviation industry today. Thanks to digital technology, companies can both stay ahead of their competitors and innovate to improve their existing business models. Digitization is transforming the expectations of consumers around the world. To improve customer interaction with digitalization, they need to re-evaluate and transform the customer experience by using and adapting to new products, applications, and tools (Richards, Seidakhmetov & Zhunussova, 2020).

Businesses that are in the process of digital transformation and that have achieved a certain amount of digitalization are faced with great risks if they cannot adapt their processes to the rapidly developing technology and cannot achieve continuity. Digital transformation can create both new opportunities and threats if the process is not well-managed for companies from all fields, regardless of the sector. According to Chanias, Myers & Hess (2019), relatively new businesses that embrace the essence of the business in their digital transformation journey will quickly outgrow their traditional competitors by applying the right strategies. In this context, the digital transformation process requires good planning and strategic management of the process. Digital transformation requires comprehensive analysis and strategic vision. Not only technology but also consumer behavior is changing rapidly. The best way to survive, progress and grow in the market with these factors is to adopt a vision of an innovative and flexible approach (Matt, Hess & Benlian, 2015). In today's world where globalization has reached its peak, businesses that can determine the needs of consumers who are hesitant about their needs and desires and the stack of information obtained in every channel and that can offer the right solutions to these needs will be preferred in the competition (Chanias, Myers & Hess, 2019).

The rapid growth in air transport creates a demand above the capacity in many airports, and as a result, the need for a reconsideration of airport policies arises. While 90% of aviation activities take place on the ground, that is, at airports, only 10% take place in the air. With the use of large aircraft, the rate of increase in the number of aircraft landings and departures decreases very slowly, while passenger and cargo traffic increase rapidly. On the other hand, rapid developments in technology have led to significant changes in the aviation industry. This change is expressed as Industry 4.0 and digital transformation. As a reflection of this change, the concept of "smart airport" has emerged for airports, which is an important element of the aviation industry. Although the technology turnover rate is the highest in the aviation sector compared to other sectors, airports need to adapt to these technological changes for their sustainability (Narongou & Sun, 2021).

Digital transformation refers to a comprehensive transformation from the operational activities of enterprises to business models, from organizational structure to customer relations. To manage this transformation process well and reduce the risk of failure, businesses need a digital business strategy in which they will determine their roadmaps within plan and control (Hájnik, Harantová & Kalašová, 2021).

In this scope, this study aims to present a new projection integrated with a digital business strategy, where businesses especially those operating in the aviation industry can successfully realize the digital transformation process and manage this process strategically. In the second part of the study after the introduction concept of knowledge management, digital transformation, process, and Industry 4.0 has been presented. Furthermore, the concept of smart airports has been defined and the digital applications in the airports have been exemplified. The case of Istanbul Airports has been analyzed and strategic management of the digital transformation process has been discussed in this part. In the conclusion part, suggestions to organizations in the aviation industry, especially airport operators have been made.

BACKGROUND

Concept of Knowledge Management

Knowledge management refers to the identification and use of collective knowledge within the organization to help organizations compete. Knowledge management is a business process that focuses on knowledge-related activities to facilitate the creation, acquisition, transformation, and use of corporate or collective knowledge to harness the intellectual capital of organizations to achieve organizational goals (De Bem Machado et al., 2022). Knowledge management should also be viewed as the critical management of knowledge to meet current and emerging needs, identify and use existing and acquired knowledge assets, and seize new opportunities. Knowledge management includes concerted, coordinated, and conscious efforts to manage the processes of knowledge creation, structuring, dissemination, and application to improve organizational performance and create value. Knowledge management is also based on the belief that significant organizational productivity improvements can be achieved through the retention and reuse of knowledge throughout the organization (Edwards, 2022).

Knowledge management is concerned with the use and development of knowledge assets to achieve the goals of the organization. It is a systematic and integrative process that involves the acquisition, creation, storage, dissemination, organization, and ultimately application of the knowledge necessary by individuals and groups to achieve organizational goals. Laurini (2021) argued that knowledge management is the process of identifying, growing, and effectively using an organization's existing knowledge to achieve organizational goals, as well as creating an organizational culture that allows more knowledge to be created. According to Cheng et al. (2023), knowledge management is an organizational capability that allows members to create, capture, share, and use their collective knowledge to improve their performance. Organizations that are successful in knowledge management are likely to view knowledge as an asset and develop organizational norms and values that support knowledge creation and sharing. Nwankpa, Roumani & Datta (2022) define knowledge management as a management function that creates knowledge, manages the flow of information within the organization, and ensures that knowledge is used effectively and efficiently for the long-term benefit of the organization.

Knowledge management involves the identification and analysis of available and required knowledge, and then the planning and control of actions to develop knowledge assets to meet organizational goals. Information assets are information about markets, products, technologies, and organizations that a business has or should have, and that enable business processes to generate profits. Knowledge management is not only about managing these information assets but also managing the processes that are effective in information assets (Karasneh, 2022). For effective knowledge management, it is essential to identify which knowledge processes represent unique and valuable capabilities (Paoloni et al., 2020). Knowledge management is largely seen as a process that includes various activities. Although there is no consensus about the components or stages of knowledge management, researchers generally draw attention to three basic components of knowledge management: knowledge acquisition, sharing, and application (Zaim et al., 2007; Obeidat et al., 2016; Chiu and Chen, 2016).

Acquiring knowledge can be defined as the process of developing and creating insights, skills, and relationships (Obeidat et al., 2016). Knowledge acquisition is about both finding knowledge and creating new knowledge from the interaction between new knowledge and previous knowledge. Information acquisition is seen as a dynamic process for capturing and examining valuable information about the organization for strategic success of the organization. Information acquisition is the interaction process of people, technology, and resources inside and outside the organization and facilitates organizations to create new skills and competencies and increase their existing knowledge stock (Chiu and Chen, 2016).

Knowledge sharing is the process in which the sharing and dissemination of information is encouraged, and the members of the organization can access the information they need from more than one source, and these sources are somehow integrated. Knowledge sharing means the dissemination and exchange of knowledge, skills, and expertise among organizational members or units. It is the information-sharing process related to the transformation or output stage, which includes the dissemination, storage, coding, and documentation of information. Knowledge sharing is the most important aspect of knowledge management that enables members of the organization to exchange their knowledge and contributes to the application of knowledge, innovation, and ultimately the competitive advantage of the organization (Zaim et al., 2007).

Knowledge application means making knowledge more active and appropriate in the organization to create values. It is the application of knowledge considered as the output aspect of knowledge management. This stage is defined as the way information is used within the organization (Song, Van Der Bij & Weggeman, 2005). Gao, Li & Clarke (2008) defined information application as business processes through which effective storage and retrieval mechanisms enable an organization to access information easily. The implementation process is about using information for organizational functions or business processes to carry out activities with visible results such as products, services, procedures, and regulations (Obeidat et al., 2016). The application of knowledge has also been recognized as a resource for organizations to achieve sustainable competitive advantage by improving performance, developing new products or services, improving quality, responding to market change, and reducing costs (Song, Van Der Bij & Weggeman, 2005).

Knowledge management supports the innovation ability of the organization, the production of new ideas increases the thinking capacity of the organization and ensures that this capacity is used to the fullest. It is a process that includes the transformation of organizational experiences into knowledge, who should do what, where, when, and how. Knowledge management provides easy access to formally recorded and explicit or implicit specialist knowledge. Knowledge management also provides collaboration, knowledge sharing, continuous learning, and development. This means that intellectual assets contribute to better quality and effective decision-making. Knowledge management aims to develop business processes in a planned and structured way for the benefit of customers. Effective knowledge management provides individuals and groups within the organization with opportunities to create, obtain and share knowledge. The innovation process includes acquiring, disseminating, and using new knowledge. Therefore, knowledge management is an undeniable building block for sustainable innovation (Migdadi, 2022).

It is thought that the knowledge management system improves the innovation process by providing faster access to new information (Du Plessis,2007). Knowledge acquisition, defined as the process of using existing knowledge or acquiring new knowledge, increases the organization's ability to achieve its goals efficiently, as well as organizational learning. According to Lai et al. (2014), knowledge is both learned and used for business development and innovation. Obtaining knowledge from the external market and internal employees provides organizations with opportunities to recombine existing knowledge and create new knowledge. Knowledge and diversity resulting from knowledge help organizational members communicate with each other and encourage innovation. Newly acquired knowledge interacting with existing knowledge increases the stocks of knowledge available to organizations, reduces uncertainty, and opens up new opportunities for both the application and use of knowledge. Thus, knowledge management encourages the creation of innovative results (Migdadi, 2022).

Analysis of Digital Transformation

The concepts of digital transformation and Industry 4.0 should be considered together. The new technologies that entered our lives with Industry 4.0 have caused many changes in our lives and ways of doing business, such as the technological developments that have been experienced before. New technologies that enter our lives bring the need for transformation with the most appropriate strategies to ensure digitalization, competitiveness, survival, and sustainability in businesses. This can be briefly called digital transformation. Industry 4.0 can be expressed as the integration of information and communication technologies (ICT) with production systems. In addition, Industry 4.0 is to develop and integrate information technologies into sectors with digitalization. The main goal is to enable them to maintain organizational processes more effectively (Tabrizi et al., 2019).

Digital transformation is a holistic transformation that takes place with human, business processes, and technology elements to serve and benefit organizations more effectively and efficiently (Fletcher & Griffiths, 2020). With the implementation of new digital technologies, market and competitive conditions are changing and existing business models may remain idle. Digital transformation radically changes conventional thoughts and attitudes, and these changes can have positive or negative consequences for businesses. It would be wrong to describe digital transformation as mere technology. It is possible to describe digital transformation as a philosophy that affects end-to-end business processes and organizational structures (Gong & Ribiere, 2021).

Digitalization has become effective primarily with the management of information in business processes with software systems. Afterward, with the developing internet network, these software system processes developed further and led to a change in the business models of the enterprises. When these changes were integrated into the organizations of the enterprises, the Industry 4.0 period started, and this period caused a transformation in the business processes, business models, and organizational structures of the enterprises. For this reason, this process has begun to be called digital transformation (Zaoui & Souissi, 2020). According to another source, digital transformation is developing new business models by using new digital technologies (IoT, artificial intelligence, social platforms, data analysis, etc.) to provide solutions to new customer needs with the changing customer habits of businesses and to gain an advantage over their competitors in the fiercely competitive environment in the market. For this, it means that businesses carry out all kinds of organizational and structural reforms to ensure competition (Lasi et al., 2014).

With digital transformation applications, industries such as goods and services or production styles are also changing. While products that were not in our lives before are now becoming a part of our lives, some products are ending their lives. However, it also causes radical changes in working life. The transition from traditional methods to new ways of working also affects businesses. Although all these changes have important advantages for humanity, there are some difficulties in the digital transformation process (Kraus et al., 2021).

With the fourth industrial revolution, it is possible to carry out production and activities more flexibly, quickly, and cost-effectively in factories established with intelligent systems. In real-time, instant, customer-specific, personalized products can be launched quickly. Another advantage and necessity of digital transformation have been understood even more during the pandemic period. Businesses have found the opportunity to carry out their business with remote working models regardless of location. This has provided a financial advantage to businesses that incorporate digital technologies into their processes and are prepared for the remote working model. Digitization and smartening of production processes is the need of today's industry. The manufacturing industry is currently transitioning from mass production to customized production. Rapid developments in production technologies and applications in industries help to increase productivity. Industry 4.0 is defined as a new level of organization and control over the entire value chain of the life cycle of products (Lasi et al., 2014). In this way, businesses can make their products and services more targeted and more accurate according to the needs of their customers with digital transformation. When digital transformation is fully implemented in businesses, the structuring process will begin in many sectors. By making the systems smart, businesses will be able to maintain competitive and profitable cooperation in the market. New investment areas will be created (Leão & da Silva, 2021).

It is possible to summarize some of the advantages of Industry 4.0 as follows. With Industry 4.0, it is possible to make predictive analyzes to diagnose possible faults in systems in advance. With Industry 4.0, there is self-awareness of systems and their components. Industry 4.0 includes environmentally friendly practices and is suitable for a sustainable structure. With Industry 4.0, high efficiency can be achieved in business processes. With Industry 4.0, a fast and flexible structure to customer demands is possible. With Industry 4.0, unnecessary costs can be eliminated, and cost advantage can be achieved. Thanks to the flexible structure of Industry 4.0, new ways of doing business and models can be developed. With Industry 4.0, new professions will be created. With Industry 4.0, there will be more ergonomic, business and production processes. In addition, with the introduction of smart systems and robots into business life, the risks that may occur in occupational health and safety are minimized (Adamik & Nowicki, 2018).

Concept of Smart Airports

"Smart airport" is a term that refers to the smart infrastructure of an airport. It is derived from the concepts of "smart cities", "smart buildings" and "smart factories". Global smart airport infrastructure is segmented into endpoint devices that include communication systems, passenger, cargo, and baggage handling, air traffic control systems, security systems, and others. Endpoint devices are further divided into sensors, tags, IP phones, and video conferencing (Alghadeir & Sakran, 2016).

The global smart airport market is dominated by key companies such as IBM Corporation, Cisco, and Siemens AG. Other companies such as Raytheon, Amadeus IT Grou,p, and QinetiQ are also defined as emerging companies in the market. Companies such as Honeywell and SITA are among the companies that have a strong position and promise for growth in the smart airport market. These leading companies are currently focusing on integrating products to build a new customer base and engaging in strategic partnerships and acquisitions as part of this strategy (Narongou & Sun, 2021).

Smart airport applications include self-service kiosks, self-boarding, autonomous vehicles, digital processing of vouchers, smart wearables, biometric services, RFID baggage tags, automated baggage delivery, lost property kiosks, advanced analytics in baggage handling, smart doors, personnel planning, and scheduling, etc.

Self Service Kiosks

Self-service check-in kiosks are computer terminals that eliminate the need for ground personnel for passenger check-in. Previously, airlines used special kiosks only for their passengers. Today, kiosks serve the check-in applications of more than one airline. Kiosks serving the check-in application of more than one airline provide many benefits, with the use of these kiosks, airports benefit from limited space usage. Airlines eliminate capital expenditures because they purchase these services directly from a ground-handling agent. Ground handling agents reduce operating costs by employing less ground personnel in passenger control, and they save time as passengers can use any kiosk instead of searching for kiosks belonging to the airline company. Ground handling agents set up self-service check-in and support their staff to encourage travelers to use self-service check-in kiosks on the land side of the entrance areas (Mohamed, Gomaa & El-Sherif, 2018).

Self-Boarding

Express boarding gates allow passengers to scan the boarding pass at the gate themselves. After the boarding pass is verified, the doors are released, and the passenger can proceed to the plane. In this application, ground personnel are not included in passenger boarding and are responsible for responding to inspection duties or special situations. This helps to reduce the need for ground personnel so ground handling agents can further reduce operating costs. Current literature suggests that personal management positively impacts customer satisfaction because it significantly reduces door-to-door processing times. Express boarding gates also record a variety of operational data that can provide further insight into customer behavior or the effectiveness of the boarding process, such as processing times by flight and gate, passenger groups using boarding gates, and passenger distribution over time (Zamorano, Fernández-Laso & de Esteban Curiel, 2020)

Autonomous Vehicles

Recent articles report some applications of autonomous, self-driving GSE vehicles. Advanced applications of autonomous driving technologies in automobiles, trucks, public transportation, and industrial and military services have also been reported. There are no articles written so far about self-driving vehicles in airport terminals. However, it is believed that the provision of self-driving cars within the airport terminal could open new possibilities in the special assistance of passengers with reduced mobility. Currently, ground personnel uses shuttles or wheelchairs to transport these passengers. It is believed that it will reduce the amount of ground personnel working by using electrically powered wheelchairs or shuttles with manual and visual control systems (Hájnik, Harantová & Kalašová, 2021).

Digital Processing of Vouchers

In the aviation industry, this term is used to mean free cash coupons for meals, hotel accommodation, and airport transfers, provided to passengers by an airline company in the event of a flight delay. Vouchers are often personalized. Usually, airlines come to a pre-existing agreement with certain hotels regarding accommodation and fares. Vouchers for meals are in many cases offered to multiple vendors and usually contain maximum cashback value. Some vendors accepting these vouchers in bulk are using electronic data processing to save airlines from this process. Businesses that do not receive many vouchers or use an electronic system often physically mail the vouchers to the airline or ground handling agent to receive payment. The digital transactions of vouchers are believed to significantly reduce transaction costs for service providers, airlines, and ground-handling agents. Vouchers related to service failure and customer satisfaction after recovery have been studied extensively in the literature. However, so far there are no publications describing the digital processing of vouchers (Kovynyov & Mikut, 2019).

Wearable Technology

Wearable technology is defined as devices connected to the same network that can respond to user requests and behaviors with the data they obtain. Although its popularity has increased with smartphones and watches, its usage area has expanded much more today. When it comes to smart bracelets, implants, smart glasses, and smart clothes, it is possible to see many applications in the fields of technology, health, fashion, and aviation (Dulhare & Rasool, 2022).

All these devices aim to create technologies that instantly respond to people's wishes and needs, improve current conditions, provide control to the user, and make life easier and follo,w these requests and changes instantly. The concept of wearable means accessories, clothes, etc. that can be easily worn on the body. corresponds to smart devices that represent the country in other words, it is all the computer technologies included in the items that can be worn comfortably on a body (Ghazal, Haneefa & Sweleh, 2016).

Today, it is possible to see wearable technologies modernized and used in aviation safety, aviation maintenance, and aviation operations to prevent worker injuries and increase operational efficiency. In particular, the primary usage areas of these technologies have been maintenance operations. With smart glasses, it makes it possible to carry out work instructions without contact with aircraft surfaces. It also offers maintenance professionals the ability to remotely stream live video to answer questions and resolve potential issues faster. With wearable technology, whether with a headset or a smart device to be worn on the arm, information about the aircraft and its parts can be obtained more quickly and easily, allowing a more planned maintenance program both for the moment and afterward, and this can prevent the aircraft from staying on the ground. Thanks to this, maintenance times are shortened, and the average daily airtime of the aircraft can be increased (Kovynyov & Mikut, 2019).

The most common use of smart wearable devices is smartwatches. Smartwatches are miniature wrist-mounted computers and a set of sensors with timekeeping functionality and are widely used by passengers at airports. With a smartwatch, passengers can receive alerts about gate changes or flight delays and scan their boarding passes in case of being late. As the smartwatch is permanently worn on your wrist, the ground handling agent can use this channel to broadcast real-time information to send messages to passengers, voice announcements, and other mobile devices other than traditional visual display monitors (Baiyere, Salmela & Tapanainen, 2020).

Biometric Systems

Today, the application areas of biometric systems are increasing day by day. While the most well-known of these are seen as applications related to airport entry-exit points, credit card systems, and the detection of criminal crimes, today they are used in insurance transactions, e-signature applications, internet banking, many smart devices, home security systems, etc. With such applications, it is possible to verify the identity of the user with only his features such as fingerprint, iris, and face recognition, and access to relevant information or approval for processing can be provided (Goode, 2018). The use of biometric systems is becoming more and more common in the aviation industry. However, this is not a system that few airports and airlines can get involved in and run. Although this is possible, the biometrics of the passengers can be processed with a joint data-based study in which all stakeholders on a sectoral basis will participate and continue, for the desired cost benefit. Today, its use is increasing, especially at airport security and crossing points (Halpern et al., 2021).

RFID Luggage Tags

RFID tags radio frequency identification (RFID) technology enables remote identification and does not require a line of sight, unlike barcode technology. The benefits of RFID luggage tags are widely discussed in the current literature. RFID tags can reduce baggage tracking, baggage route during air transport, or the amount of baggage going the wrong route. In addition, RFID tags can contain additional data such as manufacturer, and product type, and even measure environmental factors such as temperature. RFID systems can identify tags in the same general area without human assistance. RFID tags embedded in barcode tags can eliminate the need for manual inspection and guidance by ground handling agents. Currently, RFID tags are placed on paper and then added to the trunk as paper tags (Mrňa, Badánik & Novák, 2021).

Self-labeling is one of the latest ideas for luggage tagging. Passengers can tag their luggage, print their luggage tags at home, and track their luggage with their smartphones. In this context, digital luggage tags are gaining more importance. Digital luggage tags are a digital alternative to traditional paper-based luggage tags. Luggage receives a permanent luggage tag displaying the digital barcode. If the flight plan has changed or the passenger has visited again, airlines or ground handling agents can change this barcode remotely. With a tracking device inside the luggage, passengers can monitor their luggage in real-time with a smartphone (Shehieb et al., 2016)

Automatic Baggage Delivery and Lost and Found Kiosks

With labels combined with printer printing or electronic luggage tags, fully automatic machines can be used to receive passenger-labeled luggage without any interaction with ground personnel or airline employees. Some airports have already installed automatic baggage drop machines. Lost and Found kiosks are self-service computer devices that report lost luggage. It connects to the global database for lost baggage and helps travelers report delayed or lost baggage on arrival. To report lost baggage, a passenger scans the boarding pass, identifies the missing item, and enters contact information for delivery on the date the baggage is found. Passengers can get the latest information on the report by accessing a website and entering the report numbers (Kovynyov & Mikut, 2019).

Advanced Analytics in Baggage Handling

Performance-based contracts between ground handling agents and airlines require reliable data on the speed and efficiency of baggage handling systems, such as the timely delivery of bags, processing times, and baggage handling accuracy. In addition, ground handling agents collect and maintain data on operational baggage flow, and develop simulations and models to understand the past behavior and performance of baggage handling systems (Kila, 2020).

Smart Doors

Most passengers use status-based or travel class access rather than membership. Passengers with a business class or first-class tickets are required to show their boarding pass when entering the lounge. Some card members may be granted access privileges to the halls. To enter the hall, cardholders must present their cards. Also, some passengers are allowed to bring guests. Ground handling agents need to know such regulations for various airlines and lounge clubs. Additionally, lounge staff must be able to enforce these rules promptly when a particular passenger tries to enter a lounge. The access port connects to a backend application that contains the rule page. When a passenger passes or scans the boarding pass, the application applies the rule page and decides whether the passenger can reach the lounge (Lykou, Anagnostopoulou & Gritzalis, 2018).

Personnel Planning and Scheduling

Automation of personnel scheduling is a top priority for any ground handling agency, as labor costs in airport ground operations account for 60 to 80 percent of the total cost. Automated central planning in personnel planning and scheduling is the most common approach reported in the literature. This approach is based on previous demand modeling and a gradual reduction of planning understanding. Usually, the planning process starts six months in advance using the flight schedule for the next season. Total flight plan estimation is done through the production management system and can only be the distribution of flights by months, airlines, and destinations. It is used for total flight plan forecasting, vacation planning, and strategic workforce planning. Two months in advance, the total forecast is converted into a detailed flight schedule forecast. According to detailed estimates, the shift plan is compiled. The change plan is the result of the balancing demand measured against the available workforce in the flight plan forecast. The shift plan includes the distribution of different daily shifts throughout the month and the skills necessary to perform these shifts. Shift scheduling is usually accomplished using a dedicated scheduling application. Next, the shift plan is converted into a listing plan (Seo, Choi & Lee, 2012).

The staffing plan assigns employees to specific shifts and is prepared at least two weeks before their application. The staffing plan is usually completed using a time and attendance system. Low condensation is a strategy in which air traffic between peak and off-peak times is programmed to distribute traffic more evenly throughout the day. Traditional planning approaches do not include condensation by default. Ground handling agents operating at hub airports have added additional speed-reducing strategies to their planning procedures. The duty schedule assigns specific tasks to shifts. Typically, the task schedule is created using a dedicated real-time application that has the capacity to deliver it to employees' hands (Kovynyov & Mikut, 2019).

Management Process

Integrated KPI reporting shows a summary of the ratios ground handling agents use to measure and monitor corporate performance. These ratios are designed for key areas of interest, including operations, finance, human resources, safety, and quality. Calculating these rates requires a clever combination of information from multiple sources, such as the time and attendance system, the last hours of operation, and the number of flights and passengers retained in the production management system. Similarly, financial ratios require data from the payroll system, the enterprise resource planning (ERP) system, and the production management system. All rates should be calculated automatically and given to the management on a daily basis. As a result, ground-handling agents are investing in the consolidation, standardization, and active management of data pockets that provide such information. Advanced analytics and big data technologies provide the opportunity to gain more business insight (Narongou & Sun, 2021).

GSE Management

Ground support equipment (GSE) is usually located on the ramp. The GSE consists of a refueling truck, container loader, watercraft, ground power unit, air supply unit, sink service truck, catering truck, passenger boarding stairs, coaches, push vehicles, de-icing vehicles, containers, dolly, cargo pallets, and others. Automatic GSE scheduling is one of the most common applications in this field. It minimizes the total number of GSE agents required to handle flights and, as a result, reduces the ground handling agent's capital expenditure. Recent literature describes advanced scheduling methods for GSE tools and defrosting tools. Advanced programming and routing algorithms minimize general apron traffic and lower ground handling agents' fuel costs. Ground handling agents use GPS localization and tracking of GSE vehicles for planning and forecasting to collect data on effective usage (Fei, 2022).

THE CASE OF ISTANBUL AIRPORT

Istanbul New Airport is the largest infrastructure investment project in the history of the Republic of Turkey, with an estimated investment cost of 10.25 billion Euros. The airport was built on an area of 76.5 million square meters in the northern part of the European side of the city of Istanbul, where urban development and sprawl are relatively weak, 35 km from the city center (Tanrıverdi & Lezki, 2021).

In Istanbul Airport, there are 6 independent runways, 16 taxiways, 280 smart passenger bridges, 500 aircraft parking capacity, suitable for the operation of all types of aircraft, 3 separate terminal buildings, 3 technical blocks and air traffic control towers, a total of 4.5 million square meters of apron, lounge, cargo and general aviation terminal, state guest house, indoor and outdoor car park with a capacity of approximately 70,000 vehicles, health centers, hotels, fire station and garage center, and a cargo terminal building. It is expected to be the largest airport in the world with its auxiliary facilities such as maintenance hangars, in-flight catering facilities, airport support unit buildings, places of worship, power plants, and garbage disposal facilities (Meydan, 2023).

Istanbul Airport is planned to reach 200 million passenger capacity by 2033. It is approximately 110 million more than Hartsfield-Jackson Atlanta International Airport (ATL), which is the busiest airport in the world today, with 90 million passengers per year. This comparison shows to what extent Istanbul Airport represents a logistics and commercial claim in terms of capacity. The average passenger traffic of London Heathrow (LHR), which is Europe's largest transfer/transfer center airport in terms of passenger traffic, for the last ten years is 69.5 million. In this respect, Istanbul New Airport is a standard setter in its field with the potential offered by its infrastructure (Meydan, 2023).

Manuals prepared by international civil aviation and other authorized institutions on Smart Airport, industry 4.0, digital transformation, books, theses, scientific articles, periodicals, and reports obtained as a result of the literature review were evaluated qualitatively. As a result of the qualitative evaluation, an evaluation form including smart airport applications was prepared. Below is the list of digital applications used in Istanbul Airport;

- Smart Payment
- Intelligent Routing
- Self-Boarding
- Fingerprint Usage
- Smart Displays
- Face Scanning System
- Intelligent Boarding Gates
- Sensor Systems
- Self-check-in points
- Airport Mobile Applications
- Quick Pass
- Free Internet
- Lost and Found Software
- NFC Technology
- Live Support Kiosks
- Virtual Towers
- Virtual Assistants
- Lost Baggage Tracking System
- Smart Lighting
- Eco-Friendly Buildings

- Smart Tower
- Weather, Sound, and Light Tracking Sensors
- Intelligent Disaster Planning
- Security Analysis with Artificial Intelligence
- Smart Parking
- Personalized Routing
- Central Operations Management Platform
- Advanced Network Architecture
- Intelligent Expense and Income Management
- Unmanned Operation Vehicles
- Intelligent Information Systems

As seen in the list above, there are many digital information tools at Istanbul airport. In this sense, it can be said that Istanbul Airport has reached the status of being a smart airport. It is observed that Istanbul Airport, which includes many applications, has not yet been active in the applications of Intelligent Health Services and Unmanned Operation Vehicles; however, it is also an example of success in that it contains almost all the basic applications. Table 1 demonstrates the intelligent airport digital transformation tools of Istanbul Airport. Digital information tools in smart airports are shown on the vertical axis of the table, while technologies used in these tools are indicated on the horizontal axis.

Table 1 summarizes which technologies are used to create the digital services implemented at Istanbul airport. In this context, it can be said that almost all applications that can be called digital transformation exist at Istanbul airport.

The new Istanbul Airport has been able to use almost all the digital transformation tools by keeping up with the technological developments at an incredible speed. Thanks to the end-to-end technological infrastructure of the new airport, passengers' waiting times at passport, customs points and check-in counters will be reduced, while simultaneous, uninterrupted, fast, and secure internet use will be provided to 55 thousand people. Istanbul Airport will have 3 data centers, 102 integrated systems, 467 servers, 780 telecommunication provision rooms, 3257 access control systems, 3267 flight information monitors, 4549 supported computers, and 9000 security cameras. Founded by IGA Airport Operations, IGA provides all the technological infrastructure and information services of Istanbul New Airport, this service is the largest service in its field worldwide (Düzgün, 2020). Digital transformation can create both new opportunities and threats if the process is not well-managed for companies from all fields, regardless of the sector. In this context, the digital transformation process requires good planning and strategic management of the process.

Strategic Management of Digital Transformation

Businesses should adopt the concept of "strategic management "to their institutions to be superior to their competitors and have a say in the competition, and carry their businesses and organizations to a more sustainable structure. Digital transformation brings with it a deeper digitalization process than the digital technology experiences that businesses have had so far. It causes striking

Table 1. Smart airport digital transformation tools of Istanbul Airport

	Internet of Things	**Cyber-Physical Systems**	**Big Data**	**Autonomous Robots**	**Simulation**	**Integrated Systems**	**Cloud Computing Systems**	**Augmented Reality**
Smart Payment	x	x				x	x	
Intelligent Routing	x	x	x		x			x
Self-Boarding	x		x	x		x		
Fingerprint Usage	x	x	x			x	x	
Smart Displays	x					x	x	
Face Scanning System	x							
Intelligent Boarding Gates	x	x	x			x		
Sensor Systems	x	x		x				x
Self-check-in points	x	x						
Airport Mobile Applications			x			x	x	
Quick Pass		x						
Free Internet		x						
Lost and Found Software	x		x	x		x	x	
NFC Technology						x	x	
Live Support Kiosks	x	x	x			x	x	x
Virtual Towers	x	x	x		x	x	x	x
Virtual Assistants	x	x	x		x	x	x	
Lost Baggage Tracking System	x		x			x	x	
Smart Lighting	x	x				x		
Eco-Friendly Buildings	x	x	x			x		
Smart Tower	x	x	x		x	x	x	x
Weather, Sound, and Light Tracking Sensors	x	x	x			x	x	
Intelligent Disaster Planning	x	x	x			x	x	
Security Analysis with Artificial Intelligence	x	x	x		x	x	x	x
Smart Parking	x	x	x	x				
Personalized Routing	x		x		x		x	x
Central Operations Management Platform	x	x	x		x	x	x	x
Advanced Network Architecture		x				x		
Intelligent Expense and Income Management		x	x			x	x	
Unmanned Operation Vehicles								
Intelligent Information Systems	x	x	x			x	x	

transformations in customer relations, business processes, business models, and organizational structures of businesses. This transformation is possible by applying strategic management in a comprehensive way (Rêgo et al., 2021).

The digital transformation and digital technologies that we encounter with Industry 4.0 have a transformative effect on all units of enterprises. The fact that businesses can become competitive in the transformation process brings with it the need for an effective digital transformation strategy and management for due diligence, planning, coordination, and implementation. Digital technologies provide end-to-end benefits from the decision-making processes of businesses to providing high-quality products and services to customers, from intra-organizational processes to cost optimization, and from operational processes to reaching strategic goals (Grab, Olaru & Gavril,2019).

Digital transformation, in other words, using technology to radically improve the performance of businesses has made it a hot topic for companies around the world. Managers across all industries are using digital innovations such as analytics, mobility, social media, and smart embedded devices to change customer relationships, internal processes, and value propositions and improve their use of traditional technologies such as ERP (Enterprise Resource Planning). Realizing how rapidly digital technology has caused changes in all industries in the last decade, businesses argue that it is necessary to pay attention to the changes in their industries (De Bernardi, Bertello & Shams, 2019).

Businesses need a holistic digital transformation strategy that plans, implements, supervises, and measures the entire digital transformation process, as digital transformation creates an environment for disruptive changes and new challenges in businesses (Troise et al., 2022). Digital transformation management is a structured, holistic approach focused on increasing business value and reducing business risks. Companies need to take a structured approach to manage the interrelationships of the elements (products and services, organization, people, processes, applications, and infrastructure) that impact the digital transformation framework on a business's operating model. The following approach is adopted for this framework (Kontić & Vidicki, 2018);

- First, a clear vision of how Industry 4.0 is impacting your business is needed.
- Based on this vision, plans should be made to shape future operations.
- Existing operations should be modified according to these plans.
- Finally, the future working method should be determined.

This includes an effective approach to program management, stakeholder engagement, benefits, and risk management to control transformation and its outcome.

Businesses that want to realize digital transformation should strategically address this process within a plan. The business must first recognize its current situation, determine its vision, and plan and implement the necessary operations. During the operation phase, it should address the current position with continuous audit and evaluation, re-evaluate the failing points, and revise it with an agile approach. Businesses that can successfully manage, implement, and make a difference in the digital transformation process are businesses that can adapt their business processes, business models, organizational structures, and customer experience to a challenging competitive environment (Correani et al., 2020). Businesses should first prepare a plan for digital transformation and perform the process within that plan. A business aiming to initiate transformation should define its vision according to changing customer needs and competitive environment, understand its readiness and capabilities for the process of realizing business processes by reviewing it, discover opportunities to start new ventures, and restructure its operations (Mohamed Hashim, Tlemsani & Matthews, 2021).

In digital transformation, as can be experienced in major transformations, businesses often encounter difficulties in reaching their goals. In the early stages of digital transformation, the positive motivation created by rapid gains and new roles may decrease in the future. If this process is not managed well, employee motivation can become difficult, creating resistance to change, and new ways of doing business and business models may run the risk of being replaced by old work management. If they succeed in realizing the three dimensions, they will be able to provide the transformation process and speed at the optimum level. In the dimension of building basic skills, a plan and continuous improvement program are created to increase business digital competence. A well-structured digital platform and strong information technology business relationship should be established (He et al., 2020).

The success of digital transformation is related to its end-to-end control and traceability. In this context, it is important to raise awareness from the highest authority managing the process to all employees to ensure continuous improvement. This will be possible in a structure that will be formed with the participation of all parties. Increasing the digital capabilities of employees will help accelerate the digital transformation process. Actions that should be taken in the management process of a successful digital transformation are discussed under 5 headings (Ivančić, Vukšić & Spremić, 2019).

Determining the Current Situation and the Strategy: Businesses must first realize that they need to realize digital transformation and that this transformation is an inevitable necessity to compete today. However, knowing that change may come from different sectors other than their customers, competitors, and sectors, they need to take transformation steps accordingly. For this, businesses should analyze both their internal processes and the current situation of the market, determine their needs, and the steps to be taken. Businesses that scale their digital transformation strategies, set a roadmap in this framework, set goals within the scope of the strategy, and measure and evaluate with continuous feedback, are successful in their transformation journey (Nadkarni & Prügl, 2021).

Laying the Foundations Correctly: Businesses need to use the new technologies required by today's competitive environment in a way that will benefit their institutions, modernizing their existing infrastructures and transforming their previous technologies and infrastructures. While performing this transformation, the agility to implement the transformation accurately and quickly, smart applications that can make the data obtained by the enterprise meaningful in the infrastructure, business partners interacting with customers and the sector in a competitive environment, and applications related to sensors are indispensable. While laying the foundations of technology, a synchronized and consistent approach should be adopted with the transformation of business processes and business models (Baiyere, Salmela & Tapanainen, 2020).

Using Digital to Differentiate Companies: Digital transformation requires an agile structure to put the transformation on the right foundations in an increasingly competitive environment. Businesses are looking for opportunities to differentiate and gain a competitive advantage by increasing the customer experience with new value propositions due to competition. Businesses should direct their new ways of doing business in this direction and turn this experience into a business culture with a structure in which all employees are included in the process, not from the top down. Businesses may not be able to master all competencies such as user experience, digital marketing, management of digital channels, analytics, and data analysis. In these cases, efforts can be made to increase employee competencies to continue the transformation, new business models, and business processes. (Baiyere, Salmela & Tapanainen, 2020).

Ensuring the Right Management for Continuous Development: For digital transformation, the process must be embraced by the top management in businesses, and the appropriate strategy and vision must be revealed. Top management support is essential for a successful transformation. Businesses do not associate the investments they make in the transformation process with growth and productivity increase. The reason for this is that no governance structure regularly monitors the digital investments they make and will regularly convey the positive and negative results of the moves to the decision-makers with a good analysis. In this context, within the framework of the vision determined by the enterprises, the allocation of digital investments will be removed from being a financial reservation and progress toward the determined targets (Warner & Wäger, 2019).

Being aware of what needs to be done on a macro scale: To accelerate the realization of digital transformation, what businesses can do alone at some points is limited. Cooperating with non-governmental organizations, universities, official institutions, raising the necessary human resources, arranging the educational infrastructure, making the necessary incentives, and facilitating arrangements for projects and investments, and putting forth legal and legislative regulations make it important (Brelsford, 2014).

CONCLUSION

In today's world, rapid changes in the business environment have pushed organizations to seek new ways, especially with Industry 4.0, businesses have found themselves in a new and rapid digitalization process. In this process, it has been seen that businesses react very differently to digital transformation. It has been observed that businesses trying to keep up with digital transformation by using different technologies are at different levels in the digital transformation process, perhaps due to the structure of the sector they are in, or perhaps because of themselves. Even today, digital transformation, the definition of which is very difficult to put into certain patterns, is a comprehensive and profound transformation that changes the entire operation in organizations, affecting business models, strategies, organizational culture, and even leadership understanding. At this point, there is a need for a roadmap that will show this transformation and its effects on businesses. In addition, it should not be forgotten that the companies that have achieved this transformation have increased their organizational power and gained a competitive advantage over their competitors (Silahtaroğlu, 2017).

Intense and radical changes in digital technologies have led to changes in powerful paradigms in the business world. Changes in the global value chain in the business world, and changes in customer consumption habits, create new obstacles and opportunities for businesses. Businesses that want to keep up with the new order and continue their existence can successfully realize digital transformation by integrating new technologies into all their processes in a planned and strategic framework in the market with intense economic changes and competition. To develop the right digital transformation strategy, the relationship between the factors that trigger the transformation and between the factors of the digital business strategy framework and the digital transformation should be determined. Although digital transformation is mentioned in existing sources (De Bem Machado et al., 2022; Halpern et al., 2021), the link between the process and digital transformation within the framework of a digital business strategy is not examined in detail. This study has been approached from a strategic management perspective by associating digital transformation in enterprises with digital business strategy and dimensions to fill this gap in the academic literature and to help businesses, especially those operating in the aviation sector, in drawing a digital transformation roadmap.

Strategic management aims to make the organization successful, especially by running the management, production, finance, marketing, accounting, human resources management, public relations, research and development, control, and information processing systems of the enterprises in harmony. Strategic management decisions that will enable an organization to reach the determined goals are a dynamic science that provides preparation, examination, and application. In the current business conjuncture dominated by intense competition and rapid changes, the survival of businesses depends on taking fast and effective strategic decisions and taking the right steps in accordance with the rapidly changing dynamic environment. The new order of the business world requires flexibility to take and implement strategic decisions quickly.

Businesses that want to successfully realize digital transformation should be in a value-oriented thinking and activity structure, leaving the cost focus by better analyzing and understanding their demands, with products or services suitable for changing customer behaviors. It should use digital technologies with a proactive focus that enhances the customer experience in the context of accurate analysis and inferences of data to create insights into customer behavior. Another factor is to successfully realize the digital transformation by managing the digitalization process in operational processes. To increase business volume and improve efficiency, businesses should realize digital transformation. Increasing the speed, quality, cost, efficiency, and satisfaction level in the process from supplier to customer will contribute to digital transformation. Likewise, businesses can accelerate digital transformation by integrating digital technologies into their processes, from finance to human resources, from sales to accounting, and other units. Businesses should not forget that digital transformation is the basic element of human cognitive abilities, especially in using human resources efficiently in their organizations. In the stage of realizing the digital transformation, it will be important for human resources to be included in the process and adapted to the transformation process in line with the same goals.

In this study, the concept of digital transformation was examined and strategically evaluated in the management of the digital transformation process. At the same time, the concept of smart airport has been defined and Istanbul airport has been examined as a case. The following questions were tried to be answered by making use of the literature;

- What is digital transformation and what applications does it consist of?
- What are the stages of transformation in airports and what is the concept of smart airport?
- What are the results of evaluating Istanbul airport within the scope of smart airport technologies?

As a result of the evaluation, an evaluation table containing smart airport applications was prepared. As a result, it was concluded that Istanbul Airport has the status of a smart airport.

Considering the aviation industry, customers can benefit from an increasing number of new products and services introduced to the market. The communication and interaction between channels and customers are expected to develop further. Undoubtedly, there has been awareness about the products and services in the market and it has become much easier to evaluate them. In addition, the automation of the services offered to customers at the point of purchase, delivery, and post-delivery service has increased. In addition, areas where customers can benefit by creating communities and associations, such as social media, have increased and strengthened. This has pushed businesses to remain agile enough to respond to changing social and technological environments, thus investing in digital capabilities. As can be seen, the integration of the agile transformation process into digital transformation seems to be the way to ensure a strong customer focus and always be at the forefront. Finally, the following recommendations can be made to businesses:

- Invest in analytical capabilities to enable customization of products and services,
- Invest in self-service and automated customer experience across multiple channels,
- Discover and adopt a global cloud-based strategy,
- Research and training of qualified personnel should be started.

Businesses that implement these recommendations will be able to strategically manage the digital transformation process required by the technology and thus gain a competitive advantage by being one step ahead of their competitors.

QUESTIONS

1. Discuss the importance of digital transportation for organizations.
2. What are the drivers for airport operators to digitalize?
3. What are the most common digital applications in airports?
4. Why is the strategic management of digital transformation essential?
5. What technology can be applied to facilitate the procedures that customers must do at airports?
6. Discuss the actions that should be taken in the management process of a successful digital transformation.
7. Discuss the relationship between knowledge management and innovation.

REFERENCES

Adamik, A., & Nowicki, M. (2018, May). Preparedness of companies for digital transformation and creating a competitive advantage in the age of Industry 4.0. In *Proceedings of the International Conference on Business Excellence* (Vol. 12, No. 1, pp. 10-24). 10.2478/picbe-2018-0003

Alghadeir, A., & Sakran, H. A. (2016). Smart airport architecture using the Internet of Things. *International Journal of Innovative Research in Computer Science & Technology.*

Baiyere, A., Salmela, H., & Tapanainen, T. (2020). Digital transformation and the new logic of business process management. *European Journal of Information Systems*, *29*(3), 238–259. doi:10.1080/0960085X.2020.1718007

Brelsford, N. (2014). *Do middle-level managers contribute to strategic development? A study of the practices of middle-level managers In Strategic Renewal* [Doctoral dissertation]. University of Southampton.

Chanias, S., Myers, M. D., & Hess, T. (2019). Digital transformation strategy making in pre-digital organizations: The case of a financial services provider. *The Journal of Strategic Information Systems*, *28*(1), 17–33. doi:10.1016/j.jsis.2018.11.003

Cheng, Q., Liu, Y., Peng, C., He, X., Qu, Z., & Dong, Q. (2023). Knowledge digitization: Characteristics, knowledge advantage and innovation performance. *Journal of Business Research*, *163*, 113915. doi:10.1016/j.jbusres.2023.113915

Chiu, C. N., & Chen, H. H. (2016). The study of knowledge management capability and organizational effectiveness in Taiwanese public utility: The mediator role of organizational commitment. *SpringerPlus*, *5*(1), 1–34. doi:10.118640064-016-3173-6 PMID:27652093

De Bem Machado, A., Secinaro, S., Calandra, D., & Lanzalonga, F. (2022). Knowledge management and digital transformation for Industry 4.0: A structured literature review. *Knowledge Management Research and Practice*, *20*(2), 320–338. doi:10.1080/14778238.2021.2015261

De Bernardi, P., Bertello, A., & Shams, S. M. (2019). Logics hindering digital transformation in cultural heritage strategic management: An exploratory case study. *Tourism Analysis*, *24*(3), 315–327. doi:10.3727/108354219X15511864843876

Du Plessis, M. (2007). The role of knowledge management in innovation. *Journal of Knowledge Management*, *26*(4), 1367–3270. doi:10.1108/13673270710762684

Dulhare, U. N., & Rasool, S. (2022). Smart Airport System to Counter COVID-19 and Future Sustainability. In *Machine Learning and Internet of Things for Societal Issues* (pp. 55–67). Springer Nature Singapore. doi:10.1007/978-981-16-5090-1_5

Düzgün, M. (2020). Assessment Of Istanbul Grand Airport (Iga) As A Global Cargo Base By The Topsis Method. *Academic Review of Humanities and Social Sciences*, *3*(1), 125–138.

Edwards, J. S. (2022). Where knowledge management and information management meet: Research directions. *International Journal of Information Management, 63*, 102458. doi:10.1016/j.ijinfomgt.2021.102458

Fei, Y. (2022). *Smart sensing and predictive learning for optimization and simulation of airport ground equipment and staff scheduling: a cloud-based mobile integrated decision support platform* [Doctoral dissertation]. Georgia Institute of Technology.

Gao, F., Li, M., & Clarke, S. (2008). Knowledge, management, and knowledge management in business operations. *Journal of Knowledge Management, 12*(2), 3–17. doi:10.1108/13673270810859479

Ghazal, M., Ali, S., Haneefa, F., & Sweleh, A. (2016, March). Towards smart wearable real-time airport luggage tracking. In *2016 International Conference on Industrial Informatics and Computer Systems (CIICS)* (pp. 1-6). IEEE. 10.1109/ICCSII.2016.7462422

Gong, C., & Ribiere, V. (2021). Developing a unified definition of digital transformation. *Technovation, 102*, 102217. doi:10.1016/j.technovation.2020.102217

Goode, A. (2018). Biometrics for banking: Best practices and barriers to adoption. *Biometric Technology Today, 2018*(10), 5–7. doi:10.1016/S0969-4765(18)30156-5

Grab, B., Olaru, M., & Gavril, R. M. (2019). The impact of digital transformation on strategic business management. *Ecoforum Journal, 8*(1).

Hájnik, A., Harantová, V., & Kalašová, A. (2021). Use of electromobility and autonomous vehicles at airports in Europe and worldwide. *Transportation Research Procedia, 55*, 71–78. doi:10.1016/j.trpro.2021.06.008

Halpern, N., Mwesiumo, D., Suau-Sanchez, P., Budd, T., & Bråthen, S. (2021). Ready for digital transformation? The effect of organisational readiness, innovation, airport size and ownership on digital change at airports. *Journal of Air Transport Management, 90*, 101949. doi:10.1016/j.jairtraman.2020.101949 PMID:33041542

He, Q., Meadows, M., Angwin, D., Gomes, E., & Child, J. (2020). Strategic alliance research in the era of digital transformation: Perspectives on future research. *British Journal of Management, 31*(3), 589–617. doi:10.1111/1467-8551.12406

Ivančić, L., Vukšić, V. B., & Spremić, M. (2019). Mastering the digital transformation process: Business practices and lessons learned. *Technology Innovation Management Review, 9*(2), 36–50. doi:10.22215/timreview/1217

Karasneh, A. A. F. (2022). Revitalizing the BSC through knowledge management: The mediating role of intellectual capital. *Journal of Public Affairs, 22*(1), e2359. doi:10.1002/pa.2359

Kila, T. (2020). *Design and development of a governance framework for airports digitization: the case of turnaround coordinator*. Academic Press.

Kontić, L., & Vidicki, Đ. (2018). Strategy for digital organization: Testing a measurement tool for digital transformation. *Strategic Management, 23*(1), 29–35. doi:10.5937/StraMan1801029K

Kovynyov, I., & Mikut, R. (2019). Digital technologies in airport ground operations. *NETNOMICS: Economic Research and Electronic Networking, 20*(1), 1–30. doi:10.100711066-019-09132-5

Kraus, S., Schiavone, F., Pluzhnikova, A., & Invernizzi, A. C. (2021). Digital transformation in healthcare: Analyzing the current state-of-research. *Journal of Business Research, 123*, 557–567. doi:10.1016/j.jbusres.2020.10.030

Lai, Y. L., Hsu, M. S., Lin, F. J., Chen, Y. M., & Lin, Y. H. (2014). The effects of industry cluster knowledge management on innovation performance. *Journal of Business Research, 67*(5), 734–739. doi:10.1016/j.jbusres.2013.11.036

Lasi, H., Fettke, P., Kemper, H. G., Feld, T., & Hoffmann, M. (2014). Industry 4.0. *Business & Information Systems Engineering, 6*(4), 239–242. doi:10.100712599-014-0334-4

Laurini, R. (2021). A primer of knowledge management for smart city governance. *Land Use Policy, 111*, 104832. doi:10.1016/j.landusepol.2020.104832

Leão, P., & da Silva, M. M. (2021). Impacts of digital transformation on firms' competitive advantages: A systematic literature review. *Strategic Change, 30*(5), 421–441. doi:10.1002/jsc.2459

Lykou, G., Anagnostopoulou, A., & Gritzalis, D. (2018). Smart airport cybersecurity: Threat mitigation and cyber resilience controls. *Sensors (Basel), 19*(1), 19. doi:10.339019010019 PMID:30577633

Matt, C., Hess, T., & Benlian, A. (2015). Digital transformation strategies. *Business & Information Systems Engineering, 57*(5), 339–343. doi:10.100712599-015-0401-5

Meydan, C. H. (2023). Havayolu işletmelerinde dijital dönüşüm uygulamaları üzerine bir inceleme. *Journal of Aviation Research, 5*(1), 65–82.

Migdadi, M. M. (2022). Knowledge management processes, innovation capability and organizational performance. *International Journal of Productivity and Performance Management, 71*(1), 182–210. doi:10.1108/IJPPM-04-2020-0154

Mitroulis, D., & Kitsios, F. (2019, February). Digital transformation strategy: A literature review. In *Proceedings of the 6th National Student Conference of HELORS, Xanthi, Greece* (pp. 59-61). Academic Press.

Mohamed, M., Gomaa, H., & El-Sherif, N. (2018). Evaluation of current smart airport technologies implemented in Cairo international airport. International Journal of Heritage. *Tourism and Hospitality, 12*(2), 130–140.

Mohamed Hashim, M. A., Tlemsani, I., & Matthews, R. (2021). Higher education strategy in digital transformation. *Education and Information Technologies*, 1–25. PMID:34539217

Mrňa, D., Badánik, B., & Novák, A. (2021). Internet of Things as an optimization tool for smart airport concept. *European Transport-Trasporti Europei*, 82.

Nadkarni, S., & Prügl, R. (2021). Digital transformation: A review, synthesis and opportunities for future research. *Management Review Quarterly*, *71*(2), 233–341. doi:10.100711301-020-00185-7

Narongou, D., & Sun, Z. (2021). Big data analytics for smart airport management. In *Intelligent analytics with advanced multi-industry applications* (pp. 209–231). IGI Global. doi:10.4018/978-1-7998-4963-6.ch010

Nwankpa, J. K., Roumani, Y., & Datta, P. (2022). Process innovation in the digital age of business: The role of digital business intensity and knowledge management. *Journal of Knowledge Management*, *26*(5), 1319–1341. doi:10.1108/JKM-04-2021-0277

Obeidat, B., Al-Suradi, M., Masa'deh, R., & Tarhini, A. (2016). The impact of knowledge management on innovation: An empirical The Mediating Role of Innovation Speed and Quality in the Relationship 407 study on Jordanian consultancy firms. *Res. Rev*, *39*, 1214–1238.

Paoloni, M., Coluccia, D., Fontana, S., & Solimene, S. (2020). Knowledge management, intellectual capital and entrepreneurship: A structured literature review. *Journal of Knowledge Management*, *24*(8), 1797–1818. doi:10.1108/JKM-01-2020-0052

Rêgo, B. S., Jayantilal, S., Ferreira, J. J., & Carayannis, E. G. (2021). Digital transformation and strategic management: A systematic review of the literature. *Journal of the Knowledge Economy*, 1–28.

Richards, B. J., Seidakhmetov, B. K., & Zhunussova, M. A. (2020). Digital Transformation in the Aviation Industry. *Вестник академии гражданской авиации*, (2), 23-27.

Seo, S., Choi, S., & Lee, C. (2012). Security manpower scheduling for smart airports. In Computer Science and Convergence: CSA 2011 & WCC 2011 Proceedings (pp. 519-527). Springer Netherlands. doi:10.1007/978-94-007-2792-2_49

Shehieb, W., Al Sayed, H., Akil, M. M., Turkman, M., Sarraj, M. A., & Mir, M. (2016, December). A smart system to minimize mishandled luggage at airports. In *2016 International Conference on Progress in Informatics and Computing (PIC)* (pp. 154-158). IEEE. 10.1109/PIC.2016.7949485

Silahtaroğlu, G. (2017). Implementing adaptive strategies of decision support systems during crises. *Global Business Strategies in Crisis: Strategic Thinking and Development*, 287-302.

Song, M., Van Der Bij, H., & Weggeman, M. (2005). Determinants of the level of knowledge application: A knowledge-based and information-processing perspective. *Journal of Product Innovation Management*, *22*(5), 430–444. doi:10.1111/j.1540-5885.2005.00139.x

Tabrizi, B., Lam, E., Girard, K., & Irvin, V. (2019). Digital transformation is not about technology. *Harvard Business Review*, *13*(March), 1–6.

Tanrıverdi, G., & Lezki, Ş. (2021). Istanbul Airport (IGA) and quest of best competitive strategy for air cargo carriers in new competition environment: A fuzzy multi-criteria approach. *Journal of Air Transport Management*, *95*, 102088. doi:10.1016/j.jairtraman.2021.102088

Troise, C., Tani, M., Matricano, D., & Ferrara, E. (2022). Guest editorial: Digital transformation, strategic management and entrepreneurial process: dynamics, challenges and opportunities. *Journal of Strategy and Management*, *15*(3), 329–334. doi:10.1108/JSMA-08-2022-363

Warner, K. S., & Wäger, M. (2019). Building dynamic capabilities for digital transformation: An ongoing process of strategic renewal. *Long Range Planning*, *52*(3), 326–349. doi:10.1016/j.lrp.2018.12.001

Zaim, H., Tatoglu, E., & Zaim, S. (2007). Performance of knowledge management practices: A causal analysis. *Journal of Knowledge Management*, *11*(6), 54–67. doi:10.1108/13673270710832163

Zamorano, M. M., Fernández-Laso, M. C., & de Esteban Curiel, J. (2020). Smart airports: Acceptance of technology by passengers. *Cuadernos de Turismo*, (45), 567–570.

Zaoui, F., & Souissi, N. (2020). Roadmap for digital transformation: A literature review. *Procedia Computer Science*, *175*, 621–628. doi:10.1016/j.procs.2020.07.090

Chapter 10
Sharing Knowledge in Projects

Zinga Novais
ISEG, Universidade de Lisboa, Portugal

Jorge Vareda Gomes
https://orcid.org/0000-0003-0656-9284
Universidade Lusófona, Lisboa, Portugal

Mario Romão
https://orcid.org/0000-0003-4564-1883
ISEG, Universidade de Lisboa, Portugal

EXECUTIVE SUMMARY

Projects have been increasingly used in the implementation of organizations' business operations. Knowledge sharing has been considered essential in the project environment; therefore, the integration of knowledge management within project management becomes crucial for project success. The objective of this research is to study how knowledge sharing is integrated within the context of a project, and what is the perception of project team members about it. A case study was carried out in a company within the financial sector, focused on a project team of the entity. The results revealed that project managers, other professionals in project management, and the organization itself are very much aware of the importance of knowledge sharing. The results also emphasized that, regardless of the lack of incentives by top management, project team members consider that knowledge sharing highly contributes to a successful execution of projects.

INTRODUCTION

An increasing number of organizations have implemented their business operations through projects (Todorović, et al., 2015). Projects can be defined as temporary effort to create a specific product or service (PMI, 2017). Temporarily, in the sense that a project has a defined beginning and end, and is unique, in the sense that the product/service is different in some way and is distinct from other products/services (Owen & Burstein, 2005; PMI, 2017). Projects are collective endeavors, with goals based on the

DOI: 10.4018/978-1-6684-5859-4.ch010

development of common understandings, which generate personal and group knowledge that contribute to their success (Sankarasubramanian, 2009).

For many organizations, knowledge is the most important asset and its survival depends on the organization's ability to effectively use existing knowledge and to effectively create, develop, and use new knowledge (Pascoe & More, 2005). Proper knowledge is a basic prerequisite for effective project management (Gasik, 2011) and knowledge management is a vital factor for successfully undertaking projects (Sokhanvar, 2014). According to Koskinen and Pihlanto (2008), projects are often dependent on knowledge that is not in their possession. Within this context, the integration of knowledge management in project management is necessary to share information and knowledge to solve problems effectively and efficiently (Yeong & Lim, 2010). Knowledge is defined by Gao et al. (2018) as the practical and theoretical understanding of a subject, and it is considered to be an essential organizational resource (Buvik & Tvedt, 2017; Hanisch et al., 2009) and its management is considered to be a fundamental tool for the success of projects (Romani, 2017).

Generically, knowledge management represents the set of processes and practices carried out in organizations to increase the intellectual potential and of improving the effectiveness and efficiency of the management of organizational knowledge resources (Heisig, 2009; Andreeva and Kianto, 2012). The basic purpose of knowledge management is to create and share knowledge within organizations (Chen et al., 2018). Knowledge sharing is especially important in a project environment and contributes significantly to the performance of organizations (Buvik & Tvedt, 2017) and their ability to understand the best way to share knowledge between teams and between members of a project (Fernie et., 2003). Furthermore, Al Ahbabi et al. (2019) conclude that the dimensions of knowledge management have a positive impact on the innovation, quality, and operational performance of employees. Gürlek & Çemberci (2020) show that firms led by knowledge-oriented leaders have a high level of knowledge management capacity, innovation performance, and firm performance. In turn, owing to the temporary nature of projects, knowledge management in project-based organizations is not similar to functional companies (Kasvi, Vartiainen, & Hailikari, 2003). In addition, project team members split up or leave after project completion and this poses several challenges to projects and project-based organizations (Ajmal, Helo, & Kekale, 2010).

Through a case study approach, this research proves that team members use different knowledge-sharing practices and recognize their importance for the successful management of their projects.

BACKGROUND

Knowledge

"Knowledge is seen as an intangible asset, which is valuable, distinctive, path-dependent, causally ambiguous and hard to substitute or replicate" (Fang et al., 2013, p. 945). Knowledge is considered to be an essential strategic resource that allows organizations to maintain a competitive advantage in a dynamic market environment (Rashed, 2016).

There is no single definition of knowledge, it has different understandings which depend on the context in which it is defined (Ekambaram et al., 2018). For example, knowledge can be defined as the following: the practical and theoretical understanding of a subject (Gao et al., 2018); the ability to make judgments (Fernie et al., 2003); is based on reflection and human experience (De Long & Fahey,

2000); a system of connections between facts and ideas (Romani, 2017); or information combined with experience, context, interpretation, and reflection (Davenport, De Long & Beers, 1998).

De Long and Fahey (2000) believe that there are three types of knowledge: human knowledge, social knowledge, and structured knowledge. In addition, these authors posit that there are two dimensions to understanding knowledge in an organizational context: i) that knowledge can exist at the individual, group, or organizational level, and; ii) that knowledge can be tacit or explicit (De Long & Fahey, 2000). This latter dimension of knowledge is frequently mentioned in the literature (Buvik & Tvedt, 2017; Chen et al., 2018; De Long & Fahey, 2000; Fernie et al., 2003; Hoorn & Whitty, 2019; Nonaka, 1994).

Explicit knowledge consists of the following: easily accessible words and numbers (Uğurlu & Kizildağ, 2013); information defined tangibly (Gao et al., 2018; Owen & Burstein, 2005); and formal and well-structured information in the form of documentation, databases, and reports (Terzieva, 2014; Mazur et al., 2014). Explicit knowledge refers to knowledge that is transmissible in a formal and systemic language (Nonaka, 1994; Nonaka & Takeuchi, 1995).

Tacit knowledge is defined as being what we know, but cannot explain (De Long & Fahey, 2000), where the experience is rooted in the individual's mind (Koskinen et al., 2003; Chen et al., 2018). Tacit knowledge is not identifiable in a structured or documented form, but rather it is internalized by the experience, intuition, and insight of individuals who are experts within their organizations (Terzieva, 2014; Mazur et al., 2014; Davenport et al., 1998). Tacit knowledge has a personal quality, which makes it difficult to formalize and communicate (Nonaka, 1994; Nonaka & Takeuchi, 1995). According to the same author, tacit knowledge is characterized by two types of elements or dimensions: i) a cognitive dimension based on paradigms, beliefs, and points of view that provide individuals with unique perspectives, and a technical dimension supported by informal skills and know-how applied to a specific context (Nonaka, 1994; Nonaka & Konno, 1998); ii) and human action (Koskinen et al., 2003) and know-how (Bryde et al., 2018), which is complex and dynamic (Chen et al., 2018), personal, context-dependent (Fernie et al., 2003), and subjective (Hoorn & Whitty, 2019). However, according to Owen & Burstein (2005), there is also a third type of knowledge, namely: implicit knowledge, which, similar to tacit knowledge, is present in the individual's mind. The same authors explain that the main difference between implicit and tacit knowledge is the fact that whereas the latter can be captured and transferred within the organization through social networks, implicit knowledge can potentially be captured, encoded, and stored in databases or documents (Owen & Burstein, 2005).

Knowledge Management

Knowledge management has a fundamental role in the success of organizations' activities and strategies, namely in the effective support for environmental changes, in increasing productivity, in the relationships between employees, and in opening the way for development and innovation (Castrogiovanni et al., 2016; Ekambaram et al., 2018; Mueller, 2012). It is considered to be a key element for those organizations looking to obtain a competitive advantage (Wang & Ko, 2012). In a simplified way, the concept of knowledge management is based on the vision of the strategic value of organizational knowledge, using information technologies (e.g., databases and others) to facilitate the acquisition, sharing, storage, retrieval, and use of knowledge (Easterby- Smith & Lyles, 2011).

Inkinen (2016) defines knowledge management practices as being the conscious organizational and managerial practices intended to achieve organizational goals through efficient and effective management of the firm's knowledge resources.

Several studies define knowledge management processes in different ways. For example, according to Costa & Monteiro (2016) and Inkinen (2016), knowledge management is an aggregated process composed of the acquisition, creation, transfer, storage, and application of knowledge. However, in operational terms, the definition of knowledge management processes is related to the creation, sharing, and use of knowledge (Ahmad et al., 2017; Shujahat et al., 2017).

Knowledge creation is a process in which new knowledge is created through the four sub-processes of organizational knowledge creation (Andreeva & Kianto, 2011; Collins & Smith, 2006): socialization, combination, externalization, and internationalization (Collins & Smith, 2006; Lai et al., 2014).

Knowledge sharing is the donation and collection of knowledge between different knowledge units in a company (Becerra-Fernandez, Gonzalez, & Sabherwal, 2004) and is the act of transferring respective insights between fellow employees (Hooff & De Ridder, 2004). It can be categorized as formal versus informal elements, or donation versus a collection of knowledge (Hooff & De Ridder, 2004; Taminiau, Smit, & Lange, 2009). Singh et al. (2021) claim that organizations with strong knowledge-sharing practices are more competent in achieving open innovation. Abbas et al. (2019) show a substantial positive linkage between knowledge sharing and organizational innovation in Pakistani Islamic banks. Therefore, to achieve an effective knowledge exchange among employees, there must be effective knowledge sharing and helping (Singh et al., 2021). A complete process of knowledge sharing includes sharing intention, sharing behaviors, and sharing results (Akhavan &Mahdi Hosseini, 2016).

The use of knowledge is the application of knowledge that has been shared (Song, Bij, & Weggeman, 2005) and newly created knowledge becomes part of organizational behavior and the problem-solving processes through assimilation (Chen et al., 2012).

Seiner (2001) defined knowledge management as being the way the company collects, organizes, shares, and analyses the knowledge of individuals and groups, and the ways that directly affect organizational performance (Mazur et al., 2014). Mahdi et al. (2019) see knowledge as a dynamic and recurring process, in which employees must constantly connect with information and obtain new knowledge and apply that knowledge to improve their decision-making while developing knowledge and new information in the process. Knowledge management describes all the methods, instruments, and tools used in a holistic approach to generate, store, distribute, and apply knowledge, supported by the identification of knowledge and the definition of knowledge goals in all areas and levels of the organization (Mahdi et al., 2019; Rashed, 2016). Knowledge management is also considered to be a cyclical system that enables the organization to efficiently achieve its objectives by possessing the ability to transform tacit and explicit learning into habits, and thus plan and execute better (Mazur et al., 2014).

Knowledge Management Strategies

Knowledge management ensures the correct flow of knowledge through two main strategies: coding and personalization (Shujahat et al., 2017). The coding strategy is related to extracting and storing knowledge explicitly through the ICT framework, while the personalization strategy focuses on direct human interactions for the purpose of knowledge sharing (Curado & Bontis, 2006; Merat & Bo, 2013; Shujahat et al., 2017).

In the cases of coding strategy, knowledge is encrypted and stored in databases, which facilitates the access and reuse of knowledge (Hans & Skiver, 2007; Hansen et al., 1999; Kasvi et al., 2003; Ruuska & Vartiainen, 2005). Organizations that adopt coding strategy depend on the "economics of reuse", whereby once acquired or developed, knowledge assets can be used multiple times. The reuse of knowledge reduces the volume of work, reduces costs, and allows the organization to take on more projects (Hansen et al., 1999). This strategy is considered to be a good mechanism for storing large amounts of knowledge and for creating an organizational memory for all employees (Polyaninova, 2011).

The personalization strategy is the opposite of the coding strategy (Bolisani et al., 2017), in which knowledge is linked to the person who developed it (Hansen et al., 1999; Mannan et al., 2013; Polyaninova, 2011). This strategy focuses on the contribution of tacit knowledge (Bolisani et al., 2017), as a knowledge-sharing mechanism, personalization has the flexibility to transmit tacit knowledge and facilitates debate and the sharing of interpretations that may lead to the creation of new knowledge (Polyaninova, 2011).

Knowledge is transmitted and shared through personal interaction, which focuses on a dialogue between individuals via brainstorming sessions and through the building of networks of people – a "person-to-person" approach (Hansen et al., 1999; Mannan, et al., 2013; Polyaninova, 2011). Furthermore, information technologies support personalization, as their main purpose is facilitating communication and sharing tacit knowledge (Hansen et al., 1999).

The organizations that successfully generate knowledge are those that identify the knowledge management strategy out of the two that best fits their competitive strategy, using this as their main strategy and then employing the other as support (Greiner et al., 2007; Hansen et al., 1999).

Bolisani et al. (2017) present a third strategy: the sharing strategy, which refers to an approach where individuals are assumed to work better collectively, arguing that there is a need to share and socialize the elements of their private knowledge. This strategy exists under the premise that no individual possesses all the knowledge necessary to perform a complex task and that individuals should be encouraged to share their experiences and knowledge, leading to the creation of specialized islands of knowledge, where they can create and share knowledge and implement collective learning processes (Bolisani et al., 2017).

Sharing Knowledge in Project Management

Knowledge sharing refers to the dissemination of organizational knowledge with all the organization's stakeholders (Kishore, et al., 2009), and it plays a critical role in the growth of companies' businesses, through the generation of new ideas, products, and/or services (Fields, 2017), as well as by the transfer of thoughts, information, perceptions, and experiences. Consequently, knowledge sharing becomes a source of creativity and innovation in organizations (Ciulli & Kolk, 2019). Love et al. (2005) made a valuable contribution to understanding knowledge management in project environments by considering the role and processes of knowledge management in project environments, they focus on knowledge management in the context of cross-functional project teams, as well as the role of organizational learning in projects.

Knowledge is considered an essential asset for a project (Holzman, 2013), and is linked to the methodology and communication practices used in projects (Hanisch et al., 2009; Frey et al., 2009). Consequently, knowledge management is an essential tool that should be made available to the project manager for the successful completion of a project (Romani, 2017). Some researchers have linked knowledge and learning with project performance (Reich et al., 2008). Indeed, several empirical studies show a strong correlation between project management and knowledge management practices (McElroy, 2000) and also between good knowledge management practices and project performance (Leseure & Brookes, 2004).

Project knowledge management is defined as the application of concepts, tools, and techniques to complete a project within the defined time and budget, responding to the client's needs (Romani, 2017). Project knowledge management, especially in complex projects, is one of the main success factors in project management and its lack is cited as being one of the main reasons for failure (Desouza & Evaristo, 2004). Frey et al. (2009) state that project knowledge management comprises not only knowledge within projects but also knowledge between different projects and about projects. Soderlund (2010) states that in large transformation projects, it is necessary to integrate several knowledge bases in these projects. For these projects, knowledge integration depends on the ability of the participants to relate with each other to share and absorb the findings and knowledge assets that have been developed during the project and be able to adjust them to the velocity of the progress of other parts of the project. Polyaninova (2011) states that knowledge management in the project environment occurs in the transfer of experience between projects or between project teams and in the dissemination and development of new competencies from central departments to project teams.

Bassi (2014) suggested that two levels of knowledge need to be managed within an organization, namely: individual knowledge and organizational knowledge. The former refers to what individuals learn during project execution, while the latter refers to what the organization has developed and learned from managing its projects. Hanish et al. (2009) state that knowledge in projects is linked to the project management methodology and the communication practices adopted in projects, making project knowledge contribute to the overall organizational knowledge base.

According to Pretorius & Steyn (2005), the challenge of knowledge management in project environments lies in documentation and management, as well as in the distribution and sharing of newly created knowledge. Failure in this knowledge transfer within the organization leads to waste and impacts project performance (Leseure & Brookes, 2004).

Knowledge about project management, be it explicit or tacit, plays a decisive role in understanding this discipline (Morris, 2002). Knowledge increases in value when it is shared (Cabrera & Cabrera, 2002), and knowledge sharing is potentially considered to be the most important activity in knowledge management (Chen et al., 2018). Sharing is recognized as being strategically important for organizations, as it enables individuals to acquire the necessary knowledge to improve their performance (Wang & Ko, 2012). Furthermore, it is a key process in translating individual knowledge into organizational knowledge (Nesheim & Hunskaar, 2015) and is vital for innovation, increasing productivity, and maintaining competitive advantage (Mueller, 2015).

Knowledge sharing can be defined as the action of disseminating knowledge among individuals, groups, and organizations (Chen et al., 2018), where the organizational processes are associated with making knowledge available to others (Chen et al., 2018). However, some authors (e.g., Alavi & Denford, 2011) differentiate between the concepts of knowledge sharing and transfer.

Knowledge transfer is considered to be the communication of knowledge from a source to a recipient and it involves the transmission of knowledge from its original location, to where it needs to be applied (Alavi & Denford, 2011). Some authors argue that knowledge sharing is a voluntary act, suggesting that the individual presents the knowledge so that it can be used by others, and that it involves conscious action and active participation by the individual who possesses the knowledge (Wickramasinghe & Widyaratne, 2012). In turn, others suggest that knowledge sharing may not only be voluntary but is also requested, referring to the sending and receiving of requests for knowledge and the consequent fulfillment of these same requests (Wickramasinghe & Widyaratne, 2012). Knowledge sharing is especially important within the context of project management, where individuals work together and interact to perform their tasks and it is positively associated with project performance (Buvik & Tvedt, 2017).

However, it is necessary to be aware of barriers to knowledge development that may develop within the organization. These can be grouped into three homogeneous dimensions (Crupi et al., 2020):

- **Cultural Dimension:** Where the culture of an organization can be a barrier to inter-organizational knowledge sharing (Lotti Oliva, 2014). Culture can impact knowledge sharing by not implementing knowledge management tools or by not providing an adequate reward system, changing the organizational climate and relationships (Zawawi et al., 2011).
- **Structural Dimension:** Where organizational relationships seem to be an important barrier to the transfer of information from the organization to the team (Connelly & Kelloway, 2003). For this reason, organizations must promote the culture of teamwork as a knowledge-sharing generating factor, facilitating work conditions, and providing adequate infrastructure (Mariotti, 2007).
- **Strategic Dimension:** Whereby strategy development and collaborative encouragement require leadership. Knowledge is an individual resource that needs to be coordinated and integrated at the organizational level (Tiwari, 2015).

At the individual level, we highlighted certain dimensions, namely: culture (Chmielecki, 2013), emotions (Riege, 2005), trust (Park & Kim, 2018), communication skills, and the reach of social networks (Riege, 2005), and time constraints (Razmerita et al., 2016). At the inter-organizational level, various barriers exist, namely: technology issues, cross-organizational information transfer, the idea of taking tangible advantage of the information exchange, and situations where one of the organizations involved in the KS imposes the sharing of information with other organizations (Boonstra & de Vries, 2005).

CASE STUDY

Company Z

Company Z is a multinational company within the financial sector. Its subsidiary in Portugal has project teams made up of project managers and local and central project management professionals who represent the parent company.

The organization has several project teams within its departments. The target department of this study is mostly made up of project teams, whose scope applies to different areas, and, in turn, these teams employ different project management methodologies. This means that, depending on the type of project carried out by the team, several teams adopt different project management methodologies (e.g., Cascade, Agile, and Lean Six Sigma, among others).

The project team (see the structure of the team in Figure 1) under study is a team that carries out projects for internal clients, that is to say, for other business areas within the organization. It consists of a sub-team of project managers and a sub-team of PMO, which, in turn, is subdivided into two further teams: i) the coordination team, which is responsible for supporting the project managers, and ii) the PMO team, which is part of the company headquarters team.

Figure 1. Structure of the project team

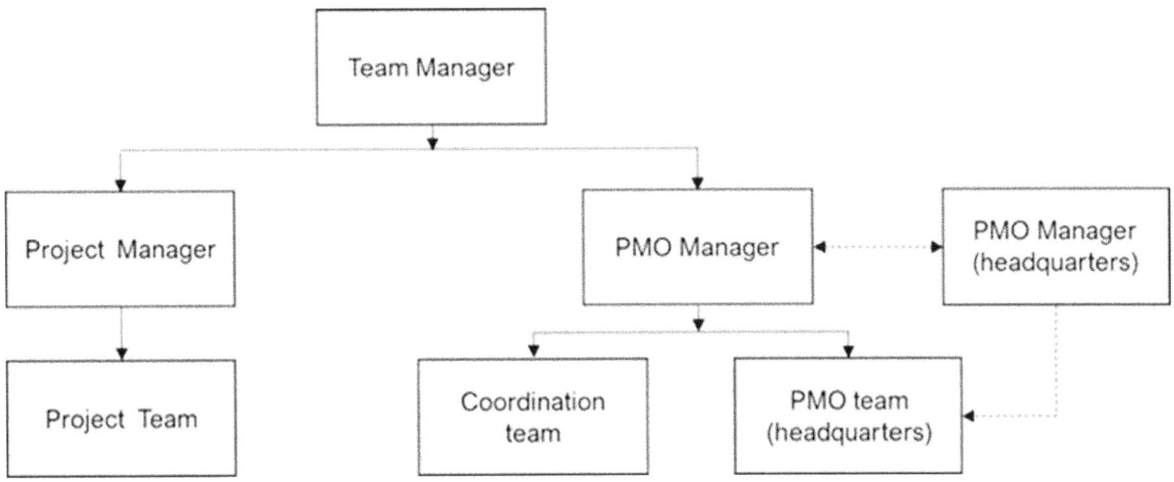

Data Collection Instrument

To understand the perception of individuals in relation to the topic of knowledge sharing, an interview was created, based on a literature review and was then applied with a project team in a financial business.

The questions created can be categorized by using the knowledge-sharing inventory developed by Liebowitz and Megbolugbe (2003) to assess how well an organization implements the knowledge management and sharing structure. This approach is divided into four categories (Liebowitz & Megbolugbe, 2003), namely:

- **Communication Flow:** How knowledge and communication exchanges are captured and disseminated by the organization.
- **Knowledge Management Environment:** Which analyses the internal cultural factors related to knowledge management within the organization.
- **Organizational Availability:** Which assesses the sophistication of the knowledge management infrastructure and the ability to share knowledge within the organization.
- **Measurement:** Which measures the likelihood of knowledge sharing and knowledge management being successful within an organization. The categorization and references are detailed in Table 1.

Table 1. The categorization of the interview (pre-validation)

Categorization	Question	References
Communication Flow	Q.3 Q.4 Q.6	(Liebowitz & Megbolugbe, 2003) (Schindler & Eppler, 2003) (Terzieva, 2014)
Knowledge Management Environment	Q.2 Q.5 Q.6a Q.9	(Bryde et al., 2018) (Chen et al., 2018) (Todorović et al.,2015) (Liebowitz & Megbolugbe, 2003)
Organizational Availability	Q.1 Q.2 Q.6b Q.6c	(Bryde et al., 2018) (Hanisch et al., 2009) (Liebowitz & Megbolugbe, 2003) (Liebowitz & Megbolugbe, 2003)
Measurement	Q.7 Q.8	(Liebowitz & Megbolugbe, 2003) (Liebowitz & Megbolugbe, 2003)

The interview script's structure asks about: the perception of the relevance of the knowledge-sharing theme within the project management; the existence of a project management methodology, knowledge sharing, and existing knowledge sources; the incentive for top management to share; and the currently used methodologies.

The responses obtained were categorized to observe the frequency of the topics mentioned by the respondents.

ANALYSIS AND DISCUSSION

The unit of analysis for this study was the members of the project and PMO teams. Answers were obtained from 10 respondents (Table 2).

Table 2. Respondents' profile

Member	Job	Age	Sex
GP01	Project Manager	30 - 40	Male
GP02	Project Manager	> 40	Male
GP03	Project Manager	> 40	Male
GP04	Project Manager	20 -30	Male
GP05	Project Manager	20 - 30	Female
PMO01	Project Manager Officer	20 - 30	Male
PMO02	Project Manager Officer	20 - 30	Female
PMO03	Project Manager Officer	20 - 30	Female
PMO04	Project Manager Officer	20 - 30	Male
L01	Coordination Team Manager	30 - 40	Male

According to the results obtained, most (7 in 10) apply Cascade Project Management methodology and most affirm that the applied methodologies incorporate knowledge management practices (6 in 10). All respondents believe it is relevant to share knowledge within a project environment. The most common sources of knowledge are guides/procedures (23%), SharePoint/Share Drive (16%), experts (13%), reports (10%), and repositories (10%).

Regarding incentives by top management, there is no consensus among respondents, with the answers indicating both the existence of incentives and the absence of them.

Notwithstanding the divergence of opinion in relation to the previous question, there is a consensus that the sharing of knowledge between project managers is a common practice among respondent teams. During their projects, most of the respondents claim to use the knowledge acquired by other project managers, as well as information from project reports, digital databases, and direct contact with project managers.

When asked about the adequacy of the currently used methodology, the general opinion is that it is indeed adequate, albeit it requires improvement.

The main problems pointed out are centered on the lack of compliance in the preparation of project documentation and on the lack of harmonization and practicality in the information storage processes.

The respondents also identified several aspects where improvement would benefit the development of their projects, namely:

- Reducing bureaucracy in general,
- Increase knowledge-sharing sessions between teams,
- Creating new tools that are easier to use,
- Increased level of contact between the various project managers,
- Greater promotion of collaborative work,
- Awareness of filling in the data associated with each project,
- Simplification and harmonisation of information sources,
- Simplification of project documentation to avoid the duplication of work,
- Simplification of reports for better understanding.

CONCLUSION

The objective of this study was to investigate the way knowledge is shared in a project environment and to ascertain how it is observed from the perspective of individuals belonging to project teams. The results obtained reveal that knowledge sharing is considered important, both by project management managers and professionals alike at the organizational level, and they identified the existence of knowledge management practices and tools which are incorporated into the methodologies adopted by the team's project management.

The study concludes that, despite the lack of incentives from top management, project managers and other members belonging to project teams consider knowledge sharing to be a relevant contribution to achieving the more successful execution of projects.

It was also concluded that, given the disparity of projects in type and dimension, knowledge-sharing practices are not yet standardized in the organization's project management methodologies. There is room for simplifying and harmonizing the documentation and information sources to enhance the dissemination of knowledge, which would benefit the results of the projects in the course.

In addition, most of the respondents seemed to be aware that it is important to define more explicit methods and practices for obtaining, storing, and sharing knowledge.

LIMITATIONS AND FUTURE WORK

The small sample size implies that this study only reflects the specific reality of the project team under study, within the specific organizational context.

For future research, it would be of interest to analyze how geographically distant project teams deal with knowledge sharing, as well as how organizational cultures and subcultures impact the sharing of knowledge in different project teams within an organization, as the culture under which projects operate has a significant impact on knowledge sharing between projects. Finally, having carried out the study on knowledge sharing, it would be of interest to study the use of knowledge in the project environment and to analyze the benefits observed by the project managers.

Discussion Questions

1. What are the reasons that lead company Z to adopt different project management methodologies (Cascade, Agile, Lean Six Sigma, among others) in terms of different projects?
2. How well organization Z implements the knowledge management and sharing structure?
3. How are knowledge and communication exchanges captured and disseminated by the Z company?
4. How company Z manages the internal cultural factors related to knowledge management within the organization?
5. Does knowledge improve the effectiveness and efficiency of managing Z organizational resources?
6. How does knowledge sharing contribute significantly to the performance of the Z company?
7. What organizational availability assesses the sophistication of the knowledge management infrastructure and the ability to share knowledge within the Z organization?
8. Why is knowledge management considered fundamental for obtaining competitive advantages in Z company?
9. How is the probability of knowledge sharing and knowledge management being successful within a Z organization measured?

REFERENCES

Abbas, J., Hussain, I., Hussain, S., Akram, S., Shaheen, I., & Niu, B. (2019). The Impact of Knowledge Sharing and Innovation on Sustainable Performance in Islamic Banks: A Mediation Analysis through an SEM Approach. *Sustainability (Basel)*, *11*(4049), 4049. Advance online publication. doi:10.3390u11154049

Ahmad, N., Lodhi, M. S., Zaman, K., & Naseem, I. (2017). Knowledge management: A gateway for organizational performance. *Journal of the Knowledge Economy*, *8*(3), 859–876. doi:10.100713132-015-0282-3

Ajmal, M. M., Helo, P., & Kekale, T. (2010). Critical factors for knowledge management in project business. *Journal of Knowledge Management, 14*(1), 156–168. doi:10.1108/13673271011015633

Akhavan, P., & Mahdi Hosseini, S. (2016). Social capital, knowledge sharing, and innovation capability, an empirical study of R&D teams in Iran. *Technology Analysis and Strategic Management, 28*(1), 96–113. doi:10.1080/09537325.2015.1072622

Al Ahbabi, S. A., Singh, S. K., Balasubramanian, S., & Gaur, S. S. (2019). Employee perception of the impact of knowledge management processes on public sector performance. *Journal of Knowledge Management, 23*(2), 351–373. doi:10.1108/JKM-08-2017-0348

Alavi, M., & Denford, J. S. (2011). Knowledge Management: Process, Practice and Web 2.0. In M. Easterby-Smith & M. A. Lyles (Eds.), Handbook of Organizational Learning & Knowledge Management (2nd ed., pp. 105–124). Academic Press.

Andreeva, T., & Kianto, A. (2011). Knowledge processes, knowledge-intensity, and innovation: A moderated mediation analysis. *Journal of Knowledge Management, 15*(6), 1016–1034. doi:10.1108/13673271111179343

Bassi, A. (2014). Human and Organizational Knowledge in a Project Management Context. *Modern Management Review, 19*(21), 7–19. doi:10.7862/rz.2014.mmr.29

Becerra-Fernandez, I., Gonzalez, A., & Sabherwal, R. (2004). *Knowledge management challenges, solutions, and technologies*. Pearson Prentice Hall.

Bolisani, E., Debei, S., & Savino, N. (2017). Renovating Project Management: Knowledge Personalization and Sharing. In M. Handzic & A. Bassi (Eds.), *Knowledge and Project Management: A Shared Approach to Improve Performance* (Vol. 5, pp. 131–153). doi:10.1007/978-3-319-51067-5_6

Bryde, D. J., Unterhitzenberger, C., Renzl, B., & Rost, M. (2018). KM and Project Management. In J. Syed, P. A. Murray, D. Hislop, & Y. Mouzughi (Eds.), *The Palgrave Handbook of Knowledge Management* (pp. 539–561). Palgrave Handbooks. doi:10.1007/978-3-319-71434-9_22

Buvik, M. P., & Tvedt, S. D. (2017). The Influence of Project Commitment and Team Commitment on the Relationship Between Trust and Knowledge Sharing in Project Teams. *Project Management Journal, 48*(2), 5–21. doi:10.1177/875697281704800202

Cabrera, Á., & Cabrera, E. F. (2002). Knowledge-sharing Dilemmas. *Organization Studies, 23*(5), 687–710. doi:10.1177/0170840602235001

Castrogiovanni, G., Ribeiro-Soriano, D., Mas-Tur, A., & Roig-Tierno, N. (2016). Where to acquire knowledge: Adapting knowledge management to financial institutions. *Journal of Business Research, 69*(5), 1812–1816. doi:10.1016/j.jbusres.2015.10.061

Chen, H., Nunes, M. B., Ragsdell, G., & An, X. (2018). Extrinsic and intrinsic motivation for experience grounded tacit knowledge sharing in Chinese software organizations. *Journal of Knowledge Management, 22*(4), 478–498. doi:10.1108/JKM-03-2017-0101

Chen, S. H., Tao, C. Q., & He, W. (2012). Empirical research on the relationship between knowledge integration and innovation ability of IT enterprise. *International Journal of Networking and Virtual Organisations, 11*(3), 315–328. doi:10.1504/IJNVO.2012.048913

Ciulli, F., & Kolk, A. (2019). Incumbents and business model innovation for the sharing economy: Implications for sustainability. *Journal of Cleaner Production, 214*, 995–1010. doi:10.1016/j.jclepro.2018.12.295

Collins, C. J., & Smith, K. G. (2006). Knowledge exchange and combination: The role of human resource practices in the performance of high-technology firms. *Academy of Management Journal, 49*(3), 544–560. doi:10.5465/amj.2006.21794671

Costa, V., & Monteiro, S. (2016). Key knowledge management processes for innovation: A systematic literature review. *VINE Journal of Information and Knowledge Management Systems, 46*(3), 386–410. doi:10.1108/VJIKMS-02-2015-0017

Curado, C., & Bontis, N. (2006). The knowledge-based view of the firm and its theoretical precursor. *International Journal of Learning and Intellectual Capital, 3*(4), 367–381. doi:10.1504/IJLIC.2006.011747

Davenport, T. H., De Long, D. W., & Beers, M. C. (1998). Successful Knowledge Management Projects. *Sloan Management Review*, 43–57.

De Long, D. W., & Fahey, L. (2000). Diagnosing cultural barriers to knowledge management. *Academy of Knowledge Executive, 14*(4), 113–127.

Desouza, K. C., & Evaristo, J. R. (2004). Managing knowledge in distributed projects. *Communications of the ACM, 47*(4), 87–91. doi:10.1145/975817.975823

Ekambaram, A., Sørensen, A. Ø., Bull-Berg, H., & Olsson, N. O. (2018). The role of big data and knowledge management in improving project-based organizations. *Procedia Computer Science, 138*, 851–858. doi:10.1016/j.procs.2018.10.111

Fang, S. C., Yang, C. W., & Hsu, W. Y. (2013). Inter-organizational knowledge transfer: The perspective of knowledge governance. *Journal of Knowledge Management, 17*(6), 943–957. doi:10.1108/JKM-04-2013-0138

Fernie, S., Green, S. D., Weller, S. J., & Newcombe, R. (2003). Knowledge sharing: Context, confusion, and controversy. *International Journal of Project Management, 21*(3), 177–187. doi:10.1016/S0263-7863(02)00092-3

Fields, Z. (Ed.). (2017). *Collective Creativity for Responsible and Sustainable Business Practice*. IGI Global. doi:10.4018/978-1-5225-1823-5

Frey, P., Lindner, F., Muller, A., & Wald, A. (2009). Project Knowledge Management Organizational Design and Success Factors - An Empirical Study in Germany. *Proceedings of 42nd Hawaii International Conference on System Sciences*, 1-14.

Gao, T., Chai, Y., & Liu, Y. (2018). A review of knowledge management about theoretical conception and designing approaches. *International Journal of Crowd Sciences, 2*(1), 42–51. doi:10.1108/IJCS-08-2017-0023

Gasik, S. (2011). A Model of Project Knowledge Management. *Project Management Journal, 42*(3), 23–44. doi:10.1002/pmj.20239

Greiner, M., Böhmann, T., & Krcmar, H. (2007). A strategy for knowledge management. *Journal of Knowledge Management, 11*(6), 3–15. doi:10.1108/13673270710832127

Gürlek, M., & Çemberci, M. (2020). Understanding the relationships among knowledge-oriented leadership, knowledge management capacity, innovation performance, and organizational performance: A serial mediation analysis. *Kybernetes, 49*(11), 2819–2846. doi:10.1108/K-09-2019-0632

Hanisch, B., Lindner, F., Mueller, A., & Wald, A. (2009). Knowledge management in project environments. *Journal of Knowledge Management, 13*(4), 148–160. doi:10.1108/13673270910971897

Hans, P. E., & Skiver, J. (2007). Organizational Culture Restraining In-House Knowledge Transfer Between Project Managers - A Case Study. *Project Management Journal, 38*(1), 110–122. doi:10.1177/875697280703800111

Hansen, M. T., Nohria, N., & Tierney, T. (1999). What's Your Strategy for Managing Knowledge? *Harvard Business Review*, 1–11. PMID:10387767

Heisig, P. (2009). Harmonisation of knowledge management – comparing 160 KM frameworks around the globe. *Journal of Knowledge Management, 13*(4), 4–31. doi:10.1108/13673270910971798

Holzman, V. (2013). A meta-analysis of brokering knowledge in project management. *International Journal of Project Management, 31*(1), 2–13. doi:10.1016/j.ijproman.2012.05.002

Hooff, B. V. D., & De Ridder, J. A. (2004). Knowledge sharing in context: The influence of organizational commitment, communication climate, and CMC use on knowledge sharing. *Journal of Knowledge Management, 8*(6), 117–130. doi:10.1108/13673270410567675

Hoorn, B., & Whitty, S. J. (2019). The five modes of comportment for project managing: Disclosing the tacit in project work. *International Journal of Project Management, 37*(3), 363–377. doi:10.1016/j.ijproman.2019.01.009

Inkinen, H. (2016). Review of empirical research on knowledge management practices and firm performance. *Journal of Knowledge Management, 20*(2), 230–257. doi:10.1108/JKM-09-2015-0336

Kasvi, J. J., Vartiainen, M., & Hailikari, M. (2003). Managing knowledge and knowledge competencies in projects and project organisations. *International Journal of Project Management, 21*(8), 571–582. doi:10.1016/S0263-7863(02)00057-1

Kishore, J. K., Sandhu, M. S., & Wai Ling, C. (2009). Knowledge sharing in an American multinational company based in Malaysia. *Journal of Workplace Learning, 21*(2), 125–142. doi:10.1108/13665620910934825

Koskinen, K. U. (2004). Knowledge Management to Improve Project Communication and Implementation. *Project Management Journal, 35*(1), 13–19. doi:10.1177/875697280403500203

Koskinen, K. U., & Pihlanto, P. (2008). Knowledge Sharing and Methods of Knowledge Sharing. In K. U. Koskinen & P. Pihlanto (Eds.), *Knowledge Management in Project-Based Companies: An Organic Perspective* (pp. 80–157). Palgrave Macmillan. doi:10.1057/9780230595071_6

Koskinen, K. U., Pihlanto, P., & Vanharanta, H. (2003). Tacit knowledge acquisition and sharing in a project work context. *International Journal of Project Management, 21*(4), 281–290. doi:10.1016/S0263-7863(02)00030-3

Lai, Y. L., Hsu, M. S., Lin, F. J., Chen, Y. M., & Lin, Y. H. (2014). The effects of industry cluster knowledge management on innovation performance. *Journal of Business Research, 67*(5), 734–739. doi:10.1016/j.jbusres.2013.11.036

Leseure, M. J., & Brookes, N. J. (2004). Knowledge management benchmarks for project management. *Journal of Knowledge Management, 8*(1), 103–116. doi:10.1108/13673270410523943

Liebowitz, J., & Megbolugbe, I. (2003). A set of frameworks to aid the project manager in conceptualizing and implementing knowledge management initiatives. *International Journal of Project Management, 21*(3), 189–198. doi:10.1016/S0263-7863(02)00093-5

Love, P., Fong, P., & Irani, Z. (2005). *Management of knowledge in project environments.* Elsevier.

Mahdi, O. R., Nassa, I. A., & Almsafir, M. K. (2019). Knowledge management processes and sustainable competitive advantage: An empirical examination in private universities. *Journal of Business Research, 94*, 320–334. doi:10.1016/j.jbusres.2018.02.013

Mannan, B., Jameel, S. S., & Haleem, A. (2013). *Knowledge Management in Project Management: An ISM Approach.* Lambert Academic Publishing.

Mazur, M., Spahić, A., Grabar, D., Grd, P., Sedlbauer, G., Sikorska, K., & Beamonte, E. P. (2014). Knowledge Management 2.0 - Handbook for companies. Lifelong Learning Programme, European Commission.

McElroy, M. W. (2000). Integrating complexity theory, knowledge management and organisational learning. *Journal of Knowledge Management, 4*(3), 195–203. doi:10.1108/13673270010377652

Merat, A., & Bo, D. (2013). Strategic analysis of knowledge firms: The links between knowledge management and leadership. *Journal of Knowledge Management, 17*(1), 3–15. doi:10.1108/13673271311300697

Morris, P. (2002). Science, objective knowledge, and the theory of project management. *Proceedings of the Institution of Civil Engineers. Civil Engineering, 150*(2), 82–90. doi:10.1680/cien.2002.150.2.82

Mueller, J. (2012). Knowledge sharing between project teams and their cultural antecedents. *Journal of Knowledge Management, 16*(3), 435–447. doi:10.1108/13673271211238751

Mueller, J. (2015). Formal and Informal Practices of Knowledge Sharing Between Project Teams and Enacted Cultural Characteristics. *Project Management Journal, 46*(1), 53–68. doi:10.1002/pmj.21471

Nesheim, T., & Hunskaar, H. M. (2015). When employees and external consultants work together on projects: Challenges of knowledge sharing. *International Journal of Project Management, 33*(7), 1417–1424. doi:10.1016/j.ijproman.2015.06.010

Nonaka, I. (1994). A Dynamic Theory of Organizational Knowledge Creation. *Organization Science, 5*(1), 14–37. doi:10.1287/orsc.5.1.14

Nonaka, I., & Konno, N. (1998). The Concept of "Ba": Building a Foundation for Knowledge Creation. *California Management Review, 40*(3), 40–54. doi:10.2307/41165942

Nonaka, I., & Takeuchi, H. (1995). *The Knowledge-creating Company – How Japanese Companies Create the Dynamics of Innovation*. Oxford University Press.

Owen, J., & Burstein, F. (2005). Where Knowledge Management Resides within Project Management. In Case Studies in Knowledge Management. doi:10.4018/978-1-59140-351-7.ch009

Pascoe, C., & More, E. (2005). Communication Climate and Organizational Knowledge Sharing. *Journal of Information and Knowledge Management*, *4*(4), 247–255. doi:10.1142/S0219649205001225

PMI. (2017). A Guide to the Project Management Body of Knowledge (PMBOK) (6th ed.). Newtown Square, PA: Project Management Institute, Inc.

Polyaninova, T. (2011). Knowledge Management in a Project Environment: Organisational CT and Project Influences. *VINE Journal of Information and Knowledge Management Systems*, *41*(3).

Pretorius, C. J., & Steyn, H. (2005). Knowledge management in project environments. *South African Journal of Business Management*, *36*(3), 41–50. doi:10.4102ajbm.v36i3.634

Rashed, M. (2016). The Readiness of Banks in Knowledge Management: A Study of Three Private Commercial Banks in Bangladesh. *Journal of Business and Financial Affairs*, *5*(2), 1–5.

Reich, B. H., Gemino, A., & Sauer, C. (2008). Modeling the knowledge perspective in IT projects. *Project Management Journal*, *39*(1_suppl), S4–S14. doi:10.1002/pmj.20056

Romani, M. (2017). Lessons Learnt Support System. In M. Handzic & A. Bassi (Eds.), *Knowledge and Project Management: A Shared Approach to Improve Performance* (Vol. 5, pp. 95–129). doi:10.1007/978-3-319-51067-5_5

Ruuska, I., & Vartiainen, M. (2005). Characteristics of knowledge sharing communities in project organizations. *International Journal of Project Management*, *23*(5), 374–379. doi:10.1016/j.ijproman.2005.01.003

Sankarasubramanian, S. (2009). Knowledge management meets project management. In *PMI® Global Congress 2009*—Asia Pacific, Kuala Lumpur, Malaysia. Newtown Square, PA: Project Management Institute.

Schindler, M., & Eppler, M. J. (2003). Harvesting project knowledge: A review of project learning methods and success factors. *International Journal of Project Management*, *21*(3), 219–228. doi:10.1016/S0263-7863(02)00096-0

Shujahat, M., Hussain, S., Javed, S., Thurasamy, R., & Ali, J. (2017). Strategic management model with lens of knowledge management and competitive intelligence: A review approach. *VINE Journal of Information and Knowledge Management Systems*, *47*(1), 55–93. doi:10.1108/VJIKMS-06-2016-0035

Singh, S. K., Gupta, S., Busso, D., & Kamboj, S. (2021). Top management knowledge value, knowledge sharing practices, open innovation, and organizational performance. *Journal of Business Research*, *128*, 788–798. doi:10.1016/j.jbusres.2019.04.040

Soderlund, J. (2010). Knowledge entrainment and project management: The case of large-scale transformation projects. *International Journal of Project Management*, *28*(2), 130–141. doi:10.1016/j.ijproman.2009.11.010

Sokhanvar, S., Matthews, J., & Yarlagadda, P. (2014). Importance of Knowledge Management Processes in a Project-based organization: A Case Study of Research Enterprise. *Procedia Engineering*, *97*, 1825–1830. doi:10.1016/j.proeng.2014.12.336

Song, M., Bij, H. V. D., & Weggeman, M. (2005). Determinants of the level of knowledge application: A knowledge-based and information-processing perspective. *Journal of Product Innovation Management*, *22*(5), 430–444. doi:10.1111/j.1540-5885.2005.00139.x

Taminiau, Y., Smit, W., & Lange, A. D. (2009). Innovation in management consulting firms through informal knowledge sharing. *Journal of Knowledge Management*, *13*(1), 42–55. doi:10.1108/13673270910931152

Terzieva, M. (2014). Project Knowledge Management: How organizations learn from experience. *Procedia Technology*, *16*, 1086–1095. doi:10.1016/j.protcy.2014.10.123

Todorović, M. L., Petrović, D. Č., Mihić, M. M., Obradović, V. L., & Bushuyev, S. D. (2015). Project success analysis framework: A knowledge-based approach in project management. *International Journal of Project Management*, *33*(4), 772–783. doi:10.1016/j.ijproman.2014.10.009

Uğurlu, Ö. Y., & Kizildağ, D. (2013). A Comparative Analysis of Knowledge Management in Banking Sector: An Empirical Research. *European Journal of Business and Management*, *5*(16), 12–19.

Wang, W.-T., & Ko, N.-Y. (2012). Knowledge sharing practices of project teams when encountering changes in project scope: A contingency approach. *Journal of Information Science*, *38*(5), 423–441. doi:10.1177/0165551512445240

Wickramasinghe, V., & Widyaratne, R. (2012). Effects of interpersonal trust, team leader support, rewards, and knowledge sharing mechanisms on knowledge sharing in project teams. *VINE Journal of Information and Knowledge Management Systems*, *42*(2), 214–236.

Yeong, A., & Lim, T. T. (2010). Integrating knowledge management with project management for project success. *Journal of Project. Program & Portfolio Management*, *1*(2), 8–19. doi:10.5130/pppm.v1i2.1735

ADDITIONAL READING

Alavi, M., & Leidner, D. (1999). Knowledge management systems: issues, challenges, and benefits. *Communications of the AIS*, *1*(2).

Alavi, M., & Leidner, D. (2001). Review: Knowledge Management and Knowledge Management Systems: Conceptual Foundations and Research Issues. *Management Information Systems Quarterly*, *25*(1), 107. doi:10.2307/3250961

Bontis, N., & Choo, C. W. (2002). *The Strategic Management of Intellectual Capital and Organizational Knowledge*. Oxford University Press.

Davenport, T. H., & Prusak, L. (1998). *Working Knowledge: How Organizations Manage What They Know*. Harvard Business School Press.

Easterby-Smith, M., & Lyles, M. A. (2011). The Evolving Field of Organizational Learning and Knowledge Management. In M. Easterby-Smith & M. A. Lyles (Eds.), Handbook of Organizational Learning & Knowledge Management (2nd ed., pp. 1–20). Academic Press.

Fong, P. S. (2005). Co-creation of knowledge by multidisciplinary project teams. In P. E. Love, P. S. Fong, & Z. Irani (Eds.), *Management of Knowledge in Project Environments* (pp. 41–36). Elsevier Butterworth-Heinemann. doi:10.1016/B978-0-7506-6251-2.50007-9

Gupta, J., & Sharma, S. (2004). *Creating Knowledge-Based Organizations*. Idea Group Publishing. doi:10.4018/978-1-59140-162-9

Kogut, B., & Zander, U. (1992). Knowledge of the firm, combinative capabilities, and the replication of technology. *Organization Science*, *3*(3), 383–397. doi:10.1287/orsc.3.3.383

Koskinen, K. U. (2000). Tacit knowledge as a promoter of project success. *European Journal of Purchasing & Supply Management*, *6*(1), 41–47. doi:10.1016/S0969-7012(99)00033-7

Maier, R. (2007). *Knowledge Management Systems: Information and Communication Technologies for Knowledge Management* (3rd ed.). Springer.

Nonaka, I. (1991). The knowledge creating company. *Harvard Business Review*, *69*(6), 96–104.

Nonaka, I., & von Krogh, G. (2009). Tacit Knowledge and Knowledge Conversion: Controversy and Advancement in Organizational Knowledge Creation Theory. *Organization Science*, *20*(3), 635–652. doi:10.1287/orsc.1080.0412

Nonaka, I., von Krogh, G., & Voelpel, S. (2006). Organizational knowledge creation theory: Evolutionary paths and future advances. *Organization Studies*, *27*(8), 1179–1208. doi:10.1177/0170840606066312

Polanyi, M. (1966). *The Tacit Dimension*. Routledge & Kegan Paul.

KEY TERMS AND DEFINITIONS

Explicit Knowledge: Refers to knowledge that is transmissible in a formal and systemic language (Nonaka, 1994; Nonaka & Takeuchi, 1995).

Knowledge: Seen as an intangible asset, which is valuable, distinctive, path-dependent, causally ambiguous, and hard to substitute or replicate (Fang et al., 2013, p. 945).

Knowledge Creation: The process in which new knowledge is created through the four sub-processes of organizational knowledge creation (Andreeva & Kianto, 2011).

Knowledge Management: The set of processes related to the creation, sharing, and use of knowledge (Ahmad et al., 2017; Shujahat et al., 2017).

Knowledge Sharing: The action of disseminating knowledge among individuals, groups, and organizations (Chen et al., 2018).

Knowledge Transfer: The communication of knowledge from a source to a recipient (Alavi & Denford, 2011).

Lessons Learned: Knowledge gained during a project that shows how project events have been addressed or should be addressed in the future, to improve future performance (PMI, 2017).

PMO (Project Management Office): Management structure that standardizes the governance processes related to the project and facilitates the sharing of resources, methodologies, tools, and techniques (PMI, 2017).

Project Knowledge Management: The application of concepts, tools, and techniques to complete a project within the defined time and budget, responding to the client's needs (Romani, 2017).

Webinars: Seminars transmitted through digital platforms, which allow sharing and interaction between individuals.

APPENDIX

Interview Guide

1. Is knowledge sharing a relevant aspect of project management?
2. What is the project management methodology applied in your team?
   a) If you have identified it above, are there specific rules for project knowledge management in it?
3. What are the existing sources of project knowledge in your team?
4. Of the sources of knowledge mentioned, which do you use most frequently?
5. Is knowledge sharing encouraged by top management?
6. In managing your projects, do you use the knowledge acquired by other project managers?
   a) Is this practice common to the project team?
   b) Is it easy to access this information?
   c) In what format is this information found? (e.g., project reports, lessons learned, direct contact with the project manager, etc.)
7. In your opinion, do you think that the knowledge-sharing methodology currently used by your team is the most appropriate?
8. In your opinion, what improvements can be applied to the methodology currently used?

Section 4
Technology Reviews and Case Studies

Chapter 11
Impact of Sustainability on Supply Chain:
Contributions and New Performance Measurements in the Disruptive Technology Era

Özden Özkanlısoy
https://orcid.org/0000-0001-7879-0733
Yeditepe University, Turkey

Füsun Bulutlar
Yeditepe University, Turkey

EXECUTIVE SUMMARY

Industry 4.0 technologies, also called disruptive, have become a part of the new world. When disruptive technologies are investigated in terms of supply chain, they have many effects on supply chain performance. Sustainability is one of the positive contributions of these technologies to supply chain performance. When measuring supply chain performance, it is necessary to keep up with the times and therefore constantly update the performance measurements. Previous studies did not address the sustainability dimension of supply chain performance measurements comprehensively. In this chapter, the authors examine supply chain sustainability performance measurements based on the existing literature and taking into account the contributions of DTs to determine them. The authors briefly explain disruptive technologies and examine the contributions of these technologies to supply chain sustainability performance separately. The main aim of the study is to guide companies and their supply chains to enhance their supply chain sustainability performance by using disruptive technologies.

DOI: 10.4018/978-1-6684-5859-4.ch011

INTRODUCTION

The evolution of technology has shown rapid development in the last 20 years. Nowadays, new technology is discovered almost every day. The main purposes of these technologies are to identify customer needs, evaluate profitability, and provide rapid solutions to process improvement (Bower & Christensen, 1995). Therefore, technologies utilized in the supply chain (SC) play a crucial role in developing operational competence and augmenting supply chain performance (SCP) (Bharadwaj et al., 2007).

Industry 4.0 (4IR), also called the Fourth Industrial Revolution, has brought with it the digital transformation of industrialization or physical manufacturing and cyber technologies by disruptive technologies (DTs), which are also called new technologies or 4IR technologies. They have significant advantages over other technologies used in SCs. Further, these technologies are called "disruptive" because they dramatically change the way consumers, industries, and businesses operate (Bower & Christensen, 1995). They destroy the systems or habits they replace because of their recognizable superior characteristics. In this respect, contrary to their name, they make significant contributions to companies and SCs in a constructive sense (Walsh et al., 2002). The implementation of them is expected to result in significant performance improvement in SCs (Fatorachian & Kazemi, 2021).

The concept of sustainability encompasses many issues, including survival and well-being. The continuity of sustainability is also crucial. Future generations should be supported as well as the current generation for continuity. Sustainability is the creation of the necessary situations for humans and nature to exist in productive conformity and the continuation of these conditions (United States Environmental Protection Agency, 2022). In other words, it is an intelligent balance between economic development, environmental management, and social equity. To establish this balance, sustainability is considered in three dimensions: Environmental, social, and economic (Panwar et al., 2006).

Environmental sustainability relates to the companies carrying out their activities with the least possible negative environmental impact (Blewitt, 2014). Social sustainability is the dimension of sustainability that requires companies to provide equal opportunities to their employees, promote social cohesion in society, and act considering their employees and society (Rogers et al., 2007). It includes people in the society, called the outer communities, and workers called the inner communities (Gimenez et al., 2012). Economic sustainability is meant to realize traditional economic goals by acting in accordance with the above-mentioned social and environmental sustainability (Carter & Rogers, 2008). Economic sustainability ensures the efficient utilization of existing resources and the long-term sustainability of profitability (Elliott, 2012).

Before addressing the affair of sustainability in SCs, supply chain management (SCM) only deals with operational and economic issues. Factors such as high-volume production, pollution, solid or waste emissions, and similar serious environmental problems in SCs (Vonderembse et al., 1997, p. 2584), environmental issues arising from SCs, acid rain, and global warming have caused environmental concerns in SCs (Moffatt, 2004; Sarkis, 2006). The significance of the concept of sustainability has been better understood with the shift of consumers towards environmentally friendly products (Nelson et al., 2012), the shift of production activities from systems focusing on economic goals to systems that also consider environmental goals, and the understanding of the significance of realizing social and environmental goals (Nahm & Vonderembse, 2002). In this way, sustainability in SCs has also been understood. The company and the SCs of which it is a member should carry out their activities by addressing social, economic, and environmental issues, and SCM should be carried out in this direction (Carter & Easton, 2011).

Sustainability performance in SCM plays a critical role not only in the survival of businesses but also in their long-term development and success (Ivanov, 2021). While DTs act an integral role in SCM, figuring out their effect on sustainability performance is critical (Markley & Davis, 2007; Rao & Holt, 2005). DTs create a cleaner environment, consumer surpluses, lower prices, and better health. Thanks to these benefits, it is estimated that it will have an economic effect from $14 trillion to $33 trillion in a year by 2025 (Manyika et al., 2013).

While the concept of sustainability in SC remains significant, SC sustainability performance measurements, including the SCOR (supply chain operations reference) performance model presented by the internationally recognized Association of Supply Chain Management (ASCM) (2022), are not comprehensively addressed. While the need to fill the gap in the literature as to these sustainability performance measurements in the SC continues, it is necessary to know which DT and which sustainability performance measurement can enhance the sustainability performance to benefit from the sustainability contributions of DTs to SCs. This chapter aims to guide companies and their SCs to measure their sustainability performances and improve their performance by utilizing DTs, determining SC sustainability performance measurements in detail, and by addressing the sustainability performance contributions of DTs to their SCs. In this direction, firstly, the authors briefly outline DTs and then present the sustainability measurements they determined based on the literature. Subsequently, they illustrate the contribution of each DT to the sustainability measurements. Finally, the authors discuss their findings.

BACKGROUND

SCM is the process of planning, coordination, and control executed to decrease costs and raise the level of service in the SC. It includes all processes from the supply of raw materials to the delivery of the final product to the customer and the return of the delivered product. The main purposes of SCM are to minimize its costs, offer the best to the customer, and utilize the resources in the SC in the most efficient way (Basu & Wright, 2008). A closer consideration of these purposes clearly shows that they are sustainability goals.

DTs, also known as 4IR technologies, will contribute to the elimination of environmental problems such as pollution and waste, demolition of nonrenewable resources, climate change, and loss of biodiversity, and thus they will improve the living standards of future generations. Scholars have started to investigate the effect of the utilization of DTs on sustainability performance in SCs (Müller et al., 2018; Stock & Seliger, 2016). Some researchers have examined whether the Fourth Industrial Revolution has an impact on sustainability in the SC (Bai et al., 2020; Bag et al., 2020; Barretto et al., 2017; Cabral et al., 2012; Fürstenau et al., 2020; Ghobakhloo, 2020; Katyar et al., 2018; Mani et al., 2018; Ramezankhani et al. 2018; Schöggl et al., 2016; Shee et al.,2018). Therefore, the following paragraphs report on some of these studies.

Ghobakhloo (2020) conducted a systematic literature review. He systematically determined the contributions of 4IR to sustainability and thus the contributions of DTs to it, contributing to the literature in this field. For this purpose, Ghobakhloo reviewed the basic design principles of 4IR and the DTs it offers. Furthermore, he modeled the contextual relationships between the 4IR and sustainability functions. As a result of this study, complex precedence relationships emerged among the various sustainability functions of 4IR. In addition, Ghobakhloo found energy sustainability, reducing harmful emissions, and improving social welfare to be functions of 4IR. The study is a guide to better figure out the benefits of DTs and evaluates their effect on sustainability performance.

Bai et al. (2020) presented a sustainability measure framework to examine DTs in detail from a sustainability perspective. They examined the technologies that have the most impact on sustainability, namely mobile technology, nanotechnology, simulation technology, and drones. They also registered the impact of DTs on sustainability by sector. While the most affected sector is automotive, the least affected sector is footwear.

Fürstenau et al. (2020) investigated the relationship between 4IR and sustainability. The researchers utilized bibliometric performance and network analysis with strategic themes between 2010 and 2019 and sought to fill research gaps to suggest future work. This study strengthens scientific efforts in this field from an economic and environmental perspective and emphasizes the lack of effort in the social field. In the conclusion, the authors presented the challenges and recommendations for further studies in this field.

Bag et al. (2020) conducted a systematic literature review to identify the contributions of 4IR to SC sustainability and to close the gap in the literature in this field. The authors identified 13 key 4IR providers that are effective in ensuring the sustainability of SC.

Kumar and Barua (2021) aimed to characterize prominent sustainability dimensions and prominent DTs. Their findings disclosed that the most prominent sustainability dimensions in oil SCs are social responsibility, business practices, safety, and technical standards. In addition, they highlighted that artificial intelligence (AI) and big data contribute dramatically to the sustainability of operations in petroleum SCs.

The following paragraphs report the studies that deal with SCP in terms of sustainability.

Ramezankhani et al. (2018) aimed to address the performance of the SC in terms of sustainability and flexibility. In line with this, they proposed a performance management system, applied it to an automotive manufacturing industry, and tested the validity of the model. They utilized a decision making trial and evaluation laboratory (better known as DEMATEL) and quality function distribution.

Mani et al. (2018) investigated social issues related to suppliers and the dimensions of social sustainability. They carried out this study in developing economies and utilized both qualitative and quantitative research methods. They conducted in-depth interviews with SC managers and a survey with manufacturing industries; they utilized structural equation modeling to analyze the survey data. The study revealed that supplier social sustainability is a significant issue. In this direction, the key points are worker rights, safety and health, social responsibility, diversity, and product responsibility. Furthermore, according to the results of the study, there is a positive relationship between the suppliers' social sustainability practices and the SCP mediated by the supplier performance.

Katyar et al. (2018) presented a distinct approach for calculating an SCP index that can be utilized by automobile companies. Based on the literature review and expert opinion, firstly, they indicated the SC operations that affect sustainability and SCP. Afterward, they designed a survey. They examined the relationship between the determined factors and SCP. In addition, they calculated the SCP index and developed an integrated model. Katyar et al. also finalized that sustainability performance mediated the relationship between SC functions and SCP.

Schöggl et al. (2016) reviewed the relevant available literature to address sustainability issues throughout the SC. Moreover, they presented a conceptual framework for SC sustainability evaluation. Finally, they investigated convenient methods and proposed three approaches for evaluating and collecting indicators of sustainability.

Shee et al. (2018) tested the hypothetical relationship of cloud-enabled SC integration with performance in a theoretical model using survey data and structural equation modeling. The results revealed that cloud-based technology has an impact on SC integration and that cloud-enabled SC integration is positively associated with SCP, which affects firm sustainability.

Some studies in the literature reveal that DTs affect SC sustainability performance through SC visibility because SC visibility and SC sustainability are interrelated concepts. For instance, while a more accurate utilization of resources provides visibility (Barretto et al., 2017), effective utilization of resources is important for SC sustainability (Global Reporting Initiative, 2011; Veleva & Ellenbecker, 2001; Zhu et al., 2011). Another example is that improving visibility into understanding procurement conditions also impacts sustainability performance (Cabral et al., 2012).

The relationship between SC visibility and SC sustainability performance has not been investigated in depth in the literature. It is necessary to evaluate the relationship between SC visibility (in terms of resources and capabilities) and economic, social, and environmental factors in the SC to fill this gap (Dubey et al. 2017). It is a significant issue to ensure and increase SC visibility. If end-to-end visibility cannot be achieved in the SC, it is not possible to predict, prevent, and administer all the problems that will occur (Kilpatrick & Barter, 2020). Therefore, visibility is significant for the sustainability of SC activities. Dubey et al. (2020) worked up a model to research the impact of SC visibility on the dimensions of SC sustainability under the regulatory influence of product complexity. They collected data through a questionnaire and analyzed them by structural equation modeling. Based on their results, SC visibility has a crucial effect on social and environmental sustainability performance.

Saqib and Zhang (2021) aimed to examine the moderator role of SC visibility in the effect of sustainable implementations on sustainable performance; they collected data through a survey and analyzed them by structural equation modeling. The study revealed that sustainable practices in production, supply, and distribution activities significantly affect the sustainability performance of the firm, and this relationship is governed by SC visibility.

Swift et al. (2018) analyzed the differences in the activity and market performance of firms to distinguish between high and low visibility companies. They performed a case study and concluded that companies with high visibility in SCs execute higher profitability than companies with less visibility. Additionally, companies with high visibility have enhanced sales performance and stock market valuations. Furthermore, this study reveals that, by increasing their visibility SCs, firms can gain operational and market benefits.

MAIN FOCUS OF THE CHAPTER

Sustainability in Supply Chains

Before the concept of sustainability emerged, the concept of environmental sensitivity gained importance, and attention was drawn to environmental destruction. Since the 2000s, sustainability has begun to be defined by its own structure, both in the business world and in the academic world. From a business perspective, sustainability is about reducing costs in every conceivable way, including future costs, to facilitate profitability, competitiveness, and longevity. The core of the sustainability mechanism is based on the elimination of waste, on prolonging the life of resources, and on adopting their best management (Scott, 2017). According to the definition of the United Nations World Commission on Environment and Development (Brundtland, 1987), it is "meeting the needs of the present without compromising the ability of future generations to meet their own needs" (p.6).

Sustainability is based on designing a vision of society utilizing all its resources in a respectful and measured way. The joint process realized by adopting this vision is called sustainability (Viederman, 1994). This concept is combined with the quality of life. In this direction, it is possible to express sustainability as "developing the quality of human life while continuing to live within the current bringing capacity of ecosystems" (Worldwide Fund for Nature, 1993, p. 32). The goal of sustainability is to achieve higher and more sustainable well-being for the entire universe, including future breeds (Caradonna, 2014). When sustainability is considered at the institutional level, it can be defined as fulfilling the needs of all stakeholders of the company without making concessions on its competence to fulfill the needs of future stakeholders (Dyllick & Hockerts, 2002).

Sustainability is an extensive notion that covers many sides of the world of humanity (Beier et al., 2017). The concept of sustainability is not limited to environmentalism. This concept, which includes the protection of economic and social sources (Choi & Ng, 2011; Ford & Despeisse, 2016), has three dimensions, namely economic, environmental, and social (Morali & Searcy, 2013). Focusing on one dimension of sustainability is a problem because it upsets its balance. For this reason, it is imperative to consider the three dimensions of sustainability with a holistic approach (Giddings et al., 2002).

There are three flows in SCs, namely product, information, and money. These flows include the processes from supplying the raw material to the production and transformation of products to the end user. SCM is the integration of these actions through enhanced SC relationships to achieve a sustainable competitive advantage (Romiguer, 2011). The significance of SCM is better understood day by day. SCM is critical in the highly competitive global business world, and well-managed SCs enable operational and strategic benefits to businesses, regions, and countries (Silvestre, 2015). With the wider SCs in modern business operations, the concept of a sustainable SC has emerged. In SCM, the issue of sustainability is crucial in terms of increasing profitability in SCs, reducing environmental impacts, and increasing social welfare. For SC sustainability performance, the management of SC operations, resources, information, and funds must be carried out (Taticchi et al., 2013).

One of the significant aspects of SC sustainability is the necessity of both trying to develop the sustainability performance of the member businesses of the SCs and making improvements in the overall sustainability performance of the entire SC. Therefore, enhancing sustainability performance in the SC is a difficult process (Vidal & Croom, 2018). For instance, moving products and services to where they are most valuable can have negative environmental and social consequences. Food production requires rare resources (i.e., soil and water). In addition, the goal of maximizing profit by reducing costs can potentially lead to problems such as low fees, poor working conditions, or child labor. This creates increasing pressure from governments, customers, or shareholders to make the SC sustainable (Eitiveni et al., 2017).

Different aspects need to be reviewed to ensure SC sustainability performance: Green design, inventory management, remanufacturing, product recovery, waste management, reverse logistics, manufacturing planning, and control activities for the reduction of energy utilization and emission (Esfahbodi et al., 2016; Ivanov, 2021; Zailani et al., 2012). Sustainability in the SC makes many contributions, involving the economic and social dimensions of sustainability, such as retaining key employees, maximizing revenue, and developing a share of the market (Büyüközkan & Berkol, 2011).

Disruptive Technologies

Today's competitive priority depends on technology superiority and especially on the effective utilization of technology (Sandström et al., 2009). For a company and its SC, a technology that looked tremendous yesterday may not be sufficient today or tomorrow. Therefore, today's technology requirements and trends are changing rapidly. Nowadays, SCs must utilize collaborative technologies that are superfast, digitally disruptive, hyper-resilient, and have high levels of superior customer service and profitable enterprise growth (Timmermans, 2016).

The identification and development of DTs are not set by strict boundaries (Manyika et al., 2013). These developing technologies have taken the title of "disruptive" because they can quickly replace the existing technology (Christensen, 1997). Contrary to what the name suggests, they are technologies that make positive contributions to SCs. Recent developments in DTs are also extremely important for businesses and their SCs to gain a competitive advantage (Das et al., 2020). These technologies encourage disruptive innovation (Sandström et al., 2009).

4IR technologies, also referred to as 4IR components, are named DTs. These technologies are generally cyber-physical systems (CPS), Internet of Things (IoT), AI, autonomous robots, big data, and analytics, blockchain, cloud computing, 3D printers, augmented reality, virtual reality (VR), autonomous (driverless) vehicles, digital twin, horizontal and vertical system/software integrations, simulation, cyber security, and 5G technologies.

4IR is a sustainability-oriented concept. The DTs offered by 4IR have enabled industrial managers to incorporate environmental protection and control initiatives into their business processes, increasing resource efficiency and the well-being of workers and society, making SCs smarter and more flexible, facilitating measurement in SCs, and increasing process security (Luthra & Mangla, 2018). In this part of the study, the authors explain DTs separately and detail their contribution to SC sustainability.

Definitions and Contributions of Disruptive Technologies

Cyber-Physical Systems (CPS): It is a technology that increases the two-way information flow between executive and decision systems in production engineering and is defined as an integrated concept that provides this (Timm & Lorig, 2015). They are next-generation systems that interact with both objects and people by integrating procedural and physical capabilities using new methods (Baheti & Gill, 2011). CPS, one of the DTs, offers enhanced connectivity and automation through boosted sharing of information. This has significantly enhanced SCP (Blome et al., 2014; Strozzi et al., 2017).

CPS utilizes information and communication technologies to monitor and understand physical processes and systems (Davies, 2015). They provide various computations, networking activities, and integration of physical processes. The main purpose of CPS is to control physical processes; the feedback fits new circumstances in real time (Liu & Xu, 2017). In addition, it enables the flexible execution of predetermined applications (Bodrow, 2017). Developing flexibility in the SC contributes to sustainability (Luthra & Mangla, 2018). The fields of application of CPS include high-reliability medical devices, traffic control and security, advanced automotive systems, process control, agriculture, health, energy saving, environmental control, critical infrastructure control (i.e., electricity, water, and communication), defense systems, manufacturing, and smart structures (Lee, 2008; Rajkumar et al., 2010).

CPS contributes to social sustainability in terms of reacting to customer needs and collaborating with people (Lasi et al.., 2014). They contribute to environmental and economic sustainability in terms of providing reliable data on material flow, energy flow, and energy consumption (Bonilla et al., 2018). CPS also contributes to the whole sustainability dimension by allowing the monitoring, control, coordination, and integration of processes (Rajkumar et al., 2010). Furthermore, they are important for sustainability, as they ensure the efficient allocation of products and materials, energy, and water resources (Müller, 2018).

Internet of Things (IoT): Things interact with both people and each other through software programs, RFID tags, sensors, triggers, and smartphones over an Internet-based communication network. In this way, they can configure themselves and have an identity and intelligence (Hermann et al., 2016; Lee, Crespi et al., 2013). The IoT connects devices so that SC information can be communicated in a meaningful way (Blanchard, 2021). This system, which provides digital functionality and automatically identifies and monitors objects, can also be defined as Internet-based information architecture (Lee & Lee, 2015). The IoT technology provides enhanced connectivity by real-time access to information. In this way, it makes significant contributions to improved SC visibility (Kache & Seuring, 2017) and SCM. The advanced automation that comes with the IoT ensures productivity, efficiency, and quality control (Yu et al., 2015) and provides improvements in operations throughout the SC.

The IoT technology is significant in terms of SC sustainability performance, as it enables processes in the SC to be more traceable, measurable, auditable, and curable (Da Xu et al., 2014; Tadejko, 2015). Providing real-time tracking of transportation activities, calculating the transportation time and delivery time according to the road condition (Lee et al., 2009), carrying the products to be moved in cold chain transportation without damage and quality, and supporting the prevention of environmental degradation (Opara, 2003) are also important issues in terms of sustainability (Aung & Chang, 2014). In addition, the IoT contributes positively to the sustainability performance of SC by reducing the possible value losses of products whose expiration date is approaching and which are at risk of deterioration. In addition, it contributes to efficient inventory counts in warehouses, reducing inventory costs. Furthermore, reducing the risks of accidents in warehouses, increasing the efficiency of handling operations, and reducing energy losses are among the contributions of this technology in terms of sustainability (Lee, 2016).

The IoT records environmental impacts. In addition, it is a significant technology in terms of SC sustainability performance, as it allows the carbon footprint of the utilized transportation and handling equipment to be recorded and the environmental impacts in the SC to be measured (Gu & Liu, 2013). The IoT has a huge capacity to transform different fields of sustainability by utilizing sensing and communication technology (Salam, 2020).

Artificial Intelligence (AI): This technology allows to perform the tasks given for increased mental phenomena such as reasoning, understanding, and learning from previous experiences, which are generally carried out by a computer or a machine under the supervision of a computer that has mostly human-specific qualities (Nabiyev, 2012). AI carries out functions that require intelligence by creating machines without humans (Kurzweil, 1992). It aims to imitate human rational activity as much as possible utilizing machines (usually electronic machines), and perhaps ultimately to improve human mental activity (Penrose, 1989).

AI can be used in miscellaneous fields, such as customer loss forecasting, demand forecasting, inventory management, purchasing, vehicle routing, logistics operation planning, logistics tracking, order picking, quality control, equipment maintenance forecasting, storage systems, and shipping in the SC (Aylak et al., 2021), and thus affect the SC sustainability performance.

Its applications are significant in terms of environmental sustainability as AI includes technologies that can support the formation of systems for renewable energy sources. In addition, it is thought that it will help reduce the effects of the global climate crisis in the future by utilizing smart agriculture systems (Jha et al., 2017). This technology can overcome complex and dynamic problems in urban studies (Wu & Silva, 2010). Indeed, AI technology is frequently used in smart city applications; in this way, it contributes to the sustainability of cities. Since smart cities also enable smart transportation systems, the utilization of AI also ensures the sustainability of transportation systems (Glasmeier & Nebiolo, 2016; Kumar Debnath et al., 2011). It is estimated that the contribution of AI technologies to the global economy will be 15 trillion USD by 2030 (Oxford Insights, 2019). Moreover, its investments in the retail sector have been estimated to reach 6 billion USD by the end of 2022 (Shankar, 2018). In this context, AI is also crucial in terms of its contribution to the economic sustainability dimension.

Autonomous Robots: Unlike static robots, autonomous robots work all the time. These robots are capable of making the fastest and most accurate instant decision analysis, thus minimizing or even completely eliminating human errors (Manyika et al., 2013; Rüßmann et al., 2015). These technologies can work close to ideal in unfavorable and/or unpredictable working conditions, and enable human-robot collaboration (Wong et al., 2018). In this way, they are flexible, collaborative, efficient, self-learning, and self-configuring systems. They are utilized in a large number of fields, such as manufacturing, assembly, maintenance and logistics, storage, material handling, and office management (Rüßmann et al., 2015). They can connect physical and cyber systems and communicate with each other in real time and expeditiously thanks to AI technology (Bekey, 2005). Autonomous robots make significant contributions to sustainability and sustainability performance, such as reducing labor costs, reducing the number of raw materials and waste, reducing the margin of error of the operators with whom they work, and increasing the quality, efficiency, and flexibility of production (Bugmann et al., 2011).

Autonomous robots are a technology utilized in a wide variety of industries such as automotive, health, education, and agriculture (Hansen, 2015; Kachouie et al., 2014; Reich-Stiebert & Eyssel, 2015; Savela et al., 2018; Schwab, 2017). It was first utilized by Amazon and Alibaba companies in SCM and has become an acceleratingly adopted technology in this field (Hofmann et al., 2019). This technology enhances efficiency and safety in warehouses, distribution centers, and factories by performing hazardous or demanding work and more intense activities (Dalmarco & Barros, 2018; Görçün, 2022). It can enhance customer satisfaction by improving deliveries. Moreover, it offers employees the opportunity to develop their competencies by leaving mundane duties (Fitzgerald, 2018; Gnambs & Appel, 2019; Ramirez-Peña et al., 2020; Shamout et al., 2022). These systems can eliminate some constraints such as the organization of manpower and the fulfillment of customer orders only during working hours. It is expected that it will lessen the need for manpower in the future, as it enables the activities in the SC to be performed autonomously. Since it ensures performance and productivity are traced, it enables the opportunity to intervene quickly in operational errors. In addition, lessening operational costs is among the potential contributions of this technology (Görçün, 2022).

Big Data Analytics: Historical data can be collected with this process, which gives signals such as vibration and pressure for correct sensor installations. With communication protocols, users can record controller signals. In this way, all data can be brought together. The combination of all these processes is called "big data." This process is a conceptual framework of a data collection and predictive production system (Witkowski, 2017). This process is very significant for SCs, as it provides in-depth information, supports more accurate decision making, and quickly extracts valuable information from various data types (Zadrozny & Kodali, 2013). One of the advantages of this technology is that data collection and data analysis can be done simultaneously and systematically. This makes a positive contribution to SCP (Davenport, 2006; Gunasekaran et al., 2017).

Making predictions about transit times and arrival times by combining data on shipment, vehicle meteorology, and traffic flow during the transportation is a sample of the fields of application of big data. Big data analytics plays a significant role in building smart transportation systems (Nguyen, 2018).

Big data technology is a tool that has a critical role in SCM. It is expected that it will make significant contributions to enhancing the sustainability performance of the SC in the future. Lagging the utilization of this technology will be considered a significant factor preventing the enhancement of sustainability performance for companies and SCs (Chalmette & Barqueros-Muñoz, 2021). It is a technology that supports the construction of a proactive SC and sustainable production. Moreover, it allows for the estimation of firm and SC performance and assessment of environmental efficiency (Chen et al., 2017; Dubey et al., 2017; Gunasekaran et al., 2017; Papadopoulos et al., 2017). This technology supports the determination of future trends through insight gain and support for decision making and enhances productivity and enables a competitive advantage. (Gao et al., 2020; Mamonov & Triantoro, 2018; Mani et al., 2018; Marjani et al., 2017; Mahmood et al., 2018; Olshannikova et al., 2017). It enables faster processes, more transparent decision making, saving time and resources, enhancing process quality, and reducing costs (Höchtl et al., 2016).

Blockchain: It is a "decentralized and distributed cryptographic digital 'ledger' technology used to record transactions" (Kim et al., 2020, p.1). With this technology, a digital record of "who owns what" can be created by people who do not recognize or count on each other (Cagigas et al., 2021). This technology, which functions as a consistent transaction history accepted by all "nodes," is a public database. It can store and transfer tangible and intangible assets such as votes, reputations, intentions, information, software, and even thoughts (Swan, 2015).

Blockchain brings contributions such as trust, transparency, traceability, security, auditability, control, cost degradation, and scalability (Correa Tavares et al., 2021). With this technology, transaction costs in the SC can be decreased and performance and communication can be improved throughout the SC. Furthermore, it is a significant technology from the standpoint of SC sustainability performance, as it protects human rights, increases healthcare patient privacy and well-being, and helps reduce carbon footprints (Upadhyay et al., 2021).

Figure 1. How blockchains work
Source: Manners-Bell and Lyon (2019)

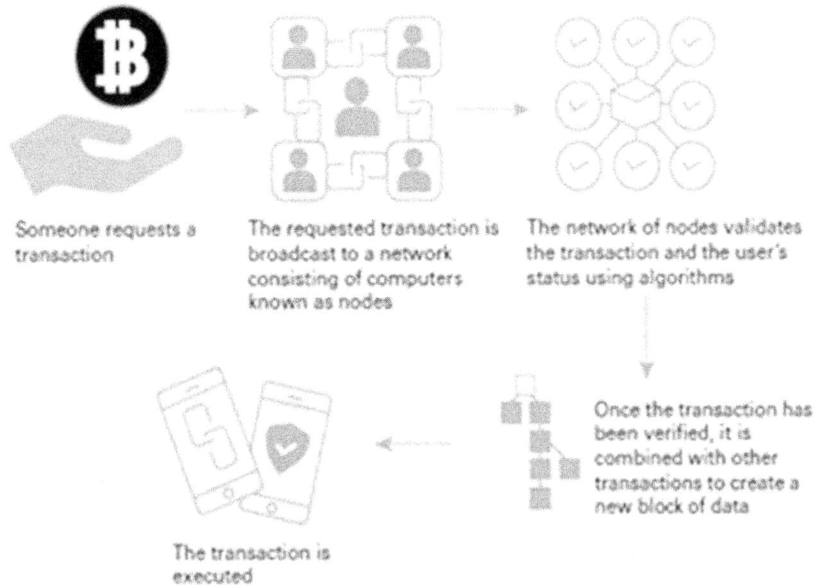

Figure 1 shows the operating process of blockchain technology. Blockchain makes a significant contribution to the SC. It is also important for increasing the accuracy of documentation and billing in the SC, given that 10% of all freight invoices contain inaccurate data, according to current industry estimates (Tanner, 2018). This technology, which also reduces conflicts in the SC, is significant regarding SC sustainability performance, as it enables the implementation of leaner and error-reducing processes (Manners-Bell & Lyon, 2019), and provides an important solution approach to security issues in commercial relations (Hawlitschek et al., 2018). Indeed, the digital execution of transactions allows to simplify processes and shorten operation times. In this regard, blockchain enhances SC sustainability performance because it provides reliable information flow and transparency, tracks processes, and allows processes to proceed correctly. In addition to enabling the detection of breaks in cold chain logistics, blockchain also contributes to sustainability by providing significant benefits in halal logistics operations (Tieman & Darun, 2017).

Cloud Computing: This technology has been improved to make on-demand network connections advantageous to a place where adjustable computing resources such as computer networking, server, and storage applications and services are shared (Atobishi et al., 2019). Cloud computing technologies create new communication platforms and new configurations of collaboration and coordination at the corporate level (Helo & Hao 2017) and provide higher integration and real-time information transferring (Chen & Deng 2015; Rashid & Tjahjono 2016). Since cloud computing has a crucial impact on sensitivity and visibility in the SC, it is significant in light of its contribution to decision-making and planning activities (Babiceanu & Seker, 2016; Tan et al., 2017).

Cloud computing contributes to environmental sustainability by making business paperless (Piyathanavong et al., 2022). It is also a green technology that enhances the operational efficiency of companies and SCs and lessens environmental impacts (Scott & Watson, 2012; Toka et al., 2013). In terms of social sustainability, it enables more effective customer support, shorter product cycle time, data transparency and easy access to data, higher data accuracy, reduction in SC response time, and better analysis of the obtained data. It ensures better inventory management and high velocity. Furthermore, it has the effect of improving the working conditions of employees by supporting work-from-home work. In terms of economic sustainability, it reduces energy costs and causes a decrease in the total cost (Piyathanavong et al., 2022).

3D Printers: This technology is also called additive manufacturing (AM). With this technology, production is carried out by superimposing very thin layers that are melted to form a physical object (Montess, 2016). 3D manufacturing is the use of digital 3D design data to build layers with additives/materials and AM. The term "3D printing" is dramatically utilized synonymously with AM. Instead of milling a workpiece from a one-piece dividing block, AM uses existing material in fine powder form to create components layer by layer. Several different metals, plastics, and composite materials can be utilized. It is an AM process that produces 3D-printed objects layer by layer (Prakash et al., 2018). This technology enables manufacturing to be carried out with the least amount of utilization of materials and energy (Kubáč, 2017). In terms of environmental sustainability, it enables a reduction in cost, material waste, CO^2 emissions, material waste, and energy supply. It also enhances the amount of recyclable waste and resource efficiency (Gebler et al., 2014; Petrovic et al., 2011). Moreover, it saves fuel by lessening the weight of the products manufactured (Wohlers, 2011).

In terms of social sustainability, 3D printer positively affects the number of qualified workers and the percentage of the locally recruited workforce (Adaloudis & Raco, 2021). It is a technology that reduces downtime. (Khajavi et al., 2014; Sutherland et al. 2014). It allows for design changes (Joshi & Sheikh, 2015). It reduces complexity in the supply chain with design consolidation (Rogers et al., 2016; Knofius et al., 2019). It enables consumers to have the opportunity to create innovative products by enhancing the potential of open design (Beltagui et al., 2020). In terms of economic sustainability, it enhances capacity utilization and reduces manufacturing costs (Baumers et al., 2011, Kreiger & Pearce, 2013). It enables lower transportation costs through localized manufacturing (Bogers et al., 2016; Schniederjans et al., 2017). It is a technology that allows cost-effective and low-volume manufacturing (Thiesse et al., 2015; Chan et al., 2018).

Augmented Reality: It is a real environment where digital media products are utilized instead of real-world objects. It is the indirect or direct way of virtual animation in the real environment by producing video, sound recording, and various graphics on digital media and augmenting them with inputs that appeal to the senses. In AR, the real world meets the virtual world in real time and attains the user in the same sensory area (Carmigniani & Furht, 2011). The adoption of AR in the logistics sector ensures that the operating environments are transferred to the virtual environment with the support of 3D graphics and that they are operated within the framework of different scenarios (Ginters & Martin-Gutierrez, 2013). AR is utilized in transportation activities and last-mile deliveries, warehousing operations, and value-added services (Glockner et al., 2014). It has contributions such as reducing costs, increasing efficiency in hands-free operations such as barcode recognition, reducing the error rate, increasing quality, providing better fuel efficiency, and increasing operational productivity and asset uptime (Büyüközkan & Güler, 2019). In this way, it contributes to the sustainability performance of the SC.

Virtual Reality (VR): It is the reconstruction of reality and allows people to communicate with objects in the environment. It is called VR because it conceives the feeling of being in a real environment in people's minds. This is achieved with 3D pictures and animations created by the computer. VR is the creation of images, holograms, sounds, locations, and similar sensory elements as an imitation of the real world. In VR, users perceive themselves in a different and 3D place, rather than their physical environment. VR environments usually involve visual experiences acquired through a computer screen (Begault & Trejo, 2000). In terms of SC sustainability performance, it has various contributions, such as shortening time to market, reducing product costs, increasing quality, facilitating new product development, and reducing risks and uncertainty (Choi et al, 2015; Mujber et al., 2004; Ottoson, 2002).

Autonomous (Driverless) Vehicles: The combination of artificial intelligence and robotics created autonomous (driverless) vehicles (Wakabayashi, 2017), and they are also called "self-driving vehicles" (Um, 2019). They make decisions by sensing environmental conditions and acting in line with the decisions they make. Thanks to the existing systems of these vehicles, the environment and traffic detection are made, and it is ensured that the vehicles can travel without the need for people (Fagnant & Kockelman, 2015). Although highway systems have been the basis of initiatives related to driverless vehicles until now, today driverless vehicles are being developed and used for railway, airway, and maritime systems. In addition, although most driverless vehicle studies and innovative developments regarding this technology are related to passenger transportation, autonomous vehicles are also used in freight transportation, due to the applications realized in urban cargo transportation. In addition, they are discussed in transportation planning and traffic survey studies (Lindholm & Behrends, 2012). Therefore, it is expected to reduce traffic congestion in freight transport and the resulting carbon gas emissions. They allow less risky transportation (Pietras, 2015).

Autonomous vehicles could adjust the driving route and velocity according to time and traffic conditions. They are technologies that support intelligent decision making (Um, 2019). They are more efficient and safer than vehicles with people behind the wheel. They can improve existing transport and logistics models (Schwab, 2017). They are vehicles that lessen traffic accidents, delivery time, and delivery cost, facilitate the transportation of large loads, lessen operational costs, enhance load traceability, and lessen maintenance costs (Perussi et al., 2019). Thanks to all these contributions, they save money. Furthermore, they enhance the mobility of children, the elderly, and the disabled (Rauniyar et al., 2018; Bagloee et al., 2016). In light of all this, it is expected that driverless vehicles will make up 50% of the automobile market by 2040 (Litman, 2017) and facilitate sustainable transportation and contribute to SC sustainability performance in the future.

Digital Twin: It is a one-to-one model of a system in a computer environment/virtual copy that mimics the behavior of a system (Tao et al., 2017). It is a virtual model of the attitude and consequences of a physical product or service in the real world. In brief, the digital twin is a virtual model of a process, product, or service (Fuller et al., 2020). It is defined as a real-time digital profile of the past and present attitude of a physical object or process that supports an optimized company's performance and is stood on large, cumulative, real-time, and real-world data measurements. This technology is considered vital for the realization of CPS, which is the most significant component of 4IR (Zhuang et al., 2018).

The digital twin aims to understand performance parameters, improve processes and carry out value-added activities effectively (Kamble, 2022; Park et al., 2019). It is a technology that supports decision making in the SC and enhances operational efficiency (Negri et al., 2017; Uhlemann et al., 2017). In addition, digital twin finds possible faults in the SC processes, reflects the data correctly, connects the processes and reduces costs (Leng et al., 2021). It enhances product design quality and energy efficiency and lessens pollution and carbon footprint (Golovina et al., 2019; Kaewunruen & Lian, 2019; Nguyen et al., 2021). It contributes to the reduction of accidents in the workplace with its utilization in vehicles (Almeaibed et al., 2021). It is also a technology utilized in the assessment of environmental risk and pollution (Zheng et al., 2020). It enables measurement of resource efficiency, recovery of secondary resources, and energy saving by utilizing it together with simulation technology (Bartie et al., 2021; Leiden et al., 2021). Because of these contributions, the digital twin is a technology that contributes to environmental, social, and economic sustainability.

Horizontal and Vertical System/Software Integrations: These technologies provide information and control flow between the horizontal and vertical elements of the company's value chain. Horizontal integration enables an uninterrupted flow of information between all stages of the production and planning process. This technology consists of steps in the production and planning processes of different companies. Vertical integration enables an uninterrupted communication and information flow in the technological infrastructure utilized in whole processes, not between processes (Sanchez et al., 2020). Since horizontal and vertical systems contribute to the establishment of information and connections and the realization of cooperation in the SC (Saucedo Martínez et al., 2018), they are significant technologies in terms of achieving the sustainability performance targets of the SC.

Horizontal and vertical system integration enhances the sustainability of business operations (Vijayan et al., 2020). In terms of environmental sustainability, it enables more efficient utilization of natural resources and supports green energy. In terms of social sustainability, it makes work sharing more equitable and supports decent work. It enhances the integration between the buyer and the seller and the cooperation in the SC. It is also a technology that supports innovation in organizations (Mabkhot et al., 2021; Phung & Pham, 2018). It ensures the participation of all employees in the processes, lessens uncertainty in the SC, and lessens the risk rate (Brettel et al., 2014). It improves product quality by enhancing SC integration (Zhao et al., 2021). Moreover, they are technologies that strengthen the position of companies in the industry (Vijayan et al., 2020). In terms of economic sustainability, it enables a reduction in production costs, labor costs, transaction costs, and marketing costs (Brettel et al., 2014; Phung & Pham, 2018). Furthermore, it enables more efficient utilization of assets (Besanko, 2000) and enhances profitability (Burn et al., 2014).

Simulation: It is a modeling technique that sets up a substructure for tracing the features of the real system by transferring the data of the physical system existing in the real world to a virtual environment (Alcácer et al., 2021). The basis for the utilization of this technology is the planning, implementation, and operation of SC processes in the context of the SC (Heckmann, 2016). It supports the analysis of various SC issues at different decision levels such as strategic, tactical, and operational (Longo, 2011). This technology enables the design of complicated and intelligent production systems, facilitating decision making, optimization, and advancement of planning and exploration models. In all these respects, it is crucial for both businesses and the SCs (De Paula Ferreira et al., 2020; Scanlan, 2019). It is a widely utilized technology in the identification and assessment of risks in SC risk management. It helps prevent SC disruptions, as it allows risks to be identified before they arise. It is also utilized to predict SCP (Heckmann, 2016; Zeigler et al., 1999).

Simulation enables high value-added solutions in SCs (Zeigler et al., 1999). It ensures enhanced market opportunities through the actualization of product customizations (Piyathanavong et al., 2022). It plays a significant role in the design of products. In addition, simulation contributes to achieving better operations, reducing waste of time and sources, and increasing productivity. The utilization of qualified workers in training is important in terms of social sustainability performance as well as its environmental and economic impact (Gunal, 2019).

Cyber Security (Smart Grids/Network Security): The high velocity and enhancing data and information exchange of SCs has also revealed "cyber criminals" who try to profit from them fraudulently today (Dupont & Lusthaus, 2021). These risks brought out by cybercriminals are called "cyber risks".

Cyber risks jeopardize the records of customers, suppliers, and employees (Riglietti & Aguada, 2018). Moreover, sensitive data breaches occur regarding processes, products, data flows, management, and operations (Boyson, 2014). In these respects, they have negative effects in terms of both social and economic sustainability. In addition, they lead to intellectual property theft, fraud, website crashes and failure of companies' information technology infrastructure and networks, and the unavailability of critical services (Riglietti & Aguada, 2018).

Cyber security technology includes many means that can be utilized to protect the cyber environment, organization, and utilizer assets. These include tools, policies, security concepts, safeguards, guidelines, risk management approaches, actions, training, best practices, assurance, and technologies (Von Solms & Van Niekerk, 2013). As a result of the 4IR, large companies believe that the threat of cyber risk will increase, so they are looking for solutions for this (Riglietti & Aguada, 2018). Cyber security technology is crucial for DTs, also called 4IR technologies, to reach their real potential (Thames & Schaefer, 2017). Cyber risks are risks that may go unnoticed until they affect the business. Therefore, they cause disruptions in SCs when they occur (Renaud et al., 2018). Consequently, they are very crucial technologies for the sustainability of SCM.

5G: It is the fifth-generation wireless technology. It is the last of the cellular communication networks created for the spread of mobile communication. In cellular communication, each region is divided into cells, and all devices in each cell are connected to an antenna in the cell by radio waves. 5G operates at higher frequencies to be faster, but this narrows the range of the waves, the cells need to be smaller and therefore more. It is foreseen that 5G technology will combine technologies such as the IoT and 3D printers with the ease it will provide in data transmission (Singh et al., 2021). It offers the opportunity to improve performance as the company develops its own resources and capabilities. It can integrate suppliers, customers, and intraorganizational logistics processes. It facilitates intrainstitutional and interinstitutional communication and information exchange (Taboada & Shee, 2020). The connectivity provided by 5G can foster the creation of cross-industry ecosystems and interconnected supply networks, thereby contributing to the sustainability of the SC (Ivanov & Dolgui 2020; Ivanov 2020; Ruel et al., 2021).

5G is a technology that enables significant energy savings (Agiwal, et al., 2019; Taboada & Shee, 2020) and enhances resource efficiency when considered in terms of whole resources (Georgakopoulos et al., 2016). Handling times, human errors, and accidents in warehouses are reduced with its utilization in warehousing activities. The risks of traffic congestion, accidents, and economic losses are reduced, while visibility and control are enhanced with their utilization in transportation and logistics activities. Moreover, transport times and waiting times of trucks are reduced. 5G is a technology that reduces CO^2 emissions and negative effects on the environment in terms of environmental sustainability. In terms of social sustainability, it is possible to contribute to social sustainability with continuous on-the-job training of employees. 5G has the effect of enhancing operational efficiency throughout the SC. Enhanced security is provided in the SC thanks to more sensitive data transmission with it (Cavalli et al., 2021). It is utilized together with technologies such as AI, cloud computing, and digital twin to enable significant SC performance improvements. Some of these performance improvements are enhanced adaptability, enhanced flexibility, shorter lead times, efficient capacity utilization, enhanced productivity, and enhanced responsiveness (Dolgui & Ivanov, 2022).

Many real-world examples have illustrated the contribution of DTs to SC sustainability performance. Using moving company technologies to cloud computing, Amazon has managed to boost its revenue significantly in 2021 compared to the previous year by reducing costs and enabling faster operational processes. It has also achieved a reduction in accidents markedly in less than a year by using AI technology in transportation activities. In this way, it also has enhanced the safety of drivers and contributes to social sustainability (Amazon, 2021, p. 60). Hellenic Bottling Company, a European bottler, has made use of IoT technology to minimize waste and energy usage, while at the same time enabling a significant increase in efficiency in the SC processes (Supply Chain Digital, 2022). Procter & Gamble has ensured that almost all capacities are traceable thanks to the use of blockchain and big data (P&G, 2019). Coca-Cola has achieved an increase in operational efficiency, better optimization, a reduction in operational risks, and more adaptation to changing market conditions by using information technologies and DTs together. AI, cloud computing, and cybersecurity are the main DTs it uses (CCI, 2021, p. 44). Unilever has enabled the company to enhance product performance and operational efficiency and shorten the time to market by using autonomous robots and AI (Unilever, 2021). Arçelik, one of the leaders in the household appliances industry, can more easily respond to changing customer needs, evaluate its processes better, and boost the efficiency of operations and customer satisfaction by using IoT, AI, robots, and big data analytics. Furthermore, the company has resulted in an improvement in product quality, a reduction in the amount of scrap and plastic consumption, and a dramatic reduction in costs by including digital twin technology in its production plan (Arçelik, 2021).

SOLUTIONS AND RECOMMENDATIONS

Sustainability Measurements in the Disruptive Technology Era

Sustainability in SCM is a key point that affects SCP (Brandenburg & Rebs, 2015; Fahimnia et al., 2017; Jabbour et al., 2012). 4IR is a sustainability-oriented concept. It does not only include environmental protection and control initiatives in processes, but it also facilitates resource efficiency, employee and community welfare, and process security in SCs (Luthra & Mangla, 2018). The main purpose of 4IR (which is called the Fourth Industrial Revolution) and the technologies it offers, is to enhance and develop companies' long-term competitiveness and SCs by raising the flexibility and productivity of production through communication, information, and rationality (Gabriel & Pessl, 2016). Simultaneously, 4IR is aimed to enhance energy and source efficiency, increase productivity, and shorten innovation and marketing cycle time (Prause, 2015). In this context, 4IR has the potential to create positive sustainability effects across the whole SC (Wagner, 2016). In this direction, it is expected that there will be a relationship between DTs (also called 4IR technologies) and SC sustainability performance.

In this study, a literature review was initially conducted to determine the SC sustainability performance measurements. It has not been considered whether it is taken as a measurement criterion in the literature. Whole studies that deal with SC sustainability performance and the effects of DTs on SCs have been considered in the literature. Since 4IR technologies constitute today's DTs, whole studies that address the effects of 4IR on sustainability in SCs and the effects discussed in these studies are within the scope of the study. First, the measurement obtained from all these studies were brought together in a measurement pool. The sources utilized during the literature review consist of research articles, review articles, and book chapters. While carrying out this study, both studies that deal with the effect of a single DT and studies that deal with whole DTs with a holistic approach were taken into account. Second, the performance measurement generated were grouped according to the dimensions of sustainability. Third, they were divided into quantitative and qualitative for convenience for further studies. The column to the right of the measure indicates whether it is a quantitative measure (QN) or a qualitative measure

(QL). Table 1, which was generated in line with the above-mentioned issues, illustrates the performance measurements prepared by the authors.

Table 1. Sustainability measurements in supply chains

Dimension of Sustainability	Measurement	QL/ QN	References
Environmental sustainability	Decrease in resource consumption (materials, energy, water).	QN	Global Reporting Initiative, 2011; Veleva & Ellenbecker, 2001; Zhu et al., 2011.
	Increase in the utilization of renewable and sustainable energy sources.	QN	Hidayatno et al., 2019.
	Increase in the amount of recycled material utilized in the manufacturing process.	QN	Zhang et al., 2018.
	Decrease in waste in the SC network.	QN	Bag et al., 2020; Gunasekaran et al., 2017.
	Decrease in CO^2 emissions.	QN	Acquaye et al., 2018.
	Decrease in carbon footprint (i.e., the carbon dioxide equivalent of greenhouse gases).	QN	Acquaye et al., 2018.
	Decrease in greenhouse gas emissions.	QN	Shaw et al., 2010.
	Decrease in the production and utilization of materials that pose a health, safety, or environmental hazard.	QN	Zhu et al. 2005.
	Increase in the traceability of reverse logistics activities.	QL	Dasaklis et al., 2020; Sufiyan et al., 2019.

Continued on following page

Table 1. Continued

Dimension of Sustainability	Measurement	QL/ QN	References
Social sustainability	Decrease in work accidents.	QN	Quang & Hara, 2019; Schöggl et al., 2016.
	Decrease in lost days.	QN	Ferreira & Silva, 2016.
	Shortening working hours by improving working conditions and work-life balance.	QN	Kurt, 2019.
	Decrease in staff turnover.	QN	Lapide, 2000.
	Decrease in the need for workforce capacity.	QN	Özkanlısoy & Akkartal, 2021.
	Increase in employee satisfaction.	QN	Saad & Patel, 2006.
	Decrease in security issues in SC processes.	QN	Stefanović & Stefanović, 2011.
	Improvement in product and service quality.	QL	Nix, 2001; Tao, 2009.
	Decrease in defective product rates.	QN	Bowersox et al., 2002.
	Decrease in product failures.	QN	Li et al., 2011.
	Ensuring improved product delivery and reliability by anticipating potential delays and disruptions.	QL	Kache & Seuring, 2017.
	Customer behavior prediction with historical data.	QL	Carbonneau et al., 2008; SAS Institute, 2014.
	Decrease in the number of products returned from the customer.	QN	Bowersox et al., 2002.
	Decrease in the number of expired products.	QN	Özkanlısoy & Akkartal, 2021.
	Resolving customer issues faster (i.e., a more agile approach to customer issues).	QN	Özkanlısoy & Akkartal, 2021.
	Increase in existing communication with customers.	QN	Özkanlısoy & Akkartal, 2021.
	Decrease in customer complaints.	QN	Chan, 2003.
	Increase in new customer acquisition.	QN	Özkanlısoy & Akkartal, 2021.
	Increase in the level of aftersales service for the customer.	QN	Yang et al., 2009; Yang, 2010.
	Decrease in errors that occur in all processes (e.g., errors in packaging, transportation, and errors in placement in the vehicle).	QN	Aramyan et al., 2007.
	Increase in coordination and cooperation in the SC.	QL	Li et al., 2019.
	Decrease in overall SC response time.	QN	Shepherd & Günter, 2010.
	Monitoring the entire SC network.	QL	Manyuni et al., 2020.
	Proactive risk warnings based on historical data.	QL	Grötsch et al, 2013; Tang, 2006.
	Increase in the documentation and billing accuracy.	QN	Bowersox et al., 2002.
	Increase in order entry accuracy.	QN	Bowersox et al., 2002.
	Decrease in damage frequency.	QN	Bowersox et al., 2002.
	Corrective and preventive actions to process faster and faster.	QL	Forslund & Jonsson, 2007.
	Increase in order fulfillment rate.	QN	Li et al., 2011.

Continued on following page

Table 1. Continued

Dimension of Sustainability	Measurement	QL/ QN	References
Economic sustainability	Increase in ROI (i.e., return on investment).	QN	Qrunfleh & Tarafdar, 2014.
	Increase in ROA (i.e., return on assets).	QN	Jothimani & Sarmah, 2014; Thakkar et al., 2009.
	Increase in return on capital employed.	QN	Thakkar et al, 2009.
	Increase in cash-to-cash cycle time.	QN	ASCM, 2022; Jothimani & Sarmah, 2014.
	Increase in net profit.	QN	Sopadang et al., 2017.
	Increase in market share growth.	QN	Thakkar et al., 2009.
	Decrease in idle capacity.	QN	Zhu et al, 2011.
	Decrease in downtime cost.	QN	Schwab, 2017.
	Decrease in recycling costs.	QN	Jun, 2009.
	Decrease in reverse logistics costs.	QN	Upadhyay & Alqassimi, 2018.
	Decrease in labor costs.	QN	Carter & Rogers, 2008; Mani et al., 2018.
	Decrease in value-at-risk (i.e., the loss that may occur within a given confidence interval in a given period).	QN	ASCM, 2022.
	Decrease in total cost.	QN	Naslund & Williamson, 2010.

In the environmental dimension, since DTs enable more fruitful utilization of sources such as energy, materials, and water at all stages of manufacturing (de Sousa Jabbour et al., 2018), these effects are considered within the scope of environmental sustainability measurements.

Social sustainability is a subject that is quite lacking in the academic literature and practice in sustainability performance (Khan et al., 2021). Considering social sustainability performance in detail is a significant difference of this study in comparison with other studies that include sustainability performance measurements. The environmental dimension of sustainability has been considered more than any other dimension until these days (D'Eusanio et al., 2019). The measurements of social sustainability performance have been lacking, so far. Sustainability should be handled with a holistic approach and whole dimensions of it (Sterling, 2009).

Since social sustainability is the dimension of sustainability that concerns employees and society, employees and customers, who are a significant part of society and SCs, are included in the scope of the study (Morals, 2017). Decreasing employee turnover, shortening working hours by improving working conditions, and reducing the need for labor are considered part of social sustainability related to employees (Welford & Frost, 2006). These sustainability measurements are a contribution of DTs to SCs. As to customers, faster resolution of customer problems, communication with customers, customer complaints, aftersales customer service level, and new customer acquisition are included in the scope of the study.

DTs have an impact on sustainability performance as they have the effect of reducing labor costs, idle capacity costs, recycling costs, and therefore the total cost (Kumar & Barua, 2021). Reverse logistics and SC are high-cost items and are significant for sustainability (Lee & Lam, 2012). Therefore, the authors included them in the study. Since DTs reduce error rates (Choi et al., 2021), the authors determined performance measurements by considering the errors that may occur in the SC activities.

The Contributions of Disruptive Technologies to Sustainability Measurements

Each DT contributes to SC sustainability performance, but each technology contributes to separate performance measurements. In this part of the study, considering the sustainability performance measurements given in Table 1 above, the contribution of each disruptive technology to these measurements was determined. While generating technology-based contributions, not all measurements in Table 1 were considered, only the technologies that DTs contributed most widely according to the literature review were regarded. While this part of the study was carried out, current academic studies were utilized, and the effect of each DT on SC sustainability performance is marked in the table. Table 2 illustrates technology-based sustainability performance contributions in the SCs.

Table 2 (a). The main contributions of disruptive technologies to sustainability in supply chains

Dimension of Sustainability	Measurement	Cyber Physical Systems (CPS)	Internet of Things (IoT)	Artificial Intelligence (AI)	Autonomous Robots	Big Data and Analytics	Blockchain	Cloud Computing
Environmental sustainability	Decrease in resource consumption (i.e., materials, energy, and water).	✓	✓	✓	✓	✓	✓	✓
	Increase in the utilization of renewable and sustainable energy sources.	✓	✓	✓	✓	✓	✓	
	Increase in the amount of recycled material utilized in the manufacturing process.	✓	✓	✓	✓			
	Decrease in waste in the SC network.		✓	✓	✓	✓	✓	✓
	Decrease in CO^2 emissions.	✓	✓	✓	✓	✓	✓	✓
	Decrease in carbon footprint (i.e., the carbon dioxide equivalent of greenhouse gases).	✓	✓	✓	✓	✓	✓	✓
	Decrease in greenhouse gas emissions.	✓	✓	✓	✓	✓	✓	✓
	Decrease in the production and use of materials that pose a health, safety, or environmental hazard.	✓	✓	✓	✓			
	Increase in the traceability of reverse logistics activities.	✓	✓		✓	✓	✓	

Continued on following page

Table 2 (a). Continued

Dimension of Sustainability	Measurement	Cyber Physical Systems (CPS)	Internet of Things (IoT)	Artificial Intelligence (AI)	Autonomous Robots	Big Data and Analytics	Blockchain	Cloud Computing
Social sustainability	Decrease in work accidents.	✓	✓		✓			
	Decrease in lost days.	✓	✓		✓			
	Shortening working hours by improving working conditions and work-life balance.			✓	✓			
	Decrease in staff turnover.			✓	✓			
	Decrease in the need for workforce capacity.			✓	✓			
	Increase in employee satisfaction.			✓	✓			
	Decrease in security issues in SC processes.	✓	✓	✓	✓		✓	
	Product and service quality improvement.	✓	✓	✓	✓	✓		
	Decrease in defective product rates.		✓	✓				
	Decrease in product failures.		✓	✓				
	Ensuring improved product delivery and reliability by anticipating potential delays and disruptions.		✓	✓	✓			
	Customer behavior prediction with historical data.					✓	✓	
	Decrease in the number of products returned from the customer.		✓					
	Decrease in the number of expired products.		✓					
	Resolving customer issues faster (i.e., a more agile approach to customer issues).	✓	✓	✓	✓			✓

Continued on following page

Table 2 (a). Continued

Dimension of Sustainability	Measurement	Cyber Physical Systems (CPS)	Internet of Things (IoT)	Artificial Intelligence (AI)	Autonomous Robots	Big Data and Analytics	Blockchain	Cloud Computing
	Increase in existing communication with customers.		✓	✓				✓
	Decrease in customer complaints.							
	Increase in new customer acquisition.							
	Increase in the level of aftersales service for the customer.	✓	✓					
	Decrease in errors that occur in all processes (e.g., errors in packaging, transportation, and errors in placement in the vehicle).	✓	✓	✓	✓		✓	✓
	Increase in coordination and cooperation in the SC.	✓	✓	✓		✓	✓	✓
	Decrease in overall SC response time.	✓	✓	✓			✓	✓
	Monitoring the entire SC network.	✓	✓			✓	✓	✓
	Proactive risk warnings based on historical data.		✓	✓		✓		✓
	Increase in the documentation and billing accuracy.						✓	
	Increase in order entry accuracy.						✓	
	Decrease in damage frequency.		✓	✓	✓		✓	
	Increase in order fulfillment rate.			✓	✓			

Continued on following page

Table 2 (a). Continued

Dimension of Sustainability	Measurement	Cyber Physical Systems (CPS)	Internet of Things (IoT)	Artificial Intelligence (AI)	Autonomous Robots	Big Data and Analytics	Blockchain	Cloud Computing
Economic sustainability	Increase in ROA (i.e., return on assets).	✓	✓	✓	✓	✓	✓	✓
	Increase in net profit.	✓	✓	✓	✓	✓	✓	✓
	Decrease in labor costs.				✓			
	Decrease in total cost.	✓	✓	✓	✓	✓	✓	✓

Source: Afolalu et al., 2021; Ahearn et al., 2016; Alizadehsalehi & Yitmen, 2023; Al-Sammarraie et al.., 2021; Azadeh & Zarrin, 2016; Bechtsis et al., 2017; Beier et al., 2017; Beier et al., 2018; Belaud et al., 2019; Berman, 2012; Bonilla et al., 2018; Brass et al., 2018; Büyüközkan & Güler, 2019; Choi et al, 2015; Chowdhury, 2013; Codinhoto et al., 2021; Corallo et al., 2020; Crosby et al., 2016; De Paula Ferreira et al., 2020; de Soto et al., 2018; de Sousa Jabbour et al., 2018; Durão et al., 2018; Dutton, 2014; Fahimi, 2009; Foster et al., 2020; Frustaci et al., 2017; Gebler et al., 2014; Ghaffar et al., 2018; Ghobakhloo, 2018; Gülşen & Özdemir, 2018; Gunal, 2019; Haar et al., 2016; Hamid et al., 2014; Hammerschmid 2017; Hawlitschek et al.., 2018; He & Bai, 2021; Howard & Dai, 2014; Humphreys et al., 2002; Indoria et al., 2021; Infosys, 2017; Joshua & Varghese, 2014; Kample et al., 2020; Khakurel et al., 2018; Khan, Koc et al., 2021; Kim et al., 2002; Lee, An et al., 2013; Liao et al., 2022; Ma et al., 2019; Margaritis et al., 2022; Martínez et al., 2018; Mois et al., 2016; Morella et al., 2020; Mourtzis et al., 2017; Mujber et al., 2004; Muñoz et al., 2021; Negri et al., 2017; Noy et al., 2018; Okwu et al., 2020; Ottoson, 2002; Pearson & Benameur, 2010; Pinho et al., 2020; PwC, 2022; Reif et al., 2010; Rejeb et al., 2021; Rose et al., 2021; Russell et al., 2015; Rüßmann et al., 2015; Sanchez et al., 2020; Saucedo Vermesan & Friess,, 2011; Scanlan, 2019; Schoettle & Sivak, 2014; Sebestyén et al., 2021; Singh et al., 2015; Söderberg et al., 2017; Su & Wang, 2021; Tanner, 2018; Tao et al., 2016; Tieman & Darun, 2017; Timčenko et al., 2016; Uhlemann et al., 2017; Upadhyay et al., 2021; Vallandingham et al., 2018; Yu et al., 2016; Yu et al., 2022; Zhou et al., 2015.

Table 2 (b). The main contributions of disruptive technologies to sustainability in supply chains

3D Printers	Augmented Reality (AR)	Virtual Reality (VR)	Autonomous Vehicles	Digital Twin	Horizontal & Vertical Systems	Simulation	Cybersecurity	5G
✓	✓	✓	✓	✓	✓	✓	✓	✓
					✓			
✓								
✓	✓	✓	✓	✓				✓
✓	✓	✓	✓				✓	✓
✓	✓	✓	✓	✓			✓	✓
✓	✓	✓	✓				✓	✓
✓								
✓	✓	✓		✓	✓			✓
✓	✓	✓	✓	✓				✓
✓	✓	✓	✓	✓				
✓								✓
								✓
			✓					
	✓	✓						✓
✓			✓	✓			✓	✓
	✓	✓			✓	✓		✓
	✓	✓			✓	✓		
	✓	✓			✓	✓		✓
	✓	✓				✓		✓
						✓		✓
	✓	✓		✓	✓			✓
					✓	✓		✓
						✓	✓	
	✓	✓				✓	✓	
	✓	✓	✓	✓	✓	✓	✓	✓
				✓	✓			✓
				✓	✓	✓		✓
				✓				✓
	✓	✓					✓	
							✓	
					✓	✓		✓
						✓		✓

Continued on following page

Table 2 (b). Continued

3D Printers	Augmented Reality (AR)	Virtual Reality (VR)	Autonomous Vehicles	Digital Twin	Horizontal & Vertical Systems	Simulation	Cybersecurity	5G
✓	✓	✓		✓	✓	✓	✓	✓
	✓	✓	✓	✓	✓	✓	✓	✓
			✓		✓			
✓	✓	✓	✓	✓	✓	✓	✓	✓

As Table 2 shows, DTs contribute to significant performance measurements in terms of sustainability in the SC. While each technology contributes to a separate performance measurement, many of the DTs contribute to many sustainability performance measurements. Since the table is formed according to contributions, only the positive effects of DTs have been considered.

When the contributions of DTs to SCs are considered according to their sustainability dimensions, the technologies that contribute the most to environmental sustainability are CPS, IoT, AI, autonomous robots, big data, and analytics, blockchain and 3D printers. When examined in terms of the social dimension, CPS, IoT, AI and autonomous robots have a significant contribution to social sustainability. In terms of economic sustainability, all technologies contribute to economic sustainability to the same extent. In terms of sustainability measurements, return on assets (ROA), increase in net profit and decrease in total cost are the measurements that these technologies contribute the most.

FUTURE RESEARCH DIRECTIONS

DTs have many positive effects, but they also have some negative effects. Before implementing a DT, the negative effects of related technologies should also be considered. Therefore, another study that addresses both positive and negative effects may be conducted in the future. In addition, the performance measurements the authors presented in this study can be prioritized according to their significance utilizing the analytical hierarchy process. Moreover, an SC sustainability performance scale can be developed using these measurements. By considering only the quantitative measurements, the data obtained from the companies, the measurements before the use of DTs, and the measurements after the use of DT can be compared on a company basis. In this way, it can be quantitatively measured how they affect sustainability performance. A certain technology can be selected and the contributions of this technology to a certain sector can be examined. Another suggestion is to examine the impact of DTs on a particular SC activity (i.e., purchasing, manufacturing, logistics). The studies can be analyzed quantitatively or qualitatively. Another suggestion is to compare the results of SC sustainability performance measurements in different industries. For this reason, according to existing research, the industries that utilize these measurements the most can be compared with the industries that utilize them the least.

CONCLUSION

4IR has enabled DTs. Contrary to their name, these technologies, which make very positive contributions, continue to create significant changes in businesses and SCs. Today, sustainability is a concept that contributes to SCs and makes a name for itself as much as DTs.

Nowadays, not only companies, but also the SCs of which they are members compete. Therefore, SCM is very significant for companies to remain alive in a global vying environment. In this context, SCs should both benefit from the availability of DTs and increase SCP by giving importance to SC sustainability practices. Both are important in terms of being the leading SCs in the respective industry. SCs should consider the contribution of DTs to sustainability performance while improving their SCP, both in terms of the utilization of these technologies and sustainability. Companies that implement these technologies should consider the sustainability performance contributions of the relevant technologies to their SCs. In summary, managers who are aware of the importance of sustainability should follow and implement technological developments and process innovations in SCs (Duarte & Cruz-Machado, 2017). Therefore, they should benefit from the contribution of DTs to sustainability.

Companies should choose suitable DTs and adapt their existing technologies to these DTs. DTs affect SCP in many ways. One of them is SC sustainability performance. Indeed, companies should select the technologies that offer significant performance improvements to the SC in terms of environmental, social, and economic aspects, and should use technologies that optimize SCP by using the right sustainability improvements.

Nowadays, not only companies, but also the SCs of which they are members compete, and for SCs to survive in this competitive environment, they need to attach significance to sustainability and enhance their sustainability performance to the highest possible level. Unfortunately, SC sustainability measurements are not comprehensive enough in the literature so far. DTs have a significant contribution to SC sustainability. In this study, the authors determined the current and potential contributions of DTs to SCs. By exploring these measurements, the authors aimed to contribute to the more comprehensive measurement of the sustainability performance of the SCs, and to improve the sustainability performance of the SC by choosing and implementing the right DTs that have low performance in terms of sustainability.

Although the concept of sustainability has emerged due to environmental concerns, SCs that make a difference in terms of sustainability performance today will be SCs that give significance to all three dimensions of sustainability at the same time and deal with them with a holistic approach. Therefore, in this study, the authors grouped SC sustainability performance measurements according to these three dimensions. So far, the studies on sustainability performance in the SC have disregarded the social dimension of sustainability. However, systems are managed and used by people. In many ways, employees are significant for sustainability performance in the age of DTs, as DTs reduce the workload of employees, provide better working conditions, enable them to develop themselves, reduce employee turnover, and increase employee satisfaction. Moreover, since the concept of social sustainability is focused on employees and society, and customers are also a part of society, customers are another factor that should be given significance in terms of SC sustainability performance.

Discussion Questions

1. What does disruptive technology mean? Which technologies make up them today?
2. What are the contributions of disruptive technologies to supply chains?

3. What does sustainability mean? What are the dimensions of sustainability?
4. Explain the significance of sustainability in supply chains.
5. What are the main contributions of disruptive technologies to the supply chain's sustainability performance?
6. Give examples of supply chain sustainability performance measures according to the dimensions of sustainability.
7. What are the technology-based contributions of disruptive technologies to supply chain sustainability performance?
8. Which disruptive technologies contribute the most to sustainability dimensions?
    a. Which disruptive technologies contribute the most to the environmental sustainability dimension in the supply chain? Why?
    b. Which disruptive technologies contribute the most to the social sustainability dimension in the supply chain? Why?
    c. Which disruptive technologies contribute the most to the economic sustainability dimension in the supply chain? Why?

ACKNOWLEDGMENT

This research received no specific grant from any funding agency in the public, commercial, or not-for-profit sectors.

REFERENCES

Acquaye, A., Ibn-Mohammed, T., Genovese, A., Afrifa, G. A., Yamoah, F. A., & Oppon, E. (2018). A quantitative model for environmentally sustainable supply chain performance measurement. *European Journal of Operational Research*, *269*(1), 188–205. doi:10.1016/j.ejor.2017.10.057

Adaloudis, M., & Roca, J. B. (2021). Sustainability tradeoffs in the adoption of 3D Concrete Printing in the construction industry. *Journal of Cleaner Production*, *307*, 1–10. doi:10.1016/j.jclepro.2021.127201

Afolalu, S. A., Ikumapayi, O. M., Abdulkareem, A., Soetan, S. B., Emetere, M. E., & Ongbali, S. O. (2021). Enviable roles of manufacturing processes in sustainable fourth industrial revolution: A case study of mechatronics. *Materials Today: Proceedings*, *44*, 2895–2901. doi:10.1016/j.matpr.2021.01.099

Agiwal, M., Saxena, N., & Roy, A. (2019). Towards connected living: 5G enabled Internet of Things (IoT). *IETE Technical Review*, *3*(2), 1–13. doi:10.1080/02564602.2018.1444516

Ahearn, M. C., Armbruster, W., & Young, R. (2016). Big data's potential to improve food supply chain environmental sustainability and food safety. *The International Food and Agribusiness Management Review*, *19*, 155–171. doi:10.22004/ag.econ.240704

Al-Sammarraie, M. A. J., Ali, A. A., & Hussein, N. M. (2021). New irrigation techniques for precision agriculture: A review. *Plant Archives*, *21*(1), 1734–1740. doi:10.51470/PLANTARCHIVES.2021.v21.S1.275

Alcácer, V., Rodrigues, C., Carvalho, H., & Cruz-Machado, V. (2021). Tracking the maturity of Industry 4.0: The perspective of a real scenario. *International Journal of Advanced Manufacturing Technology*, *116*(7), 2161–2181. doi:10.100700170-021-07550-0 PMID:34248244

Alizadehsalehi, S., & Yitmen, I. (2023). Digital twin-based progress monitoring management model through reality capture to extended reality technologies (DRX). *Smart and Sustainable Built Environment*, *12*(1), 200–236. doi:10.1108/SASBE-01-2021-0016

Amazon. (2021). *Delivering progress every day: Amazon's 2021 sustainability report.* Retrieved March 14, 2023, from https://sustainability.aboutamazon.com/2021-sustainability-report.pdf

Aramyan, L. H., Oude Lansink, A. G. J. M., van der Vorst, J. G. A. J., & van Kooten, O. (2007). Performance measurement in agri-food supply chains: A case study. *Supply Chain Management*, *12*(4), 304–315. doi:10.1108/13598540710759826

Arçelik. (2021). *Lead the change: Sustainability report 2021*. Retrieved March 16, 2023, from https://www.arcelikglobal.com/media/6938/arcelik21_sustainability_report.pdf

Association for Supply Chain Management. (2022). *Introduction to processes*. Retrieved April 14, 2022, from https://scor.ascm.org/performance/introduction

Aung, M. M., & Chang, Y. S. (2014). Traceability in a food supply chain: Safety and quality perspectives. *Food Control*, *39*, 172–184. doi:10.1016/j.foodcont.2013.11.007

Aylak, B., Oral, O., & Yazıcı, K. (2021). Using artificial intelligence and machine learning applications in logistics [Yapay zeka ve makine öğrenmesi tekniklerinin lojistik sektöründe kullanımı]. *El-Cezeri Journal of Science and Engineering*, *8*(1), 79–88. doi:10.31202/ecjse.776314

Azadeh, A., & Zarrin, M. (2016). An intelligent framework for productivity assessment and analysis of human resource from resilience engineering, motivational factors, HSE, and ergonomics perspectives. *Safety Science*, *89*, 55–71. doi:10.1016/j.ssci.2016.06.001

Babiceanu, R. F., & Seker, R. (2016). Big data and virtualization for manufacturing cyber-physical systems: A survey of the current status and future outlook. *Computers in Industry*, *81*(128), 128–137. doi:10.1016/j.compind.2016.02.004

Bag, S., Wood, L. C., Xu, L., Dhamija, P., & Kayikci, Y. (2020). Big data analytics as an operational excellence approach to enhance sustainable supply chain performance. *Resources, Conservation and Recycling*, *153*(February), 1–10. doi:10.1016/j.resconrec.2019.104559

Bagloee, S. A., Tavana, M., Asadi, M., & Oliver, T. (2016). Autonomous vehicles: Challenges, opportunities, and future implications for transportation policies. *Journal of Modern Transportation*, *24*(4), 284–303. doi:10.100740534-016-0117-3

Bartie, N. J., Cobos-Becerra, Y. L., Fröhling, M., Schlatmann, R., & Reuter, M. A. (2021). The resources, exergetic and environmental footprint of the silicon photovoltaic circular economy: Assessment and opportunities. *Resources, Conservation and Recycling*, *169*, 1–24. doi:10.1016/j.resconrec.2021.105516

Basu, R., & Wright, N. (2008). *Total supply chain management*. Elsevier Press. doi:10.1016/B978-0-7506-8426-2.50006-X

Baumers, M., Tuck, C., Wildman, R., Ashcroft, I., & Hague, R. (2011). Energy inputs to additive manufacturing: does capacity utilization matter? In *2011 International Solid Freeform Fabrication Symposium*. University of Texas at Austin. 10.26153/tsw/15275

Bechtsis, D., Tsolakis, N., Vlachos, D., & Iakovou, E. (2017). Sustainable supply chain management in the digitalisation era: The impact of automated guided vehicles. *Journal of Cleaner Production*, *142*, 3970–3984. doi:10.1016/j.jclepro.2016.10.057

Begault, D. R., & Trejo, L. J. (2000). *3-D sound for virtual reality and multimedia*. NASA Center for AeroSpace Information.

Beier, G., Niehoff, S., & Xue, B. (2018). More sustainability in industry through industrial Internet of Things? *Applied Sciences (Basel, Switzerland)*, *8*(2), 1–12. doi:10.3390/app8020219

Beier, G., Niehoff, S., Ziems, T., & Xue, B. (2017). Sustainability aspects of a digitalized industry: A comparative study from China and Germany. *International Journal of Precision Engineering and Manufacturing - Green Technology*, *4*, 227-234. doi:10.1007/s40684-017-0028-8

Bekey, G. A. (2005). *Autonomous robots: From biological inspiration to implementation and control*. MIT Press.

Belaud, J. P., Prioux, N., Vialle, C., & Sablayrolles, C. (2019). Big data for agri-food 4.0: Application to sustainability management for by-products supply chain. *Computers in Industry*, *111*, 41–50. doi:10.1016/j.compind.2019.06.006

Beltagui, A., Kunz, N., & Gold, S. (2020). The role of 3D printing and open design on adoption of socially sustainable supply chain innovation. *International Journal of Production Economics*, *221*, 1–16. doi:10.1016/j.ijpe.2019.07.035

Benz, M., & Chatterjee, D. (2020). Calculated risk? A cybersecurity evaluation tool for SMEs. *Business Horizons*, *63*(4), 531–540. doi:10.1016/j.bushor.2020.03.010

Berman, B. (2012). 3-D printing: The new industrial revolution. *Business Horizons*, *55*(2), 155–162. doi:10.1016/j.bushor.2011.11.003

Besanko, D., Dranove, D., & Shandley, M. (2000). *The economics of strategy* (2nd ed.). John Wiley & Sons.

Bharadwaj, S., Bharadwaj, A., & Bendoly, E. (2007). The performance effects of complementarities between information systems, marketing, manufacturing, and supply chain processes. *Information Systems Research*, *18*(4), 437–453. doi:10.1287/isre.1070.0148

Blanchard, D. (2021). *Supply chain management best practices*. John Wiley & Sons.

Blasco Puchades, J., & Portolés Griñan, L. (2011). Additive layered manufacturing: Sectors of industrial application shown through case studies. *International Journal of Production Research*, *49*(4), 1061–1079. doi:10.1080/00207540903479786

Blewitt, J. (2014). *Understanding sustainable development* (2nd ed.). Routledge. doi:10.4324/9781315886459

Blome, C., Paulraj, A., & Schuetz, K. (2014). Supply chain collaboration and sustainability: A profile deviation analysis. *International Journal of Operations & Production Management*, *34*(5), 639–663. doi:10.1108/IJOPM-11-2012-0515

Bodrow, W. (2017). Impact of Industry 4.0 in service-oriented firm. *Advances in Manufacturing*, *5*(4), 394–400. doi:10.100740436-017-0196-3

Bogers, M., Hadar, R., & Bilberg, A. (2016). Additive manufacturing for consumer-centric business models: Implications for supply chains in consumer goods manufacturing. *Technological Forecasting and Social Change*, *102*, 225–239. doi:10.1016/j.techfore.2015.07.024

Bonilla, S. H., Silva, H. R. O., da Silva, M. T., Gonçalves, R. F., & Sacomano, J. B. (2018). Industry 4.0 and sustainability implications: A scenario-based analysis of the impacts and challenges. *Sustainability*, *10*(10), 1–24. doi:10.3390u10103740

Bower, J. L., & Christensen, C. M. (1995). Disruptive technologies: Catching the wave. *Harvard Business Review*, (Jan-Feb), 43–53.

Bowersox, D., Closs, D., & Cooper, M. B. (2002). *Supply chain logistics management*. McGraw-Hill.

Boyson, S. (2014). Cyber supply chain risk management: Revolutionizing the strategic control of critical IT systems. *Technovation*, *34*(7), 342–353. doi:10.1016/j.technovation.2014.02.001

Brass, I., Tanczer, L., Carr, M., Elsden, M., & Blackstock, J. (2018). Standardising a moving target: The development and evolution of IoT security standards. In *Living in the Internet of Things: Cybersecurity of the IoT* (pp. 1–9). IET., doi:10.1049/cp.2018.0024

Brettel, M., Friederichsen, N., Keller, M., & Rosenberg, M. (2014). How virtualization, decentralization and network building change the manufacturing landscape: An industry 4.0 perspective. *International Journal of Information and Communication Engineering*, *8*(1), 37–44.

Brundtland, G. H. (1987). *The United Nations World Commission on Environment and Development: Our common future*. Oxford University Press.

Bugmann, G., Siegel, M., & Burcin, R. (2011). A role for robotics in sustainable development? In *IEEE Africon'11* (pp. 1–4). IEEE. doi:10.1109/AFRCON.2011.6072154

Burns, L. R., Goldsmith, J. C., & Sen, A. (2014). Horizontal and vertical integration of physicians: A tale of two tails. *Advances in Health Care Management*, *15*, 39–117. doi:10.1108/S1474-8231(2013)0000015009 PMID:24749213

Büyüközkan, G., & Berkol, C. (2011). Designing a sustainable supply chain using an integrated analytic network process and goal programming approach in quality function deployment. *Expert Systems with Applications*, *38*, 13731–13748. doi:10.1016/j.eswa.2011.04.171

Büyüközkan, G., & Güler, M. (2019). Lojistik 4.0 teknolojilerinin analizi için metodolojik yaklaşım. *Journal of Entrepreneurship and Innovation Management*, *8*(1), 21–47.

Cagigas, D., Clifton, J., Diaz-Fuentes, D., & Fernández-Gutiérrez, M. (2021). Blockchain for public services: A systematic literature review. *IEEE Access : Practical Innovations, Open Solutions*, *9*, 13904–13921. doi:10.1109/ACCESS.2021.3052019

Carbonneau, R., Laframboise, K., & Vahidov, R. (2008). Application of machine learning techniques for supply chain demand forecasting. *European Journal of Operational Research*, *184*(3), 1140–1154. doi:10.1016/j.ejor.2006.12.004

Carmigniani, J., & Furht, B. (2011). Augmented reality: An overview. In B. Furth (Ed.), *Handbook of augmented reality* (pp. 3–46). Springer. doi:10.1007/978-1-4614-0064-6_1

Carter, C. R., & Easton, P. L. (2011). Sustainable supply chain management: Evolution and future directions. *International Journal of Physical Distribution & Logistics Management*, *41*(1), 46–62. doi:10.1108/09600031111101420

Carter, C. R., & Rogers, D. (2008). A framework of sustainable supply chain management: Moving toward new theory. *International Journal of Physical Distribution & Logistics Management*, *38*(5), 360–387. doi:10.1108/09600030810882816

Cavalli, L., Lizzi, G., Guerrieri, L., Querci, A., De Bari, F., Barbieri, G., Ferrini, S., Di Meglio, R., Cardone, R., Tardo, A., Pagano, P., Tesei, A., & Lattuca, D. (2021). Addressing efficiency and sustainability in the port of the future with 5G: The experience of the Livorno port. a methodological insight to measure innovation technologies' benefits on port operations. *Sustainability (Basel)*, *13*(21), 1–21. doi:10.3390u132112146

CCI. (2021). *Coca-Cola İçecek 2021 integrated annual report.* Retrieved March 14, 2023, from https://www.cci.com.tr/Portals/3/CCI_Integrated_Report_2021.pdf

Chalmeta, R., & Barqueros-Muñoz, J. E. (2021). Using big data for sustainability in supply chain management. *Sustainability (Basel)*, *13*(13), 1–25. doi:10.3390u13137004

Chan, F. T. S. (2003). Performance measurement in a supply chain. *International Journal of Advanced Manufacturing Technology*, *21*(7), 534–548. doi:10.1007001700300063

Chan, H. K., Griffin, J., Lim, J. J., Zeng, F., & Chiu, A. S. (2018). The impact of 3D Printing Technology on the supply chain: Manufacturing and legal perspectives. *International Journal of Production Economics*, *205*, 156–162. doi:10.1016/j.ijpe.2018.09.009

Chen, L., & Jia, G. (2017). Environmental efficiency analysis of China's regional industry: A data envelopment analysis (DEA) based approach. *Journal of Cleaner Production*, *142*, 846–853. doi:10.1016/j.jclepro.2016.01.045

Chen, Y. J., & Deng, M. (2015). Information sharing in a manufacturer: Supplier relationship: suppliers' incentive and production efficiency. *Production and Operations Management*, *24*(4), 619–633. doi:10.1111/poms.12261

Choi, S., Jung, K., & Nog, S. D. (2015). Virtual reality applications in manufacturing industries: Past research, present findings, and future directions. *Concurrent Engineering, Research and Applications, 21*(1), 565–572. doi:10.1177/1063293X14568814

Choi, S., & Ng, A. (2011). Environmental and economic dimensions of sustainability and price effects on consumer responses. *Journal of Business Ethics, 104*(2), 269–282. doi:10.100710551-011-0908-8

Choi, T. M., Kumar, S., Yue, X., & Chan, H. L. (2021). Disruptive technologies and operations management in the Industry 4.0 era and beyond. *Production and Operations Management, 31*(1), 1–23. doi:10.1111/poms.13622

Chowdhury, G. (2013). Sustainability of digital information services. *The Journal of Documentation, 69*(5), 602–622. doi:10.1108/JD-08-2012-0104

Christensen, C. M. (1997). *The innovator's dilemma: When new technologies cause great firms to fail.* Harvard University Press.

Codinhoto, R., Becher, O., Heron, J. N., & Donato, V. (2021). BIM bin: Waste management through BIM and digital twin. In M. Del Giudice & A. Osello (Eds.), *Handbook of research on developing smart cities based on digital twins* (pp. 265–294). IGI Global. doi:10.4018/978-1-7998-7091-3.ch013

Cohen, D., Sargeant, M., & Somers, K. (2014). 3-D printing takes shape. *The McKinsey Quarterly, 1*, 1–6.

Corallo, A., Lazoi, M., & Lezzi, M. (2020). Cybersecurity in the context of Industry 4.0: A structured classification of critical assets and business impacts. *Computers in Industry, 114*, 1–15. doi:10.1016/j.compind.2019.103165

Correa Tavares, E., Meirelles, F. D. S., Tavares, E. C., Cunha, M. A., & Schunk, L. M. (2021). Blockchain in the Amazon: Creating public value and promoting sustainability. *Information Technology for Development, 27*(3), 579–598. doi:10.1080/02681102.2020.1848772

Crosby, M., Pattanayak, P., Verma, S., & Kalyanaraman, V. (2016). Blockchain technology: Beyond bitcoin. *Applied Innovation Review, 2*, 6–19.

D'Eusanio, M., Zamagni, A., & Petti, L. (2019). Social sustainability and supply chain management: Methods and tools. *Journal of Cleaner Production, 235*, 178–189. doi:10.1016/j.jclepro.2019.06.323

Da Xu, L., He, W., & Li, S. (2014). Internet of things in industries: A survey. *IEEE Transactions on Industrial Informatics, 10*(4), 2233–2243. doi:10.1109/TII.2014.2300753

Dalmarco, G., & Barros, A. C. (2018). Adoption of Industry 4.0 technologies in supply chains. In A. C. Moreira, L. Miguel, D. F. Ferreira, & R. A. Zimmermann (Eds.), *Innovation and Supply Chain Management* (pp. 303–319). Springer., doi:10.1007/978-3-319-74304-2_14

Das, R., Banerjee, M., & De, S. (Eds.). (2020). *Emerging trends in disruptive technology management for sustainable development*. CRC Press.

Dasaklis, T. K., Casino, F., & Patsakis, C. (2020). A traceability and auditing framework for electronic equipment reverse logistics based on blockchain: The case of mobile phones. In *Proceedings of the 2020 11th International Conference on Information, Intelligence, Systems and Applications (IISA)* (pp. 1-7). IEEE. 10.1109/IISA50023.2020.9284394

Davenport, T. H. (2006). Competing on analytics. *Harvard Business Review, 84*(1), 98–107. PMID:16447373

Davies, R. (2015). *Industry 4.0: Digitalisation for productivity and growth.* European Parliament.https://www.europarl.europa.eu/thinktank/en/document/EPRS_BRI(2015)568337

De, A., Wang, J., & Tiwari, M. K. (2019). Hybridizing basic variable neighborhood search with particle swarm optimization for solving sustainable ship routing and bunker management problem. *IEEE Transactions on Intelligent Transportation Systems, 21*(3), 986–997. doi:10.1109/TITS.2019.2900490

De Paula Ferreira, W., Armellini, F., & De Santa-Eulalia, L. (2020). Simulation in Industry 4.0: A state-of-the-art review. *Computers & Industrial Engineering, 149. Computers & Industrial Engineering, 106868*, 1–17. doi:10.1016/j.cie.2020.106868

de Soto, B. G., Agustí-Juan, I., Hunhevicz, J., Joss, S., Graser, K., Habert, G., & Adey, B. T. (2018). Productivity of digital fabrication in construction: Cost and time analysis of a robotically built wall. *Automation in Construction, 92*, 297–311. doi:10.1016/j.autcon.2018.04.004

de Sousa Jabbour, A. B. L., Jabbour, C. J. C., Foropon, C., & Filho, M. G. (2018). When titans meet: Can Industry 4.0 revolutionise the environmentally sustainable manufacturing wave? The role of critical success factors. *Technological Forecasting and Social Change, 132*, 18–25. doi:10.1016/j.techfore.2018.01.017

Dolgui, A., & Ivanov, D. (2022). 5G in Digital supply chain and operations management: Fostering flexibility, end-to-end connectivity and real-time visibility through internet-of-everything. *International Journal of Production Research, 60*(2), 442–451. doi:10.1080/00207543.2021.2002969

Duarte, S., & Cruz-Machado, V. (2017). Exploring linkages between lean and green supply chain and the industry 4.0. In *Proceedings of the International Conference on Management Science Engineering Management* (pp. 1242-1252). Springer.

Dubey, R., Gunasekaran, A., Papadopoulos, T., Childe, S. J., Shibin, K. T., & Wamba, S. F. (2017). Sustainable supply chain management: Framework and further research directions. *Journal of Cleaner Production, 142*(2), 1119–1130. doi:10.1016/j.jclepro.2016.03.117

Dupont, B., & Lusthaus, J. (2022). Countering distrust in illicit online networks: The dispute resolution strategies of cybercriminals. *Social Science Computer Review, 40*(4), 892–913. doi:10.1177/0894439321994623 PMID:35971389

Durão, L. F., Haag, S., Anderl, R., Schützer, K., & Zancul, E. (2018). Digital twin requirements in the context of Industry 4.0. In *Proceedings of the IFIP International Conference on Product Lifecycle Management* (pp. 204-214). Springer. 10.1007/978-3-030-01614-2_19

Dutton, H. W. (2014). Putting things to work: Social and policy challenges for the Internet of things. *Info, 16*(3), 1–21. doi:10.1108/info-09-2013-0047

Eitiveni, I., Kurnia, S., & Buyya, R. (2017). Sustainable supply chain management: Taxonomy, gaps, and future directions. *PACIS 2017 Proceedings*, 121. https://aisel.aisnet.org/pacis2017/121

Elliott, J. A. (2012). *An introduction to sustainable development* (4th ed.). Routledge. doi:10.4324/9780203844175

Esfahbodi, A., Zhang, Y., & Watson, G. (2016). Sustainable supply chain management in emerging economies: Trade-offs between environmental and cost performance. *International Journal of Production Economics, 181*, 350–366. doi:10.1016/j.ijpe.2016.02.013

Fagnant, D. J., & Kockelman, K. (2015). Preparing a nation for autonomous vehicles: Opportunities, barriers, and policy recommendations. *Transportation Research Part A, Policy and Practice, 77*, 167–181. doi:10.1016/j.tra.2015.04.003

Fahimi, F. (2009). *Autonomous robots: Modeling, path planning and control.* Springer Nature., doi:10.1007/978-0-387-09538-7

Ferreira, L. M. D. F., & Silva, C. (2016). Integrating sustainability metrics in the supply chain performance measurement system. In L. M. D. F. Ferreira & C. Silva (Eds.), *Multiple Helix Ecosystems for Sustainable Competitiveness: Innovation* (pp. 113–132). Technology, and Knowledge Management., doi:10.1007/978-3-319-29677-7_8

Fitzgerald, J. (2018). *Using autonomous robots to drive supply chain innovation.* Deloitte. Retrieved June 27, 2022, from https://www2.deloitte.com/content/dam/Deloitte/us/Documents/manufacturing/us-manufacturing-autonomous-robots-supply-chain-innovation.pdf

Forslund, H., & Jonsson, P. (2007). The impact of forecast information quality on supply chain performance. *International Journal of Operations & Production Management, 27*(1), 90–107. doi:10.1108/01443570710714556

Foster, T., Mieno, T., & Brozović, N. (2020). Satellite-based monitoring of irrigation water use: Assessing measurement errors and their implications for agricultural water management policy. *Water Resources Research, 56*(11), 1–19. doi:10.1029/2020WR028378

Frustaci, M., Pace, P., Aloi, G., & Fortino, G. (2017). Evaluating critical security issues of the IoT world: Present and future challenges. *IEEE Internet of Things Journal, 5*(4), 2483–2495. doi:10.1109/JIOT.2017.2767291

Fuller, A., Fan, Z., Day, C., & Barlow, C. (2020). Digital twin: Enabling technology, challenges, and open research. *IEEE Access : Practical Innovations, Open Solutions, 8*, 108952–108971. doi:10.1109/ACCESS.2020.2998358

Gao, Q., Guo, S., Liu, X., Manogaran, G., Chilamkurti, N., & Kadry, S. (2020). Simulation analysis of supply chain risk management system based on IoT information platform. *Enterprise Information Systems, 14*(9-10), 1354–1378. doi:10.1080/17517575.2019.1644671

Garvey, M. D. (2021). A philosophical examination on the definition of cyberspace. In S. Carnovale & S. Yeniyurt (Eds.), *Cyber Security and Supply Chain Management: Risks, Challenges, and Solutions* (pp. 1–11). World Scientific Publishing. doi:10.1142/9789811233128_0001

Gebler, M., Uiterkamp, A. J. S., & Visser, C. (2014). A global sustainability perspective on 3D printing technologies. *Energy Policy, 74*, 158–167. doi:10.1016/j.enpol.2014.08.033

Georgakopoulos, A., Margaris, A., Tsagkaris, K., & Demestichas, P. (2016). Resource sharing in 5G contexts: Achieving sustainability with energy and resource efficiency. *IEEE Vehicular Technology Magazine, 11*(1), 40–49. doi:10.1109/MVT.2015.2508319

Ghaffar, S. H., Corker, J., & Fan, M. (2018). Additive manufacturing technology and its implementation in construction as an eco-innovative solution. *Automation in Construction, 93*, 1–11. doi:10.1016/j.autcon.2018.05.005

Ghobakhloo, M. (2018). The future of manufacturing industry: A strategic roadmap toward Industry 4.0. *Journal of Manufacturing Technology Management, 29*(6), 910–936. doi:10.1108/JMTM-02-2018-0057

Ghobakhloo, M. (2020). Industry 4.0, digitization, and opportunities for sustainability. *Journal of Cleaner Production, 252*(2020). *Journal of Cleaner Production, 119869*, 1–21. doi:10.1016/j.jclepro.2019.119869

Giddings, B., Hopwood, B., & O'brien, G. (2002). Environment, economy and society: Fitting them together into sustainable development. *Sustainable Development (Bradford), 10*(4), 187–196. doi:10.1002d.199

Gimenez, C., Sierra, V., & Rodon, J. (2012). Sustainable operations: Their impact on the triple bottom line. *International Journal of Production Economics, 140*(1), 149–159. doi:10.1016/j.ijpe.2012.01.035

Ginters, E., & Martin-Gutierrez, J. (2013). Low cost augmented reality and RFID application for logistics items visualization. *Procedia Computer Science, 26*, 3–13. doi:10.1016/j.procs.2013.12.002

Glasmeier, A. K., & Nebiolo, M. (2016). Thinking about smart cities: The travels of a policy idea that promises a great deal, but so far has delivered modest results. *Sustainability (Basel), 8*(11), 1–11. doi:10.3390u8111122

Global Reporting Initiative. (2011). *Sustainability reporting guidelines*. GRI.

Glockner, H., Jannek, K., Mahn, J., & Theis, B. (2014). *Augmented reality in logistics. Changing the way we see logistics: A DHL perspective*. DHL Customer Solutions & Innovation.

Gnambs, T., & Appel, M. (2019). Are robots becoming unpopular? Changes in attitudes towards autonomous robotic systems in Europe. *Computers in Human Behavior, 93*, 53–61. doi:10.1016/j.chb.2018.11.045

Golovina, T., Polyanin, A., Adamenko, A., Khegay, E., & Schepinin, V. (2020). Digital twins as a new paradigm of an industrial enterprise. *International Journal of Technology, 11*(6), 1115–1124. doi:10.14716/ijtech.v11i6.4427

Görçün, Ö. F. (2022). Autonomous robots and utilization in logistics process. In İ. İyigün & Ö. F. Görçün (Eds.), *Logistics 4.0 and Future of Supply Chains* (pp. 83–93). Springer. doi:10.1007/978-981-16-5644-6_6

Grötsch, V. M., Blome, C., & Schleper, M. C. (2013). Antecedents of proactive supply chain risk management: A contingency theory perspective. *International Journal of Production Research, 51*(10), 2842–2867. doi:10.1080/00207543.2012.746796

Gu, Y., & Liu, Q. (2013). Research on the application of the Internet of things in reverse logistics information management. *Journal of Industrial Engineering and Management, 6*(4), 963–973. doi:10.3926/jiem.793

Gülşen, İ., & Özdemir, Ş. (2018). Perakendecilikte Teknolojik Yenilikler ve Uygulamalar. *Pazarlama Teorisi ve Uygulamaları Dergisi, 4*(1), 103–138.

Gunal, M. (2019). Simulation for the better: The future in industry 4.0. In M. Gunal (Ed.), *Simulation for Industry 4.0* (pp. 275–283). Springer. doi:10.1007/978-3-030-04137-3_16

Gunasekaran, A., Papadopoulos, T., Dubey, R., Wamba, S. F., Childe, S. J., Hazen, B., & Akter, S. (2017). Big data and predictive analytics for supply chain and organizational performance. *Journal of Business Research, 70*, 308–317. doi:10.1016/j.jbusres.2016.08.004

Haar, J. M., de Fluiter, A., & Brougham, D. (2016). Abusive supervision and turnover intentions: The mediating role of perceived organisational support. *Journal of Management & Organization, 22*(2), 139–153. doi:10.1017/jmo.2015.34

Hamid, N. S. S., Abdul Azziz, F., & Azizi, A. (2014). Virtual reality applications in manufacturing system. In *Science and Information Conference* (pp. 1034-1037). IEEE. https://doi.org/10.1109/SAI.2014.6918317

Hansen, B. G. (2015). Robotic milking-farmer experiences and adoption rate in Jæren, Norway. *Journal of Rural Studies, 41*, 109–117. doi:10.1016/j.jrurstud.2015.08.004

Hawlitschek, F., Notheisen, B., & Teubner, T. (2018). The limits of trust-free systems: A literature review on blockchain technology and trust in the sharing economy. *Electronic Commerce Research and Applications, 29*, 50–63. doi:10.1016/j.elerap.2018.03.005

He, B., & Bai, K. J. (2021). Digital twin-based sustainable intelligent manufacturing: A review. *Advances in Manufacturing, 9*(1), 1–21. doi:10.100740436-020-00302-5

Heckmann, I. (2016). *Towards supply chain risk analytics*. Springer Nature. doi:10.1007/978-3-658-14870-6

Helo, P., & Hao, Y. (2017). Cloud manufacturing system for sheet metal processing. *Production Planning and Control, 28*(6–8), 524–537. doi:10.1080/09537287.2017.1309714

Hermann, M., Pentek, T., & Otto, B. (2016). Design principles for industry 4.0 scenarios. In *Proceedings of the 2016 49th Hawaii International Conference on System Sciences (HICSS)* (pp. 3928-3937). IEEE Computer Society. 10.1109/HICSS.2016.488

Hidayatno, A., Destyanto, A. R., & Hulu, C. A. (2019). Industry 4.0 technology implementation impact to industrial sustainable energy in Indonesia: A model conceptualization. *Energy Procedia, 156*, 227–233. doi:10.1016/j.egypro.2018.11.133

Höchtl, J., Parycek, P., & Schöllhammer, R. (2016). Big data in the policy cycle: Policy decision making in the digital era. *Journal of Organizational Computing and Electronic Commerce, 26*(1-2), 147–169. doi:10.1080/10919392.2015.1125187

Hofmann, E., Sternberg, H., Chen, H., Pflaum, A., & Prockl, G. (2019). Supply chain management and Industry 4.0: Conducting research in the digital age. *International Journal of Physical Distribution & Logistics Management, 9*(10), 945–955. doi:10.1108/IJPDLM-11-2019-399

Howard, D., & Dai, D. (2014). Public perceptions of self-driving cars: The case of Berkeley, California. *Transportation Research Board 93rd Annual Meeting, 14*(4502), 1-16.

Humphreys, P., Huang, G., & McIvor, R. (2002). An expert system for evaluating the make or buy decision. *Computers & Industrial Engineering, 42*(2/4), 567–585. doi:10.1016/S0360-8352(02)00052-9

Indoria, M., Kumar, P., Panwar, Y., & Sharma, T. (2021). Implementation of Industry 4.0 to achieve sustainable manufacturing in steel industry: A case study. *Systematic Literature Review and Meta Analysis Journal, 2*(1), 1–9. doi:10.54480lrm.v2i1.10

Infosys. (2017). *AI: The promise of a great future for retailers.* Retrieved April 12, 2022, from https://www.infosys.com/human-amplification/Documents/retail-ai-perspective.pdf

Ivanov, D. (2020). Viable supply chain model: Integrating agility, resilience and sustainability perspectives – Lessons from and thinking beyond the COVID-19 pandemic. *Annals of Operations Research,* 1–21. doi:10.100710479-020-03640-6 PMID:32836614

Ivanov, D. (2021). *Introduction to supply chain resilience: Management, modelling, technology.* Springer Nature.

Ivanov, D., & Dolgui, A. (2020). Viability of intertwined supply networks: Extending the supply chain resilience angles towards survivability. A position paper motivated by COVID-19 outbreak. *International Journal of Production Research, 58*(10), 2904–2915. doi:10.1080/00207543.2020.1750727

Jha, S. K., Bilalovic, J., Jha, A., Patel, N., & Zhang, H. (2017). Renewable energy: Present research and future scope of artificial intelligence. *Renewable & Sustainable Energy Reviews, 77,* 297–317. doi:10.1016/j.rser.2017.04.018

Joshi, S. C., & Sheikh, A. A. (2015). 3D printing in aerospace and its long-term sustainability. *Virtual and Physical Prototyping, 10*(4), 175–185. doi:10.1080/17452759.2015.1111519

Joshua, L., & Varghese, K. (2014). Automated recognition of construction labour activity using accelerometers in field situations. *International Journal of Productivity and Performance Management, 67*(3), 841–862. doi:10.1108/IJPPM-05-2013-0099

Jothimani, D., & Sarmah, S. P. (2014). Supply chain performance measurement for third party logistics. *Benchmarking, 21*(6), 944–963. doi:10.1108/BIJ-09-2012-0064

Jun, X. (2009). Model Of cluster green supply chain performance evaluation based on circular economy. In *Proceedings of the 2009 Second International Conference on Intelligent Computation Technology and Automation* (vol. 3, pp. 941-944). IEEE. 10.1109/ICICTA.2009.692

Kache, F., & Seuring, S. (2017). Challenges and opportunities of digital information at the intersection of big data analytics and supply chain management. *International Journal of Operations & Production Management, 37*(1), 10–36. doi:10.1108/IJOPM-02-2015-0078

Kachouie, R., Sedighadeli, S., Khosla, R., & Chu, M. T. (2014). Socially assistive robots in elderly care: A mixed-method systematic literature review. *International Journal of Human-Computer Interaction, 30*(5), 369–393. doi:10.1080/10447318.2013.873278

Kaewunruen, S., & Lian, Q. (2019). Digital twin aided sustainability-based lifecycle management for railway turnout systems. *Journal of Cleaner Production, 228*, 1537–1551. doi:10.1016/j.jclepro.2019.04.156

Kamble, S. S., Gunasekaran, A., Parekh, H., Mani, V., Belhadi, A., & Sharma, R. (2022). Digital twin for sustainable manufacturing supply chains: Current trends, future perspectives, and an implementation framework. *Technological Forecasting and Social Change, 176*, 1–13. doi:10.1016/j.techfore.2021.121448

Khajavi, S. H., Partanen, J., & Holmstrom, J. (2014). Additive manufacturing in the spare parts supply chain. *Computers in Industry, 65*(1), 50–63. doi:10.1016/j.compind.2013.07.008

Khakurel, J., Penzenstadler, B., Porras, J., Knutas, A., & Zhang, W. (2018). The rise of artificial intelligence under the lens of sustainability. *Technologies, 6*(4), 1–18. doi:10.3390/technologies6040100

Khan, S. A., Koc, M., & Al-Ghamdi, S. G. (2021). Sustainability assessment, potentials, and challenges of 3D printed concrete structures: A systematic review for built environmental applications. *Journal of Cleaner Production, 303. Journal of Cleaner Production, 127027*, 1–14. doi:10.1016/j.jclepro.2021.127027

Khan, S. A. R., Zkik, K., Belhadi, A., & Kamble, S. S. (2021). Evaluating barriers and solutions for social sustainability adoption in multi-tier supply chains. *International Journal of Production Research, 59*(11), 3378–3397. doi:10.1080/00207543.2021.1876271

Kilpatrick, J., & Barter, L. (2020). *COVID-19: Managing supply chain risk and disruption*. Deloitte.

Kim, B., Graves, R., Heragu, S., & Onge, A. (2002). Intelligent agent modeling of an industrial warehousing problem. *IIE Transactions, 34*(7), 601–612. doi:10.1080/07408170208928897

Kim, S., Park, H., & Lee, J. (2020). Word2vec-based latent semantic analysis (W2V-LSA) for topic modeling: A study on blockchain technology trend analysis. *Expert Systems with Applications, 152*, 1–12. doi:10.1016/j.eswa.2020.113401

Knofius, N., van der Heijden, M. C., & Zijm, W. H. (2019). Consolidating spare parts for asset maintenance with additive manufacturing. *International Journal of Production Economics, 208*, 269–280. doi:10.1016/j.ijpe.2018.11.007

Kreiger, M., & Pearce, J. M. (2013). Environmental life cycle analysis of distributed three-dimensional printing and conventional manufacturing of polymer products. *ACS Sustainable Chemistry & Engineering, 1*(12), 1511–1519. doi:10.1021c400093k

Kubáč, L. (2017). 3D printing in logistics. *Acta Logistica Moravica Periodický Internetový ČasopisV Oboru Logistiky, 7*(1), 8-15.

Kumar, S., & Barua, M. K. (2021). Sustainability of operations through disruptive technologies in the petroleum supply chain. *Benchmarking, 29*(5), 1–37. doi:10.1108/BIJ-02-2021-0086

Kumar Debnath, A., Haque, M. M., Chin, H. C., & Yuen, B. (2011). Sustainable urban transport: Smart technology initiatives in Singapore. *Transportation Research Record: Journal of the Transportation Research Board, 2243*(1), 38–45. doi:10.3141/2243-05

Kurt, R. (2019). Industry 4.0 in terms of industrial relations and its impacts on labour life. *Procedia Computer Science, 158*, 590–601. doi:10.1016/j.procs.2019.09.093

Kurzweil, R. (1992). *The age of intelligent machines*. MIT Press.

Lapide, L. (2000). What about measuring supply chain performance. *Achieving Supply Chain Excellence Through Technology*, 2(2), 287–297.

Lasi, H., Fettke, P., Kemper, H. G., Feld, T., & Hoffmann, M. (2014). Industry 4.0. *Business & Information Systems Engineering*, *6*(4), 239–242. doi:10.100712599-014-0334-4

Lee, A. H., Kang, H. Y., Hsu, C. F., & Hung, H. C. (2009). A green supplier selection model for high-tech industry. *Expert Systems with Applications, 36*(4), 7917–7927. doi:10.1016/j.eswa.2008.11.052

Lee, C. K. M., & Lam, J. S. L. (2012). Managing reverse logistics to enhance sustainability of industrial marketing. *Industrial Marketing Management, 41*(4), 589–598. doi:10.1016/j.indmarman.2012.04.006

Lee, E. A. (2008). Cyber physical systems: Design challenges. In *Proceedings of the 11th IEEE International Symposium on Object and Component-Oriented Real-Time Distributed Computing (ISORC)* (pp. 363-369). IEEE. 10.1109/ISORC.2008.25

Lee, G. M., Crespi, N., Choi, J. K., & Boussard, M. (2013). Internet of things. In E. Bertin, N. Crespi, & T. Magedanz (Eds.), *Evolution of telecommunication services* (pp. 257–282). Springer. doi:10.1007/978-3-642-41569-2_13

Lee, I., & Lee, K. (2015). The Internet of Things (IoT): Applications, investments, and challenges for enterprises. *Business Horizons, 58*(4), 431–440. doi:10.1016/j.bushor.2015.03.008

Lee, K. (2016). How the Internet of things will change your world. *IdeaBook 2016, 5*(1). Retrieved April 10, 2022, from http://digital.supplychainquarterly.com/supplychain/ideabook_2016/?folio=50&sub_id=Hxh5qJH8aRP9&pg=1#pg1

Lee, Y. M., An, L., Liu, F., Horesh, R., Chae, Y. T., & Zhang, R. (2013). Applying science and mathematics to big data for smarter buildings. *Annals of the New York Academy of Sciences, 1295*(1), 18–25. doi:10.1111/nyas.12193 PMID:23819911

Leiden, A., Herrmann, C., & Thiede, S. (2021). Cyber-physical production system approach for energy and resource efficient planning and operation of plating process chains. *Journal of Cleaner Production, 280*, 1–17. doi:10.1016/j.jclepro.2020.125160

Leng, J., Zhou, M., Xiao, Y., Zhang, H., Liu, Q., Shen, W., Su, Q., & Li, L. (2021). Digital twins-based remote semi-physical commissioning of flow-type smart manufacturing systems. *Journal of Cleaner Production, 306*. *Article*, *127278*, 1–17. doi:10.1016/j.jclepro

Li, L., Su, Q., & Chen, X. (2011). Ensuring supply chain quality performance through applying the SCOR model. *International Journal of Production Research, 49*(1), 33–57. doi:10.1080/00207543.2010.508934

Li, S., Cui, X., Huo, B., & Zhao, X. (2019). Information sharing, coordination, and supply chain performance: The moderating effect of demand uncertainty. *Industrial Management & Data Systems, 119*(5), 1046–1071. doi:10.1108/IMDS-10-2018-0453

Liao, M., Lan, K., & Yao, Y. (2022). Sustainability implications of artificial intelligence in the chemical industry: A conceptual framework. *Journal of Industrial Ecology, 26*(1), 164–182. doi:10.1111/jiec.13214

Lindholm, M., & Behrends, S. (2012). Challenges in urban freight transport planning–a review in the Baltic Sea Region. *Journal of Transport Geography, 22*, 129–136. doi:10.1016/j.jtrangeo.2012.01.001

Litman, T. (2017). *Autonomous vehicle implementation predictions*. Victoria Transport Policy Institute.

Liu, C., & Xu, X. (2017). Cyber-physical machine tool: The era of machine tool 4.0. *The 50th CIRP Conference on Manufacturing Systems. Procedia CIRP, 63*, 70–75. doi:10.1016/j.procir.2017.03.078

Longo, F. (2011). Advances of modeling and simulation in supply chain and industry. *Simulation, 87*(8), 651–656. doi:10.1177/0037549711418033

Luthra, S., & Mangla, S. K. (2018). Evaluating challenges to Industry 4.0 initiatives for supply chain sustainability in emerging economies. *Process Safety and Environmental Protection, 117*, 168–179. doi:10.1016/j.psep.2018.04.018

Ma, S., Zhang, Y., Lv, J., Yang, H., & Wu, J. (2019). Energy-cyber-physical system enabled management for energy-intensive manufacturing industries. *Journal of Cleaner Production, 226*, 892–903. doi:10.1016/j.jclepro.2019.04.134

Mabkhot, M. M., Ferreira, P., Maffei, A., Podržaj, P., Mądziel, M., Antonelli, D., ... Lohse, N. (2021). Mapping Industry 4.0 enabling technologies into united nations sustainability development goals. *Sustainability, 13*(5), 1–33. doi:10.3390u13052560

Mahmood, A., Zen, H., & Hilles, S. M. S. (2018). Big data and privacy issues for connected vehicles in intelligent transportation systems. In S. Sakr & A. Zomaya (Eds.), *Encyclopedia of Big Data Technologies*. Springer. doi:10.1007/978-3-319-63962-8_234-1

Mamonov, S., & Triantoro, T. M. (2018). The strategic value of data resources in emergent industries. *International Journal of Information Management, 39*, 146–155. doi:10.1016/j.ijinfomgt.2017.12.004

Mani, V., Gunasekaran, A., & Delgado, C. (2018). Enhancing supply chain performance through supplier social sustainability: An emerging economy perspective. *International Journal of Production Economics, 195*, 259–272. doi:10.1016/j.ijpe.2017.10.025

Manners-Bell, J., & Lyon, K. (2019). *The logistics and supply chain innovation handbook: Disruptive technologies and new business models*. Kogan Page Publishers.

Manyika, J., Chui, M., Bughin, J., Dobbs, R., Bisson, P., & Marrs, A. (2013). *Disruptive technologies: Advances that will transform life, business, and the global economy*. McKinsey Global Institute.

Marjani, M., Nasaruddin, F., Gani, A., Karim, A., Hashem, I. A. T., Siddiqa, A., & Yaqoob, I. (2017). Big IoT data analytics: Architecture, opportunities, and open research challenges. *IEEE Access : Practical Innovations, Open Solutions, 5*, 5247–5261. doi:10.1109/ACCESS.2017.2689040

Markley, M. J., & Davis, L. (2007). Exploring future competitive advantage through sustainable supply chains. *International Journal of Physical Distribution & Logistics Management*, *9*(37), 763–774. doi:10.1108/09600030710840859

Moffatt, I. (2004). Global warming: Scientific modeling and its relationship to the economic dimensions of policy. In A. D. Owen & N. Hanley (Eds.), *The economics of climate change* (pp. 6–34). Routledge.

Mois, G., Sanislav, T., & Folea, S. C. (2016). A cyber-physical system for environmental monitoring. *IEEE Transactions on Instrumentation and Measurement*, *65*(6), 1463–1471. doi:10.1109/TIM.2016.2526669

Montes, J. O. (2016). Impacts of 3D printing on the development of new business models. In *Proceedings of the 2016 IEEE European Technology and Engineering Management Summit (E-TEMS)* (1-9). IEEE. 10.1109/E-TEMS.2016.7912605

Morali, O., & Searcy, C. (2013). A review of sustainable supply chain management practices in Canada. *Journal of Business Ethics*, *117*(3), 635–658. doi:10.100710551-012-1539-4

Morella, P., Lambán, M. P., Royo, J., Sánchez, J. C., & Ng Corrales, L. D. C. (2020). Development of a new green indicator and its implementation in a cyber–physical system for a green supply chain. *Sustainability (Basel)*, *12*(20), 1–19. doi:10.3390u12208629

Mourtzis, D., Vlachou, A., & Zogopoulos, V. (2017). Cloud-based augmented reality remote maintenance through shop-floor monitoring: A product-service system approach. *Journal of Manufacturing Science and Engineering*, *139*(061011), 1–11. doi:10.1115/1.4035721

Mujber, T. S., Szecsi, T., & Hashmi, M. S. J. (2004). Virtual reality applications in manufacturing process simulation. *Journal of Materials Processing Technology*, *155-156*, 1834–1838. doi:10.1016/j.jmatprotec.2004.04.401

Müller, J. M., Kiel, D., & Voigt, K. I. (2018). What drives the implementation of Industry 4.0? The role of opportunities and challenges in the context of sustainability. *Sustainability (Basel)*, *10*(1), 247. doi:10.3390u10010247

Muñoz, I., Alonso-Madrid, J., Menéndez-Muñiz, M., Uhart, M., Canou, J., Martin, C., Fabritius, M., Calvo, L., Poudelet, L., Cardona, R., Lombois-Burger, H., Vlasopoulos, N., Bouyssou, C., Dirrenberger, J., Papacharalampopoulos, A., & Stavropoulos, P. (2021). Life cycle assessment of integrated additive-subtractive concrete 3D printing. *International Journal of Advanced Manufacturing Technology*, *112*(7), 2149–2159. doi:10.100700170-020-06487-0

Nabiyev, V. (2012). *Yapay zeka*. Seçkin Yayıncılık.

Nahm, A. Y., & Vonderembse, M. A. (2002). Theory development: An industrial/post- industrial perspective on manufacturing. *International Journal of Production Research*, *40*(9), 2067–2095. doi:10.1080/00207540210128233

Naslund, D., & Williamson, S. (2010). What is management in supply chain management? A critical review of definitions, frameworks, and terminology. *Journal of Management Policy and Practice*, *11*(4), 11–28.

Negri, E., Fumagalli, L., & Macchi, M. (2017). A review of the roles of digital twin in SFS-based production systems. *Procedia Manufacturing*, *11*, 939–948. doi:10.1016/j.promfg.2017.07.198

Nelson, D. M., Marsillac, E., & Rao, S. S. (2012). Antecedents and evolution of the green supply chain. *Journal of Operations and Supply Chain Management*, 29-43. DOI: doi:10.12660/joscmv1n1p29-43

Nguyen, T., Duong, Q. H., Van Nguyen, T., Zhu, Y., & Zhou, L. (2021). Knowledge mapping of digital twin and physical internet in supply chain management: A systematic literature review. *International Journal of Production Economics*, *244*, 1–20. doi:10.1016/j.ijpe.2021.108381

Nix, N. (2001). Customer service in supply chain management context. In J. T. Mentzer (Ed.), *Supply chain management* (pp. 358–359). Sage Publications.

Noy, I. Y., Shinar, D., & Horrey, W. J. (2018). Automated driving: Safety blind spots. *Safety Science*, *102*, 68–78. doi:10.1016/j.ssci.2017.07.018

Okwu, M. O., Tartibu, L., & Machesa, M. (2020). Fourth industrial revolution and sustainable impact in autonomous fleets for effective supply chain network in manufacturing systems. In *Proceedings of the 31st Annual Conference of Southern African Institute for Industrial Engineering* (pp. 5-7). Muldersdrift, South Africa: SAIIE.

Olshannikova, E., Olsson, T., Huhtamäki, J., & Kärkkäinen, H. (2017). Conceptualizing big social data. *Journal of Big Data*, *4*(3), 1–19. doi:10.118640537-017-0063-x

Opara, L. U. (2003). Traceability in agriculture and food supply chain: A review of basic concepts, technological implications, and future prospects. *Food. Agriculture & Environment*, *1*(1), 101–106.

Ottoson, S. (2002). Virtual reality in the product development process. *Journal of Engineering Design*, *13*(2), 159–172. doi:10.1080/09544820210129823

Oxford Insights. (2019). *Government artificial intelligence*. Retrieved August 13, 2022, from https://www.oxfordinsights.com/ai-readiness2019

Özkanlısoy, Ö., & Akkartal, E. (2021). Digital transformation in supply chains: Current applications, contributions, and challenges. *Business & Management Studies: An International Journal*, *9*(1), 32–55. doi:10.15295/bmij.v9i1.1673

Panwar, R., Rinne, T., Hansen, E., & Juslin, H. (2006). Corporate responsibility: Balancing economic, environmental, and social issues in the forest products industry. *Forest Products Journal*, *56*(2), 4–13.

Papadopoulos, T., Gunasekaran, A., Dubey, R., Altay, N., Childe, S. J., & Fosso-Wamba, S. (2017). The role of Big Data in explaining disaster resilience in supply chains for sustainability. *Journal of Cleaner Production*, *142*, 1108–1118. doi:10.1016/j.jclepro.2016.03.059

Park, K. T., Nam, Y. W., Lee, H. S., Im, S. J., Noh, S. D., Son, J. Y., & Kim, H. (2019). Design and implementation of a digital twin application for a connected micro smart factory. *International Journal of Computer Integrated Manufacturing*, *32*(6), 596–614. doi:10.1080/0951192X.2019.1599439

Pearson, S., & Benameur, A. (2010). Privacy, security, and trust issues arising from cloud computing. In *Proceedings of the 2010 IEEE Second International Conference on Cloud Computing Technology and Science* (pp. 693-702). IEEE. 10.1109/CloudCom.2010.66

Penrose, R. (1989). *The emperor's new mind: Concerning computers, minds, and the laws of physics*. Oxford University Press. doi:10.1093/oso/9780198519737.001.0001

Perussi, J. B., Gressler, F., & Seleme, R. (2019). Supply chain 4.0: Autonomous vehicles and equipment to meet demand. *International Journal of Supply Chain Management*, *8*(4), 33–41.

P&G. (2019). *Environmental sustainability report 2019*. Retrieved March 14, 2023, from https://downloads.ctfassets.net/oggad6svuzkv/7nSofG7XXtcYERIz5Vm3Xc/c8f716206225387fc9f7fe14ffbbac07/updated_citizenship_report_2019_environmental_sustainability.pdf

Phung, H. G., & Pham, D. B. (2018). Effects of integrated shrimp farming in Vietnam. *Journal of the World Aquaculture Society*, *49*(4), 664–675. doi:10.1111/jwas.12465

Pietras, B. (2015). New frontiers in driverless vehicles. *Engineering & Technology*, *10*(3), 64–67. doi:10.1049/et.2015.0326

Pinho, A. C., Amaro, A. M., & Piedade, A. P. (2020). 3D printing goes greener: Study of the properties of post-consumer recycled polymers for the manufacturing of engineering components. *Waste Management (New York, N.Y.)*, *118*, 426–434. doi:10.1016/j.wasman.2020.09.003 PMID:32966947

Piyathanavong, V., Huynh, V. N., Karnjana, J., & Olapiriyakul, S. (2022). Role of project management on sustainable supply chain development through industry 4.0 technologies and circular economy during the COVID-19 pandemic: A multiple case study of Thai metals industry. *Operations Management Research*, 1-25. doi:10.1007/s12063-022-00283-7

Prakash, K. S., Nancharaih, T., & Rao, V. S. (2018). Additive manufacturing techniques in manufacturing-an overview. *Materials Today: Proceedings*, *5*(2), 3873–3882. doi:10.1016/j.matpr.2017.11.642

Qrunfleh, S., & Tarafdar, M. (2014). Supply chain information systems strategy: Impacts on supply chain performance and firm performance. *International Journal of Production Economics*, *147*, 340–350. doi:10.1016/j.ijpe.2012.09.018

Quang, H. T., & Hara, Y. (2019). The push effect of risks on supply chain performance: Service-oriented firms. *Business Process Management Journal*, *25*(7), 1734–1758. doi:10.1108/BPMJ-12-2017-0343

Rajkumar, R., Lee, I., Sha, L., & Stankovic, J. (2010). Cyber-physical systems: The next computing revolution. In *Proceedings of the Design Automation Conference* (pp. 731-736), IEEE. 10.1145/1837274.1837461

Ramirez-Peña, M., Sotano, A. J. S., Pérez-Fernandez, V., Abad, F. J., & Batista, M. (2020). Achieving a sustainable shipbuilding supply chain under I4. 0 perspective. *Journal of Cleaner Production*, *244*, 1–11. doi:10.1016/j.jclepro.2019.118789

Rao, P., & Holt, D. (2005). Do green supply chains lead to competitiveness and economic performance? *International Journal of Operations & Production Management*, *25*(9), 898–916. doi:10.1108/01443570510613956

Rashid, A., & Tjahjono, B. (2016). Achieving manufacturing excellence through the integration of enterprise systems and simulation. *Production Planning and Control, 27*(10), 837–852. doi:10.1080/09537287.2016.1143132

Rauniyar, A., Hagos, D. H., & Shrestha, M. (2018). A crowd-based intelligence approach for measurable security, privacy, and dependability in internet of automated vehicles with vehicular fog. *Mobile Information Systems, 2018*, 1–14. doi:10.1155/2018/7905960

Reich-Stiebert, N., & Eyssel, F. (2015). Learning with educational companion robots? Toward attitudes on education robots, predictors of attitudes, and application potentials for education robots. *International Journal of Social Robotics, 7*(5), 875–888. doi:10.100712369-015-0308-9

Reif, R., Günthner, W. A., Schwerdtfeger, B., & Klinker, G. (2010). Evaluation of an augmented reality supported picking system under practical conditions. *Computer Graphics Forum, 29*(1), 2–12. doi:10.1111/j.1467-8659.2009.01538.x

Rejeb, A., Keogh, J. G., Wamba, S. F., & Treiblmaier, H. (2021). The potentials of augmented reality in supply chain management: A state-of-the-art review. *Management Review Quarterly, 71*(4), 819–856. doi:10.100711301-020-00201-w

Renaud, K., Flowerday, S., Warkentin, M., Cockshott, P., & Orgeron, C. (2018). Is the responsibilization of the cyber security risk reasonable and judicious? *Computers & Security, 78*, 198–211. doi:10.1016/j.cose.2018.06.006

Riglietti, G., & Aguada, L. (2018). *Supply chain resilience report*. The Business Continuity Institute.

Rogers, H., Baricz, N., & Pawar, K. S. (2016). 3D printing services: Classification, supply chain implications and research agenda. *International Journal of Physical Distribution & Logistics Management, 46*(10), 886–907. doi:10.1108/IJPDLM-07-2016-0210

Rogers, P. P., Jalal, K. F., & Boyd, J. A. (2007). *An Introduction to Sustainable Development*. Routledge. doi:10.4324/9781849770477

Rose, D. C., Lyon, J., de Boon, A., Hanheide, M., & Pearson, S. (2021). Responsible development of autonomous robotics in agriculture. *Nature Food, 2*(5), 306–309. doi:10.103843016-021-00287-9 PMID:37117726

Ruel, S., El Baz, J., Ivanov, D., & Das, A. (2021). Supply chain viability: Conceptualization, measurement, and nomological validation. *Annals of Operations Research*, 1–30. doi:10.100710479-021-03974-9 PMID:33716370

Russell, S., Dewey, D., & Tegmark, M. (2015). Research priorities for robust and beneficial artificial intelligence. *AI Magazine, 36*(4), 105–114. doi:10.1609/aimag.v36i4.2577

Rüßmann, M., Lorenz, M., Gerbert, P., Waldner, M., Justus, J., Engel, P., & Harnisch, M. (2015). Industry 4.0: The future of productivity and growth in manufacturing industries. *Boston Consulting Group, 9*(1), 1-14.

Saad, M., & Patel, B. (2006). An investigation of supply chain performance measurement in the Indian automotive sector. *Benchmarking, 13*(1/2), 36–53. doi:10.1108/14635770610644565

Salam, A. (2020). Internet of things for sustainability: Perspectives in privacy, cybersecurity, and future trends. In A. Salam (Ed.), *Internet of Things for Sustainable Community Development: Wireless Communications, Sensing, and Systems* (pp. 299–327). Springer Nature. doi:10.1007/978-3-030-35291-2_10

Sanchez, M., Exposito, E., & Aguilar, J. (2020). Industry 4.0: Survey from a system integration perspective. *International Journal of Computer Integrated Manufacturing*, *33*(10-11), 1017–1041. doi:10.1080/0951192X.2020.1775295

Sandström, C., Magnusson, M., & Jörnmark, J. (2009). Exploring factors influencing incumbents' response to disruptive innovation. *Creativity and Innovation Management*, *18*(1), 8–15. doi:10.1111/j.1467-8691.2009.00507.x

Sarkis, J. (2006). *Greening the Supply Chain*. Springer. doi:10.1007/1-84628-299-3

SAS Institute. (2014). *SAS for: Demand-driven forecasting and planning*. Retrieved May 17, 2022, from https://www.sas.com/content/dam/SAS/en_us/doc/overviewbrochure/sas-for-demand-driven-planning-optimization-107293.pdf

Saucedo Martínez, J., Pérez Lara, M., Marmolejo Saucedo, J., Salais Fierro, T., & Vasant, P. (2018). Industry 4.0 framework for management and operations: A review. *Journal of Ambient Intelligence and Humanized Computing*, *9*(3), 789–801. doi:10.100712652-017-0533-1

Savela, N., Turja, T., & Oksanen, A. (2018). Social acceptance of robots in different occupational fields: A systematic literature review. *International Journal of Social Robotics*, *10*(4), 493–502. doi:10.100712369-017-0452-5

Schniederjans, D. G. (2017). Adoption of 3D-printing technologies in manufacturing: A survey analysis. *International Journal of Production Economics*, *183*, 287–298. doi:10.1016/j.ijpe.2016.11.008

Schoettle, B., & Sivak, M. (2014). A survey of public opinion about connected vehicles in the U.S., the UK, and Australia. In *Proceedings of the 2014 International Conference on Connected Vehicles and Expo (ICCVE)* (pp. 687-692). IEEE. 10.1109/ICCVE.2014.7297637

Schöggl, J. P., Fritz, M. M. C., & Baumgartner, R. J. (2016). Toward supply chain-wide sustainability assessment: A conceptual framework and an aggregation method to assess supply chain performance. *Journal of Cleaner Production*, *131*, 1–14. doi:10.1016/j.jclepro.2016.04.035

Schwab, K. (2017). *The fourth industrial revolution*. Currency Books.

Scott, J. T. (2017). *The sustainable business: A practitioner's guide to achieving long-term profitability and competitiveness*. Routledge. doi:10.4324/9781351276603

Sebestyén, V., Czvetkó, T., & Abonyi, J. (2021). The applicability of Big Data in climate change research: The importance of system of systems thinking. *Frontiers in Environmental Science*, *9*(70), 1–26. doi:10.3389/fenvs.2021.619092

Shamout, M., Ben-Abdallah, R., Alshurideh, M., Alzoubi, H., Kurdi, B., & Hamadneh, S. (2022). A conceptual model for the adoption of autonomous robots in supply chain and logistics industry. *Uncertain Supply Chain Management*, *10*(2), 577–592. doi:10.5267/j.uscm.2021.11.006

Shankar, V. (2018). How artificial intelligence (AI) is reshaping retailing. *Journal of Retailing*, *94*(4), 5–11. doi:10.1016/S0022-4359(18)30076-9

Shaw, S., Grant, D. B., & Mangan, J. (2010). Developing environmental supply chain performance measures. *Benchmarking*, *17*(3), 320–339. doi:10.1108/14635771011049326

Shepherd, C., & Günter, H. (2010). Measuring supply chain performance: Current research and future directions. In J. C. Fransoo, T. Waefler, & J. R. Wilson (Eds.), *Behavioral Operations in Planning and Scheduling* (pp. 105–121). Springer. doi:10.1007/978-3-642-13382-4_6

Singh, A., Mishra, N., Ali, S. I., Shukla, N., & Shankar, R. (2015). Cloud computing technology: Reducing carbon footprint in beef supply chain. *International Journal of Production Economics*, *164*, 462–471. doi:10.1016/j.ijpe.2014.09.019

Singh, R., Gehlot, A., Akram, S. V., Gupta, L. R., Jena, M. K., Prakash, C., Singh, S., & Kumar, R. (2021). Cloud manufacturing, internet of things-assisted manufacturing and 3D printing technology: Reliable tools for sustainable construction. *Sustainability (Basel)*, *13*(13), 1–20. doi:10.3390u13137327

Söderberg, R., Wärmefjord, K., Carlson, J. S., & Lindkvist, L. (2017). Toward a digital twin for real-time geometry assurance in individualized production. *CIRP Annals*, *66*(1), 137–140. doi:10.1016/j.cirp.2017.04.038

Sopadang, A., Wichaisri, S., & Banomyong, R. (2017, April). Sustainable supply chain performance measurement a case study of the sugar industry. In *Proceedings of the International Conference on Industrial Engineering and Operations Management* (pp. 1-12). IEOM Society International.

Stefanović, N., & Stefanović, D. (2011). Supply chain performance measurement system based on scorecards and web portals. *Computer Science and Information Systems*, *8*(1), 167–192. doi:10.2298/CSIS090608018S

Sterling, S. (2009). The ecological and environmental dimensions of the holistic curriculum. In G. Papagiannis (Ed.), *Education for sustainability* (pp. 309–322). Eolss Publishers.

Stock, T., & Seliger, G. (2016). Opportunities of sustainable manufacturing in Industry 4.0. *Procedia CIRP*, *40*, 536–541. doi:10.1016/j.procir.2016.01.129

Strozzi, F., Colicchia, C., Creazza, A., & Noe, C. (2017). Literature review on the "smart factory" concept using bibliometric tools. *International Journal of Production Research*, *55*(22), 6572–6591. doi:10.1080/00207543.2017.1326643

Su, Y., & Wang, X. (2021). Innovation of agricultural economic management in the process of constructing smart agriculture by big data. *Sustainable Computing: Informatics and Systems*, *31*, 1–7. doi:10.1016/j.suscom.2021.100579

Sufiyan, M., Haleem, A., Khan, S., & Khan, M. I. (2019). Evaluating food supply chain performance using hybrid fuzzy MCDM technique. *Sustainable Production and Consumption*, *20*, 40–57. doi:10.1016/j.spc.2019.03.004

Supply Chain Digital. (2022). *Top 10: Innovative & ESG-friendly global supply chains.* Retrieved December 17, 2022, from https://supplychaindigital.com/sustainability/top-10-innovative-esg-friendly-global-supply-chains

Sutherland, W. J., Aveling, R., Brooks, T. M., Clout, M., Dicks, L. V., Fellman, L., Fleishman, E., Gibbons, D. W., Keim, B., Lickorish, F., Monk, K. A., Mortimer, D., Peck, L. S., Pretty, J., Rockström, J., Rodríguez, J. P., Smith, R. K., Spalding, M. D., Tonneijck, F. H., & Watkinson, A. R. (2014). A horizon scan of global conservation issues for 2014. *Trends in Ecology & Evolution*, *29*(1), 15–22. doi:10.1016/j.tree.2013.11.004 PMID:24332318

Swan, M. (2015). *Blockchain: Blueprint for a new economy* (1st ed.). O'Reilly.

Taboada, I., & Shee, H. (2020). Understanding 5G technology for future supply chain management. *International Journal of Logistics*, *24*(4), 1–15. doi:10.1080/13675567.2020.1762850

Taboada, I., & Shee, H. (2021). Understanding 5G technology for future supply chain management. *International Journal of Logistics*, *24*(4), 392–406. doi:10.1080/13675567.2020.1762850

Tadejko, P. (2015). Application of Internet of Things in logistics: Current challenges. *Ekonomia i Zarządzanie*, *7*(4), 54–64. doi:10.12846/j.em.2015.04.07

Tan, K. H., Ji, G., Lim, C. P., & Tseng, M. L. (2017). Using big data to make better decisions in the digital economy. *International Journal of Production Research, 55*(17), 4998–5000. https://doi.org/.2017.1331051 doi:10.1080/00207543

Tang, C. S. (2006). Robust strategies for mitigating supply chain disruptions. *International Journal of Logistics*, *9*(1), 33–45. doi:10.1080/13675560500405584

Tanner, M. (2018). *Why China will drive blockchain and four related myths*. Forbes. Retrieved May 7, 2022, from www.forbes.com/sites/tannermark/2018/08/01/blockchain-china-misunderstandings/#a65d29213c85

Tao, F., Cheng, J., Qi, Q., Zhang, M., Zhang, H., & Sui, F. (2017). Digital twin-driven product design, manufacturing, and service with big data. *International Journal of Advanced Manufacturing Technology*, *94*(9-12), 3563–3576. doi:10.100700170-017-0233-1

Tao, F., Wang, Y., Zuo, Y., Yang, H., & Zhang, M. (2016). Internet of Things in product life-cycle energy management. *Journal of Industrial Information Integration*, *1*, 26–39. doi:10.1016/j.jii.2016.03.001

Tao, X. (2009, December). Performance evaluation of supply chain based on fuzzy matter-element theory. In *Proceedings of the 2009 International Conference on Information Management, Innovation Management, and Industrial Engineering* (vol. 1, pp. 549-552). IEEE. 10.1109/ICIII.2009.138

Taticchi, P., Tonelli, F., & Pasqualino, R. (2013). Performance measurement of sustainable supply chains: A literature review and a research agenda. *International Journal of Productivity and Performance Management*, *62*(8), 782–804. doi:10.1108/IJPPM-03-2013-0037

Thakkar, J., Kanda, A., & Deshmukh, S. G. (2009). Supply chain performance measurement framework for small and medium scale enterprises. *Benchmarking*, *16*(5), 702–723. doi:10.1108/14635770910987878

Thames, L., & Schaefer, D. (2017). Industry 4.0: An overview of key benefits, technologies, and challenges. In L. Thames & D. Schaefer (Eds.), *Cybersecurity for Industry 4.0: Analysis for design and manufacturing* (pp. 1–33). Springer. doi:10.1007/978-3-319-50660-9_1

Thiesse, F., Wirth, M., Kemper, H. G., Moisa, M., Morar, D., Lasi, H., Piller, F., Buxmann, P., Mortara, L., Ford, S., & Minshall, T. (2015). Economic implications of additive manufacturing and the contribution of MIS. *Business & Information Systems Engineering*, *57*(2), 139–148. doi:10.100712599-015-0374-4

Tieman, M., & Darun, M. R. (2017). Leveraging blockchain technology for halal supply chains. *ICR Journal*, *8*(4), 547–550. doi:10.52282/icr.v8i4.167

Timčenko, V., Zogović, N., Jevtić, M., & Đorđević, B. (2016). Assessing cloud computing sustainability. In *Proceedings of the 6th International Conference on Information Society and Technology, ICIST* (pp. 40-45). ICIST2016.

Timm, I. J., & Lorig, F. (2015). Logistics 4.0: A Challenge for Simulation. In *Proceedings of the Winter Simulation Conference (WSC)* (pp. 3118-3119). IEEE. 10.1109/WSC.2015.7408428

Timmermans, K. (2016). *Digital trendsetters: Secrets of the most successful supply chains*. Retrieved August 13, 2022, from https://www.mhlnews.com/global-supply-chain/article/22051791/digital-trendsetters-secrets-of-the-most-successful-supply-chains

Toka, A., Aivazidou, E., Antoniou, A., & Arvanitopoulos-Darginis, K. (2013). Cloud computing in supply chain management: an overview. In D. Garaham, I. Manikas, & D. K. Folinas (Eds.), *E-Logistics and E-Supply Chain Management: Applications for Evolving Business* (pp. 218–231). IGI Global. doi:10.4018/978-1-4666-3914-0.ch012

Uhlemann, T. H. J., Schock, C., Lehmann, C., Freiberger, S., & Steinhilper, R. (2017). The digital twin: Demonstrating the potential of real time data acquisition in production systems. *Procedia Manufacturing*, *9*, 113–120. doi:10.1016/j.promfg.2017.04.043

Um, J. S. (2019). *Drones as cyber-physical systems*. Springer. doi:10.1007/978-981-13-3741-3

Unilever. (2021). *Purpose-led, future-fit: Unilever annual report and accounts 2021*. Retrieved March 16, 2023, from https://www.unilever.com/files/92ui5egz/production/e582e46a7f7170fd10be32cf65113b738f19f0c2.pdf

United States Environmental Protection Agency. (2022). *Home*. Retrieved February 10, 2022, from www.epa.gov

Upadhayay, S., & Alqassimi, O. (2018). Transition from linear to circular economy. *Westcliff International Journal of Applied Research*, *2*(2), 62–74. doi:10.47670/wuwijar201822OASU

Upadhyay, A., Mukhuty, S., Kumar, V., & Kazancoglu, Y. (2021). Blockchain technology and the circular economy: Implications for sustainability and social responsibility. *Journal of Cleaner Production, 293*(2021). *Journal of Cleaner Production, 126130*, 1–7. doi:10.1016/j.jclepro.2021.126130

Vallandingham, L. R., Yu, Q., Sharma, N., Strandhagen, J. W., & Strandhagen, J. O. (2018). Grocery retail supply chain planning and control: Impact of consumer trends and enabling technologies. *IFAC-PapersOnLine*, *51*(11), 612–617. doi:10.1016/j.ifacol.2018.08.386

Veleva, V., & Ellenbecker, M. (2001). Indicators of sustainable production: Framework and methodology. *Journal of Cleaner Production*, *9*(6), 519–549. doi:10.1016/S0959-6526(01)00010-5

Vermesan, O., & Friess, P. (2011). *Internet of things strategic research roadmap*. River Publishers.

Viederman, S. (1994). Five capitals and three pillars of sustainability. *The Newsletter of PEGS*, *4*(1), 5–12.

Vijayan, G., Kamarulzaman, N. H., Mukherjee, A., & Vaiappuri, S. K. (2020). Strategic value creation in a supply chain. In *Supply Chain and Logistics Management: Concepts, Methodologies, Tools, and Applications* (pp. 1–19). IGI Global., doi:10.4018/978-1-7998-0945-6.ch001

Von Solms, R., & Van Niekerk, J. (2013). From information security to cyber security. *Computers & Security*, *38*, 97–102. doi:10.1016/j.cose.2013.04.004

Wakabayashi, Y., Kamioka, M., Kinugawa, J., & Kosuge, K. (2017). KitPaDy: Robot co-worker in kitting process: Basic concept and computation of working time. In *2017 13th IEEE Conference on Automation Science and Engineering (CASE)* (pp. 320-327). IEEE.

Walsh, S. T., Kirchhoff, B. A., & Newbert, S. (2002). Differentiating market strategies for disruptive technologies. *IEEE Transactions on Engineering Management*, *49*(4), 341–351. doi:10.1109/TEM.2002.806718

Welford, R., & Frost, S. (2006). Corporate social responsibility in Asian supply chains. *Corporate Social Responsibility and Environmental Management*, *13*(3), 166–176. doi:10.1002/csr.121

Witkowski, K. (2017). Internet of things, big data, industry 4.0: Innovative solutions in logistics and supply chains management. *Procedia Engineering*, *182*, 763–769. doi:10.1016/j.proeng.2017.03.197

Wohlers, T. (2011). Making products by using additive manufacturing. *Manufacturing Engineering*, *146*(4), 70–77.

Wong, C., Yang, E., Yan, X. T., & Gu, D. (2018). Autonomous robots for harsh environments: A holistic overview of current solutions and ongoing challenges. *Systems Science & Control Engineering*, *6*(1), 213–219. doi:10.1080/21642583.2018.1477634

Worldwide Fund for Nature. (1993). *Sustainable use of natural resources: Concepts, issues and criteria.* Gland.

Wu, N., & Silva, E. A. (2010). Artificial intelligence solutions for urban land dynamics: A review. *Journal of Planning Literature*, *24*(3), 246–265. doi:10.1177/0885412210361571

Yang, J. (2010). On the construction and implementation methods for performance measurement of reverse supply chain. In *Proceedings of the Seventh International Conference on Fuzzy Systems and Knowledge Discovery* (vol. 1, pp. 899-903). IEEE. 10.1109/FSKD.2010.5569111

Yang, J., Zang, L., & Hao, Z. (2009). Study on the performance evaluation system of reverse supply chain based on BSC and triangular fuzzy number AHP. In *Proceedings of the 2009 International Conference on Information Engineering and Computer Science (ICIECS 2009)* (pp. 1-3). IEEE. 10.1109/ICIECS.2009.5364327

Yu, J., Bang, H. C., Lee, H., & Lee, Y. S. (2016). Adaptive Internet of Things and Web of Things convergence platform for Internet of reality services. *The Journal of Supercomputing*, *72*(1), 84–102. doi:10.100711227-015-1489-6

Yu, S., Mishra, A. N., Gopal, A., Slaughter, S., & Mukhopadhyay, T. (2015). E-procurement infusion and operational process impacts in MRO procurement: Complementary or substitutive effects? *Production and Operations Management*, *24*(7), 1054–1107. doi:10.1111/poms.12362

Yu, W., Patros, P., Young, B., Klinac, E., & Walmsley, T. G. (2022). Energy digital twin technology for industrial energy management: Classification, challenges, and future. *Renewable & Sustainable Energy Reviews*, *112407*, 1–14. doi:10.1016/j.rser.2022.112407

Zadrozny, P., & Kodali, R. (2013). Big data and splunk. In P. Zadrozny & R. Kodali (Eds.), *Big data analytics using Splunk: Deriving operational intelligence from social media, machine data, existing data warehouses, and other real-time streaming sources* (pp. 1–7). Apress.

Zailani, S., Jeyaraman, K., Vengadasan, G., & Premkumar, R. (2012). Sustainable supply chain management (SSCM) in Malaysia: A survey. *International Journal of Production Economics*, *140*(1), 330–340. doi:10.1016/j.ijpe.2012.02.008

Zeigler, B. P., Kim, D., & Buckley, S. J. (1999). Distributed supply chain simulation in a DEVS/CORBA execution environment. In *Proceedings of the 31st Conference on Winter Simulation: Simulation---A Bridge to The Future-Volume 2* (pp. 1333-1340). 10.1145/324898.325274

Zhang, M., Tse, Y. K., Doherty, B., Li, S., & Akhtar, P. (2018). Sustainable supply chain management: Confirmation of a higher-order model. *Resources, Conservation and Recycling*, *128*, 206–221. doi:10.1016/j.resconrec.2016.06.015

Zhao, X., Wang, P., & Pal, R. (2021). The effects of agro-food supply chain integration on product quality and financial performance: Evidence from Chinese agro-food processing business. *International Journal of Production Economics*, *231*, 1–16. doi:10.1016/j.ijpe.2020.107832

Zheng, J., Dai, Y., Liang, Y., Liao, Q., & Zhang, H. (2020). An online real-time estimation tool of leakage parameters for hazardous liquid pipelines. *International Journal of Critical Infrastructure Protection*, *31*, 1–10. doi:10.1016/j.ijcip.2020.100389

Zhou, K., Liu, T., & Zhou, L. (2015, August). Industry 4.0: Towards future industrial opportunities and challenges. In *Proceedings of the 2015 12th International Conference on Fuzzy Systems and Knowledge Discovery (FSKD)* (pp. 2147-2152). IEEE. 10.1109/FSKD.2015.7382284

Zhu, Q., Geng, Y., Sarkis, J., & Lai, K. H. (2011). Evaluating green supply chain management among Chinese manufacturers from the ecological modernization perspective. *Transportation Research Part E, Logistics and Transportation Review*, *47*(6), 808–821. doi:10.1016/j.tre.2010.09.013

Zhu, Q., Sarkis, J., & Geng, Y. (2005). Green supply chain management in China: Pressures, practices, and performance. *International Journal of Operations & Production Management*, *25*(5), 449–468. doi:10.1108/01443570510593148

Zhuang, C., Liu, J., & Xiong, H. (2018). Digital twin-based smart production management and control framework for the complex product assembly shopfloor. *International Journal of Advanced Manufacturing Technology, 96*(1-4), 1149–1163. doi:10.100700170-018-1617-6

KEY TERMS AND DEFINITIONS

Disruptive Technology: It is a technology that makes a positive contribution to the SCs, which have received the title of "disruptive" because they can quickly replace the existing technology.

Economic Sustainability: It is the sustainability dimension that ensures the efficient use of existing resources and the long-term sustainability of profitability.

Environmental Sustainability: It is a dimension of sustainability that relates to the companies carrying out their activities with the least possible negative environmental impact.

Industry 4.0: Industry 4.0 (4IR), also called the Fourth Industrial Revolution, is the industrial revolution that brings digital transformation with the combination of new technologies or disruptive technologies (DTs), also called 4IR technologies, and industrialization or physical production and cyber technologies.

Performance Measurement: It is the process of measuring the effectiveness and efficiency of undertaken action.

Social Sustainability: It is the dimension of sustainability that requires companies to provide equal opportunities to their employees, promote social cohesion in society, and act considering their employees and society. It also includes people in the society, called the outer communities, and workers, called the inner communities.

Supply Chain: It consists of businesses, suppliers, and customers. These are the three key factors of the supply chain. Suppliers of suppliers, customers of customers, logistics service providers such as storage, distribution, and transportation, financial institutions, independent marketing institutions, and communication and information service providers can be added to these. Therefore, supply chain members can be listed as suppliers, manufacturers, distributors, retailers, and customers.

Supply Chain Management: Supply chain management is the ability for businesses to work with their suppliers to provide high quality materials and components at competitive prices.

Supply Chain Performance: The entire supply chain can meet end-customer needs, associated with ensuring the availability of products, delivering them on time in the right way, ensuring appropriate inventory levels. It also exceeds the functional boundaries of organizations, i.e., production, distribution, marketing and sales, research, and development.

Sustainability: It is the creation of the necessary situations for humans and nature to exist in productive conformity and the continuation of these conditions.

Chapter 12
Enhancing DevOps Using Intelligent Techniques:
Application of Artificial Intelligence and Machine Learning Techniques to DevOps

Sahana P. Shankar
M.S. Ramaiah University of Applied Sciences, India

Deepak Varadam
M.S. Ramaiah University of Applied Sciences, India

Aryan Bharadwaj
M.S. Ramaiah University of Applied Sciences, India

Shraddha Dayananda
M.S. Ramaiah University of Applied Sciences, India

Sarthak Agrawal
M.S. Ramaiah University of Applied Sciences, India

Ayush Jha
M.S. Ramaiah University of Applied Sciences, India

Surya Tejas V.
M.S. Ramaiah University of Applied Sciences, India

EXECUTIVE SUMMARY

Change is an inevitable part of any business. Customer satisfaction and building good will is the primary goal. The real success lies in the above two factors rather than money. Different businesses operate in different ways. Each one focuses on a different set of criteria and thus follows a different set of models. There are various models in the software development life cycle, such as the waterfall model, spiral model, V-model, and so on. These models have advantages and disadvantages and aid in the improvement of a company's workforce. They overcome the disadvantages of the previous model with each model. DevOps is the most recent model that is widely used. This chapter deals with DevOps, including the need, working, and how it differs from other models. This also looks into how intelligent techniques can be used to enhance the DevOps process for better productivity in the businesses (i.e., AIOps). It summarizes the different phases in DevOps, the corresponding machine learning or artificial algorithms that can be applied in the phases.

DOI: 10.4018/978-1-6684-5859-4.ch012

INTRODUCTION

DevOps is a software development model that has been recently in high demand as of around 2009 (Subramanya et al., 2022). As the name suggests DevOps derived from the words development and operation, aims to combine the development and operations parts of a software development life cycle (Faustino et al., 2022). It includes a set of activities or procedures and the necessary tools required to combine the responsibilities of both the processes of software development and its operation in the same team as shown in Figure 1.

Figure 1. A system view of DevOps

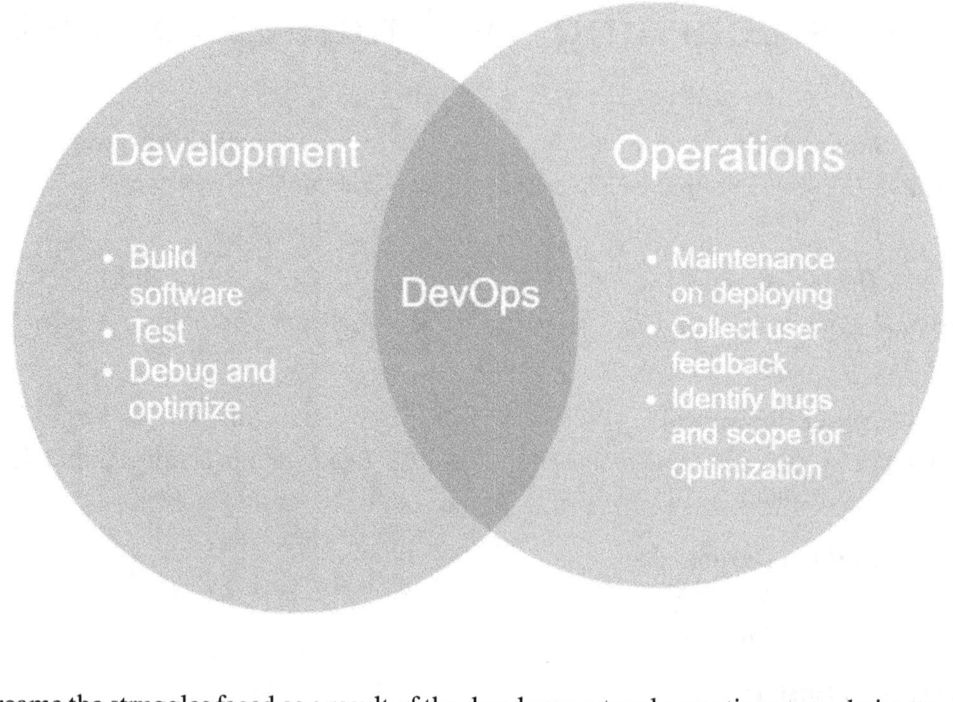

It overcame the struggles faced as a result of the development and operations team being two separate entities where one was not concerned with the activities of the other creating an obstacle to the smooth rollout of software (Subramanya et al., 2022). DevOps allows cross-functional team synchronization based on the company's philosophy and culture, hence it's more than just a set of practices. A major feature of DevOps is that it need not have major technological changes but instead focuses on team culture and coordination (Arvanitou et al., 2022). The development side of DevOps focuses on developing the software based on the client's requirements, continuously testing, debugging, and optimizing the software based on the continuous feedback received from the operations side that helps identify bugs and provides the parameters to be optimized. The simultaneous and synchronized working of the development and operations teams results in cutting down the effort required for software development and the expenditure required for its maintenance after deployment (Faustino et al., 2022).

DevOps allows the faster introduction of software into the market in a more stable manner for the company. However, since it consists of new methods and ideas which haven't been practiced by companies until recently it is still underdeveloped and consists of obstacles. These obstacles are being overcome as many companies use, study, improve, and implement DevOps while producing their software products (Wiedemann et al., 2019).

An ethnographic study on three companies that implemented DevOps methods consistently concluded that it provides the advantages of easy and rapid iteration and deployment, increased reliability, and reduced burden (Zhou et al., 2022). The DevOps model allows companies to have frequent releases and rapid bug fixing. New update releases that are less prone to bugs and improved with rapid iterations are possible with lesser effort with the DevOps model.

DevOps is inclusive of the culture, process, and technology that is required to be executed and implemented. Different companies and their software products have different implementations and maturity, therefore, the creation and implementation of the DevOps models are difficult between teams. Apart from these aspects the continuous software delivery and feedback cycles demand the need for automation as it is new and difficult for teams to cope and collaborate with it (Wiedemann et al., 2019).

The main challenges are the unavailability of proper infrastructure, knowledge, skill, and management, lack of collaboration and communication, and the lack of confidence and trust in the DevOps method as this approach of software development is new to the market. These challenges exist despite the results that the companies that have implemented DevOps have shown. However, over time these obstacles would be overcome as the practice and study of this model develop (Bijwe & Shankar, 2022).

The increased speed of delivery of software and its maintenance has demanded the need for automation to be involved in this field. Machine Learning Operations (MLOps) refers to the process of designing, developing, testing, and maintaining scalable Machine Learning models. MLOps integrates Machine Learning features into the DevOps model that helps to prevent the conflict of completing tasks between developer and operations by allowing faster and smoother workflow. The MLOps design is however specific to the application being developed and cannot be implemented for other applications. Modularity and the main principles of DevOps are considered to be the important features of MLOps. MLOps is used in iterative design, model development, and operations parts of the software to maximize the advantages of Machine Learning implementation for the above activities (Subramanya et al., 2022).

LITERATURE REVIEW OF DEVOPS

DevOps discusses the necessary cultural and organizational changes, as well as the automation technologies for implementation. It discusses how a typical company or organization is made up of multiple units/teams such as architects, project managers, system owners, developers, and so on, each with their own set of policies and procedures, which leads to organizational pains such as outages, slow IT, infighting, knowledge waste, motion waste, and so on. The emphasis is on adding customer value, eliminating waste, reducing cycle time, and identifying and removing bottlenecks. Employees are happier with a DevOps approach, and systems have fewer flaws that can be solved faster by utilizing automation technologies like issue tracking tools, collaboration tools, management tools, and source control tools (Katal et al., 2019).

The article focuses on setting up a cloud-based DevOps process and utilizing services. It discusses the difficulties encountered, such as maintaining various application settings and versions across servers, slow deployment between development and test environments, and inconsistency between development and operations environments. It discusses the process/phases for putting DevOps into practice on cloud platforms, which is described by continuous processes including planning, integration, testing, deployment, and feedback & monitoring. Phases don't have boundaries between them, and they don't start until the last one has finished. According to the article, DevOps reduces outages by 80%. It discusses how pilot projects can be successful in terms of collaboration, innovation, efficiency, decreased failures, and job satisfaction (Agrawal & Rawat, 2019).

DevOps allows quick, continuous release cycles and rapid adaptability to change user requirements, as well as the need for continuous system monitoring to discover errors and simplify the debugging process. It discusses a feedback-receiving system that blends operational and development data to detect abnormal behavior. It links the continuous operating system to the continuous development process, which generates real-time feedback. The provided input is included in the development process to achieve higher system quality. According to the study, two unsupervised Machine Learning algorithms, k-means clustering, and archetypal analysis, are used to characterize the set of data and determine if the new data points are anomalous or typical. The DevOps feedback mechanism, which employs Machine Learning, aids in the proactive monitoring of the system for any anomalies (Figalist et al., 2019).

The incorporation of DevOps culture and methods into industrial production settings are for small and medium-sized businesses which quickly implement Industry 4.0 technologies. The essential premise of this strategy is a continuous process of operation, observation, and evolution of the whole production environment to integrate all stakeholders and systems and make rapid modifications. It also addresses the Titan Platform, which helps in the integration and monitoring of industrial production environments through the use of industrial DevOps (Hasselbring et al., 2019).

The Cluster orchestration frameworks like Kubernetes and Docker Swarm are developed to accommodate the high turnover application cycle caused by DevOp's quick and frequent releases. It discusses how infrastructure problems may have a direct influence on the application. It examines proactive application deployment methods as well as the prediction of infrastructure breakdown. The method employs failure-risk metrics, such as the Failure-Index, calculated from application turnover rates and infrastructure failure prediction. It also claims that the algorithms decrease application disruption by 20%. In terms of application disruption count, the suggested algorithms outperform the existing techniques (Suk et al., 2019).

The article focuses on performance analysis and examines the uncertainties that may affect performance analysis, such as workload functions and resource availability (Trubiani et al., 2018). Its mission is to find and quantify these unknown factors. To make better decisions, DevOps teams must be aware of the potential difficulties that may arise during the DevOps life cycle to properly understand data, models, and outcomes. These uncertainties are generally detected by identifying the source, explaining how various uncertainties exist in input data, operational outcomes, and design models, and doing a vulnerability analysis to assess the influence of these uncertainty sources on results interpretation. The article makes developers aware of the uncertainties and does a sensitivity analysis to highlight the primary system flaws that cause performance concerns.

The article examines the methods of integration and maintenance of IT products by design teams throughout their life cycle. It discusses DevOps aspects such as the principle of shared responsibility, openness, and rapid feedback. It analyses the important independent factors that influence DevOps deployment through a case study of a higher education institution's Information Management System project. It explores how DevOps ideas aid in the optimization and productivity of developers. Employees accompany the whole lifespan of the IT product, regardless of the organizational structure of the firms that apply the DevOps approach (Veres et al., 2019).

The primary objective is to analyze modern DevOps technologies for strategizing execution models and monetizing business model innovation. It describes how DevOps improves collaboration across different teams and reduces cultural inequalities, allowing for faster delivery of apps or solutions. It addresses how DevOps can bridge the gap between Continuous Integration and Deployment. Modern DevOps approaches promote automation for all segments, minimizing human participation and improving organizational performance. Technology businesses discover a new method to solve limits and modify the operational environment by modernizing the technology architecture and planning the DevOps frameworks (Koilada, 2019)

The use of AI and DevOps and how they are interconnected is elucidated clearly in this article. They have explained how DevOps aids in the rapid delivery of high-quality software and how AI aids in the enhancement of functionality. This article explains how AI has improved DevOps and can help businesses, as well as the practical implications and importance of AI in DevOps (Mboweni et al., 2022).

DevOps and blockchain are interconnected because DevOps focuses on automation, measurement, and sharing, whereas blockchain focuses on security and thus plays important roles. This study enlightens how blockchain works in a DevOps environment, what factors aid in blockchain involvement in DevOps, and how blockchain and DevOps can be combined. This article's findings aid industry experts and the research and development community in developing a roadmap and guidelines for incorporating blockchain into the DevOps framework (Akbar et al., 2022).

A combination of Agile and DevOps has resulted in addressing the increasing complexity of customer requirements and requests (Almeida et al., 2022). It explicates how this combination can replace the Waterfall models used in software development and operations. This study describes the benefits of this combined framework by citing 12 case studies about international software companies, each of which cites different benefits such as improved team communication, reduced time, etc.

Figure 2. Graphical abstract

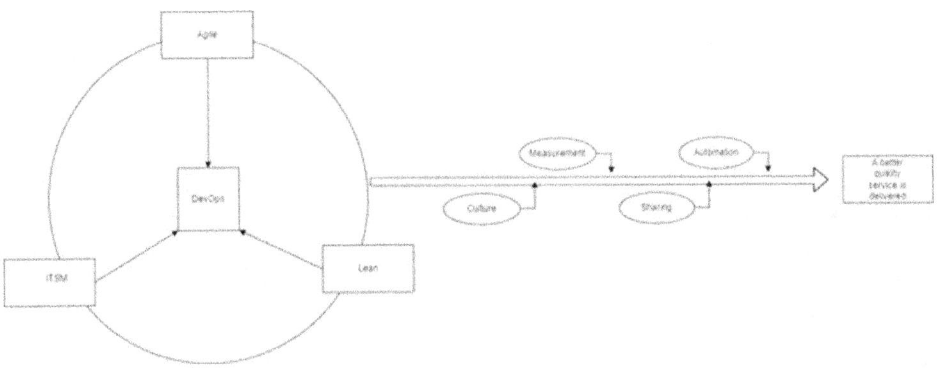

As a result of the coronavirus outbreak, most software companies' work environments changed dramatically, as software practitioners began to work remotely. To address the challenges of working remotely, organizations began to automate the software process. The authors have mentioned how it is done using DevOps in this article by referencing other articles (Khan et al., 2022).

With digital transformation rapidly gaining importance over the last few decades, organizations must ensure that they compete amongst themselves to be one step ahead while ensuring a smooth process. As a result, they adopted Agile methodologies to respond quickly to changing times. This is accomplished through the use of DevOps. This article's authors explained how DevOps can measure a team's performance, which is critical, by providing 13 key performance identifiers that ensure better quality and faster results as shown in Figure 2 (Gomes et al., 2022). DevOps and microservices are used to ensure that businesses meet software demands and provide capabilities through rapid and dependable software development. Although these are widely used, technical and organizational requirements have created an efficiency issue. This article discusses the advantages and disadvantages of software teams that use DevOps and microservices (De Bayser et al., 2022).

The development, security, operations, and maintenance, or DecSecOps, automatically integrates security into all stages of the software development lifecycle. All teams in this process share responsibility for application and infrastructure. This study emphasizes the importance of increasing efficiency in research and development and automated security (Chen & Suo, 2022). A cloud-based simulation is created for R&D, which opens all features such as testing, production, and so on; builds enterprise-level online DevOps systems; automates testing, and deployment, which improves the environment and shortens the overall cycle of R&D testing, and so on (Li et al., 2022)

A localizing change in the system by loosely coupling microservices, which in turn accelerates changes in trends, business changes such as legal matters, and user environment changes. Because it is difficult to adapt to these constant changes, the authors have proposed a new type of DevOps called DevFemOps. It is used to improve the maintainability and quality of the system. This paper discusses how close the goal of DevFemOps is to the DevOps cycle, with QA engineers at the center (Fukuzaki et al., 2022). To improve existing ML (Machine Learning) and DL (Deep Learning)-based systems that are used to solve complex real-world problems by applying DevOps practices to these systems. This will boost the deliverability and quality of the system (John et al., 2022).

WORKING OF DEVOPS

DevOps is an advanced version of the Agile model that unites the Development and Operations team. The diagram below illustrates the four areas involved in DevOps. The basic model for software development was the Waterfall model. It was simple, old, and took a lot of time to complete a simple project. To overcome these issues, the concept of the Agile model was introduced. The Agile model was fast and facilitated better interaction between the different teams. DevOps is a new discipline, thus it comes with its difficulties and risks of mistakes. In terms of integration, security, and continuous delivery, the cloud is crucial. A team must be knowledgeable and adaptable to implement DevOps effectively (Gokarna & Singh, 2021).

This illustrates the many difficulties the software development team has while utilizing the DevOps methodology as opposed to more conventional methods like the Waterfall model and iterative development, among others. It demonstrates many methods for addressing the issues; one of them involves leveraging AI and Machine Learning to automate everything and quicken the pace of development (Battina, 2021).

The DevOps technique is shifting toward leveraging AI for development, such as continuous monitoring, modifying, and analyzing the data, as we enter the new age where everything is digitally driven and everyone lives in a cyber-physical environment. Software and system engineering can be done more quickly and simply with the help of AI, which may offer a model-based framework (Bruneliere et al., 2022). This is an era of AI, Data Science, and Machine Learning. Data science is continuously being used in the application of Machine Learning (ML) to solve problems for the real world, industries are continuously increasing and expanding and the value of certain fields is also getting increased. To increase the overall business value by utilizing effective and predictive models, many science teams are working in the data science and Machine Learning fields. A concept is put out that uses Deep Learning and Artificial Intelligence to speed up DevOps (Development and Operations). The initialization, Software development, and operations are combined in DevOps (Lwakatare et al., 2020).

As per a recent survey, the scope of AI applications has suddenly increased in recent years. Source code production, maintenance, and user-related problems are addressed by the coupling of Artificial Intelligence (AI). The advancements made in Natural Language Processing (NLP) may be used to explain a large chunk of this increased interest. These techniques have a dual relationship with domains. Many of these beliefs have been put into practice thanks to the natural hypothesis, which claims that "software is a sort of human communication" and that code exhibits patterns resembling those of (human) natural languages (Matsui & Goya, 2021).

Recent research and this article have demonstrated the potential for high-stakes Artificial Intelligence (AI) development to improve people and the environments in which they live. Today's evolving procedures, however, come with a higher risk of critical errors, such as overuse, disuse, and abuse, which can lead to loss of life and liberty. To ensure that AI-enabled technology is delivered on schedule, software designers must focus on preventing these possible usage issues. A cost-effective examination of the human machine and its interactions is discussed comprehensively in the following paper (Gil et al., 2020).

AI is a modern technology that will be integrated into the system so that performance can be improved, and DevOps can be used as an effective method for delivering software when they are interconnected. For instance, DevOps teams may utilize AI, to test the data, code for the system, can do continuous releases, and monitor the software. AI in DevOps can also improve the automation of the software, it can quickly identify the issues, and foster the corporation. With AI, DevOps can produce software more efficiently. It can also be used to boost speed by enabling rapid development and providing features for operation cycles. In addition, Machine learning techniques can also assist with the guiding principles of the DevOps system components. The DevOps environment also contains data produced by continuous integration and tool deployment. Metrics that are evaluated and connected, such as the number of integrations, their success rate, the intervals between them, and the number of defects per integration, may all be of genuine benefit. AI is made possible at scale by using DevOps tools to operationalize Machine Learning models from conception to production. DevOps uses AI to make sure that the right delivery methods are in place and are flexible. These days of quick technological development, it is crucial to develop a "fail fast" mindset. The continuous supply, deployment, and monitoring of models via DevOps AI will essentially be possible as shown below in Figure 3.

Speed Cut back on non-value-added tasks while delivering AI to save time to market. Quality to speed up dataset cleansing, improve the quality of AI models, and encourage continuous learning. Scalability considers the problems and ensures AI models can expand or contract as necessary. Stability maintains the dependability and accuracy of deployed digital AI models (Rafi et al., 2022).

Figure 3. Monitoring of models via DevOps AI

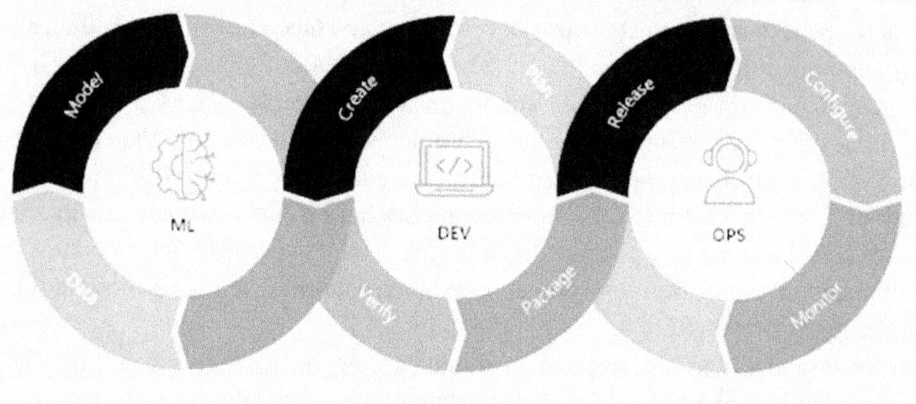

ENHANCING DEVOPS USING INTELLIGENT TECH

DevOps is a branch of software engineering that entails the collaboration of a team of specialists (operations team and development team) to concurrently build and deliver software systems (Bankar & Shah, 2023). With the aid of DevOps, repetitive human labor that is susceptible to errors may be eliminated. According to studies, implementing DevOps results in higher quality goods in less time, with more security, and at a lower cost. DevOps may be thought of as an extension of Agile in which functionality is produced at a quicker rate. It also adheres to the concept that people and relationships are more essential than processes and instruments (Ali et al., 2022).

When integrated, the two teams responsible for development and operations may do marvels for the company as shown below in Figure 4. Today's growing corporate phenomenon is the combination of teams known as DevOps. Making software systems using Machine Learning-based components is a very difficult task. The main goal of a Machine Learning process is to find the best prediction model through training cycles. Advanced software development approaches like DevOps have been widely utilized to highlight the quick development cycles and continuous delivery of software upgrades. There is currently no accepted method for merging Machine Learning processes; nevertheless, DevOps and Machine Learning may be utilized to develop solutions (Wang et al., 2020).

Figure 4. Intelligent tech to enhance DevOps

According to research, it is very difficult to govern information technology systems without Artificial Intelligence and DevOps. It is difficult for the DevOps team to organize and digest the data while also resolving customer complaints as a result of the increasing volume of data.

ADVANTAGES OF USING INTELLIGENT TECH WITH DEVOPS

There are several advantages to integrating AI with DevOps, some of which are discussed here. The ability of AI in DevOps to improve software program security is of primary importance. The idea of Artificial Intelligence accelerates the pace at which security checks may be run. AI does this by enhancing the efficacy of false identifications and greatly decreasing the threat of vector identification delays.

The current shortage of qualified cybersecurity specialists that most businesses are now experiencing may also be managed with AI. It creates personalized secure code patterns that correct any errors it has found. The majority of the difficulties DevOps teams have may be resolved by an AI-based DevOps amalgamation. Here are some examples of how AI is changing DevOps:

1. Artificial Intelligence has enhanced the accessibility of data. As a result, the DevOps team collaborates better and is made more effective.
2. AI may be used to gather material from diverse sources and formally organize it (Macarthy & Bass, 2020)
3. The manual setup and automation of security components are geared toward lowering the likelihood of errors and administration configuration issues when AI and ML are involved. Exploring vulnerabilities by an attacker results in improvisation, which is done to lessen downtime & possible breaches. Analyzing and decision-making become efficient and data-backed using AI & ML computing.

4. Since developing software is their primary function, AI and DevOps are intertwined. AI alone is unable to accomplish this. As a result, an app for learning a foreign language incorporates AI-based technologies like natural language processing (NLP).
5. DevOps teams may become more productive by using AI to support them throughout the whole testing, developing, releasing, and showcasing of programs process as shown in Table 1 (Hemon et al., 2020).

Table 1. Comparison between industry trends and pillars of DevOps

Industry Trends	Pillars of DevOps
DevOps to DevSecOps and NoOps Single click deployment for the cloud with security first focus in the software development lifecycle	Collaborative culture Reduced IT boundaries across organizational functions and businesses
Monolithic to Microservices The catalyst to DevOps/ NoOps adoption with containerized development, testing, and deployment	Flexible infrastructure Integrated IaaS resources to support variable workload demands and customer requirements
Hyper-automation Accelerating DevOps adoption through cognitive automation and analytics	Leadership and governance Directional vision and policies driving scale and scope of enterprise DevOps

INTRODUCTION TO AIOPS

The tech sector is progressively taking measures to include security in the different phases of the DevOps lifecycle in response to the massive breach of personal and private data. DevSecOps is the process of incorporating security as a crucial component into the DevOps life cycle. Figure 5 clearly illustrates the different phases of the DevSecOps process. By optimizing the transition from development to production, forecasting the consequences of deployment on production settings, and automatically reacting to changes in the environment, recent advancements in Artificial Intelligence and Machine Learning methods might enhance DevOps procedures. AIOps is the name given to the process of integrating AI into the DevOps life cycle (Sen, 2019)

Based on the sector considered, IT staff or developers, differ from AIOps depending on various firms. Ops personnel seek comprehensive system insight to better understand the potential causes of problems in a whole manufacturing process (Myrbakken & Colomo, 2017). IT firms will fully utilize DevOps when deployment automation techniques and an automated data analysis approach are applied. The advantages of automation include streamlined delivery, very few setbacks, and increased customer satisfaction. More businesses are adopting this business strategy over time. Artificial Intelligence will be a big help to DevOps.

Figure 5. Different phases of the DevSecOps process

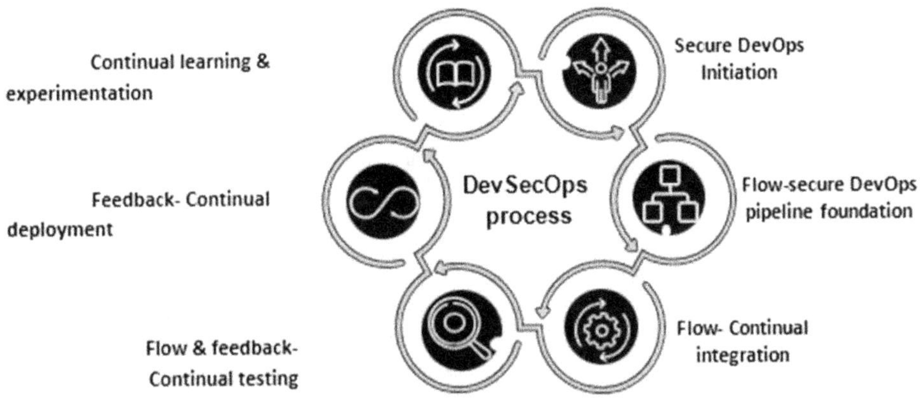

AIOps have the potential to revolutionize how IT operations teams manage alerts and address issues. Through incident management and constant alerts, IT may change a DevOps pipeline. It can ingest measurements, use inference models to derive useful insights from data, and automate common and regular operational operations by leveraging data science and computational methodologies. AIOps not only provides a contextual perspective of service health, but also streamlines procedures for monitoring, alerting, and correction (Sánchez & Colomo, 2020).

DevOps uses various tools in each phase presenting the results as shown in Table 2.

Table 2. Tools used in different phases of DevOps

Phases	Tools/Methods	Result
Continuous Development	• Laravel Digital Ocean • Ruby on Rails • Docker • Craft CMS • Ghost CMS • Google Web Starter Kit • Grunt Gulp • Slack • Python • Heroku	This is the stage where the software is "planned" and "coded." During the planning stage, the project's vision is chosen, and the developers
Continuous Integration	• Surge • Jenkins • Travis • Selenium	The developers must make changes to the source code regularly in this software development practice. This could occur every day or week. Every commit is afterward constructed, enabling early problem diagnosis, if any. Code construction also entails code review, unit testing, integration testing, and packaging in addition to compilation.
Continuous Testing	• Smoke testing: • Unit testing • Integration testing • System testing • Acceptance testing	In comparison to manually running the tests, automation testing saves a significant amount of time, effort, and labor. Additionally, creating reports is a huge benefit. It becomes easier to assess the test cases in a test suite that failed. The execution of the test cases can also be scheduled for specific times. The code is continually integrated with the current code after testing.
Continuous Monitoring	• Akamai mPulse • AppDynamics • BMC Helix Operations Management • ChaosSearch • Dynatrace • Elastic Observability • New Relic One • Splunk • Sumo Logic	The DevOps life cycle helps in keeping a regular check on the performance of the application, which is highly important. Here, crucial data about the software's usage is documented. To determine the application's correct operation, this data is processed. In this stage, the system faults, such as low memory and unavailable servers, are fixed. In this phase, the underlying source of any problem is identified. It keeps the services safe and readily available. Additionally, any network problems are fixed during this period. It enables us to automatically address issues as soon as they are discovered.
Continuous Feedback	• GetFeedback • Slack • Jira Service Management • Pendo	As it assesses the impact of every release on the user experience and then relays that assessment to the DevOps team to optimize future releases, continuous feedback is crucial to application release and deployment.
Continuous Deployment	• DeployBot • GitLab • AWS CodeDeploy • Octopus Deploy • Bamboo Deploy • CircleCI • Jenkins • TeamCity	At this point, the code is deployed to the servers used for production. Making sure that the code is correctly deployed on all of the servers is also crucial. The code is directly deployed to a live environment rather than being provided to a staging environment.
Continuous Operations	• Jira Service Management • Jira Software • Opsgenie • Statuspage	This phase allows us to rectify any errors or faults in the previous version and might help in better efficiency

USAGE OF DEVOPS

DevOps is important because it is a software development and operation approach that enables faster product generation and easier maintenance of existing installations. DevOps can primarily be used to reduce production time while increasing reliability and stability. Because of improved communication and consistency between the Development and Operations teams, the process becomes more fluid and error-free. DevOps is more concerned with test and delivery automation. The purpose of DevOps is to provide value and enhance the flow of the organization. Development and operations teams have been integrated, and engineers now work throughout the whole application lifecycle rather than being constrained to a specific role. The emphasis is on adding customer value, eliminating waste, reducing cycle time, and identifying and removing bottlenecks. Employees are happier with a DevOps approach, and systems have fewer flaws that can be solved faster by utilizing automation technologies like issue tracking tools, collaboration tools, management tools, and source control tools. DevOps fills in the gaps for enterprises struggling with Agile, allowing them to achieve the results they desired.

DevOps is a preferred strategy due to the following factors as shown in Figure 6:

- **Brings Teams Together for Quicker Product Software Delivery:** DevOps brings together the development and operations teams, resulting in improved communication and cooperation and faster product delivery.
- **Focus on Customers:** The switch to DevOps is important because it forces the team to think about customers first. DevOps naturally puts engineers in the shoes of consumers since it focuses on smaller releases and allows for more quick feedback. Additionally, it enables the operation team to hear what the users have to say and add any necessary features or improvements.
- **Rapid Delivery:** The most time-consuming process is continually being improved upon and sped up by the DevOps team, resulting in more frequent and better software product releases.
- **Quality:** DevOps prioritizes testing throughout the Software Development Life Cycle and assigns tasks to all engineers involved. It promotes exploratory testing, which can enhance software quality by identifying how to properly test built software components.
- **Reliability and Security:** Adoption of DevOps improves service dependability by boosting the availability and connectivity of services essential for an organization's efficient operation. Strengthened security is another important benefit of a solid DevOps strategy. DevSecOps expands on the basic components of DevOps, development, and operations, by including security as a separate component in the pipeline. DevSecOps adheres to the principle of continuous iterative improvement, which simplifies the entire security management process.
- **Optimized and Streamlined Process:** Teams learn to move faster, release small changes more often, notice difficulties in near real-time, and respond by rolling forward by utilizing a continuous pipeline from development to operations. Every day, DevOps assists a company in becoming its finest version. The advantage of DevOps is more concentrated on optimizing the most critical business operations.
- **Maintenance:** The DevOps approach is ideal for sustaining a product over time and making sure it continues to function for generations. DevOps teams may avoid long-lasting problems by placing a significant emphasis on performance across the whole lifecycle.
- **Cost:** The cost of operation is decreased over time since the development and operation teams cooperate as a whole.

Figure 6. Benefits of DevOps

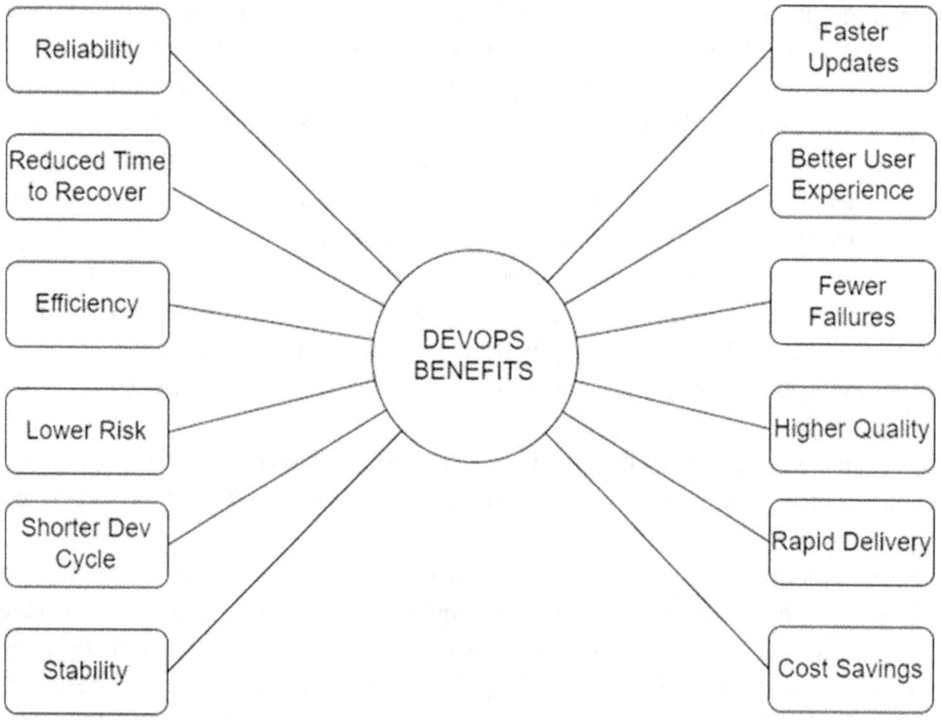

The following are the difficulties encountered when switching to DevOps:

- Because DevOps is all about breaking down boundaries between development and operations teams, the first difficulty is a lack of cooperation and communication between the two.
- The second most visible barrier is a lack of management and trust issues due to a lack of knowledge and abilities. This might be a concern if automation initiatives need extensive integration effort.
- The third major problem is the proper continuous integration of all tools for testing, development, and operation to all function together in a continuous way.
- Moving from conventional infrastructure to DevOps affects the entire business and requires the acquisition of new technologies. Enterprises must invest in new tools and teach their employees how to utilize them.
- Adopting DevOps can occasionally increase complexity since new tools and technologies might result in a more complicated production environment.
- Adoption of Devops increases expenses since new hardware and software resources are required, as well as the hire of skilled Devops engineers.
- Because there is no industry-wide standardization for DevOps, it might be challenging to incorporate the culture and may need the development of their process and tool-set.

DevOps comes with its perks but it's not always an ideal fit for an enterprise, the following reasons discuss further:

- When a company does not require regular product releases. For example, if a company has a business plan that does not need often updated software to match client demand. Such a company is unlikely to gain from the quick and continuous rollout that DevOps has to offer.
- Many organizations are resistant to change if the currently established technique works well. Many organizations prefer to stick with the traditional method since it works for them, and they don't bother transitioning to DevOps if the outcomes are expected to be similar.
- Highly regulated businesses, like healthcare, put safety over speed; these companies do not prioritize DevOps.
- Sometimes even If the business is highly dependent on frequent software releases, shifting to DevOps is not a good option in the middle of a merger and acquisition. With many changes going on inside the company during the merger, it is simply not the correct timing for significant shifts in how the IT teams work.

DEVOPS IS NOT IDEAL FOR USE

Implementing the DevOps model might not always be successful and efficient. At times trying to implement DevOps is faced with obstacles which makes it less ideal for use in such cases. Implementing DevOps implies a change in current communicational patterns, an organizational culture that is deeply rooted in a company and not malleable, and different constraints and environments than the existing ones. In cases where an organization has a deep-rooted culture and environment, changing it to adopt DevOps is extremely challenging and may cost more overheads than implementing a regular development method. In such cases, it is better to not opt for DevOps. In certain cases where an environment used in the production system can be complex making it difficult to replicate such environments for testing and verification. In such cases automated testing is less trusted, therefore, for such heterogeneous environments or complex environments, DevOps is not preferred (Riungu et al., 2016). Apart from an organization's change to uncertainty due to deep-rooted culture other factors such as having workers with the right technical skills, undeveloped technology and tools, and uncertainty in responsibilities and cultural changes suggest that using other development models is more feasible than implementing DevOps (Senapathi et al., 2018). There is a lack of industry consensus on how to measure software delivery and there is a lack of experts who can design such surveys. There is also a lack of trained professionals to implement DevOps since its methods are continuously evolving and new methods and tools are being introduced. Apart from this, the difficulties in redesigning the current systems to accommodate continuous delivery make DevOps practically difficult to implement. Due to all these challenges and limitations, DevOps is not currently ideal for use. However, with further development in the field, its usage can turn more practical and ideal (Leite et al., 2019)

KNOWLEDGE MANAGEMENT IN AI

Artificial Intelligence (AI) knowledge management is the act of gathering, compiling, and preserving the information required to develop and run AI systems. This can incorporate a variety of knowledge kinds, including unstructured text, pictures, and audio as well as organized data. Knowledge management in AI is to make sure that the information required to train and run AI systems is precise, current, and conveniently available.

A set of rules and best practices for gathering, arranging, and managing knowledge for AI systems makes up a knowledge management framework for AI. This can include rules for gathering and annotating data, techniques for classifying and archiving information, and methods for guaranteeing the accuracy and applicability of the knowledge used to develop and run AI systems. For AI-based systems to successfully gather, represent, and disseminate information, knowledge management is essential. Knowledge representation, knowledge acquisition, and knowledge dissemination are the three key parts of knowledge management. The process of expressing knowledge in a way that an AI system can readily comprehend and modify involves knowledge representation. The process of obtaining new knowledge, whether from internal or external sources, is referred to as knowledge acquisition. Dissemination of knowledge is the process of making knowledge accessible to users and the AI system. Many AI-based systems, including expert systems, decision support systems, and intelligent agents, make use of knowledge management approaches. Because these systems rely on knowledge to make judgments and offer suggestions, knowledge management strategies might be useful. Additionally, knowledge management may assist these systems become more effective and efficient by enabling them to learn new information and adjust to changing conditions (De Bem Machado et al., 2022).

Knowledge is represented in a formal ontology, which is a structured representation of ideas and connections, as part of ontology-based knowledge management. Rule-based knowledge management includes encoding knowledge as rules that an AI system may use to decide what to do and how to do it. Case-based thinking entails applying prior knowledge to new situations. In AI-based systems, there are both possibilities and difficulties for knowledge management. The development of efficient methods for expressing, obtaining, and sharing information that can be utilized by AI-based systems in a range of disciplines is one of the primary problems. The development of knowledge management methods that can be utilized to raise the functionality and effectiveness of AI-based systems is one of the primary potentials for knowledge management in these systems (Olan et al., 2022).

DEVOPS FOR SUSTAINABLE SOFTWARE

More of an attitude than a practice, sustainable software development. It is a technique for creating software that seeks to maximize overall application effectiveness while minimizing energy and resource consumption needs. The consequence of long-term task prioritization, and well-maintained software is the secret to effective short-term responsiveness in sustainable software development.

Case Study 1: Netflix

Netflix is a well-known entertainment company that streams TV shows, movies, and documentaries from a variety of genres and social groups. A large distributed system called Amazon Web Services hosts Netflix's streaming service (AWS). Netflix developers had to put a lot of emphasis on the dependability and robustness of both server-side and client-side components since there are so many parts that need to operate together to deliver dependable video streams to users across a variety of devices. They came to a simple conclusion that practicing failure repeatedly, is the best way to become comfortable in managing failure. In typical DevOps fashion, Netflix developers started automating failure to reach the necessary level of confidence and quality. Being a large company, Netflix has to deal with issues like managing a heavy user load at once and managing resources to give their users better performance. To accomplish this task, Netflix adopted a new technology called DevOps, but they did not prioritize DevOps over innovation which increased their profit and usability. Netflix is currently the major streaming service in the world just now, with about 215 million subscribers and distribution in over 190 nations. And a large part of this success can be attributed to its capacity for embracing more modern technology as well as its DevOps culture, which enables them to develop swiftly to satisfy customer requests and enhance consumer interactions. Netflix, however, disagrees with DevOps.

To achieve this goal, Netflix launched the Chaos Monkey tool, the first in a collection of tools known as the Netflix Simian Army. This device completely changed Netflix's engineering. Chaos Monkey is essentially an algorithm that runs continually in all Netflix systems and causes chaos by randomly shutting down servers. As a result, when developing algorithms, Netflix developers are always dealing with erratic services and unplanned outages. DevOps, which stands for testing and creating concurrently, pushes developers to construct fault-tolerant systems to minimize the irritation of their everyday job as developers. This chaos not only provides developers a rare opportunity to test their software under unexpected failure situations. When automation is utilized to create a setting where behavioral economics supports the creation of applications with the necessary level of quality, DevOps is at its finest. Despite being a very data-driven organization, they do not have even one office monitor that shows them their metrics in real time. Instead, they give algorithms the task of data analysis and only receive notifications when anything goes wrong. This allows their engineers to focus on the products they want to create rather than wasting time trying to understand the data. Once more, not every company may be able to achieve this, especially if their goods are dependent on a certain set of KPIs. To write code in this sort of situation, Netflix developers will design their systems from the bottom - up to be incredibly resilient to spine service failures, tested, and adaptive (Ebert & Hochstein, 2022).

For adopting this technology Netflix switched itself from a monolithic, data center application to a cloud-based Java microservices architecture. It brought up the following changes:

- Using NoSQL databases and a deformalized data model.
- Allowed Netflix teams to be freely connected to facilitate the team's ability to develop and implement improvements at their own pace.
- Centralized release coordination.
- Continuous delivery was made possible by multi-week hardware provisioning processes.

Case Study 2: Etsy

Etsy, Inc., an American Internet shop, specializes in unique things and vintage or handcrafted goods. These goods fall into several sectors, including jewelry, bags, garments, home furnishings, toys, and supplies for making art. Over 120 million products were available in the internet marketplace for handmade and vintage goods, which brought together 7.5 million sellers and 96.3 million buyers. In its first public offering (IPO) in 2015, Etsy raised $100 million. By 2020, it generated a net income of $349.25 million. In today's highly competitive business climate, obtaining high technological quality and speed to market is of utmost importance. Fees for services like "Promoted Listings," payment processing, and the gathering of shipping information through the website make up Etsy's revenue stream with the fastest pace of growth; additional revenue includes payments from outside payment processors.

Etsy provides global creative industries communities with e-commerce on a massive scale with close to 4.4 million suppliers and 81.9 million customers. Early on, in 2009, Etsy adopted DevOps best practices and has been actively pursuing the approach ever since. Etsy is hence commonly praised as the embodiment of DevOps for demonstrating to the world what outcome measures are feasible by forgoing conventional software development methodologies. Programmers, supervisors of operational procedures, and database administrators made up the technical staff of Etsy in 2005. Despite having just roughly 35 people, the team nonetheless struggled greatly to work together. This barrier was standing in the way of Etsy's growth as a business. Etsy's engineers recognized the drawbacks of Waterfall business models and monolithic architecture in 2008: Having a lot of data changes, releasing incorrect information, losing faith in the release, deploying slowly, and having fewer opportunities for research and development (Kim et al., 2021).

After adopting DevOps the lessons that any other software firm can take from Etsy are:

- The process of changing a company's culture is not simple. One must interact with stakeholders at various levels who can have divergent opinions on the subject as a whole. It may be necessary to illustrate the advantages of cultural change throughout the entire process. Make an honest evaluation of where your team and codebase are concerning releases as well as your desires to take them forward.
- Focus on writing short, manageable sections of code. The best approach to advance is to go slowly and be able to iterate. Instead of concentrating on the reliability of the deployment platform, emphasize the quality of the code. The aforementioned objective can be achieved by delivering smaller pieces of code more frequently. It is simpler to check the quality of the code when there are smaller deployment pieces.
- Full use of automation is recommended to achieve improved precision, dependability, consistency, and speed. Use visuals to test your strategy and delivery procedure. Making wise business selections will be made easier for the company.
- To bring about cultural and transformative changes inside the business, emphasize enhancing value-based learning and teamwork. To create transformative change inside the firm, promote value-based learning and teamwork (Gall & Pigni, 2022).

Case Study 3: Health Organization

Businesses nowadays are competing with one another for clients who will buy their products. However, teams occasionally run into issues due to jargon specific to their profession. For instance, the IT team may use a different slang term for a word that the development team would use a different term for. DevOps is advantageous for the organization in this situation since all of the teams predefine their vernacular, so there is no need for the teams to suffer as a result of that issue.

- A healthcare organization has distinct teams for IT, compliance, and clinical operations. Each team had its language and procedures, which caused misunderstandings and delays in putting new software into place. The company chose to use a DevOps methodology to boost productivity and communication.
- The clinical, IT, and compliance teams collaborated with the DevOps team to expedite the software development and operations procedures. To assure correctness and consistency across many

teams, they employed a shared set of tools and procedures, such as version control and automated testing. The group also established a common vocabulary and lexicon, which made it easier for everyone to grasp one another's terminology (Yarlagadda, 2021).

- The healthcare organization was able to cut the time required for software deployment by 50% as a consequence of implementing DevOps. In addition to enhancing cooperation and communication within teams, the DevOps methodology also helped teams to better grasp one another's languages and work processes.
- Automated testing decreased the likelihood of mistakes and enhanced the caliber of software releases. The healthcare organization was also able to swiftly make software upgrades, which enhanced patient care and cut expenses. Due to the compliance team's ability to give feedback early in the software development process, the organization also increased compliance with regulatory standards (Gupta et al., 2019).

LIMITATIONS OF DEVOPS

Level of Adoption of AI in DevOps in the Industry

- The adoption of DevOps in the industry varies depending on the organization, industry, and location. However, DevOps has gained significant momentum in recent years, with more and more organizations adopting DevOps practices to streamline their software development and delivery processes.
- According to GitLab's survey, 24% of respondents claimed AI/ML is used in their DevOps methods, which is more than twice the number in 2021. AI/ML is used by 31% of teams for code review and 37% of teams for software testing (Rzig et al., 2022).

CONCLUSION

This paper clearly shows that DevOps is the next breakthrough in an organization's operations. This type of model not only improves the company's efficiency but also helps to maintain accuracy through the use of automated tools. Another distinction is that, unlike other models, DevOps can employ any automated tool that aids organizations. When compared to the most popular software development model, the DevOps model focuses more on testing and integration, whereas Agile focuses on incremental development. DevOps is much faster than Agile; prioritizes documentation; has fewer bugs, and so on. As a result, implementing DevOps may reduce the likelihood of organizations losing time, money, and resources. It may take some time and effort to incorporate DevOps into your existing process. However, it will eventually help to create an Agile and scalable system that is ready for rapid change and growth.

QUESTIONS

1. DevOps relies on the participation of all team members, if there is a problem with the data in any phase, it provides inaccurate information. How can this be avoided?
2. With layoffs becoming more common in the current climate, removing an employee who has vital information from the company may pose an inefficiency issue. What should be done in this situation to keep the information safe?
3. With so many automated tools, it is possible that the tool used in one company is not used in the other. As a result, when data is exchanged between companies, the results may differ or be more efficient than the received report. Would the use of DevOps not be a major issue if companies could not stop using this tool because they have used it for a long time and it could cause an internal issue?
4. In the above scenario, Agile may be a better model because it relies heavily on automation tools such as Jira, JunoOne, and others for testing. So, why use DevOps when automation is used in all phases?
5. If there is a security breach, it will affect not only a team or a team member but the entire organization because all teams share their insights and results. How can this be avoided with the growth of MNCs and large organizations?
6. Documentation is the most basic requirement in any model. Because the DevOps workflow or the representation of the DevOps phases is an infinite symbol, even the smallest change must be documented in every team. Because there is a lot of documentation, there is a chance that there will be less storage, and increasing the space will be expensive. Is it necessary to document at each stage?
7. If a company decides to implement a new tool, it must also find a corresponding tool for the other teams. The reason for this is that if the new tool increases efficiency, it must be maintained or improved if the results of the other tools are integrated. Another issue is attempting to teach these tools to team members, which wastes time. Should new tools be integrated into the company's workforce to improve efficiency and performance, or should they continue to save time and money?
8. The request for a user to send to a load balancer in a microservice architecture analyzes the request and routes it to the appropriate microservice. Consider the following scenario: the machine abruptly stops working. In this scenario, propose a DevOps-related solution.

REFERENCES

Agrawal, P., & Rawat, N. (2019, September). DevOps, a new approach to cloud development & testing. In *2019 International Conference on Issues and Challenges in Intelligent Computing Techniques (ICICT)* (Vol. 1, pp. 1-4). IEEE. 10.1109/ICICT46931.2019.8977662

Akbar, M. A., Mahmood, S., & Siemon, D. (2022, June). Toward effective and efficient DevOps using blockchain. In *Proceedings of the International Conference on Evaluation and Assessment in Software Engineering 2022* (pp. 421-427). 10.1145/3530019.3531344

Ali, S., Riasat, H., Zubair, S., & Arif, S. (2022). DevOps in Practice a Systematic Literature Review. *Journal of Information & Communication Technology, 16*(1).

Almeida, F., Simões, J., & Lopes, S. (2022). Exploring the benefits of combining DevOps and agile. *Future Internet, 14*(2), 63. doi:10.3390/fi14020063

Arvanitou, E. M., Ampatzoglou, A., Bibi, S., Chatzigeorgiou, A., & Deligiannis, I. (2022). Applying and Researching DevOps: A Tertiary Study. *IEEE Access : Practical Innovations, Open Solutions, 10*, 61585–61600. doi:10.1109/ACCESS.2022.3171803

Bankar, S., & Shah, D. (2023). Decentralized Framework to Strengthen DevOps Using Blockchain. In *Computational Intelligence: Select Proceedings of InCITe 2022* (pp. 517–525). Springer Nature Singapore. doi:10.1007/978-981-19-7346-8_44

Battina, D. S. (2021). The Challenges and Mitigation Strategies of Using DevOps during Software Development. *International Journal of Creative Research Thoughts.*

Bijwe, A., & Shankar, P. (2022, October). Challenges of Adopting DevOps Culture on the Internet of Things Applications-A Solution Model. In *2022 2nd International Conference on Technological Advancements in Computational Sciences (ICTACS)* (pp. 638-645). IEEE. 10.1109/ICTACS56270.2022.9988182

Bruneliere, H., Muttillo, V., Eramo, R., Berardinelli, L., Gomez, A., Bagnato, A., Sadovykh, A., & Cicchetti, A. (2022). AIDOaRt: AI-augmented Automation for DevOps, a model-based framework for continuous development in Cyber–Physical Systems. *Microprocessors and Microsystems, 94*, 104672. doi:10.1016/j.micpro.2022.104672

Chen, T., & Suo, H. (2022, October). Design and Practice of Security Architecture via DevSecOps Technology. In *2022 IEEE 13th International Conference on Software Engineering and Service Science (ICSESS)* (pp. 310-313). IEEE. 10.1109/ICSESS54813.2022.9930212

De Bayser, M., Segura, V., Azevedo, L. G., Tizzei, L. P., Thiago, R., Soares, E., & Cerqueira, R. (2022, April). DevOps and Microservices in Scientific System development: experience on a multi-year industry research project. In *Proceedings of the 37th ACM/SIGAPP Symposium on Applied Computing* (pp. 1452-1455). 10.1145/3477314.3507317

De Bem Machado, A., Secinaro, S., Calandra, D., & Lanzalonga, F. (2022). Knowledge management and digital transformation for Industry 4.0: A structured literature review. *Knowledge Management Research and Practice, 20*(2), 320–338. doi:10.1080/14778238.2021.2015261

Ebert, C., & Hochstein, L. (2022). DevOps in Practice. *IEEE Software, 40*(1), 29–36. doi:10.1109/MS.2022.3213285

Faustino, J., Adriano, D., Amaro, R., Pereira, R., & da Silva, M. M. (2022). DevOps benefits: A systematic literature review. *Software, Practice & Experience, 52*(9), 1905–1926. doi:10.1002pe.3096

Figalist, I., Biesdorf, A., Brand, C., Feld, S., & Kiermeier, M. (2019, July). Supporting the DevOps feedback loop using unsupervised machine learning. In *2019 IEEE International Symposium on Innovations in Intelligent Systems and Applications (INISTA)* (pp. 1-6). IEEE. 10.1109/INISTA.2019.8778283

Fukuzaki, T., Liu, S., & Butler, M. (2022). DevFemOps: Enhancing maintainability based on microservices using formal engineering methods. *Connection Science*, *34*(1), 2125–2138. doi:10.1080/09540091.2022.2099347

Gall, M., & Pigni, F. (2022). Taking DevOps mainstream: A critical review and conceptual framework. *European Journal of Information Systems*, *31*(5), 548–567. doi:10.1080/0960085X.2021.1997100

Gil, D., Hobson, S., Mojsilović, A., Puri, R., & Smith, J. R. (2020). AI for management: An overview. *The future of management in an AI world: Redefining purpose and strategy in the fourth industrial revolution*, 3-19.

Gokarna, M., & Singh, R. (2021, February). DevOps: a historical review and future works. In *2021 International Conference on Computing, Communication, and Intelligent Systems (ICCCIS)* (pp. 366-371). IEEE. 10.1109/ICCCIS51004.2021.9397235

Gomes, M., Pereira, R., Silva, M., de Vasconcelos, J. B., & Rocha, Á. (2022). KPI's for Evaluation of DevOps Teams. In *Information Systems and Technologies: WorldCIST 2022* (Vol. 3, pp. 142–156). Springer International Publishing. doi:10.1007/978-3-031-04829-6_13

Gupta, R. K., Venkatachalapathy, M., & Jeberla, F. K. (2019, May). Challenges in adopting continuous delivery and DevOps in a globally distributed product team: a case study of a healthcare organization. In *2019 ACM/IEEE 14th International Conference on Global Software Engineering (ICGSE)* (pp. 30-34). IEEE 10.1109/ICGSE.2019.00020

Hasselbring, W., Henning, S., Latte, B., Möbius, A., Richter, T., Schalk, S., & Wojcieszak, M. (2019, March). Industrial develops. In *2019 IEEE International Conference on Software Architecture Companion (ICSA-C)* (pp. 123-126). IEEE. 10.1109/ICSA-C.2019.00029

Hemon, A., Lyonnet, B., Rowe, F., & Fitzgerald, B. (2020). From Agile to DevOps: Smart skills and collaborations. *Information Systems Frontiers*, *22*(4), 927–945. doi:10.100710796-019-09905-1

John, M. M., Olsson, H. H., & Bosch, J. (2022). Towards an AI-driven business development framework: A multi-case study. *Journal of Software (Malden, MA)*, 2432. doi:10.1002mr.2432

Katal, A., Bajoria, V., & Dahiya, S. (2019, March). DevOps: Bridging the gap between Development and Operations. In *2019 3rd International Conference on Computing Methodologies and Communication (ICCMC)* (pp. 1-7). IEEE.

Khan, A. A., Abrahamsson, P., & Niazi, M. (2022). Introduction to the special issue of managing software processes using soft computing techniques. *Information and Software Technology*, *152*, 107055. doi:10.1016/j.infsof.2022.107055 PMID:36034520

Kim, G., Humble, J., Debois, P., Willis, J., & Forsgren, N. (2021). *The DevOps handbook: How to create world-class agility, reliability, & security in technology organizations*. IT Revolution.

Koilada, D. K. (2019, June). Business model innovation using modern DevOps. In 2019 IEEE Technology & Engineering Management Conference (TEMSCON) (pp. 1-6). IEEE. doi:10.1109/TEMSCON.2019.8813557

Leite, L., Rocha, C., Kon, F., Milojicic, D., & Meirelles, P. (2019). A survey of DevOps concepts and challenges. *ACM Computing Surveys, 52*(6), 1–35. doi:10.1145/3359981

Li, J., Li, W., Zhang, X., Duan, J., & Wang, H. (2022, March). Design of DevOps environment based on cloud platform architecture. In *2022 IEEE 6th Information Technology and Mechatronics Engineering Conference (ITOEC)* (Vol. 6, pp. 95-99). IEEE. 10.1109/ITOEC53115.2022.9734518

Lwakatare, L. E., Crnkovic, I., & Bosch, J. (2020, September). DevOps for AI–Challenges in the Development of AI-enabled Applications. In *2020 International Conference on Software, Telecommunications and Computer Networks (SoftCOM)* (pp. 1-6). IEEE. 10.23919/SoftCOM50211.2020.9238323

Macarthy, R. W., & Bass, J. M. (2020, August). An empirical taxonomy of DevOps in practice. In *2020 46th Euromicro Conference on Software Engineering and Advanced Applications (SEAA)* (pp. 221-228). IEEE. 10.1109/SEAA51224.2020.00046

Matsui, B. M. A., & Goya, D. H. (2021, November). Applying DevOps to machine learning processes: A systematic mapping. In *Anais do XVIII Encontro Nacional de Inteligência Artificial e Computacional* (pp. 559–570). SBC. doi:10.5753/eniac.2021.18284

Mboweni, T., Masombuka, T., & Dongmo, C. (2022, July). A Systematic Review of Machine Learning DevOps. In *2022 International Conference on Electrical, Computer and Energy Technologies (ICECET)* (pp. 1-6). IEEE.

Myrbakken, H., & Colomo-Palacios, R. (2017). DevSecOps: a multivocal literature review. In *Software Process Improvement and Capability Determination: 17th International Conference, SPICE 2017, Palma de Mallorca, Spain, October 4–5, 2017, Proceedings* (pp. 17-29). Springer International Publishing.

Olan, F., Arakpogun, E. O., Suklan, J., Nakpodia, F., Damij, N., & Jayawickrama, U. (2022). Artificial intelligence and knowledge sharing: Contributing factors to organizational performance. *Journal of Business Research, 145*, 605–615. doi:10.1016/j.jbusres.2022.03.008

Rafi, S., Akbar, M. A., Mahmood, S., Alsanad, A., & Alothaim, A. (2022). Selection of DevOps best test practices: A hybrid approach using ISM and fuzzy TOPSIS analysis. *Journal of Software (Malden, MA), 34*(5), e2448. doi:10.1002mr.2448

Riungu-Kalliosaari, L., Mäkinen, S., Lwakatare, L. E., Tiihonen, J., & Männistö, T. (2016). DevOps adoption benefits and challenges in practice: A case study. *Product-Focused Software Process Improvement: 17th International Conference, PROFES 2016, Trondheim, Norway, November 22-24, 2016 Proceedings, 17*, 590–597.

Rzig, D. E., Hassan, F., & Kessentini, M. (2022). An empirical study on ML DevOps adoption trends, efforts, and benefits analysis. *Information and Software Technology, 152*, 107037. doi:10.1016/j.infsof.2022.107037

Sánchez-Gordón, M., & Colomo-Palacios, R. (2020, June). Security as culture: a systematic literature review of DevSecOps. In *Proceedings of the IEEE/ACM 42nd International Conference on Software Engineering Workshops* (pp. 266-269). 10.1145/3387940.3392233

Sen, A. (2021). DevOps, DevSecOps, AIOPS-paradigms to IT operations. *Evolving Technologies for Computing, Communication, and Smart World Proceedings of ETCCS, 2020*, 211–221.

Senapathi, M., Buchan, J., & Osman, H. (2018, June). DevOps capabilities, practices, and challenges: Insights from a case study. In *Proceedings of the 22nd International Conference on Evaluation and Assessment in Software Engineering 2018* (pp. 57-67). 10.1145/3210459.3210465

Subramanya, R., Sierla, S., & Vyatkin, V. (2022). From DevOps to MLOps: Overview and Application to Electricity Market Forecasting. *Applied Sciences (Basel, Switzerland)*, *12*(19), 9851. doi:10.3390/app12199851

Suk, T., Hwang, J., Bulut, M. F., & Zeng, Z. (2019, July). Failure-aware application placement modeling and optimization in high turnover DevOps environment. In *2019 IEEE 12th International Conference on Cloud Computing (CLOUD)* (pp. 115-123). IEEE. 10.1109/CLOUD.2019.00030

Trubiani, C., Jamshidi, P., Cito, J., Shang, W., Jiang, Z. M., & Borg, M. (2018). Performance issues? Hey DevOps, mind the uncertainty. *IEEE Software*, *36*(2), 110–117. doi:10.1109/MS.2018.2875989

Veres, O., Kunanets, N., Pasichnyk, V., Veretennikova, N., Korz, R., & Leheza, A. (2019, September). Development and Operations-The Modern Paradigm of the Work of IT Project Teams. In *2019 IEEE 14th International Conference on Computer Sciences and Information Technologies (CSIT)* (Vol. 3, pp. 103-106). IEEE. 10.1109/STC-CSIT.2019.8929861

Wang, Z., Shi, M., & Li, C. (2020, December). An Intelligent DevOps Platform Research and Design Based on Machine Learning. In *2020 Eighth International Conference on Advanced Cloud and Big Data (CBD)* (pp. 42-47). IEEE. 10.1109/CBD51900.2020.00017

Wiedemann, A., Forsgren, N., Wiesche, M., Gewald, H., & Krcmar, H. (2019). The DevOps Phenomenon: An executive crash course. *ACM Queue; Tomorrow's Computing Today*, *17*(2), 93–112. doi:10.1145/3329781.3338532

Yarlagadda, R. T. (2017). Implementation of DevOps in healthcare systems. *Implementation of DevOps in Healthcare Systems, International Journal of Emerging Technologies and Innovative Research.*

Zhou, X., Huang, H., Zhang, H., Huang, X., Shao, D., & Zhong, C. (2022, May). A cross-company ethnographic study on software teams for DevOps and microservices: organization, benefits, and issues. In *Proceedings of the 44th International Conference on Software Engineering: Software Engineering in Practice* (pp. 1-10). 10.1145/3510457.3513054

Chapter 13
Socio-Ecological and Green Innovation Management System Performance:
An Approach Towards Green Enterprises

José G. Vargas-Hernandez
Instituto Tecnológico Mario Molina, Mexico

Muhammad Mahboob Ali
Dhaka School of Economics, University of Dhaka, Bangladesh

Omar C. Vargas-González
Tecnológico Nacional de México, Ciudad Guzmán, Mexico

EXECUTIVE SUMMARY

This study has the aim to analyze the implications of socio-ecological and green innovation management system performance. It begins from the assumption that the socio-ecological system in any national, regional, local, organizational, group, and personal green innovation in system performance leads to the system performance. The method employed is a meta-analytical reflection based on theoretical and empirical literature review of the literature. It is concluded that the green innovation management system performance is determined by the socio-ecological strategies and policymaking.

INTRODUCTION

Sociology-ecological balance and green innovation of a country have been a great status starting from the micro and macroeconomic scenario along with complimentary support from the behavioral economics which must be supported by green investment, green financing, green marketing, green management, green entrepreneur, and green customer. Baah, Agyabeng-Mensah, Afum, & Lascano Armas (2023) commented that corporate environmental ethics and green creativity are critical antecedents to green

DOI: 10.4018/978-1-6684-5859-4.ch013

competitive advantage, sustainable production, and financial performance. Climate change results from the emissions of greenhouse gases due to industrial agroecology practices developing an ecological crisis and leading to the degradation of land (Intergovernmental Panel on Climate Change, 2014; Bot et al., 2000). Even in the case of digitization, e-waste management needs to be cautious so that sociology-ecological balances do not hamper. Terzi (2022) argued that the green industrial revolution has two impacts: accelerating the green change-making economic and planned cleverness, still devoid of weather deliberation; this speedy economic alteration at the comprehensive stage determination goes away several countries at the back, particularly persons to say no to become accustomed to this technical move. As such implementation of the green industrial revolution is much more important for advanced, emerging, and underdeveloped countries.

As such the research question of this study is how a sociolect-ecological and green innovation management system can perform well for the betterment of the people on the planet. In line with the previously mentioned research question, the objective of this study is to analyze the implications of sociolect-ecological and green innovation system performance, beginning from the assumption that the sociolect-ecological system in any national, regional, local, organizational, group, and personal green innovation in system performance leads to the system performance. This study is based on secondary sources. The study emphasized qualitative analysis. As such the study will use different books, and journals and conduct a literature review. Exact sources will be mentioned. The period of the study is from 1st January 2023 to 7th May 2023.

BACKGROUND

Leal Filho, Azul, Brandli, özuyar, & Wall (2022) emphasized on nurtures of information towards sustenance which works towards the UN Sustainable development goal to safeguard sustainable consumption and production processes. The impacts of sociolect-ecological transformation on labor markets are expected in job substitutions with sectorial employment shifts from fossil fuel to renewable energies, job elimination without replacement such as in the coal and oil refining sectors, redefinition, and transformation of existing jobs such as in energy and resources saving and job displacement due to relocation of firms moving to other territories with laxer constraints on environmental regulations and greenhouse gas emissions (Gouverneur, & Netzer, 2014). Research and development in systems transformation lead to the internal generation of innovative power (Törnberg, 2018).

According to ILO (Viewed on 5th May 2023) green enterprise development results in greener, environment-friendly, safe, and more productive workplaces. Performance management needs to be supported by creating green enterprises for human welfare, and social and worldwide countries value creation for human benefits. Industry 5.0 is creating opportunities for more human well-being-related industrialization processes by helping to keep sociolect-ecological balances and green innovation may lead to helping humanity. Complexity thinking and interactive human-nature ecosystems, insights, concepts, and tools lead to produce spontaneous and emergent properties of complex sociolect-ecological systems applied to describe the morphology of these complex systems, although it is a questionable argument (Corley, & Tinker, 2003).

Quintuple helix socio ecosystems innovation models are a structural process. The theoretical propositions framework of the quintuple helix model and the analysis of urban green living labs as a practice-based concept that leads to innovation diplomacy concept and knowledge production and transfer in the innovation ecosystem and sociolect-ecological transition. The quintuple helix innovation model drives the societal interactions and exchanges promoted by a cooperation system of knowledge, innovation, and expertise for sustainable development (Carayannis, & Campbell, 2010).

Knowledge creation in the economic systems can create new green products and services and new green jobs promoting green economic growth for economic benefits with performance management so that innovative and creative values can assist corporate social responsibility and corporate governance so that both can act. While many countries are still working to process expertise interlinked with innovative technologies to change skillfulness and productiveness through Industry 4.0 which does not consider human-centric development for which Industry 5.0 is necessary to communities of the earth to do their jobs besides robots and smart machines. The use of Industry 5.0 is still in its comparative immaturity. In this regard, Russ (2021) said that the changing Padkos environment has created a new complex ecosystem, unknowable and confronting the Homo Sapiens on a global scale as individuals and as societies, one that would question and challenge almost every assumption that was taken for granted and accepted in the natural, social, economic and political space. The political economy should work for superb leadership of the earth which will work for peace and tranquility and the welfare of the people of diversified countries in an integrated manner. As such countries of the earth should need to take proper strategies to develop structures that incorporate human and machine persons bidding to tap the specific welfare which can be reaped as the motion continues to develop namely 'One Earth, One Family, One Future.' To advance a Green Industrial Revolution refers to end-to-end innovative fresh measures to apply clean energy and increase environment-friendly socioeconomic systems while protecting the earth's physical resources and reversing harm to geographical damages. The green industrial revolution and Industry 5.0 should work as complementary for the welfare of the human being and compensation management must work for the survival of the human being.

The ecological burden has been racketed to the biosphere as a phenomenon of unpredictable changes in ecosystems in terms of climate change, crashing biodiversity, pollution, destruction of habitat, the evolution of species into viral outbreaks, etc. (Myers & Frumkin, 2020; Whitmee, 2008). Georgieva (2023) argued that to achieve the goals of 'One Earth, One Family, One Future', the world needs to find common ground even as geopolitical tensions are rising and countries need to avoid zero-sum policies that would only leave the world poorer and less secure. As such, the political economy may act for attaining sociolect-ecological balances, and green investment with the help of green enterprises can be established.

MAIN FOCUS OF THE CHAPTER

The sociolect-ecological and green innovation management system is highly interrelated with the sustainable development of a country as it brings the welfare of the society through attaining a Pareto optimal situation. To achieve the previously mentioned objective, the analysis starts with the sociolect-ecological system innovation to concentrate on green innovation leading to the innovation management system performance in the Literature review part. This will be followed by the methodology of the study. The study also contributes solutions and recommendations for the betterment of the planet's scenarios in the section of Solutions and Recommendations. Future research directions will be discussed in the following section, Finally, there is a conclusion of the chapter followed by references and acknowledgment, and key terms and definitions will be included.

ISSUES, CONTROVERSIES, PROBLEMS

Global warming is one of the key issues to maintaining the sociology-ecological balance. Deforestation and forest degradation are a great threat to biodiversity. Balanced development between agriculture and industry is required but most of the countries are not taking any such steps. A political economy with humanitarian leadership in diversified countries of the planet is required but most of the countries have not taken any such steps. Allocative efficiency and performance management are valuable tools. The integral energy shortage is leading Earth towards in search for renewable energies. Hydrogen peroxide may be an alternative energy for continuing sustainable development. The shortage of pure water for drinking and inefficient irrigation system is also a great hindrance for the planet. A political economy with humanitarian leadership in diversified countries of the planet is required. To sustain the ready-made garments industry business in Bangladesh, the country has been developing sustainable green investment culture through green enterprises.

The need for growing urban innovation green areas pressures the sociology-ecological innovation systems emerging multifaceted and complex challenges to be tackled by distributive and collaborative innovation processes. Urban green innovation areas are related to the sociolect-ecological contexts co-developed with the socio-political future. Green urban innovations and evolution as sociology-ecological systems approach are changes that integrate with the human environment systems thinking in an integrated approach to assess system threats (Berkes et al., 2000; Young et al., 2006). Sociology-ecological innovation is a dimension contextualized in a broad environment that fits with the implementation urban green living lab innovation model approach for the quintuple helix. An urban green living innovation lab generates and evolves a tacit codified exchange of knowledge and innovation within a natural and urban sociology-ecological environment transition system becoming sustainable balance and ensuring quality of life. Urban and rural sociology-ecological systems change with time through the complex dynamics of development and re-development, urbanization, de-urbanization, and ex-urbanization forces (Seta et al., 2011; Vercoe, et al., 2014).

Urban and rural green living innovation lab is an instrument to include a variety of stakeholders and actors searching to meet innovations in sociology-ecological challenges (Franz, 2014). The fourth helix is a conceptual framework to assess sociology-ecological innovation in urban green areas and the environment, encouraging the integration of analytical dimensions. The urban living lab is a practical framework to implement quintuple helix innovation into practice in the context of sociology-ecological transition in green urban innovation areas. In rural areas also, green labs must be set up to arrange the green industrial revolution.

The context of a sociolect-ecological transition aims to lay the foundation for sustainable green growth and development. Economic growth needs to be reconciled with ecological integrity support systems to avoid concerns about the disturbance of previously separated ecosystems for the improvement of quality of life (Myers & Frumkin, 2020; Whitmee, et al., 2015). The anthropology dimensions of disturbance coincide with natural and human systems to generate discoveries to transform recoveries and reassembly. Green growth has effects on employment which may not differ from economic growth. Contextual innovation development in a sociolect-ecological innovation environment is in line with the green urban living lab theoretical framework leading to an implementation of the quintuple helix model for innovation.

A sociolect-ecological innovation system framework provides insights into regional innovative Eco-industrial development strategies focusing on changing the relationships between urban green governance, land uses, renewable energies, time use, etc. Only considering resources, assets, and processes of localized knowledge, learning, and innovation is a limited analytical scope leading to the analysis of regional innovation systems to become attuned to the linkages of the non-local networks and extra-regional institutions (Cooke, 2005; Martin & Moodysson, 2013; Moodysson, et al., 2008) Regional innovation systems have been criticized for one-size-fits-all models (Coenen et al., 2017; Todtling, &Trippl, 2005) while offering an analytical framework to include the contextual, place-based nature and typologies of innovation processes (Asheim et al., 2015; Cooke, 2005). Worldwide heating is probable to affect the regular climate forms by regular vicissitudes in climate shapes.

The sociology-ecological components of innovative processes of green urban gardening and peri-urban agriculture have a behavioral change of social transformations aimed at the solution of environmental sustainability problems. Urban and rural settlements with contrasting qualities stimulate socio-ecological and technical innovations to achieve environmental sustainability governance as the emergence of transformation processes of new forms of urban and peri-urban green areas to further rural and urban development. This transformation of innovations requires a specific time to absorb so that sociology-ecological and economic-natural creativity together adding knowledge, skill, aptitude, and human resources can confront the challenges of local, regional, and global modifications for economic development (Carayannis, et al., 2012). Urban and rural land uses have been under continuous pressure to develop urban and rural respectively green innovation, adapt to social and environmental changes, and experiment, formulate, and implement strategies for social learning in the innovative transformation to sociolect-ecosystem sustainability.

The framing conditions of peri-urban and urban green agricultural projects and programs are different. This leads to urbanization in long-term social transition interrelated with the associated knowledge and ecological concerns. Social capital generated within the urban green living lab innovation leverages to sustain a sociology-ecological innovation transition through experiments of the quintuple helix innovation model to stimulate solutions to the challenges and to foster long-term changes. Urban green living innovation labs develop and work with temporary collectives supported by collaboration between the different stakeholders and actors. Green finance is critical in validating a mechanism influencing green innovation. Transformation of the traditional financial system is required to achieve a more efficient allocation of green finance and investment. The green finance system can be improved to facilitate green innovation developments for which balanced development between rural and urban sectors are being required.

Creating and developing a more comprehensive financial system to meet the most diverse financial needs of small, medium, and generous-sized firms in a more convenient form to alleviate the increasing capacities of green innovation. Green finance has spatial spillover effects across different regions and requires a cross-country analysis to validate findings. Drought and water shortage are one of the key weather alterations' negative influences. Performance dimensions are the procedure used to measure the competence and efficacy of schemes, agendas, and creativity. The definition and the concept of sustainable green wealth and its distribution between and within generations is the main concern. The sustainability concerns of green growth and development are related to immaterial and intangible green wealth components such as natural environment capital.

The development of innovative ideas generates feasible solutions to achieve the sustainable development goals and their targets so that socioeconomic and sociology-ecological sustainable development issues of fragile sociolect ecosystems can be resolved through vertical and horizontal development planning execution. Sustainable development implies eco-innovation and eco-entrepreneurship of active human agents involved in the circulation of knowledge between societal systems, know-how, and innovation changes for the knowledge economy and society (Barth, 2011; Carayannis, & Campbell, 2010). The systemic character of eco-innovations in the context of sociology-ecological transitions and green systemic social and institutional changes take a long-time lag for investors to sustain until the generation of outcomes, products, or services yield returns (Arundel, Kanerva, & Kemp, 2011). The risks and costs of environmental investments of ventures may be shared through external financing. Sociology-ecological systems are more tightly coupled and interdependent increasing the risks of systemic risks for failures at global scales to spread rapidly across the economic and social domains and geographies (Homer-Dixon, et al.,2015).

Recognizing the interactions of sociology-ecological and human-natural systems could benefit the wildfire risk. Human actors' governance system of fire-prone forests resists changes that require learning better to manage. Wildfire risk in forests is characterized as a sociology-ecological pathology of complex ecological and social systems interactions across multiple temporal and spatial scales leading to the governance system with strategies (Kline et al., 2016). The governance system of wildfire risk design and implementation strategies to mitigate the sociology-ecological pathology through innovative planning systems, analytical tools, and policies approached (Kline et al., 2016). Green credit is the ratio between total green credit and the total credit of listed companies. Green credit of firms and their total stock market value of listed firms. Green securities are the ratio between the total stock market value in the environmental protection industry and the total market value of listed companies. Green insurance is the ratio between agricultural and property insurance. However, most of the underdeveloped and emerging economic countries do not have a green insurance system.

The generic model of local innovation systems with the participation of research centers and universities can play a relevant role as a decisive component of economic performance and must reflect the local conditions marked by the participation of the innovative performance of firms. The innovative flow through the interactions between the actors of the innovation system, human resources, and infrastructure leads to the successful firm that will migrate to the innovation center to receive financial resources and exploit its growth potential which guarantees the performance of the links between the university and its resources, proximity to entrepreneurs in a stage of growth, attention from venture capital interested in technology-based start-ups that had passed the source entrepreneurial stage. The research on tertiary education models may emphasize the clusters formed by different actors, entrepreneurs, government institutions and agencies, firms, research, and academic institutions in a cluster resulting in innovative performance.

Different university-based local innovation models share similar objectives but have different origins and characteristics associated with the performance of firms, encourage the development of entrepreneurial cultures of students and researchers in their communities, generate quality employment, promote mechanisms to protect intellectual property, and facilitate technology transfer and commercialization to the market. Sociology-ecological innovation processes tackle environmental sustainability and ecosystems challenges involving market failure and public value tackled in innovation management theory through eco-entrepreneurship and public-private interactions. As such green industrial revolution is inevitable. There are some issues related to the effective promotion by the government creating the conditions of local innovation systems to increase innovations, productivity, and performance of firms (Porter, 1998). Innovation performance has an impact on diverse environmental regulations. Strong environmental policies and regulations improve public environmental awareness and strengthen the power of consumers to pressure ventures to implement green product and service innovations.

The dynamic assessments of sociology-ecological services are relevant to analyze drivers and future effects of the changes (Wagner, & Gobster, 2007). The volatility of investment and its performance in the measurement of social finance are relevant factors for Grabenwarter, & Liechtenstein (2012). Strategies and policies of adaptation and transition to sociology-ecological sustainability innovation to connect land uses of rural and urban land lead to different forms of urban green areas, agro-ecology, and gardening, the possibilities, and difficulties to transition to innovative social infrastructure for transformation for large-scale projects of sustainability governance (Luz, & Pires, 2014). The regional governance system must be opened to stakeholder groups from civil society fostering cultures of constructive challenges of regional and local status quo (European Commission,2012).

The state government must provide high levels of support for research and development investing in foundations of science, technology, and innovation to facilitate the creation of state universities-based tech parks and business incubators and specialized technical schools and training centers, encouraging local innovation system development, promote the location of firms and coordinate innovation activities, creation of regional scaling for regional economic development, improve infrastructure, transport and communications activities, training programs, development of regional innovation strategies and benchmarking, promote convergence of objectives and collaboration, the establishment of incubators and technology parks based on technological innovation, collect data on innovation performance, provide funds for local, regional, global economic development strategies focused on innovation, improvement of local, regional, global information systems based on technological innovation (Porter, 2001).

The incremental changes cope with the challenges in the domains of energy production, greenhouse gas emissions, pollution, water supply, weather events, and multi-dimensional transformation processes (Fischer-Kowalski, & Rotmans, 2009; Markard et al., 2012). The use of liquefied petroleum gas is an effective innovation in energy saving in human and forest resources and least polluting and smokeless in socio ecosystems with positive effects on the environment and human life., with the contribution towards better health (Nautiyal, 2011). Stimulating technological innovation with the management of scientific knowledge and technological institutions involved in research leads to new contracting forms to facilitate mobility from public institutions to the creation of research projects in private technology-based firms to increase performance.

In the multilevel governance architecture, the upper levels set the strategic goals, ten performance standards, and the institutions or rules of the game and the lower levels are freer to advance the ends (Barca, 2009). Ali(2018) argued that to establish a green economy as a super goal, a new green investment bank ought to be established in Bangladesh with the following purposes: substitute old technologies to reduce carbon emission; supply human fundamental needs by reducing environmental risk; inclusive green economic development and growth; acquaint with renewable energy sources; procedure of surface water; world-wide collaboration to protect environment and climate change is required; Dohlaikhal area in Bangladesh may be acknowledged as an industrial belt, and financing through the Green investment bank after establishment may be conducted; Microinsurance may be arranged for generating green product in Bangladesh and also other countries of the planet. Rutkowska, & Sulich (2021) argued that green labor management and its management technique can seek jointly decrease the consumption of natural resources, create less waste, reduction of greenhouse gas releases, and, on top of all, get rid of social inequalities.

LITERATURE REVIEW

Complex ecosystem dynamics (Holling, 1973) is a concept used to explain the capacity to adapt and shape change. Sustainable transitions theories consider that innovation niches deviate from the dominant socio-technical regimes to create change trajectories leading to sociolect-ecological systemic transformations (Geels, 2004). The innovation ecosystem is related to the production and circulation of knowledge in the sociolect-ecological innovation transition to analyzing the urban green living innovation lab approach. Sustainable transition theories of sociolect-ecological innovation tend to deviate in innovation niches from the dominant socio-technical regime creating change trajectories that lead to systemic transformations (Geels, 2004). The sociolect-ecological innovation approach is an integrated complex unit and holistic system to exchange resources and assess the threats (Berkes et al., 2000) to be regulated (Berkes et al., 2002; Machlis et al., 1997).

Logical moral individualism conflicts with the perspectives of complex systems on sociolect-ecological changes in cross-scale dynamics the cycles of growth and creative destruction (Quilley, 2020). The individual project innovation sociology-ecological analysis is used in this design in specific research cases focused on Eco-entrepreneurship and urban environment, open to shape through action research and become collaborative in nature to encompass the innovation development process in urban sociolect-ecosystems, the relationships between mediators emerge with the stimulus of sociolect-environmental change and sociolect-ecological innovation (Dennis et al., 2016). Urban sociolect-ecological systems tend to change at temporal and spatial scales following a patchwork non-homogenous dynamic, such as the case of a residential parcel re-owned after years. Green modernity urges progress, improvements, novelty, and innovations to transform for more sustainable arrangements (Nordhaus, & Shallenberger, 2007).

The sociology-ecological innovation development is a process facilitated by the steering commitments leveraging social capital, planning, implementation, and coaching of resources, and knowledge transfer between the ecosystem stakeholders. A relational ontological approach considers socio-agroecological systems as sociotechnical and sociology-ecological relationships as networks locating marginal and isolated socio-agroecological practitioners. Solutions to problems of economic and sociology-ecological integrated dimensions to socio-humanitarian systems require mathematical modeling of economic growth and socio-environmental and innovation factors. Human involvement in some ecosystems may be an expression of colonialism and standing as enduring relationships of sociology-ecological resistance in the form of community initiative through the leverage of resources and power for a vision of landscape transformation, coalitions of small-scale producers that continue to resist, challenge and re-directing interventions to promote sociology-ecological change and development (Watkins, 2018).

Sentiments of farmers may remain pervasive in enduring the self-organized multispecies and sociology-ecological connections with local and regional human-nature geographies and ecosystems synergized through interactions among the humans, flora, fauna, soils, fire, physio-chemical environments, etc.

In the socio-economic, geopolitical, geo-economics, and sociology-ecological framework of exploitation, agricultural plantations are export-oriented monocultures at the expense of more complex agroecological systems favored by Indigenous communities with traditional knowledge characterized by segregated landscapes and disarticulation of socio-biodiversity landscapes and economies (Manson, 2001). Monocultures remain the socio-economic and sociology-ecological ecosystems of the historical context of coloniality and modernity (Blaut, 1993; Mignolo, 2005; Wolf, 1982).

Violent insurrections lead to more routine bargaining forms, the sociology-ecological and socio-economic forms frame humans to become innovative and calculating economic agents and socio-political actors. Resistance to colonial governance cultures can be violent or mundane and shrewd to contribute to integrating agro-ecosystems and innovating sociology-ecological knowledge and cultures based on the fundamental ecologies and epistemes in indigenous landscapes (Araujo, 2013; Carney & Voeks, 2003; Reis & Azevedo, 2012; Schwartz, 1992; Van Norman, 2013). Agro-ecosystems may create a network of tradition and innovation to adapt and innovate knowledge and cultures of sociology-ecological change supported by indigenous socio-ecosystems and epistemes to construct the landscape that contributes to creating the economic conditions.

Some agro-ecological landscapes remain in the type of colonial violent monoculture generating socio-ecological systems with socio-politics-economic, cultural, and nutritional abundance with the neoliberal dispossessions schemes including the traditional knowledge and socio-ecological relations in local and regional landscapes remaining illegible to science, policymaking, and development agencies (Watkins, 2018). Dimensions of the innovation ecosystem of the quintuple helix model and other socio-ecological systems are the elements of innovation diplomacy to bridge the barriers between the separated fields and actors (Carayannis, & Campbell, 2011; Yin, 1984). The quintuple helix model has the elements of innovative sociology-ecological transition systems as the sources of contribution to the integration of natural environments under the assumption of creating synergies between the economy, universities, society, and democracy (Carayannis, & Campbell, 2011).

The Quintuple Helix innovation model is a nonlinear interdisciplinary and trans-disciplinary framework, suitable in theory and practices to analyze the link between knowledge and technical know-how to lead to natural environmental and innovation systems aimed to analyze quality management, the natural balance, and the diversity and plurality and promote a lasting development (Barth, 2011; Carayannis & Campbell, 2010). There is not enough empirical evidence to explore the limitations and possibilities of this analytical framework, only applied in assessing national and regional innovation ecosystems and not to analyze the sociology-ecological innovation development process.

The evolution of the regional innovation system is a responsive and admirably adapted theory of the innovation geography to change knowledge pattern flows resulting from globalization. Regional innovation systems have a capacity framework in placed-based structures conditioned by innovation identified with regional advantages, although have been criticized for their conception of space and being bounded (Bathelt et al., 2004; Bunnell, & Coe, 2001). The analytical framework for socio-ecological innovation ecosystems is structured based on innovation democracy concepts leading to knowledge production to be applied in transition to interactions of urban living lab models governed in such a way to be able to connect to the traditional top-down and bottom-up or grassroots approaches.

Mechanisms of knowledge link natural and human communities in post-trauma reassembly under conditions of sociology-ecological systems to adapt and innovate long-term outcomes including responses intended to reduce threats by sociology-ecological reassembly. The severity of extreme weather-related events needs conceptual frameworks for traumas and post-traumas and sociological transformations (IPCC, 2012; Leaning, & Guha-Sapir, 2013). The knowledge production exchange process and open innovation diplomacy take place in collaborative innovation socio-ecosystems. Knowledge production makes it relevant to the system of innovation networks and clusters. Clusters and networks in regional innovation systems and most recently smart specialization about research, development, and innovation embedded in regional innovation policy are distinct conceptual foundations of the innovation policy in trans-formative policy thinking with structural specialization effects on weak regions with the potential to transform regional economic structures (Foray, 2015).

The analytical framework of an urban green living innovation lab as a sociology-ecological innovation transition model is structured with the concepts of innovation democracy, knowledge creation and transfer, and innovation ecosystem. Sociology-ecological innovation transition interacts with environmental goals making sense of the conceptual model of an innovation ecosystem model framework. Complex sociology-ecological systems located in dynamic and rooted territories and landscapes, across scales and places, emerge as eco-systems from human environmental collaborations (Rangan & Kull, 2009; Rocheleau, 2011). The sociology-ecological innovation ecosystems are used in the quintuple helix model related to green urban innovation regarding the sociology-ecological context to co-develop the sociotechnical advances multi-level perspective to sociotechnical innovation (Geels, & Schot, 2007) is a tool to analyze the transition in economies as in the energy system of wood fuel in the transition to an uncertain sociotechnical scope.

An analysis outline for collaborative innovation and knowledge production network is the triple helix model expanded to the fourth helix for innovation processes in partnerships between university-government-industry and civil society The fifth helix model of socio-ecosystem innovation adds the natural environment into account (Carayannis & Campbell, 2009, 2010, 2012; Etzkowitz & Leydesdorff, 1995, 2000). The alternative socio-ecological systems embodied by prefigurative groups are the ones rooted in ontologies and innovation practices such as people taking the power of production to fill the gaps in supply chains. Sociology-ecological innovation and production systems under crisis conditions signal the danger of external dependence on a finite natural resource, the ecological and biophysical costs that limit growth at the expense of ecological spaces, and the challenges of cooperation benefits.

Imbalance change in the earth among developed, emerging, and undeveloped countries, deforestation is rising alarmingly along with the rise of global temperature has created trauma which may coincidence human well-being and natural systems will create reciprocal responses to disruption (Gotham et al., 2014). A pathway to address the metalevel design objective, the system-level objective can be based on the systemic leverage for the emergence of a global Eco-civilization. The design based on ways from experiential, presentational, propositional, and practical knowledge through local and virtual conversation based on systemic inquiry offers an example of systemic sociology-ecological innovation supported by collective intelligence. A team working on the design of international events addressing issues of livability and throw ability in systemic sociology-ecological innovation focuses on systemic intervention levels of meta-level on curating the conditions for a throwable planet (Laszlo, et al., 2012).

Reversing the degradation of socio-ecosystems can partially meet the increasing demands for services ecosystems. Pollution impacts the socio-ecosystems through natural resource management. The waste emissions of firms restricted by governments rely on compulsory systems more than their initiatives. The analysis of a socio-ecosystem management system can be approached by historical and structural perspectives based on variables such as social capital, trust building, strategic collaboration, sense-making, knowledge generation, etc. (McAllister, & Kornet,2002). The socio-ecosystem management approaches facilitate collaboration on achieving objectives and enhancing socio-ecosystem values. The adaptive ecomanagement approach addresses many issues related to socio-ecosystem management (Boyle et al., 2001; Dale et al., 2000).

The local legitimacy enhances the sociology-ecological management and the identification and creation of conflict resolution and positive situations. Integrating community development and sociology-ecological management, the stakeholders create collective meaning, promote public participation, and enhance empowerment by reinforcing power structures (Agrawal and Gibson, 1999, Brown, 2003; Pretty, 1995). Collaboration requires communication skills for voluntary participation supported by formal institutions to reduce vulnerability of the sociology-ecological management. Horizontal collaboration coordinates and engages local actors and associations in knowledge generation and the sociology-ecological management process. Social networks are an instrument for mobilizing social memory, generating social capital, and legal, political, and financial support to ecosystem management initiatives.

Horizontal collaboration coordinates and engages local actors and associations in knowledge generation and the sociology-ecological management process. Innovation networking of producers engages in both top-down and bottom-up approaches aimed at developing competencies, capabilities, and resources for the sociology-ecological and agroecological systems. The integration of economic, sociology-ecological cultural, and spiritual dimensions in a modeling method ensures the stability and viability of an entire system (Ramazanov, 2009, 2018). The use of mixed methods is used to analyze reconstructions of sociology-ecological and eco-systems changes to scrutinize development initiatives to transform landscapes and socio-economies (Watkins, 2018). The less developed global South is becoming the future of global cities with few developments and small-scale social and ecological innovations in renewable energies, transportation systems, and scarce natural resources to mention a few practices.

Socio-ecological transition systems are unpredictable, difficult to manage and control and generate unexpected results (Helbing, 2013). Socio-psychological analysis of socio-ecological system transitions and transformation processes departs from the traditional structural innovation systems based on capital accumulation driving to the global arrangements of political economy and power (McMichael, 2009). Neoliberal capitalism is an economic system that has been at the center of ecological degradation since the industrial revolution and will continue unless socio-ecological transformations reduce it (Harvey, 1996; Kallis, 2011; Klein, 2015; Moore, 2015; Smith, 1984). Socio-ecological innovation niche systems focus on the process of transition at socio-technical infrastructure, knowledge, institutions, norms, and rules (Geels, 2011). Overriding the ecological complexity by advancing the Fordist industrial process based on agroecological production and agri-food systems was the result of integrating genetics, chemicals, and machinery (Wolf & Buttel, 1996).

In an agroforestry system, planting annuals with perennials is an innovative idea for maximizing outputs from the cultivation of land (Nautiyal et al.,1998). The interstitial change occurs with learning, experimentation, and innovation within the sociology-ecological context drawing on resources, stress responses, and changes with the potential to catalyze systemic changes (Allen, 2004; Wright, 2010). Transitions from the traditional agriculture sector to the socio-agroecological sector must be facilitated by social and not isolated activities such as attending presential learning and experimentation activities or through the reliance on the Internet, based on common socio-agroecological knowledge systems supporting place-based innovation management compensating the research gaps on agroecology (Rosmann, 1994). Scientific and sociology-ecological knowledge blended with historical wisdom and experiential developments of resourceful practitioners supported with selected farms and resources working with efficient innovation management transition from traditional agriculture to socio-agroecological systems.

The socio-agroecological management transformations are complex systemic farming changes leading to psychological, socio-ecological, socioeconomic, and political processes shaping the farm enterprises. Traditional farming and agriculture systems research in developing and industrialized settings can be blended in an integrated and complex socio-agroecological agri-food systems analysis across economics, sociology, and geography (Altieri, & Nicholls, 2008; Campbell, 2009; Gliessman, 2007; Goodman, et al. 1987; Perfecto, et al., 2009). Building the socio-ecological innovation knowledge base and infrastructure to give support to the socio-agroecology facilitates the cooperation of projects occurring in some spaces with the growing presence of organic manufacturing and industrial socio-agroecology, evolving, creating, and generating more creative spaces for socio-agroecological knowledge and agro-food production systems (Guthman, 2004; Pratt, 2009).

Farming sociology-ecological strategies are transition-oriented towards environmental management systems, biodiversity, reliance on resources, and cycling in closing loops. Innovation management of biodiversity in sociolect-agroecological systems requires in-depth technical knowledge related to the life-cycling processes of soil nutrients in response to the environmental viability of place-based particularities with knowledge and information. Overcoming the systemic innovation barriers requires insisting on applications of place-based approaches predicated on the experimental perspective (Barca, 2009). The sociology-ecological green transition results of a shift expected to have implications for the different dimensions of work that are relevant for the macro-economics for sustainability in the relevant relationship between growth, work, and productivity (Jackson, & Victor, 2011).

Islam, Ali, &Medhekar (2017) found that consumers who buy green products frequently are willing to pay higher prices, compared to the consumer who buys green products occasionally; a good percentage of business firms have no plans to produce and sell green products. As such, government and financial institutions can take a more active role in providing encouragement and tangible incentives to the businesses to produce and sell green products in the country; those who purchased frequently could be more sensitive to climate change issues and are willing to support the production and sale of green products even at the expense of paying higher prices. This could be (i) Green regulation, (ii) Green financing, and (iii) Green public-private-foreign partnerships. Inclusive green economic development and growth (i) Green production;(ii) Green marketing;(iii) Green distribution;(iv) Green consumption -interpreted as a good sign in the sense that businesses should feel more confident to produce more green products, supported by government subsidies (Islam, Ali, &Medhekar,2017). Zhang, Xu, & Wang (2020) opined that if companies want to achieve outstanding green creativity, especially to "turn crises into opportunities" for environmental challenges, affects creative process engagement from an organizational level and implications for public policy.

SOLUTIONS AND RECOMMENDATIONS

Sociology-ecological innovation schemes smear the urban and rural green living test center with the area to ease agile and flexible testing with solutions connected to schemes pressure and confrontation. Sociology-ecological innovation changes by urban and rural green innovation prevailing test center can subsidize to sustainability enabled by trans-disciplinary trial endorsing participants' assignation and cooperative knowledge. Green enterprises can benefit by upgrading the performance dimension of sustainability issues. Making decisions through research and develop to create and develop innovations matching humans and environmental concerns are related to environmental sustainability leading to becoming more effective and feasible if the structure and functions of the system are concurrent with planning integrally and holistically including biological and cultural relations (Hjortsø et al. 2006; Ramakrishnan, 2003, 2008; Rogers, 2003).

Global, regional, and national innovation systems in policy-making circles are the result of a holistic strategy (Camagni, & Capello, 2013; Coenen et al., 2017; Morgan, 2017; Uyarra et al. 2017). An integrated approach to sustainability systems thinking responds to sociolect-ecological policy innovation agenda reflecting the broader international sustainable development urging for the creation of transformation niches aimed to promote sociology-ecological transformations in terms of ideas and actions (Moore et al., 2014). The identification of policy instruments and implications is a challenge in alternative innovation forms in contrast to policy prescriptions of market system failures in orthodox innovation. Damage to the longstanding growing of forests has of late mainly been exaggerated by deforestation processes. Waste and junk are shared views in urban and rural areas of diversified countries. This has been rising in e-waste worldwide as the use of the digitization process is gradually rising.

Rules of innovation and creativity in the strategy-making processes and innovation governance are relevant to be expanded for the research on innovation geography (Flanagan, & Uyarra, 2016). Sociology-ecological innovation policy instruments for urban green growth control and zoning provide methodologies to determine effectiveness compared to other models and interventions of climate action planning. Some climate action planning is innovative besides relying on conventional urban planning techniques. Sociology-ecological innovation modeling and climate action planning and policy instruments in urban green areas reveal differences in development patterns such as urban land use changes, mitigate emissions, and aggregate climate impacts, including actions of renewable energy, waste emissions management, land uses, transportation, etc. (Bassett, & Shandas, 2010). The planet's innovation and creativity systems are place-sensitive smart specialization strategies and an analysis tool of the local, regional, and global innovation and creativity conditions.

The place-blind innovation policy emulates and transfers best practices from successful regional innovation systems in efforts to build high-tech developments in the desert (Barca et al.,2012). Sociology-ecological innovation modeling should compare urban and rural green areas to reveal the deep-rooted behavioral and cultural relationships and preferences, the institutional and socio-technical regimes, anthropology and their links and impacts on gas emissions making it possible to measure the urban-rural extent, sprawl, and low-density development. Sociology-ecological innovation concept is well known but used in the context of transition and design of economic green growth and development is difficult to define in a shortcut manner. Local, regional, and global eco-industrial innovation should have policies for the low-carbon strategies that need to be implemented in both urban and rural green areas. Green gardening and entrepreneurship are satisfactory desires since it works like business, in that one has preparation, idea, and guidance, gratifying in their closeness. This is because green gardening helps to have plants in, the scenery from place to place is closely changing --and sociology-ecological performance may be affected through the alternation. Russ's (2021) comment is very much implied in the present context of the Earth where the ecological turbulence system of the earth prevails and where green enterprises may act as a solution.

Densely populated countries like Bangladesh need to take strong measures to curtail drastic population growth to balance development between the human development index and environment-friendly development. Green enterprises need to play a vital role in green innovation and sociolect-ecological balances to ensure a green industrial revolution. A green insurance system must be developed in Bangladesh and other countries of the earth. Awareness among green producers and green consumers must be raised so that market equilibrium for green products can be attained. Deforestation must be stopped, and new forests must be created. Clean water for drinking may be arranged through an integrated water management system. Industry 5.0 will play a vital role all over the planet considering the 'One Earth, One Family, One Future' idea. But to implement 'One Earth, One Family, One Future' will need strong political will by the global leaders.

Geo-economics and geopolitical activities must be strengthened for human welfare ideas which require political economics to be used for the welfare criterion of the human being. Any failure of any factor would lead to failure in the management of the system with a direct negative impact on the human being. Acute shortage of energy may be mitigated by the rise of the use of hydrogen peroxide. In the fuel lockups, hydrogen peroxide aids two characters: the situation stands "catholyte," sense of both the electrolyte – a liquid that ways electricity and lets the reaction happen – besides the cathode or the share of the battery that attracts electrons. Hydrogen is well-thought-out alternative fuel attention to hydrogen as a substitute conveyance fuel stems from its aptitude to power fuel cells in zero-emission vehicles, it is possible for domestic production, and the fuel cell's profligate filling time and in height competence.

Hydrogen can be used by fuel cells to produce electricity, or power and heat. Nowadays hydrogen is the greatest used in petroleum refining and fertilizer production, while transportation and values are developing markets. However, hydrogen is an incompetent usage of clean electricity. A political economy with humanitarian leadership on the earth is necessary to create growth with equity which generates employment opportunities and ensures social justice. Destruction of nature must be stopped for industrialization alternative arrangements need to be established. Big Data, Internet of Thinking (IOT), Artificial intelligence, and blockchain technology may be used by green enterprises for the betterment of their organizations. Green industrial revolution is nowadays the most important to sustain overall. Performance management of green enterprises will be helpful to attain the best quality output of the organizations and it should be distributed with equity consideration.

FUTURE RESEARCH DIRECTIONS

The future research study must examine the diverse types of intensity of environmental regulations and hindrances to executing these regulations in diversified countries. Forthcoming research work should focus on experiences in the sociology-ecological management strategies and dealing with change and uncertainty as well as the applicability of corporate governance to ensure the implementation of good environmental policies for the betterment of the societies and use of green environment so that pro-people well-being can be achieved.

A depth study to ensure 'One Earth, One Family, One Future' needs sociology-ecological balances along with green innovation which requires a wider range of quantitative analysis supported by qualitative analysis among diversified countries through using Artificial intelligence and big data with sustainable development characteristics so that policymakers can get a right direction and through the implementation of those directions in multi-faced arenas may be able to create 'One Earth, One Family, One Future' in future in true sense. Green enterprises ought to work for allocative efficiency for the planet so that removing income inequality and social justice can be arranged by creating an efficient market so that commodities and facilities can be optimally circulated between consumers and producers in an economy. Green industrial revolution among the countries of the planet needs to be more aggressively attained to sustain in the world for which a comparative study among the developed, emerging, and underdeveloped nations may be done.

CONCLUSION

A green innovation management system can be performed as a system under a design of policies and strategies considering its local, domestic, or regional even the planet as a whole problem in an integrated manner. Green enterprises need to be developed worldwide by each country's leaders who must be transformation leaders and as such government policy must be in favor of creating green enterprises. This will in turn arrange better performance of sociology-ecological balances accompanied by green investment. In this same order of ideas, both policies and human beings directly impact the performance of the green innovation management system, since the first factor generates the guidelines or lines to follow for the correct management of the system, and for the second factor, human beings, are those who apply the actions that the policies to determine. Sociology-ecological innovation becomes a process of social transformation, change, and problem-solving related to environmental sustainability problems, which have an impact on allocative efficiency. Bangladesh should go for industry 5.0, besides, the green industrial revolution procedure's implementation to expedite her economic development programs to maintain socio-economic betterment and welfare of the human being at large.

The sociology-ecological innovation system is a way of thinking applied to urban green living labs that may resist the urban sociology-ecological system. Sociology-ecological innovation transition should be considered in a broad sense through project-based experiments of quintuple helix innovation for long-term changes and stimulating urban green solutions and challenges. Implications of the performance of the system, understood as the level of use of the management of green sociology-ecological innovation, considering its main factors such as a sociology-ecological system at the national, regional, local, organizational, group, personal performance, sociology-ecological strategies, and policy formulation. Fulfillment of sustainable development goals needs sociology-ecological balances and green investment through creating green enterprises on the planet so that one world, one vision for the welfare of human beings can be possible if greediness, corruption, and nepotism among the member countries of the planet can be reduced and equal treatment with social justice and advancement of community development at par can be developed.

Re-localization of green health, green products, green consumers, green financing, green marketing, green management, green education, and sociology-ecological focused activities in emerging landscapes controlled by political actors, requires a societal approach in a more prosocial trajectory to community and family well-being and community development in a wider sense. An asymmetric information system may be arranged. Environmentally sustainable strategies have proven to be insufficient for sociology-ecological innovation systematic changes and transformations. Transitions to innovation management of sociology-ecological systems require internal cognitive changes through new patterns of thought of holistic ecological systems thinking of nature. The sociology-ecological transition must envisage strategies to improve the relationship between green economic growth and employment.

The radical foundation and formation involving the co-emergence of research and development innovation and business activities within the regional innovation systems is an entire creation and development of a new and distinct domain of the firm. Complex models of economic and sociology-ecological innovation systems are integrated into stochastic sociology-ecological dynamics of growth and development in an innovative economy. It is continuously more well-organized to use renewable power straight than to convert renewable energy to hydrogen aimed at energy use. This is factual cross ways segments then finish usages. Bangladesh and other developed and less developed nations must be aware of alternative sources of renewable energy for better performance for suitable development.

The integration of several domains, dimensions, and sectors of activities of sociology-ecological-economic systems with elements of humanitarian variables leads to the development of multifaceted system types that functions under conditions of instability and disasters which may be removed by arranging green enterprises worldwide. Lagging local and regional innovation systems must have an innovation policy portfolio supporting vertical smart strategic specialization joint to horizontal research on innovation capabilities required to prevent future innovation actions and avoid the risks inherent to knowledge and the digital economy. Citizens' well-being is more dependable on the foundational consumption based on social infrastructure, delivery networks, systems, and consumption more than individual consumption which depends on the market income of essential goods and services.

Governance of sociology-ecological innovation policies become relevant in societies and states with some levels of risk in their responses to global pressures and sociology-ecological development targeting local communities be considered too high value. Creation of green enterprise development discourses growth tasks with equity through creating employment opportunities, emphasizing sustainable development and green livelihoods foundation, and reducing poverty. Worldwide policymakers necessary to lay highlight generating green enterprises. This will lead to building capacity and improvement of performance through sociolect-ecological and green innovation management systems with the assistance of the green industrial revolution where the nucleus will be green enterprises.

QUESTIONS

1. What do you understand by system performance?
2. What are the main factors involved in the sociolect-ecological and green innovation management system performance?
3. How can you evaluate the term green enterprises' performance?
4. What is the role of human beings to influence the green innovation management system performance?
5. What is the role of policymaking in influencing the green enterprise's performance?
6. Is it undisputed that policymakers and human actions still have the potential to determine the future activities of the sociology-ecological system performance?
7. "Recommendations and conclusions of this paper are of value to inform policymakers in its efforts to promote management system performance to achieve sustainable development goals." Justify.
8. How to conduct a better sociolect-ecological and green innovation management system performance that may bring more benefits for the well-being of the human being and better life on the planet?
9. What do you mean by One Earth, One Family, One Future? How is it related to sustainable development?
10. Why is green enterprise creation necessary? Does it create growth with equity? If so, how? If not, why?
11. What can be the most effective renewable energy? Explain.
12. Why Industry 5.0 is necessary to imply all over the earth now?
13. Evaluate the green industrial revolution.
14. How do you prepare a scientific plan for creating employment opportunities and growth with equity through green enterprises?

ACKNOWLEDGMENT

This research received no specific grant from any public, commercial, or not-for-profit sector funding.

REFERENCES

Agrawal, A., & Gibson, A. (1999). Enchantment and Disenchantment: The Role of Community in Natural Resource Conservation. *World Development*, *27*(4), 629–649. doi:10.1016/S0305-750X(98)00161-2

Ali, M. M. (2018). Existing situation and prospects of the green economy: Evidence from Bangladesh. *Environment and Ecology*, *9*(2), 7–21. doi:10.21511/ee.09(2).2018.01

Allen, P. (2004). *Together at the table: Sustainability and sustenance in the American agrifood system*. The Pennsylvania State University Press.

Altieri, M., & Nicholls, C. (2008). Scaling up agroecological approaches for food sovereignty in Latin America. *Development*, *51*(4), 472–480. doi:10.1057/dev.2008.68

Araujo, A. L. (2013). Introduction to Atlantic approaches to resistance against slavery in the Americas. *Journal of African Diaspora Archaeological Heritage*, *2*(1), 1–5. doi:10.1179/2161944113Z.0000000001

Arundel, A., Kanerva, M., & Kemp, R. (2011). *Integrated innovation policy for an integrated problem: Addressing climate change, resource scarcity and demographic change to 2030*. European Commission.

Asheim, B. T., Coenen, L., & Moodysson, J. (2015). Methods and applications of regional innovation systems analysis. In Handbook of Research Methods and Applications in Economic Geography (pp. 272–290). Edward Elgar. doi:10.4337/9780857932679.00020

Baah, C., Agyabeng-Mensah, Y., Afum, E., & Lascano Armas, J. A. (2023). Exploring corporate environmental ethics and green creativity as antecedents of green competitive advantage, sustainable production, and financial performance: empirical evidence from manufacturing firms. Benchmarking: An International Journal. doi:10.1108/BIJ-06-2022-0352

Barca, F. (2009). *Agenda for a Reformed Cohesion Policy: A Place-based Approach to Meeting European Union Challenges and Expectations*. https://www.europarl.europa.eu/meetdocs/2009_2014/documents/regi/dv/barca_report_/barca_report_en.pdf

Barca, F., McCann, P., & Rodríguez-Pose, A. (2012). The case for regional development intervention: Place-based versus place-neutral approaches. *Journal of Regional Science*, *52*(1), 134–152. doi:10.1111/j.1467-9787.2011.00756.x

Barth, T. D. (2011). The idea of a green new deal in a Quintuple Helix Model of knowledge, expertise, and innovation. *International Journal of Social Ecology and Sustainable Development*, *1*(2), 1–14. doi:10.4018/jsesd.2011010101

Bassett, E., & Shandas, V. (2010). Innovation and climate action planning: Perspectives from municipal plans. *Journal of the American Planning Association*, *76*(4), 435–450. doi:10.1080/01944363.2010.509703

Bathelt, H., Malmberg, A., & Maskell, P. (2004). Clusters and knowledge: Local buzz, global pipelines, and the process of knowledge creation. *Progress in Human Geography*, *28*(1), 31–56. doi:10.1191/0309132504ph469oa

Berkes, F., Colding, J., & Folke, C. (Eds.). (2002). *Navigating Social–Ecological Systems*. Cambridge University Press.

Berkes, F., Folke, C., & Colding, J. (Eds.). (2000). *Linking Social and Ecological Systems: Management Practices and Social Mechanisms for Building Resilience*. Cambridge University Press.

Blaut, J. M. (1993). *The Colonizer's Model of the World: Geographical Diffusionism and Eurocentric History*. The Guilford Press.

Bot, A., Nachtergaele, F., & Young, A. (2000). *Land resource potential and constraints at regional and country levels*. Food & Agriculture Organization.

Boyle, M., Kay, J., & Pond, B. (2001). Monitoring in support of policy: an adaptive ecosystem approach. In T. Munn (Ed.), *Encyclopedia of Global Environmental Change* (Vol. 4, pp. 116–137). Wiley and Son.

Brown, K. (2003). Integrating Conservation and Development: A Case of Institutional Misfit. *Frontiers in Ecology and the Environment, 1*(9), 479–487. doi:10.1890/1540-9295(2003)001[0479:ICADAC]2.0.CO;2

Bruckmeier, K., & Olsson, G. (2014). An attempt to clarify the resilience concept for renewed strategies of farm modernization. *11th European IFSA Symposium, Farming Systems Facing Global Challenges: Capacities and Strategies Proceedings.*

Bunnell, T. G., & Coe, N. M. (2001). Spaces and scales of innovation. *Progress in Human Geography, 25*(4), 569–589. doi:10.1191/030913201682688940

Camagni, R., & Capello, R. (2013). Regional innovation patterns and the EU regional policy reform: Toward smart innovation policies. *Growth and Change, 44*(2), 355–389. doi:10.1111/grow.12012

Campbell, H. (2009). Breaking new ground in food regime theory: Corporate environmentalism, ecological feedbacks and the 'food from somewhere' regime? *Agriculture and Human Values, 26*(4), 309–319. doi:10.100710460-009-9215-8

Carayannis, E. G., & Campbell, D. F. (2009). Mode 3 and Quadruple Helix: Toward a 21st Century Fractal Innovation Ecosystem. *International Journal of Technology Management, 46*(3), 201–234. doi:10.1504/IJTM.2009.023374

Carayannis, E. G., & Campbell, D. F. (2010). Triple Helix, Quadruple Helix, and Quintuple Helix and How Do Knowledge, Innovation, and the Environment Relate To Each Other? A Proposed Framework for a Trans-disciplinary Analysis of Sustainable Development and Social Ecology. *International Journal of Social Ecology and Sustainable Development, 1*(1), 41–69. doi:10.4018/jsesd.2010010105

Carayannis, E. G., & Campbell, D. F. J. (2011). Open Innovation Diplomacy and a 21st Century Fractal Research, Education, and Innovation (FREIE) Ecosystem: Building on the Quadruple and Quintuple Helix Innovation Concepts and the "Mode 3" Knowledge Production System. *Journal of the Knowledge Economy, 2*(3), 327–372. doi:10.100713132-011-0058-3

Carayannis, E. G., & Campbell, D. F. J. (2012). *Mode 3 Knowledge Production in Quadruple Helix Innovation Systems*. Springer New York., doi:10.1007/978-1-4614-2062-0

Carney, J. A., & Voeks, R. A. (2003). Landscape legacies of the African diaspora in Brazil Prog. *Progress in Human Geography, 27*(2), 139–152. doi:10.1191/0309132503ph418oa

Coenen, L., Asheim, B., Bugge, M. M., & Herstad, S. J. (2017). Advancing regional innovation systems: What does evolutionary economic geography bring to the policy table? *Environment and Planning C. Politics and Space*, *35*(4), 600–620.

Cooke, P. (2005). Regionally asymmetric knowledge capabilities and open innovation: Exploring 'Globalisation 2'—A new model of industrial organization. *Research Policy*, *34*(8), 1128–1149. doi:10.1016/j.respol.2004.12.005

Corley, R. H. V., & Tinker, P. B. H. (2003). *The Oil Palm*. Wiley-Blackwell. doi:10.1016/j.respol.2004.12.005

Dale, V. H., Brown, S., Hauer, R. A., Hobbs, N. T., Huntly, N., Naima, R. J., Ribosome, W. E., Turner, M. G., & Valene, T. J. (2000). Ecological Principles and Guidelines for Managing the Use of Land. *Ecological Applications*, *10*(3), 639–670. doi:10.2307/2641032

Dennis, M., Armitage, R. P., & James, P. (2016). Social-ecological innovation: Adaptive responses to urban environmental conditions. *Urban Ecosystems*, *19*(3), 1063–1082. doi:10.100711252-016-0551-3

Etzkowitz, H., & Leydesdorff, L. (1995). The Triple Helix — University-Industry-Government Relations: A Laboratory for Knowledge Based Economic Development. *EASST Review, 14*(1), 14-19. https://ssrn.com/abstract=2480085

Etzkowitz, H., & Leydesdorff, L. (2000). The Dynamics of Innovation: From National Systems and "Mode 2" to a Triple Helix of University–Industry–Government Relations. *Research Policy*, *29*(2), 109–123. doi:10.1016/S0048-7333(99)00055-4

European Commission. (2012). *Guide to Research and Innovation Strategies for Smart Specialisations (RIS 3)*. Publications Office of the European Union.

Fischer-Kowalski, M., & Rotmans, J. (2009). Conceptualizing, observing, and influencing social-ecological transitions. *Ecology and Society*, *14*(2), 3. doi:10.5751/ES-02857-140203

Flanagan, K., & Uyarra, E. (2016). Four dangers in innovation policy studies – and how to avoid them. *Industry and Innovation*, *23*(2), 177–188. doi:10.1080/13662716.2016.1146126

Franz, Y. (2014). Chances and Challenges for Social Urban Living Labs in urban research. *ENoLLOpenLivingLab Days. Conference Proceedings,* 105-114.

Geels, F. W. (2004). From sectoral systems of innovation to socio-technical systems: Insights about dynamics and change from sociology and institutional theory. *Research Policy*, *33*(6-7), 897–920. doi:10.1016/j.respol.2004.01.015

Geels, F. W., & Schot, J. (2007). Typology of sociotechnical transition pathways. *Research Policy*, *36*(3), 399–417. doi:10.1016/j.respol.2007.01.003

Georgieva, K. (2023). *Policy Priorities for the G20: One Earth, One Family, One Future*. IMF Blog. https://www.imf.org/en/Blogs/Articles/2023/02/22/policy-priorities-for-the-g20-one-earth-one-family-one-future

Gliessman, S. R. (2007). *Agroecology: The ecology of sustainable food systems*. CRC Press.

Goodman, D., Sorj, B., & Wilkinson, J. (1987). *From farming to biotechnology*. Basil Blackwell.

Gotham, K. F., Blum, M., & Campanella, R. (2014). Toward a new normal: Trauma, diversity, and the New Orleans Urban Long-Term Research Area Exploratory (ULTRA-Ex) Project. *Cities and the Environment*, *7*(4), 31–43.

Gouverneur, J., & Netzer, N. (2014). Take the Wheel and Steer! Trade Unions and the Just Transition. In *State of the World 2014*. Island Press. doi:10.5822/978-1-61091-542-7_21

Grabenwarter, U., & Liechtenstein, H., (2012). *In search of gamma: an unconventional perspective on impact investing,* IESE Business School, University of Navarra, and Family Office Circle Foundation.

Guthman, J. (2004). The trouble with 'organic lite' in California: A rejoinder to the 'conventionalisation' debate. *Sociologia Ruralis*, *44*(3), 301–316. doi:10.1111/j.1467-9523.2004.00277.x

Harvey, D. (1996). Justice, Nature, and the Geography of Difference. Blackwell.

Helbing, D. (2013). Globally networked risks and how to respond. *Nature*, *497*(7447), 51–59. doi:10.1038/nature12047 PMID:23636396

Hjortsø, C. N., Stræde, S., & Helles, F. (2006). Applying multi-criteria decision-making to protected areas and buffer zone management: A case study in the Royal Chitwan National Park, Nepal. *Journal of Forest Economics*, *12*(2), 91–108. doi:10.1016/j.jfe.2006.03.001

Holling, C. S. (1973). Resilience and Stability of Ecological Systems. *Annual Review of Ecology and Systematics*, *4*(1), 1–23. doi:10.1146/annurev.es.04.110173.000245

Homer-Dixon, T., Walker, B., Biggs, R., Crépin, A.-S., Folke, C., Lambin, E., Peterson, G., Rockström, J., Scheffer, M., Steffen, W., & Troell, M. (2015). Synchronous failure: The emerging causal architecture of global crisis. *Ecology and Society*, *2015*(3), 20. doi:10.5751/ES-07681-200306

Intergovernmental Panel on Climate Change (IPCC). (2012). *Managing the Risks of Extreme Events and Disasters to Advance Climate Change Adaptation: Special Report of the Intergovernmental Panel on Climate Change*. IPCC/Cambridge University Press.

Intergovernmental Panel on Climate Change (IPCC). (2014). Summary for policymakers. In *Climate change 2014: impacts, adaptation, and vulnerability. part A: global and sectoral aspects*. Contribution of working group II to the fifth assessment report of the intergovernmental panel on climate change. Cambridge University Press ILO. https://www.ilo.org/global/topics/green-jobs/areas-of-work/WCMS_461943/lang--en/index.htm

Islam, A. M., Ali, M. M., & Medhekar, A. (2017). Exploratory results of green production, sale, willing to pay and financing: Case of Bangladesh. *Environment and Ecology*, *8*(3), 8–17. doi:10.21511/ee.08(3).2017.01

Jackson, T., & Victor, P. (2011). Productivity and Work in the 'Green Economy'. Some Theoretical Reflections and Empirical Tests. *Environmental Innovation and Societal Transitions*, *1*(1), 101–108. doi:10.1016/j.eist.2011.04.005

Kallis, G. (2011). In defense of degrowth. *Ecological Economics*, *70*(5), 873–880. doi:10.1016/j.ecolecon.2010.12.007

Klein, N. (2015). *This Changes Everything: Capitalism vs. The Climate. Simon*. Schuster.

Kline, D., Leahy, J. E., Littell, J. S., Millington, J. D. A., Nielsen-Pincus, M., & Olsen, C. S., Paveglio, T. B., Roos, C. I., Steen-Adams, M. M., Stevens, F. R., Vukomanovic, J., White, E. M., & Bowman, D. M. J. S. (2016). Wildfire risk as a socioecological pathology. *Frontiers in Ecology and the Environment*, *4*, 276–284.

Laszlo, A., Blachfellner, S., Bosch, O., Nguyen, N., Bulc, V., Edson, M., Wilby, J., & Pór, G. (2012). *Proceedings of the International Federation for Systems Research Conversations*. https://hdl.handle.net/2440/77156

Leal Filho, W., Azul, A. M., Brandli, L., Özuyar, P.G., & Wall, T. (Eds.). (2022). Responsible Consumption and Production. Encyclopedia of the UN Sustainable Development Goals. In Socio-ecological balance. Springer. doi:10.1007/978-3-319-95726-5_300136

Leaning, J., & Guha-Sapir, D. (2013). Natural Disasters, Armed Conflict, and Public Health. *The New England Journal of Medicine*, *369*(19), 1836–1842. doi:10.1056/NEJMra1109877 PMID:24195550

Luz, A., & Pires, I. (2014). Regularização das Hortas Urbanasna Cidade de Lisboa - as Hortas Sociais do Vale de Chelas. Livro de Atas do 1° Congresso da AssociaçãoInternacional de CiênciasSociais e Humanas me Língua Portuguesa, 6935–6952.

Machlis, G., Force, J., & Burch, W. J. Jr. (1997). The Human Ecosystem Part I: The Human Ecosystem as an Organizing Concept in Ecosystem Management. *Society & Natural Resources*, *10*(4), 347–367. doi:10.1080/08941929709381034

Manson, S. M. (2001). Simplifying complexity: A review of complexity theory. *Geoforum*, *32*(3), 405–414. doi:10.1016/S0016-7185(00)00035-X

Markard, J., Raven, B., & Truffer, B. (2012). Sustainability transitions: An emerging field of research and its prospects. *Research Policy*, *41*(6), 955–967. doi:10.1016/j.respol.2012.02.013

Martin, R., & Moodysson, J. (2013). Comparing knowledge bases: On the geography and organization of knowledge sourcing in the regional innovation system of Scania, Sweden. *European Urban and Regional Studies*, *20*(2), 170–187. doi:10.1177/0969776411427326

McAllister, J. W., & Kornet, D. J. (2002). Historical and Structural Approaches in the Natural and Human Sciences In *Four Analytical Essays and a Critical Debate on the Future of Scholastic Endeavour.* Amsterdam University Press. https://www.jstor.org/stable/j.ctt46mzw4.5

McMichael, P. (2009). A food regime genealogy. *The Journal of Peasant Studies*, *36*(1), 139–169. doi:10.1080/03066150902820354

Moodysson, J., Coenen, L., & Asheim, B. (2008). Explaining spatial patterns of innovation: Analytical and synthetic modes of knowledge creation in the Medicon Valley life-science cluster. *Environment and Planning A. Environment & Planning A*, *40*(5), 1040–1056. doi:10.1068/a39110

Moore, J. W. (2015). *Capitalism in the Web of Life: Ecology and the Accumulation of Capital*. Verso.

Moore, M., Tjornbo, O., Enfors, E., Knapp, C., Hodbod, J., Baggio, J., Norström, A., Olsson, P., & Biggs, D. (2014). Studying the Complexity of Change: Toward an Analytical Framework for Understanding Deliberate Social-Ecological Transformations. *Ecology and Society*, *19*(4), 54. doi:10.5751/ES-06966-190454

Morgan, K. (2017). Nurturing novelty: Regional innovation policy in the age of smart specialisation. *Environment and Planning C. Politics and Space*, *35*(4), 569–583.

Myers, S., & Frumkin, H. (2020). *Planetary Health: Protecting Nature to Protect Ourselves*. Island Press. doi:10.5822/978-1-61091-966-1

Nautiyal, S. (2011). Can conservation and development interventions in the Indian Central Himalaya ensure environmental sustainability? A socioecological evaluation. *Sustainability Science*, *6*(2), 151–167. doi:10.100711625-011-0126-4

Nordhaus, T., & Shellenberger, M. (2007). *Break Through: From the Death of Environmentalism to the Politics of Possibility*. Houghton Mifflin Company.

Perfecto, I., Vandermeer, J., & Wright, A. (2009). *Nature's matrix: Linking agriculture, conservation, and food sovereignty*. Earthscan. doi:10.4324/9781849770132

Porter, M. (1998, November–December). Clusters and the new economics of competition. *Harvard Business Review*, *76*(6), 77–90. PMID:10187248

Porter, M. (2001). *Clusters of Innovation: regional foundations of U. S. competitiveness*. Council on Competitiveness. Monitor Group.

Pratt, J. (2009). Incorporation and resistance: Analytical issues in the conventionalization debate and alternative food chains. *Journal of Agrarian Change*, *9*, 155–174.

Pretty, J. (1995). Participatory Learning for Sustainable Agriculture. *World Development*, *23*(8), 1247–1263. doi:10.1016/0305-750X(95)00046-F

Quilley, S. (2020). Can progressives' shimmy? *Institute for Policy Public Research Progressive Review.*, *27*, 179–185.

Ramakrishnan, P. S. (2003). Conserving the sacred: the protective impulse and the origins of modern protected areas. In D. Harmon & A. D. Putney (Eds.), *The full value of parks: from economics to the intangible* (pp. 26–41). Rowman & Littlefield.

Ramakrishnan, P. S. (2008). *The cultural cradle of biodiversity*. National Book Trust.

Ramazanov, S. K., Nadyon, G. A., Krishtal, N. I., Stepanenko, O. P., & Timashova, L. A. (2009). Innovative technologies of crisis management of economic systems, Monograph. SNU named V. Dalya.

Rangan, H., & Kull, C. A. (2009). What makes ecology 'political'? Rethinking 'scale' in political ecology. *Progress in Human Geography*, *33*(1), 28–45. doi:10.1177/0309132508090215

Reis, J. J., & Azevedo, E. (Eds.). (2012). *Escravidão e suas sombras*. EDUFBA. doi:10.7476/9788523211882

Rocheleau, D. E. (2011). Rooted networks, webs of relation, and the power of situated science: Bringing the models back down to Earth. In Knowing Nature: Conversations at the Intersection of Political Ecology and Science Studies. University of Chicago Press.

Rogers, E. M. (2003). *Diffusion of innovations*. Free Press.

Rosmann, R. L. (1994). Farmer initiated on-farm research. *American Journal of Alternative Agriculture*, *9*(1-2), 34–37. doi:10.1017/S0889189300005531

Russ, M. (2021). Knowledge management for sustainable development in the era of continuously accelerating technological revolutions: A framework and models. *Sustainability (Basel)*, *13*(6), 3353. doi:10.3390u13063353

Schwartz, S. B. (1992). *Slaves, Peasants, and Rebels: Reconsidering Brazilian Slavery*. University of Illinois Press.

Seta, K. C., & … . (2011). A Meta-Analysis of Global Urban Land Expansion. *PLoS One*, *6*(8), e23777. doi:10.1371/journal.pone.0023777 PMID:21876770

Smith, N. (1984). *Uneven development: Nature, capital, and the Production of Space*. Blackwell.

Tödtling, F., & Trippl, M. (2005). One size fit all. Towards a differentiated regional innovation policy approach. *Research Policy*, *34*(8), 1203–1219. doi:10.1016/j.respol.2005.01.018

Törnberg, A. (2018). Combining transition studies and social movement theory: Towards a new research agenda. *Theory and Society*, *47*(3), 381–408. doi:10.100711186-018-9318-6

Uyarra, E., Flanagan, K., Magro, E., Wilson, J. R., & Sotarauta, M. (2017). Understanding regional innovation policy dynamics: Actors, agency, and learning. *Environment and Planning C. Politics and Space*, *35*(4), 559–568.

Van Norman, W. C. (2013). *Shade Grown Slavery: The Lives of Slaves on Coffee Plantations in Cuba*. Vanderbilt University Press. doi:10.2307/j.ctv167554g

Vercoe, R. A., Welch-Devine, M., Hardy, D., Demoss, J. A., Bonney, S. N., Allen, K., Brosius, P., Charles, D., Crawford, B., Heisel, S., Heynen, N., de Jesús-Crespo, R. G., Nibbelink, N., Parker, L., Pringle, C., Shaw, A., & Van Sant, L. (2014). Acknowledging trade-offs and understanding complexity: Exurbanization issues in Macon County, North Carolina. *Ecology and Society*, *19*(1), 23–32. doi:10.5751/ES-05970-190123

Wagner, M. M., & Gobster, P. H. (2007). Interpreting landscape change: Measured biophysical change and surrounding social context. *Landscape and Urban Planning*, *81*(1-2), 67–80. doi:10.1016/j.landurbplan.2006.10.019

Watkins, C. (2018). Landscapes and resistance in the African diaspora: Five centuries of palm oil on Bahia's Dendê Coast. *Journal of Rural Studies*, *61*, 137–154. doi:10.1016/j.jrurstud.2018.04.009

Whitmee, S., Haines, A., Beyrer, C., Boltz, F., Capon, A. G., Dias, B. F. S., Ezeh, A., Frumkin, H., Gong, P., Head, P., & ... . (2015). Safeguarding human health in the Anthropocene epoch: Report of The Rockefeller Foundation–Lancet Commission on planetary health. *Lancet, 386*(10007), 1973–2028. doi:10.1016/S0140-6736(15)60901-1 PMID:26188744

Wolf, E. (1982). *Europe and the People without History*. University of California Press.

Wolf, S., & Buttel, F. (1996). The political economy of precision farming. *American Journal of Agricultural Economics, 78*(5), 1269–1274. doi:10.2307/1243505

Wright, E. O. (2010). *Envisioning real utopias*. Verso.

Yin, R. (1984). *Case Study Research*. Sage Publications.

Young, O. R., Berkhout, F., Gallopin, G. C., Janssen, M. A., Ostrom, E., & van der Leeuw, S. (2006). The Globalization of Socio-Ecological Systems: An Agenda for Scientific Research. *Global Environmental Change, 16*(3), 304–316. doi:10.1016/j.gloenvcha.2006.03.004

Zhang, W., Xu, F., & Wang, X. (2020). How Green Transformational Leadership Affects Green Creativity: Creative Process Engagement as Intermediary Bond and Green Innovation Strategy as Boundary Spanner. *Sustainability, 12*(9), 3841. doi:10.3390/su12093841

KEY TERMS AND DEFINITIONS

Allocative Efficiency: Allocative efficiency refers to a situation where a good or service falls at the price and quantity through the intersection of the supply and demand curves.

Economic Benefit: An economic benefit arises through investment or doing business when the real rate of return can be positive.

Employment Opportunities: When recruitment occurs and those who intend to do a job can get an opportunity to join in the job of an organization or a company.

Government Policy: Refers to decisions, schemes, projects, or programs initiated by the government sector.

Green Industrial Revolution: Green industrial revolution refers to a situation that challenges reconciling economic and environmental hazards including the growth of low-carbon hydrogen, zero-emission vehicles, green public transport such as rickshaw vans used in Bangladesh, bicycles, green buildings, green innovation and green finance, green marketing, etc.

Industry 5.0: Refers to the industrial advancement for the betterment of the laborers at the focus of the manufacturing procedures and usages of innovative skills to deliver successes including their professional advancement through the manufacturing restrictions or limitations on the earth has been happening.

Knowledge: To get ideas and or learn from formal or informal experiences with enthusiasm.

Performance Management: Refers to generating an atmosphere wherever individuals can accomplish the finest of their capacities and can function at the best worth of their job utmost competently and successfully.

Skill: Skill is the ability to do capably methodological acquaintance efficiently and effectively.

Compilation of References

Abbas, A. A., Badawi, S., & Almahdi, M. H. (2021). Toward Successful Social Media Viral Marketing: A Knowledge Management Approach. In *International Conference on Business and Technology* (pp. 377-389). Springer. 10.1007/978-3-030-69221-6_28

Abbas, J., Hussain, I., Hussain, S., Akram, S., Shaheen, I., & Niu, B. (2019). The Impact of Knowledge Sharing and Innovation on Sustainable Performance in Islamic Banks: A Mediation Analysis through an SEM Approach. *Sustainability (Basel)*, *11*(4049), 4049. Advance online publication. doi:10.3390u11154049

Abdul-Jalal, H., Toulson, P., & Tweed, D. (2013). Knowledge sharing success for sustaining organizational competitive advantage. *Procedia Economics and Finance*, *7*, 150–157. doi:10.1016/S2212-5671(13)00229-3

Abley, B. (2014a). *Advocate Technical Services Televate Proposal for Ohio SLIGP.* Academic Press.

Abley, B. (2014b). *OH Project Plan.* Academic Press.

Abley, B. (2016). *What is FirstNet?* YouTube. https://www.youtube.com/watch?v=w94UCxI-QuE

Abley, B. (2017). *OhioFirst.Net Next Generation FireFighter Demo.* YouTube. https://www.youtube.com/watch?v=4xmBUVoCKS8

Abubakar, A. M., Behravesh, E., Rezapouraghdam, H., & Yildiz, S. B. (2019). Applying artificial intelligence techniques to predict knowledge-hiding behavior. *International Journal of Information Management*, *49*, 45–57. doi:10.1016/j.ijinfomgt.2019.02.006

Accenture. (2015, March 25). *U.S. retailers struggling to meet consumer expectations around mobile and in-store experience, Accenture study finds* [Press Release]. https://newsroom.accenture.com/news/us-retailers-struggling-to-meet-consumer-expectations-around-mobile-and-in-store-experience-accenture-study-finds.htm

Acquaye, A., Ibn-Mohammed, T., Genovese, A., Afrifa, G. A., Yamoah, F. A., & Oppon, E. (2018). A quantitative model for environmentally sustainable supply chain performance measurement. *European Journal of Operational Research*, *269*(1), 188–205. doi:10.1016/j.ejor.2017.10.057

Adaloudis, M., & Roca, J. B. (2021). Sustainability tradeoffs in the adoption of 3D Concrete Printing in the construction industry. *Journal of Cleaner Production*, *307*, 1–10. doi:10.1016/j.jclepro.2021.127201

Adamik, A., & Nowicki, M. (2018, May). Preparedness of companies for digital transformation and creating a competitive advantage in the age of Industry 4.0. In *Proceedings of the International Conference on Business Excellence* (Vol. 12, No. 1, pp. 10-24). 10.2478/picbe-2018-0003

Adams, R., Bessant, J., & Phelps, R. (2006). Innovation management measurement: A review. *International Journal of Management Reviews*, *8*(1), 21–47. doi:10.1111/j.1468-2370.2006.00119.x

Adeyemi, I. O., Uzamot, W. O., & Temim, F. M. (2022). Knowledge Transfer and Use as Predictors of Law Firm Performance: Nigerian Lawyer's Perspectives. *International Journal of Knowledge Management*, *18*(1), 1–17. doi:10.4018/IJKM.291097

Afolalu, S. A., Ikumapayi, O. M., Abdulkareem, A., Soetan, S. B., Emetere, M. E., & Ongbali, S. O. (2021). Enviable roles of manufacturing processes in sustainable fourth industrial revolution: A case study of mechatronics. *Materials Today: Proceedings*, *44*, 2895–2901. doi:10.1016/j.matpr.2021.01.099

Agiwal, M., Saxena, N., & Roy, A. (2019). Towards connected living: 5G enabled Internet of Things (IoT). *IETE Technical Review*, *3*(2), 1–13. doi:10.1080/02564602.2018.1444516

Agrawal, A., & Gibson, A. (1999). Enchantment and Disenchantment: The Role of Community in Natural Resource Conservation. *World Development*, *27*(4), 629–649. doi:10.1016/S0305-750X(98)00161-2

Agrawal, P., & Rawat, N. (2019, September). DevOps, a new approach to cloud development & testing. In *2019 International Conference on Issues and Challenges in Intelligent Computing Techniques (ICICT)* (Vol. 1, pp. 1-4). IEEE. 10.1109/ICICT46931.2019.8977662

Aguilera, R. V., Rupp, D. E., Williams, C. A., & Ganapathi, J. (2007). Putting the S back in corporate social responsibility: A multilevel theory of social change in organizations. *Academy of Management Review*, *32*(3), 836–863. doi:10.5465/amr.2007.25275678

Ahearn, M. C., Armbruster, W., & Young, R. (2016). Big data's potential to improve food supply chain environmental sustainability and food safety. *The International Food and Agribusiness Management Review*, *19*, 155–171. doi:10.22004/ag.econ.240704

Ahmad, N., Lodhi, M. S., Zaman, K., & Naseem, I. (2017). Knowledge management: A gateway for organizational performance. *Journal of the Knowledge Economy*, *8*(3), 859–876. doi:10.100713132-015-0282-3

Ahn, S., Kim, J., & Kim, J. (2022). The Bifold Triadic Relationships Framework: A Theoretical Primer for Advertising Research in the Metaverse. *Journal of Advertising*, *51*(5), 592–607. doi:10.1080/00913367.2022.2111729

Ajmal, M. M., Helo, P., & Kekale, T. (2010). Critical factors for knowledge management in project business. *Journal of Knowledge Management*, *14*(1), 156–168. doi:10.1108/13673271011015633

Akbar, M. A., Mahmood, S., & Siemon, D. (2022, June). Toward effective and efficient DevOps using blockchain. In *Proceedings of the International Conference on Evaluation and Assessment in Software Engineering 2022* (pp. 421-427). 10.1145/3530019.3531344

Akhavan, P., & Mahdi Hosseini, S. (2016). Social capital, knowledge sharing, and innovation capability, an empirical study of R&D teams in Iran. *Technology Analysis and Strategic Management*, *28*(1), 96–113. doi:10.1080/09537325.2015.1072622

Al Ahbabi, S. A., Singh, S. K., Balasubramanian, S., & Gaur, S. S. (2019). Employee perception of the impact of knowledge management processes on public sector performance. *Journal of Knowledge Management*, *23*(2), 351–373. doi:10.1108/JKM-08-2017-0348

Alavi, M., & Denford, J. S. (2011). Knowledge Management: Process, Practice and Web 2.0. In M. Easterby-Smith & M. A. Lyles (Eds.), Handbook of Organizational Learning & Knowledge Management (2nd ed., pp. 105–124). Academic Press.

Alavi, M., & Leidner, D. E. (2001). Knowledge management and knowledge management systems: Conceptual foundations and research issues. *Management Information Systems Quarterly*, *25*(1), 107–136. doi:10.2307/3250961

Alcácer, V., Rodrigues, C., Carvalho, H., & Cruz-Machado, V. (2021). Tracking the maturity of Industry 4.0: The perspective of a real scenario. *International Journal of Advanced Manufacturing Technology*, *116*(7), 2161–2181. doi:10.100700170-021-07550-0 PMID:34248244

Alghadeir, A., & Sakran, H. A. (2016). Smart airport architecture using the Internet of Things. *International Journal of Innovative Research in Computer Science & Technology.*

Ali, A. A., Paris, L., & Gunasekaran, A. (2019). Key factors influencing knowledge-sharing practices and its relationship with organizational performance within the oil and gas industry. *Journal of Knowledge Management*, *23*(9), 1806–1837. doi:10.1108/JKM-06-2018-0394

Ali, M. M. (2018). Existing situation and prospects of the green economy: Evidence from Bangladesh. *Environment and Ecology*, *9*(2), 7–21. doi:10.21511/ee.09(2).2018.01

Ali, S., Riasat, H., Zubair, S., & Arif, S. (2022). DevOps in Practice a Systematic Literature Review. *Journal of Information & Communication Technology*, *16*(1).

Alizadehsalehi, S., & Yitmen, I. (2023). Digital twin-based progress monitoring management model through reality capture to extended reality technologies (DRX). *Smart and Sustainable Built Environment*, *12*(1), 200–236. doi:10.1108/SASBE-01-2021-0016

Allen, P. (2004). *Together at the table: Sustainability and sustenance in the American agrifood system.* The Pennsylvania State University Press.

Almeida, F., Simões, J., & Lopes, S. (2022). Exploring the benefits of combining DevOps and agile. *Future Internet*, *14*(2), 63. doi:10.3390/fi14020063

Alpala, L., Quiroga-Parra, D., Torres, J., & Peluffo-Ordóñez, D. (2022). Smart Factory Using Virtual Reality and Online Multi-User: Towards a Metaverse for Experimental Frameworks. *Applied Sciences (Basel, Switzerland)*, *12*(12), 6258. doi:10.3390/app12126258

Al-Sammarraie, M. A. J., Ali, A. A., & Hussein, N. M. (2021). New irrigation techniques for precision agriculture: A review. *Plant Archives*, *21*(1), 1734–1740. doi:10.51470/PLANTARCHIVES.2021.v21.S1.275

Alshehhi, A., Nobanee, H., & Khare, N. (2018). The impact of sustainability practices on corporate financial performance: Literature trends and future research potential. *Sustainability (Basel)*, *10*(2), 494. doi:10.3390u10020494

Altieri, M., & Nicholls, C. (2008). Scaling up agroecological approaches for food sovereignty in Latin America. *Development*, *51*(4), 472–480. doi:10.1057/dev.2008.68

Alves, H., Fernandes, C., & Raposo, M. (2016). Social media marketing: A literature review and implications. *Psychology and Marketing*, *33*(12), 1029–1038. doi:10.1002/mar.20936

Amabile, T. M. (1998). How to kill creativity. *Harvard Business Review on Breakthrough Thinking*, *76*(5), 76–87. PMID:10185433

Amazon. (2021). *Delivering progress every day: Amazon's 2021 sustainability report.* Retrieved March 14, 2023, from https://sustainability.aboutamazon.com/2021-sustainability-report.pdf

Anatan, L. (2021). Interorganizational Knowledge Transfer Practices Toward MSMEs 4.0: A Proposed Conceptual Framework. *Review of Integrative Business and Economics Research, 10*, 409–418. https://search.proquest.com/openview/2051203ec44ceeaedc2ebd8f7b81325a/1?pq-origsite=gscholar&cbl=2032316

Anderson, D. (2014). *OhioFirst.Net State and Local Implementation Grant Program Support Request for Quotation # OITRFQ093.* State of Ohio Procurement Services. https://procure.ohio.gov/bidders-and-suppliers/resources/03_OB_Solicitations_Contracts

Andreeva, T., & Kianto, A. (2011). Knowledge processes, knowledge-intensity, and innovation: A moderated mediation analysis. *Journal of Knowledge Management, 15*(6), 1016–1034. doi:10.1108/13673271111179343

Ansari, J. A. N., & Khan, N. A. (2020). Exploring the role of social media in collaborative learning the new domain of learning. *Smart Learning Environments, 7*(1), 1-16. https://slejournal.springeropen.com/articles/10.1186/s40561-020-00118-7

Antunes, H. D. J. G., & Pinheiro, P. G. (2020). Linking knowledge management, organizational learning and memory. *Journal of Innovation & Knowledge, 5*(2), 140–149. doi:10.1016/j.jik.2019.04.002

Aramyan, L. H., Oude Lansink, A. G. J. M., van der Vorst, J. G. A. J., & van Kooten, O. (2007). Performance measurement in agri-food supply chains: A case study. *Supply Chain Management, 12*(4), 304–315. doi:10.1108/13598540710759826

Araujo, A. L. (2013). Introduction to Atlantic approaches to resistance against slavery in the Americas. *Journal of African Diaspora Archaeological Heritage, 2*(1), 1–5. doi:10.1179/2161944113Z.0000000001

Arçelik. (2021). *Lead the change: Sustainability report 2021.* Retrieved March 16, 2023, from https://www.arcelikglobal.com/media/6938/arcelik21_sustainability_report.pdf

Archambault, L., Wetzel, K., Foulger, T. S., & Kim Williams, M. (2010). Professional development 2.0: Transforming teacher education pedagogy with 21st-century tools. *J. Digital Learn. Teach. Educ., 27*(1), 4–11. doi:10.1080/21532974.2010.10784651

Arundel, A., Kanerva, M., & Kemp, R. (2011). *Integrated innovation policy for an integrated problem: Addressing climate change, resource scarcity and demographic change to 2030.* European Commission.

Arvanitou, E. M., Ampatzoglou, A., Bibi, S., Chatzigeorgiou, A., & Deligiannis, I. (2022). Applying and Researching DevOps: A Tertiary Study. *IEEE Access : Practical Innovations, Open Solutions, 10*, 61585–61600. doi:10.1109/ACCESS.2022.3171803

Asheim, B. T., Coenen, L., & Moodysson, J. (2015). Methods and applications of regional innovation systems analysis. In Handbook of Research Methods and Applications in Economic Geography (pp. 272–290). Edward Elgar. doi:10.4337/9780857932679.00020

Asibong, U., Okafor, C. J., Asibong, I., Ayi, E., Omoronyia, O., & Owoidoho, U. (2020). Psychological distress and social media usage: A survey among undergraduates of a university in Calabar, Nigeria. *The Nigerian Postgraduate Medical Journal, 27*(2), 115–126. doi:10.4103/npmj.npmj_169_19 PMID:32295942

Association for Supply Chain Management. (2022). *Introduction to processes.* Retrieved April 14, 2022, from https://scor.ascm.org/performance/introduction

Atchison, E. (2023). *What's a Helpdesk Ticket? The Complete Guide.* Capacity. https://capacity.com/learn/helpdesk/helpdesk-ticket/#:~:text=A%20helpdesk%20ticket%20is%20an%20automated%20request%20for%20tracking%20and,to%20their%20product%20or%20service

Aung, M. M., & Chang, Y. S. (2014). Traceability in a food supply chain: Safety and quality perspectives. *Food Control, 39*, 172–184. doi:10.1016/j.foodcont.2013.11.007

Awasthi, S., Ahuja, R., & Sharma, S. (2022). Leadership and Emotional Intelligence: A Comparative Study. In D. Bathla & A. Singh (Eds.), *Applying Metalytics to Measure Customer Experience in the Metaverse* (pp. 99–110). IGI Global. doi:10.4018/978-1-6684-6133-4.ch009

Aylak, B., Oral, O., & Yazıcı, K. (2021). Using artificial intelligence and machine learning applications in logistics [Yapay zeka ve makine öğrenmesi tekniklerinin lojistik sektöründe kullanımı]. *El-Cezeri Journal of Science and Engineering, 8*(1), 79–88. doi:10.31202/ecjse.776314

Ayuso, S., Rodríguez, M. Á., García-Castro, R., & Ariño, M. Á. (2011). Does stakeholder engagement promote sustainable innovation orientation? *Industrial Management & Data Systems, 111*(9), 1399–1417. doi:10.1108/02635571111182764

Azadeh, A., & Zarrin, M. (2016). An intelligent framework for productivity assessment and analysis of human resource from resilience engineering, motivational factors, HSE, and ergonomics perspectives. *Safety Science, 89*, 55–71. doi:10.1016/j.ssci.2016.06.001

Baah, C., Agyabeng-Mensah, Y., Afum, E., & Lascano Armas, J. A. (2023). Exploring corporate environmental ethics and green creativity as antecedents of green competitive advantage, sustainable production, and financial performance: empirical evidence from manufacturing firms. Benchmarking: An International Journal. doi:10.1108/BIJ-06-2022-0352

Babiceanu, R. F., & Seker, R. (2016). Big data and virtualization for manufacturing cyber-physical systems: A survey of the current status and future outlook. *Computers in Industry, 81*(128), 128–137. doi:10.1016/j.compind.2016.02.004

Baghalzadeh Shishehgarkhaneh, M., Keivani, A., Moehler, R., Jelodari, N., & Roshdi Laleh, S. (2022). Internet of Things (IoT), Building Information Modeling (BIM), and Digital Twin (DT) in Construction Industry: A Review, Bibliometric, and Network Analysis. *Buildings, 12*(10), 1503. doi:10.3390/buildings12101503

Bagloee, S. A., Tavana, M., Asadi, M., & Oliver, T. (2016). Autonomous vehicles: Challenges, opportunities, and future implications for transportation policies. *Journal of Modern Transportation, 24*(4), 284–303. doi:10.100740534-016-0117-3

Bag, S., Wood, L. C., Xu, L., Dhamija, P., & Kayikci, Y. (2020). Big data analytics as an operational excellence approach to enhance sustainable supply chain performance. *Resources, Conservation and Recycling, 153*(February), 1–10. doi:10.1016/j.resconrec.2019.104559

Bai, C., Dallasega, P., Orzes, G., & Sarkis, J. (2020). Industry 4.0 technologies assessment: A sustainability perspective. *International Journal of Production Economics, 229*, 107776. doi:10.1016/j.ijpe.2020.107776

Bai, H., & Lehman, J. (2003). *Impact of a professional development project on university faculty members' perceptions and use of technology.* In D. Lassner & C. McNaught (Eds.), *Proceedings of ED-MEDIA–World Conference on Educational Multimedia, Hypermedia & Telecommunications, 2003* (pp. 1927–1934). Association for the Advancement of Computing in Education. Available online at https://www.learntechlib.org/p/14126/

Baiyere, A., Salmela, H., & Tapanainen, T. (2020). Digital transformation and the new logic of business process management. *European Journal of Information Systems, 29*(3), 238–259. doi:10.1080/0960085X.2020.1718007

Bankar, S., & Shah, D. (2023). Decentralized Framework to Strengthen DevOps Using Blockchain. In *Computational Intelligence: Select Proceedings of InCITe 2022* (pp. 517–525). Springer Nature Singapore. doi:10.1007/978-981-19-7346-8_44

Bansal, P., & DesJardine, M. R. (2014). Business sustainability: It is about time. *Strategic Organization*, *12*(1), 70–78. doi:10.1177/1476127013520265

Barca, F. (2009). *Agenda for a Reformed Cohesion Policy: A Place-based Approach to Meeting European Union Challenges and Expectations.* https://www.europarl.europa.eu/meetdocs/2009_2014/documents/regi/dv/barca_report_/barca_report_en.pdf

Barca, F., McCann, P., & Rodríguez-Pose, A. (2012). The case for regional development intervention: Place-based versus place-neutral approaches. *Journal of Regional Science*, *52*(1), 134–152. doi:10.1111/j.1467-9787.2011.00756.x

Barth, T. D. (2011). The idea of a green new deal in a Quintuple Helix Model of knowledge, expertise, and innovation. *International Journal of Social Ecology and Sustainable Development*, *1*(2), 1–14. doi:10.4018/jsesd.2011010101

Bartie, N. J., Cobos-Becerra, Y. L., Fröhling, M., Schlatmann, R., & Reuter, M. A. (2021). The resources, exergetic and environmental footprint of the silicon photovoltaic circular economy: Assessment and opportunities. *Resources, Conservation and Recycling*, *169*, 1–24. doi:10.1016/j.resconrec.2021.105516

Bartley, D. (2022). *World Aquaculture 2020–A brief overview*. FAO.

Barton, J. R., Baeza-González, S., Hopp, J. Z., & Román, Á. (2023). Neostructural innovation and directionality in Chilean salmon aquaculture. *Marine Policy*, *150*, 105518. doi:10.1016/j.marpol.2023.105518

Baskerville, R., & Dulipovici, A. (2006). The theoretical foundations of knowledge management. *Knowledge Management Research and Practice*, *4*(2), 83–105. doi:10.1057/palgrave.kmrp.8500090

Bassett, E., & Shandas, V. (2010). Innovation and climate action planning: Perspectives from municipal plans. *Journal of the American Planning Association*, *76*(4), 435–450. doi:10.1080/01944363.2010.509703

Bassi, A. (2014). Human and Organizational Knowledge in a Project Management Context. *Modern Management Review*, *19*(21), 7–19. doi:10.7862/rz.2014.mmr.29

Basten, D., & Haamann, T. (2018). Approaches for organizational learning: A literature review. *SAGE Open*, *8*(3). Advance online publication. doi:10.1177/2158244018794224

Basu, R., & Wright, N. (2008). *Total supply chain management*. Elsevier Press. doi:10.1016/B978-0-7506-8426-2.50006-X

Batat, W., & Hammedi, W. (2022). The extended reality technology (ERT) framework for designing customer and service experiences in phygital settings: a service research agenda. *Journal of Service Management*. doi:10.1108/JOSM-08-2022-0289

Bathelt, H., Malmberg, A., & Maskell, P. (2004). Clusters and knowledge: Local buzz, global pipelines, and the process of knowledge creation. *Progress in Human Geography*, *28*(1), 31–56. doi:10.1191/0309132504ph469oa

Batool, F., Mohammad, J., Awang, S. R., & Ahmad, T. (2022). The effect of knowledge sharing and systems thinking on organizational sustainability: The mediating role of creativity. *Journal of Knowledge Management*. https://www.emerald.com/insight/content/doi/10.1108/JKM-10-2021-0785/full/html

Battina, D. S. (2021). The Challenges and Mitigation Strategies of Using DevOps during Software Development. *International Journal of Creative Research Thoughts*.

Baumers, M., Tuck, C., Wildman, R., Ashcroft, I., & Hague, R. (2011). Energy inputs to additive manufacturing: does capacity utilization matter? In *2011 International Solid Freeform Fabrication Symposium*. University of Texas at Austin. 10.26153/tsw/15275

Baumgartner, R. J., & Rauter, R. (2017). Strategic perspectives of corporate sustainability management to develop a sustainable organization. *Journal of Cleaner Production*, *140*, 81–92. doi:10.1016/j.jclepro.2016.04.146

Becerra-Fernandez, I., Gonzalez, A., & Sabherwal, R. (2004). *Knowledge management challenges, solutions, and technologies*. Pearson Prentice Hall.

Bechtsis, D., Tsolakis, N., Vlachos, D., & Iakovou, E. (2017). Sustainable supply chain management in the digitalisation era: The impact of automated guided vehicles. *Journal of Cleaner Production*, *142*, 3970–3984. doi:10.1016/j.jclepro.2016.10.057

Begault, D. R., & Trejo, L. J. (2000). *3-D sound for virtual reality and multimedia*. NASA Center for AeroSpace Information.

Beier, G., Niehoff, S., Ziems, T., & Xue, B. (2017). Sustainability aspects of a digitalized industry: A comparative study from China and Germany. *International Journal of Precision Engineering and Manufacturing - Green Technology, 4*, 227-234. doi:10.1007/s40684-017-0028-8

Beier, G., Niehoff, S., & Xue, B. (2018). More sustainability in industry through industrial Internet of Things? *Applied Sciences (Basel, Switzerland)*, *8*(2), 1–12. doi:10.3390/app8020219

Bekey, G. A. (2005). *Autonomous robots: From biological inspiration to implementation and control*. MIT Press.

Belaud, J. P., Prioux, N., Vialle, C., & Sablayrolles, C. (2019). Big data for agri-food 4.0: Application to sustainability management for by-products supply chain. *Computers in Industry*, *111*, 41–50. doi:10.1016/j.compind.2019.06.006

Beltagui, A., Kunz, N., & Gold, S. (2020). The role of 3D printing and open design on adoption of socially sustainable supply chain innovation. *International Journal of Production Economics*, *221*, 1–16. doi:10.1016/j.ijpe.2019.07.035

Benz, M., & Chatterjee, D. (2020). Calculated risk? A cybersecurity evaluation tool for SMEs. *Business Horizons*, *63*(4), 531–540. doi:10.1016/j.bushor.2020.03.010

Berkes, F., Colding, J., & Folke, C. (Eds.). (2002). *Navigating Social–Ecological Systems*. Cambridge University Press.

Berkes, F., Folke, C., & Colding, J. (Eds.). (2000). *Linking Social and Ecological Systems: Management Practices and Social Mechanisms for Building Resilience*. Cambridge University Press.

Berman, B. (2012). 3-D printing: The new industrial revolution. *Business Horizons*, *55*(2), 155–162. doi:10.1016/j.bushor.2011.11.003

Berquist, G. (2014). FirstNet Communication. Public Safety Agency.

Berry, T. (2023). *How to do a SWOT analysis for better strategic planning*. Bplans.com. https://www.bplans.com/business-planning/how-to-write/marketing-sales/swot-analysis/

Besanko, D., Dranove, D., & Shandley, M. (2000). *The economics of strategy* (2nd ed.). John Wiley & Sons.

Bharadwaj, S., Bharadwaj, A., & Bendoly, E. (2007). The performance effects of complementarities between information systems, marketing, manufacturing, and supply chain processes. *Information Systems Research, 18*(4), 437–453. doi:10.1287/isre.1070.0148

Bibri, S. (2022). The Social Shaping of the Metaverse as an Alternative to the Imaginaries of Data-Driven Smart Cities: A Study in Science, Technology, and Society. *Smart Cities, 5*(3), 832–874. doi:10.3390martcities5030043

Biering, E., Boxaspen, K. K., & Næsje, T. F. (2021). *Styringsgruppens oppsummering og vurdering av lakseluspåvirkning på ville laksefisk 2021*. Havforskningsinstituttet.

Bijwe, A., & Shankar, P. (2022, October). Challenges of Adopting DevOps Culture on the Internet of Things Applications-A Solution Model. In *2022 2nd International Conference on Technological Advancements in Computational Sciences (ICTACS)* (pp. 638-645). IEEE. 10.1109/ICTACS56270.2022.9988182

Binkley, C. (2022, October 24). *Test scores show how COVID set kids back across the US PBS*. Retrieved January 6, 2023, from https://www.pbs.org/newshour/education/test-scores-show-how-covid-set-kids-back-across-the-u-s

Blanchard, D. (2021). *Supply chain management best practices*. John Wiley & Sons.

Blasco Puchades, J., & Portolés Griñan, L. (2011). Additive layered manufacturing: Sectors of industrial application shown through case studies. *International Journal of Production Research, 49*(4), 1061–1079. doi:10.1080/00207540903479786

Blaut, J. M. (1993). *The Colonizer's Model of the World: Geographical Diffusionism and Eurocentric History*. The Guilford Press.

Blewitt, J. (2014). *Understanding sustainable development* (2nd ed.). Routledge. doi:10.4324/9781315886459

Blome, C., Paulraj, A., & Schuetz, K. (2014). Supply chain collaboration and sustainability: A profile deviation analysis. *International Journal of Operations & Production Management, 34*(5), 639–663. doi:10.1108/IJOPM-11-2012-0515

Bodrow, W. (2017). Impact of Industry 4.0 in service-oriented firm. *Advances in Manufacturing, 5*(4), 394–400. doi:10.100740436-017-0196-3

Bogers, M., Hadar, R., & Bilberg, A. (2016). Additive manufacturing for consumer-centric business models: Implications for supply chains in consumer goods manufacturing. *Technological Forecasting and Social Change, 102*, 225–239. doi:10.1016/j.techfore.2015.07.024

Bolisani, E., Debei, S., & Savino, N. (2017). Renovating Project Management: Knowledge Personalization and Sharing. In M. Handzic & A. Bassi (Eds.), *Knowledge and Project Management: A Shared Approach to Improve Performance* (Vol. 5, pp. 131–153). doi:10.1007/978-3-319-51067-5_6

Bonilla, S. H., Silva, H. R. O., da Silva, M. T., Gonçalves, R. F., & Sacomano, J. B. (2018). Industry 4.0 and sustainability implications: A scenario-based analysis of the impacts and challenges. *Sustainability, 10*(10), 1–24. doi:10.3390u10103740

Börner, K., Chen, C., & Boyack, K. W. (2003). Visualizing knowledge domains. *Annual Review of Information Science & Technology, 37*(1), 179–255. doi:10.1002/aris.1440370106

Bossle, M. B., de Barcellos, M. D., Vieira, L. M., & Sauvée, L. (2016). The drivers for adoption of eco-innovation. *Journal of Cleaner Production, 113*, 861–872. doi:10.1016/j.jclepro.2015.11.033

Boston Consulting Group (BCG). (2021, December 5). *Teachers know best - Bill & Melinda Gates Foundation*. Retrieved June 23, 2022, from https://usprogram.gatesfoundation.org/-/media/dataimport/resources/pdf/2016/11/gates-pdmarketresearch-dec5.pdf

Bot, A., Nachtergaele, F., & Young, A. (2000). *Land resource potential and constraints at regional and country levels*. Food & Agriculture Organization.

Bower, J. L., & Christensen, C. M. (1995). Disruptive technologies: Catching the wave. *Harvard Business Review*, (Jan-Feb), 43–53.

Bowersox, D., Closs, D., & Cooper, M. B. (2002). *Supply chain logistics management*. McGraw-Hill.

Boyle, M., Kay, J., & Pond, B. (2001). Monitoring in support of policy: an adaptive ecosystem approach. In T. Munn (Ed.), *Encyclopedia of Global Environmental Change* (Vol. 4, pp. 116–137). Wiley and Son.

Boyson, S. (2014). Cyber supply chain risk management: Revolutionizing the strategic control of critical IT systems. *Technovation*, *34*(7), 342–353. doi:10.1016/j.technovation.2014.02.001

Brass, I., Tanczer, L., Carr, M., Elsden, M., & Blackstock, J. (2018). Standardising a moving target: The development and evolution of IoT security standards. In *Living in the Internet of Things: Cybersecurity of the IoT* (pp. 1–9). IET., doi:10.1049/cp.2018.0024

Brelsford, N. (2014). *Do middle-level managers contribute to strategic development? A study of the practices of middle-level managers In Strategic Renewal* [Doctoral dissertation]. University of Southampton.

Brettel, M., Friederichsen, N., Keller, M., & Rosenberg, M. (2014). How virtualization, decentralization and network building change the manufacturing landscape: An industry 4.0 perspective. *International Journal of Information and Communication Engineering*, *8*(1), 37–44.

Brown, K. (2003). Integrating Conservation and Development: A Case of Institutional Misfit. *Frontiers in Ecology and the Environment*, *1*(9), 479–487. doi:10.1890/1540-9295(2003)001[0479:ICADAC]2.0.CO;2

Bruckmeier, K., & Olsson, G. (2014). An attempt to clarify the resilience concept for renewed strategies of farm modernization. *11th European IFSA Symposium, Farming Systems Facing Global Challenges: Capacities and Strategies Proceedings*.

Brundtland, G. H. (1987). *The United Nations World Commission on Environment and Development: Our common future*. Oxford University Press.

Bruneliere, H., Muttillo, V., Eramo, R., Berardinelli, L., Gomez, A., Bagnato, A., Sadovykh, A., & Cicchetti, A. (2022). AIDOaRt: AI-augmented Automation for DevOps, a model-based framework for continuous development in Cyber–Physical Systems. *Microprocessors and Microsystems*, *94*, 104672. doi:10.1016/j.micpro.2022.104672

Bryde, D. J., Unterhitzenberger, C., Renzl, B., & Rost, M. (2018). KM and Project Management. In J. Syed, P. A. Murray, D. Hislop, & Y. Mouzughi (Eds.), *The Palgrave Handbook of Knowledge Management* (pp. 539–561). Palgrave Handbooks. doi:10.1007/978-3-319-71434-9_22

Bugmann, G., Siegel, M., & Burcin, R. (2011). A role for robotics in sustainable development? In *IEEE Africon'11* (pp. 1–4). IEEE. doi:10.1109/AFRCON.2011.6072154

Buhalis, D., O'Connor, P., & Leung, R. (2023). Smart hospitality: From smart cities and smart tourism towards agile business ecosystems in networked destinations. *International Journal of Contemporary Hospitality Management, 35*(1), 369–393. doi:10.1108/IJCHM-04-2022-0497

Bunnell, T. G., & Coe, N. M. (2001). Spaces and scales of innovation. *Progress in Human Geography, 25*(4), 569–589. doi:10.1191/030913201682688940

Burns, L. R., Goldsmith, J. C., & Sen, A. (2014). Horizontal and vertical integration of physicians: A tale of two tails. *Advances in Health Care Management, 15*, 39–117. doi:10.1108/S1474-8231(2013)0000015009 PMID:24749213

Buvik, M. P., & Tvedt, S. D. (2017). The Influence of Project Commitment and Team Commitment on the Relationship Between Trust and Knowledge Sharing in Project Teams. *Project Management Journal, 48*(2), 5–21. doi:10.1177/875697281704800202

Büyüközkan, G., & Berkol, C. (2011). Designing a sustainable supply chain using an integrated analytic network process and goal programming approach in quality function deployment. *Expert Systems with Applications, 38*, 13731–13748. doi:10.1016/j.eswa.2011.04.171

Büyüközkan, G., & Güler, M. (2019). Lojistik 4.0 teknolojilerinin analizi için metodolojik yaklaşım. *Journal of Entrepreneurship and Innovation Management, 8*(1), 21–47.

Cabrera, Á., & Cabrera, E. F. (2002). Knowledge-sharing Dilemmas. *Organization Studies, 23*(5), 687–710. doi:10.1177/0170840602235001

Cagigas, D., Clifton, J., Diaz-Fuentes, D., & Fernández-Gutiérrez, M. (2021). Blockchain for public services: A systematic literature review. *IEEE Access : Practical Innovations, Open Solutions, 9*, 13904–13921. doi:10.1109/ACCESS.2021.3052019

Callon, M., Courtial, J., & Laville, F. (1991). Co-word analysis as a tool for describing the network of interactions between basic and technological research: The case of polymer chemistry. *Scientometrics, 22*(1), 155–205. doi:10.1007/BF02019280

Callon, M., Courtial, J., Turner, W. A., & Bauin, S. (1983). From translations to problematic networks: An introduction to co-word analysis. *Social Sciences Information. Information Sur les Sciences Sociales, 22*(2), 191–235. doi:10.1177/053901883022002003

Camagni, R., & Capello, R. (2013). Regional innovation patterns and the EU regional policy reform: Toward smart innovation policies. *Growth and Change, 44*(2), 355–389. doi:10.1111/grow.12012

Campbell, H. (2009). Breaking new ground in food regime theory: Corporate environmentalism, ecological feedbacks and the 'food from somewhere' regime? *Agriculture and Human Values, 26*(4), 309–319. doi:10.100710460-009-9215-8

Cappannari, L., & Vitillo, A. (2022). XR and Metaverse Software Platforms. In Roadmapping Extended Reality (pp. 135-156). doi:10.1002/9781119865810.ch6

Carayannis, E. G., & Campbell, D. F. (2009). Mode 3 and Quadruple Helix: Toward a 21st Century Fractal Innovation Ecosystem. *International Journal of Technology Management, 46*(3), 201–234. doi:10.1504/IJTM.2009.023374

Carayannis, E. G., & Campbell, D. F. (2010). Triple Helix, Quadruple Helix, and Quintuple Helix and How Do Knowledge, Innovation, and the Environment Relate To Each Other? A Proposed Framework for a Trans-disciplinary Analysis of Sustainable Development and Social Ecology. *International Journal of Social Ecology and Sustainable Development, 1*(1), 41–69. doi:10.4018/jsesd.2010010105

Carayannis, E. G., & Campbell, D. F. J. (2011). Open Innovation Diplomacy and a 21st Century Fractal Research, Education, and Innovation (FREIE) Ecosystem: Building on the Quadruple and Quintuple Helix Innovation Concepts and the "Mode 3" Knowledge Production System. *Journal of the Knowledge Economy*, *2*(3), 327–372. doi:10.100713132-011-0058-3

Carayannis, E. G., & Campbell, D. F. J. (2012). *Mode 3 Knowledge Production in Quadruple Helix Innovation Systems*. Springer New York., doi:10.1007/978-1-4614-2062-0

Carbonneau, R., Laframboise, K., & Vahidov, R. (2008). Application of machine learning techniques for supply chain demand forecasting. *European Journal of Operational Research*, *184*(3), 1140–1154. doi:10.1016/j.ejor.2006.12.004

Carmela Annosi, M., Brunetta, F., Capo, F., & Heideveld, L. (2020). Digitalization in the agri-food industry: The relationship between technology and sustainable development. *Management Decision*, *58*(8), 1737–1757. doi:10.1108/MD-09-2019-1328

Carmigniani, J., & Furht, B. (2011). Augmented reality: An overview. In B. Furth (Ed.), *Handbook of augmented reality* (pp. 3–46). Springer. doi:10.1007/978-1-4614-0064-6_1

Carney, J. A., & Voeks, R. A. (2003). Landscape legacies of the African diaspora in Brazil Prog. *Progress in Human Geography*, *27*(2), 139–152. doi:10.1191/0309132503ph418oa

Carter, C. R., & Easton, P. L. (2011). Sustainable supply chain management: Evolution and future directions. *International Journal of Physical Distribution & Logistics Management*, *41*(1), 46–62. doi:10.1108/09600031111101420

Carter, C. R., & Rogers, D. (2008). A framework of sustainable supply chain management: Moving toward new theory. *International Journal of Physical Distribution & Logistics Management*, *38*(5), 360–387. doi:10.1108/09600030810882816

Castro, G. D. R., Fernandez, M. C. G., & Colsa, A. U. (2021). Unleashing the convergence amid digitalization and sustainability towards pursuing the sustainable development goals (SDGs): A holistic review. *Journal of Cleaner Production*, *280*, 122204. doi:10.1016/j.jclepro.2020.122204

Castrogiovanni, G., Ribeiro-Soriano, D., Mas-Tur, A., & Roig-Tierno, N. (2016). Where to acquire knowledge: Adapting knowledge management to financial institutions. *Journal of Business Research*, *69*(5), 1812–1816. doi:10.1016/j.jbusres.2015.10.061

Cauthen, L. L. (2021). *The 2020 digital transition survey results are in: Just how large is the K12 ed-tech market?* The Learning Counsel. Retrieved August 12, 2022, from https://thelearningcounsel.com/article/2020-digital-transition-survey-results-are-just-how-large-k12-ed-tech-market

Cavalli, L., Lizzi, G., Guerrieri, L., Querci, A., De Bari, F., Barbieri, G., Ferrini, S., Di Meglio, R., Cardone, R., Tardo, A., Pagano, P., Tesei, A., & Lattuca, D. (2021). Addressing efficiency and sustainability in the port of the future with 5G: The experience of the Livorno port. a methodological insight to measure innovation technologies' benefits on port operations. *Sustainability (Basel)*, *13*(21), 1–21. doi:10.3390u132112146

CCI. (2021). *Coca-Cola İçecek 2021 integrated annual report.* Retrieved March 14, 2023, from https://www.cci.com.tr/Portals/3/CCI_Integrated_Report_2021.pdf

Cervellon, M. C., & Wernerfelt, A. S. (2012). Knowledge sharing among green fashion communities online: Lessons for the sustainable supply chain. *Journal of Fashion Marketing and Management*, *16*(2), 176–192. doi:10.1108/13612021211222860

Chalmers, R., & Brannan, G. (2022). *Organizational Culture.* National Library of Medicine. StatPearls. https://www.ncbi.nlm.nih.gov/books/NBK560543/

Chalmeta, R., & Barqueros-Muñoz, J. E. (2021). Using big data for sustainability in supply chain management. *Sustainability (Basel)*, *13*(13), 1–25. doi:10.3390u13137004

Cham, T. H., Lim, Y. M., Cheng, B. L., & Lee, T. H. (2016). Determinants of knowledge management systems success in the banking industry. *VINE Journal of Information and Knowledge Management Systems*, *46*(1), 2–20. doi:10.1108/VJIKMS-03-2014-0021

Chan, F. T. S. (2003). Performance measurement in a supply chain. *International Journal of Advanced Manufacturing Technology*, *21*(7), 534–548. doi:10.1007001700300063

Chang, T. W., & Hung, C. Z. (2021). How to shape the employees' organization sustainable green knowledge sharing: Cross-level effect of green organizational identity effect on green management behavior and performance of members. *Sustainability (Basel)*, *13*(2), 626–645. doi:10.3390u13020626

Chang, T.-C., & Chuang, S.-H. (2009). Performance effects of knowledge management: Corporate management characteristics and competitive strategy enablers. *Asian Journal of Management and Humanity Sciences*, *4*(4), 181–199. doi:10.6413/AJMHS.200910.0181

Chan, H. K., Griffin, J., Lim, J. J., Zeng, F., & Chiu, A. S. (2018). The impact of 3D Printing Technology on the supply chain: Manufacturing and legal perspectives. *International Journal of Production Economics*, *205*, 156–162. doi:10.1016/j.ijpe.2018.09.009

Chanias, S., Myers, M. D., & Hess, T. (2019). Digital transformation strategy making in pre-digital organizations: The case of a financial services provider. *The Journal of Strategic Information Systems*, *28*(1), 17–33. doi:10.1016/j.jsis.2018.11.003

ChatGPT. (2022). *How can school systems use autopoietic epistemology to improve knowledge management strategies?* Retrieved from https://openai.com/chatgpt/

Chatterjee, S., Chaudhuri, R., Vrontis, D., & Piccolo, R. (2021). Enterprise social network for knowledge sharing in MNCs: Examining the role of knowledge contributors and knowledge seekers for cross-country collaboration. *Journal of International Management*, *27*(1), 100827. doi:10.1016/j.intman.2021.100827

Chebbi, H., Yahiaoui, D., Thrassou, A., & Vrontis, D. (2013). The exploration activity's added value into the innovation process. *Global Business and Economics Review*, *15*(2–3), 265–278. doi:10.1504/GBER.2013.053073

Chen, T., & Suo, H. (2022, October). Design and Practice of Security Architecture via DevSecOps Technology. In *2022 IEEE 13th International Conference on Software Engineering and Service Science (ICSESS)* (pp. 310-313). IEEE. 10.1109/ICSESS54813.2022.9930212

Chen, F. W., Fu, L. W., Wang, K., Tsai, S. B., & Su, C. H. (2018). The influence of entrepreneurship and social networks on economic growth—From a sustainable innovation perspective. *Sustainability (Basel)*, *10*(7), 2510–2539. doi:10.3390u10072510

Cheng, C. C., & Shiu, E. C. (2012). Validation of a proposed instrument for measuring eco-innovation: An implementation perspective. *Technovation*, *32*(6), 329–344. doi:10.1016/j.technovation.2012.02.001

Cheng, Q., Liu, Y., Peng, C., He, X., Qu, Z., & Dong, Q. (2023). Knowledge digitization: Characteristics, knowledge advantage and innovation performance. *Journal of Business Research*, *163*, 113915. doi:10.1016/j.jbusres.2023.113915

Chen, H., Nunes, M. B., Ragsdell, G., & An, X. (2018). Extrinsic and intrinsic motivation for experience grounded tacit knowledge sharing in Chinese software organizations. *Journal of Knowledge Management*, *22*(4), 478–498. doi:10.1108/JKM-03-2017-0101

Chen, L., & Jia, G. (2017). Environmental efficiency analysis of China's regional industry: A data envelopment analysis (DEA) based approach. *Journal of Cleaner Production, 142*, 846–853. doi:10.1016/j.jclepro.2016.01.045

Chen, Q., & Lee, S. (2021). Research Status and Trend of Digital Twin: Visual Knowledge Mapping Analysis. *International Journal of Advanced Smart Convergence, 10*(4), 84–97. doi:10.7236/IJASC.2021.10.4.84

Chen, S. H., Tao, C. Q., & He, W. (2012). Empirical research on the relationship between knowledge integration and innovation ability of IT enterprise. *International Journal of Networking and Virtual Organisations, 11*(3), 315–328. doi:10.1504/IJNVO.2012.048913

Chen, Y. J., & Deng, M. (2015). Information sharing in a manufacturer: Supplier relationship: suppliers' incentive and production efficiency. *Production and Operations Management, 24*(4), 619–633. doi:10.1111/poms.12261

Chesbrough, H., Vanhaverbeke, W., & West, J. (2006). *Open innovation: Researching a new paradigm.* Oxford University Press.

Chgbesjp, P. V. (2018). *9 essential tips leading a multicultural team.* Personnel Communication. LinkedIn.

Chiu, C. N., & Chen, H. H. (2016). The study of knowledge management capability and organizational effectiveness in Taiwanese public utility: The mediator role of organizational commitment. *SpringerPlus, 5*(1), 1–34. doi:10.118640064-016-3173-6 PMID:27652093

Choi, S., Jung, K., & Nog, S. D. (2015). Virtual reality applications in manufacturing industries: Past research, present findings, and future directions. *Concurrent Engineering, Research and Applications, 21*(1), 565–572. doi:10.1177/1063293X14568814

Choi, S., & Ng, A. (2011). Environmental and economic dimensions of sustainability and price effects on consumer responses. *Journal of Business Ethics, 104*(2), 269–282. doi:10.100710551-011-0908-8

Choi, T. M., Kumar, S., Yue, X., & Chan, H. L. (2021). Disruptive technologies and operations management in the Industry 4.0 era and beyond. *Production and Operations Management, 31*(1), 1–23. doi:10.1111/poms.13622

Chopra, M., Saini, N., Kumar, S., Varma, A., Mangla, S. K., & Lim, W. M. (2021). Past, present, and future of knowledge management for business sustainability. *Journal of Cleaner Production, 328*, 129592. doi:10.1016/j.jclepro.2021.129592

Chowdhury, G. (2013). Sustainability of digital information services. *The Journal of Documentation, 69*(5), 602–622. doi:10.1108/JD-08-2012-0104

Christensen, C. M. (2013). *The innovator's dilemma: When new technologies cause great firms to fail.* Harvard Business Review Press.

Ciganke, A. P., Mao, E., & Srite, M. (2008). Organizational culture for knowledge management systems: A study of corporate users. *International Journal of Knowledge Management, 4*(1), 1–16. doi:10.4018/jkm.2008010101

Ciulli, F., & Kolk, A. (2019). Incumbents and business model innovation for the sharing economy: Implications for sustainability. *Journal of Cleaner Production, 214*, 995–1010. doi:10.1016/j.jclepro.2018.12.295

Clarkson, M. B. E. (1995). A stakeholder framework for analyzing and evaluating corporate social performance. *Academy of Management Review, 20*(1), 92. doi:10.2307/258888

Cobo, M. J., López-Herrera, A. G., Herrera-Viedma, E., & Herrera, F. (2011). An approach for detecting, quantifying, and visualizing the evolution of a research field: A practical application to the fuzzy sets theory field. *Journal of Informetrics, 5*(1), 146–166. doi:10.1016/j.joi.2010.10.002

Cobo, M. J., López-Herrera, A. G., Herrera-Viedma, E., & Herrera, F. (2012). SciMAT: A new science mapping analysis software tool. *Journal of the American Society for Information Science and Technology*, *63*(8), 1609–1630. doi:10.1002/asi.22688

Cochran, P. L., & Wood, R. A. (1984). Corporate social responsibility and financial performance. *Academy of Management Journal, 27*(1), 42.

Codinhoto, R., Becher, O., Heron, J. N., & Donato, V. (2021). BIM bin: Waste management through BIM and digital twin. In M. Del Giudice & A. Osello (Eds.), *Handbook of research on developing smart cities based on digital twins* (pp. 265–294). IGI Global. doi:10.4018/978-1-7998-7091-3.ch013

Coenen, L., Asheim, B., Bugge, M. M., & Herstad, S. J. (2017). Advancing regional innovation systems: What does evolutionary economic geography bring to the policy table? *Environment and Planning C. Politics and Space*, *35*(4), 600–620.

Cohen, D. (2006). What is your return on knowledge? *Harvard Business Review*. https://hbr.org/2006/12/whats-your-return-on-knowledge

Cohen, D., Sargeant, M., & Somers, K. (2014). 3-D printing takes shape. *The McKinsey Quarterly*, *1*, 1–6.

Collins, C. J., & Smith, K. G. (2006). Knowledge exchange and combination: The role of human resource practices in the performance of high-technology firms. *Academy of Management Journal*, *49*(3), 544–560. doi:10.5465/amj.2006.21794671

Comcast. (n.d.). *Our Company*. https://corporate.comcast.com/company

Compton, M. (2012). *President Obama Signs the Payroll Tax Cut*. The Obama White House Archives. https://obamawhitehouse.archives.gov/blog/2012/02/22/president-obama-signs-payroll-tax-cut

Cooke, P. (2005). Regionally asymmetric knowledge capabilities and open innovation: Exploring 'Globalisation 2'—A new model of industrial organization. *Research Policy*, *34*(8), 1128–1149. doi:10.1016/j.respol.2004.12.005

Corallo, A., Lazoi, M., & Lezzi, M. (2020). Cybersecurity in the context of Industry 4.0: A structured classification of critical assets and business impacts. *Computers in Industry*, *114*, 1–15. doi:10.1016/j.compind.2019.103165

Correa Tavares, E., Meirelles, F. D. S., Tavares, E. C., Cunha, M. A., & Schunk, L. M. (2021). Blockchain in the Amazon: Creating public value and promoting sustainability. *Information Technology for Development*, *27*(3), 579–598. doi:10.1080/02681102.2020.1848772

Costa, V., & Monteiro, S. (2016). Key knowledge management processes for innovation: A systematic literature review. *VINE Journal of Information and Knowledge Management Systems*, *46*(3), 386–410. doi:10.1108/VJIKMS-02-2015-0017

Coulter, N., Monarch, I., & Konda, S. (1998). Software engineering as seen through its research literature: A study in co-word analysis. *Journal of the American Society for Information Science*, *49*(13), 1206–1223. doi:10.1002/(SICI)1097-4571(1998)49:13<1206::AID-ASI7>3.0.CO;2-F

Creating America's Public Safety Broadband Network Building a Network with First Responders (2016). Academic Press.

Crosby, M., Pattanayak, P., Verma, S., & Kalyanaraman, V. (2016). Blockchain technology: Beyond bitcoin. *Applied Innovation Review*, *2*, 6–19.

Curado, C., & Bontis, N. (2006). The knowledge-based view of the firm and its theoretical precursor. *International Journal of Learning and Intellectual Capital*, *3*(4), 367–381. doi:10.1504/IJLIC.2006.011747

Curran, M. A. (2009). Wrapping our brains around sustainability. *Sustainability (Basel)*, *1*(1), 5–13. doi:10.3390u1010005

D'Eusanio, M., Zamagni, A., & Petti, L. (2019). Social sustainability and supply chain management: Methods and tools. *Journal of Cleaner Production*, *235*, 178–189. doi:10.1016/j.jclepro.2019.06.323

Da Xu, L., He, W., & Li, S. (2014). Internet of things in industries: A survey. *IEEE Transactions on Industrial Informatics*, *10*(4), 2233–2243. doi:10.1109/TII.2014.2300753

Dahan, N., Al-Razgan, M., Al-Laith, A., Alsoufi, M., Al-Asaly, M., & Alfakih, T. (2022). Metaverse Framework: A Case Study on E-Learning Environment (ELEM). *Electronics (Basel)*, *11*(10), 1616. doi:10.3390/electronics11101616

Dai, Y., Wang, J., & Gao, S. (2022). Advanced Electronics and Artificial Intelligence: Must-Have Technologies Toward Human Body Digital Twins. *Advanced Intelligent Systems*, *4*(7), 2100263. doi:10.1002/aisy.202100263

Dale, V. H., Brown, S., Hauer, R. A., Hobbs, N. T., Huntly, N., Naima, R. J., Ribosome, W. E., Turner, M. G., & Valene, T. J. (2000). Ecological Principles and Guidelines for Managing the Use of Land. *Ecological Applications*, *10*(3), 639–670. doi:10.2307/2641032

Dalkir, K. (2011). *Knowledge Management in Theory and Practice* (2nd ed.). MIT Press.

Dalmarco, G., & Barros, A. C. (2018). Adoption of Industry 4.0 technologies in supply chains. In A. C. Moreira, L. Miguel, D. F. Ferreira, & R. A. Zimmermann (Eds.), *Innovation and Supply Chain Management* (pp. 303–319). Springer., doi:10.1007/978-3-319-74304-2_14

Dasaklis, T. K., Casino, F., & Patsakis, C. (2020). A traceability and auditing framework for electronic equipment reverse logistics based on blockchain: The case of mobile phones. In *Proceedings of the 2020 11th International Conference on Information, Intelligence, Systems and Applications (IISA)* (pp. 1-7). IEEE. 10.1109/IISA50023.2020.9284394

Das, R., Banerjee, M., & De, S. (Eds.). (2020). *Emerging trends in disruptive technology management for sustainable development*. CRC Press.

Davenport, T. H. (2006). Competing on analytics. *Harvard Business Review*, *84*(1), 98–107. PMID:16447373

Davenport, T. H., De Long, D. W., & Beers, M. C. (1998). Successful Knowledge Management Projects. *Sloan Management Review*, 43–57.

Davidow, W., & Malone, M. (1992). *The virtual corporation, structuring and revitalizing the corporation for the 21st century*. HarperBusiness.

Davies, R. (2015). *Industry 4.0: Digitalisation for productivity and growth*. European Parliament.https://www.europarl.europa.eu/thinktank/en/document/EPRS_BRI(2015)568337

Davis, F. D. (1985). *A technology acceptance model for empirically testing new end-user information systems: Theory and results* [Doctoral dissertation, Massachusetts Institute of Technology]. https://dspace.mit.edu/bitstream/handle/1721.1/15192/14927137-MIT.pdf

Dawson, P. M., & Andriopoulos, C. (2014). Managing change, creativity & innovation. *Sage (Atlanta, Ga.)*.

De Bayser, M., Segura, V., Azevedo, L. G., Tizzei, L. P., Thiago, R., Soares, E., & Cerqueira, R. (2022, April). DevOps and Microservices in Scientific System development: experience on a multi-year industry research project. In *Proceedings of the 37th ACM/SIGAPP Symposium on Applied Computing* (pp. 1452-1455). 10.1145/3477314.3507317

De Bem Machado, A., Secinaro, S., Calandra, D., & Lanzalonga, F. (2022). Knowledge management and digital transformation for Industry 4.0: A structured literature review. *Knowledge Management Research and Practice*, *20*(2), 320–338. doi:10.1080/14778238.2021.2015261

De Bernardi, P., Bertello, A., & Shams, S. M. (2019). Logics hindering digital transformation in cultural heritage strategic management: An exploratory case study. *Tourism Analysis*, *24*(3), 315–327. doi:10.3727/108354219X15511864843876

De Ketelaere, B., Smeets, B., Verboven, P., Nicolaï, B., & Saeys, W. (2022). Digital twins in quality engineering. *Quality Engineering*, *34*(3), 404–408. doi:10.1080/08982112.2022.2052731

De Long, D. W., & Fahey, L. (2000). Diagnosing cultural barriers to knowledge management. *Academy of Knowledge Executive*, *14*(4), 113–127.

De Long, D. W., & Fahey, L. (2000). Diagnosing cultural barriers to knowledge management. *The Academy of Management Perspectives*, *14*(4), 113–127. doi:10.5465/ame.2000.3979820

De Paula Ferreira, W., Armellini, F., & De Santa-Eulalia, L. (2020). Simulation in Industry 4.0: A state-of-the-art review. *Computers & Industrial Engineering, 149. Computers & Industrial Engineering*, *106868*, 1–17. doi:10.1016/j.cie.2020.106868

de Soto, B. G., Agustí-Juan, I., Hunhevicz, J., Joss, S., Graser, K., Habert, G., & Adey, B. T. (2018). Productivity of digital fabrication in construction: Cost and time analysis of a robotically built wall. *Automation in Construction*, *92*, 297–311. doi:10.1016/j.autcon.2018.04.004

de Sousa Jabbour, A. B. L., Jabbour, C. J. C., Foropon, C., & Filho, M. G. (2018). When titans meet: Can Industry 4.0 revolutionise the environmentally sustainable manufacturing wave? The role of critical success factors. *Technological Forecasting and Social Change*, *132*, 18–25. doi:10.1016/j.techfore.2018.01.017

De, A., Wang, J., & Tiwari, M. K. (2019). Hybridizing basic variable neighborhood search with particle swarm optimization for solving sustainable ship routing and bunker management problem. *IEEE Transactions on Intelligent Transportation Systems*, *21*(3), 986–997. doi:10.1109/TITS.2019.2900490

Dennis, M., Armitage, R. P., & James, P. (2016). Social-ecological innovation: Adaptive responses to urban environmental conditions. *Urban Ecosystems*, *19*(3), 1063–1082. doi:10.100711252-016-0551-3

Derting, T. L., Ebert-May, D., Henkel, T. P., Maher, J. M., Arnold, B., & Passmore, H. A. (2016). Assessing faculty professional development in STEM higher education: Sustainability of outcomes. *Science Advances*, *2*(3), e1501422. doi:10.1126ciadv.1501422 PMID:27034985

Desouza, K. C., & Evaristo, J. R. (2004). Managing knowledge in distributed projects. *Communications of the ACM*, *47*(4), 87–91. doi:10.1145/975817.975823

Di Vaio, A., Palladino, R., Hassan, R., & Escobar, O. (2020). Artificial intelligence and business models in the sustainable development goals perspective: A systematic literature review. *Journal of Business Research*, *121*, 283–314. doi:10.1016/j.jbusres.2020.08.019

Dilmaghani, M., Fahimnia, F., Ardakan, M. A., & Naghshineh, N. (2015). Function of knowledge culture in the effectiveness of knowledge management procedures: A case study of a knowledge-based organization. *Webology*, *12*(1).

Djimesah, I. E., Zhao, H., Okine, A. N. D., Li, Y., Duah, E., & Mireku, K. K. (2022). Analyzing the technology of acceptance model of Ghanaian crowdfunding stakeholders. *Technological Forecasting and Social Change*, *175*, 121323. doi:10.1016/j.techfore.2021.121323

Dolgui, A., & Ivanov, D. (2022). 5G in Digital supply chain and operations management: Fostering flexibility, end-to-end connectivity and real-time visibility through internet-of-everything. *International Journal of Production Research*, *60*(2), 442–451. doi:10.1080/00207543.2021.2002969

Douglas, J. (2019). *These American workers are the most afraid of A.I. taking their jobs.* CNBC. https://www.cnbc.com/2019/11/07/these-american-workers-are-the-most-afraid-of-ai-taking-their-jobs.html

Du Plessis, M. (2007). The role of knowledge management in innovation. *Journal of Knowledge Management, 26*(4), 1367–3270. doi:10.1108/13673270710762684

Duarte, S., & Cruz-Machado, V. (2017). Exploring linkages between lean and green supply chain and the industry 4.0. In *Proceedings of the International Conference on Management Science Engineering Management* (pp. 1242-1252). Springer.

Dubey, R., Gunasekaran, A., Papadopoulos, T., Childe, S. J., Shibin, K. T., & Wamba, S. F. (2017). Sustainable supply chain management: Framework and further research directions. *Journal of Cleaner Production, 142*(2), 1119–1130. doi:10.1016/j.jclepro.2016.03.117

Dubey, R., Gupta, M., Mikalef, P., & Akter, S. (2022). Incorporating blockchain technology in information systems research. *International Journal of Information Management, 102573.* Advance online publication. doi:10.1016/j.ijinfomgt.2022.102573

Dubois, D., Niessing, J., & Kachan, K. (2020). A*nalytics-Driven Transformation at Majid Al Futtaim: Building a Data-Led, Test-&-Learn Culture to Generate Customer Value in the Middle East.* Insead, The Business School for the World. https://www.insead.edu/

Dulhare, U. N., & Rasool, S. (2022). Smart Airport System to Counter COVID-19 and Future Sustainability. In *Machine Learning and Internet of Things for Societal Issues* (pp. 55–67). Springer Nature Singapore. doi:10.1007/978-981-16-5090-1_5

Dupont, B., & Lusthaus, J. (2022). Countering distrust in illicit online networks: The dispute resolution strategies of cybercriminals. *Social Science Computer Review, 40*(4), 892–913. doi:10.1177/0894439321994623 PMID:35971389

Durão, L. F., Haag, S., Anderl, R., Schützer, K., & Zancul, E. (2018). Digital twin requirements in the context of Industry 4.0. In *Proceedings of the IFIP International Conference on Product Lifecycle Management* (pp. 204-214). Springer. 10.1007/978-3-030-01614-2_19

Dutton, H. W. (2014). Putting things to work: Social and policy challenges for the Internet of things. *Info, 16*(3), 1–21. doi:10.1108/info-09-2013-0047

Düzgün, M. (2020). Assessment Of Istanbul Grand Airport (Iga) As A Global Cargo Base By The Topsis Method. *Academic Review of Humanities and Social Sciences, 3*(1), 125–138.

Dwivedi, Y. K., Ismagilova, E., Hughes, D. L., Carlson, J., Filieri, R., Jacobson, J., . . . Wang, Y. (2021). Setting the future of digital and social media marketing research: Perspectives and research propositions. *International Journal of Information Management, 59*, 102168. https://www.sciencedirect.com/science/article/pii/S0268401220308082

Dwivedi, Y., Hughes, L., Baabdullah, A., Ribeiro-Navarrete, S., Giannakis, M., Al-Debei, M., Dennehy, D., Metri, B., Buhalis, D., Cheung, C. M. K., Conboy, K., Doyle, R., Dubey, R., Dutot, V., Felix, R., Goyal, D. P., Gustafsson, A., Hinsch, C., Jebabli, I., ... Wamba, S. (2022). Metaverse beyond the hype: Multidisciplinary perspectives on emerging challenges, opportunities, and agenda for research, practice and policy. *International Journal of Information Management, 66*, 102542. doi:10.1016/j.ijinfomgt.2022.102542

Ebert, C., & Hochstein, L. (2022). DevOps in Practice. *IEEE Software, 40*(1), 29–36. doi:10.1109/MS.2022.3213285

Edwards, J. S. (2022). Where knowledge management and information management meet: Research directions. *International Journal of Information Management, 63*, 102458. doi:10.1016/j.ijinfomgt.2021.102458

Edwards, J. S., Shaw, D., & Collier, P. M. (2005). Knowledge management systems: Finding a way with technology. *Journal of Knowledge Management*, *9*(1), 113–125. doi:10.1108/13673270510583009

Eitiveni, I., Kurnia, S., & Buyya, R. (2017). Sustainable supply chain management: Taxonomy, gaps, and future directions. *PACIS 2017 Proceedings*, 121. https://aisel.aisnet.org/pacis2017/121

Ekambaram, A., Sørensen, A. Ø., Bull-Berg, H., & Olsson, N. O. (2018). The role of big data and knowledge management in improving project-based organizations. *Procedia Computer Science*, *138*, 851–858. doi:10.1016/j.procs.2018.10.111

Elliott, J. A. (2012). *An introduction to sustainable development* (4th ed.). Routledge. doi:10.4324/9780203844175

Ellison, N. B., Gibbs, J. L., & Weber, M. S. (2015). The use of enterprise social network sites for knowledge sharing in distributed organizations: The role of organizational affordances. *The American Behavioral Scientist*, *59*(1), 103–123. doi:10.1177/0002764214540510

Eom, S. (2022). The Emerging Digital Twin Bureaucracy in the 21st Century. *Perspectives on Public Management and Governance*, *5*(2), 174–186. doi:10.1093/ppmgov/gvac005

Equinix. (n.d.). *Who we are*. https://www.equinix.com/about

Esfahbodi, A., Zhang, Y., & Watson, G. (2016). Sustainable supply chain management in emerging economies: Trade-offs between environmental and cost performance. *International Journal of Production Economics*, *181*, 350–366. doi:10.1016/j.ijpe.2016.02.013

Etzkowitz, H., & Leydesdorff, L. (1995). The Triple Helix — University-Industry-Government Relations: A Laboratory for Knowledge Based Economic Development. *EASST Review*, *14*(1), 14-19. https://ssrn.com/abstract=2480085

Etzkowitz, H., & Leydesdorff, L. (2000). The Dynamics of Innovation: From National Systems and "Mode 2" to a Triple Helix of University–Industry–Government Relations. *Research Policy*, *29*(2), 109–123. doi:10.1016/S0048-7333(99)00055-4

European Commission. (2001). *Green paper. promoting a European framework for corporate social responsibility*. European Commission.

European Commission. (2012). *Guide to Research and Innovation Strategies for Smart Specialisations (RIS 3)*. Publications Office of the European Union.

European Commission. (2022). *Eco-innovation at the heart of European policies*. Retrieved from https://green-business.ec.europa.eu/eco-innovation_en

Fagerberg, J., Mowery, D. C., & Nelson, R. R. (2005). *The Oxford handbook of innovation*. Oxford University Press.

Fagnant, D. J., & Kockelman, K. (2015). Preparing a nation for autonomous vehicles: Opportunities, barriers, and policy recommendations. *Transportation Research Part A, Policy and Practice*, *77*, 167–181. doi:10.1016/j.tra.2015.04.003

Fahimi, F. (2009). *Autonomous robots: Modeling, path planning and control*. Springer Nature., doi:10.1007/978-0-387-09538-7

Fang, S. C., Yang, C. W., & Hsu, W. Y. (2013). Inter-organizational knowledge transfer: The perspective of knowledge governance. *Journal of Knowledge Management*, *17*(6), 943–957. doi:10.1108/JKM-04-2013-0138

Fan, J. S. (2019). Woke Capital: The Role of Corporations in Social Movements. *Harvard Business Law Review*, *9*(2), 441–494.

FAO. (2018). *The future of food and agriculture—Alternative pathways to 2050*. FAO.

FAO. (2020). *The state of world fisheries and aquaculture 2020 (sustainability in action)*. FAO.

FAO. (2021). *Strategic framework 2022-2031. Documents C 2021/7*. FAO.

Faraboschi, P., Frachtenberg, E., Laplante, P., Milojicic, D., & Saracco, R. (2022). Virtual Worlds (Metaverse): From Skepticism, to Fear, to Immersive Opportunities. *Computer*, *55*(10), 100–106. doi:10.1109/MC.2022.3192702

Faustino, J., Adriano, D., Amaro, R., Pereira, R., & da Silva, M. M. (2022). DevOps benefits: A systematic literature review. *Software, Practice & Experience*, *52*(9), 1905–1926. doi:10.1002pe.3096

FCC. (2022). *911 Reliability, Network Outages, and Related Reporting Obligations*. Federal Communications Commission. https://www.fcc.gov/enforcement/areas/911-outages-reporting

Fei, Y. (2022). *Smart sensing and predictive learning for optimization and simulation of airport ground equipment and staff scheduling: a cloud-based mobile integrated decision support platform* [Doctoral dissertation]. Georgia Institute of Technology.

Fernandez, R., Abdullahi, A., Shacklett, M., Greenberg, K., & Stone, B. (2022, July 28). *Most technology purchases come with high degree of Regret, Gartner says*. TechRepublic. Retrieved January 6, 2023, from https://www.techrepublic.com/article/most-technology-purchases-come-with-high-degree-of-regret-gartner-says/

Fernie, S., Green, S. D., Weller, S. J., & Newcombe, R. (2003). Knowledge sharing: Context, confusion, and controversy. *International Journal of Project Management*, *21*(3), 177–187. doi:10.1016/S0263-7863(02)00092-3

Ferreira, L. M. D. F., & Silva, C. (2016). Integrating sustainability metrics in the supply chain performance measurement system. In L. M. D. F. Ferreira & C. Silva (Eds.), *Multiple Helix Ecosystems for Sustainable Competitiveness: Innovation* (pp. 113–132). Technology, and Knowledge Management., doi:10.1007/978-3-319-29677-7_8

Fields, Z. (Ed.). (2017). *Collective Creativity for Responsible and Sustainable Business Practice*. IGI Global. doi:10.4018/978-1-5225-1823-5

Figalist, I., Biesdorf, A., Brand, C., Feld, S., & Kiermeier, M. (2019, July). Supporting the DevOps feedback loop using unsupervised machine learning. In *2019 IEEE International Symposium on Innovations in Intelligent Systems and Applications (INISTA)* (pp. 1-6). IEEE. 10.1109/INISTA.2019.8778283

FirstNet: The History of our Nation's Public Safety Network. (2022). FirstNet Authority. https://www.firstnet.gov/about/history

Fischer-Kowalski, M., & Rotmans, J. (2009). Conceptualizing, observing, and influencing social-ecological transitions. *Ecology and Society*, *14*(2), 3. doi:10.5751/ES-02857-140203

Fiskeridirektoratet. (2017). *Utviklingstillatelser*. Bergen: Fiskeridirektoratet.

Fiskeridirektoratet. (2021). *Nøkkeltall fra norsk havbruksnæring 2020*. Bergen: Fiskeridirektoratet.

Fitzgerald, J. (2018). *Using autonomous robots to drive supply chain innovation*. Deloitte. Retrieved June 27, 2022, from https://www2.deloitte.com/content/dam/Deloitte/us/Documents/manufacturing/us-manufacturing-autonomous-robots-supply-chain-innovation.pdf

Flanagan, K., & Uyarra, E. (2016). Four dangers in innovation policy studies – and how to avoid them. *Industry and Innovation*, *23*(2), 177–188. doi:10.1080/13662716.2016.1146126

Forslund, H., & Jonsson, P. (2007). The impact of forecast information quality on supply chain performance. *International Journal of Operations & Production Management, 27*(1), 90–107. doi:10.1108/01443570710714556

Foster, T., Mieno, T., & Brozović, N. (2020). Satellite-based monitoring of irrigation water use: Assessing measurement errors and their implications for agricultural water management policy. *Water Resources Research, 56*(11), 1–19. doi:10.1029/2020WR028378

Franz, Y. (2014). Chances and Challenges for Social Urban Living Labs in urban research. *ENoLLOpenLivingLab Days. Conference Proceedings,* 105-114.

Freeman, R. E. (1984). *Strategic management: A stakeholder approach.* Pittman.

Frey, P., Lindner, F., Muller, A., & Wald, A. (2009). Project Knowledge Management Organizational Design and Success Factors - An Empirical Study in Germany. *Proceedings of 42nd Hawaii International Conference on System Sciences*, 1-14.

Frustaci, M., Pace, P., Aloi, G., & Fortino, G. (2017). Evaluating critical security issues of the IoT world: Present and future challenges. *IEEE Internet of Things Journal, 5*(4), 2483–2495. doi:10.1109/JIOT.2017.2767291

FTC (2022, June 23). *Children's Online Privacy Protection Rule ("COPPA").* Federal Trade Commission.

Fuglsang, L., & Olsen, P. (2007). *Videnskabsteori i samfunnsvidenskaberne.* Roskilde Universitetsforlag.

Fukuzaki, T., Liu, S., & Butler, M. (2022). DevFemOps: Enhancing maintainability based on microservices using formal engineering methods. *Connection Science, 34*(1), 2125–2138. doi:10.1080/09540091.2022.2099347

Fuller, A., Fan, Z., Day, C., & Barlow, C. (2020). Digital twin: Enabling technology, challenges, and open research. *IEEE Access : Practical Innovations, Open Solutions, 8*, 108952–108971. doi:10.1109/ACCESS.2020.2998358

Gall, M., & Pigni, F. (2022). Taking DevOps mainstream: A critical review and conceptual framework. *European Journal of Information Systems, 31*(5), 548–567. doi:10.1080/0960085X.2021.1997100

Gao, F., Li, M., & Clarke, S. (2008). Knowledge, management, and knowledge management in business operations. *Journal of Knowledge Management, 12*(2), 3–17. doi:10.1108/13673270810859479

Gao, Q., Guo, S., Liu, X., Manogaran, G., Chilamkurti, N., & Kadry, S. (2020). Simulation analysis of supply chain risk management system based on IoT information platform. *Enterprise Information Systems, 14*(9-10), 1354–1378. doi:10.1080/17517575.2019.1644671

Gao, T., Chai, Y., & Liu, Y. (2018). A review of knowledge management about theoretical conception and designing approaches. *International Journal of Crowd Sciences, 2*(1), 42–51. doi:10.1108/IJCS-08-2017-0023

Garriga, E., & Melé, D. (2004). Corporate social responsibility theories: Mapping the territory. *Journal of Business Ethics, 53*(1-2), 51–71. doi:10.1023/B:BUSI.0000039399.90587.34

Garvey, M. D. (2021). A philosophical examination on the definition of cyberspace. In S. Carnovale & S. Yeniyurt (Eds.), *Cyber Security and Supply Chain Management: Risks, Challenges, and Solutions* (pp. 1–11). World Scientific Publishing. doi:10.1142/9789811233128_0001

Gasik, S. (2011). A Model of Project Knowledge Management. *Project Management Journal, 42*(3), 23–44. doi:10.1002/pmj.20239

Gebler, M., Uiterkamp, A. J. S., & Visser, C. (2014). A global sustainability perspective on 3D printing technologies. *Energy Policy, 74*, 158–167. doi:10.1016/j.enpol.2014.08.033

GeeksforGeeks. (2023). *Difference between Circuit Switching and Packet Switching*. GeeksforGeeks. https://www.geeksforgeeks.org/difference-between-circuit-switching-and-packet-switching/

Geels, F. W. (2004). From sectoral systems of innovation to socio-technical systems: Insights about dynamics and change from sociology and institutional theory. *Research Policy, 33*(6-7), 897–920. doi:10.1016/j.respol.2004.01.015

Geels, F. W., & Schot, J. (2007). Typology of sociotechnical transition pathways. *Research Policy, 36*(3), 399–417. doi:10.1016/j.respol.2007.01.003

Georgakopoulos, A., Margaris, A., Tsagkaris, K., & Demestichas, P. (2016). Resource sharing in 5G contexts: Achieving sustainability with energy and resource efficiency. *IEEE Vehicular Technology Magazine, 11*(1), 40–49. doi:10.1109/MVT.2015.2508319

Georgieva, K. (2023). *Policy Priorities for the G20: One Earth, One Family, One Future*. IMF Blog. https://www.imf.org/en/Blogs/Articles/2023/02/22/policy-priorities-for-the-g20-one-earth-one-family-one-future

Ghaffar, S. H., Corker, J., & Fan, M. (2018). Additive manufacturing technology and its implementation in construction as an eco-innovative solution. *Automation in Construction, 93*, 1–11. doi:10.1016/j.autcon.2018.05.005

Ghazal, M., Ali, S., Haneefa, F., & Sweleh, A. (2016, March). Towards smart wearable real-time airport luggage tracking. In *2016 International Conference on Industrial Informatics and Computer Systems (CIICS)* (pp. 1-6). IEEE. 10.1109/ICCSII.2016.7462422

Ghobakhloo, M. (2018). The future of manufacturing industry: A strategic roadmap toward Industry 4.0. *Journal of Manufacturing Technology Management, 29*(6), 910–936. doi:10.1108/JMTM-02-2018-0057

Ghobakhloo, M. (2020). Industry 4.0, digitization, and opportunities for sustainability. *Journal of Cleaner Production, 252*, 119869. doi:10.1016/j.jclepro.2019.119869

Giddings, B., Hopwood, B., & O'brien, G. (2002). Environment, economy and society: Fitting them together into sustainable development. *Sustainable Development (Bradford), 10*(4), 187–196. doi:10.1002d.199

Gil, D., Hobson, S., Mojsilović, A., Puri, R., & Smith, J. R. (2020). AI for management: An overview. *The future of management in an AI world: Redefining purpose and strategy in the fourth industrial revolution*, 3-19.

Gimenez, C., Sierra, V., & Rodon, J. (2012). Sustainable operations: Their impact on the triple bottom line. *International Journal of Production Economics, 140*(1), 149–159. doi:10.1016/j.ijpe.2012.01.035

Ginters, E., & Martin-Gutierrez, J. (2013). Low cost augmented reality and RFID application for logistics items visualization. *Procedia Computer Science, 26*, 3–13. doi:10.1016/j.procs.2013.12.002

Giovannoni, E., & Fabietti, G. (2013). What is sustainability? A review of the concept and its applications. *Integrated Reporting*, 21-40. https://link.springer.com/chapter/10.1007/978-3-319-02168-3_2

Glasmeier, A. K., & Nebiolo, M. (2016). Thinking about smart cities: The travels of a policy idea that promises a great deal, but so far has delivered modest results. *Sustainability (Basel), 8*(11), 1–11. doi:10.3390u8111122

Gliessman, S. R. (2007). *Agroecology: The ecology of sustainable food systems*. CRC Press.

Global Reporting Initiative. (2011). *Sustainability reporting guidelines*. GRI.

Glockner, H., Jannek, K., Mahn, J., & Theis, B. (2014). *Augmented reality in logistics. Changing the way we see logistics: A DHL perspective*. DHL Customer Solutions & Innovation.

Gnambs, T., & Appel, M. (2019). Are robots becoming unpopular? Changes in attitudes towards autonomous robotic systems in Europe. *Computers in Human Behavior, 93*, 53–61. doi:10.1016/j.chb.2018.11.045

Gokarna, M., & Singh, R. (2021, February). DevOps: a historical review and future works. In *2021 International Conference on Computing, Communication, and Intelligent Systems (ICCCIS)* (pp. 366-371). IEEE. 10.1109/ICCCIS51004.2021.9397235

Golovina, T., Polyanin, A., Adamenko, A., Khegay, E., & Schepinin, V. (2020). Digital twins as a new paradigm of an industrial enterprise. *International Journal of Technology, 11*(6), 1115–1124. doi:10.14716/ijtech.v11i6.4427

Gomes, M., Pereira, R., Silva, M., de Vasconcelos, J. B., & Rocha, Á. (2022). KPI's for Evaluation of DevOps Teams. In *Information Systems and Technologies: WorldCIST 2022* (Vol. 3, pp. 142–156). Springer International Publishing. doi:10.1007/978-3-031-04829-6_13

Gond, J., & Crane, A. (2010). Corporate social performance disoriented: Saving the lost paradigm? *Business & Society, 49*(4), 677–703. doi:10.1177/0007650308315510

Gong, C., & Ribiere, V. (2021). Developing a unified definition of digital transformation. *Technovation, 102*, 102217. doi:10.1016/j.technovation.2020.102217

González-Alcaide, G. (2021). Bibliometric studies outside the information science and library science field: Uncontainable or uncontrollable? *Scientometrics, 126*(8), 6837–6870. doi:10.100711192-021-04061-3

González-Masip, J. (2020). Corporate sustainability, business sustainability, or corporate social responsibility: Some relevant criteria for choosing the right one. In G. Martín-de Castro, & J. González-Masip (Eds.), Knowledge management for corporate social responsibility (pp. 45-62). Business Science Reference (IGI Global). doi:10.4018/978-1-7998-4833-2.ch003

Goode, A. (2018). Biometrics for banking: Best practices and barriers to adoption. *Biometric Technology Today, 2018*(10), 5–7. doi:10.1016/S0969-4765(18)30156-5

Goodman, D., Sorj, B., & Wilkinson, J. (1987). *From farming to biotechnology*. Basil Blackwell.

Google. (n.d.). *Classroom Management Tools & Resources*. Google for Education. Retrieved November 20, 2022, from https://edu.google.com/workspace-for-education/classroom/

Görçün, Ö. F. (2022). Autonomous robots and utilization in logistics process. In İ. İyigün & Ö. F. Görçün (Eds.), *Logistics 4.0 and Future of Supply Chains* (pp. 83–93). Springer. doi:10.1007/978-981-16-5644-6_6

Gotham, K. F., Blum, M., & Campanella, R. (2014). Toward a new normal: Trauma, diversity, and the New Orleans Urban Long-Term Research Area Exploratory (ULTRA-Ex) Project. *Cities and the Environment, 7*(4), 31–43.

Gouverneur, J., & Netzer, N. (2014). Take the Wheel and Steer! Trade Unions and the Just Transition. In *State of the World 2014*. Island Press. doi:10.5822/978-1-61091-542-7_21

Grab, B., Olaru, M., & Gavril, R. M. (2019). The impact of digital transformation on strategic business management. *Ecoforum Journal, 8*(1).

Grabenwarter, U., & Liechtenstein, H., (2012). *In search of gamma: an unconventional perspective on impact investing*, IESE Business School, University of Navarra, and Family Office Circle Foundation.

Graham, E. (2021, December 14). *Who is behind the attacks on educators and public schools?* NEA. Retrieved June 23, 2022, from https://www.nea.org/advocating-for-change/new-from-nea/who-behind-attacks-educators-and-public-schools

Greco, M., Grimaldi, M., & Hanandi, M. (2013). How to select knowledge management systems: A framework to support managers. *International Journal of Engineering Business Management*, *5*, 6. doi:10.5772/56003

Grefsrud, E. S., Karlsen, Ø., Kvamme, B. O., Glover, K. A., Husa, V., Hansen, P. K., & Stien, L. H. (2021). *Risikorapport norsk fiskeoppdrett 2021-risikovurdering*. Havforskningsinstituttet.

Greiner, M., Böhmann, T., & Krcmar, H. (2007). A strategy for knowledge management. *Journal of Knowledge Management*, *11*(6), 3–15. doi:10.1108/13673270710832127

Gross, B. (2022a). *Worldwide connectivity solutions final project* [Unpublished paper]. Franklin University.

Gross, B. (2022b). *Worldwide connectivity solutions organizational analysis* [Unpublished paper]. Franklin University.

Gross, B. (2022c). *Worldwide connectivity solutions vision and roadmap* [Unpublished paper]. Franklin University.

Grötsch, V. M., Blome, C., & Schleper, M. C. (2013). Antecedents of proactive supply chain risk management: A contingency theory perspective. *International Journal of Production Research*, *51*(10), 2842–2867. doi:10.1080/00207543.2012.746796

Grover, V., & Davenport, T. (2001). General perspectives on knowledge management: Fostering a research agenda. *Journal of Management Information Systems*, *18*(1), 5–21. doi:10.1080/07421222.2001.11045672

Guggina, D. (2022). *A new era of fulfillment: Introducing Walmart's next generation fulfillment centers*. Walmart. https://corporate.walmart.com/newsroom/2022/06/03/a-new-era-of-fulfillment-introducing-walmarts-next-generation-fulfillment-centers

Gülşen, İ., & Özdemir, Ş. (2018). Perakendecilikte Teknolojik Yenilikler ve Uygulamalar. *Pazarlama Teorisi ve Uygulamaları Dergisi*, *4*(1), 103–138.

Gunal, M. (2019). Simulation for the better: The future in industry 4.0. In M. Gunal (Ed.), *Simulation for Industry 4.0* (pp. 275–283). Springer. doi:10.1007/978-3-030-04137-3_16

Gunasekaran, A., Papadopoulos, T., Dubey, R., Wamba, S. F., Childe, S. J., Hazen, B., & Akter, S. (2017). Big data and predictive analytics for supply chain and organizational performance. *Journal of Business Research*, *70*, 308–317. doi:10.1016/j.jbusres.2016.08.004

Gupta, R. K., Venkatachalapathy, M., & Jeberla, F. K. (2019, May). Challenges in adopting continuous delivery and DevOps in a globally distributed product team: a case study of a healthcare organization. In *2019 ACM/IEEE 14th International Conference on Global Software Engineering (ICGSE)* (pp. 30-34). IEEE 10.1109/ICGSE.2019.00020

Gupta, S., Rudd, J., & Lee, N. (2014). Business sustainability through successful integration of marketing and operations. *Industrial Marketing Management*, *43*(1), 3–5. doi:10.1016/j.indmarman.2013.10.004

Gürlek, M., & Çemberci, M. (2020). Understanding the relationships among knowledge-oriented leadership, knowledge management capacity, innovation performance, and organizational performance: A serial mediation analysis. *Kybernetes*, *49*(11), 2819–2846. doi:10.1108/K-09-2019-0632

Guthman, J. (2004). The trouble with 'organic lite' in California: A rejoinder to the 'conventionalisation' debate. *Sociologia Ruralis*, *44*(3), 301–316. doi:10.1111/j.1467-9523.2004.00277.x

Gu, Y., & Liu, Q. (2013). Research on the application of the Internet of things in reverse logistics information management. *Journal of Industrial Engineering and Management*, *6*(4), 963–973. doi:10.3926/jiem.793

Haar, J. M., de Fluiter, A., & Brougham, D. (2016). Abusive supervision and turnover intentions: The mediating role of perceived organisational support. *Journal of Management & Organization, 22*(2), 139–153. doi:10.1017/jmo.2015.34

Hacklin, F., & Wallnöfer, M. (2012). The business model in the practice of strategic decision making: Insights from a case study. *Management Decision, 50*(2), 166–188. doi:10.1108/00251741211203515

Haenlein, M., & Kaplan, A. (2019). A brief history of artificial intelligence: On the past, present, and future of artificial intelligence. *California Management Review, 61*(4), 5–14. doi:10.1177/0008125619864925

Hájnik, A., Harantová, V., & Kalašová, A. (2021). Use of electromobility and autonomous vehicles at airports in Europe and worldwide. *Transportation Research Procedia, 55*, 71–78. doi:10.1016/j.trpro.2021.06.008

Halpern, N., Mwesiumo, D., Suau-Sanchez, P., Budd, T., & Bråthen, S. (2021). Ready for digital transformation? The effect of organisational readiness, innovation, airport size and ownership on digital change at airports. *Journal of Air Transport Management, 90*, 101949. doi:10.1016/j.jairtraman.2020.101949 PMID:33041542

Hamid, N. S. S., Abdul Azziz, F., & Azizi, A. (2014). Virtual reality applications in manufacturing system. In *Science and Information Conference* (pp. 1034-1037). IEEE. https://doi.org/10.1109/SAI.2014.6918317

Hanafizadeh, P., & Mehrabioun, M. (2018). Application of SSM in tackling problematical situations from academicians' viewpoints. *Systemic Practice and Action Research, 31*(2), 179–220. doi:10.100711213-017-9422-y

Handa, P., Pagani, J., & Bedford, D. (2019). *Knowledge assets and knowledge audits*. Emerald. doi:10.1108/9781789737714

Handisyde, N., Telfer, T. C., & Ross, L. G. (2017). Vulnerability of aquaculture-related livelihoods to changing climate at the global scale. *Fish and Fisheries, 18*(3), 466–488. doi:10.1111/faf.12186

Hanisch, B., Lindner, F., Mueller, A., & Wald, A. (2009). Knowledge management in project environments. *Journal of Knowledge Management, 13*(4), 148–160. doi:10.1108/13673270910971897

Hansen, B. G. (2015). Robotic milking-farmer experiences and adoption rate in Jæren, Norway. *Journal of Rural Studies, 41*, 109–117. doi:10.1016/j.jrurstud.2015.08.004

Hansen, M. T., Nohria, N., & Tierney, T. (1999). What's Your Strategy for Managing Knowledge? *Harvard Business Review*, 1–11. PMID:10387767

Hans, P. E., & Skiver, J. (2007). Organizational Culture Restraining In-House Knowledge Transfer Between Project Managers - A Case Study. *Project Management Journal, 38*(1), 110–122. doi:10.1177/875697280703800111

Hariharan, A., Risling, M., Felic, A., & Ostertag, T. (2023). *Integration of Smart Glasses for Knowledge Transfer in Industrial Remote Maintenance: Learnings from Practice.* Paper presented at the Extended Reality and Metaverse, Cham, Switzerland.

Harisanty, D., Anna, N., Putri, T., Firdaus, A., & Noor Azizi, N. (2022). Leaders, practitioners and scientists' awareness of artificial intelligence in libraries: a pilot study. *Library Hi Tech.* doi:10.1108/LHT-10-2021-0356

Harper, M. (2019). *What are the best four components of knowledge management?* American Productivity & Quality Center (APQC). https://www.apqc.org/blog/what-are-best-four-components-knowledge-management#:~:text=The%20best%20four%20components%20of%20knowledge%20management%20are%20people%2C%20process,manage%20and%20measure%20knowledge%20flows

Harrigan, P., Daly, T. M., Coussement, K., Lee, J. A., Soutar, G. N., & Evers, U. (2021). Identifying influencers on social media. *International Journal of Information Management, 56*, 102246. doi:10.1016/j.ijinfomgt.2020.102246

Harvey, D. (1996). Justice, Nature, and the Geography of Difference. Blackwell.

Harwell, D. (2019). As Walmart turns to robots, it's the human workers who feel like machines. *The Washington Post*. https://www.washingtonpost.com/technology/2019/06/06/walmart-turns-robots-its-human-workers-who-feel-like-machines/

Hashem, I. A. T., Chang, V., Anuar, N. B., Adewole, K., Yaqoob, I., Gani, A., Ahmed, E., & Chiroma, H. (2016). The role of big data in a smart city. *International Journal of Information Management*, *36*(5), 748–758. doi:10.1016/j.ijinfomgt.2016.05.002

Hassani, H., Huang, X., & MacFeely, S. (2022). Impactful Digital Twin in the Healthcare Revolution. *Big Data and Cognitive Computing*, *6*(3), 83. doi:10.3390/bdcc6030083

Hasselbring, W., Henning, S., Latte, B., Möbius, A., Richter, T., Schalk, S., & Wojcieszak, M. (2019, March). Industrial develops. In *2019 IEEE International Conference on Software Architecture Companion (ICSA-C)* (pp. 123-126). IEEE. 10.1109/ICSA-C.2019.00029

Hawlitschek, F., Notheisen, B., & Teubner, T. (2018). The limits of trust-free systems: A literature review on blockchain technology and trust in the sharing economy. *Electronic Commerce Research and Applications*, *29*, 50–63. doi:10.1016/j.elerap.2018.03.005

Heater, B. (2022, May 23). Walmart adding Symbotic robots to warehouses throughout US. *TechCrunch*. https://social.techcrunch.com/2022/05/23/walmart-is-adding-symbotic-robots-to-warehouses-across-the-country/

He, B., & Bai, K. J. (2021). Digital twin-based sustainable intelligent manufacturing: A review. *Advances in Manufacturing*, *9*(1), 1–21. doi:10.100740436-020-00302-5

Heckmann, I. (2016). *Towards supply chain risk analytics*. Springer Nature. doi:10.1007/978-3-658-14870-6

Heisig, P. (2009). Harmonisation of knowledge management – comparing 160 KM frameworks around the globe. *Journal of Knowledge Management*, *13*(4), 4–31. doi:10.1108/13673270910971798

Helbing, D. (2013). Globally networked risks and how to respond. *Nature*, *497*(7447), 51–59. doi:10.1038/nature12047 PMID:23636396

Helo, P., & Hao, Y. (2017). Cloud manufacturing system for sheet metal processing. *Production Planning and Control*, *28*(6–8), 524–537. doi:10.1080/09537287.2017.1309714

Helpjuice. (2022). *Helpjuice*. https://helpjuice.com/

Hemon, A., Lyonnet, B., Rowe, F., & Fitzgerald, B. (2020). From Agile to DevOps: Smart skills and collaborations. *Information Systems Frontiers*, *22*(4), 927–945. doi:10.100710796-019-09905-1

Hemsley, J., & Mason, R. M. (2012). The nature of knowledge in the social media age: Implications for knowledge management models. In *2012 45th Hawaii International Conference on System Sciences* (pp. 3928-3937). IEEE.

Henderson, R. M., & Clark, K. B. (1990). Architectural innovation: The reconfiguration of existing product technologies and the failure of established firms. *Administrative Science Quarterly*, *35*(1), 9–30. doi:10.2307/2393549

Henriques, I., & Sadorsky, P. (1999). The relationship between environmental commitment and managerial perceptions of stakeholder importance. *Academy of Management Journal*, *42*(1), 87–99. doi:10.2307/256876

He, Q., Meadows, M., Angwin, D., Gomes, E., & Child, J. (2020). Strategic alliance research in the era of digital transformation: Perspectives on future research. *British Journal of Management*, *31*(3), 589–617. doi:10.1111/1467-8551.12406

Hermann, M., Pentek, T., & Otto, B. (2016). Design principles for industry 4.0 scenarios. In *Proceedings of the 2016 49th Hawaii International Conference on System Sciences (HICSS)* (pp. 3928-3937). IEEE Computer Society. 10.1109/HICSS.2016.488

Herrmann, S. M., & Hutchinson, C. F. (2005). The changing contexts of the desertification debate. *Journal of Arid Environments, 63*(3), 538–555. doi:10.1016/j.jaridenv.2005.03.003

Hidayatno, A., Destyanto, A. R., & Hulu, C. A. (2019). Industry 4.0 technology implementation impact to industrial sustainable energy in Indonesia: A model conceptualization. *Energy Procedia, 156*, 227–233. doi:10.1016/j.egypro.2018.11.133

Hill, K. (2015). *Ohio uses FirstNet video games to showcase public safety LTE potential.* RCR Wireless News. https://www.rcrwireless.com/20160517/featured/ohio-uses-firstnet-video-game-to-showcase-lte-potential-tag6

Hislop, D. (2013). *Knowledge management in organizations: A critical introduction.* Oxford University Press.

Hjortsø, C. N., Stræde, S., & Helles, F. (2006). Applying multi-criteria decision-making to protected areas and buffer zone management: A case study in the Royal Chitwan National Park, Nepal. *Journal of Forest Economics, 12*(2), 91–108. doi:10.1016/j.jfe.2006.03.001

Höchtl, J., Parycek, P., & Schöllhammer, R. (2016). Big data in the policy cycle: Policy decision making in the digital era. *Journal of Organizational Computing and Electronic Commerce, 26*(1-2), 147–169. doi:10.1080/10919392.2015.1125187

Hodgkins, K. (2014). Daily app: GoodGuide helps you find green, healthy and socially responsible products. *Engadget.* https://www.engadget.com/2014-04-22-daily-app-goodguide-helps-you-find-green-healthy- and-socially.html

Hofmann, E., Sternberg, H., Chen, H., Pflaum, A., & Prockl, G. (2019). Supply chain management and Industry 4.0: Conducting research in the digital age. *International Journal of Physical Distribution & Logistics Management, 9*(10), 945–955. doi:10.1108/IJPDLM-11-2019-399

Hofstede, G. (1991). *Cultures and organizations: Software of the mind.* McGraw-Hill.

Holling, C. S. (1973). Resilience and Stability of Ecological Systems. *Annual Review of Ecology and Systematics, 4*(1), 1–23. doi:10.1146/annurev.es.04.110173.000245

Holon, I. Q. (2021, October 12). *K-12 digital instruction and assessment market to reach $42b by 2025.* HolonIQ. Global Impact Intelligence. Retrieved August 12, 2022, from https://www.holoniq.com/notes/k-12-digital-instruction-and-assessment-market-to-reach-42b-by-2025

Holzman, V. (2013). A meta-analysis of brokering knowledge in project management. *International Journal of Project Management, 31*(1), 2–13. doi:10.1016/j.ijproman.2012.05.002

Homer-Dixon, T., Walker, B., Biggs, R., Crépin, A.-S., Folke, C., Lambin, E., Peterson, G., Rockström, J., Scheffer, M., Steffen, W., & Troell, M. (2015). Synchronous failure: The emerging causal architecture of global crisis. *Ecology and Society, 2015*(3), 20. doi:10.5751/ES-07681-200306

Hooff, B. V. D., & De Ridder, J. A. (2004). Knowledge sharing in context: The influence of organizational commitment, communication climate, and CMC use on knowledge sharing. *Journal of Knowledge Management, 8*(6), 117–130. doi:10.1108/13673270410567675

Hoorn, B., & Whitty, S. J. (2019). The five modes of comportment for project managing: Disclosing the tacit in project work. *International Journal of Project Management, 37*(3), 363–377. doi:10.1016/j.ijproman.2019.01.009

Hosen, M., Ogbeibu, S., Giridharan, B., Cham, T. H., Lim, W. M., & Paul, J. (2021). Individual motivation and social media influence on student knowledge sharing and learning performance: Evidence from an emerging economy. *Computers & Education, 172*, 104262. doi:10.1016/j.compedu.2021.104262

Howard, D., & Dai, D. (2014). Public perceptions of self-driving cars: The case of Berkeley, California. *Transportation Research Board 93rd Annual Meeting, 14*(4502), 1-16.

Huang, J. C., & Newell, S. (2003). Knowledge integration processes and dynamics within the context of cross-functional projects. *International Journal of Project Management, 21*(3), 167–176. doi:10.1016/S0263-7863(02)00091-1

Huang, P., & Shih, L. (2009). Effective environmental management through environmental knowledge management. *International Journal of Environmental Science and Technology, 6*(1), 35–50. doi:10.1007/BF03326058

Humphreys, P., Huang, G., & McIvor, R. (2002). An expert system for evaluating the make or buy decision. *Computers & Industrial Engineering, 42*(2/4), 567–585. doi:10.1016/S0360-8352(02)00052-9

Hung, S. W., Chen, P. C., & Chung, C. F. (2014). Gaining or losing? The social capital perspective on supply chain members' knowledge sharing of green practices. *Technology Analysis and Strategic Management, 26*(2), 189–206. doi:10.1080/09537325.2013.850475

Huynh-The, T., Pham, Q., Pham, X., Nguyen, T., Han, Z., & Kim, D. (2023). Artificial intelligence for the metaverse: A survey. *Engineering Applications of Artificial Intelligence, 117*, 105581. doi:10.1016/j.engappai.2022.105581

Hwang, Y. (2023). When makers meet the metaverse: Effects of creating NFT metaverse exhibition in maker education. *Computers & Education, 194*, 104693. doi:10.1016/j.compedu.2022.104693

Inder, S. (2023). Entrepreneurial Opportunities in Metaverse. In M. Gupta, P. Jindal, & S. Bansal (Eds.), *Promoting Consumer Engagement Through Emotional Branding and Sensory Marketing* (pp. 52–62). IGI Global.

Indoria, M., Kumar, P., Panwar, Y., & Sharma, T. (2021). Implementation of Industry 4.0 to achieve sustainable manufacturing in steel industry: A case study. *Systematic Literature Review and Meta Analysis Journal, 2*(1), 1–9. doi:10.54480lrm.v2i1.10

Infosys. (2017). *AI: The promise of a great future for retailers.* Retrieved April 12, 2022, from https://www.infosys.com/human-amplification/Documents/retail-ai-perspective.pdf

Inkinen, H. (2016). Review of empirical research on knowledge management practices and firm performance. *Journal of Knowledge Management, 20*(2), 230–257. doi:10.1108/JKM-09-2015-0336

Institutional Shareholder Services, Inc. (2023). *ESG ratings & rankings.* https://www.issgovernance.com/esg/ratings/

Intergovernmental Panel on Climate Change (IPCC). (2012). *Managing the Risks of Extreme Events and Disasters to Advance Climate Change Adaptation: Special Report of the Intergovernmental Panel on Climate Change.* IPCC/Cambridge University Press.

Intergovernmental Panel on Climate Change (IPCC). (2014). Summary for policymakers. In *Climate change 2014: impacts, adaptation, and vulnerability. part A: global and sectoral aspects.* Contribution of working group II to the fifth assessment report of the intergovernmental panel on climate change. Cambridge University Press ILO. https://www.ilo.org/global/topics/green-jobs/areas-of-work/WCMS_461943/lang--en/index.htm

Invest Northern Ireland. (n.d.). *Knowledge management and business growth: Advantages and disadvantages of knowledge management.* Nibusinessinfo.co.uk. https://www.nibusinessinfo.co.uk/content/advantages-and-disadvantages-knowledge-management

Islam, A. M., Ali, M. M., & Medhekar, A. (2017). Exploratory results of green production, sale, willing to pay and financing: Case of Bangladesh. *Environment and Ecology, 8*(3), 8–17. doi:10.21511/ee.08(3).2017.01

ISO. (2018). *ISO 30401:2018. Knowledge management systems—Requirements.*

ISO. (2018). *Knowledge management systems.* https://www.iso.org

Israilidis, J., Odusanya, K., & Mazhar, M. U. (2021). Exploring knowledge management perspectives in smart city research: A review and future research agenda. *International Journal of Information Management, 56,* 101989. doi:10.1016/j.ijinfomgt.2019.07.015

Ivančić, L., Vukšić, V. B., & Spremić, M. (2019). Mastering the digital transformation process: Business practices and lessons learned. *Technology Innovation Management Review, 9*(2), 36–50. doi:10.22215/timreview/1217

Ivanov, D. (2021). *Introduction to supply chain resilience: Management, modelling, technology.* Springer Nature.

Ivanov, D. (2020). Viable supply chain model: Integrating agility, resilience and sustainability perspectives – Lessons from and thinking beyond the COVID-19 pandemic. *Annals of Operations Research,* 1–21. doi:10.100710479-020-03640-6 PMID:32836614

Ivanov, D., & Dolgui, A. (2020). Viability of intertwined supply networks: Extending the supply chain resilience angles towards survivability. A position paper motivated by COVID-19 outbreak. *International Journal of Production Research, 58*(10), 2904–2915. doi:10.1080/00207543.2020.1750727

Jackson, T., & Victor, P. (2011). Productivity and Work in the 'Green Economy'. Some Theoretical Reflections and Empirical Tests. *Environmental Innovation and Societal Transitions, 1*(1), 101–108. doi:10.1016/j.eist.2011.04.005

Jacob, A., & Teuteberg, F. (2020). Towards a Taxonomy for Design options of social networking technologies in sustainable business models. *Sustainability (Basel), 13*(1), 81–100. doi:10.3390u13010081

Jamil, S., Rahman, M., & Fawad, M. (2022). A Comprehensive Survey of Digital Twins and Federated Learning for Industrial Internet of Things (IIoT), Internet of Vehicles (IoV) and Internet of Drones (IoD). *Applied System Innovation, 5*(3), 56. doi:10.3390/asi5030056

Jelenic, D. The importance of knowledge management in Organizations–with emphasis on the balanced scorecard learning and growth Perspective. *Knowledge and Learning, International Conference,* 453-483.

Jensen, H. S. (2008). Knowledge Management in the Knowledge Economy. *The Journal of Regional Analysis & Policy, 38*(2), 130–137.

Jeon, J. (2023). The impact of XR applications' user experience-based design innovativeness on loyalty. *Cogent Business & Management, 10*(1), 2161761. doi:10.1080/23311975.2022.2161761

Jha, S. K., Bilalovic, J., Jha, A., Patel, N., & Zhang, H. (2017). Renewable energy: Present research and future scope of artificial intelligence. *Renewable & Sustainable Energy Reviews, 77,* 297–317. doi:10.1016/j.rser.2017.04.018

Jilani, M. M. A. K., Fan, L., Islam, M. T., & Uddin, M. A. (2020). The influence of knowledge sharing on sustainable performance: A moderated mediation study. *Sustainability (Basel), 12*(3), 908–926. doi:10.3390u12030908

Jin, J., Xu, H., & Leng, B. (2022). Adaptive Points Sampling for Implicit Field Reconstruction of Industrial Digital Twin. *Sensors (Basel)*, *22*(17), 6630. doi:10.339022176630 PMID:36081088

Joffre, O. M., Klerkx, L., Dickson, M., & Verdegem, M. (2017). How is innovation in aquaculture conceptualized and managed? A systematic literature review and reflection framework to inform analysis and action. *Aquaculture (Amsterdam, Netherlands)*, *470*, 129–148. doi:10.1016/j.aquaculture.2016.12.020

John, M. M., Olsson, H. H., & Bosch, J. (2022). Towards an AI-driven business development framework: A multi-case study. *Journal of Software (Malden, MA)*, 2432. doi:10.1002mr.2432

Johnson, M. P. (2015). Sustainability management and small and medium-sized enterprises: Managers' awareness and implementation of innovative tools. *Corporate Social Responsibility and Environmental Management*, *22*(5), 271–285. doi:10.1002/csr.1343

Joshi, S. C., & Sheikh, A. A. (2015). 3D printing in aerospace and its long-term sustainability. *Virtual and Physical Prototyping*, *10*(4), 175–185. doi:10.1080/17452759.2015.1111519

Joshua, L., & Varghese, K. (2014). Automated recognition of construction labour activity using accelerometers in field situations. *International Journal of Productivity and Performance Management*, *67*(3), 841–862. doi:10.1108/IJPPM-05-2013-0099

Jothimani, D., & Sarmah, S. P. (2014). Supply chain performance measurement for third party logistics. *Benchmarking*, *21*(6), 944–963. doi:10.1108/BIJ-09-2012-0064

Jotkoff, E. (2022, February 1). *NEA survey: Massive staff shortages in schools leading to educator burnout; alarming number of educators indicating they plan to leave the profession.* NEA. Retrieved June 23, 2022, from https://www.nea.org/about-nea/media-center/press-releases/nea-survey-massive-staff-shortages-schools-leading-educator

Julian, H., Chung, T., & Wang, Y. (2023). Adoption of Metaverse in South East Asia: Vietnam, Indonesia, Malaysia. In P. C. Lai (Ed.), *Strategies and Opportunities for Technology in the Metaverse World* (pp. 196–234). IGI Global. doi:10.4018/978-1-6684-5732-0.ch012

Jun, X. (2009). Model Of cluster green supply chain performance evaluation based on circular economy. In *Proceedings of the 2009 Second International Conference on Intelligent Computation Technology and Automation* (vol. 3, pp. 941-944). IEEE. 10.1109/ICICTA.2009.692

Kache, F., & Seuring, S. (2017). Challenges and opportunities of digital information at the intersection of big data analytics and supply chain management. *International Journal of Operations & Production Management*, *37*(1), 10–36. doi:10.1108/IJOPM-02-2015-0078

Kachouie, R., Sedighadeli, S., Khosla, R., & Chu, M. T. (2014). Socially assistive robots in elderly care: A mixed-method systematic literature review. *International Journal of Human-Computer Interaction*, *30*(5), 369–393. doi:10.1080/10447318.2013.873278

Kaewunruen, S., & Lian, Q. (2019). Digital twin aided sustainability-based lifecycle management for railway turnout systems. *Journal of Cleaner Production*, *228*, 1537–1551. doi:10.1016/j.jclepro.2019.04.156

Kallis, G. (2011). In defense of degrowth. *Ecological Economics*, *70*(5), 873–880. doi:10.1016/j.ecolecon.2010.12.007

Kamble, S. S., Gunasekaran, A., Parekh, H., Mani, V., Belhadi, A., & Sharma, R. (2022). Digital twin for sustainable manufacturing supply chains: Current trends, future perspectives, and an implementation framework. *Technological Forecasting and Social Change*, *176*, 1–13. doi:10.1016/j.techfore.2021.121448

Kande, M., & Sonmez, M. (2020). *Don't fear AI: The tech will lead to long-term job growth.* World Economic Forum. https://www.weforum.org/agenda/2020/10/dont-fear-ai-it-will-lead-to-long-term-job-growth/

Karasneh, A. A. F. (2022). Revitalizing the BSC through knowledge management: The mediating role of intellectual capital. *Journal of Public Affairs*, *22*(1), e2359. doi:10.1002/pa.2359

Kasvi, J. J., Vartiainen, M., & Hailikari, M. (2003). Managing knowledge and knowledge competencies in projects and project organisations. *International Journal of Project Management*, *21*(8), 571–582. doi:10.1016/S0263-7863(02)00057-1

Katal, A., Bajoria, V., & Dahiya, S. (2019, March). DevOps: Bridging the gap between Development and Operations. In *2019 3rd International Conference on Computing Methodologies and Communication (ICCMC)* (pp. 1-7). IEEE.

Kelly, P., Tejeda-Delgado, C., & Slate, J. R. (2008). Superintendents' Views on Financial and Non-Financial Incentives on Teacher Recruitment and Retention. *The International Journal of Educational Leadership Preparation*, *3*(1), n1.

Keshmiri Neghab, H., Jamshidi, M., & Keshmiri Neghab, H. (2022). Digital Twin of a Magnetic Medical Microrobot with Stochastic Model Predictive Controller Boosted by Machine Learning in Cyber-Physical Healthcare Systems. *Information (Basel)*, *13*(7), 321. doi:10.3390/info13070321

Kesselman, M., & Esquivel, W. (2022). Technology on the move, Consumer Electronics Show 2022: The evolving metaverse and much more. *Library Hi Tech News*, *39*(5), 1–4. doi:10.1108/LHTN-03-2022-0038

Khajavi, S. H., Partanen, J., & Holmstrom, J. (2014). Additive manufacturing in the spare parts supply chain. *Computers in Industry*, *65*(1), 50–63. doi:10.1016/j.compind.2013.07.008

Khakurel, J., Penzenstadler, B., Porras, J., Knutas, A., & Zhang, W. (2018). The rise of artificial intelligence under the lens of sustainability. *Technologies*, *6*(4), 1–18. doi:10.3390/technologies6040100

Khan, A. A., Abrahamsson, P., & Niazi, M. (2022). Introduction to the special issue of managing software processes using soft computing techniques. *Information and Software Technology*, *152*, 107055. doi:10.1016/j.infsof.2022.107055 PMID:36034520

Khandelwal, K., & Upadhyay, A. K. (2021). Virtual reality interventions in developing and managing human resources. *Human Resource Development International*, *24*(2), 219–233. doi:10.1080/13678868.2019.1569920

Khan, S. A. R., Zkik, K., Belhadi, A., & Kamble, S. S. (2021). Evaluating barriers and solutions for social sustainability adoption in multi-tier supply chains. *International Journal of Production Research*, *59*(11), 3378–3397. doi:10.1080/00207543.2021.1876271

Khan, S. A., Koc, M., & Al-Ghamdi, S. G. (2021). Sustainability assessment, potentials, and challenges of 3D printed concrete structures: A systematic review for built environmental applications. *Journal of Cleaner Production, 303. Journal of Cleaner Production, 127027*, 1–14. doi:10.1016/j.jclepro.2021.127027

Kila, T. (2020). *Design and development of a governance framework for airports digitization: the case of turnaround coordinator*. Academic Press.

Kilpatrick, J., & Barter, L. (2020). *COVID-19: Managing supply chain risk and disruption.* Deloitte.

Kim, B., Graves, R., Heragu, S., & Onge, A. (2002). Intelligent agent modeling of an industrial warehousing problem. *IIE Transactions*, *34*(7), 601–612. doi:10.1080/07408170208928897

Kim, G., Humble, J., Debois, P., Willis, J., & Forsgren, N. (2021). *The DevOps handbook: How to create world-class agility, reliability, & security in technology organizations*. IT Revolution.

Kim, S., Park, H., & Lee, J. (2020). Word2vec-based latent semantic analysis (W2V-LSA) for topic modeling: A study on blockchain technology trend analysis. *Expert Systems with Applications*, *152*, 1–12. doi:10.1016/j.eswa.2020.113401

Kishore, J. K., Sandhu, M. S., & Wai Ling, C. (2009). Knowledge sharing in an American multinational company based in Malaysia. *Journal of Workplace Learning*, *21*(2), 125–142. doi:10.1108/13665620910934825

Kleine, A., & von Hauff, M. (2009). Sustainability-driven implementation of corporate social responsibility: Application of the integrative sustainability triangle. *Journal of Business Ethics*, *85*(S3), 517–533. doi:10.100710551-009-0212-z

Klein, N. (2015). *This Changes Everything: Capitalism vs. The Climate. Simon*. Schuster.

Kline, D., Leahy, J. E., Littell, J. S., Millington, J. D. A., Nielsen-Pincus, M., & Olsen, C. S., Paveglio, T. B., Roos, C. I., Steen-Adams, M. M., Stevens, F. R., Vukomanovic, J., White, E. M., & Bowman, D. M. J. S. (2016). Wildfire risk as a socioecological pathology. *Frontiers in Ecology and the Environment*, *4*, 276–284.

Knofius, N., van der Heijden, M. C., & Zijm, W. H. (2019). Consolidating spare parts for asset maintenance with additive manufacturing. *International Journal of Production Economics*, *208*, 269–280. doi:10.1016/j.ijpe.2018.11.007

Koenig, M. E. D. (2012, May 4). *What is KM? Knowledge management explained.* KMWorld.

Koilada, D. K. (2019, June). Business model innovation using modern DevOps. In 2019 IEEE Technology & Engineering Management Conference (TEMSCON) (pp. 1-6). IEEE. doi:10.1109/TEMSCON.2019.8813557

Kontić, L., & Vidicki, Đ. (2018). Strategy for digital organization: Testing a measurement tool for digital transformation. *Strategic Management*, *23*(1), 29–35. doi:10.5937/StraMan1801029K

Koskinen, K. U. (2004). Knowledge Management to Improve Project Communication and Implementation. *Project Management Journal*, *35*(1), 13–19. doi:10.1177/875697280403500203

Koskinen, K. U., & Pihlanto, P. (2008). Knowledge Sharing and Methods of Knowledge Sharing. In K. U. Koskinen & P. Pihlanto (Eds.), *Knowledge Management in Project-Based Companies: An Organic Perspective* (pp. 80–157). Palgrave Macmillan. doi:10.1057/9780230595071_6

Koskinen, K. U., Pihlanto, P., & Vanharanta, H. (2003). Tacit knowledge acquisition and sharing in a project work context. *International Journal of Project Management*, *21*(4), 281–290. doi:10.1016/S0263-7863(02)00030-3

Kovynyov, I., & Mikut, R. (2019). Digital technologies in airport ground operations. *NETNOMICS: Economic Research and Electronic Networking*, *20*(1), 1–30. doi:10.100711066-019-09132-5

KPMG. (2022). *Taxation of Aquaculture 2022*. KPMG.

Kraus, S., Kumar, S., Lim, W., Kaur, J., Sharma, A., & Schiavone, F. (2023). From moon landing to metaverse: Tracing the evolution of Technological Forecasting and Social Change. *Technological Forecasting and Social Change*, *189*, 122381. doi:10.1016/j.techfore.2023.122381

Kraus, S., Schiavone, F., Pluzhnikova, A., & Invernizzi, A. C. (2021). Digital transformation in healthcare: Analyzing the current state-of-research. *Journal of Business Research*, *123*, 557–567. doi:10.1016/j.jbusres.2020.10.030

Kreiger, M., & Pearce, J. M. (2013). Environmental life cycle analysis of distributed three-dimensional printing and conventional manufacturing of polymer products. *ACS Sustainable Chemistry & Engineering, 1*(12), 1511–1519. doi:10.1021c400093k

Kubáč, L. (2017). 3D printing in logistics. *Acta Logistica Moravica Periodický Internetový ČasopisV Oboru Logistiky, 7*(1), 8-15.

Kujala, J., Sachs, S., Leinonen, H., Heikkinen, A., & Laude, D. (2022). Stakeholder engagement: Past, present, and future. *Business & Society, 61*(5), 1136–1196. doi:10.1177/00076503211066595

Kumar Debnath, A., Haque, M. M., Chin, H. C., & Yuen, B. (2011). Sustainable urban transport: Smart technology initiatives in Singapore. *Transportation Research Record: Journal of the Transportation Research Board, 2243*(1), 38–45. doi:10.3141/2243-05

Kumar, S., & Barua, M. K. (2021). Sustainability of operations through disruptive technologies in the petroleum supply chain. *Benchmarking, 29*(5), 1–37. doi:10.1108/BIJ-02-2021-0086

Kurt, R. (2019). Industry 4.0 in terms of industrial relations and its impacts on labour life. *Procedia Computer Science, 158*, 590–601. doi:10.1016/j.procs.2019.09.093

Kurzweil, R. (1992). *The age of intelligent machines*. MIT Press.

Kuykendall, K. (2022, April 12). Report: Students used 74 different Ed Tech tools in fall 2021 semester, educators used 86. *THE Journal*. Retrieved June 23, 2022, from https://thejournal.com/articles/2022/04/12/students-used-74-different-ed-tech-tools-in-fall-2021-semester-while-educators-used-86.aspx

Kwanya, T., Stilwell, C., & Underwood, P. (2012). Intelligent libraries and apomediators: Distinguishing between Library 3.0 and Library 2.0. *Journal of Librarianship and Information Science, 45*(3), 187–197. doi:10.1177/0961000611435256

Lai, Y. L., Hsu, M. S., Lin, F. J., Chen, Y. M., & Lin, Y. H. (2014). The effects of industry cluster knowledge management on innovation performance. *Journal of Business Research, 67*(5), 734–739. doi:10.1016/j.jbusres.2013.11.036

Lapide, L. (2000). What about measuring supply chain performance. *Achieving Supply Chain Excellence Through Technology, 2*(2), 287–297.

Lasi, H., Fettke, P., Kemper, H., Feld, T., & Hoffmann, M. (2014). Industry 4.0. *Business & Information Systems Engineering, 6*(4), 239–242. doi:10.100712599-014-0334-4

Laszlo, A., Blachfellner, S., Bosch, O., Nguyen, N., Bulc, V., Edson, M., Wilby, J., & Pór, G. (2012). *Proceedings of the International Federation for Systems Research Conversations*. https://hdl.handle.net/2440/77156

Laurini, R. (2021). A primer of knowledge management for smart city governance. *Land Use Policy, 111*, 104832. doi:10.1016/j.landusepol.2020.104832

Leal Filho, W., Azul, A. M., Brandli, L., Özuyar, P.G., & Wall, T. (Eds.). (2022). Responsible Consumption and Production. Encyclopedia of the UN Sustainable Development Goals. In Socio-ecological balance. Springer. doi:10.1007/978-3-319-95726-5_300136

Leal Filho, W., Manolas, E., & Pace, P. (2015). The future we want: Key issues on sustainable development in higher education after Rio and the UN decade of education for sustainable development. *International Journal of Sustainability in Higher Education, 16*(1), 112–129. doi:10.1108/IJSHE-03-2014-0036

Leaning, J., & Guha-Sapir, D. (2013). Natural Disasters, Armed Conflict, and Public Health. *The New England Journal of Medicine, 369*(19), 1836–1842. doi:10.1056/NEJMra1109877 PMID:24195550

Leão, P., & da Silva, M. M. (2021). Impacts of digital transformation on firms' competitive advantages: A systematic literature review. *Strategic Change, 30*(5), 421–441. doi:10.1002/jsc.2459

Lee, K. (2016). How the Internet of things will change your world. *IdeaBook 2016, 5*(1). Retrieved April 10, 2022, from http://digital.supplychainquarterly.com/supplychain/ideabook_2016/?folio=50&sub_id=Hxh5qJH8aRP9&pg=1#pg1

Lee, A. H., Kang, H. Y., Hsu, C. F., & Hung, H. C. (2009). A green supplier selection model for high-tech industry. *Expert Systems with Applications, 36*(4), 7917–7927. doi:10.1016/j.eswa.2008.11.052

Lee, C. K. M., & Lam, J. S. L. (2012). Managing reverse logistics to enhance sustainability of industrial marketing. *Industrial Marketing Management, 41*(4), 589–598. doi:10.1016/j.indmarman.2012.04.006

Lee, E. A. (2008). Cyber physical systems: Design challenges. In *Proceedings of the 11th IEEE International Symposium on Object and Component-Oriented Real-Time Distributed Computing (ISORC)* (pp. 363-369). IEEE. 10.1109/ISORC.2008.25

Lee, G. M., Crespi, N., Choi, J. K., & Boussard, M. (2013). Internet of things. In E. Bertin, N. Crespi, & T. Magedanz (Eds.), *Evolution of telecommunication services* (pp. 257–282). Springer. doi:10.1007/978-3-642-41569-2_13

Lee, I., & Lee, K. (2015). The Internet of Things (IoT): Applications, investments, and challenges for enterprises. *Business Horizons, 58*(4), 431–440. doi:10.1016/j.bushor.2015.03.008

Lee, Y. M., An, L., Liu, F., Horesh, R., Chae, Y. T., & Zhang, R. (2013). Applying science and mathematics to big data for smarter buildings. *Annals of the New York Academy of Sciences, 1295*(1), 18–25. doi:10.1111/nyas.12193 PMID:23819911

Leiden, A., Herrmann, C., & Thiede, S. (2021). Cyber-physical production system approach for energy and resource efficient planning and operation of plating process chains. *Journal of Cleaner Production, 280*, 1–17. doi:10.1016/j.jclepro.2020.125160

Leite, L., Rocha, C., Kon, F., Milojicic, D., & Meirelles, P. (2019). A survey of DevOps concepts and challenges. *ACM Computing Surveys, 52*(6), 1–35. doi:10.1145/3359981

Leng, J., Zhou, M., Xiao, Y., Zhang, H., Liu, Q., Shen, W., Su, Q., & Li, L. (2021). Digital twins-based remote semi-physical commissioning of flow-type smart manufacturing systems. *Journal of Cleaner Production, 306. Article, 127278*, 1–17. doi:10.1016/j.jclepro

Leseure, M. J., & Brookes, N. J. (2004). Knowledge management benchmarks for project management. *Journal of Knowledge Management, 8*(1), 103–116. doi:10.1108/13673270410523943

Lestari, N. D. I., & Subriadi, A. P. (2021, September). EdTech Investment: Optimism, Pessimism, and Uncertainty. In *2021 International Conference on Electrical and Information Technology (IEIT)* (pp. 239-245). IEEE. 10.1109/IEIT53149.2021.9587429

Li, J., Li, W., Zhang, X., Duan, J., & Wang, H. (2022, March). Design of DevOps environment based on cloud platform architecture. In *2022 IEEE 6th Information Technology and Mechatronics Engineering Conference (ITOEC)* (Vol. 6, pp. 95-99). IEEE. 10.1109/ITOEC53115.2022.9734518

Liao, M., Lan, K., & Yao, Y. (2022). Sustainability implications of artificial intelligence in the chemical industry: A conceptual framework. *Journal of Industrial Ecology*, *26*(1), 164–182. doi:10.1111/jiec.13214

Liao, S. (2003). Knowledge management technologies and applications: A literature review from 1995 to 2002. *Expert Systems with Applications*, *25*(2), 155–164. doi:10.1016/S0957-4174(03)00043-5

Liberatore, M. J., & Pollack-Johnson, B. (2013). Improving project management decision-making by modeling quality, time, and cost continuously. *IEEE Transactions on Engineering Management*, *60*(3), 518–528. doi:10.1109/TEM.2012.2219586

Lichtenthaler, U., & Lichtenthaler, E. (2009). A capability-based framework for open innovation: Complementing absorptive capacity. *Journal of Management Studies*, *46*(8), 1315–1338. doi:10.1111/j.1467-6486.2009.00854.x

Liebowitz, J. (2001). Knowledge management and its link to artificial intelligence. *Expert Systems with Applications*, *20*(1), 1–6. doi:10.1016/S0957-4174(00)00044-0

Liebowitz, J., & Megbolugbe, I. (2003). A set of frameworks to aid the project manager in conceptualizing and implementing knowledge management initiatives. *International Journal of Project Management*, *21*(3), 189–198. doi:10.1016/S0263-7863(02)00093-5

Li, L., Su, Q., & Chen, X. (2011). Ensuring supply chain quality performance through applying the SCOR model. *International Journal of Production Research*, *49*(1), 33–57. doi:10.1080/00207543.2010.508934

Lindholm, M., & Behrends, S. (2012). Challenges in urban freight transport planning–a review in the Baltic Sea Region. *Journal of Transport Geography*, *22*, 129–136. doi:10.1016/j.jtrangeo.2012.01.001

Li, S., Cui, X., Huo, B., & Zhao, X. (2019). Information sharing, coordination, and supply chain performance: The moderating effect of demand uncertainty. *Industrial Management & Data Systems*, *119*(5), 1046–1071. doi:10.1108/IMDS-10-2018-0453

Litman, T. (2017). *Autonomous vehicle implementation predictions*. Victoria Transport Policy Institute.

Little, M. (2019). *Building an agile KM roadmap*. KM Institute. https://www.kminstitute.org/blog/building-agile-km-roadmap

Liu, C., & Xu, X. (2017). Cyber-physical machine tool: The era of machine tool 4.0. *The 50th CIRP Conference on Manufacturing Systems. Procedia CIRP*, *63*, 70–75. doi:10.1016/j.procir.2017.03.078

Loafman, J. (2020). *Choice and convenience: Omnichannel around the world, today and into the future*. Walmart. https://corporate.walmart.com/newsroom/2020/12/09/choice-and-convenience-omnichannel-around-the-world-today-and-into-the-future

Longo, F. (2011). Advances of modeling and simulation in supply chain and industry. *Simulation*, *87*(8), 651–656. doi:10.1177/0037549711418033

López-Robles, J. R., Cobo, M. J., Gutiérrez-Salcedo, M., Martínez-Sánchez, M., Gamboa-Rosales, N. K., & Herrera-Viedma, E. (2021). 30th anniversary of applied intelligence: A combination of bibliometrics and thematic analysis using SciMAT. *Applied Intelligence*, *51*(9), 6547–6568. doi:10.100710489-021-02584-z

Lovdata. (2021). *Forskrift om endring av laksetildelingsforskriften - Fastsatt av Nærings- og fiskeridepartementet 1. juli 2021 med hjemmel i lov 17. juni 2005 nr. 79 om akvakultur (akvakulturloven) § 4, § 5, § 6 og § 7*. Oslo: Lovdata.

Love, P., Fong, P., & Irani, Z. (2005). *Management of knowledge in project environments*. Elsevier.

Lubberink, R., Blok, V., Van Ophem, J., & Omta, O. (2017). Lessons for responsible innovation in the business context: A systematic literature review of responsible, social and sustainable innovation practices. *Sustainability (Basel)*, *9*(5), 721. doi:10.3390u9050721

Lundvall, B.-Å. (2010). *National systems of innovation: Toward a theory of innovation and interactive learning*. Anthem press. doi:10.7135/UPO9781843318903

Luthra, S., & Mangla, S. K. (2018). Evaluating challenges to Industry 4.0 initiatives for supply chain sustainability in emerging economies. *Process Safety and Environmental Protection*, *117*, 168–179. doi:10.1016/j.psep.2018.04.018

Luz, A., & Pires, I. (2014). Regularização das Hortas Urbanasna Cidade de Lisboa - as Hortas Sociais do Vale de Chelas. Livro de Atas do 1° Congresso da AssociaçãoInternacional de CiênciasSociais e Humanas me Língua Portuguesa, 6935–6952.

Lwakatare, L. E., Crnkovic, I., & Bosch, J. (2020, September). DevOps for AI–Challenges in the Development of AI-enabled Applications. In *2020 International Conference on Software, Telecommunications and Computer Networks (SoftCOM)* (pp. 1-6). IEEE. 10.23919/SoftCOM50211.2020.9238323

Lykou, G., Anagnostopoulou, A., & Gritzalis, D. (2018). Smart airport cybersecurity: Threat mitigation and cyber resilience controls. *Sensors (Basel)*, *19*(1), 19. doi:10.339019010019 PMID:30577633

Mabkhot, M. M., Ferreira, P., Maffei, A., Podržaj, P., Mądziel, M., Antonelli, D., ... Lohse, N. (2021). Mapping Industry 4.0 enabling technologies into united nations sustainability development goals. *Sustainability*, *13*(5), 1–33. doi:10.3390u13052560

Macarthy, R. W., & Bass, J. M. (2020, August). An empirical taxonomy of DevOps in practice. In *2020 46th Euromicro Conference on Software Engineering and Advanced Applications (SEAA)* (pp. 221-228). IEEE. 10.1109/SEAA51224.2020.00046

Machlis, G., Force, J., & Burch, W. J. Jr. (1997). The Human Ecosystem Part I: The Human Ecosystem as an Organizing Concept in Ecosystem Management. *Society & Natural Resources*, *10*(4), 347–367. doi:10.1080/08941929709381034

Maddahi, Y., & Chen, S. (2022). Applications of Digital Twins in the Healthcare Industry: Case Review of an IoT-Enabled Remote Technology in Dentistry. *Virtual Worlds*, *1*(1), 20–41. doi:10.3390/virtualworlds1010003

Maguire, M., & Bevan, N. (2002). User requirements analysis: A review of supporting methods. In J. Hammond, T. Gross, & J. Wesson (Eds.), Usability. Gaining a Competitive Edge (pp. 133-148). Springer Science+Business Media. doi:10.1007/978-0-387-35610-5

Mahajan, R., & Bose, M. (2018). Business sustainability: Exploring the meaning and significance. *ImiKonnect, 7*(2), 8-13. https://www.researchgate.net/profile/Montu-Bose-2/publication/333078727_Business_Sustainability_Exploring_the_Meaning_and_Significance/links/5cda460f458515712ea950ba/Business-Sustainability-Exploring-the-Meaning-and-Significance.pdf

Mahdi, O. R., Nassa, I. A., & Almsafir, M. K. (2019). Knowledge management processes and sustainable competitive advantage: An empirical examination in private universities. *Journal of Business Research*, *94*, 320–334. doi:10.1016/j.jbusres.2018.02.013

Mahmood, A., Zen, H., & Hilles, S. M. S. (2018). Big data and privacy issues for connected vehicles in intelligent transportation systems. In S. Sakr & A. Zomaya (Eds.), *Encyclopedia of Big Data Technologies*. Springer. doi:10.1007/978-3-319-63962-8_234-1

Majchrzak, A., Faraj, S., Kane, G. C., & Azad, B. (2013). The contradictory influence of social media affordances on online communal knowledge sharing. *Journal of Computer-Mediated Communication, 19*(1), 38–55. doi:10.1111/jcc4.12030

Mamonov, S., & Triantoro, T. M. (2018). The strategic value of data resources in emergent industries. *International Journal of Information Management, 39*, 146–155. doi:10.1016/j.ijinfomgt.2017.12.004

Manavalan, E., & Jayakrishna, K. (2019). A review of Internet of Things (IoT) embedded sustainable supply chain for industry 4.0 requirements. *Computers & Industrial Engineering, 127*, 925–953. doi:10.1016/j.cie.2018.11.030

Manika, J., Lund, S., Chui, M., Bughin, J., Woetzel, J., Brata, P., Ko, R., & Sanghvi, S. (2017). *Jobs lost, jobs gained: Workforce transitions in a time of automation*. McKinsey Global Institute.

Mani, V., Gunasekaran, A., & Delgado, C. (2018). Enhancing supply chain performance through supplier social sustainability: An emerging economy perspective. *International Journal of Production Economics, 195*, 259–272. doi:10.1016/j.ijpe.2017.10.025

Mannan, B., Jameel, S. S., & Haleem, A. (2013). *Knowledge Management in Project Management: An ISM Approach*. Lambert Academic Publishing.

Manners-Bell, J., & Lyon, K. (2019). *The logistics and supply chain innovation handbook: Disruptive technologies and new business models*. Kogan Page Publishers.

Manson, S. M. (2001). Simplifying complexity: A review of complexity theory. *Geoforum, 32*(3), 405–414. doi:10.1016/S0016-7185(00)00035-X

Mansourian, S. (2017). Governance and forest landscape restoration: A framework to support decision-making. *Journal for Nature Conservation, 37*, 21–30. doi:10.1016/j.jnc.2017.02.010

Manyika, J., Chui, M., Bughin, J., Dobbs, R., Bisson, P., & Marrs, A. (2013). *Disruptive technologies: Advances that will transform life, business, and the global economy*. McKinsey Global Institute.

Marjani, M., Nasaruddin, F., Gani, A., Karim, A., Hashem, I. A. T., Siddiqa, A., & Yaqoob, I. (2017). Big IoT data analytics: Architecture, opportunities, and open research challenges. *IEEE Access : Practical Innovations, Open Solutions, 5*, 5247–5261. doi:10.1109/ACCESS.2017.2689040

Markard, J., Raven, B., & Truffer, B. (2012). Sustainability transitions: An emerging field of research and its prospects. *Research Policy, 41*(6), 955–967. doi:10.1016/j.respol.2012.02.013

Markley, H. (2021). *Remembering 9/11 and how it changed public safety communications*. FirstNet. https://www.firstnet.gov/newsroom/blog/remembering-911-and-how-it-changed-public-safety-communications

Markley, M. J., & Davis, L. (2007). Exploring future competitive advantage through sustainable supply chains. *International Journal of Physical Distribution & Logistics Management, 9*(37), 763–774. doi:10.1108/09600030710840859

Marr, B. (2021). *Walmart: Big data analytics at the world's biggest retailer*. https://bernardmarr.com/walmart-big-data-analytics-at-the-worlds-biggest-retailer/

Martín-de Castro, G., Amores-Salvadó, J., & Díez-Vial, I. (2022). Framing the evolution of the "environmental strategy" concept: Exploring a key construct for the environmental policy agenda. *Business Strategy and the Environment*.

Martin, R., & Moodysson, J. (2013). Comparing knowledge bases: On the geography and organization of knowledge sourcing in the regional innovation system of Scania, Sweden. *European Urban and Regional Studies, 20*(2), 170–187. doi:10.1177/0969776411427326

Martins, V. W. B., Rampasso, I. S., Anholon, R., Quelhas, O. L. G., & Leal Filho, W. (2019). Knowledge management in the context of sustainability: Literature review and opportunities for future research. *Journal of Cleaner Production*, *229*, 489–500. doi:10.1016/j.jclepro.2019.04.354

Marwick, A. D. (2001). Knowledge management technology. *IBM Systems Journal*, *40*(4), 814–830. doi:10.1147j.404.0814

Ma, S., Zhang, Y., Lv, J., Yang, H., & Wu, J. (2019). Energy-cyber-physical system enabled management for energy-intensive manufacturing industries. *Journal of Cleaner Production*, *226*, 892–903. doi:10.1016/j.jclepro.2019.04.134

Massingham, P. (2019). *Knowledge Management*. SAGE Publications, Ltd.

Matsui, B. M. A., & Goya, D. H. (2021, November). Applying DevOps to machine learning processes: A systematic mapping. In *Anais do XVIII Encontro Nacional de Inteligência Artificial e Computacional* (pp. 559–570). SBC. doi:10.5753/eniac.2021.18284

Matt, C., Hess, T., & Benlian, A. (2015). Digital transformation strategies. *Business & Information Systems Engineering*, *57*(5), 339–343. doi:10.100712599-015-0401-5

Mazur, M., Spahić, A., Grabar, D., Grd, P., Sedlbauer, G., Sikorska, K., & Beamonte, E. P. (2014). Knowledge Management 2.0 - Handbook for companies. Lifelong Learning Programme, European Commission.

Mboweni, T., Masombuka, T., & Dongmo, C. (2022, July). A Systematic Review of Machine Learning DevOps. In *2022 International Conference on Electrical, Computer and Energy Technologies (ICECET)* (pp. 1-6). IEEE.

McAllister, J. W., & Kornet, D. J. (2002). Historical and Structural Approaches in the Natural and Human Sciences In *Four Analytical Essays and a Critical Debate on the Future of Scholastic Endeavour.* Amsterdam University Press. https://www.jstor.org/stable/j.ctt46mzw4.5

McAllister, W. (2023). *Circuit terminology*. Khan Academy. https://www.khanacademy.org/science/electrical-engineering/ee-circuit-analysis-topic/circuit-elements/a/ee-circuit-terminology

McElroy, M. W. (2000). Integrating complexity theory, knowledge management and organisational learning. *Journal of Knowledge Management*, *4*(3), 195–203. doi:10.1108/13673270010377652

McMichael, P. (2009). A food regime genealogy. *The Journal of Peasant Studies*, *36*(1), 139–169. doi:10.1080/03066150902820354

Mehdikhani, R., & Valmohammadi, C. (2019). Strategic collaboration and sustainable supply chain management: The mediating role of internal and external knowledge sharing. *Journal of Enterprise Information Management*, *32*(5), 778–806. doi:10.1108/JEIM-07-2018-0166

Merat, A., & Bo, D. (2013). Strategic analysis of knowledge firms: The links between knowledge management and leadership. *Journal of Knowledge Management*, *17*(1), 3–15. doi:10.1108/13673271311300697

Metaxiotis, K., Ergazakis, K., Samouilidis, E., & Psarras, J. (2003). Decision support through knowledge management: The role of the artificial intelligence. *Information Management & Computer Security*, *11*(5), 216–221. doi:10.1108/09685220310500126

Meydan, C. H. (2023). Havayolu işletmelerinde dijital dönüşüm uygulamaları üzerine bir inceleme. *Journal of Aviation Research*, *5*(1), 65–82.

Meza-Ruiz, I. D., Rocha-Lona, L., del Rocío Soto-Flores, M., Garza-Reyes, J. A., Kumar, V., & Lopez-Torres, G. C. (2017). Measuring business sustainability maturity-levels and best practices. *Procedia Manufacturing*, *11*, 751–759. doi:10.1016/j.promfg.2017.07.176

Middle-Class Tax Relief and Job Creation Act of 2012. (2012). http://catalog.gpo.gov/fdlpdir/locate.jsp?ItemNumber=0575&SYS=000869737

Midt-NorskHavbruk. (2020). *Installasjon og testing før utsett av fisk i Aquatraz G3–Driftserfaring fra Aquatraz G1, G2 og G3*. Rørvik.

Midt-NorskHavbruk. (2021). *Aquatraz: Sluttrapport for biologiprogram og tetthetsprogram – merdgenerasjon 3 på Årsetfjorden*. Rørvik.

Midt-NorskHavbruk. (2022). *Aquatrazprosjektet - Sluttrapport. Utvikling av semi-lukket stålmerd fra konsept til kommersielt produkt*. Rørvik.

Migdadi, M. M. (2022). Knowledge management processes, innovation capability and organizational performance. *International Journal of Productivity and Performance Management*, *71*(1), 182–210. doi:10.1108/IJPPM-04-2020-0154

Miljødirektoratet. (2022). *Miljøstatus.no, Påvirkning fra fiskeoppdrett*. Miljødirektoratet.

Mitroulis, D., & Kitsios, F. (2019, February). Digital transformation strategy: A literature review. In *Proceedings of the 6th National Student Conference of HELORS, Xanthi, Greece* (pp. 59-61). Academic Press.

Moffatt, I. (2004). Global warming: Scientific modeling and its relationship to the economic dimensions of policy. In A. D. Owen & N. Hanley (Eds.), *The economics of climate change* (pp. 6–34). Routledge.

Mohamed Hashim, M. A., Tlemsani, I., & Matthews, R. (2021). Higher education strategy in digital transformation. *Education and Information Technologies*, 1–25. PMID:34539217

Mohamed, M., Gomaa, H., & El-Sherif, N. (2018). Evaluation of current smart airport technologies implemented in Cairo international airport. International Journal of Heritage. *Tourism and Hospitality*, *12*(2), 130–140.

Mohamed, M., Stankosky, M., & Mohamed, M. (2009). An empirical assessment of knowledge management criticality for sustainable development. *Journal of Knowledge Management*, *13*(5), 271–286. doi:10.1108/13673270910988105

Mois, G., Sanislav, T., & Folea, S. C. (2016). A cyber-physical system for environmental monitoring. *IEEE Transactions on Instrumentation and Measurement*, *65*(6), 1463–1471. doi:10.1109/TIM.2016.2526669

Montes, J. O. (2016). Impacts of 3D printing on the development of new business models. In *Proceedings of the 2016 IEEE European Technology and Engineering Management Summit (E-TEMS)* (1-9). IEEE. 10.1109/E-TEMS.2016.7912605

Moodysson, J., Coenen, L., & Asheim, B. (2008). Explaining spatial patterns of innovation: Analytical and synthetic modes of knowledge creation in the Medicon Valley life-science cluster. *Environment and Planning A. Environment & Planning A*, *40*(5), 1040–1056. doi:10.1068/a39110

Moore, J. W. (2015). *Capitalism in the Web of Life: Ecology and the Accumulation of Capital*. Verso.

Moore, M., Tjornbo, O., Enfors, E., Knapp, C., Hodbod, J., Baggio, J., Norström, A., Olsson, P., & Biggs, D. (2014). Studying the Complexity of Change: Toward an Analytical Framework for Understanding Deliberate Social-Ecological Transformations. *Ecology and Society*, *19*(4), 54. doi:10.5751/ES-06966-190454

Morali, O., & Searcy, C. (2013). A review of sustainable supply chain management practices in Canada. *Journal of Business Ethics*, *117*(3), 635–658. doi:10.100710551-012-1539-4

Morella, P., Lambán, M. P., Royo, J., Sánchez, J. C., & Ng Corrales, L. D. C. (2020). Development of a new green indicator and its implementation in a cyber–physical system for a green supply chain. *Sustainability (Basel), 12*(20), 1–19. doi:10.3390u12208629

Morgan, K. (2017). Nurturing novelty: Regional innovation policy in the age of smart specialisation. *Environment and Planning C. Politics and Space, 35*(4), 569–583.

Morris, M., Schindehutte, M., & Allen, J. (2005). The entrepreneur's business model: Toward a unified perspective. *Journal of Business Research, 58*(6), 726–735. doi:10.1016/j.jbusres.2003.11.001

Morrison, J. R., Ross, S. M., & Cheung, A. C. K. (2019). From the market to the classroom: How ed-tech products are procured by school districts interacting with vendors. *Educational Technology Research and Development, 67*(2), 389–421. doi:10.100711423-019-09649-4

Morris, P. (2002). Science, objective knowledge, and the theory of project management. *Proceedings of the Institution of Civil Engineers. Civil Engineering, 150*(2), 82–90. doi:10.1680/cien.2002.150.2.82

Mourtzis, D., Angelopoulos, J., & Panopoulos, N. (2023). Blockchain Integration in the Era of Industrial Metaverse. *Applied Sciences (Basel, Switzerland), 13*(3), 1353. doi:10.3390/app13031353

Mourtzis, D., Vlachou, A., & Zogopoulos, V. (2017). Cloud-based augmented reality remote maintenance through shop-floor monitoring: A product-service system approach. *Journal of Manufacturing Science and Engineering, 139*(061011), 1–11. doi:10.1115/1.4035721

Mrňa, D., Badánik, B., & Novák, A. (2021). Internet of Things as an optimization tool for smart airport concept. *European Transport-Trasporti Europei*, 82.

Mueller, J. (2012). Knowledge sharing between project teams and their cultural antecedents. *Journal of Knowledge Management, 16*(3), 435–447. doi:10.1108/13673271211238751

Mueller, J. (2015). Formal and Informal Practices of Knowledge Sharing Between Project Teams and Enacted Cultural Characteristics. *Project Management Journal, 46*(1), 53–68. doi:10.1002/pmj.21471

Mujber, T. S., Szecsi, T., & Hashmi, M. S. J. (2004). Virtual reality applications in manufacturing process simulation. *Journal of Materials Processing Technology, 155-156*, 1834–1838. doi:10.1016/j.jmatprotec.2004.04.401

Müller, J. M., Kiel, D., & Voigt, K. I. (2018). What drives the implementation of Industry 4.0? The role of opportunities and challenges in the context of sustainability. *Sustainability (Basel), 10*(1), 247. doi:10.3390u10010247

Multi-Agency Radio Communication System . (2022). Ohio Department of Administrative Services. https://das.ohio.gov/technology-and-strategy/marcs

Muñoz, I., Alonso-Madrid, J., Menéndez-Muñiz, M., Uhart, M., Canou, J., Martin, C., Fabritius, M., Calvo, L., Poudelet, L., Cardona, R., Lombois-Burger, H., Vlasopoulos, N., Bouyssou, C., Dirrenberger, J., Papacharalampopoulos, A., & Stavropoulos, P. (2021). Life cycle assessment of integrated additive-subtractive concrete 3D printing. *International Journal of Advanced Manufacturing Technology, 112*(7), 2149–2159. doi:10.100700170-020-06487-0

Muñoz-Pascual, L., Galende, J., & Curado, C. (2019). Human resource management contributions to knowledge sharing for a sustainability-oriented performance: A mixed methods approach. *Sustainability (Basel), 12*(1), 161–180. doi:10.3390u12010161

Mura, M., Longo, M., Micheli, P., & Bolzani, D. (2018). The evolution of sustainability measurement research. *International Journal of Management Reviews, 20*(3), 661–695. doi:10.1111/ijmr.12179

Myers, S., & Frumkin, H. (2020). *Planetary Health: Protecting Nature to Protect Ourselves*. Island Press. doi:10.5822/978-1-61091-966-1

Myrbakken, H., & Colomo-Palacios, R. (2017). DevSecOps: a multivocal literature review. In *Software Process Improvement and Capability Determination: 17th International Conference, SPICE 2017, Palma de Mallorca, Spain, October 4–5, 2017, Proceedings* (pp. 17-29). Springer International Publishing.

Mystakidis, S. (2023). Sustainable Engagement in Open and Distance Learning With Play and Games in Virtual Reality: Playful and Gameful Distance Education in VR. In I. R. Management Association (Ed.), Research Anthology on Virtual Environments and Building the Metaverse (pp. 297-312). IGI Global.

Nabiyev, V. (2012). *Yapay zeka*. Seçkin Yayıncılık.

Nadkarni, S., & Prügl, R. (2021). Digital transformation: A review, synthesis and opportunities for future research. *Management Review Quarterly*, *71*(2), 233–341. doi:10.100711301-020-00185-7

Nærings-ogfiskeridepartementet. (2015). *Meld. St. 16 (2014-2015) - Forutsigbar og miljømessig bærekraftig vekst i norsk lakse- og ørretoppdrett*. Oslo: Nærings-og fiskeridepartementet

Nahm, A. Y., & Vonderembse, M. A. (2002). Theory development: An industrial/post- industrial perspective on manufacturing. *International Journal of Production Research*, *40*(9), 2067–2095. doi:10.1080/00207540210128233

Narongou, D., & Sun, Z. (2021). Big data analytics for smart airport management. In *Intelligent analytics with advanced multi-industry applications* (pp. 209–231). IGI Global. doi:10.4018/978-1-7998-4963-6.ch010

Naslund, D., & Williamson, S. (2010). What is management in supply chain management? A critical review of definitions, frameworks, and terminology. *Journal of Management Policy and Practice*, *11*(4), 11–28.

Nautiyal, S. (2011). Can conservation and development interventions in the Indian Central Himalaya ensure environmental sustainability? A socioecological evaluation. *Sustainability Science*, *6*(2), 151–167. doi:10.100711625-011-0126-4

Nazaretsky, T., Ariely, M., Cukurova, M., & Alexandron, G. (2022). Teachers' trust in AI-powered educational technology and a professional development program to improve it. *British Journal of Educational Technology*, *53*(4), 914–931. doi:10.1111/bjet.13232

Negri, E., Fumagalli, L., & Macchi, M. (2017). A review of the roles of digital twin in SFS-based production systems. *Procedia Manufacturing*, *11*, 939–948. doi:10.1016/j.promfg.2017.07.198

Nelson, D. M., Marsillac, E., & Rao, S. S. (2012). Antecedents and evolution of the green supply chain. *Journal of Operations and Supply Chain Management*, 29-43. Doi:10.12660/joscmv1n1p29-43

Nemati, H. R., Steiger, D. M., Iyer, L. S., & Herschel, R. T. (2002). Knowledge warehouse: An architectural integration of knowledge management, decision support, artificial intelligence and data warehousing. *Decision Support Systems*, *33*(2), 143–161. doi:10.1016/S0167-9236(01)00141-5

Nesheim, T., & Hunskaar, H. M. (2015). When employees and external consultants work together on projects: Challenges of knowledge sharing. *International Journal of Project Management*, *33*(7), 1417–1424. doi:10.1016/j.ijproman.2015.06.010

Nguyen, T., Duong, Q. H., Van Nguyen, T., Zhu, Y., & Zhou, L. (2021). Knowledge mapping of digital twin and physical internet in supply chain management: A systematic literature review. *International Journal of Production Economics*, *244*, 1–20. doi:10.1016/j.ijpe.2021.108381

Nguyen, V. M., Young, N., & Cooke, S. J. (2017). A roadmap for knowledge exchange and mobilization research in conservation and natural resource management. *Conservation Biology*, *31*(4), 789–798. doi:10.1111/cobi.12857 PMID:27767241

Nicolopoulou, K. (2011). Towards a theoretical framework for knowledge transfer in the field of CSR and sustainability. *Equality, Diversity and Inclusion*, *30*(6), 524–538. doi:10.1108/02610151111157738

Nishant, R., Kennedy, M., & Corbett, J. (2020). Artificial intelligence for sustainability: Challenges, opportunities, and a research agenda. *International Journal of Information Management*, *53*, 102104. doi:10.1016/j.ijinfomgt.2020.102104

Nix, N. (2001). Customer service in supply chain management context. In J. T. Mentzer (Ed.), *Supply chain management* (pp. 358–359). Sage Publications.

Njoku, J., Nwakanma, C., Amaizu, G., & Kim, D. (2022). Prospects and challenges of Metaverse application in data-driven intelligent transportation systems. *IET Intelligent Transport Systems*. doi:10.1049/itr2.12252

Nonaka, I. (1994). A Dynamic Theory of Organizational Knowledge Creation. *Organization Science*, *5*(1), 14–37. doi:10.1287/orsc.5.1.14

Nonaka, I., & Konno, N. (1998). The Concept of "Ba": Building a Foundation for Knowledge Creation. *California Management Review*, *40*(3), 40–54. doi:10.2307/41165942

Nonaka, I., & Takeuchi, H. (1995). *The Knowledge-creating Company – How Japanese Companies Create the Dynamics of Innovation*. Oxford University Press.

Nordhaus, T., & Shellenberger, M. (2007). *Break Through: From the Death of Environmentalism to the Politics of Possibility*. Houghton Mifflin Company.

Noy, I. Y., Shinar, D., & Horrey, W. J. (2018). Automated driving: Safety blind spots. *Safety Science*, *102*, 68–78. doi:10.1016/j.ssci.2017.07.018

Noyons, E. C. M., Moed, H. F., & Luwel, M. (1999). Combining mapping and citation analysis for evaluative bibliometric purposes: A bibliometric study. *Journal of the American Society for Information Science*, *50*(2), 115–131. doi:10.1002/(SICI)1097-4571(1999)50:2<115::AID-ASI3>3.0.CO;2-J

Noyons, E. C. M., Moed, H., & Van Raan, A. (1999). Integrating research performance analysis and science mapping. *Scientometrics*, *46*(3), 591–604. doi:10.1007/BF02459614

Nwankpa, J. K., Roumani, Y., & Datta, P. (2022). Process innovation in the digital age of business: The role of digital business intensity and knowledge management. *Journal of Knowledge Management*, *26*(5), 1319–1341. doi:10.1108/JKM-04-2021-0277

O'Dwyer, B., Unerman, J., & Hession, E. (2005). User needs in sustainability reporting: Perspectives of stakeholders in Ireland. *European Accounting Review*, *14*(4), 759–787. doi:10.1080/09638180500104766

Obeidat, B., Al-Suradi, M., Masa'deh, R., & Tarhini, A. (2016). The impact of knowledge management on innovation: An empirical The Mediating Role of Innovation Speed and Quality in the Relationship 407 study on Jordanian consultancy firms. *Res. Rev*, *39*, 1214–1238.

OECD. (2009). *Eco-innovation, Framework, Practices and Measurement*. OECD.

OECD. (2020). *Guidelines for collecting and interpreting innovation data, 2005*. OECD.

Okwu, M. O., Tartibu, L., & Machesa, M. (2020). Fourth industrial revolution and sustainable impact in autonomous fleets for effective supply chain network in manufacturing systems. In *Proceedings of the 31st Annual Conference of Southern African Institute for Industrial Engineering* (pp. 5-7). Muldersdrift, South Africa: SAIIE.

Olan, F., Arakpogun, E. O., Suklan, J., Nakpodia, F., Damij, N., & Jayawickrama, U. (2022). Artificial intelligence and knowledge sharing: Contributing factors to organizational performance. *Journal of Business Research*, *145*, 605–615. doi:10.1016/j.jbusres.2022.03.008

Olawumi, T. O., & Chan, D. W. (2018). A scientometric review of global research on sustainability and sustainable development. *Journal of Cleaner Production*, *183*, 231–250. doi:10.1016/j.jclepro.2018.02.162

Oliver, S., & Kandadi, K. R. (2006). How to develop knowledge culture in organizations? A multiple case study of large distributed organizations. *Journal of Knowledge Management*, *10*(4), 6–24. doi:10.1108/13673270610679336

Olshannikova, E., Olsson, T., Huhtamäki, J., & Kärkkäinen, H. (2017). Conceptualizing big social data. *Journal of Big Data*, *4*(3), 1–19. doi:10.118640537-017-0063-x

Oostervink, N., Agterberg, M., & Huysman, M. (2016). Knowledge sharing on enterprise social media: Practices to cope with institutional complexity. *Journal of Computer-Mediated Communication*, *21*(2), 156–176. doi:10.1111/jcc4.12153

Opara, L. U. (2003). Traceability in agriculture and food supply chain: A review of basic concepts, technological implications, and future prospects. *Food. Agriculture & Environment*, *1*(1), 101–106.

OpenAI. (2020). *ChatGPT: OpenAI's language model for conversation*. https://openai.com/research/chatgpt

Oracle. (2023). *What is big data?* https://www.oracle.com/big-data/what-is-big-data/

Oragui, D. (2022). *Tacit knowledge: Definition, examples, and importance*. https://helpjuice.com/blog/tacit-knowledge

Orlando, B., Ballestra, L. V., Scuotto, V., Pironti, M., & Del Giudice, M. (2022). The impact of R&D investments on eco-innovation: A cross-cultural perspective of green technology management. *IEEE Transactions on Engineering Management*, *69*(5), 2275–2284. doi:10.1109/TEM.2020.3005525

Orr, D. (2021). *How 9/11 Changed Me and First Responder Communications*. NIST. https://www.nist.gov/blogs/taking-measure/how-911-changed-me-and-first-responder-communications

Ottoson, S. (2002). Virtual reality in the product development process. *Journal of Engineering Design*, *13*(2), 159–172. doi:10.1080/09544820210129823

Owen, J., & Burstein, F. (2005). Where Knowledge Management Resides within Project Management. In Case Studies in Knowledge Management. doi:10.4018/978-1-59140-351-7.ch009

Oxford Insights. (2019). *Government artificial intelligence*. Retrieved August 13, 2022, from https://www.oxfordinsights.com/ai-readiness2019

Özkanlısoy, Ö., & Akkartal, E. (2021). Digital transformation in supply chains: Current applications, contributions, and challenges. *Business & Management Studies: An International Journal*, *9*(1), 32–55. doi:10.15295/bmij.v9i1.1673

P&G. (2019). *Environmental sustainability report 2019*. Retrieved March 14, 2023, from https://downloads.ctfassets.net/oggad6svuzkv/7nSofG7XXtcYERIz5Vm3Xc/c8f716206225387fc9f7fe14ffbbac07/updated_citizenship_report_2019_environmental_sustainability.pdf

Pamucar, D., Deveci, M., Gokasar, I., Tavana, M., & Köppen, M. (2022). A metaverse assessment model for sustainable transportation using ordinal priority approach and Aczel-Alsina norms. *Technological Forecasting and Social Change*, *182*, 121778. doi:10.1016/j.techfore.2022.121778

Panwar, R., Rinne, T., Hansen, E., & Juslin, H. (2006). Corporate responsibility: Balancing economic, environmental, and social issues in the forest products industry. *Forest Products Journal*, *56*(2), 4–13.

Paoloni, M., Coluccia, D., Fontana, S., & Solimene, S. (2020). Knowledge management, intellectual capital and entrepreneurship: A structured literature review. *Journal of Knowledge Management*, *24*(8), 1797–1818. doi:10.1108/JKM-01-2020-0052

Papadopoulos, T., Gunasekaran, A., Dubey, R., Altay, N., Childe, S. J., & Fosso-Wamba, S. (2017). The role of Big Data in explaining disaster resilience in supply chains for sustainability. *Journal of Cleaner Production*, *142*, 1108–1118. doi:10.1016/j.jclepro.2016.03.059

Park, C., Jeong, S., Joshi, M., Osborn, T. J., Ho, C., Piao, S., ... Park, H. (2018). Keeping global warming within 1.5 C constrains the emergence of aridification. *Nature Climate Change*, *8*(1), 70–74. doi:10.103841558-017-0034-4

Parker, K. (2022, November 9). Why explicit instruction matters, according to neuroscience. *Tes Magazine*.

Park, K. T., Nam, Y. W., Lee, H. S., Im, S. J., Noh, S. D., Son, J. Y., & Kim, H. (2019). Design and implementation of a digital twin application for a connected micro smart factory. *International Journal of Computer Integrated Manufacturing*, *32*(6), 596–614. doi:10.1080/0951192X.2019.1599439

Park, S., & Kim, Y. (2022). A Metaverse: Taxonomy, Components, Applications, and Open Challenges. *IEEE Access : Practical Innovations, Open Solutions*, *10*, 4209–4251. doi:10.1109/ACCESS.2021.3140175

Pascoe, C., & More, E. (2005). Communication Climate and Organizational Knowledge Sharing. *Journal of Information and Knowledge Management*, *4*(4), 247–255. doi:10.1142/S0219649205001225

Patyal, V. S., Sarma, P., Modgil, S., Nag, T., & Dennehy, D. (2022). Mapping the links between industry 4.0, circular economy and sustainability: A systematic literature review. *Journal of Enterprise Information Management*, *35*(1), 1–35. doi:10.1108/JEIM-05-2021-0197

Pearson, S., & Benameur, A. (2010). Privacy, security, and trust issues arising from cloud computing. In *Proceedings of the 2010 IEEE Second International Conference on Cloud Computing Technology and Science* (pp. 693-702). IEEE. 10.1109/CloudCom.2010.66

Penrose, R. (1989). *The emperor's new mind: Concerning computers, minds, and the laws of physics*. Oxford University Press. doi:10.1093/oso/9780198519737.001.0001

Perfecto, I., Vandermeer, J., & Wright, A. (2009). *Nature's matrix: Linking agriculture, conservation, and food sovereignty*. Earthscan. doi:10.4324/9781849770132

Perussi, J. B., Gressler, F., & Seleme, R. (2019). Supply chain 4.0: Autonomous vehicles and equipment to meet demand. *International Journal of Supply Chain Management*, *8*(4), 33–41.

Phung, H. G., & Pham, D. B. (2018). Effects of integrated shrimp farming in Vietnam. *Journal of the World Aquaculture Society*, *49*(4), 664–675. doi:10.1111/jwas.12465

Pietras, B. (2015). New frontiers in driverless vehicles. *Engineering & Technology*, *10*(3), 64–67. doi:10.1049/et.2015.0326

Pine, B. J., Pine, J., & Gilmore, J. H. (1999). *The experience economy: Work is theatre & every business a stage*. Harvard Business Press.

Pinho, A. C., Amaro, A. M., & Piedade, A. P. (2020). 3D printing goes greener: Study of the properties of post-consumer recycled polymers for the manufacturing of engineering components. *Waste Management (New York, N.Y.)*, *118*, 426–434. doi:10.1016/j.wasman.2020.09.003 PMID:32966947

Pinzone, M., Albè, F., Orlandelli, D., Barletta, I., Berlin, C., Johansson, B., & Taisch, M. (2020). A framework for operative and social sustainability functionalities in human-centric cyber-physical production systems. *Computers & Industrial Engineering*, *139*, 105132. doi:10.1016/j.cie.2018.03.028

Piyathanavong, V., Huynh, V. N., Karnjana, J., & Olapiriyakul, S. (2022). Role of project management on sustainable supply chain development through industry 4.0 technologies and circular economy during the COVID-19 pandemic: A multiple case study of Thai metals industry. *Operations Management Research*, 1-25. doi:10.1007/s12063-022-00283-7

PMI. (2017). A Guide to the Project Management Body of Knowledge (PMBOK) (6th ed.). Newtown Square, PA: Project Management Institute, Inc.

Polyaninova, T. (2011). Knowledge Management in a Project Environment: Organisational CT and Project Influences. *VINE Journal of Information and Knowledge Management Systems*, *41*(3).

Popescu, D., Dragomir, M., Popescu, S., & Dragomir, D. (2022). Building Better Digital Twins for Production Systems by Incorporating Environmental Related Functions—Literature Analysis and Determining Alternatives. *Applied Sciences (Basel, Switzerland)*, *12*(17), 8657. doi:10.3390/app12178657

Porter, M. (1998, November–December). Clusters and the new economics of competition. *Harvard Business Review*, *76*(6), 77–90. PMID:10187248

Porter, M. (2001). *Clusters of Innovation: regional foundations of U. S. competitiveness*. Council on Competitiveness. Monitor Group.

Powell, W. W., & Snellman, K. (2004). The knowledge economy. *Annual Review of Sociology*, *30*(1), 199–220. doi:10.1146/annurev.soc.29.010202.100037

Power, D. J. (2014). Using ‘Big data for analytics and decision support. *Journal of Decision Systems*, *23*(2), 222–228. doi:10.1080/12460125.2014.888848

Prakash, K. S., Nancharaih, T., & Rao, V. S. (2018). Additive manufacturing techniques in manufacturing-an overview. *Materials Today: Proceedings*, *5*(2), 3873–3882. doi:10.1016/j.matpr.2017.11.642

Pratt, J. (2009). Incorporation and resistance: Analytical issues in the conventionalization debate and alternative food chains. *Journal of Agrarian Change*, *9*, 155–174.

Pretorius, C. J., & Steyn, H. (2005). Knowledge management in project environments. *South African Journal of Business Management*, *36*(3), 41–50. doi:10.4102ajbm.v36i3.634

Pretty, J. (1995). Participatory Learning for Sustainable Agriculture. *World Development*, *23*(8), 1247–1263. doi:10.1016/0305-750X(95)00046-F

Qamar, S., Anwar, Z., & Afzal, M. (2023). A systematic threat analysis and defense strategies for the metaverse and extended reality systems. *Computers & Security*, *128*, 103127. doi:10.1016/j.cose.2023.103127

Qi, Y., Wang, X., Li, Y., Zhang, G., & Jin, H. (2021). The effects of inter-organizational compatibility on knowledge transfer in cross-border M&As. *Management Decision*, *59*(9), 2123–2142. doi:10.1108/MD-03-2020-0349

Qrunfleh, S., & Tarafdar, M. (2014). Supply chain information systems strategy: Impacts on supply chain performance and firm performance. *International Journal of Production Economics*, *147*, 340–350. doi:10.1016/j.ijpe.2012.09.018

Quang, H. T., & Hara, Y. (2019). The push effect of risks on supply chain performance: Service-oriented firms. *Business Process Management Journal*, *25*(7), 1734–1758. doi:10.1108/BPMJ-12-2017-0343

Quilley, S. (2020). Can progressives’ shimmy? *Institute for Policy Public Research Progressive Review.*, *27*, 179–185.

Rafi, S., Akbar, M. A., Mahmood, S., Alsanad, A., & Alothaim, A. (2022). Selection of DevOps best test practices: A hybrid approach using ISM and fuzzy TOPSIS analysis. *Journal of Software (Malden, MA), 34*(5), e2448. doi:10.1002mr.2448

Rahaman, T. (2022). Into the Metaverse – Perspectives on a New Reality. *Medical Reference Services Quarterly, 41*(3), 330–337. doi:10.1080/02763869.2022.2096341 PMID:35980623

Rahman, N. A., Yaacob, Z., & Radzi, R. M. (2016). An overview of technological innovation on SME survival: A conceptual paper. *Procedia: Social and Behavioral Sciences, 224*, 508–515. doi:10.1016/j.sbspro.2016.05.427

Rajkumar, R., Lee, I., Sha, L., & Stankovic, J. (2010). Cyber-physical systems: The next computing revolution. In *Proceedings of the Design Automation Conference* (pp. 731-736), IEEE. 10.1145/1837274.1837461

Rajput, S., & Singh, S. P. (2019). Connecting circular economy and industry 4.0. *International Journal of Information Management, 49*, 98–113. doi:10.1016/j.ijinfomgt.2019.03.002

Ramakrishnan, P. S. (2003). Conserving the sacred: the protective impulse and the origins of modern protected areas. In D. Harmon & A. D. Putney (Eds.), *The full value of parks: from economics to the intangible* (pp. 26–41). Rowman & Littlefield.

Ramakrishnan, P. S. (2008). *The cultural cradle of biodiversity*. National Book Trust.

Ramazanov, S. K., Nadyon, G. A., Krishtal, N. I., Stepanenko, O. P., & Timashova, L. A. (2009). Innovative technologies of crisis management of economic systems, Monograph. SNU named V. Dalya.

Ramirez-Peña, M., Sotano, A. J. S., Pérez-Fernandez, V., Abad, F. J., & Batista, M. (2020). Achieving a sustainable shipbuilding supply chain under I4. 0 perspective. *Journal of Cleaner Production, 244*, 1–11. doi:10.1016/j.jclepro.2019.118789

Rangan, H., & Kull, C. A. (2009). What makes ecology 'political'? Rethinking 'scale' in political ecology. *Progress in Human Geography, 33*(1), 28–45. doi:10.1177/0309132508090215

Rao, P., & Holt, D. (2005). Do green supply chains lead to competitiveness and economic performance? *International Journal of Operations & Production Management, 25*(9), 898–916. doi:10.1108/01443570510613956

Rashed, M. (2016). The Readiness of Banks in Knowledge Management: A Study of Three Private Commercial Banks in Bangladesh. *Journal of Business and Financial Affairs, 5*(2), 1–5.

Rashid, A., & Tjahjono, B. (2016). Achieving manufacturing excellence through the integration of enterprise systems and simulation. *Production Planning and Control, 27*(10), 837–852. doi:10.1080/09537287.2016.1143132

Rastegar, R., & Ruhanen, L. (2021). A safe space for local knowledge sharing in sustainable tourism: An organisational justice perspective. *Journal of Sustainable Tourism*, 1–17. https://www.tandfonline.com/doi/abs/10.1080/09669582.2021.1929261

Raudeliūnienė, J., Davidavičienė, V., & Jakubavičius, A. (2018). Knowledge management process model. *Entrepreneurship and Sustainability Issues, 5*(3), 542–554. doi:10.9770/jesi.2018.5.3(10)

Rauniyar, A., Hagos, D. H., & Shrestha, M. (2018). A crowd-based intelligence approach for measurable security, privacy, and dependability in internet of automated vehicles with vehicular fog. *Mobile Information Systems, 2018*, 1–14. doi:10.1155/2018/7905960

Razmerita, L., Kirchner, K., & Nielsen, P. (2016). What factors influence knowledge sharing in organizations? A social dilemma perspective of social media communication. *Journal of Knowledge Management, 20*(6), 1225–1246. doi:10.1108/JKM-03-2016-0112

Reed, M. S., Buenemann, M., Atlhopheng, J., Akhtar-Schuster, M., Bachmann, F., Bastin, G., ... Essahli, W. (2011). Cross-scale monitoring and assessment of land degradation and sustainable land management: A methodological framework for knowledge management. *Land Degradation & Development*, *22*(2), 261–271. doi:10.1002/ldr.1087

Rêgo, B. S., Jayantilal, S., Ferreira, J. J., & Carayannis, E. G. (2021). Digital transformation and strategic management: A systematic review of the literature. *Journal of the Knowledge Economy*, 1–28.

Reich, B. H., Gemino, A., & Sauer, C. (2008). Modeling the knowledge perspective in IT projects. *Project Management Journal*, *39*(1_suppl), S4–S14. doi:10.1002/pmj.20056

Reich-Stiebert, N., & Eyssel, F. (2015). Learning with educational companion robots? Toward attitudes on education robots, predictors of attitudes, and application potentials for education robots. *International Journal of Social Robotics*, *7*(5), 875–888. doi:10.100712369-015-0308-9

Reif, R., Günthner, W. A., Schwerdtfeger, B., & Klinker, G. (2010). Evaluation of an augmented reality supported picking system under practical conditions. *Computer Graphics Forum*, *29*(1), 2–12. doi:10.1111/j.1467-8659.2009.01538.x

Reis, J. J., & Azevedo, E. (Eds.). (2012). *Escravidão e suas sombras*. EDUFBA. doi:10.7476/9788523211882

Rejeb, A., Keogh, J. G., Wamba, S. F., & Treiblmaier, H. (2021). The potentials of augmented reality in supply chain management: A state-of-the-art review. *Management Review Quarterly*, *71*(4), 819–856. doi:10.100711301-020-00201-w

Renaud, K., Flowerday, S., Warkentin, M., Cockshott, P., & Orgeron, C. (2018). Is the responsibilization of the cyber security risk reasonable and judicious? *Computers & Security*, *78*, 198–211. doi:10.1016/j.cose.2018.06.006

Ribeiro, J. (2016). Educational technology decision-making: Technology acquisition for 746,000 Ontario students. *Canadian Journal of Educational Administration and Policy*, 176.

Richards, B. J., Seidakhmetov, B. K., & Zhunussova, M. A. (2020). Digital Transformation in the Aviation Industry. *Вестник академии гражданской авиации*, (2), 23-27.

Riege, A., & Lindsay, N. (2006). Knowledge management in the public sector: Stakeholder partnerships in the public policy development. *Journal of Knowledge Management*, *10*(3), 24–39. doi:10.1108/13673270610670830

Riglietti, G., & Aguada, L. (2018). *Supply chain resilience report*. The Business Continuity Institute.

Riungu-Kalliosaari, L., Mäkinen, S., Lwakatare, L. E., Tiihonen, J., & Männistö, T. (2016). DevOps adoption benefits and challenges in practice: A case study. *Product-Focused Software Process Improvement: 17th International Conference, PROFES 2016, Trondheim, Norway, November 22-24, 2016 Proceedings*, *17*, 590–597.

Rocheleau, D. E. (2011). Rooted networks, webs of relation, and the power of situated science: Bringing the models back down to Earth. In Knowing Nature: Conversations at the Intersection of Political Ecology and Science Studies. University of Chicago Press.

Rodríguez-Rebés, L., Navío-Marco, J., & Ibar-Alonso, R. (2021). Influence of organisational innovation and innovation in general on eco-innovation in European companies. *Journal of Intellectual Capital*, *22*(5), 840–867. doi:10.1108/JIC-06-2020-0203

Rogers, E. M. (2003). *Diffusion of innovations*. Free Press.

Rogers, H., Baricz, N., & Pawar, K. S. (2016). 3D printing services: Classification, supply chain implications and research agenda. *International Journal of Physical Distribution & Logistics Management*, *46*(10), 886–907. doi:10.1108/IJPDLM-07-2016-0210

Rogers, P. P., Jalal, K. F., & Boyd, J. A. (2007). *An Introduction to Sustainable Development*. Routledge. doi:10.4324/9781849770477

Romani, M. (2017). Lessons Learnt Support System. In M. Handzic & A. Bassi (Eds.), *Knowledge and Project Management: A Shared Approach to Improve Performance* (Vol. 5, pp. 95–129). doi:10.1007/978-3-319-51067-5_5

Romford, J. (2021). *Knowledge culture in knowledge management*. Agility Online Ltd. https://agilityportal.io/blog/knowledge-culture-in-knowledge-management#:~:text=in%20Knowledge%20Management-,Knowledge%20Culture%20in%20Knowledge%20Management,managing%20knowledge%20within%20an%20organizations

Rosa, P., Sassanelli, C., Urbinati, A., Chiaroni, D., & Terzi, S. (2020). Assessing relations between circular economy and industry 4.0: A systematic literature review. *International Journal of Production Research*, *58*(6), 1662–1687. doi:10.1080/00207543.2019.1680896

Rose, D. C., Lyon, J., de Boon, A., Hanheide, M., & Pearson, S. (2021). Responsible development of autonomous robotics in agriculture. *Nature Food*, *2*(5), 306–309. doi:10.103843016-021-00287-9 PMID:37117726

Rosmann, R. L. (1994). Farmer initiated on-farm research. *American Journal of Alternative Agriculture*, *9*(1-2), 34–37. doi:10.1017/S0889189300005531

Roth, H. (2022). *Knowledge Culture — Its meaning in marketing & branding*. Neuroflash GmbH. https://neuroflash.com/blog/knowledge-culture-meaning-in-marketing-branding/

Rouse, M. (2013). *What does network redundancy mean?* Techopedia. https://www.techopedia.com/definition/29305/network-redundancy

Ruel, S., El Baz, J., Ivanov, D., & Das, A. (2021). Supply chain viability: Conceptualization, measurement, and nomological validation. *Annals of Operations Research*, 1–30. doi:10.100710479-021-03974-9 PMID:33716370

Ruppel, C. P., & Harrington, S. J. (2001). Sharing knowledge through intranets: A study of organizational culture and intranet implementation. *IEEE Transactions on Professional Communication, 44*(1), 37-52.

Russ, M., Fineman, R., & Jones, J.K. (2009). Conceptual theory: What do you know? *Knowledge Management Strategies for Business Development*, 1-22. . doi:10.4018/978-1-60566-348-7.ch001

Russell, S., Dewey, D., & Tegmark, M. (2015). Research priorities for robust and beneficial artificial intelligence. *AI Magazine*, *36*(4), 105–114. doi:10.1609/aimag.v36i4.2577

Russ, M. (2010). *How Do We Get There? Strategy Action Framework–"Action Engine"*. IGI Global. doi:10.4018/978-1-60566-348-7.ch009

Russ, M. (2016). The probable foundations of sustainabilism: Information, energy and entropy based definition of capital, Homo Sustainabiliticus and the need for a "new gold". *Ecological Economics*, *130*, 328–338. doi:10.1016/j.ecolecon.2016.07.013

Russ, M. (2021). Knowledge management for sustainable development in the era of continuously accelerating technological revolutions: A framework and models. *Sustainability (Basel)*, *13*(6), 3353. doi:10.3390u13063353

Russ, M. (2021). The individual and the organizational model of quantum decision-making and learning: An introduction and the application of the quadruple loop learning. *Merits*, *1*(1), 34–46. doi:10.3390/merits1010005

Russ, M., Fineman, R., Paterni, R., & Jones, J. K. (2012). How do we get there? Strategy action framework-"Action engine.". In *Organizational learning and knowledge: Concepts, methodologies, tools and applications* (pp. 442–476). IGI Global. doi:10.4018/978-1-60960-783-8.ch204

Rüßmann, M., Lorenz, M., Gerbert, P., Waldner, M., Justus, J., Engel, P., & Harnisch, M. (2015). Industry 4.0: The future of productivity and growth in manufacturing industries. *Boston Consulting Group, 9*(1), 1-14.

Ruuska, I., & Vartiainen, M. (2005). Characteristics of knowledge sharing communities in project organizations. *International Journal of Project Management, 23*(5), 374–379. doi:10.1016/j.ijproman.2005.01.003

Rzig, D. E., Hassan, F., & Kessentini, M. (2022). An empirical study on ML DevOps adoption trends, efforts, and benefits analysis. *Information and Software Technology, 152*, 107037. doi:10.1016/j.infsof.2022.107037

Saad, M., & Patel, B. (2006). An investigation of supply chain performance measurement in the Indian automotive sector. *Benchmarking, 13*(1/2), 36–53. doi:10.1108/14635770610644565

Saito, A., Umemoto, K., & Ikeda, M. (2007). A strategy-based ontology of knowledge management technologies. *Journal of Knowledge Management, 11*(1), 97–114. doi:10.1108/13673270710728268

Salam, A. (2020). Internet of things for sustainability: Perspectives in privacy, cybersecurity, and future trends. In A. Salam (Ed.), *Internet of Things for Sustainable Community Development: Wireless Communications, Sensing, and Systems* (pp. 299–327). Springer Nature. doi:10.1007/978-3-030-35291-2_10

Salisbury, M., & Plass, J. (2001). A conceptual framework for a knowledge management system. *Human Resource Development International, 4*(4), 451–464. doi:10.1080/13678860010016913

Sánchez-Gordón, M., & Colomo-Palacios, R. (2020, June). Security as culture: a systematic literature review of DevSecOps. In *Proceedings of the IEEE/ACM 42nd International Conference on Software Engineering Workshops* (pp. 266-269). 10.1145/3387940.3392233

Sanchez, M., Exposito, E., & Aguilar, J. (2020). Industry 4.0: Survey from a system integration perspective. *International Journal of Computer Integrated Manufacturing, 33*(10-11), 1017–1041. doi:10.1080/0951192X.2020.1775295

Sandström, C., Magnusson, M., & Jörnmark, J. (2009). Exploring factors influencing incumbents' response to disruptive innovation. *Creativity and Innovation Management, 18*(1), 8–15. doi:10.1111/j.1467-8691.2009.00507.x

Sanguankaew, P., & Vathanophas Ractham, V. (2019). Bibliometric review of research on knowledge management and sustainability, 1994–2018. *Sustainability (Basel), 11*(16), 4388. doi:10.3390u11164388

Sanji, M., Behzadi, H., & Gomroki, G. (2022). Chatbot: An intelligent tool for libraries. *Library Hi Tech News, 39*(3), 17–20. doi:10.1108/LHTN-01-2021-0002

Sankarasubramanian, S. (2009). Knowledge management meets project management. In *PMI® Global Congress 2009—* Asia Pacific, Kuala Lumpur, Malaysia. Newtown Square, PA: Project Management Institute.

Santana, M., & Lopez-Cabrales, A. (2019). Sustainable development and human resource management: A science mapping approach. *Corporate Social Responsibility and Environmental Management, 26*(6), 1171–1183. doi:10.1002/csr.1765

Santoro, G., Vrontis, D., Thrassou, A., & Dezi, L. (2018). The Internet of Things: Building a knowledge management system for open innovation and knowledge management capacity. *Technological Forecasting and Social Change, 136*, 347–354. doi:10.1016/j.techfore.2017.02.034

Sarkis, J. (2006). *Greening the Supply Chain.* Springer. doi:10.1007/1-84628-299-3

Şarlıoğlu, G., Boyacı, E., & Akca, M. (2023). Information and Communication Technologies in Logistics and Supply Chain Management in Turkey: Human Resource Practices and New Challenges. In N. Sharma & K. Shalender (Eds.), *Managing Technology Integration for Human Resources in Industry 5.0* (pp. 174–197). IGI Global. doi:10.4018/978-1-6684-6745-9.ch011

SAS Institute. (2014). *SAS for: Demand-driven forecasting and planning*. Retrieved May 17, 2022, from https://www.sas.com/content/dam/SAS/en_us/doc/overviewbrochure/sas-for-demand-driven-planning-optimization-107293.pdf

Saucedo Martínez, J., Pérez Lara, M., Marmolejo Saucedo, J., Salais Fierro, T., & Vasant, P. (2018). Industry 4.0 framework for management and operations: A review. *Journal of Ambient Intelligence and Humanized Computing*, *9*(3), 789–801. doi:10.100712652-017-0533-1

Saura, J. R., Palos-Sanchez, P., & Rodríguez Herráez, B. (2020). Digital marketing for sustainable growth: Business models and online campaigns using sustainable strategies. *Sustainability (Basel)*, *12*(3), 1003–1023. doi:10.3390u12031003

Savage, J., & Savage, J. (2011). *Cross-curricular teaching and learning in the secondary school*. Routledge.

Savela, N., Turja, T., & Oksanen, A. (2018). Social acceptance of robots in different occupational fields: A systematic literature review. *International Journal of Social Robotics*, *10*(4), 493–502. doi:10.100712369-017-0452-5

Schindler, M., & Eppler, M. J. (2003). Harvesting project knowledge: A review of project learning methods and success factors. *International Journal of Project Management*, *21*(3), 219–228. doi:10.1016/S0263-7863(02)00096-0

Schmidheiny, S., WBCSD, & Unotec Holding Ag. (1992). Changing course. A global business perspective on development and the environment. The MIT Press.

Schniederjans, D. G. (2017). Adoption of 3D-printing technologies in manufacturing: A survey analysis. *International Journal of Production Economics*, *183*, 287–298. doi:10.1016/j.ijpe.2016.11.008

Schoettle, B., & Sivak, M. (2014). A survey of public opinion about connected vehicles in the U.S., the UK, and Australia. In *Proceedings of the 2014 International Conference on Connected Vehicles and Expo (ICCVE)* (pp. 687-692). IEEE. 10.1109/ICCVE.2014.7297637

Schöggl, J. P., Fritz, M. M. C., & Baumgartner, R. J. (2016). Toward supply chain-wide sustainability assessment: A conceptual framework and an aggregation method to assess supply chain performance. *Journal of Cleaner Production*, *131*, 1–14. doi:10.1016/j.jclepro.2016.04.035

Schumpeter, J. A. (1934). *The theory of economic development: an inquiry into profits, capital, credit, interest, and the business cycle*. Harvard University Press.

Schwab, K. (2017). *The fourth industrial revolution*. Currency Books.

Schwartz, S. B. (1992). *Slaves, Peasants, and Rebels: Reconsidering Brazilian Slavery*. University of Illinois Press.

Scott, J. T. (2017). *The sustainable business: A practitioner's guide to achieving long-term profitability and competitiveness*. Routledge. doi:10.4324/9781351276603

Searcy, C. (2012). Corporate sustainability performance measurement systems: A review and research agenda. *Journal of Business Ethics*, *107*(3), 239–253. doi:10.100710551-011-1038-z

Sebestyén, V., Czvetkó, T., & Abonyi, J. (2021). The applicability of Big Data in climate change research: The importance of system of systems thinking. *Frontiers in Environmental Science*, *9*(70), 1–26. doi:10.3389/fenvs.2021.619092

Sen, A. (2021). DevOps, DevSecOps, AIOPS-paradigms to IT operations. *Evolving Technologies for Computing, Communication, and Smart World Proceedings of ETCCS, 2020*, 211–221.

Senapathi, M., Buchan, J., & Osman, H. (2018, June). DevOps capabilities, practices, and challenges: Insights from a case study. In *Proceedings of the 22nd International Conference on Evaluation and Assessment in Software Engineering 2018* (pp. 57-67). 10.1145/3210459.3210465

Seo, S., Choi, S., & Lee, C. (2012). Security manpower scheduling for smart airports. In Computer Science and Convergence: CSA 2011 & WCC 2011 Proceedings (pp. 519-527). Springer Netherlands. doi:10.1007/978-94-007-2792-2_49

Seta, K. C., & … . (2011). A Meta-Analysis of Global Urban Land Expansion. *PLoS One*, *6*(8), e23777. doi:10.1371/journal.pone.0023777 PMID:21876770

Sezen, B., & Cankaya, S. Y. (2013). Effects of green manufacturing and eco-innovation on sustainability performance. *Procedia: Social and Behavioral Sciences*, *99*, 154–163. doi:10.1016/j.sbspro.2013.10.481

Shahzad, M., Qu, Y., Zafar, A. U., Ding, X., & Rehman, S. U. (2020). Translating stakeholders' pressure into environmental practices–The mediating role of knowledge management. *Journal of Cleaner Production*, *275*, 124163. doi:10.1016/j.jclepro.2020.124163

Shamout, M., Ben-Abdallah, R., Alshurideh, M., Alzoubi, H., Kurdi, B., & Hamadneh, S. (2022). A conceptual model for the adoption of autonomous robots in supply chain and logistics industry. *Uncertain Supply Chain Management*, *10*(2), 577–592. doi:10.5267/j.uscm.2021.11.006

Shankar, V. (2018). How artificial intelligence (AI) is reshaping retailing. *Journal of Retailing*, *94*(4), 5–11. doi:10.1016/S0022-4359(18)30076-9

Sharma, A., Iyer, G. R., Mehrotra, A., & Krishnan, R. (2010). Sustainability and business-to-business marketing: A framework and implications. *Industrial Marketing Management*, *39*(2), 330–341. doi:10.1016/j.indmarman.2008.11.005

Shaw, S., Grant, D. B., & Mangan, J. (2010). Developing environmental supply chain performance measures. *Benchmarking*, *17*(3), 320–339. doi:10.1108/14635771011049326

Sheehan, P., & Houghton, J. W. (2000). *A primer on the knowledge economy*. Centre for Strategic Economic Studies.

Shehieb, W., Al Sayed, H., Akil, M. M., Turkman, M., Sarraj, M. A., & Mir, M. (2016, December). A smart system to minimize mishandled luggage at airports. In *2016 International Conference on Progress in Informatics and Computing (PIC)* (pp. 154-158). IEEE. 10.1109/PIC.2016.7949485

Shen, B., Tan, W., Guo, J., Zhao, L., & Qin, P. (2021). How to Promote User Purchase in Metaverse? A Systematic Literature Review on Consumer Behavior Research and Virtual Commerce Application Design. *Applied Sciences (Basel, Switzerland)*, *11*(23), 11087. doi:10.3390/app112311087

Shepherd, C., & Günter, H. (2010). Measuring supply chain performance: Current research and future directions. In J. C. Fransoo, T. Waefler, & J. R. Wilson (Eds.), *Behavioral Operations in Planning and Scheduling* (pp. 105–121). Springer. doi:10.1007/978-3-642-13382-4_6

Shiffrin, R. M., & Borner, K. (2004). Mapping knowledge domains. *Proceedings of the National Academy of Sciences of the United States of America, 101*(Suppl 1), 5183-5185. 10.1073/pnas.0307852100

Shujahat, M., Hussain, S., Javed, S., Thurasamy, R., & Ali, J. (2017). Strategic management model with lens of knowledge management and competitive intelligence: A review approach. *VINE Journal of Information and Knowledge Management Systems*, *47*(1), 55–93. doi:10.1108/VJIKMS-06-2016-0035

Silahtaroğlu, G. (2017). Implementing adaptive strategies of decision support systems during crises. *Global Business Strategies in Crisis: Strategic Thinking and Development*, 287-302.

Singh, A., Mishra, N., Ali, S. I., Shukla, N., & Shankar, R. (2015). Cloud computing technology: Reducing carbon footprint in beef supply chain. *International Journal of Production Economics*, *164*, 462–471. doi:10.1016/j.ijpe.2014.09.019

Singh, R., Gehlot, A., Akram, S. V., Gupta, L. R., Jena, M. K., Prakash, C., Singh, S., & Kumar, R. (2021). Cloud manufacturing, internet of things-assisted manufacturing and 3D printing technology: Reliable tools for sustainable construction. *Sustainability (Basel)*, *13*(13), 1–20. doi:10.3390u13137327

Singh, S. K., Gupta, S., Busso, D., & Kamboj, S. (2021). Top management knowledge value, knowledge sharing practices, open innovation and organizational performance. *Journal of Business Research*, *128*, 788–798. doi:10.1016/j.jbusres.2019.04.040

Siyaev, A., & Jo, G. (2021). Towards Aircraft Maintenance Metaverse Using Speech Interactions with Virtual Objects in Mixed Reality. *Sensors (Basel)*, *21*(6), 2066. doi:10.339021062066 PMID:33804253

Smith, M. (2019). *Walmart's new Intelligent Retail Lab shows a glimpse into the future of retail, IRL*. Walmart. https://corporate.walmart.com/newsroom/2019/04/25/walmarts-new-intelligent-retail-lab-shows-a-glimpse-into-the-future-of-retail-irl

Smith, N. (1984). *Uneven development: Nature, capital, and the Production of Space*. Blackwell.

Smuts, H., & Van der Merwe, A. (2022). Knowledge management in society 5.0: A sustainability perspective. *Sustainability (Basel)*, *14*(11), 6878. doi:10.3390u14116878

Sneesl, R., Jusoh, Y. Y., Jabar, M. A., & Abdullah, S. (2022). Revising technology adoption factors for IoT-based smart campuses: A systematic review. *Sustainability (Basel)*, *14*(8), 4840. doi:10.3390u14084840

Söderberg, R., Wärmefjord, K., Carlson, J. S., & Lindkvist, L. (2017). Toward a digital twin for real-time geometry assurance in individualized production. *CIRP Annals*, *66*(1), 137–140. doi:10.1016/j.cirp.2017.04.038

Soderlund, J. (2010). Knowledge entrainment and project management: The case of large-scale transformation projects. *International Journal of Project Management*, *28*(2), 130–141. doi:10.1016/j.ijproman.2009.11.010

Sokhanvar, S., Matthews, J., & Yarlagadda, P. (2014). Importance of Knowledge Management Processes in a Project-based organization: A Case Study of Research Enterprise. *Procedia Engineering*, *97*, 1825–1830. doi:10.1016/j.proeng.2014.12.336

Song, M., Van Der Bij, H., & Weggeman, M. (2005). Determinants of the level of knowledge application: A knowledge-based and information-processing perspective. *Journal of Product Innovation Management*, *22*(5), 430–444. doi:10.1111/j.1540-5885.2005.00139.x

Sopadang, A., Wichaisri, S., & Banomyong, R. (2017, April). Sustainable supply chain performance measurement a case study of the sugar industry. In *Proceedings of the International Conference on Industrial Engineering and Operations Management* (pp. 1-12). IEOM Society International.

Spicer, A., & Hyatt, D. (2017). Walmart's emergent low-cost sustainable product strategy. *California Management Review*, *59*(2), 116–141. doi:10.1177/0008125617695287

Stead, S. M. (2019). Using systems thinking and open innovation to strengthen aquaculture policy for the United Nations Sustainable Development Goals. *Journal of Fish Biology*, *94*(6), 837–844. doi:10.1111/jfb.13970 PMID:30887512

Stefanović, N., & Stefanović, D. (2011). Supply chain performance measurement system based on scorecards and web portals. *Computer Science and Information Systems*, *8*(1), 167–192. doi:10.2298/CSIS090608018S

Sterling, S. (2009). The ecological and environmental dimensions of the holistic curriculum. In G. Papagiannis (Ed.), *Education for sustainability* (pp. 309–322). Eolss Publishers.

Stobierski, T. (2020). *Emergent vs. deliberate strategy: How & when to use each.* https://online.hbs.edu/blog/post/emergent-vs-deliberate-strategy#:~:text=What%20Is%20an%20Emergent%20Strategy,initiatives%20from%20within%20an%20organization

Stobierski, T. (2020). *How to calculate ROI to justify a project.* Harvard Business School Online Business Insights Blog. https://online.hbs.edu/blog/post/how-to-calculate-roi-for-a-project

Stock, T., & Seliger, G. (2016). Opportunities of sustainable manufacturing in Industry 4.0. *Procedia CIRP, 40*, 536–541. doi:10.1016/j.procir.2016.01.129

Stoddard, C. (2022). Give Your Employees the Tools They Need to be Productive. *Harvard Business Review.* https://hbr.org/sponsored/2022/11/give-your-employees-the-tools-they-need-to-be-productive

Stomski, L. (2022). *Walmart launches one global Walmart Academy to help 2.3 million associates build and grow their careers.* Walmart. https://corporate.walmart.com/newsroom/2022/06/02/walmart-launches-one-global-walmart-academy-to-help-2-3-million-associates-build-and-grow-their-careers

Storper, M. (1997). *The regional world: territorial development in a global economy.* Routledge.

Strand, R., Freeman, R. E., & Hockerts, K. (2015). Corporate social responsibility and sustainability in Scandinavia: An overview. *Journal of Business Ethics, 127*(1), 1–15. doi:10.100710551-014-2224-6

Strivr. (2022). *Elevate performance through immersive experience.* https://www.strivr.com/lp/elevate-performance/

Strozzi, F., Colicchia, C., Creazza, A., & Noe, C. (2017). Literature review on the "smart factory" concept using bibliometric tools. *International Journal of Production Research, 55*(22), 6572–6591. doi:10.1080/00207543.2017.1326643

Subramani, M. R., & Rajagopalan, B. (2003). Knowledge-sharing and influence in online social networks via viral marketing. *Communications of the ACM, 46*(12), 300–307. doi:10.1145/953460.953514

Subramanya, R., Sierla, S., & Vyatkin, V. (2022). From DevOps to MLOps: Overview and Application to Electricity Market Forecasting. *Applied Sciences (Basel, Switzerland), 12*(19), 9851. doi:10.3390/app12199851

Sufiyan, M., Haleem, A., Khan, S., & Khan, M. I. (2019). Evaluating food supply chain performance using hybrid fuzzy MCDM technique. *Sustainable Production and Consumption, 20*, 40–57. doi:10.1016/j.spc.2019.03.004

Suk, T., Hwang, J., Bulut, M. F., & Zeng, Z. (2019, July). Failure-aware application placement modeling and optimization in high turnover DevOps environment. In *2019 IEEE 12th International Conference on Cloud Computing (CLOUD)* (pp. 115-123). IEEE. 10.1109/CLOUD.2019.00030

Sulaiman, K. A., Adeyemi, I. O., & Ayegun, I. (2020). Information sharing and evaluation as determinants of spread of fake news on social media among Nigerian youths: Experience from COVID-19 pandemic. *International Journal of Knowledge Content Development & Technology, 10*(4), 65–82. https://www.koreascience.or.kr/article/JAKO202009252118722.page

Sullivan, E. T. (2022, June 23). *Schools are looking for evidence from their Edtech. are companies ready to provide it?* EdSurge. Retrieved January 6, 2023, from https://www.edsurge.com/news/2022-06-23-schools-are-looking-for-evidence-from-their-edtech-are-companies-ready-to-provide-it)

Supply Chain Digital. (2022). *Top 10: Innovative & ESG-friendly global supply chains.* Retrieved December 17, 2022, from https://supplychaindigital.com/sustainability/top-10-innovative-esg-friendly-global-supply-chains

Sutherland, W. J., Aveling, R., Brooks, T. M., Clout, M., Dicks, L. V., Fellman, L., Fleishman, E., Gibbons, D. W., Keim, B., Lickorish, F., Monk, K. A., Mortimer, D., Peck, L. S., Pretty, J., Rockström, J., Rodríguez, J. P., Smith, R. K., Spalding, M. D., Tonneijck, F. H., & Watkinson, A. R. (2014). A horizon scan of global conservation issues for 2014. *Trends in Ecology & Evolution, 29*(1), 15–22. doi:10.1016/j.tree.2013.11.004 PMID:24332318

Suwandi, D. (2015). *Km roadmap & strategy*. SlideShare. https://www.slideshare.net/djatmikosuwandi/km-roadmap-strategy.to

Su, Y., & Wang, X. (2021). Innovation of agricultural economic management in the process of constructing smart agriculture by big data. *Sustainable Computing: Informatics and Systems, 31*, 1–7. doi:10.1016/j.suscom.2021.100579

Swan, M. (2015). *Blockchain: Blueprint for a new economy* (1st ed.). O'Reilly.

Taboada, I., & Shee, H. (2020). Understanding 5G technology for future supply chain management. *International Journal of Logistics, 24*(4), 1–15. doi:10.1080/13675567.2020.1762850

Tabrizi, B., Lam, E., Girard, K., & Irvin, V. (2019). Digital transformation is not about technology. *Harvard Business Review, 13*(March), 1–6.

Tadejko, P. (2015). Application of Internet of Things in logistics: Current challenges. *Ekonomia i Zarządzanie, 7*(4), 54–64. doi:10.12846/j.em.2015.04.07

Tait, E., & Pierson, C. (2022). Artificial Intelligence and Robots in Libraries: Opportunities in LIS Curriculum for Preparing the Librarians of Tomorrow. *Journal of the Australian Library and Information Association, 71*(3), 256–274. doi:10.1080/24750158.2022.2081111

Tajpour, M., Hosseini, E., Mohammadi, M., & Bahman-Zangi, B. (2022). The effect of knowledge management on the sustainability of technology-driven businesses in emerging markets: The mediating role of social media. *Sustainability (Basel), 14*(14), 8602. doi:10.3390u14148602

Taminiau, Y., Smit, W., & Lange, A. D. (2009). Innovation in management consulting firms through informal knowledge sharing. *Journal of Knowledge Management, 13*(1), 42–55. doi:10.1108/13673270910931152

Tan, K. H., Ji, G., Lim, C. P., & Tseng, M. L. (2017). Using big data to make better decisions in the digital economy. *International Journal of Production Research, 55*(17), 4998–5000. https://doi.org/.2017.1331051 doi:10.1080/00207543

Tang, C. S. (2006). Robust strategies for mitigating supply chain disruptions. *International Journal of Logistics, 9*(1), 33–45. doi:10.1080/13675560500405584

Tanner, M. (2018). *Why China will drive blockchain and four related myths*. Forbes. Retrieved May 7, 2022, from www.forbes.com/sites/tannermark/2018/08/01/blockchain-china-misunderstandings/#a65d29213c85

Tanrıverdi, G., & Lezki, Ş. (2021). Istanbul Airport (IGA) and quest of best competitive strategy for air cargo carriers in new competition environment: A fuzzy multi-criteria approach. *Journal of Air Transport Management, 95*, 102088. doi:10.1016/j.jairtraman.2021.102088

Tao, F., Cheng, J., Qi, Q., Zhang, M., Zhang, H., & Sui, F. (2017). Digital twin-driven product design, manufacturing, and service with big data. *International Journal of Advanced Manufacturing Technology, 94*(9-12), 3563–3576. doi:10.100700170-017-0233-1

Tao, F., Wang, Y., Zuo, Y., Yang, H., & Zhang, M. (2016). Internet of Things in product life-cycle energy management. *Journal of Industrial Information Integration, 1*, 26–39. doi:10.1016/j.jii.2016.03.001

Tao, X. (2009, December). Performance evaluation of supply chain based on fuzzy matter-element theory. In *Proceedings of the 2009 International Conference on Information Management, Innovation Management, and Industrial Engineering* (vol. 1, pp. 549-552). IEEE. 10.1109/ICIII.2009.138

Taticchi, P., Tonelli, F., & Pasqualino, R. (2013). Performance measurement of sustainable supply chains: A literature review and a research agenda. *International Journal of Productivity and Performance Management, 62*(8), 782–804. doi:10.1108/IJPPM-03-2013-0037

Terzieva, M. (2014). Project Knowledge Management: How organizations learn from experience. *Procedia Technology, 16*, 1086–1095. doi:10.1016/j.protcy.2014.10.123

Teubner, T., & Camacho, S. (2023). Facing Reciprocity: How Photos and Avatars Promote Interaction in Micro-communities. *Group Decision and Negotiation*. Advance online publication. doi:10.100710726-023-09814-4

Thakkar, J., Kanda, A., & Deshmukh, S. G. (2009). Supply chain performance measurement framework for small and medium scale enterprises. *Benchmarking, 16*(5), 702–723. doi:10.1108/14635770910987878

Thames, L., & Schaefer, D. (2017). Industry 4.0: An overview of key benefits, technologies, and challenges. In L. Thames & D. Schaefer (Eds.), *Cybersecurity for Industry 4.0: Analysis for design and manufacturing* (pp. 1–33). Springer. doi:10.1007/978-3-319-50660-9_1

The BetterUp Team. (2019). *Q&A with Equinix: Personalized development for employees through coaching.* BetterUp. https://www.betterup.com/blog/qanda-with-equinix-personalized-development-for-employees-through-coaching

The CASEL Guide to schoolwide social and emotional learning. (2023). CASEL. Retrieved December 3, 2022, from https://schoolguide.casel.org/

The FirstNet Network Expands Across Ohio to Advance Public Safety Communications Capabilities . (2020). AT&T. https://about.att.com/story/2020/fn_ohio.html

The Revolution in Emergency Communications . (2017). https://www.policeforum.org/assets/EmergencyCommunications.pdf

The visual collaboration platform for every team: Miro. (n.d.). Retrieved November 20, 2022, from https://miro.com/

Thiesse, F., Wirth, M., Kemper, H. G., Moisa, M., Morar, D., Lasi, H., Piller, F., Buxmann, P., Mortara, L., Ford, S., & Minshall, T. (2015). Economic implications of additive manufacturing and the contribution of MIS. *Business & Information Systems Engineering, 57*(2), 139–148. doi:10.100712599-015-0374-4

Tidd, J., & Bessant, J. R. (2020). *Managing innovation: Integrating technological, market and organizational change.* John Wiley & Sons.

Tieman, M., & Darun, M. R. (2017). Leveraging blockchain technology for halal supply chains. *ICR Journal, 8*(4), 547–550. doi:10.52282/icr.v8i4.167

Timčenko, V., Zogović, N., Jevtić, M., & Đorđević, B. (2016). Assessing cloud computing sustainability. In *Proceedings of the 6th International Conference on Information Society and Technology, ICIST* (pp. 40-45). ICIST2016.

Timmermans, K. (2016). *Digital trendsetters: Secrets of the most successful supply chains*. Retrieved August 13, 2022, from https://www.mhlnews.com/global-supply-chain/article/22051791/digital-trendsetters-secrets-of-the-most-successful-supply-chains

Timm, I. J., & Lorig, F. (2015). Logistics 4.0: A Challenge for Simulation. In *Proceedings of the Winter Simulation Conference (WSC)* (pp. 3118-3119). IEEE. 10.1109/WSC.2015.7408428

Tlili, A., Huang, R., Shehata, B., Liu, D., Zhao, J., Metwally, A., Wang, H., Denden, M., Bozkurt, A., Lee, L.-H., Beyoglu, D., Altinay, F., Sharma, R. C., Altinay, Z., Li, Z., Liu, J., Ahmad, F., Hu, Y., Salha, S., ... Burgos, D. (2022). Is Metaverse in education a blessing or a curse: A combined content and bibliometric analysis. *Smart Learning Environments*, *9*(1), 24. doi:10.118640561-022-00205-x

Todorović, M. L., Petrović, D. Č., Mihić, M. M., Obradović, V. L., & Bushuyev, S. D. (2015). Project success analysis framework: A knowledge-based approach in project management. *International Journal of Project Management*, *33*(4), 772–783. doi:10.1016/j.ijproman.2014.10.009

Tödtling, F., & Trippl, M. (2005). One size fit all. Towards a differentiated regional innovation policy approach. *Research Policy*, *34*(8), 1203–1219. doi:10.1016/j.respol.2005.01.018

Toka, A., Aivazidou, E., Antoniou, A., & Arvanitopoulos-Darginis, K. (2013). Cloud computing in supply chain management: an overview. In D. Garaham, I. Manikas, & D. K. Folinas (Eds.), *E-Logistics and E-Supply Chain Management: Applications for Evolving Business* (pp. 218–231). IGI Global. doi:10.4018/978-1-4666-3914-0.ch012

Törnberg, A. (2018). Combining transition studies and social movement theory: Towards a new research agenda. *Theory and Society*, *47*(3), 381–408. doi:10.100711186-018-9318-6

Troise, C., Tani, M., Matricano, D., & Ferrara, E. (2022). Guest editorial: Digital transformation, strategic management and entrepreneurial process: dynamics, challenges and opportunities. *Journal of Strategy and Management*, *15*(3), 329–334. doi:10.1108/JSMA-08-2022-363

Tromp, J. (2022). Extended Reality & The Backbone: Towards a 3D Mirrorworld. In Roadmapping Extended Reality (pp. 193-227). Academic Press.

Trubiani, C., Jamshidi, P., Cito, J., Shang, W., Jiang, Z. M., & Borg, M. (2018). Performance issues? Hey DevOps, mind the uncertainty. *IEEE Software*, *36*(2), 110–117. doi:10.1109/MS.2018.2875989

Tsalis, T. A., Malamateniou, K. E., Koulouriotis, D., & Nikolaou, I. E. (2020). New challenges for corporate sustainability reporting: United Nations' 2030 agenda for sustainable development and the sustainable development goals. *Corporate Social Responsibility and Environmental Management*, *27*(4), 1617–1629. doi:10.1002/csr.1910

Uğurlu, Ö. Y., & Kizildağ, D. (2013). A Comparative Analysis of Knowledge Management in Banking Sector: An Empirical Research. *European Journal of Business and Management*, *5*(16), 12–19.

Uhlemann, T. H. J., Schock, C., Lehmann, C., Freiberger, S., & Steinhilper, R. (2017). The digital twin: Demonstrating the potential of real time data acquisition in production systems. *Procedia Manufacturing*, *9*, 113–120. doi:10.1016/j.promfg.2017.04.043

Ullah, H., Wang, Z., Bashir, S., Khan, A. R., Riaz, M., & Syed, N. (2021). Nexus between IT capability and green intellectual capital on sustainable businesses: Evidence from emerging economies. *Environmental Science and Pollution Research International*, *28*(22), 27825–27843. doi:10.100711356-020-12245-2 PMID:33515153

Umar, T. (2022). Challenges of BIM implementation in GCC construction industry. *Engineering, Construction, and Architectural Management*, *29*(3), 1139–1168.

Um, J. S. (2019). *Drones as cyber-physical systems*. Springer. doi:10.1007/978-981-13-3741-3

UNCCD. (2023). *United Nations convention to combat desertification*. Retrieved from https://www.unccd.int/

Unglesbee, B. (2022). Walmart plots 4 new "next generation" fulfillment centers. *Retail Dive*. https://www.retaildive.com/news/walmart-plots-fulfillment-centers-jobs/624868

Unilever. (2021). *Purpose-led, future-fit: Unilever annual report and accounts 2021.* Retrieved March 16, 2023, from https://www.unilever.com/files/92ui5egz/production/e582e46a7f7170fd10be32cf65113b738f19f0c2.pdf

United Nations. (2020). *Sustainable development goals.* Retrieved from https://www.un.org/sustainabledevelopment/sustainable-development-goals/

United States Environmental Protection Agency. (2022). *Home.* Retrieved February 10, 2022, from www.epa.gov

Upadhayay, S., & Alqassimi, O. (2018). Transition from linear to circular economy. *Westcliff International Journal of Applied Research, 2*(2), 62–74. doi:10.47670/wuwijar201822OASU

Upadhyay, A., Mukhuty, S., Kumar, V., & Kazancoglu, Y. (2021). Blockchain technology and the circular economy: Implications for sustainability and social responsibility. *Journal of Cleaner Production, 293*(2021). *Journal of Cleaner Production, 126130*, 1–7. doi:10.1016/j.jclepro.2021.126130

Uyan, U., Şanal, M., & Ibin, A. (2022). A Theoretical Investigation on Intra-Firm Knowledge Sharing: The Roles of Contextual, Relational, and Socio-Cognitive Factors. In Understanding, Implementing, and Evaluating Knowledge Management in Business Settings (pp. 14-41). IGI Global.

Uyarra, E., Flanagan, K., Magro, E., Wilson, J. R., & Sotarauta, M. (2017). Understanding regional innovation policy dynamics: Actors, agency, and learning. *Environment and Planning C. Politics and Space, 35*(4), 559–568.

Vallandingham, L. R., Yu, Q., Sharma, N., Strandhagen, J. W., & Strandhagen, J. O. (2018). Grocery retail supply chain planning and control: Impact of consumer trends and enabling technologies. *IFAC-PapersOnLine, 51*(11), 612–617. doi:10.1016/j.ifacol.2018.08.386

Van den Besselaar, P., & Heimeriks, G. (2006). Mapping research topics using word-reference co-occurrences: A method and an exploratory case study. *Scientometrics, 68*(3), 377–393. doi:10.100711192-006-0118-9

Van Norman, W. C. (2013). *Shade Grown Slavery: The Lives of Slaves on Coffee Plantations in Cuba.* Vanderbilt University Press. doi:10.2307/j.ctv167554g

Van Raan, A. F. J., & Noyons, E. C. M. (2002). Discovery of patterns of scientific and technological development and knowledge transfer. *Proceedings of the 6th International Conference on Current Research Information Systems,* 105-112.

Varsei, M., Soosay, C., Fahimnia, B., & Sarkis, J. (2014). Framing sustainability performance of supply chains with multidimensional indicators. *Supply Chain Management, 19*(3), 242–257. doi:10.1108/SCM-12-2013-0436

Veleva, V., & Ellenbecker, M. (2001). Indicators of sustainable production: Framework and methodology. *Journal of Cleaner Production, 9*(6), 519–549. doi:10.1016/S0959-6526(01)00010-5

Venkatesan, S. (2021). *How Walmart is using A.I. to make smarter substitutions in online grocery orders.* Walmart. https://corporate.walmart.com/newsroom/2021/06/24/headline-how-walmart-is-using-a-i-to-make-smarter-substitutions-in-online-grocery-orders

Vercoe, R. A., Welch-Devine, M., Hardy, D., Demoss, J. A., Bonney, S. N., Allen, K., Brosius, P., Charles, D., Crawford, B., Heisel, S., Heynen, N., de Jesús-Crespo, R. G., Nibbelink, N., Parker, L., Pringle, C., Shaw, A., & Van Sant, L. (2014). Acknowledging trade-offs and understanding complexity: Exurbanization issues in Macon County, North Carolina. *Ecology and Society, 19*(1), 23–32. doi:10.5751/ES-05970-190123

Veres, O., Kunanets, N., Pasichnyk, V., Veretennikova, N., Korz, R., & Leheza, A. (2019, September). Development and Operations-The Modern Paradigm of the Work of IT Project Teams. In *2019 IEEE 14th International Conference on Computer Sciences and Information Technologies (CSIT)* (Vol. 3, pp. 103-106). IEEE. 10.1109/STC-CSIT.2019.8929861

Vermesan, O., & Friess, P. (2011). *Internet of things strategic research roadmap*. River Publishers.

Viederman, S. (1994). Five capitals and three pillars of sustainability. *The Newsletter of PEGS*, *4*(1), 5–12.

Vijayan, G., Kamarulzaman, N. H., Mukherjee, A., & Vaiappuri, S. K. (2020). Strategic value creation in a supply chain. In *Supply Chain and Logistics Management: Concepts, Methodologies, Tools, and Applications* (pp. 1–19). IGI Global., doi:10.4018/978-1-7998-0945-6.ch001

Vinuesa, R., Azizpour, H., Leite, I., Balaam, M., Dignum, V., Domisch, S., Felländer, A., Langhans, S. D., Tegmark, M., & Fuso Nerini, F. (2020). The role of artificial intelligence in achieving the sustainable development goals. *Nature Communications*, *11*(1), 233. doi:10.103841467-019-14108-y PMID:31932590

Virji, H., Padgham, J., & Seipt, C. (2012). Capacity building to support knowledge systems for resilient development—Approaches, actions, and needs. *Current Opinion in Environmental Sustainability*, *4*(1), 115–121. doi:10.1016/j.cosust.2012.01.005

Von Solms, R., & Van Niekerk, J. (2013). From information security to cyber security. *Computers & Security*, *38*, 97–102. doi:10.1016/j.cose.2013.04.004

Vuori, V., & Okkonen, J. (2012). Knowledge sharing motivational factors of using an intra-organizational social media platform. *Journal of Knowledge Management*, *16*(4), 592–603. doi:10.1108/13673271211246167

Wagner, M. M., & Gobster, P. H. (2007). Interpreting landscape change: Measured biophysical change and surrounding social context. *Landscape and Urban Planning*, *81*(1-2), 67–80. doi:10.1016/j.landurbplan.2006.10.019

Wakabayashi, Y., Kamioka, M., Kinugawa, J., & Kosuge, K. (2017). KitPaDy: Robot co-worker in kitting process: Basic concept and computation of working time. In *2017 13th IEEE Conference on Automation Science and Engineering (CASE)* (pp. 320-327). IEEE.

Walmart. (2017). *What is a Walmart Academy? How they're building confidence and careers*. https://corporate.walmart.com/newsroom/opportunity/20170417/what-is-a-walmart-academy-how-theyre-building-confidence-and-careers

Walmart. (2022). *Human capital: Good jobs and advancement for associates*. https://corporate.walmart.com/esgreport/esg-issues/human-capital

Walsh, S. T., Kirchhoff, B. A., & Newbert, S. (2002). Differentiating market strategies for disruptive technologies. *IEEE Transactions on Engineering Management*, *49*(4), 341–351. doi:10.1109/TEM.2002.806718

Wang, W.-T., & Ko, N.-Y. (2012). Knowledge sharing practices of project teams when encountering changes in project scope: A contingency approach. *Journal of Information Science*, *38*(5), 423–441. doi:10.1177/0165551512445240

Wang, W., Zhang, D., Wang, H., Zhu, Q., & Morabbi Heravi, H. (2022). How do businesses achieve sustainable success and gain a competitive advantage in the green era? *Kybernetes*, 1–20. doi:10.1108/K-07-2021-0614

Wang, Z., Shi, M., & Li, C. (2020, December). An Intelligent DevOps Platform Research and Design Based on Machine Learning. In *2020 Eighth International Conference on Advanced Cloud and Big Data (CBD)* (pp. 42-47). IEEE. 10.1109/CBD51900.2020.00017

Warner, K. S., & Wäger, M. (2019). Building dynamic capabilities for digital transformation: An ongoing process of strategic renewal. *Long Range Planning*, *52*(3), 326–349. doi:10.1016/j.lrp.2018.12.001

Watkins, C. (2018). Landscapes and resistance in the African diaspora: Five centuries of palm oil on Bahia's Dendê Coast. *Journal of Rural Studies*, *61*, 137–154. doi:10.1016/j.jrurstud.2018.04.009

Weinand, D. (2019). *Lessons from Walmart: Smart strategies for retailers of all sizes*. Incisiv. https://www.incisiv.com/blog/lessons-from-walmart-smart-strategies-for-retailers-of-all-sizes

Weking, J., Desouza, K., Fielt, E., & Kowalkiewicz, M. (2023). Metaverse-enabled entrepreneurship. *Journal of Business Venturing Insights*, *19*, e00375. doi:10.1016/j.jbvi.2023.e00375

Welford, R., & Frost, S. (2006). Corporate social responsibility in Asian supply chains. *Corporate Social Responsibility and Environmental Management*, *13*(3), 166–176. doi:10.1002/csr.121

Westeren, K. I. (2016). How transfer of knowledge can be linked to productivity and competitiveness of the firm-theoretical considerations and case study. *Informe Gepec*, *20*(2), 156–171.

Westeren, K. I. (2020). Innovation processes in aquaculture: Comparing companies in Norway and Chile. In *Entrepreneurship-Contemporary Issues*. IntechOpen.

Westeren, K. I., Cader, H., de Fátima Sales, M., Similä, J. O., & Staduto, J. (2018). *Competitiveness and knowledge: An international comparison of traditional firms*. Routledge. doi:10.4324/9781315625331

What is Appreciative Inquiry? Examples & Resources for the Appreciative Inquiry Process. (2020, December 10). Benedictine University CVDL.

Whitmee, S., Haines, A., Beyrer, C., Boltz, F., Capon, A. G., Dias, B. F. S., Ezeh, A., Frumkin, H., Gong, P., Head, P., & … . (2015). Safeguarding human health in the Anthropocene epoch: Report of The Rockefeller Foundation–Lancet Commission on planetary health. *Lancet*, *386*(10007), 1973–2028. doi:10.1016/S0140-6736(15)60901-1 PMID:26188744

Wickramasinghe, V., & Widyaratne, R. (2012). Effects of interpersonal trust, team leader support, rewards, and knowledge sharing mechanisms on knowledge sharing in project teams. *VINE Journal of Information and Knowledge Management Systems*, *42*(2), 214–236.

Wiedemann, A., Forsgren, N., Wiesche, M., Gewald, H., & Krcmar, H. (2019). The DevOps Phenomenon: An executive crash course. *ACM Queue; Tomorrow's Computing Today*, *17*(2), 93–112. doi:10.1145/3329781.3338532

Wikipedia. (2023a). Comcast. In *Wikipedia*. https://en.wikipedia.org/wiki/Comcast

Wikipedia. (2023b). Lumen Technologies. In *Wikipedia*. https://en.wikipedia.org/wiki/Lumen_Technologies

Wikipedia. (2023c). SWOT analysis. In *Wikipedia*. https://en.wikipedia.org/wiki/SWOT_analysis

Wikipedia. (2023d). Tacit knowledge. In *Wikipedia*. Wikipedia.

Wilson, M. (2003). Corporate sustainability: What is it and where does it come from? *Ivey Business Journal*, *67*(6), 1–5.

Witkowski, K. (2017). Internet of things, big data, industry 4.0: Innovative solutions in logistics and supply chains management. *Procedia Engineering*, *182*, 763–769. doi:10.1016/j.proeng.2017.03.197

Wohlers, T. (2011). Making products by using additive manufacturing. *Manufacturing Engineering*, *146*(4), 70–77.

Wolf, E. (1982). *Europe and the People without History*. University of California Press.

Wolf, S., & Buttel, F. (1996). The political economy of precision farming. *American Journal of Agricultural Economics*, *78*(5), 1269–1274. doi:10.2307/1243505

Wong, C., Yang, E., Yan, X. T., & Gu, D. (2018). Autonomous robots for harsh environments: A holistic overview of current solutions and ongoing challenges. *Systems Science & Control Engineering*, *6*(1), 213–219. doi:10.1080/21642583.2018.1477634

Wong, P. K., Ho, Y. P., & Autio, E. (2005). Entrepreneurship, innovation and economic growth: Evidence from GEM data. *Small Business Economics*, *24*(3), 335–350. doi:10.100711187-005-2000-1

Wong, S. K. S. (2013). Environmental requirements, knowledge sharing and green innovation: Empirical evidence from the electronics industry in China. *Business Strategy and the Environment*, *22*(5), 321–338. doi:10.1002/bse.1746

World Commission on Environment and Development. (1987). *Our common future*. United Nations.

Worldwide Fund for Nature. (1993). *Sustainable use of natural resources: Concepts, issues and criteria.* Gland.

Wright, E. O. (2010). *Envisioning real utopias*. Verso.

Wu, N., & Silva, E. A. (2010). Artificial intelligence solutions for urban land dynamics: A review. *Journal of Planning Literature*, *24*(3), 246–265. doi:10.1177/0885412210361571

Xiong, M., & Wang, H. (2022). Digital twin applications in aviation industry: A review. *International Journal of Advanced Manufacturing Technology*, *121*(9), 5677–5692. doi:10.100700170-022-09717-9

Xu, Y. (2008). *Widget Communication Architecture with Emphasis on Mobile Devices*. Academic Press.

Yang, C., Tu, X., Autiosalo, J., Ala-Laurinaho, R., Mattila, J., Salminen, P., & Tammi, K. (2022). Extended Reality Application Framework for a Digital-Twin-Based Smart Crane. *Applied Sciences (Basel, Switzerland)*, *12*(12), 6030. doi:10.3390/app12126030

Yang, J. (2010). On the construction and implementation methods for performance measurement of reverse supply chain. In *Proceedings of the Seventh International Conference on Fuzzy Systems and Knowledge Discovery* (vol. 1, pp. 899-903). IEEE. 10.1109/FSKD.2010.5569111

Yang, J., Zang, L., & Hao, Z. (2009). Study on the performance evaluation system of reverse supply chain based on BSC and triangular fuzzy number AHP. In *Proceedings of the 2009 International Conference on Information Engineering and Computer Science (ICIECS 2009)* (pp. 1-3). IEEE. 10.1109/ICIECS.2009.5364327

Yarlagadda, R. T. (2017). Implementation of DevOps in healthcare systems. *Implementation of DevOps in Healthcare Systems, International Journal of Emerging Technologies and Innovative Research.*

Ye, N., Kueh, T., Hou, L., Liu, Y., & Yu, H. (2020). A bibliometric analysis of corporate social responsibility in sustainable development. *Journal of Cleaner Production*, *272*, 122679. doi:10.1016/j.jclepro.2020.122679

Yeong, A., & Lim, T. T. (2010). Integrating knowledge management with project management for project success. *Journal of Project. Program & Portfolio Management*, *1*(2), 8–19. doi:10.5130/pppm.v1i2.1735

Yin, R. (1984). *Case Study Research*. Sage Publications.

Young, O. R., Berkhout, F., Gallopin, G. C., Janssen, M. A., Ostrom, E., & van der Leeuw, S. (2006). The Globalization of Socio-Ecological Systems: An Agenda for Scientific Research. *Global Environmental Change*, *16*(3), 304–316. doi:10.1016/j.gloenvcha.2006.03.004

Yu, J. (2022). Exploration of Educational Possibilities by Four Metaverse Types in Physical Education. *Technologies*, *10*(5), 104. doi:10.3390/technologies10050104

Yu, J., Bang, H. C., Lee, H., & Lee, Y. S. (2016). Adaptive Internet of Things and Web of Things convergence platform for Internet of reality services. *The Journal of Supercomputing*, *72*(1), 84–102. doi:10.100711227-015-1489-6

Yu, S., Mishra, A. N., Gopal, A., Slaughter, S., & Mukhopadhyay, T. (2015). E-procurement infusion and operational process impacts in MRO procurement: Complementary or substitutive effects? *Production and Operations Management, 24*(7), 1054–1107. doi:10.1111/poms.12362

Yu, W., Patros, P., Young, B., Klinac, E., & Walmsley, T. G. (2022). Energy digital twin technology for industrial energy management: Classification, challenges, and future. *Renewable & Sustainable Energy Reviews, 112407*, 1–14. doi:10.1016/j.rser.2022.112407

Zadrozny, P., & Kodali, R. (2013). Big data and splunk. In P. Zadrozny & R. Kodali (Eds.), *Big data analytics using Splunk: Deriving operational intelligence from social media, machine data, existing data warehouses, and other real-time streaming sources* (pp. 1–7). Apress.

Zailani, S., Jeyaraman, K., Vengadasan, G., & Premkumar, R. (2012). Sustainable supply chain management (SSCM) in Malaysia: A survey. *International Journal of Production Economics, 140*(1), 330–340. doi:10.1016/j.ijpe.2012.02.008

Zaim, H., Tatoglu, E., & Zaim, S. (2007). Performance of knowledge management practices: A causal analysis. *Journal of Knowledge Management, 11*(6), 54–67. doi:10.1108/13673270710832163

Zamorano, M. M., Fernández-Laso, M. C., & de Esteban Curiel, J. (2020). Smart airports: Acceptance of technology by passengers. *Cuadernos de Turismo*, (45), 567–570.

Zaoui, F., & Souissi, N. (2020). Roadmap for digital transformation: A literature review. *Procedia Computer Science, 175*, 621–628. doi:10.1016/j.procs.2020.07.090

Zeigler, B. P., Kim, D., & Buckley, S. J. (1999). Distributed supply chain simulation in a DEVS/CORBA execution environment. In *Proceedings of the 31st Conference on Winter Simulation: Simulation---A Bridge to The Future-Volume 2* (pp. 1333-1340). 10.1145/324898.325274

Železný-Green, D. R., Kagawa, F., & Giri, R. (2022, April 29). *Three reasons why the boost EdTech got from the COVID-19 pandemic may be short-lived.* Global Partnership for Education. Retrieved January 6, 2023, from https://www.globalpartnership.org/blog/three-reasons-why-boost-edtech-got-covid-19-pandemic-may-be-short-lived

Zhang, W., Xu, F., & Wang, X. (2020). How Green Transformational Leadership Affects Green Creativity: Creative Process Engagement as Intermediary Bond and Green Innovation Strategy as Boundary Spanner. *Sustainability, 12*(9), 3841. doi:10.3390/su12093841

Zhang, M., Tse, Y. K., Doherty, B., Li, S., & Akhtar, P. (2018). Sustainable supply chain management: Confirmation of a higher-order model. *Resources, Conservation and Recycling, 128*, 206–221. doi:10.1016/j.resconrec.2016.06.015

Zhang, Y., Moe, W. W., & Schweidel, D. A. (2017). Modeling the role of message content and influencers in social media rebroadcasting. *International Journal of Research in Marketing, 34*(1), 100–119. doi:10.1016/j.ijresmar.2016.07.003

Zhang, Z., Wen, F., Sun, Z., Guo, X., He, T., & Lee, C. (2022). Artificial Intelligence-Enabled Sensing Technologies in the 5G/Internet of Things Era: From Virtual Reality/Augmented Reality to the Digital Twin. *Advanced Intelligent Systems, 4*(7), 2100228. doi:10.1002/aisy.202100228

Zhao, J., & de Pablos, P. O. (2010). Regional knowledge management: The perspective of management theory. *Behaviour & Information Technology, 7*(3), 39–49.

Zhao, X., Wang, P., & Pal, R. (2021). The effects of agro-food supply chain integration on product quality and financial performance: Evidence from Chinese agro-food processing business. *International Journal of Production Economics, 231*, 1–16. doi:10.1016/j.ijpe.2020.107832

Zheng, J., Dai, Y., Liang, Y., Liao, Q., & Zhang, H. (2020). An online real-time estimation tool of leakage parameters for hazardous liquid pipelines. *International Journal of Critical Infrastructure Protection*, *31*, 1–10. doi:10.1016/j.ijcip.2020.100389

Zhou, K., Liu, T., & Zhou, L. (2015, August). Industry 4.0: Towards future industrial opportunities and challenges. In *Proceedings of the 2015 12th International Conference on Fuzzy Systems and Knowledge Discovery (FSKD)* (pp. 2147-2152). IEEE. 10.1109/FSKD.2015.7382284

Zhou, X., Huang, H., Zhang, H., Huang, X., Shao, D., & Zhong, C. (2022, May). A cross-company ethnographic study on software teams for DevOps and microservices: organization, benefits, and issues. In *Proceedings of the 44th International Conference on Software Engineering: Software Engineering in Practice* (pp. 1-10). 10.1145/3510457.3513054

Zhuang, C., Liu, J., & Xiong, H. (2018). Digital twin-based smart production management and control framework for the complex product assembly shopfloor. *International Journal of Advanced Manufacturing Technology*, *96*(1-4), 1149–1163. doi:10.100700170-018-1617-6

Zhu, Q., Geng, Y., Sarkis, J., & Lai, K. H. (2011). Evaluating green supply chain management among Chinese manufacturers from the ecological modernization perspective. *Transportation Research Part E, Logistics and Transportation Review*, *47*(6), 808–821. doi:10.1016/j.tre.2010.09.013

Zhu, Q., Sarkis, J., & Geng, Y. (2005). Green supply chain management in China: Pressures, practices, and performance. *International Journal of Operations & Production Management*, *25*(5), 449–468. doi:10.1108/01443570510593148

About the Contributors

* * *

Ismail Adeyemi is currently an Assistant Lecturer in the Departments of Library and Information Science, Kwara State University, Malete, Kwara State, Nigeria. He was a former Librarian at Pinheiro LP, Ilupeju, Lagos State with branches in Abuja and Port-Harcourt. He holds a bachelor's and master's degrees in Library and Information Science from the Department of Library and Information Science, University of Ilorin. He was the General Secretary of National Association of Library and Information Science Students (University of Ilorin) in the 2012/2013 session. He interned at Kwara State Public Library and was part of the team that developed Roemichs International School Library in Ilorin, Nigeria. He has worked with Olusegun Obasanjo Presidential Library (Library Officer/Admin Assistant) and Lamp Bearer Islamic School (School Librarian).

Muhammad Mahboob Ali, PhD, Post Doctorate, is currently working as a Professor of Economics, Entrepreneurship and ICT in Dhaka School of Economics (Constituent Institution of the University of Dhaka), Bangladesh. His passion is teaching and doing research work. His articles have been publishing in different international journals and peer reviewed book chapters and number of published research based articles were around 160.He also authored several books which is totaling 25 including research based, novels, dramas, short stories, rhymes. Professor Ali is contributing regularly post editorial in different dailies and also giving expert comments in diversified TV and Radio channels.

Füsun Bulutlar received the MBA degree from the Middle East Technical University, Turkey, in 2001 and a PhD degree in Organizational Behaviour from the Marmara University, Turkey, in 2005. She currently works as a full professor at Yeditepe University, Department of International Trade and Business. Her current research interests include disruptive technologies. supply chain visibility, scale development, business ethics, leadership and managerialism.

Mohammad Daradkeh is an Associate Professor of Business Analytics and Data Science at the College of Engineering & IT, University of Dubai. He has extensive experience in innovation and entrepreneurship research and management, having worked at Yarmouk University in Jordan and Lincoln University in New Zealand before joining the University of Dubai. Dr. Daradkeh's research interests focus on Business Intelligence, Data Analytics, and Innovation Management, which he has published extensively in reputed academic publishers such as Elsevier, Springer, Emerald MDPI, and IGI. He is also a member of the editorial board of several renowned journals. Dr. Daradkeh's expertise in innovation and entrepreneurship makes him an invaluable contributor to the field, and he is dedicated to inspiring the next generation of aspiring business leaders through his work. In particular, he is interested in the application of Business Intelligence and Data Analytics in the development and implementation of metaverse technologies, and related practices to support innovation and entrepreneurship in education.

Jorge Gomes is a researcher at ADVANCE, ISEG, School of Economics & Management of the Universidade de Lisboa. He holds a PhD in Management from ISEG and a Masters in Management Sciences from ISCTE-IUL, He also have a post-graduation in Project Management from INDEG/ISCTE, and a degree in Geographic Engineering from the Faculty of Sciences of the Universidade de Lisboa. During the past 30 years, he has worked as an engineer, project manager, quality auditor and consultant. Teaches Management at ULHT, Lisboa. His research interests include Benefits Management, Project Management, Project Success, Maturity Models, IS/IT Investments, IS/IT in Healthcare and IS/IT Management.

Jaime J. González-Masip is Lecturer in Business Management and Corporate Sustainability at Universidad Politécnica de Madrid (Spain). He got his Ph.D. focused on Business Management and CSR from Universidad Complutense de Madrid in 2017, where he earned the Best Doctoral Thesis Award of 2017 from the Economics and Business School. He holds a degree in Computer Science Engineering and in Marketing. His research interests include CSR, Corporate Sustainability, Sustainable Entrepreneurship and Business Ethics. He made his postdoctoral research stays at Copenhagen Business School (Denmark) and University of Edinburgh Business School (UK).

Brenda Gross, after earning an Associate of Applied Science degree in Computer Information Systems, entered an internship program at Wright-Patterson Air Force Base as a Computer Specialist. At the same time, she worked on completing my Bachelor of Science degree in Computer Science. In 2017, she completed her Master of Science degree in Health Informatics, and in January 2022, she began the Doctor of Professional Studies – Instructional Design Leadership program at Franklin University. Before completing her BS degree, she transitioned from a civilian employee at Wright Patterson Air Force Base to a government contractor supporting the Air Force. During her 22 years supporting the Air Force, she has worked on several projects supporting the Air Force in various roles, including software analyst, software developer, database developer, programmer, and technical lead. Additionally, after earning her BS degree, she worked as an adjunct at Clark State Community College for about two years. Her passion is lifelong learning, as there is something to learn every day. She genuinely enjoys reading, research, and collaborative learning experiences in academics. After completing her Doctor of Professional Studies program, her long-term goal is to teach online courses at a university. Her BS and MS degrees were online programs, as is her Doctor of Professional Studies program; therefore, she understands the potential challenges that online learning may present.

Liz Kheng is a doctoral candidate working towards her DBA at Franklin University in Columbus, Ohio, where she also earned her MBA in 2019. Liz's dissertation research topic closely aligns with her professional role as an IT consultant and small business owner and partner at TSG Partners Ltd. She is exploring systems theory to understand organizational systems to identify the component that may promote the financial independence of foster youth. Liz has worked as an IT consultant for almost twenty years in the health and human services sector. She specializes in contract management and IT services for state, local government, and educational institutions (SLED). Her most notable projects include the Ohio FirstNet Project, during the knowledge management, requirements gathering, and the public outreach phase of the first responders' priority 5G broadband network. As a partner with TSG, Liz worked with Accenture to build a development team for the Ohio Gateway Modernization Project, a digital platform for Ohio businesses to apply for licensures and pay commercial and sales taxes. Liz has also partnered with CBTS to provide Chromebooks to students at Columbus City Schools, the largest school district in Ohio. The project also included developing an inventory knowledge management system to manage and track assets.

Beth Kiernan Ferrigno has been working in instructional technology for 25 years, having supported both school systems and educational technology companies in implementation, project management, change management and more. She is a respected implementation expert with extensive leadership on fast-moving, complicated projects from early stages through to scalable execution. Proven ability to build trusted relationships with stakeholder groups and confidently advocate, influence and negotiate across various levels of the organization. Beth is a doctoral student at Franklin University pursuing her DPS in Instructional Design Leadership.

Zinga Novais is a project manager. She holds a Master's in Project Management from ISEG, School of Economics & Management of the University of Lisbon. She also holds a post-graduation in Project Management and a post-graduation in Management & Business Consulting, both from ISEG - University of Lisbon; and a degree in Public Administration from ISCSP, School of Social and Political Sciences of the University of Lisbon.

Özden Özkanlısoy is a PhD candidate in the field of international trade and logistics management at Yeditepe University. She hold a M.Sc. in supply chain and logistics management from Bahçeşehir University. She worked as research assistant for five years. Her research fields focus on digital tranformation, risk management and sustainability in supply chains. She has conducted three different scale development and validation studies for her doctoral program on the field of supply chain management. The first of them, the using disruptive technology scale, they developed with Prof. Bulutlar has been published in the Web of Science database. .

Mário José Batista Romão is an Associate Professor of Information Systems, with Aggregation, at ISEG – University of Lisbon. He is Director of the Masters program in Computer Science and Management. He holds a PhD in Management Sciences by ISCTE-IUL and by Computer Integrated Manufacturing at Cranfiel University (UK). He also holds a MsC in Telecommunications and Computer Science, at IST - Instituto Superior Técnico, University of Lisbon. He is Pos-Graduated in Project Management and holds the international certification Project Management Professional (PMP), by PMI – Project Management International. He has a degree in Electrotecnic Engineer by IST.

Sahana. P. Shankar completed her B.E in Information Science and Engineering and MTech in Software Engineering from Ramaiah Institute of Technology, Bangalore. She is a third rank holder in B.E and a first rank holder with gold medal in MTech. She has worked with Unisys as Associate Engineer in the Software Product Testing domain for three years. She holds a US Patent bearing patent number

US20160034382. She has worked with RIT as a Teaching Assistant for 6 months under the TEQIP-II scholarship program. She has published papers in various national and international journals and conferences. She has also authored several book chapters. She is an ISTQB certified software tester. She is currently working with Ramaiah University of Applied Sciences, Bangalore as an Assistant Professor in the Department of Computer Science and Engineering.

Deepak Varadam holds a Masters Degree in Microsystems Engineering from Heriot-Watt University, Edinburgh (Scotland), U.K. and P.G.Diploma in ECE from Napier University, U.K. He worked as a Postgraduate Masters Research Scientist under Biomedical Microengineering Group (BMG) at Heriot-Watt University. He is currently working as an Assistant Professor in Faculty of Engineering and Technology, Computer Science and Engineering Department at Ramaiah University of Applied Sciences (RUAS) since 2010. He has been actively participating in delivering corporate trainings, seminars and have publications in national, international journals and conferences. His research interests is in MEMS, Embedded Systems, Software Engineering, Computer Graphics and Embedded Networking.

Omar Vargas-González is professor and Head of Systems and Computing Department at Tecnologico Nacional de Mexico Campus Ciudad Guzman, professor at Telematic Engineering at Centro Universitario del Sur Universidad de Guadalajara with a master degree in Computer Systems. Has been trained in Innovation and Multidisciplinary Entrepreneurship at Arizona State University (2018) and a Generation of Ecosystems of Innovation, Entrepreneurship and Sustainability for Jalisco course by Harvard University T.H. Chan School of Health. At present conduct research on diverse fields such as Entrepreneurship, Economy, Statistics, Mathematics and Information and Computer Sciences. Has colaborated in the publication of over 20 scientific articles and conducted diverse Innovation and Technological Development projects.

Index

A

B

D

E

S

T

U

V

W

www.ingramcontent.com/pod-product-compliance
Lightning Source LLC
LaVergne TN
LVHW060409300926
849162LV00006B/1377